CRITICAL SURVEY
OF
LONG FICTION

CRITICAL SURVEY
OF
LONG FICTION

English Language Series

Revised Edition

Hann-Law

4

Edited by
FRANK N. MAGILL

SALEM PRESS
Pasadena, California   Englewood Cliffs, New Jersey

SECOND PRINTING

Library of Congress Cataloging-in-Publication Data
Critical survey of long fiction. English language series/
    edited by Frank N. Magill. — Rev. ed.
        p.   cm.
    Includes bibliographical references and index.
    1. English fiction—Dictionaries. 2. American
fiction—Dictionaries. 3. English fiction—
Bio-bibliography. 4. American fiction—
Bio-bibliography. 5. Novelists, English—
Biography—Dictionaries. 6. Novelists, American—
Biography—Dictionaries.
I. Magill, Frank Northen, 1907-   .
PR821.C7   1991
823.009′03—dc20   91-19694
ISBN 0-89356-825-2 (set)   CIP
ISBN 0-89356-829-5 (volume 4)

PRINTED IN THE UNITED STATES OF AMERICA

LIST OF AUTHORS IN VOLUME 4

CRITICAL SURVEY
OF
LONG FICTION

BARRY HANNAH

Born: Clinton, Mississippi; April 23, 1942

Principal long fiction
Geronimo Rex, 1972; *Nightwatchmen*, 1973; *Ray*, 1980; *The Tennis Handsome*, 1983; *Hey Jack!*, 1987; *Boomerang*, 1989; *Never Say Die*, 1991.

Other literary forms
Barry Hannah has published short stories in *Esquire* magazine; some of these have been collected in *Airships* (1978) and *Captain Maximus* (1985).

Achievements
Because his fiction is often set in the contemporary South and is characterized by violence and gothic humor, Barry Hannah has most often been compared to William Faulkner, Flannery O'Connor, and Carson McCullers, other Southern writers who have explored violent and eccentric human behavior in Southern settings. Yet Hannah has a style and an energy that set him apart from others as a highly original American writer. His much-acclaimed first novel, *Geronimo Rex*, was awarded the William Faulkner Prize for Fiction and was nominated for a National Book Award, while *Airships*, his first book of short stories, received the Arnold Gingrich Short Fiction Award (Gingrich was founder and editor of *Esquire* magazine). Hannah has also received a Bellaman Foundation Award in Fiction (1970) and a Bread Loaf Fellowship (1971), and has been honored by the American Academy of Arts and Letters.

Biography
Barry Hannah was born on April 23, 1942, in Clinton, Mississippi, a town near Jackson, the state capital. He attended the public schools in Clinton, playing trumpet in the school band, and went on to Mississippi College, where he received his A.B. degree. He continued his education at the University of Arkansas, where he received both an M.A. and an M.F.A. in creative writing. Hannah began writing his first novel, *Geronimo Rex*, while he was working toward his creative writing degree, and an early version of a chapter from that novel appeared in the first issue of *Intro*, a journal that presented the best work from the nation's university writing programs. Much like Hannah, the protagonist of *Geronimo Rex*, Harry Monroe, is a young man searching for identity in a socially troubled South, and his name, Harry (Barry) Monroe, suggests that the author drew heavily from his own experience. Other fictional work, such as *Boomerang*, also seems to draw upon Hannah's personal life: the narrator of *Boomerang* is named Barry, and the novel is set in Clinton.

Much of Hannah's early fiction was published in *Esquire* magazine, where it received critical acclaim and wide readership. Nine of these stories were among the twenty collected in *Airships*, his finest and best-known collection of short fiction. Hannah is often at his best in short works, and sometimes his novels seem more collections of vignettes and short pieces than expanded unified narratives. Following *Airships* came four novels: *Ray*, *The Tennis Handsome*, *Hey Jack!*, and *Boomerang*. A second volume of short stories, *Captain Maximus*, was published in 1985.

Except for a brief period in California, where he worked on film scripts for director Robert Altman, Hannah has for the most part remained in the South, teaching creative writing and literature at Clemson University in South Carolina, at the University of Alabama, and at the University of Mississippi. He has also taught creative writing at the University of Iowa and the University of Montana, and was a writer-in-residence at Middlebury College in Vermont. He is the father of three children, two sons and a daughter, and lives with his third wife, Susan, in Oxford, Mississippi.

Analysis

Barry Hannah's fiction is populated with the Confederate soldiers, redneck idlers, gifted liars, failed intellectuals, desperate women, and violent men that readers of American literature have come to expect from Southern writers, but Hannah's comic inventiveness, dazzling prose, and lopsided view of life make them highly original portraits. Hannah writes like a juiced-up Faulkner, and the reader is often swept along by the sheer manic energy of his narratives. While his fiction is often short on plot, it is full of loopy twists and turns, imaginative surprises, and hilarious nonsense.

Hannah's highly acclaimed first novel, *Geronimo Rex*, is a good example. Owing much to the *Bildungsroman*, the novel of experience that chronicles a young person's rise to maturity, and to picaresque tales of adventurous rogues, *Geronimo Rex* is Hannah's portrait of the artist as a young punk. Growing up in a Southern mill town during the 1950's, Harry Monroe, Hannah's principal character, is a complexity of self-hatred and egotism, sensitivity and self-righteousness, artistry and violence. He sees himself in an old photograph of Apache chieftain Geronimo as a rebel warrior in a wild and savage country; he even starts wearing an Indian kerchief, boots, and a snakeskin jacket, does war dances on top of parked cars, and carries a gun. What he likes about Geronimo, he muses at one point, is that the Indian had "cheated, lied, stolen, usurped, killed, burned, raped, pillaged, razed, trapped, ripped, mashed," and Harry decides that he "would like to go into that line of work." Unlike other fictional depictions of youth in the 1950's—J. D. Salinger's Holden Caulfield in *The Catcher in the Rye* (1951), for example—Harry is no idealist surrounded by hypocritical adults. Harry *is* the world around him— hypocritical, violent, self-centered, and cynical.

In college, Harry becomes involved with mad racist Peter Lepoyster, whose hatred and sexual obsessions have driven him in and out of Whitfield, the local insane asylum. Harry's college roommate, Bobby Dove Fleece, has stolen from Lepoyster a bundle of erotic love letters written to a woman named Catherine, and Harry and Fleece become as obsessed with Lepoyster as he was with his woman. Lepoyster stalks the streets, spouting racial and anti-Semitic filth, breaking up civil rights demonstrations, and even becoming incensed when a black marching band shows up in a local parade. Harry and Fleece, equally obsessed, stalk Lepoyster and even sneak up on his house one night to take a shot at him, wounding him in the knee. Lepoyster is clearly what Harry himself could become, a comically frightening racist driven out of his mind by sexual desire and hatred, a mad pervert who has succumbed to the irrational drives of death, violence, and despair.

Opposed to Lepoyster, however, is Harley Butte, a black man who once worked in the mattress factory owned by Harry's father. Butte, who worships John Philip Sousa and writes march music of his own, is the director of a high school band modeled on the incredible Dream of Pines Colored High School Band, the best band in the state. If Lepoyster represents Southern racial hatred, Butte clearly represents racial harmony, the desire to see both blacks and whites marching to the same music. A musician like Butte, Harry plays the trumpet, but he likes blues and jazz, not Sousa. Harry, it is clear, improvises his own tunes and marches to his own drummer.

Yet it is the pathetic Lepoyster, not Harry, who is the true Geronimo, the savage killer in a country not his own. Lepoyster dies violently, shot to death in a gunfight with Fleece, a gentle soul who has never before even fired a gun. By the end of the novel, Harry has married Prissy Lombardo, a young girl who looks like a "pubescent Arab," writes poetry as well as plays the trumpet, and pursues an academic career as an English teacher. Although he is a poet and musician, Harry is still partly Geronimo Rex, the rebel with a streak of violence. Still, the novel, which begins and ends with brilliant descriptions of marching bands (Hannah writes about marching bands better than any other American writer), ends with harmony and hope.

While *Geronimo Rex* may not be a great American novel, it is a very good one, and an exceptional first novel for a beginning author. The story is told with a memorably comic and exuberant first-person narrative voice that Hannah skillfully employs in all of his later novels, and it is full of memorable scenes and characters: the death of an old dog and mule that wander into the Monroe yard when Harry is a boy; the rambling, sexually obsessed monologues of Bobby Dove Fleece, Harry's college roommate; the comic and pathetic Mother Rooney, who runs a boardinghouse where Harry stays.

Hannah's second novel, *Nightwatchmen*, continues the exploits of Harry Monroe, but he is not the central character. That distinction goes to Thorpe Trove, a striking figure who wears purple prescription glasses perched on his long nose beneath a wild shock of orange hair. In this novel of many voices, Trove is the central narrative voice, and it is he who tape-records the others for the reader. The central plot of *Nightwatchmen*, a kind of surreal mystery thriller, takes place at mythical Southwestern Mississippi University, where an unknown assailant called The Knocker is clubbing graduate students and faculty as they work in their offices late at night. When Conrad, a nightwatchman, and Spell, a janitor, are not only knocked but also beheaded, it becomes apparent that The Knocker may also be The Killer. Trove becomes obsessed with finding this mysterious figure (actually, two mysterious figures, as it turns out) and begins tape-recording anyone who might have clues—such as graduate student Harry Monroe. Harry and fellow graduate student Lawrence Head theorize that The Knocker intends only to conk pedants and bores, but when Didi Sweet, a fellow graduate student and an attractive divorcée, is knocked, that theory falls into doubt. The murders of Conrad and Spell, and the later murder of graduate student William Tell, dispel it entirely. Other clues come from part-time plumber Frank Theron Knockre and Douglas David "Dougie" Lotrieux, a film projectionist in a local theater.

Independently wealthy, Trove hires aging private detective Howard Hunter, and together they track down and destroy The Killer during the onslaught of Hurricane Camille. All of this takes place during some memorable scenes of storm and destruction: Dougie being swept along the countryside by 150-mile-per-hour winds, Head's landlady being decapitated by the tin roof of her house, the dead being blown by the hurricane from a local graveyard and found hanging in the trees.

Deciding upon corporal punishment for Dougie Lotrieux, who has known all along the identity of The Killer and now wants to die, Trove and his associates bring in Harry Monroe as executioner. Harry is by now completing his Ph.D. in English at Clemson and is about to bring out a second volume of poetry, but he still carries his gun and has wanted throughout the novel to kill something. Harry, who shoots Dougie through the head and buries his body on the beach, remains the divided Harry Monroe of the first novel: a sensitive artist, a judgmental observer of life, and a violent man.

Exactly what issue *Nightwatchmen* is trying to address is unclear. "A nightwatchman," Lawrence Head meditates at one point, "ought to be rather hungry for conversation. He ought to be dying to flood you with talk." The novel is, above all, a flood of talk from lonely and tormented people. Nightwatchmen keep lonely vigils, like these isolated and lonely night people, and Hurricane Camille seems an appropriate metaphor for the swirling turbulence of emotions within the characters, whose lives also cause death and destruction.

Hannah's third novel, *Ray*, is a departure from his first two. Condensed from a manuscript that was originally four hundred pages, *Ray* is a book of little more than a hundred pages and sixty-two short sections, some of them consisting of only a sentence or two. Furthermore, the novel is more upbeat than the previous two, for the title is a hearty cheer for life ("Hoo! Ray") as well as the narrator's name. Ray is an Alabama doctor and a former Vietnam fighter pilot whose fantasies of the Civil War, in which heat-seekers and phosphorus bombs battle sabers and horsemen, equate one war with another. An alcoholic, Ray administers drugs to addicted patients and practices selective euthanasia on the hurtful and depraved. The divorced father of three children, Ray seeks comfort from Sister, the daughter of the poor and hopeless Hooch family. Sister leaves home to become a prostitute and model for pornographic photographs and is eventually shot to death by Baptist preacher Maynard Castro, while her father is almost killed when his propane lantern explodes.

Ray confronts these tragedies, ministers to the needy, and meets a woman with whom he falls in love and marries. The victim of life's suffering—"I am infected with every disease I ever tried to cure," he says—Ray survives war, the poverty-ridden South, the loss of friends and lovers, and his own self-pity to become a heroic figure. By the end of the novel, he is plunging forward, saber raised, like the Confederate officers of his Civil War fantasies. A Christ-figure—he is thirty-three and, as he states in the opening sentence, "born of religious parents"—Ray suffers so that others may live (old man Hooch survives to become, under Ray's guidance, a gifted poet) and is himself resurrected.

Ray is Hannah's most concise novel, a carryover perhaps from the volume of short stories that constituted his previously published book, and in it Hannah comes to grips with the historical past of the Civil War and the grinding poverty of Southern families like the Hooches. Ray is in many ways a personification of the United States itself during the 1970's: haunted by war, divided by violent emotions and yearnings for peace, and searching for historical roots. Like his country, Ray lives through the worst of times and survives, perhaps even stronger than ever.

The Tennis Handsome, Hannah's fourth novel, first appeared in *Esquire* magazine and was later collected in *Airships*. The wildly improbable tale of a charismatic but brain-damaged tennis professional, his companion, and his high school tennis coach, the novel is a return to Hannah's comic exuberance and expansive style. French Edward, the "tennis handsome" of the title, is a kind of idiot savant, a brilliant tennis player but a vegetable off the court, having survived a plunge from a bridge with only part of his faculties intact. While in high school, French comes home one afternoon to find his mother in bed with his tennis coach, Jimmy Word, who, previously gay, has apparently rediscovered the joys of heterosexuality. Riddled with Freudian hatred, French gets even with Word by challenging the older man to a tennis match; hoping for a heart attack, French succeeds in giving the coach only a stroke, but it is enough to make Word partially blind and to give him a frightful voice ("like that of a man in a cave of wasps"). Such is French's charisma that

Word loves him all the more, following him from tournament to tournament, his voice bleating above the crowd and—"crazed with partisanship"— pinching French with pride after each victory. Even worse, French's mother still loves Word, a fact that drives French to desperation. Grappling with Word above a river, French drops off the bridge with the old man. Word is no worse for the experience, but French is brain-damaged.

Now cared for by Dr. Baby Levaster, a former high school tennis teammate and another admirer of tennis handsomes, French wanders the tennis circuit in search of the ineffable. During a match in Boston, lightning strikes his metal racket, turning French "radiant as a silver-plated statue" and somewhat psychic and, for a time, clearing his damaged brain. He even begins to write poetry, though only bawdy doggerel. French continues to seek these crystalline moments. Meanwhile, separated from his wife Cecelia, French finds comfort with a crippled woman named Inez, a Cuban polio victim who becomes pregnant with his child. In spite of being in a wheelchair, Inez also comforts Levaster. In fact, Levaster finds carnal comfort with practically anyone he can, including French's mother, Olive, and a woman named Beth Battrick, who has been having an affair with her nephew, Bobby Smith, a Vietnam veteran haunted by his past.

Smith's story, previously published in both *Esquire* and *Airships* as "Midnight and I'm Not Famous Yet," recounts his capture and subsequent killing of Li Dap, a North Vietnamese general, and the loss of Smith's friend Tubby Wooten. Returned from the war and in love with his aunt, Smith has become entwined in the lives of French and Levaster. The aunt, after nearly being raped by a walrus, runs off with a Southern senator. Inez dies in childbirth. Word dies of natural causes in Smith's car, and Smith dumps him off a bridge near Vicksburg. French, looking for the ultimate fix, almost electrocutes himself by clamping onto battery cables. Cecelia, angered at Levaster's refusal to give up French's baby (which has passed from Inez to Smith to Levaster), murders Levaster with a crossbow. Smith, having seen senseless devastation before, somehow survives along with French.

The zaniness of Hannah's narrative—Carson McCullers rewritten by Groucho Marx, as one reviewer put it—is entertainment enough, but there may even be message in his madness. The American reverence for athletic prowess, Hannah suggests, is a kind of misplaced religious awe with a dose of sexual longing, as slightly off-center as Bobby Smith's passion for his own aunt. French Edward, a Christ-figure in shorts and sneakers, is both saintly and visionary, capable of arousing desire in both sexes, and tennis, like war, is a field of combat where courage, victory, and defeat are exhibited. Like all athletes, French helps the spectator to define himself through the athlete's continual Christlike struggles.

Between *The Tennis Handsome* and Hannah's next two novels came his second volume of short stories, *Captain Maximus*. In some of those stories he pays homage to Ernest Hemingway and Richard Hugo, two American authors who confront personal experience directly and write about it with honest sentiment. Hannah attempts to do the same in *Hey Jack!* and *Boomerang*, and both novels are a radical departure from his earlier work. Hannah abandons the wildly exuberant comic style of the earlier works for a more measured and direct prose, his narrator seems closer to Hannah himself (the narrator of *Boomerang* is called Barry), and his characters seem drawn more directly from experience than from the imagination.

The Jack of *Hey Jack!* is a seventy-seven-year-old café owner, a former war correspondent, Kentucky sheriff, college professor of criminal science, and Mississippi cattleman. The plot of the novel involves Jack's daughter, a forty-year-old schoolteacher named Alice, who is seeing rock star Ronnie Foot against her father's wishes. Foot, a kind of Elvis Presley from Hell, is a cocaine-snorting egotist who lives in a large mansion with Gramps, an alcoholic redneck who likes to shoot his .22 rifle at the chickens and people outside. Foot, who has a history of using and destroying women, abuses and humiliates Alice, turns her into a drug addict, and kills her with Gramps's .22 while trying to shoot a Coca-Cola bottle off her head. On trial for murder, Foot hangs himself in his cell. The novel is a tribute to men such as Jack and the narrator, Homer, who are like the First Marine Division at Chosin, site of the great Korean War battle in which Homer fought thirty years earlier and which still haunts his dreams: they dig in, attack when they can, bury their dead, and learn to survive.

Boomerang, another novel of survival, again attempts to deal with life's past and present pains. Like the actual boomerang that the narrator finds and learns how to control, past experiences that one has tried to cast away come back to strengthen and instruct the narrator, whose name by this sixth novel has become "Barry." From Harry to Barry, Hannah's voice has been at the center of his narratives, connecting past with present, viewing life's experiences with black humor and irreverence, and involving the reader in his hatreds, loves, failures, and many moods. By this sixth novel, that voice is hard to distinguish from that of the author, for it confronts the reader directly with shared experiences in straightforward, unadorned prose. While Hannah's writing gains strength from the realistic characters and situations, *Boomerang* as a whole lacks the unpredictability and lyric humor of his earlier writings, and the sentiment often teeters into the maudlin.

Nevertheless, Barry Hannah remains one of America's most original talents, a Southern regionalist whose hilarious, weird, and very human characters shock readers into recognition of themselves, a lover of the English language who, as he has said, is always trying to get as much as he can out of words.

Kenneth Seib

Other major works

SHORT FICTION: *Airships*, 1978; *Captain Maximus*, 1985.

Bibliography

Hannah, Barry. "The Spirits Will Win Through." Interview by R. Vanarsdall. *The Southern Review* 19 (Spring, 1983): 317-341. An indispensable interview conducted April 27, 1982, in Oxford, Mississippi, where Hannah is writer-in-residence at the University of Mississippi. Hannah talks of his influences—Walker Percy, Hemingway, Faulkner, James Joyce, Thomas Wolfe—and his friendships with Jimmy Buffet, Thomas McGuane, Richard Brautigan, and others, as well as voicing his thoughts on writing and life.

Hill, Robert. "Barry Hannah." *South Carolina Review* 9 (November, 1976): 25-29. Hill finds that, in the midst of "some of the most baroque plots this side of *Titus Andronicus*," Hannah is one of the United States' best stylists, a writer whose works are filled with memorable characters and meaningful, though random, experiences.

Madden, David. "Barry Hannah's *Geronimo Rex* in Retrospect." *The Southern Review* 19 (Spring, 1983): 309-316. Madden once found *Geronimo Rex* "the best first novel I've ever reviewed." Considering it again ten years later, he agrees with his original assessment, but now finds it lacking an intellectual framework and a "conceptualizing imagination."

Noble, Donald R. "'Tragic and Meaningful to an Insane Degree': Barry Hannah." *Southern Literary Journal* 15 (Fall, 1982): 37-44. Noble finds Hannah's vision split: while he believes that the world is chaotic and disconnected, Hannah still seems to have an abundant comic spirit and love of life. Hannah holds his readers not by his vision but by the power of his voice, that of a "jazz speaker" who plays with words the way a musician plays with notes.

Updike, John. "From Dyna Domes to Turkey-Pressing." *The New Yorker* 48 (September 9, 1972): 121-124. Updike, one of the United States' best novelists in the late twentieth century, places Hannah's *Geronimo Rex* in the 1950's tradition of "the whining adolescent novel." Nevertheless, he admires Hannah's energy, style, and "morbid zest."

ELIZABETH HARDWICK

Born: Lexington, Kentucky; July 27, 1916

Principal long fiction
The Ghostly Lover, 1945; *The Simple Truth*, 1955; *Sleepless Nights*, 1979.

Other literary forms
Elizabeth Hardwick's book reviews and literary and cultural criticism have been her most influential work. Her frank, fresh, intellectually audacious, and emotionally engaging comments provided a comprehensive critique of literary and popular culture. Her baroque style and contextual approach, yoking history with art, was formative in developing the particular brand of progressive criticism characteristic of *The New York Review of Books* and in the tradition of the *Partisan Review*, bent upon restoring texture and depth to reviewing. Her most influential essays from 1952 to 1961 were collected from the *Partisan Review*, *Harper's*, *Encounter*, *The New Republic*, and *The New York Times Book Review*, as well as *The New York Review of Books*, in a volume entitled *A View of My Own: Essays on Literature and Society* (1962), suggesting in the allusion to Virginia Woolf her intensely personal approach to criticism. Hardwick's long-standing interest in feminist issues is reflected in her second collection of essays, *Seduction and Betrayal: Women and Literature* (1974). A third collection, *Bartleby in Manhattan and Other Essays*, appeared in 1983.

An important Hardwick essay, "Domestic Manners in a New America," perhaps best illustrates the connections between the public and the private self which she defined as "style," a key concept which informs both her cultural criticism and her fiction. Appearing first in *Daedalus* (Winter, 1978), and later in an anthology of influential articles by social commentators—*A New America?* (1979), edited by Stephen R. Graubard—Hardwick's essay delineates the alterations in contemporary culture brought about by "the power of external forces" and a particular sort of inner change, a new expectation for the private life. The interior perception of life as a long process, one governed by cycles and seasons, is transformed by the deviation and dislocation of contemporary urban life, "the shortened life of the feelings" evidenced in the prevalent failure of will in human relationships, rules, customs, and habits. Hardwick sees in personal "style" the traumatic effects of modernity; for her, as for Jane Austen, style defines moral condition.

Achievements
Hardwick's criticism engaged not only literary culture but also the wider group of committed intellectuals seeking synthesis between the diverse, ap-

parently dislocated, aspects of contemporary life. Prominent in her critical ideology is the assumption that a substructure of history, biology, and psychology underlies the complex edifice of contemporary culture, a foundation which the critic must show as informing, though not determining, the work. Coupled with this multidisciplinary approach is that process of dynamically yoking together disparate thoughts and feelings in such a way that a new synthesis or a hidden foundation is revealed. This juxtaposition, similar in so many ways to that of the metaphysical poets, has the effect of constantly recombining and transforming experience.

The matter of style seems a crucial point in Hardwick's work, both style as a concept and Hardwick's own yoking of dissimilarities, startling the reader with its expressive, mercurial quality, capturing the play of a mind at work. Her writing frequently has a baroque quality—loose passages coupled with short, pithy statements. Capturing the qualities of supreme thoughtfulness along with engaged feeling, her work creates a sharp effect, combining an almost audacious assertiveness with demure understatement. Her conversational colloquialisms, playful and expressive, appear in Hardwick's conceptual framework as "style," that self-presentation by which the interior, one's relationship to history, is revealed.

The other key concept in her thought and practice is that of the "radical," not in the political sense, but meaning a return, often an intellectually jarring return, to the crux of a creative work or a received idea. Certain writers such as Mary McCarthy possess what Hardwick called a "radical" vision, always unconventional, often involving a moral stance. Characters become emblems of these root qualities, as in the "radical innocence" of Rudy Peck in *The Simple Truth*. The ability of a writer or a critic to go to the crux of a problem, to perceive something not marked before, to have a genuinely new thought which brings together known facts in surprising ways, was for Hardwick the hallmark of the intellectual and creative life.

Hardwick was the recipient of many awards for creative and critical achievement, including a Guggenheim Fellowship and the George Jean Nathan Award for drama criticism.

Biography

Elizabeth Hardwick's own life provides a model of the committed intellectual, demonstrating the dialectic between history and the imagination, thought and feeling, which informs her essays and fiction. Born in Lexington, Kentucky, on July 27, 1916, one of the eleven children of Eugene Allen and Mary Ramsey Hardwick, she attended public schools and then the University of Kentucky. The sense of place so strong in Hardwick appears especially in her early work, the substructure of Kentucky rootedness juxtaposed to the restless, mobile style of middle-class yearnings. The opposite pole is New York, the "Lourdes" of cities, which educates and informs the self. Although alert to and appreciative of Southern literature, Hardwick nevertheless spoke of herself, in a letter of September, 1982, as never having felt drawn to being a Southern writer, but instead toward "the vague, but somewhat meaningful notion of the 'intellectual.'" In her later work, far from the dreamy Southern settings of her first novel, with its matriarchal, mythical grandmother, the interwoven lives of black and white, the cockfights, the wild youth, and, finally, the journey to the wider world of the university and the city itself, Hardwick perhaps epitomizes for many the urban intellectual style.

Hardwick's radical criticism and progressive aesthetic developed from her study of literature and culture, from graduate study at Columbia and the early influence of the *Partisan Review*, an intellectual milieu which she describes as a "combination of radical political ideas of a complicated kind and avant-garde literature." This method was not formalistic or belletristic but always represented the paradoxical product of the progressive politics of the *Partisan Review* and the particular intellectuality and wit of the metaphysical poetry which enjoyed a revival at the time. Hardwick's aesthetic was also influenced by her long teaching career, at Barnard and at other places, including Columbia Graduate School of the Arts, where she taught creative writing. Many of her essays have the flavor of classroom interchange, a flash of contact between mentor and student, a dynamic oral quality, and a sense of extemporaneous composition, sometimes with inserts and headings like a teacher's lecture notes.

Much of Hardwick's later creative work is an imaginative reconstruction of personal experience, the encounter of the individual with others and the world in modern history. Her marriage to the poet Robert Lowell in July, 1949, exemplified in some ways that special relationship between two creative people which the two of them found in George Eliot and Henry Lewes. Lowell and Hardwick shared not only their intellectual background but also their political commitment, evident in Lowell's indictment for conscientious objection to militarism. In his *Notebook 1967-68* (1969), Lowell writes of Eliot and Lewes: "Writers marry/their kind still, true and one and clashing," and upon his own twenty-year marriage: "We stand set; two trees, their roots," recalling shared lives, age, friendships, illness, and war, and many cities—Boston, Maine, and New York. "I was then a 'we,'" Hardwick says in *Sleepless Nights*. Her marriage to Lowell ended in divorce in 1972, to be followed by his death in 1977. Of their only child, Harriet Winslow Lowell, Hardwick spoke of feeling a "passion almost criminal."

Analysis

In her three published novels, Elizabeth Hardwick demonstrates the complex interplay between the buried life of the emotions, "the cemetery of home, education, nerves, heritage, and tics," and the emerging life in which the individual seeks self-definition by her own consciousness, her sense of autonomy and transcendence. The protagonist of *The Ghostly Lover*, Hardwick's first novel, is an obviously autobiographical figure. Marian, slowly coming to terms with family and hometown boyfriend, pursues her somewhat foggy destiny far from her Southern home in a city university. She has depended on two illusions: that she can only be supported by some outside force, usually a man, and that she must herself support her two rootless parents, who have abandoned her and her brother since childhood. Parents, powerful in the imagination but in life weak and absent, first the "savage's totem" from which "being and power" are derived, are lost in pursuit of the American dream. Her mother, who has "been in too many places, had lives in too many houses, and been neighbor to too many people," represents in her unformed femininity that immanence of which Simone de Beauvoir speaks, a "guide for the preordained destiny of the daughter" from which Marian must extricate herself at the end, when she is asked to loan the inheritance money on which her journey to the city depends. Likewise she must reject Bruce, the father-lover of her adolescence who, replacing her own father, pays for her tuition, and then Leo, the city boyfriend, more a peer, but yet representing an escape into marriage and safety. The grandmother, who has reared the children, is an inscrutable matriarch in whom the archaic powers of home and family are located. She personifies that "animal nature," "the hidden violence of union between the two sexes"; her experience, unredeemed by thought and judgment, is found to be not mysterious but simply illiterate.

In a reversal of the traditional scheme, the shy, repressed girl escapes, while the wild, resourceful brother, Albert, is trapped in the family home, conveniently married to a dumpy, unimaginative town girl. Hattie, the black servant girl, is Marian's black double, the frightening other whose stubborn autonomy is at once fearful ("black sinfulness") and attractive. Other women complete her initiation into the underworld of female possibility—neighbor Mary, mother's friend, with her secret abortion; Gertrude, the German library-science student, lost in the anonymous city; another woman friend who attaches herself pathetically to a man. Moving from the deceptive paradise of childhood to the necessary reality of the adult world, she arrives finally at Grand Central again, meeting the objective correlative of her condition, an "icy ray of light," no man to meet her, "separated . . . forever from him [Leo] and his shelter like the forbidden gates of Eden," self-created at last.

Published in 1955 and dedicated to her mother, Hardwick's second novel, *The Simple Truth*, concerns moral initiation in a Midwestern university town, a location symbolic of American culture and Midwestern space and disconnection, marked by psychological introspection and personal anonymity. Rudy Peck, a university student and the son of Finnish immigrants, himself an "anonymous creation" aspiring to selfhood, has murdered his upper-class girl friend. The girl friend was an adventurer, self-created in her own uniqueness and style, a quality well noted by Doris Parks, whose Austenesque "true sturdiness" and acute moral sensibility involve her at once as evaluator of the moral landscape in which Rudy, "innocently guilty," is acquitted. In this variation on the traditional seduction and betrayal motif, Rudy, a serious, thoughtful young man, is, like Theodore Dreiser's Clyde Griffiths, finally not morally accountable. The trial draws the obsessive attention of Doris' husband Joseph, a bumbling, sensitive, aspiring writer of ambiguous possibilities, and Anita Mitchell, a small-town faculty wife seeking escape from her limiting environment of "beefsteak, peas, and whiskey"; both Joseph and Anita see in Rudy an expression of their own unresolved condition. At the close of the novel, Doris, whose perspective has gradually become that of the narrator, recognizes the distinct moral spheres she and Joseph occupy and, with a few tears, accepts her own independence and aloneness, one of the "new women" setting out in the politically and psychologically ambivalent American landscape.

Hardwick's third novel, *Sleepless Nights*, published in 1979, reconstructs personal experience not in the confessional mode associated with Robert Lowell, but as a piece of "transformed and even distorted memory," in a series of communications to a friend, "Mary McC" (Mary McCarthy). From contemplation of her rag rug, "product of a broken old woman in a squalid nursing home," the narrator examines the combination of deprivation and survival, loss and preservation in the histories of the "unfortunate ones"— Juanita the prostitute, bag ladies, spinsters, cleaning women, Billie Holiday, and the new woman Marie—with a mixture of "sympathy and bewilderment" at their shared "fateful fertility" on the one hand, and, on the other, "the old, profound acceptance of the things of life." In an aura of intimate conversation, they confront broken veins, disease, backbreaking work, selfdestruction, divorce, separation, boredom, and perhaps autonomy.

Hardwick's perspective demands connection and sympathy, not the detachment of either irony or sentimentality. Submerged female life, the other side of time-conscious, outer-directed material culture, becomes emblematic, as female weeping becomes the "weeping sores" of the ulcerated legs, the shame and poverty lurking under the intricate surface detail. Hardwick's own childhood, her Columbia homesickness and friends, the life in Maine, Boston, and New York, the "lifetime of worrying and reading," are fused in memory with the paradoxical power and tenacity of the buried life, as the woman, now no longer young, traverses the final sections of the journey into "strange parts of town" fundamental to her creativity and connectedness.

Janet Polansky

Other major works

NONFICTION: *Selected Letters of William James*, 1961 (edited); *A View of My Own: Essays on Literature and Society*, 1962; *Seduction and Betrayal:*

Women and Literature, 1974; *Rediscovered Fiction by American Women: A Personal Selection*, 1977 (edited, 18 volumes); *Bartleby in Manhattan and Other Essays*, 1983.

Bibliography

Bryfonski, Dedria, ed. *Contemporary Literary Criticism*. Vol. 13. Detroit: Gale Research, 1980. Presents a sampling of reviews from such sources as *The Sewanee Review* for Hardwick's second novel, *The Simple Truth*; *The New York Times Book Review* for *Sleepless Nights*; and several reviews on her work *Seduction and Betrayal: Women and Literature*, for which she received much praise.

Kibler, James E., Jr., ed. *Dictionary of Literary Biography*. Vol. 6. Detroit: Gale Research, 1980. Discusses Hardwick's novels, from *The Ghostly Lover* to *Sleepless Nights*. Includes background information on Hardwick's upbringing in Kentucky and the effect on her writing after her move to the sophistication of New York. Mentions her long and successful career as a social and literary critic, but also notes the lack of development in her novels. A useful introduction to Hardwick, as there is currently no full-length study on her work.

Miller, Jane. *Women Writing About Men*. London: Virago Press, 1986. In her chapter, "Resisting the Bullies," Miller mentions Hardwick's book, *Seduction and Betrayal: Women and Literature*, and its reference to women who become heroes by gaining mastery over their husbands. In so doing, she places Hardwick in the genre of women writers—such as Virginia Woolf— who write about women striving for recognition in their own right.

Stone, Laurie. "Hardwick's Way." *The Village Voice*, May 7, 1979, 98-100. "I have almost nothing negative to say about this book," says Stone in this appreciative review of Hardwick's novel *Sleepless Nights*. Also comments on the feminist theme in Hardwick's work *Seduction and Betrayal: Women and Literature*.

THOMAS HARDY

Born: Higher Bockhampton, England; June 2, 1840
Died: Dorchester, England; January 11, 1928

Principal long fiction

Desperate Remedies, 1871; *Under the Greenwood Tree*, 1872; *A Pair of Blue Eyes*, 1872-1873; *Far from the Madding Crowd*, 1874; *The Hand of Ethelberta*, 1875-1876; *The Return of the Native*, 1878; *The Trumpet-Major*, 1880; *A Laodicean*, 1880-1881; *Two on a Tower*, 1882; *The Mayor of Casterbridge*, 1886; *The Woodlanders*, 1886-1887; *Tess of the D'Urbervilles*, 1891; *Jude the Obscure*, 1895; *The Well-Beloved*, 1897.

Other literary forms

In addition to his novels, Thomas Hardy published four collections of short stories, *Wessex Tales* (1888), *A Group of Noble Dames* (1891), *Life's Little Ironies* (1894), and *A Changed Man* (1913). In the latter part of his life, after he had stopped writing novels altogether, he published approximately a thousand poems in eight separate volumes which have since been collected in one volume by his publisher, Macmillan & Company. In addition to this staggering body of work, Hardy also published an epic-drama of the Napoleonic wars in three parts between 1903 and 1908 entitled *The Dynasts*, a play entitled *The Famous Tragedy of the Queen of Cornwall* (1923), and a series of essays on fiction and other topics, which have been collected in individual volumes. All the novels and stories are available in a uniform library edition in eighteen volumes, published in the early 1960's by Macmillan & Company. Finally, *The Early Life of Thomas Hardy* (1928) and *The Later Years of Thomas Hardy* (1930), although ostensibly a two-volume biography of Hardy by his second wife, Florence Hardy, is generally recognized to be Hardy's own autobiography compiled from his notes in his last few years.

Achievements

Hardy is second only to Charles Dickens as the most written-about and discussed writer of the Victorian era. At least one new book and dozens of articles appear on his work every year. Certainly in terms of volume and diversity alone, Hardy is a towering literary figure with two admirable careers—one as novelist and one as poet—to justify his position.

Interest in Hardy's work has followed two basic patterns. The first was philosophical, with many critics creating metaphysical structures that supposedly underlay his fiction. In the last two decades, however, interest has shifted to that aspect of Hardy's work most scorned before—his technical facility and generic experimentation. Only in the last few years has what once was termed fictional clumsiness been reevaluated in terms of poetic technique.

Furthermore, Hardy's career as a poet, which has always been under the shadow of his fiction, has been reevaluated. Hardy was a curious blend of the old-fashioned and the modern. With a career that began in the Victorian era and did not end until after World War I, Hardy was contemporary both with Matthew Arnold and with T. S. Eliot. Critics such as Babette Deutsch and Vivian De Sola Pinto claim that Hardy bridged the gulf between the Victorian sensibility and the modern era. In his unflinching confrontation with meaninglessness in the universe, Hardy embodied Albert Camus' description of the absurd creator in *The Myth of Sisyphus* (1942); he rebelled against the chaos of the world by asserting his own freedom to persist in spite of that meaninglessness.

Hardy was a great existential humanist. His hope for humanity was that man would realize that creeds and conventions which presupposed a god-oriented center of value were baseless. He hoped that man would loosen himself from those foolish hopes and creeds and become aware of his freedom to create his own value. If man would only realize, Hardy felt, that all people were equally alone and without hope for divine help, then perhaps man would realize also that it was the height of absurdity for such lost and isolated creatures to fight among themselves.

Biography

Thomas Hardy was born in the small hamlet of Higher Bockhampton in Stinsford parish on June 2, 1840. His father was a master mason, content with his low social status and at home in his rural surroundings. His mother, however, who Hardy once called "a born bookworm," made Hardy aware of his low social status and encouraged his education. John Hicks, a friend of Hardy's father and a Dorchester architect, took the boy on as a pupil at the age of sixteen. The well-known poet William Barnes had a school next door to Hicks's office, and Hardy developed an influential friendship with the older man that remained with him. Another early influence on the young Hardy was Horace Moule, a classical scholar with a Cambridge education who was an essayist and reviewer. Moule introduced Hardy to intellectual conversation about Greek literature as well as contemporary issues; it was at Moule's suggestion that Hardy read John Stuart Mill as well as the infamous *Essays and Reviews* (1860, Reverend Henry Bristow Wilson, editor), both of which contributed to the undermining of Hardy's simple religious faith.

Hardy was twenty-two when he went to London to pursue his architectural training. By that time he also entertained literary ambitions and had begun writing poetry. The publication of A. C. Swinburne's *Poems and Ballads* in 1866 so influenced Hardy that he began a two-year period of intensive study and experimentation in writing poetry; none of the many poems he sent out was accepted, however, and he returned to Bockhampton in 1867. It was at this point that Hardy decided to turn to writing fiction. In his old age, he wrote in a letter that he never wanted to write novels at all, but that circumstances compelled him to turn them out.

Hardy's first fictional effort, *The Poor Man and the Lady*, based on the contrast between London and rural life, received some favorable responses from publishers, but after a discussion with George Meredith, Hardy decided not to publish it, and instead, on Meredith's advice, wrote *Desperate Remedies* in imitation of the detective style of Wilkie Collins. Later, eager to publish works that would establish his career as a writer, Hardy took the advice of a reader who liked the rural scenes in his unpublished novel and wrote the pastoral idyll, *Under the Greenwood Tree*. The book was well received by the critics, but sales were poor. One editor advised him to begin writing serials for periodical publication. With the beginning of *A Pair of Blue Eyes*, Hardy said good-bye to architecture as a profession and devoted the rest of his life to writing.

In 1874, Hardy married Emma Lavinia Gifford, a dynamic and socially ambitious young woman who shared his interests in books. In the meantime, *Far from the Madding Crowd* had appeared to many favorable reviews, and editors began asking for Hardy's work. While living with his wife in a cottage at Sturminster Newton, Hardy composed *The Return of the Native* and enjoyed what he later called the happiest years of his life. Hardy and his wife began a social life in London until he became ill and they decided to return to Dorset, where, while writing *The Mayor of Casterbridge*, he had his home, "Max Gate," built. For the next several years, Hardy continued his writing, traveled with his wife, and read German philosophy.

His enthusiasm for *Tess of the D'Urbervilles* was dampened when it was turned down by two editors before being accepted for serial publication by a third. The publication of the work brought hostile reaction and notoriety— a notoriety that increased after the publication of *Jude the Obscure*. Hardy was both puzzled and cynical about these reactions, but he was by then financially secure and decided to return to his first love: for the rest of his life he wrote no more fiction, but concentrated solely on poetry. His volumes of poetry were well received, and his experiment with metaphysics in the epic-drama, *The Dynasts*, brought him even more respect, honor, and fame. These final years of Hardy's life appear to have been spoiled only by the death of his wife in 1912. Within four years, however, he married Florence Dugdale, who had been a friend of the family and had done secretarial work for him. She cared for him for the remainder of his life. Hardy continued to write poetry regularly. His final volume of poems, *Winter Words*, was ready to be published when he died on January 11, 1928. His ashes were placed in Westminster Abbey.

Analysis

In *The Courage to Be* (1952), Paul Tillich has said that "the decisive event which underlies the search for meaning and the despair of it in the twentieth century is the loss of God in the nineteenth century." Most critics of the literature of the nineteenth century have accepted this notion and have established a new perspective for studying the period by demonstrating that what is now referred to as the "modern situation" or the "modern artistic dilemma" actually began with the breakup of a value-ordered universe in the Romantic period. Thomas Hardy, both in philosophical attitude and artistic technique, firmly belongs in this modern tradition.

It is a critical commonplace that at the beginning of his literary career Hardy experienced a loss of belief in a divinely ordered universe. The impact of this loss on Hardy cannot be overestimated. In his childhood recollections he appears as an extremely sensitive boy who attended church so regularly that he knew the service by heart, and who firmly believed in a personal and just God who ruled the universe and took cognizance of the situation of man. Consequently, when he came to London in his twenties and was exposed to the concept of a demythologized religion in the *Essays and Reviews* and the valueless nontelelogical world of Charles Darwin's *On the Origin of Species by Means of Natural Selection* (1859), the loss of his childhood god was a traumatic experience.

What is often called Hardy's philosophy can be summed up in one of his earliest notebook entries in 1865: "The world does not despise us; it only neglects us." An interpretation of any of Hardy's novels must begin with this assumption. The difference between Hardy and other nineteenth century artists who experienced a similar loss of belief is that while others were able to achieve a measure of faith—William Wordsworth reaffirmed an organic concept of nature and of the creative mind which can penetrate it, and Thomas Carlyle finally entered the Everlasting Yea with a similar affirmation of nature as alive and progressive—Hardy never made such an affirmative leap to transcendent value. Hardy was more akin to another romantic figure, Samuel Taylor Coleridge's Ancient Mariner, who, having experienced the nightmarish chaos of a world without meaning or value, can never fully get back into an ordered world again.

Hardy was constantly trying to find a way out of his isolated dilemma, constantly trying to find a value to which he could cling in a world of accident, chance, and meaningless indifference. Since he refused to give in to hope for an external value, however, he refused to submit to illusions of transcendence; the only possibility for him was to find some kind of value in the emptiness itself. Like the Ancient Mariner, all Hardy had was his story of loss and despair, chaos and meaninglessness. If value were to be found at all, it lay in the complete commitment to this story—"facing the worst," and playing it back over and over again, exploring its implications, making others aware of its truth. Consequently, Hardy's art can be seen as a series of variations in form on this one barren theme of loss and chaos—"questionings in the exploration of reality."

While Hardy could imitate popular forms and create popular novels such as *Desperate Remedies*, an imitation of Wilkie Collins' detective novel, or *The Hand of Ethelberta*, an imitation of the social comedy popular at the time, when he wished to write a serious novel, one that would truly express his vision of man's situation in the universe, he could find no adequate model in the novels of his contemporaries. He solved this first basic problem in his search for form by returning to the tragic drama of the Greek and Elizabethan ages—a mode with which he was familiar through extensive early reading. Another Greek and Elizabethan mode he used, although he was less conscious of its literary tradition, was the pastoral narrative—a natural choice because of its surface similarity to his own subject matter of isolated country settings and innocent country people.

Hardy's second problem in the search for form arose from the incompatibility between the classical tragic vision and his own uniquely modern view. The classical writers saw man within a stable and ordered religious and social context, while Hardy saw man isolated, alone, searching for meaning in a world that offered none. Because Hardy denied the static and ordered worldview of the past, he was in turn denied the broad context of myth, symbol, and ritual which stemmed from that view. Lost without a God-ordered mythos, Hardy had to create a modern myth that presupposed the absence of God; he needed a pattern. Hardy's use of the traditional patterns of tragedy and pastoral, combined with his rejection of the old mythos that formerly gave meaning to these patterns, resulted in a peculiar distortion as his novels transcended their original patterns.

Nature in Hardy's "pastoral" novels, *The Woodlanders* and *Far from the Madding Crowd*, is neither benevolent nor divinely ordered. Similarly, the human dilemma in his "tragic" novels, *The Return of the Native* and *The Mayor of Casterbridge*, is completely antithetical to what it was for the dramatists of the past. The Greek hero was tragic because he violated a cosmic order; Hardy's heroes are tragic precisely because there is no such order. For the Greek hero there is a final reconciliation which persuades him to submit to the world. For Hardy's hero there is only the never-ending dialectic between man's nostalgia for value and the empty, indifferent world.

In *Tess of the D'Urbervilles* and *Jude the Obscure*, Hardy rejected the traditional tragic and pastoral patterns and allowed the intrinsic problem of his two protagonists to order the chaotic elements of the works. The structure of these novels can be compared to that of the epic journey of Wordsworth in *The Prelude* (1850) and Coleridge in *The Rime of the Ancient Mariner* (1798). As the critic Morse Peckham has said in *Beyond the Tragic Vision: The Quest for Identity in the Nineteenth Century* (1962), the task of the nineteenth century artist was no longer to find an external controlling form, but to "symbolize the orientative drive itself, the power of the individual to maintain his identity by creating order which would maintain his gaze at the world as it is, at things as they are." The loss of order is reflected in the structure of *Tess of the D'Urbervilles*, as the young heroine is literally evicted from the familiarity of her world and must endure the nightmarish wandering process of trying to get back inside. The structuring drive of *Jude the Obscure* is Jude's search for an external order that will rid him of the anguish of his own gratuitousness.

Hardy's first important novel, *Far from the Madding Crowd*, was the first in which he successfully adapted a traditional form, the pastoral, to his own purposes, greatly altering it in the process. In *Elizabethan Poetry: A Study in Conventions, Meaning and Expression* (1952), Hallet Smith has described the pastoral as constituting the ideal of the good life: in the pastoral world, nature is the true home of man; the gods take an active concern in man's welfare; the inhabitants of this world are content and self-sufficient. The plot complications of the pastoral usually arise by the intrusion of an aspiring mind from the outside, an antipastoral force which seeks to overthrow the idyllic established order. On the surface, *Far from the Madding Crowd* conforms perfectly to this definition of the pastoral. The story is set in an agricultural community; the main character is a shepherd; the bulk of the inhabitants are content with their lives. The plot complications arise from the intrusion of the antipastoral Sergeant Troy and the love of three different men for the pastoral maid, Bathsheba. To see the novel as a true pastoral, however, is to ignore living form in order to see a preestablished pattern. The pastoral ideal cannot be the vision of this novel because Hardy was struggling with the active tension between man's hopes and the world's indifference.

Far from the Madding Crowd begins in a lighthearted mood with the comic situation of Gabriel Oak's unsuccessful attempts to woo the fickle maid Bathsheba, but Oak, often called the stabilizing force in the novel, is an ambiguous figure. Although he is described as both a biblical and a classical shepherd, he is unequivocally neither. Moreover, the first section of the novel hovers between tragedy and comedy. Even the "pastoral tragedy," the "murder" of all of Gabriel's sheep by the foolish young dog, is equivocal; the dog is not so much destroyed for his crime as he is executed. Gabriel's character, as well as the entire tone of the novel, shifts after this short prologue. When he next appears he is no longer the contented shepherd with modest ambitions; rather, he has developed the indifference to fate and fortune which, Hardy says, "though it often makes a villain of a man, is the basis of his sublimity when it does not."

The change that takes place in Gabriel is caused by his loss and is more significant than the change in Bathsheba because of her gain of an inheritance. Bathsheba, a typical pastoral coquette in the prologue of the novel, makes an ostensible shift when she inherits a farm of her own, but she is still coquettish and vain enough to be piqued by Farmer William Boldwood's indifference to her charms and to send him the valentine saying "Marry Me." Boldwood, "the nearest approach to aristocracy that this remote quarter of the parish could boast of," is a serious, self-sufficient man who sees "no absurd side to the follies of life." The change the valentine causes in him is so extreme as to be comic.

The Bathsheba-Gabriel relationship is complicated by this new wooer. In this section of the novel, until the appearance of Sergeant Troy, there appears a series of scenes in which Gabriel, Boldwood, and Bathsheba are frozen into a tableau with the ever-present sheep in the background. The death and physical suffering of the sheep take on a sinister, grotesque imagery to make an ironic commentary on the absurdity of man's ephemeral passions in a world dominated by cruelty and death. The irrationality of physical passion is more evident when Bathsheba is overwhelmed by Troy. Their relationship begins with the feminine frill of her dress being caught in his masculine spur and blossoms with her submission to his dazzling sword exercises. After Boldwood's complete demoralization and the marriage of Bathsheba and Troy, the antipastoral Troy corrupts the innocent harvest festival until it becomes a wild frenzy and then a drunken stupor. The pastoral world of the "good life" is turned upside down as the approaching storm transforms the landscape into something sinister. It is significant that the rustics are asleep during the storm, for they are truly unaware of the sickness of the world and its sinister aspect. Troy, too, is unaware of the storm, as he is always unaware of an incongruity between man and the indifferent world. Only Gabriel, Bathsheba, and Boldwood, the involved and suffering characters of the novel, react to this symbolic storm.

Just as the death of the sheep formed the ever-present background to the first two parts of the novel, the death of Fanny Robin dominates the third section. From the time her body begins its journey in Joseph Poorgrass' wagon until the "Gurgoyle" washes Troy's flowers off her grave, death becomes the most important character in the book. By far the most important effect of Fanny Robin's death is on Bathsheba. When she opens the coffin to find out that Fanny was pregnant with Troy's child, the scene is "like an illusion raised by some fiendish incantation." Her running away to seclude herself in the wood is called by many critics her reconciliation with the natural world of the pastoral, but this view is wholly untenable: her retreat is on the edge of a swamp of which the "general aspect was malignant." There is no pastoral goodness about the hollow in which she hides. It is a "nursery of pestilences. . . . From its moist and poisonous coat seemed to be exhaled the essences of evil things in the earth." This is one of those grotesque situations in which man becomes aware of his isolated state, when his need for solace in the natural world is met with only indifference, when he becomes aware of the absurdity of his demands on a barren and empty world. Bathsheba changes after her experience in this "boundary situation"; she gains the awareness which has characterized Gabriel all along.

After this climactic scene of confrontation with the indifferent world, the book loses its focus. In a diffuse and overlong denouement, Boldwood presses his advantage with Bathsheba until the night of the party, when she is on the point of giving in. Troy's return at this moment and his murder by Boldwood seems forced and melodramatic. Bathsheba's return to marry Gabriel is a concession to the reading public as much as it is to the pastoral pattern of the novel itself. *Far from the Madding Crowd*, a fable of the barrenness and death of the pastoral world and the tragic results of wrong choice through the irrationality of sexual attraction, truly ends with Bathsheba's isolation and painful new awareness in the pestilent swamp.

The Woodlanders, although more explicit in its imagistic presentation of the unhealthy natural world and more complex in its conflicts of irrational sexual attraction, manifests much of the same kind of formal distortion as is found in *Far from the Madding Crowd*. The world of Little Hintock, far from being the ideal pastoral world, is even more valueless, more inimical a world than Weatherbury. Instead of the grotesque death of sheep, trees become the symbolic representation of man's absurd situation in an empty world. Little Hintock is a wasteland, a world of darkness, isolation, guilt, and human cross-purposes. One's nostrils are always filled with the odor of dead leaves, fermenting cider, and heavy, blossomy perfume. One cannot breathe or stretch out one's arms in this world. The so-called "natural" inhabitants of the Wood are dissatisfied with the nature of the world around them. Grace's father, Mr. Melbury, cramped and crippled by his lifetime struggle to make his living from the trees, wants his daughter to be able to escape such a world by marrying an outsider. A conflict is created, though, by the guilt he feels for a wrong he did to Giles Winterborne's father; he tries to atone for it by promising Grace to Giles. John South, Marty's father, on whose life the landholdings of Giles depend, is neurotically afraid of the huge tree in his yard. The tree takes on a symbolic aura as representative of the uncontrollable force of the natural world.

Furthermore, the sophisticated outsiders in the novel are cut off from the world they inhabit and are imaged as "unnatural." Strange unnatural lights can be seen from the house of the young Dr. Fitzpiers, who is said to be in league with the devil. The bored Felice Charmond is so unnatural that she must splice on the luxuriance of natural beauty by having a wig made of Marty South's hair. The isolated and cramped Hintock environment creates a boredom and ennui in these two characters that serve to further the narrative drive of the novel.

Grace, the most equivocal character in the novel, is the active center of its animating conflicts. Her wavering back and forth between the natural world and the antinatural is the central tension that crystallizes the tentative and uncomfortable attitude of all the characters. It is her dilemma of choice that constitutes the major action, just as it was Bathsheba's choice that dominated *Far from the Madding Crowd*. The choices that the characters make to relieve themselves of tension are made through the most irrational emotion, love, in a basically irrational world. Grace marries Fitzpiers in an effort to commit herself to a solid world of value. Fitzpiers sees in Grace the answer to a Shelleyean search for a soul mate. To commit oneself to a line of action that assumes the world is ordered and full of value, to choose a course of action that hopes to lessen the tentativeness of life, to deceive oneself into thinking that there is solidarity—these are the tragic errors that Hardy's characters repeatedly make.

The marriage begins to break up when Fitzpiers, aware that Grace is not the ideal he desired, goes to the lethargic Mrs. Charmond, and when Grace, aware that her hope for solidarity was misdirected, tries to go back to the natural world through the love of Giles. Social conventions, however, which Hardy says are holdovers from outworn creeds, interfere. Grace is unable to obtain a divorce, for the law makes her irrational first choice inflexible. Despairing of the injustice of natural law as well as of social law, she runs away to Giles, who, too self-effacing to rebel against either code, lets her have his house while he spends the night in an ill-sheltered hut. At this point, confused and in anguish about what possibility there is left for her, uncertain of the value of any action, Grace confronts the true nature of the world and the absurdity of her past hopes for value in it. The storm that catches Grace alone in the house is a climactic representation for her of the inimical natural world, just as the pestilent swamp was for Bathsheba. "She had never before been so struck with the devilry of a gusty night in the wood, because she had never been so entirely alone in spirit as she was now. She seemed almost to be apart from herself—a vacuous duplicate only." Grace's indecision and absurd hopes have been leading to this bitter moment of realization in which she is made aware of the ephemeral nature of human existence and the absurdity of human hopes in a world without intrinsic value.

Just as in *Far from the Madding Crowd*, the tension of the action collapses after this confrontation. Giles dies and Fitzpiers returns after having ended his affair with Mrs. Charmond. After a short period of indifference, Grace, still his wife by law, returns to him. In his customary ironic way, however, Hardy does not allow this reconciliation to be completely satisfying, for it is physical only. Grace, having narrowly missed being caught in a mantrap set for Fitzpiers, is enticingly undressed when Fitzpiers rushes to her and asks to be taken back. This physical attraction is the only reason that Fitzpiers desires a reconciliation. Grace is still indifferent to him, but it is now this very indifference that makes their reunion possible. Seeing no one reaction as more valuable than another, she takes the path of least resistance. The rural chorus ends the novel by commenting that they think the union will not last.

Although many critics have pointed out the formal framework of *The Return of the Native*—the classical five-act division, the unity of time, place, and line of action, and the character similarities to Oedipus and Prometheus—other studies have struggled with the book's ambiguities and the difficulties involved in seeing it as a classical tragedy. Certainly, the pattern is classical, but the distortion of the pattern becomes the more significant structuring principle. Egdon Heath is the landscape from which God has departed. Man in such an empty world will naturally begin to feel an affinity with the wasteland, such as islands, moors, and dunes. Little more needs to be said here about the part the Heath plays in the action, for critics have called it the principal actor in the drama. Indeed, it does dominate the scene, for the actions of all the characters are reactions in some way to the indifference the Heath represents.

As in *Far from the Madding Crowd*, there is a chorus of rustics in *The Return of the Native*. They belong on the Heath because of their ignorance of the incongruity between man's longing for meaning and the intractable indifference of the world. They still maintain a mythical, superstitious belief in a pagan animism and fatalistically accept the nature of things. The Druidical rites of the opening fires, the unimportance of Christian religion, the black mass and voodoo doll of Susan Nonesuch: all these characterize the pagan fatalism of the rustics.

The main characters, however, do not belong with the rustics. They make something other than a fatalistic response to the Heath and are characterized by their various reactions to its indifference. Mrs. Yeobright is described as having the very solitude exhaled from the Heath concentrated in her face. Having lived with its desolation longer than any of the others, she no longer can escape, but she is desperate to see that Clym does. Damon Wildeve does not belong to the Heath but has taken over a patch of land a former tenant died in trying to reclaim. Although he is dissatisfied, he is not heroic; he is involved in no search, no vital interaction with the indifferent world. Tomasin Yeobright is characterized in a single image, as she is in the house loft, selecting apples: "the sun shone in a bright yellow patch upon the figure of the maiden as she knelt and plunged her naked arms into the soft brown fern." She aligns herself with the natural world through her innocence and consequently perceives no incongruity. Diggory Venn, the most puzzling figure in the novel, is an outcast. The most typical image of him is by his campfire alone, the red glow reflecting off his own red skin. He simply wanders on the open Heath, minding other people's business, and waiting for his chance to marry Tomasin.

These characters, regardless of their conflicts with the irrationality of human choice or the indifference of the Heath, are minor in comparison with the two antithetical attitudes of Eustacia Vye and Clym Yeobright. The most concrete image of Eustacia is of her wandering on the Heath, carrying an hourglass in her hand, gazing aimlessly out over the vast wasteland. Her search for value, her hope for escape from the oppressive indifference of the Heath, lies in being "loved to madness." Clym, however, sees friendliness and geniality written on the Heath. He is the disillusioned intellectual trying to make a return to the mythic simplicity of the natural world. Clym would prefer not to think, not to grapple with the incongruities he has seen. The very disease of thought that forces him to see the "coil of things" makes him desire to teach rather than to think. He is indeed blind, as his mother tells him, in thinking he can instill into the peasants the view that "life is a thing to be put up with," for they have always known it and fatalistically accepted it. Furthermore, he shows his blindness by marrying Eustacia, thinking she will remain with him on the Heath, while Eustacia reveals that she is as misdirected as he is by idealizing him and thinking that he will take her away from the Heath. Both characters search for a meaning and basis for value, but both are trapped by the irrationality of love and vain hopes in an irrational world.

At the beginning of Book Four, Clym literally goes blind because of his studying and must actually look at the world through smoked glasses. He welcomes the opportunity to ignore the incongruities of the world by sub-suming himself in the Heath and effacing himself in his furze-cutting. In his selfish attempt to "not think" about it, he ignores what this means to Eustacia. She can find no meaning at all in such self-effacing indifference; it is the very thing against which she is rebelling. She returns again to her old pagan ways at the village dance and considers the possibility of Wildeve once more.

Mrs. Yeobright's journey across the Heath, a trip colored by grotesque images of the natural world—the tepid, stringy water of nearly dried pools where "maggoty" shapes cavort; the battered, rude, and wild trees whose limbs are splintered, lopped, and distorted by the weather—is a turning point in the action of the book. In a concatenation of chance events and human misunderstanding, Eustacia turns Mrs. Yeobright away from the door and the old woman dies as a result. At this point, Eustacia blames some "colossal Prince of the world for framing her situation and ruling her lot."

Clym, still selfish, ignores the problems of the living Eustacia and concentrates on the "riddle of death" of his mother. Had he been able to practice what he professed—human solidarity—he might have saved Eustacia and himself, but instead he bitterly blames her for his mother's death and is the immediate cause of Eustacia's flight. Eustacia's trip across the Heath to her death is similar to Mrs. Yeobright's in that the very natural world seems antagonistic to her. She stumbles over "twisted furze roots, tufts of rushes, or oozing lumps of fleshly fungi, which at this season lay scattered about the Heath like the rotten liver and lungs of some colossal animal." Her leap into the pool is a noble suicide. It is more a rebellion against the indifference of the world around her than it is a submission to its oppressiveness. It is the admission of the absurdity of man's hopes by a romantic temperament that refuses to live by such absurdity.

The tragic pattern of *The Mayor of Casterbridge* has been said by most critics to be more explicit than that of *The Return of the Native*; more recently, however, critics have been quick to point out that there are serious difficulties involved in seeing *The Mayor of Casterbridge* as an archetypal tragic ritual. Although Henchard is Oedipus-like in his opposition to the rational, Creon-like Farfrae, the plot of the novel, like that of *The Return of the Native*, involves the reactions of a set of characters to the timeless indifference of the world. In this case, the mute and intractable world is imaged in the dead myths and classical legends of Casterbridge. Secluded as much as Little Hintock, the world of *The Woodlanders*, Casterbridge is "huddled all together, shut in by a square wall of trees like a plot of garden by a box-edging." The town is saturated with the old superstitions and myths of the past. The primary image of the desolate world of the town and its dead and valueless past is the Casterbridge Ring, a relic of an ancient Roman amphitheatre. The Ring is a central symbol which embodies the desolation of the old myths of human value. It formerly had been the gallows site, but now it is a place for illicit meetings of all kinds, except, Hardy notes, those of happy lovers. A place of man's inhumanity to man is no place for the celebration of love.

The inhumanity of one person to another and the human need for love play an important part in the action of the novel. While the classical Oedipus is guilty of breaking a cosmic law, Henchard is guilty of breaking a purely human one. By selling his wife, he treats her as a thing, not a human being. He rejects human relationships and violates human interdependence and solidarity. This is the sin that begins to find objectification years later when the blight of the bread agitates the townspeople and when his wife, Susan, returns.

It is not this sin alone that means tragedy for Henchard, just as it is not Oedipus' violation alone that brings his downfall. Henchard's character—his irrational behavior, his perverse clinging to the old order and methods, his rash and impulsive nature—also contributes to his defeat. Henchard is an adherent of the old ways. Though he is ostensibly the mayor, an important man, he is actually closer to the rustic, folk characters than the hero of any other Hardy novel. He is not a rebel against the indifference of the world so much as he is a simple hay-stacker, trying desperately to maintain a sense of value in the worn-out codes and superstitions of the past. In the oft-quoted "Character is Fate" passage in the novel, Hardy makes explicit Henchard's problem. He calls him a Faust-like character, "a vehement, gloomy being who had quitted the ways of vulgar men without light to guide him on a better way." Thus, Henchard is caught between two worlds, one of them dead and valueless, the other not worthy enough to be a positive replacement. The levelheaded business sense of Farfrae, the social climbing and superficiality of Lucetta, the too-strict rationality of Elizabeth-Jane—all who represent the new order of human attitudes—appear anemic and self-deceived in the face of Henchard's dynamic energy.

It often seems that the nature of things is against Henchard, but the nature of things is that events occur which cannot be predicted, and that they often occur just at the time when one does not want them to. Many such unpredicted and ill-timed events accumulate to cause Henchard's tragedy. For example, just when he decides to marry Lucetta, his wife Susan returns; just at the time of Susan's death, he is once more reminded of his obligation to Lucetta; just at the time when he tells Elizabeth-Jane that she is his daughter, he discovers that she is not; just at the time when he calls on Lucetta to discuss marriage, she has already met and found a better mate in Farfrae.

Many of the events that contribute to his own downfall are a combination of this "unholy brew" and his impulsive nature. That the weather turned bad during his planned entertainment he could not prevent, but he could have been more prepared for the rain had he not been in such a hurry to best Farfrac. The unpredictable nature of the weather at harvest time was also beyond his control, but again had he not been so intent on ruining Farfrae he might have survived. He begins to wonder if someone is roasting a waxen image of him or stirring an "unholy brew" to confound him. Moreover, the attitudes of other characters accumulate to contribute to Henchard's downfall. Farfrae, as exacting as a machine, rejects Henchard's fatherly love and makes few truly human responses at all. Lucetta, once dependent on Henchard, becomes so infatuated with her new wealth that she no longer needs him. At the beginning of the novel, Susan's simple nature is incapable of realizing that Newsom's purchase of her is not valid, and at the end, her daughter, Elizabeth-Jane, is so coldly rational that she can cast Henchard off without possibility of reconciliation. None of these characters faces the anguish of being human as Henchard does.

The ambiguity that arises from the combination of all these forces makes it difficult to attribute Henchard's tragedy to any one of them. His death in the end marks the inevitable disappearance of the old order, but it is also the only conclusion possible for the man who has broken the only possible existing order when a cosmic order is no longer tenable—the human order of man himself. The reader is perhaps made to feel that Henchard has suffered more than he deserved. As a representative of the old order, his fall must be lamented even as the search is carried on for a new foundation of value and order. At the death of the old values in *The Mayor of Casterbridge*, a new order is not available.

The form and meaning of *Tess of the D'Urbervilles* springs from Tess's relation to the natural world. At the beginning of the novel she is a true child of nature who, although sensitive to painful incongruities in her experience, is confident that the natural world will provide her with a basis of value and will protect and sustain her. When nature fails her, her perplexity throws her out of the comfortable world of innocence and natural rapport. Tess then begins a journey both inward and outward in search of a stable orientation and a reintegration into a relationship with the natural world.

Tess first appears in her "natural home" in the small hamlet of Marlott, where her innocence is dramatized as she takes part in the May-Day dance. There is a sensitivity in Tess that sets her apart from the other inhabitants. Shame for her father's drunken condition makes her volunteer to take the beehives to market, and despair for the laziness of her parents makes her dreamily watch the passing landscape and ignore where she is going. When, as a result, the horse Prince is killed, Tess's sense of duty to her family, now in economic difficulties, overcomes her pride and she agrees to go to her aristocratic relatives for help. It is her first journey outside the little world of Marlott and her first real encounter with corruption. Alec, her cousin, is a stock figure of the sophisticated, antinatural world. Their first scene together is formalized into an archetypal image of innocence in the grasp of the corrupt.

Just as it is Tess's natural luxuriance and innocence that attracts Alec, it is also her innocence that leads to her fall. When he takes her into the woods, strangely enough she is not afraid of him as before. She feels that she is in her natural element. She so trusts the natural world to protect her that she innocently falls asleep and is seduced by Alec. The antinatural force that began with her father's alleged nobility, coupled with Tess's own innocence and sensitivity and her naïve trust in the world, all work together to make her an outcast. When her illegitimate child dies and the church refuses it a Christian burial, Tess unequivocally denies the validity of organized religion. She probes within herself to try to find some meaning in her despair. Suddenly she becomes quite consciously aware of the abstract reality of death: "Almost at a leap Tess thus changed from simple girl to complex woman." The facing of the idea of death without a firm hope for transcendence is the conclusion of Tess's inward search in this second phase of her experience, when, still maintaining a will to live and enjoy, she has hopes of submerging herself into the natural world again.

The Valley of the Great Dairies where Tess goes next is the natural world magnified, distorted, thrown out of proportion. It is so lush and fertile as to become a symbolic world. As Tess enters the valley, she feels hope for a new reintegration. For the time being, she dismisses the disturbing thought of her doubt in her childhood God and is satisfied to immerse herself within the purely physical world of the farm's lushness. She manages to ignore her moral plight until she meets the morally ambiguous Angel Clare. In contrast to Tess, Angel's moral perplexity arises from intellectual questioning rather than from natural disillusionment. Intellectually convinced that he has lost faith, Angel rebels against the conventions of society and the church and goes to the Valley of the Great Dairies where he believes innocence and uncontaminated purity and goodness prevail. For Angel, Tess represents the idealistic goal of natural innocence, but the natural world no more affirms this relationship than it did condemn the former one. On the first night of their marriage, Tess confesses to Angel her relationship with Alec. Angel, the idealist, has desired to see a natural perfection in Tess. Doubting that perfection, he rejects her as anti-natural. Angel cannot accept the reality of what nature is truly like; he is tied to a conventional orientation more than he realizes.

After Angel leaves her, Tess wanders about the countryside doing farm work at various places until one morning on the road she awakes to find dead pheasants around her. At this point, Tess becomes aware that in a Darwinistic universe, without teleological possibility and without inherent goodness, violation, injury, even death, are innate realities. Tess realizes that she is not guilty by the laws of such a world. After this realization she can go to the barren world of Chalk-Newton and not feel so much the incongruity of the place. With its "white vacuity of countenance with the lineaments gone," Chalk-Newton represents the wasteland situation of a world without order or value. Tess can remain indifferent to it because of her new realization of its indifference to her.

Cold indifference, however, offers no escape from her moral conflict. Alec D'Urberville comes back into her life, proclaiming that he has accepted Christianity and exorting her not to "tempt" him again. Ironically, by trying to convince him of her own realization of a world without God and by propounding Angel's uncommitted humanism to him, she only succeeds in reconverting Alec back to his old demonic nature and thus creates another threat to herself. When her father dies and the family loses its precarious freehold, Tess gives in to Alec's persistent urging once more. When Angel, in the rugged South American mountains, comes to the same realization that Tess experienced on the road, he returns to find that Tess has renounced life and self completely, allowing her body to drift, "like a corpse upon the current, in a direction dissociated from the living will." After the return of Angel, when Tess finds her last hopes dashed, she sees in Alec all the deception and meaninglessness of a world she trusted. When she kills him, she is transformed by her rebellion. Like Percy Bysshe Shelley's Beatrice Cenci, she is aware of no guilt; she transcends any kind of moral judgment. She acknowledges her absolute freedom, and in that fearful moment, she is willing to accept the human penalties for such freedom.

In the last part of the novel, when Angel and Tess wander without any real hope of escape, Tess is already condemned to die. Isolated in the awareness of her own ephemerality in a valueless world, Tess vows she is "not going to think of anything ouside of now." The final scene at Stonehenge is a triumph of symbolic realization of place; the silent, enigmatic stones, mysterious and implacable, resist any attempt at explanation. Tess, in saying that she likes to be there, accepts the indifferent universe. Lying on the altar of a heathen temple, she is the archetypal sacrifice of man's rebellion against an empty world. When the carriers of the law of nature and society arrive, Tess, having rebelled against these laws and rejected them, can easily say, "I am ready."

Tess's real tragedy springs from her insistent hope throughout the novel to find external meaning and justification for her life. Only at the end of the novel, when she rebels by killing Alec, does she achieve true awareness. Unlike the classical tragic hero, she is not reconciled to the world through an acceptance of universal justice. Her very salvation, the only kind of salvation in Hardy's world, lies in her denial of such a concept.

With some significant differences, *Jude the Obscure* is concerned with the same problem that animates *Tess of the D'Urbervilles*—the absurdity and tragedy of man's hopes for value in an indifferent universe. As a literary creation, it is a "process" through which Hardy tries to structure the symbolic journey of every man who searches for a foundation, a basis for meaning and value. The problem, however, is that all the symbols that represent meaning to Jude—the colleges, the church, the ethereal freedom of Sue Bridehead, and even the physical beauty of his wife Arabella—are illusory. By contrast, those things that have real symbolic value in the world are the forbidding, sacrosanct walls of the college complex, which Jude cannot enter; the decaying materiality of the churches which he tries to restore; the neurotic irrationality of Sue, which he fails to understand; and his own body, to which he is inextricably tied. It is precisely Jude's "obscurity," his loss of "at-homeness" in the world, with which the novel is concerned. He is obscure because he is without light, because he tries in every way possible to find an illumination of his relation to the world, but without success.

It is significant that the novel opens with the departure of the schoolmaster Phillotson, for to Jude, orphaned and unwanted by his aunt, the teacher has been the center of the world. His leaving marks the necessity of Jude's finding a new center and a new hope to relieve his loneliness. The first projection of his hopes fo find value is naturally toward Christminster, the destination of his teacher. In the first part of the book his dream is seen only as an indefinable glow in the distance that offers all possibilities by its very unknown nature. Although he consciously devotes himself to the Christian framework, one night after having read a classical poem, he kneels and prays to Diana, the goddess of the moon. Both of these value systems—Christian faith and Greek reason—are projected on his vision of Christminster, but both of them are temporarily forgotten when he meets Arabella, "a substantial female animal." Later, when she tells him that she is pregnant, although it destroys all his former plans, he idealizes the marriage state, calls his hopes for Christminster "dreams about books, and degrees and impossible fellowships," and dedicates himself to home, family, and the pedestrian values of Marygreen. His discovery that Arabella has deceived him is only the first reversal in his search for unity and value.

In the second phase of Jude's development, the long-planned journey to Christminster is prompted by the immediacy of seeing a picture of Sue Bridehead; she becomes a concrete symbol of his vision. His first glimpse of Sue has the quality of idealistic wish-fulfillment. His growing desire for her expresses a need for an "anchorage" to his thoughts. He goes to the church she attends, and this church, associated with his vision of Sue, temporarily becomes that anchorage. Sue is not, however, representative of Christian values; she is rather the classical pagan. This dichotomy of values creates a recurring tension in Jude's search throughout the book.

Jude's first major disillusionment at Christminster comes when he is turned down by all five colleges to which he has applied. After this disappointment, he shifts his hopes from the reason and knowledge of the schools to the faith of the Church. This religious impulse dominates Jude's hopes in the third phase of his development. He practices the rituals of the Church in the hope that he can find a meaning for himself, but Sue, who laughed at his idealistic notions of the intellectual life, tells him that the Church is not the way either. Sue, who changes in Jude's eyes as his goals change, is always important to him as a symbol of his aspirations and ideals. When he loses her to Phillotson, he is struck even more by the "scorn of Nature for man's finer emotions and her lack of interest in his aspirations."

Phase four of Jude's search is a transition section presenting the decay of the values of the past. Jude, studying theology and church ritual with a last weakening hope, is only vaguely aware of the decay and aridity around him. His need for Sue, an ambiguous mixture of desire for the ideal and the physical, begins to take on more importance for him until he decides that he is unfit "to fill the part of a propounder of accredited dogma" and burns all his theology books. Sue, a spiritual creture, cannot live with Phillotson any longer. She goes to Jude, who, having rejected everything else, is ready to project his desires for meaning entirely on an ambiguous union with her as both physical wife and Shelleyan soul mate.

The fifth part of the novel is a phase of movement as Jude and Sue wander from town to town, living as man and wife in all respects except the sexual. Not until Arabella returns and Sue fears she will lose Jude, does she give in to him, but with infinite regret. In the final phase of Jude's development, after the birth of his children, including the mysterious child named "Father Time," the family moves back to Christminster. Instead of being optimistic, Jude is merely indifferent. He recognizes himself as an outsider, a stranger to the universe of ideals and hopes of other men. He has undergone a process that has slowly stripped him of such hopes for meaning. He sees man's desire for meaning as absurd in a world that has no concern for man, a universe that cannot fulfill dreams of unity or meaning.

The tragedy of Father Time causes Sue to alter her belief that she can live by instinct, abjuring the laws of society. She makes an extreme shift, accepting a supreme deity against whose laws she feels she has transgressed; her self-imposed penance for her "sin" of living with Jude is to go back to Phillotson. After Sue leaves, Jude goes to "a dreary, strange flat scene, where boughs dripped, and coughs and consumption lurked, and where he had never been before." This is a typical Hardy technique for moments of realization: the natural world becomes an inimical reflection of the character's awareness of the absurd. After this, Jude's reaction to the world around him is indifference: he allows himself to be seduced by Arabella again and marries her. Jude's final journey to see Sue is a journey to death and a final rejection of the indifferent universe of which his experiences have made him aware.

In his relentless vision of a world stripped of transcendence, Hardy is a distinctly modern novelist. As Nathan A. Scott has said of him, "not only does he lead us back to that trauma in the nineteenth century out of which the modern existentialist imagination was born, but he also brings us forward to our own time."

Charles E. May

Other major works

SHORT FICTION: *Wessex Tales*, 1888; *A Group of Noble Dames*, 1891; *Life's Little Ironies*, 1894; *A Changed Man*, 1913.

PLAYS: *The Dynasts: A Drama of the Napoleonic Wars*, 1903, 1906, 1908; *The Famous Tragedy of the Queen of Cornwall*, 1923.

POETRY: *Wessex Poems*, 1898; *Poems of the Past and Present*, 1901; *Time's Laughingstocks and Other Verses*, 1909; *Satires of Circumstances*, 1914; *Moments of Vision*, 1917; *Late Lyrics and Earlier*, 1922; *Human Shows, Far Phantasies*, 1925; *Winter Words*, 1928.

NONFICTION: *Life and Art*, 1925 (E. Brennecke, editor); *Personal Writings*, 1966 (Harold Orel, editor).

Bibliography

Bayley, John. *An Essay on Hardy*. Cambridge, England: Cambridge University Press, 1978. Gives a close reading of most of Hardy's major novels, stressing the instability in his style. Hardy's writing was often ambiguous and, by arousing uncertain expectations in the reader, he was able to enhance suspense. His later novels, culminating in *Jude the Obscure*, were more tightly organized, a feature not to Bayley's liking, who prefers the adventitious and unplanned. Also notes that Hardy's attitude toward his male heroes is often determined by their relations with the novel's central female personality.

Gregor, Ian. *The Great Web*. London: Faber & Faber, 1974. Stresses coherence, arguing that the novels from *Far from the Madding Crowd* to *Jude the Obscure* should be read together as the expression of a journal of mental development and that each of the major novels is itself an unfolding. A general proposition about life gradually becomes evident as the action in each of the novels is set forward. Supports this controversial view through discussion of the major novels.

Miller, J. Hillis. *Thomas Hardy: Distance and Desire*. Cambridge, Mass.: Harvard University Press, 1970. Miller is one of the leading critical theorists in the United States, and this book has been very influential. In contrast with those who emphasize development in Hardy's career, Miller thinks that the basic approach characteristic of Hardy's fiction was established early and remained constant. Each of the novels expresses a strong desire on the part of the main character. At the same time, the novel distances itself from the emotional proclivities of the protagonist. The interplay between what the main character wants and the detachment of the author energizes the stories.

Southerington, F. R. *Hardy's Vision of Man*. London: Chatto & Windus, 1971. Defends at considerable length a revolutionary account of Hardy. Most authorities see Hardy as a pessimist: His "President of the Immortals" is indifferent to human concerns. However, for Southerington, he is an optimist; his novels show that given appropriate attitudes, one need not be overcome by adversity. The novels also contain many autobiographical passages, which the book traces in detail.

Stewart, J. I. M. *Thomas Hardy: A Critical Biography*. London: Longman, 1971. This exceptionally well-written book is an excellent introductory study. Gives an account of both Hardy's life and works and, although relatively short, covers all the essentials. A chapter on Hardy's poetry gives an analysis of *The Dynasts*, a long verse drama that brings out his philosophy more clearly than most of his novels. Tends to be critical of Hardy's religious views and also looks on American critics with a jaundiced eye. The author is himself a successful novelist and, under the pen name "Michael Innes," an even more successful detective-story writer.

MARK HARRIS
Mark Harris Finkelstein

Born: Mount Vernon, New York; November 19, 1922

Principal long fiction

Trumpet to the World, 1946; *City of Discontent*, 1952; *The Southpaw*, 1953; *Bang the Drum Slowly*, 1956; *A Ticket for a Seamstitch*, 1957; *Something About a Soldier*, 1957; *Wake Up, Stupid*, 1959; *The Goy*, 1970; *Killing Everybody*, 1973; *It Looked Like For Ever*, 1979; *Lying in Bed*, 1984; *Speed*, 1990.

Other literary forms

Mark Harris has written an autobiography, *Best Father Ever Invented* (1976), and a number of other books "carved" out of his journals which are essentially autobiographical, though they are tied in with larger historical events. Even his *Saul Bellow: Drumlin Woodchuck* (1980) is largely about Harris himself. He has written a play, *Friedman and Son* (1962), and did the screenplay for the film made from his novel *Bang the Drum Slowly*. Other screenplays include *Boswell for the Defence* (1983) and *Boswell's London Journal* (1984). He has also written television adaptations of fiction, notably *The Man That Corrupted Hadleyburg* (1980), based on Mark Twain's story.

Achievements

Harris is a serious writer whose novels have been widely and for the most part favorably reviewed, and some of which have achieved modestly good sales. Curiously, however, literary critics who have lavished articles and books on many lesser writers have virtually ignored Harris. There are reasons, perhaps, why this is so. First, four of his novels—including his best-known books—have as their protagonist a semiliterate professional baseball player. For this reason alone, Harris has frequently been dismissed as a superficial talent, although baseball is merely the setting of the novels; Harris' themes— maturity, aging, and death—are the themes of much great literature. Harris' reputation has also suffered for extraliterary reasons: he is outspoken politically, and he never seems to be on the side that is currently in vogue. A pacifist, he attacked American involvement in World War II and the Korean War when it was not popular to do so. Whatever the reasons, Harris' work has not received the attention it deserves. Nevertheless, the few English teachers who offer one of his books in American novel classes regularly find that is the students' favorite book of the semester. Harris' novels—funny, readable, intelligent, and unlike anyone else's—have made for their author a small but secure and respectable place in American letters, a place that will remain when a number of the current blockbusters have been forgotten.

Biography

Mark Harris Finkelstein was born November 19, 1922, in Mt. Vernon, New York, of a well-to-do family. When he went out as a young man looking for work, he dropped the Finkelstein, since Jews were not being hired. He never reassumed the name, and he has from time to time agonized over whether he was fleeing from his Jewish heritage. In 1943, he went into the army and was sent to the South for basic training. He was appalled at the treatment of blacks, and also at the way the whole generation of young men were being trained to kill or be killed in order to destroy "evil." At a point of personal crisis, he deserted the army, was arrested, thrown in the stockade, and finally discharged as "psychoneurotic." His first novel (written while he was in the army hospital), *A Trumpet to the World*, has a black soldier as its protagonist. He wrote about this experience again in *Something About a Soldier*, this time with a character like himself as protagonist. Clearly, the extreme experiences of that time marked his entire life, and must have gone some way toward forming his political attitudes, particularly his pacifism, and also his championing of the individual against society. After his discharge, he did newspaper work while writing his second novel, *City of Discontent*, a novelized biography of Vachel Lindsay, which has as its thesis the criticism of the crass American society that trapped him with money and destroyed him as a poet.

Harris loved sports, but was physically small and bespectacled. Perhaps, then, there is an element of wish-fulfillment in his creation of Henry Wiggen, the southpaw pitcher for the New York Mammoths, whose career he followed throughout four novels. He wrote the first Wiggen book, *The Southpaw*, while he was working on his M. A. at the University of Denver in the late 1940's. The novel turned out to be one of his most popular; it no doubt helped him get the teaching job at San Francisco State University which he held from 1954 to 1967. While teaching there, he completed his Ph.D. work at the University of Minnesota, where he came under the influence of pacifist Mulford Sibley and solidified his political views.

Harris was perhaps feeling complacent about his career when he suffered two setbacks. He wrote *Something About a Soldier*, one of the best books he has written, sent it to his publisher, and—for one of the few times in his life—had it rejected. The novel, paralleling closely his experiences in 1943, made heroes of the young men who used any means to avoid being in the army, and made the American war effort itself seem senseless and evil. In 1955, the country was not ready, the publishers may have felt, for such a radical attack on one of its basic institutions. Harris was shaken by the rejection and did something he felt was a kind of retreat. He went back to his earlier success and wrote a new novel about Henry Wiggen. Ironically, that novel, *Bang the Drum Slowly*, has become perhaps his most popular book. At around the same time, *Life* magazine offered him what was in those days an enormous amount of money to do a long story for them. They warned him only to remember that *Life* was a "family" magazine. He thought they meant that he should stay away from sex and religious controversy; he wrote long and hard and sent them an intricately wrought story. They rejected it and published instead a meretricious piece of fiction by a hack writer. Harris concluded that it was not merely controversy which the mass media wished to avoid but also craft. The work they published explained itself to the reader, whereas Harris' made the reader think for himself. Shortly afterward, *Something About a Soldier* was finally published, and even the rejected *Life* story came out as a book, *A Ticket for Seamstitch*. Harris' experiences with *Life* and with writing for television confirmed for him his belief that craft was anathema to the mass media, and yet he was aware of the lure of the mass media, the big audiences, the big money. These became themes in his next novel, *Wake Up, Stupid*, about a college teacher somewhat like Harris, who has dreams of making a fortune by taking his serious play to Broadway, and the disillusionment he suffers when his dreams are realized. The book was well received, sold very well, and ironically, resulted in many offers to do writing projects for the very mass media he had satirized.

For a decade, Harris wrote no more novels. Gradually, he realized that he was in the midst of a crisis in his writing. He turned inward at this time, producing two autobiographical works, *Mark the Glove Boy: Or, The Last Days of Richard Nixon* (1964) and *Twentyone Twice: A Journal* (1966), and a play, *Friedman and Son*, about a writer who has dropped his Jewish surname. The play was printed with a long autobiographical introduction in which Harris discussed his fears that without realizing it he had been denying his Jewish roots. After a decade-long hiatus, Harris published his next novel, *The Goy*. The goy of the title is a Gentile who wants to become a Jew, but is rebuffed by the Jews, who distrust his motives. Conceivably, Harris thought of himself at this time as virtually a goy: he was trying to reestablish his ethnic ties, seeing in his heritage the source of his strength.

A professor of creative writing at Arizona State University, Harris continued to write steadily throughout the 1970's and 1980's. His interest in the father-son bond, explored in *Friedman and Son* and *Best Father Ever Invented* (1976) influenced his choice of a publisher for his 1990 novel: a piece by Donald I. Fine about his own memories of his father prompted Harris to send Fine the manuscript of *Speed*.

Analysis

Of Mark Harris' major books, most have been novels, and the rest have been more or less autobiographical works. What is curious is how similar the fiction and nonfiction books have been in structure and theme. While Harris has spoken of himself as the "disguised" person in his novels, his autobiographical works often seem to mimic the plots of his novels. Indeed, one of the obvious points in common between the two kinds of books is an interest in autobiography, for even in the novels many of the protagonists seem to be writing their biographies, or to be centrally concerned with searching their own lives for a pattern that will make their experience coherent to them—regularly the theme of the nonfiction works as well. Henry Wiggen, for example, ostensibly the writer of the four baseball books (his teammates call him "Author" Wiggen), is, with his own brand of spelling and grammar, engaged in writing his autobiography. The black protagonist of *Trumpet to the World* becomes a writer in order to put down his experience. *City of Discontent*, a different kind of blending of fiction and biography, is a novelized biography of Vachel Lindsay. The novel *Wake Up, Stupid* consists mainly of the letters the protagonist, Lee Youngdahl, writes to his friends, and the replies he gets, self-conscious written documents through which he tries to understand himself. Westrum, the protagonist of *The Goy*, has a massive, nearly lifelong journal; Harris himself has steadily kept a journal since childhood, from which he has "carved" much of his autobiographical writing.

Perhaps the significance Harris finds in this constant attention to the self can be most clearly seen in the character of Westrum in *The Goy*. Westrum is firmly convinced that simply by writing down in detail the daily events of his life, he will in effect be writing a history of the world in his time. The experience of a man, or any man, Harris seems to be saying, is the experience of all mankind. Therefore, careful attention to a single life, even his own, is justified, because that single life comes to represent everyone's life.

There is as well a philosophical reason for Harris' close attention to the individual. Harris is committed absolutely to the value of the individual as opposed to society or any other collective entity. This conviction is at the basis of his pacifism, for he believes that no individual should be sacrificed for some larger "good," as young men are sacrificed when they are sent off to war. It is at the heart, as well, of his concern over racism, for when someone is placed in a class in order to be discriminated against, it is his individual humanity that is being overlooked.

While in theory, then, any man is a representative of Everyman, for his fictional purposes Harris has found the professional athlete and the gifted writer to be particularly good representatives, since they not only—as showmen—must live in the real world, and be subject to its temptations, but also are driven by a strong inner discipline to excel in their craft. Indeed, Harris makes his baseball player Henry Wiggen a writer as well (however questionable his literacy), and later makes his writer-characters, Lee Youngdahl and Westrum, powerful athletes.

The gifts, the discipline, and the temptations are all important ingredients in the novels. Since Harris is granting supreme importance to the individual, the individual has a responsibility to be worthy of that importance. He has an existential need to excel. Because he has great gifts, and because he strives so single-mindedly to be all that he possibly can be, he can be led into temptation. He can try to be too much, or naïvely try to be what will ultimately be detrimental. Typically, in a Harris novel, the protagonist is introduced to the reader as an individual with enormous potential. His friends expect greatness from him, as he does of himself. He then goes out into the real world to fulfill his promise, where he meets a number of characters who began like him but have sold their talents for money, or out of fear or self-deception. The protagonist, seeking a role model, imitates first one, then the other of these characters, while his friends wait with diminishing patience for him to come to his senses. At last, there is a moment of "definition" when painful experience brings him to himself and back into reconciliation with his real friends.

When Harris began working on *The Southpaw*, his first novel about baseball pitcher Henry Wiggen, his friends were worried. "Baseball was for boys, they said, not for literature, but I wrote my book anyhow, out of the faith that if I was moved and amused by what I was writing somebody else was bound to be, betting on my humanity that way." The configuration of the novel, indeed, is no different from that of a baseball story for boys. Henry plays ball in high school, is discovered, gets his chance, goes into the major league, wins twenty-six games in his first season, and leads his team to victory in the World Series. What makes it a serious novel is the growing up Henry has to do, and the speed with which he must do it. His extraordinary talents bring with them extraordinary temptations. In the brutally competitive world of the professional athlete (he has already noticed that every step up the ladder he takes is at the expense of someone else, only slightly older, who is cut from the team to make room for him), he has to get his life together quickly, or ruin it for good.

Henry is essentially decent and honest and has sensible values, but he is very young. The characters surrounding him can be divided into three categories, each representing one of the directions Henry can take in his own life. First there are Henry's true friends, above all his father. At an early point in his own professional baseball career, Henry's father was asked to compromise his principles. He refused and took a humble job driving a school bus and tending the grounds of the observatory. There is Aaron, director of the observatory, tough, cranky, outspoken politically (in a widely publicized conflict during World War II, he had refused the army permission to use his observatory for military purposes), and full of wise advice for Henry, which Henry never has time to listen to: "Only sorely troubled human beings need success in the accepted sense; the wise are content to own the love and respect of a few neighbors of moderate means, little 'success' and no visible ambition." Aaron's niece Holly is just as independent, just as sure of the few important things she wants. Among them is Henry, whom she picks out early to be her man. When as a teenager Henry tells her of his first bumbling attempts at sex with Thedabara Brown, Holly quickly takes him to her own bed, to stake her claim, but later, when he is riding high in his career and constantly proposing to her, she continues to put him off. She wants to see first if he will weather his sea of temptations.

In the second set of characters, Henry observes Sad Sam Yale, the master pitcher, Henry's boyhood idol. Sam is aging, and in fact, Henry eventually replaces him, yet Sam still represents everything Henry thinks he wants to be. Sam has selfishly and ruthlessly pulled himself to the top, his goal being to win fame, lots of money, and sex with glamorous women. Having great ability, and dedicating his life single-mindedly to these pursuits, he attains them; in the end, however, they melt in his hands, leaving him empty and disillusioned. The third class of characters is represented by Patricia Moors, daughter of the wealthy car-manufacturing Moors family, which owns the team. Henry's family and friends admire only integrity and genuine values; Sad Sam wants only what he can get out of the world for himself; Patricia is entirely a company person, giving up her integrity to serve the Moors empire— even spending a night in a motel with the team's ugliest player to get him to sign a contract for a couple of thousand dollars less.

Young Henry, separated from the good advice of Holly, Aaron, and his father, admires and wants to imitate Sad Sam, and finds himself sexually attracted to Patricia, who represents all that is spuriously glamorous. Henry's team leads the league all season, but toward the end they go into a slump. Everyone is nervous, the players annoy one another, and Henry develops a psychosomatic back problem that inteferes with his pitching motion. At a crucial moment in a game that might determine the pennant, Henry, worried that his curve is not breaking, throws a spitball. Such a pitch is outlawed. If it breaks wildly, it could kill a player. It works properly, however, and Henry is not caught; he wins the game and the approval of the team. He learns later that his father, while watching the game on television, had wept, and Holly had almost given up on him. When the team wins the World Series, all the backbiting is gone. Teammates who had hated each other share a drink in friendship. Everyone loves everyone, but suddenly Henry's basic good sense asserts itself. He has achieved all his dreams, and somehow found them empty. He realizes that if a few games had gone differently, they would still all be enemies; if he had won fewer games himself, he would not be the apple of his owner's eye. Friendship and respect based merely on winning, he realizes, are worthless and transitory. Patricia Moors, beautiful and jingling with expensive jewelry, calls for him. He turns and leaves the party, returning home, where Holly is waiting for him, at last certain that Henry the Navigator, as she calls him, has found his true course.

Before entering the army, young Jacob Epstein, the protagonist of *Something About a Soldier*, has changed his name to Epp so that he can find employment in Gentile business establishments. His father is a well-to-do "financier," he has boasted (actually a pawnbroker). Epp has carried his membership card in the Young Republicans Club, has campaigned against Roosevelt, and has been co-captain of the high school debating team, convincingly debating such issues as "Resolved: Irish Neutrality Endangers Allied Power." He is a naïve and sheltered young man of seventeen from upstate New York when he enters the army in 1943 and is sent to the South for basic training.

He is just such a young man as Harris himself was when he entered the army, and, just as with Harris himself, the experience is decisive. The change comes slowly. At first, Epp works hard to excel at being a soldier. He meets a young girl and dances with her, but her father is a member of a leftist union, and the union meeting hall is a shabby place, not upstanding and proudly American like the big department store he has had to change his name to work in. Thus, he is rather patronizing of the old man. Like other bright young men (when the army psychologist tests him, his IQ goes off the charts), he can be insufferable.

Epp is fortunate to find a friend in his company commander, Captain Dodd—who also befriends Epp's girl friend. While Epp is still wondering if he dares kiss Joleen goodnight, Captain Dodd is already taking her to a hotel. She and Dodd talk about Epp. Dodd asks if Epp loves her. She says Epp loves all mankind, that he has joined the army to defeat evil in order to save the world. Dodd says that one cannot love abstractions, one can only love individuals. By this time, Epp, living away from his affluent home for the first time, has begun to see blacks ruthlessly discriminated against, has seen among his fellow soldiers the disenfranchised poor. He meets Nathan, a member of the union to which Joleen's father belongs. Nathan is an even better debater than Epp, and convinces him that capitalism is the real evil in the world. Epp joins the Communist Party (putting his membership card in his wallet next to his Young Republicans card), but he is still caught up in abstractions: fighting the war for Communism is no different from fighting the war for capitalism.

Dodd, discussing Epp with Joleen, says that he will learn how to love properly one day, if he lives long enough, "which he will, if I can swing it." Dodd knows that their whole company is going over to its death. He tells Epp that if he runs away, he will not die. This is unthinkable to Epp, until word reaches him that his best friend in high school has been killed in the war. Now he sees the skull beneath the flesh, and he flees. It is not only fear of death, but it is also more than that. Though a debater and a logician, his final decision is sublogical, preverbal. He resolves in his heart not to die, not to kill, but to love only. He is arrested and thrown in the stockade, but Dodd, as his last act before going overseas to his death, gets him discharged as psychoneurotic.

Most of this action is presented in flashback, because when the novel begins it is fifteen years later. Epp, the only survivor, a teacher now, has been living quietly with the guilt of betraying his country. Slowly, however, it comes to him: one cannot betray a country, since that is an abstraction. One can only betray men, and the man he betrayed was Dodd. Dodd had saved him, and he had saved him for love, which again is only an abstraction, since only a woman can be loved. He goes then and finds Joleen, who, not hearing of his discharge, has lived the fifteen years thinking he has been killed with the rest of the company.

The novel quietly, uninsistently has its allegorical dimension. Jacob, as his name suggests, is that Old Testament promise of future generations that is about to be sacrificed when miraculously the lamb intervenes, and is sacrificed in his place (Dodd—whose name rhymes with God—is thirty-three when he saves Jacob and goes off to his own death; he has other Christ-like attributes as well). Some feel that this is Harris' finest novel. He has written many autobiographical books which yet have features of his novels, and many of his novels have strong autobiographical elements, but only in this one case has he been able to write a pure novel which is at the same time deeply autobiographical.

After Harris had written three Henry Wiggen novels, he came increasingly to feel that the persona of his semiliterate hero was too great a limitation. Henry did not have the vocabulary to say all that Harris knew. On the other hand, while Jacob could express himself intellectually, he was too small to express himself very well physically. In Lee Youngdahl, the protagonist of *Wake Up, Stupid*, Harris fused Henry Wiggen and Jacob Epp. Youngdahl is a college professor, novelist, and playwright who began his career as a professional boxer. This superhero, however, is not a mere figure of wish fulfillment. All of Youngdahl's exceptional gifts have in the end increased his dissatisfaction with life, and as the novel begins, he is on the point of taking impulsive actions that may permanently damage what is good in him.

Youngdahl is a teacher at a reputable college, he has a circle of good friends who admire his work, his novels have been well received, even if he has not made much money from them, and he has just completed a play that one of his colleagues wants to direct, lovingly and understandingly, for the college theater group. He has a good wife, who is perfect for him. He has health and physical strength.

Youngdahl is up for tenure, and he is evaluated by a philistine committee, the members of which jot down notes on whether he dresses tidily or organizes his lectures methodically. They are rather like a comic Greek chorus, but they have their effect: they turn Youngdahl inward. He is not only worried that perhaps they will find him lacking and turn him down for tenure, but also, as he turns inward and examines himself, he wonders if he is doing the right things. Is life passing him by? Is he living up to his immense potential? He decides he is not. He sets out to be a great romantic lover by having an affair with a glamorous actress; a great scholar, by becoming a teacher at Harvard; a commercial as well as critical success, by taking his play to Broadway; and a famous athlete, first by buying an interest in a professional boxer, and next by getting in the ring with him to show him how to box.

Wake Up, Stupid is, like most of Harris' novels, a novel of coming-of-age. As in earlier novels, there is a very rich cast of supporting characters: his wife and friends, who wait with decreasing patience for him to find himself, and the flawed characters who embody the various temptations he is facing and provide examples against which he can measure himself. The actress whom he chases knows that he is at heart a happily married man, and easily discourages him. Youngdahl has an old friend, a romantic hippie who lives in various parts of the world. He shows up and instantly has a torrid, short-lasting affair with the actress—just what Youngdahl thought he wanted. Youngdahl looks more closely, however, and realizes that his friend's complete lack of discipline in life and love has led to the failure of his own marriage, of his friendships, and of his writing, despite his initial potential. Youngdahl applies for the job at Harvard, and his friends there champion his application but also urge him to tidy up his dress and stress his scholarly rather than his creative writing. In the end, he realizes what a misfit he would be at Harvard, and he stands up the selection committee. He takes his play to Broadway, but finds himself surrounded by inane and grasping hacks who want everything in his play explained so that the simplest person in the audience can understand it; at last, he sees the light and withdraws. The final moment of definition comes when he climbs into the ring with his boxer and wakes up on the floor of the gym. "He hit me with his right hand, and I was further defined." The best life, finally, is to work quietly and with unremitting discipline to bring out the very best of one's talent, to bring it out without compromise for one's own satisfaction, and for the approval of a small but discerning group of genuine friends. The committee meets and approves him for tenure in one minute, recognizing his true value, as he himself has come to do.

Youngdahl's acceptance of himself and his confidence in the value of his work reflect Harris' own convictions as a writer whose devotion to his craft does not depend on fame or on material rewards. If the writer writes well and truly, Harris suggests, the moral statement will be there, and if it achieves nothing directly, in some small, gradual way the world will be made better.

Norman Lavers

Other major works
   PLAY: *Friedman and Son*, 1962.
   SCREENPLAYS: *Bang the Drum Slowly*, 1973; *Boswell for the Defence*, 1983; *Boswell's London Journal*, 1984.
   TELEPLAY: *The Man That Corrupted Hadleyburg*, 1980.

NONFICTION: *Mark the Glove Boy: Or, The Last Days of Richard Nixon*, 1964; *Twentyone Twice: A Journal*, 1966; *Best Father Ever Invented*, 1976; *Short Work of It: Selected Writing*, 1979; *Saul Bellow: Drumlin Woodchuck*, 1980.

Bibliography

Harris, Mark. "Three On: An Interview with David Carkeet, Mark Harris, and W. P. Kinsella." Interview by Brooke K. Horvath and William J. Palmer. *Modern Fiction Studies* 33 (Spring, 1987): 183-194. The focus of the interview is sports and literature. Harris speaks of some of the reasons he chose to write about baseball, describing the game as representing a cross section of America and having comic possibilities. He also had some experience as a ballplayer in his youth.

Lavers, Norman. "Mark Harris." In *Dictionary of Literary Biography: Yearbook: 1980*, edited by Jean W. Ross, 1981. A very brief biography of Harris and a list of his major works up until 1981.

_____. *Mark Harris*. Boston: Twayne, 1978. A life-and-works treatment of Harris in the Twayne authors series. Discusses each of Harris' novels in detail and speaks of his autobiographical characters and plots. Includes a bibliography of primary and secondary works.

Schafer, William J. "Versions of (American) Pastoral." *Critique: Studies in Modern Fiction* 19, no. 1 (1977): 28-48. Sees Harris' baseball novels as versions of a distinctly American pastoral and his use of myth and typically American characters as central to his best fiction.

WILSON HARRIS

Born: New Amsterdam, British Guiana; March 24, 1921

Principal long fiction

Palace of the Peacock, 1960; *The Far Journey of Oudin*, 1961; *The Whole Armour*, 1962; *The Secret Ladder*, 1963; *Heartland*, 1964; *The Eye of the Scarecrow*, 1965; *The Waiting Room*, 1967; *Tumatumari*, 1968; *Ascent to Omai*, 1970; *Black Marsden*, 1972; *Companions of the Day and Night*, 1975; *Da Silva da Silva's Cultivated Wilderness and Genesis of the Clowns*, 1977; *The Tree of the Sun*, 1978; *The Angel at the Gate*, 1982; *Carnival*, 1985; *The Guiana Quartet*, 1985 (includes *Palace of the Peacock, The Far Journey of Oudin, The Whole Armour*, and *The Secret Ladder*); *The Infinite Rehearsal*, 1987.

Other literary forms

Wilson Harris' first published novel appeared in 1960, when he was thirty-nine. Before this, his creative efforts were mainly in poetry, which, given the poetic-prose of his novels, is not surprising. He has published two slim volumes of poems: *Fetish* (1951), issued under the pseudonym Kona Waruk, and *Eternity to Season* (1954). While the first collection is perceived as apprenticeship material, the second is generally praised and seen as complementary to his early novels; it anticipates the novels' symbolic use of the Guyanese landscape to explore the various antinomies that shape the artist and his community. Harris has published two volumes of short stories, *The Sleepers of Roraima* (1970), with three stories, and *The Age of the Rainmakers* (1971), with four. These stories are drawn from the myths and legends of the Aborigines of the Guyanese hinterland. Harris does not simply relate these myths and legends; as in his novels, he imbues them with symbolic and allegorical significance. Harris, conscious of how unconventional and difficult are his novels, has attempted to elucidate his theories of literature in several critical works. His language here, however, is as densely metaphorical as in his novels. Harris' ideas are outlined in *Tradition, the Writer, and Society* (1967), a group of short exploratory essays on the West Indian novel, and *History, Fable, and Myth in the Caribbean and Guianas* (1970), a series of three lectures. These ideas are developed in his two later volumes of essays, *Explorations: A Selection of Tales and Articles* (1981) and *The Womb of Space: The Cross-Cultural Imagination* (1983), in which Harris analyzes the works of a wide range of writers, including Ralph Ellison, William Faulkner, Paule Marshall, Christopher Okigbo, Edgar Allan Poe, Raja Rao, Jean Rhys, Derek Walcott, and Patrick White.

Achievements

From the publication of his very first novel, Harris' work has attracted much attention. Though many readers are puzzled by his innovative techniques and his mystical ideas, his works have received lavish praise. While firmly established as a major Caribbean novelist, Harris is not seen as simply a regional writer. Critics outside the Caribbean perceive him as one of the most original and significant writers of the second half of the twentieth century, and, in trying to come to grips with his ideas and techniques, have compared him with William Blake, Joseph Conrad, William Faulkner, Herman Melville, and W. B. Yeats. As would be expected of one who eschews the conventional realistic novel, Harris is not without his detractors. Some readers have pounced on his work for being idiosyncratic, obscure, and farraginous. Those who defend him indicate that Harris' novels demand more of the reader than the conventional work and that what initially appears to be merely obscure and confused is intended to shock the reader and force him to deconstruct his habitual perceptions and responses. His importance has been acknowledged by the many awards he has received from cultural and academic institutions: He received the English Arts Council Award twice (in 1968 and in 1970) and a Guggenheim Fellowship (in 1972), and has held many visiting professorships and fellowships at such institutions as Aarhus University (Denmark), Mysore University (India), Newcastle University (Australia), the University of Toronto, the University of the West Indies, the University of Texas, and Yale University. In 1984, he received an honorary doctorate from the University of the West Indies, and subsequently he was awarded the 1985-1987 Guyana Prize for Fiction.

Biography

Theodore Wilson Harris was born in New Amsterdam, British Guiana (now known as Guyana), on March 24, 1921. He attended Queen's College, a prestigious high school staffed by English expatriates, from 1934 to 1939. He went on to study land surveying and geomorphology, and in 1942 became an assistant government surveyor and made the first of many expeditions into the interior of Guyana. Between 1944 and 1953, he led several expeditions into other interior and coastal areas. The interior, with its dense tropical jungles, vast savannahs, and treacherous rivers, and the coastal region, with its mighty estuaries and extensive irrigation system, had a strong effect on Harris, later reflected in his novels. These expeditions also made Harris aware of the life of the Amerindians and of the various peoples of Guyana of African, Asian, and European ancestry, who have come to populate his novels. While working as a surveyor, he nurtured his artistic talents by writing numerous poems, stories, and short essays for the little magazine *Kyk-over-al*, edited by the poet A. J. Seymour. In 1950, he visited Europe for the first time, touring England and the Continent, and in 1959 he emigrated to Great Britain. That year, he married Margaret Burns, a Scottish writer. (He was married in 1945 to Cecily Carew, but the marriage ended in divorce.) With the publication of his first novel in 1960, Harris became a full-time writer. He settled in London but constantly traveled to take up fellowships and professorships in Europe, Australia, India, the Caribbean, Canada, and the United States.

Analysis

Wilson Harris' novels are variations on one theme. He believes that polarization in any community is destructive in any form it takes, whether it is between the imperial and the colonial, the human and the natural, the physical and the spiritual, the historical and the contemporary, the mythic and the scientific, or even the living and the dead. The healthy community should be in a constant state of evolution or metamorphosis, striving to reconcile these static opposites. The artist himself must aspire to such a unifying perception if he is to be truly creative, and his art must reflect his complementary, reconciling vision. He should reject, for example, the rigid conventional demarcation between past and present, corporeal and incorporeal, literal and allegorical. Time past, present, and future should be interlaced. The dead should exist side by side with the living. The literal should be indistinguishable from the metaphorical. In adhering to such ideas of fictional form, Harris has produced innovative novels that some see as complex and challenging, others as obscure and idiosyncratic.

This perception of society and the artist and of the form his fiction should take informs all of Harris' novels, with gradations in emphasis, scope, and complexity. Some novels, for example, emphasize the polarization rather than the integration of a community. Some accent the allegorical rather than the realistic. Some juxtapose the living with the dead. There are shifts in setting from novel to novel. Harris' artistic psyche is embedded in Guyana, and, though he has lived in Great Britain since 1959, in his fiction he constantly returns to his native land, making use of the varied landscape of coastland, estuaries, jungles, waterfalls, mountains, and savannahs. In his later novels, the range of his settings expands to include the Caribbean, Great Britain, and Latin America.

Palace of the Peacock, Harris' first novel, is the first of *The Guiana Quartet*, four sequential novels which are set in different regions of Guiana. The novel is a perfect introduction to Harris' canon: It establishes the ideas and forms that are found in subsequent works. Of all of his novels, this is the one which has received the most extensive critical scrutiny and explication. Set in the Guyanese interior, the novel recounts the journey upriver of Donne, an efficient and ruthless captain, and his multiracial crew. They are looking for a settlement where they hope to find the Amerindian laborers who earlier fled Donne's harsh treatment. The account of the journey is provided by a shadowy first-person narrator, Donne's brother, who accompanies them. After an arduous journey, Donne and his crew reach the settlement, only to find that the Amerindians have left. They again set out in search of them and, as they travel further upriver, several of the crew meet their deaths—some of them accidentally, some not. Eventually, Donne and two members of the crew reach the source of the river, a waterfall, and, abandoning their boat, begin climbing the cliff, only to fall to their deaths. The narrative is quite thin, and is not given in as linear and realistic a way as this outline suggests. The novel, for example, begins with Donne being shot and killed before undertaking his journey, then proceeds to tell of the entire crew drowning but coming alive just before they reach the Amerindian settlement, and concludes with Donne falling to his death but reaching the mountaintop where stands the Palace of the Peacock.

The novel clearly is allegorical. Critics agree that Harris employs Donne and his strange crew as representations of antithetical yet complementary aspects of human experience. Yet their interpretations of what precisely these characters represent are quite diverse, and the novel accommodates them all. The novel is seen as examining the brotherhood of invader and invaded, the common destiny of the diverse races of Guyana, and the complementary and interdependent relationship between the material and the spiritual, the historical and the contemporary, and the living and the dead. The novel could be interpreted also as an allegorical study of the growth of the artist in an environment inhospitable to art. Drawing from his own experience in the challenging Guyanese hinterland, where he wrote his early pieces while working as a land surveyor, Harris shows that harsh surroundings put the aspiring artist in a quandary, for he is forced to look to his physical well-being by developing a materialistic, aggressive outlook that works against his contemplative, humane, artistic nature. At the end of the novel, Harris' narrator comes to realize that as an artist he must accept that he is the sum total of all the diverse antithetical experiences and impulses that coexist tensely but creatively in his psyche.

A cursory explication of the novel as such an allegorical *Bildungsroman* will provide an insight into Harris' unconventional artistry. Harris examines his narrator-protagonist's progression toward acceptance of the polarities of his artistic psyche in four broad phases which correspond to the four books of the novel. In book 1, the narrator, aspiring toward artistic and humane goals, suppresses his assertive and dictatorial tendencies. From the opening paragraph, it is evident that the narrator and Donne are alter egos: They represent antithetical aspects of one individual, who could be termed the protagonist. Their oneness is emphasized as much as their polarities. The protagonist's rejection of his Donnean qualities is signified by Donne's death in the novel's opening section and by the awakening of the narrator in a maternity ward, suggestive of a birth. After this scene, the journey upriver begins and Donne is found aboard the boat with his crew, but it is the narrator whose voice is prominent. At the end of book 1, Donne is described as being a shadow of his former self.

In book 2, the protagonist discovers that he cannot totally suppress his Donnean qualities, for to survive as an artist in his harsh environment he must be both the humane, contemplative observer and the assertive, forceful participant. This shift is indicated by the narrator's mellowing attitude toward Donne, who reappears as his former assertive self in book 2. Donne himself, however, mellows toward the narrator, admitting that he is caught up in "material slavery" and that he hates himself for being "a violent taskmaster." Their gradual adjustment to each other is shown in the relationships among the eight members of the crew, who, described by Harris as "agents of personality," represent overlapping but distinct impulses of the divided protagonist. Their personalities tend to run the scale from Donne's to the narrator's. They have their own alter egos. In book 3, as Donne and the narrator adjust to each other—that is, as the protagonist tries to resolve the inner conflict between his contemplative and active natures—various pairs of the crew die.

In book 4, the protagonist attains a new conception of himself as an artist—a conception that accommodates his antithetical feelings and attitudes. He now perceives that though as an artist he must resist the qualities of Donne and members of the crew close to him, he cannot deny them, for the artist incorporates all of their characteristics no matter how unrelated to art they may appear to be. The artist must acquire the all-embracing vision. A host of metaphors suggests this complementary conception. The protagonist reaches the Palace of the Peacock, with its panoramic perspective of the savannah, by falling back into the savannah. The Palace of the Peacock is also El Dorado, which Harris describes as "City of Gold, City of God"; it encompasses both material and spiritual riches. The Palace, moreover, has many windows offering an encompassing view of the world below and stands in contrast to Donne's one-windowed prisonhouse of the opening chapter. Taken together with the peacock's color spectrum, the many eyes of the peacock's tail, and the harmonious singing which pervades the many palatial rooms, the Palace paradoxically suggests both oneness and multiplicity. Such a perception of the artistic vision offered in this interpretation of *Palace of the Peacock* is not unique; it is found, for example, in the works of Yeats and Blake, whom Harris quotes several times in the novel. The uniqueness of the novel is to be found in the form and setting Harris employs to explore this familiar theme.

The Guyanese hinterland is most evocatively depicted in the novel, though realistic description recedes before the symbolic and allegorical functions of the setting. Though the characters occasionally emerge as living individuals and though their conversations have the authentic ring of Guyanese dialect and speech rhythm, they do not appear primarily as human figures but as allegorical forms. As a result, the protagonist's conflicts are not dramatized in any particularly credible, realistic situation. (*The Secret Ladder*, the last novel of *The Guiana Quartet*, which describes a similar river journey and a similarly ambivalent, tormented protagonist, provides a slightly more realistic, less allegorical study.)

The Far Journey of Oudin, Harris' second novel, is set in the riverain Abary district of Guyana, which is not too far inland from the Atlantic coast. The setting is as evocatively portrayed as is the Guyanese interior in *Palace of the Peacock*. The inhabitants of this community are East Indian farmers whose forefathers came to Guyana as indentured laborers. A few of these farmers have accumulated material wealth and have established a contemporary version of the master-laborer relationship with the less fortunate. *The Far Journey of Oudin* emphasizes the community's greed. It tells of Rajah's conspiring with his cousins to murder their illegitimate half brother, to whom their father left his property. The murderers suffer for their crime: Ram, a powerful, ruthless moneylender, brings about their ruin, with the help of Oudin, a drifter, who resembles the murdered half brother. Ram orders Oudin to abduct Rajah's daughter, Beti. Oudin, however, elopes with her. Thirteen years later, when Oudin is dying, Ram seeks to make Oudin and Beti's unborn child his heir.

The narrative is slightly more substantial in this novel than in *Palace of the Peacock*, but it is similarly submerged beneath Harris' allegorical emphasis. The characters, fluctuating between allegorical and literal functions, do not really come alive. The novel begins with Oudin's death and his vision of the past, which merges with the present and the future. He exists on several levels; he appears, for example, to be the murdered half brother. The novel emphasizes the polarized relationship between Ram, the unscrupulous materialist, and the sensitive, spiritual Oudin, whose unborn child to whom Ram lays claim symbolizes the possibility in the dichotomized community of reintegration—a factor which is underscored by the novel's circular structure and the recurring images of the union of opposites, such as the reference to the marriage of the sun and moon, to the juxtaposition of fire and water, and to the natural cycle of death and rebirth. Oudin, who strives to be an integrated individual, refers to "the dreadful nature in every compassionate alliance one has to break gradually in order to emerge into one's ruling constructive self."

The Whole Armour, the third novel of *The Guiana Quartet*, examines the fragmentation and integration of another Guyanese community, that of the riverain-coastal Pomeroon region. While the society of *The Far Journey of Oudin* is disrupted by greedy materialists, whom Harris perceives as the contemporary equivalents of the exploitative colonizers, that of *The Whole Armour* is disturbed by unbridled passion which erupts into violence and murder. Harris does not want to suppress passion, but he believes that it should be counterbalanced by discipline and control. This complementary Dionysian-Apollonian relationship is suggested by a series of betrothal images and particularly by the image of the tiger (the word used for what in the novel is actually a jaguar), which connotes the antithetical but complementary aspects of Blake's tiger.

The plot is difficult to extract because of the virtual inseparability of the actual and the allegorical, the living and the dead, and because of the elusive metaphors, described by Harris as his "fantastication of imagery." The novel, in bare outline, tells of the protagonist Cristo's fleeing the law, having been accused, apparently without justification, of the murder of Sharon's sweetheart. Cristo is sheltered from the law by his mother, Magda, a prostitute, and Abram, who falsely claims to be his father. Cristo and Sharon become lovers and are fugitives together. Eventually, they are caught but view the future hopefully because of the child Sharon has conceived. Cristo, who is linked with both the tiger and Christ, and the virginal Sharon are set against the passionate older generation. The two constantly yearn for regeneration and perceive themselves as being the founders of a new social order. The explicit discussion of this need for a new order has encouraged some critics to see *The Whole Armour* as Harris' most obviously political novel.

The Secret Ladder could be considered a restatement of and a sequel to *Palace of the Peacock*; it has, however, more plausible characterization and straightforward structuring. Like Donne, the protagonist, Fenwick, is in charge of a crew of men that reflect the racial mixture of Guyana. They are on a government hydrographic expedition that is surveying a stretch of the Canje river as the first step in a planned water conservation scheme. Poseidon, the patriarchal head of a primitive community of descendants of runaway slaves, violently resents their intrusion. Fenwick tries, with the help of Bryant, one of his crew, and Catalena, Bryant's mistress, to win him over. There is much misunderstanding and confrontation. In the end, Poseidon is accidentally killed.

Fenwick, like the protagonist of *Palace of the Peacock*, is torn between "imagination and responsibility," between dominating and accommodating. His boat significantly is named *Palace of the Peacock*. Evidently, he is aware of the importance of integrating his contrary impulses. He is attempting to live in the world of men with the insight his counterpart, Donne, has gained in the Palace of the Peacock. This attempt leads to inner turmoil and disturbing ambivalence, which the novel underscores with numerous images and metaphors. Fenwick frequently mentions the need to unify the head and the heart. His inner contradiction, like Donne's, is externalized in the relationship among his crew: For example, Weng the hunter is compared with Chiung the hunted; Bryant the thoughtful is juxtaposed with Catalena the emotional. Despite the more conventional plot, characterization, and structure, the novel is clearly Harris'. Its theme is polarization and reconciliation, and it is charged with allegorical and symbolic implications.

Harris' next five novels—*Heartland, The Eye of the Scarecrow, The Wait-*

ing Room, *Tumatumari*, and *Ascent to Omai*—are also set in Guyana and provide further explorations of community and creativity imperiled by various confrontations and polarizations. Yet he places the emphasis now on individuals and on deep probing of their consciousness. The protagonists become progressively more internalized. Subtler dichotomies are examined, such as concrete and abstract realities, scientific and mythic truths, fiction reflecting and being reality, individual and communal aspirations. And in *The Waiting Room* and *Tumatumari*, Harris examines for the first time the psyche of female protagonists. He portrays Prudence of *Tumatumari*, for example, as engaged in an imaginative reconstruction of her brutal past, which she metamorphoses into something meaningful to her present. *Ascent to Omai* similarly affirms the possibility of creativity in catastrophe. In these five novels, Harris' audacious experiments with form continue. In *The Eye of the Scarecrow*, which is perhaps the Harris novel that is structurally furthest removed from conventional form, and *The Waiting Room*, he introduces the disjointed diary form.

In the later novels—*Black Marsden*, *Companions of the Day and Night*, *Da Silva da Silva's Cultivated Wilderness and Genesis of the Clowns*, *The Tree of the Sun*, *The Angel at the Gate*, and *Carnival*—Harris shifts the emphasis from portraying society's fragmentation, as he did in the early novels, to its possibilities for reintegration. Rebirth and resurrection are common motifs. If the Caribbean's brutal colonial history and its multiracial population provide the ideal context for a heightened consideration of communal disintegration, its "cross-cultural imagination" is similarly suited to an exploration of communal integration. These later novels all feature cross-cultural Caribbean or South American protagonists. In so doing, they are not restrictively regional in scope; they are concerned with the human community at large. This is pointed up by their larger canvases. They are set not simply in the Caribbean and Guyana but in Great Britain, India, and Latin America as well. An increasingly common form of these novels is the employment of narrators as editors and biographers who seek to piece together the protagonists' lives and raise questions about the polarities of art and life and about the literal and representational functions of language itself.

The polarization in the assessment of Wilson Harris' work continues unabated. His advocates lavish praise on him, some perceiving him as a candidate for the Nobel Prize. Many appreciative articles and several book-length studies have been written on him. His upbraiders continue to complain that his novels are strange, with, as David Ormerod observes, "no discernible yardstick for meaning—just a simple bland identification, where X is symbolic of something, perhaps Y or Z, because the author has just this minute decided that such will be the case." Shirley Chew, speaking of *The Tree of the Sun*, states: "Harris has failed to rise to some of the more common expectations one brings to the reading of a novel." It is possible that such criticism is indicative of an inability to respond to the demands of Harris' challenging innovations; on the other hand, it is perhaps a reminder to Harris of his own rejection of the static polarization in community and creativity, a warning to him to heed the conventional in his pursuit of the innovative.

Victor J. Ramraj

Other major works

SHORT FICTION: *The Sleepers of Roraima*, 1970; *The Age of the Rainmakers*, 1971.

POETRY: *Fetish*, 1951 (as Kona Waruk); *Eternity to Season*, 1954.

NONFICTION: *Tradition, the Writer, and Society*, 1967; *History, Fable, and Myth in the Caribbean and Guianas*, 1970; *Fossil and Psyche*, 1974; *Explorations: A Selection of Tales and Articles*, 1981; *The Womb of Space: The Cross-Cultural Imagination*, 1983.

Bibliography

Drake, Sandra. *Wilson Harris and the Modern Tradition: A New Architecture of the World*. Westport, Conn.: Greenwood Press, 1986. Places Harris in the modernist tradition and shows how his fiction comprises a "third-world modernism." The reading of four novels—*Palace of the Peacock, Tumatumari, Ascent to Omai*, and *Genesis of the Clowns*—in this light rounds out the discussion. The accompanying bibliographical essay provides a valuable survey of the critical response to Harris' work.

Gilkes, Michael, ed. *The Literate Imagination: Essays on the Novels of Wilson Harris*. London: Macmillan, 1989. This collection includes Harris' discussion of "Literacy and the Imagination," as well as eleven essays by international critics whose work is divided into three sections: "Phenomenal Space," "Language and Perception," and "The Dialectical Imagination."

Howard, W. J. "Wilson Harris's *Guiana Quartet*: From Personal Myth to National Identity." *Ariel* 1 (1970): 46-60. Placing the novels that compose *The Guiana Quartet—Palace of the Peacock, The Far Journey of Oudin, The Whole Armour*, and *The Secret Ladder*—into the symbolist tradition, the essay links Harris' work with the poetry of William Blake and W. B. Yeats. Concludes that, like these earlier poets, Harris transforms history into myth.

Mackey, Nathaniel. "The Unruly Pivot: Wilson Harris's *The Eye of the Scarecrow*." *Texas Studies in Literature and Language* 20 (1978): 633-659. Offers a perceptive analysis of *The Eye of the Scarecrow* and helps to elucidate Harris' fiction in general. Emphasis is placed on the self-reflexive nature that characterizes all of Harris' writing.

Maes-Jelinek, Hena. "Wilson Harris." In *West Indian Literature*, edited by

Bruce King. London: Macmillan, 1979. The discussion comprises a general introduction to Harris' fiction and traces his literary development through its various phases. Also helps to define Harris' place in West Indian literature and the way he relates to other West Indian writers, whose work is discussed in additional chapters.

_____. *Wilson Harris*. Boston: Twayne, 1982. An excellent introduction to a complex body of fiction, the study provides biographical materials and traces the progress of Harris' fiction through detailed analyses of theme and technique. Includes extensive primary and secondary bibliographies and a chronology. Overall, a good book for the beginning reader of Harris' work.

World Literature Written in English 22 (Spring, 1983). Entitled "Symposium on Wilson Harris," this special issue includes an interview with Harris and his essay on William Faulkner's *Intruder in the Dust*. Articles by international critics on Harris' poetry, early writing, major novels, and literary theory are also included.

JIM HARRISON

Born: Grayling, Michigan; December 11, 1937

Principal long fiction

Wolf: A False Memoir, 1971; *A Good Day to Die*, 1973; *Farmer*, 1976; *Legends of the Fall*, 1979; *Warlock*, 1981; *Sundog: The Story of an American Foreman*, 1984; *Dalva*, 1988; *The Woman Lit by Fireflies*, 1990.

Other literary forms

To appreciate fully the lyrical voice which dominates Jim Harrison's best novels, it is helpful to bear in mind that he began his career as a poet. His first two volumes, *Plain Song* (1965) and *Locations* (1968), received very little attention, and the reviews were mixed. With the publication of *Outlyer and Ghazals* (1971), critics began to give Harrison his due, but his next two volumes, *Letters to Yesenin* (1973) and *Returning to Earth* (1977), both issued by small publishing houses, were again, for the most part, overlooked even after they were reissued in a single volume in 1979. *Selected and New Poems: 1961-1981* (1982), a volume which included the best of his previous work, demonstrated Harrison's range and complexity and established his as a major voice in American poetry. His collection, *The Theory and Practice of Rivers: Poems* (1986), only served to demonstrate more fully both his breadth of interests and his mastery of the poetic form.

In addition to novels and poetry, Harrison has published numerous essays, predominantly in *Sports Illustrated* and *Esquire*. In his essays, Harrison emerges as an amateur naturalist who denounces fish-and-game violators, sings praises to seasoned guides and to ardent canoe racers, and laments the passing of the wilderness in the face of developmentalism.

Achievements

Harrison is a venturesome and talented writer who has proven himself an able poet, novelist, and journalist. He has been able to revitalize the territories and boundaries explored by others and to make them new. Both northern Michigan and Key West, the Hemingway provinces, are re-created in Harrison's work. Also present are the subterranean worlds and the connecting roads which the Beats had earmarked, the relatively unsullied outback celebrated by Edward Abbey and Theodore Roethke, and the predominantly masculine worlds explored by writers such as Tom McGuane and Larry McMurtry.

By refusing to limit himself to a single genre and by attending to "audible things, things moving at noon in full raw light," Harrison has been able to appeal to a diversified audience and to portray an integrated vision that reflects the subtler nuances of the physical and natural world. While his references are often esoteric, he is a masterful storyteller who easily blends primitive and naturalistic images with arcane literary allusions. The reader is thus able to hear and feel simultaneously the meaning and motion of objects and experiences.

Biography

James Thomas Harrison was born December 11, 1937, in Grayling, Michigan; soon after his birth, his family moved to Reed City and then to the East Lansing area when Harrison was twelve. While he has repeatedly stated that his childhood was unremarkable, he clearly assimilated the spirit of the land and people found in northern Michigan and was deeply affected by the emotional bonds which held his family together. Perhaps because so much of this land has been ravaged by development, northern Michigan has come to constitute Harrison's Yoknapatawpha County, peopled by figures drawn from his German and Swedish ancestral lines.

Convinced that "you couldn't be an artist in Michigan," he made a number of treks to various metropolitan areas in search of the "right setting" in which to write; not surprisingly, these forays, described in *Wolf*, were unsuccessful. It was not until after his father and sister were killed in a head-on crash that he began to write in earnest. This personal loss, all the greater because it was unexpected, informs several of his novels and poems.

As the allusions which pepper Harrison's writing make clear, he is a prodigious reader. Not surprisingly, his graduate work was in comparative literature, and he considers himself an "internationalist" as far as his literary tastes and influences are concerned. Harrison is also an avid outdoorsman who uses fishing as a counterweight to the time he devotes to writing; he is committed to a code of ethics and way of life which discourage superfluous self-indulgence and encourage husbanding of resources.

Analysis

What is perhaps most striking about Jim Harrison's novels is the range of emotions which they encompass. While he consistently assumes a masculine point of view and revels in violence and debauchery, he is able to capture the romantic spirit which energizes his protagonists. He also avoids the bathetic trap that undermines the artistry of so many novels written from an aggressively male perspective. His central characters, though often wantonly callous in their attitudes toward women, are propelled by a youthful wanderlust and are always extremely affable.

In his novels, Harrison often routinely suspends the narrative sequence and deletes causal explanation. In this way, he constructs a seamless web and traps reader and character alike in a world inhabited by legendary figures who are attuned to primeval nuances and thrive on epic adventure. His penchant for the episodic is complemented by his metaphorical language and lyric sensibilities, which enhance his ability to shift scenes rapidly without sacrificing artistic control or obscuring the qualitative aspects of his various milieus.

By subtitling *Wolf* "A False Memoir," Harrison properly alerts the reader to the poetic license that he has taken in reconstructing his biography. Much of what is included is factual, but he has embellished it and transformed it into art. The work is "false" in that it merges time and place in such a way as to convey a gestalt of experiences rather than a sequence of events. It is also "false" because he succumbs to his "constant urge to reorder memory" and indulges himself in "all those oblique forms of mental narcissism." What results is a compelling odyssey of Swanson's impetuous flirtation with decadence and debauchery.

In his relatively obtuse "author's note," Harrison provides some biographical data to flesh out the Swanson persona. Also included is an admission that the romance he is about to unfold is somewhat of a self-indulgence which, like his desire to see a wolf in broad daylight, is central to no one but himself. Having thus offered his apologia, he proceeds to enmesh the reader in the tangles of people and places that have affected his narrator, Swanson. When Swanson is introduced, he is on a week-long camping trip in northern Michigan's Huron Mountains. In the course of the novel, he is alternately lost in the woods and lost in his own mental mires as he reflects on the "unbearably convulsive" life he had led between 1956 and 1960.

Swanson's wilderness excursions constitute a correlative for his sallies into the mainstream. When he is in the woods, his hikes produce a configuration resembling a series of concentric circles; he is guided largely by his instincts and his familiarity with certain reference points. Similarly, his treks to Boston, New York City, and San Francisco have a cyclical cadence and his itineraries are dictated more by his primal emotions than by conscious planning. In both environments, he assumes the stance of a drifter who is searching, against the odds, to discover an ordering principle around which to unscramble his conflicting longings.

A careful reading of *Wolf* reveals that the tension between the free-wheeling and nostalgic selves energizes the entire book. By coming to the woods, Swanson is attempting somehow to resolve the dualistic longings that have colored his first thirty-three years, to "weigh the mental scar tissue" acquired during his various rites of passage. While in the woods, he is constantly recalling the head-on crash which killed both his father and his sister; the pain of this memory is undisguised and serves as a counterweight to the bravado with which he depicts his adventuring.

Appropriately, the dominant chord in *Wolf,* as in most of Harrison's work, is a sense of dispossession and loss. Throughout the book, he emphasizes the ways in which greed, technology, and stupidity have led to the despoliation of the wilderness and endangered not only species but ways of life as well. Noting that the "continent was becoming Europe in my own lifetime," Swanson recognizes that the "merest smell of profit would lead us to gut any beauty left." It is this understanding that leads him to depict governments as "azoological beasts," to conceive of the history of the United States in terms of rapine and slaughter, and to indulge himself in fantasies of depredation which come to fruition in *A Good Day to Die.*

When one reaches the end of the novel, however, one senses that Swanson has resolved very little. During his week in the woods, he has not only failed to see the wolf but has also failed to illuminate a route "out of the riddle that only leads to another"; even as he labels his urban adventures "small and brutally stupid voyages" and accepts the fact that he longs for the permanence once provided by the remote family homesteads, he acknowledges that he will continue to drift, to "live the life of an animal" and to "transmute my infancies, plural because I always repeat never conquer, a circle rather than a coil or spiral."

A Good Day to Die, as William Crawford Wood observes, constitutes the second part of the song begun in *Wolf.* The novel, which takes its title from a Nez Percé Indian saying regarding war, chronicles the journey of the nameless narrator (who bears a marked resemblance to Swanson) from Key West to northern Arizona and on to Orofino, Idaho. As in *Wolf,* Harrison relies heavily on flashbacks and melds the narrator's memories with ongoing events; the novel is then less a correspondence between two periods than the route by which the narrator comes to accept life's capriciousness as a matter of course.

The nascent urge to avenge nature present in *Wolf* comes to fruition in *A Good Day to Die.* While the narrator, in retreat from his domestic woes, is vacationing and fishing in Key West, he is befriended by Tim, a Vietnam veteran whose philosophy of life is fatalistic and whose life-style is hedonistic. In the midst of an intoxicating evening, the two formulate a vague plan to go west and save the Grand Canyon from damnation. En route, they stop in Valdosta, Georgia, to pick up Sylvia, Tim's childhood sweetheart, who is the epitome of idealized womanhood—beautiful, innocent, and vulnerable—and who, in the course of the journey, unwittingly evokes the basest emotions and reactions from both of her cohorts.

The improbability that such a threesome could long endure is mitigated by Harrison's ability to capture the conflicting urges and needs of all three. While Sylvia may be too homey to be entirely credible, she does assume a very real presence. Throughout the novel, she functions as a counterweight to her companions and serves to underscore the risks inherent in not controlling one's romanticism. While all three have a tendency to delude themselves, she seems the most incapable of grounding herself and perceiving her situation clearly.

In *Farmer,* Harrison frees himself from his tendency to write false memoirs in lieu of novels. There are passing references to a nephew who resembles the author, but these serve to underscore Harrison's familiarity with the people and the milieu he is depicting. The portraits are especially sharp and clear in the cases of Joseph, a forty-three-year-old farmer schoolteacher, and Dr. Evans, a seventy-three-year-old country physician. Equally crystalline is Harrison's portrayal of the northern Michigan environs in which Joseph's long overdue "coming of age" occurs.

Against the advice of his twin sister, Arlice, and his best friend, Orin, Joseph has remained on the family homestead in northern Michigan "not wanting to expose himself to the possible cruelties of a new life." Crippled in a farm accident at the age of eight, he has used various pretexts to avoid travel; he has lived through books rather than opening himself to firsthand experience. While his reading has kept him abreast, it has done little to sate his hunger for a fuller existence. In fact, his preference for books dealing with the ocean, marine biology, distant wars, and the Orient has contributed to his growing dissatisfaction; he longs to visit the ocean, to partake more fully of the life about which he has only read and dreamed.

Against this backdrop Harrison develops a strain which was present in both of his previous novels: the counterpointing of characters. In this case, the restrained but steadfast Rosealee is set in contrast to the urbanized and impetuous Catherine. Rosealee and Joseph, both reared in the provincial backwaters, have been about to be married for approximately six years. Joseph, who has made love to only a few women in his lifetime, impulsively enters into an affair with Catherine, his seventeen-year-old student, who is attractive, experienced, and willing.

Structurally, the novel moves from June, 1956, back to the events which transpired between October, 1955, and the following June. The affair begins as a self-indulgence, but Joseph becomes increasingly lightheaded and child-like, revelling in a swell of sensations and previously unknown emotions; he becomes embroiled in the kind of sexual morass which he had previously associated with the fictional worlds of Henry Miller and D. H. Lawrence. Only in retrospect does he understand the risks he has taken in order to free himself from his spiritual torpor; he has nearly destroyed Rosealee's love.

In the hands of a lesser writer, the story which Harrison unfolds could quickly become melodrama, the tone maudlin. That it does not is a measure of Harrison's talent. The book, far from lacking ironic distance, as some critics have charged, constitutes a parody of the Romantic novel; throughout the book, Harrison burlesques Joseph's inability to attain "a peace that refused to arrive" and with mock-seriousness describes self-pity as "an emotion [Joseph] had never allowed himself." Using Dr. Evans as a foil, Harrison unearths Joseph's buried resentments and fears and concludes the novel in such a way as to confirm the doctor's earlier statement that Catherine "is not even a person yet" and that the dallying has simply served as a diversion for both of them. The fact that Joseph cannot come firmly to this conclusion on his own clearly distinguishes him from the protagonists in *Legends of the Fall*.

Legends of the Fall, a collection of three novellas, confirms Harrison's fascination with those elemental and primal emotions which defy logic, are atavistic, and propel one into the "nether reaches of human activity" despite the attendant risks. Cochran in *Revenge*, Nordstrom in *The Man Who Gave Up His Name* and Tristan in *Legends of the Fall* operate in defiance of consensual reality; each builds his own fate, guided more by inner compulsions and a taste for the quintessential mystery of existence than by rational planning.

All three of the main characters are blessed with "supernatural constitutions" and a wariness which allows them to survive against the odds and to perform feats of strength and cunning. Running like a chord through all three of these novellas is Harrison's sense of the gratuitousness of any life plan, his belief that events are "utterly wayward, owning all the design of water in the deepest and furthest reaches of the Pacific." There are countless chance meetings and abrupt turns of plot and any number of catalytic conversions. While in novels such confluences might have strained the reader's ability to suspend disbelief, in the novellas one is swept along and becomes a willing co-conspirator.

Revenge is, in some respects, the weakest of the three pieces because the reader is asked to believe that Cochran, who spent twenty years in the Navy as a fighter pilot, is so transported by his affair with Miryea that he is blind to the warnings issued by her husband, whose nickname, Tibey, means shark. In the service, Cochran had earned a reputation for being "enviably crazier and bolder than anyone else," but he had also maintained the instinctual mindfulness of the Japanese samurai, insisting on understanding "as completely as possible where he was and why." Once he meets Miryea, however, his circumspection is superseded by his romanticism and his "visionary energy." He conceives of her in terms of a Modigliani painting, the quintessence of female beauty and charm; he is plummeted into a "love trance" which "ineluctably peels back his senses." Failing to comprehend the meaning of Tibey's gift of a one-way ticket to Madrid and seven thousand dollars, Cochran sets out heedlessly on a weekend tryst to Agua Prieta, where he and Miryea are beaten unmercifully by Tibey and his henchmen.

Opening with a visage of the badly wounded Cochran lying in the desert, Harrison neatly discounts the pertinence of biographical data and summarily explains how Cochran arrived at his unenviable state. The focus of *Revenge* then comes squarely to rest on Cochran's attempts to avenge himself and recover Miryea. Despite the novella's sparsity, the reader is given sufficient information to comprehend the separate agonies which Cochran, Miryea, and Tibey are experiencing and to understand the emotional flux which resulted in the die being "cast so deeply in blood that none of them would be forgiven by their memories."

The events which transpire are a mix of the comic and the deadly serious, which come to a head when Miryea, succumbing to her own agony, becomes comatose—a development which allows Cochran to discover her whereabouts. The denouement follows quickly; Cochran and Tibey journey together to perform what amounts to a death watch. The epilogue is deftly understated so as to capture the enormity of Cochran's loss—he mechanically digs a grave "with terrible energy, methodical, inevitable"—and the meaning of the Sicilian adage "Revenge is a dish better served cold" becomes clear and indisputable.

Harrison's ability to write economic and yet sufficiently comprehensive novellas is more fully realized in *The Man Who Gave Up His Name*. While again Harrison provides minimal biographical data to explain how Nordstrom, once a prominent Standard Oil executive, has come to be a cook in a modest restaurant in Islamorada, Florida, he focuses the novel in such a way as to make Nordstrom's conversion convincing and compelling. Nordstrom, like Joseph in *Farmer*, gradually awakens to his lassitude and, unlike Joseph, decides to do something positive to change his life and to get back in touch with the elemental pleasures which had sustained him when he was growing up in Reinlander, Wisconsin. What enables Nordstrom to make the transition is the fact that he has retained a healthy capacity for wonder. The novella opens with the image of Nordstrom dancing alone so as to recapture the metaphysical edginess which his years of success have denied him. Harrison then provides an overview of the pivotal experiences which have left Nordstrom dissatisfied with himself "for so perfectly living out all of his mediocre assumptions about life." In the course of two short chapters, Harrison introduces Laura, Nordstrom's former wife, and their daughter Sonia who, when she was sixteen, had jolted Nordstrom out of his lethargy with the observation that he and Laura were both "cold fish." This observation prompted Nordstrom to resign his Standard Oil job and take a less demanding job as vice president of a large book wholesaler and to seek fulfillment through any number of expensive purchases and avocations.

Nordstrom's quest for the "volume and intensity" which had been lacking in his corporate existence is accelerated when his father unexpectedly passes away in October of 1977. As he is grappling with his own sense of loss and "the unthinkable fact of death," he is compelled to question why he has conformed to all of the normative expectations which have so little to do with the essence of life. To the amazement and horror of friends and family, he resigns his position and tries to give his money away, even making a contribution of twenty-five thousand dollars to the National Audubon Society "though he had no special fascination for birds." At the behest of his broker and his ex-wife, he sees a psychiatrist and it becomes clear that he has exchanged the inessential insanities fostered by the American Dream for the essential insanities which will allow him to free himself from stasis and fulfill personal desires.

The defiance of social expectations which lies at the heart of Nordstrom's transition is even more central to an understanding of Tristan, the main character in *Legends of the Fall*. Unlike Nordstrom, however, Tristan has never paid obeisance to anyone. Having abandoned any sense of cosmic justice at the age of twelve, Tristan has steadfastly made his own rules and run his life according to personal design. He emerges as a legendary voyager, propelled by a seemingly genetic compulsion to wander; spiritually he is the direct descendant of his grandfather who at the age of eighty-four is still engaged in high seas adventuring. Like Cochran and Nordstrom, Tristan has chosen to "build his own fate with gestures so personal that no one in the family ever knew what was on his seemingly thankless mind." Accordingly, Tristan is fated to live out certain inevitabilities.

Legends of the Fall is an episodic saga with perimeters which are staggering in their breadth. In the course of eighty-one pages, Harrison manages to imagine into being a multigenerational extended family, recount several complete cycles of events, and examine the ramifications of these sequences as they affect each member. The action spans several decades and several continents and it is a measure of Harrison's mastery that he can cover this range without sacrificing context or character delineation.

The tale opens in 1914 with the departure of Tristan and his brothers, Alfred and Samuel, from the family homestead in Choteau, Montana; accompanied by One Stab, they travel to Canada to enlist in the war effort. Using several complementary techniques, Harrison economically contrasts the personalities of the three brothers; it quickly becomes clear that Tristan and Alfred are polar opposites and that Samuel, a romantic naturalist in the tradition of Jean Louis Rodolphe Agassiz, is fated to die in World War I.

Just how opposed Tristan and Alfred are becomes a central thread in the novel. After Samuel is killed, Harrison makes a point of underlining the grief and guilt experienced by Tristan and Ludlow; Alfred's response is virtually nonexistent since "as a child of consensual reality" he alone escaped feelings of guilt. Equally important for understanding the distance between the two is that Tristan's career moves him from the status of horse wrangler to outlaw, while Alfred goes through all of the proper channels beginning as an officer and ending as a United States senator. Finally, the response of Susannah, who is first married to Tristan and then to Alfred, is telling; her breakdown and ultimate suicide are a response, in part, to the impossibility of ever regaining Tristan's love.

The "legends" which constitute the heart of the novella are Tristan's, but the dominating spirit is One Stab's "Cheyenne sense of fatality." Samuel's death is the first turning point and, while Ludlow is consumed by his own powerlessness, Tristan is compelled to act. That Samuel's death was the product of the Germans' use of mustard gas not only serves to justify Tristan's revenge—scalping several German soldiers—but also to convey Harrison's antipathy for the grotesqueries justified in the name of modernization.

Tristan's legendary status is enhanced by his joining and then succeeding his grandfather as the pilot of a schooner which trafficks in munitions, ivory, and drugs. Rather than dwelling on the specifics of the seven years which Tristan spends at sea, Harrison merely provides a glimpse of the first year and an outline of the next six, noting that the substance of these years is known only to Tristan and his crew. The next leg of Tristan's journey is also neatly understated. It begins when he returns home "still sunblasted, limping, unconsoled and looking at the world with the world's coldest eye." It soon becomes evident, however, that the wounds which the sea could not assuage are virtually washed away by his marriage to Two, the half-Indian daughter of Ludlow's foreman, Decker. The seven-year grace period which Tristan experiences is elliptically treated because "there is little to tell of happiness"; Harrison quickly shifts to the *coup de grâce* which kills Two and leaves Tristan inconsolable, "howling occasionally in a language not known on earth."

With a growing realization that he could never even the score with the world, that his losses far exceeded his ability to avenge the capriciousness of either Samuel or Two's death, Tristan nevertheless becomes embroiled in a final sequence of death-defying events. Again the denouement is quick, but it involves an unexpected turn as Ludlow assumes the active role. As in the other novellas, the epilogue adds a sense of completeness and juxtaposes the modernized ranch owned by Alfred's heirs with the family graveyard in the canyon where they once had found "the horns of the full curl ram." It comes as no surprise that, "always alone, apart, somehow solitary, Tristan is buried up in Alberta." So ends the legend.

In his 1981 novel, *Warlock*, Harrison melds the tone and techniques of the "false memoir" with those associated with the genre of detective fiction; what initially appears to be a marked unevenness in the pacing of the book is a direct result of this unconventional wedding. The first part of the novel contains minimal action and is used primarily to develop the central characters; the second and third parts, on the other hand, are packed with action and abrupt turns of plot. What unifies the work is Harrison's adept use of several comic devices, including a great deal of what Sigmund Freud called "harmless" wit and humor.

When he is introduced, Warlock, at the age of forty-two, has recently lost his forty-five-thousand-dollar foundation executive position and expends much of his time in self-indulgent reverie and experiments in creative cookery. He is a Keatsian romantic who began his career as an artist "on the tracks of the great Gauguin," finds resonance in the nobility and idealism of works such as *Doctor Zhivago* (1958) and *Don Quixote de la Mancha* (1605, 1615), and spends countless hours dreaming of a new beginning. He and Diana have moved north to Michigan's Lake Leelanau Peninsula to maintain "the illusion that one lived in a fairy tale, and everything would work out," a motive which makes him an unlikely candidate for top-secret sleuthing.

Diana, on the other hand, appears to be relatively stable with a nature almost antithetical to Warlock's. Yet, it becomes clear that she is not really any more able to decode the enigmas of reality than he. Although she is repeatedly depicted as a pragmatist, this trait is counterbalanced by her affinity for Oriental mysticism and her infatuation with genius. While she is an ardent feminist and an excellent surgical nurse, she is equally drawn to the charades that animate their sexual life and constitute a variant of the living theater in which Warlock later becomes the unwitting star.

It is the dynamic tension between Diana and Warlock which leads him to accept a position as a troubleshooter for Diana's associate, Dr. Rabun; while both acknowledge that Rabun is an eccentric, neither knows the extent of his idiosyncrasies. From the onset, Rabun lets it be known that he does not like to reveal all that he knows; it is his very elusive nature that energizes the last two parts of the novel. How little either Diana or Warlock knows about him becomes clear only after both have been sufficiently beguiled to prostitute themselves and do his bidding.

The initial meeting between Warlock and Rabun and its immediate aftermath resemble slapstick comedy. In addition to the absurdist context into which Harrison implants their clandestine meeting, there is the brusque repartee and the importance each attaches to the inessentials. The contents of a briefcase, which Rabun entrusts to Warlock, are telling; in addition to two folders outlining Rabun's holdings, there are copies of *Modern Investigative Techniques*, a guide to tax law regulations, and a sensationalized, paperback best-seller on business crime. Warlock is given two days and instructed to study the material and to write a brief reaction to it. Warlock's behavior is no less comic; he arrives home and promptly secretes the briefcase into the refrigerator for safe keeping and deludes himself with grandiose dreams that his life is beginning to merge "with a larger scheme of affairs," a truth which, unknown to him, constitutes a pithy double entendre.

Warlock's father, a top detective in Minneapolis, tries to warn his son away from the position and, failing at that, offers a good deal of advice and assistance. Their conversations are peppered throughout and serve to infuse the novel with a droll Midwestern humor and to underline Warlock's comic naïveté. Warlock's unpreparedness and vulnerability quickly become a dominant chord; while he conceives of himself as one of the "knights of the surrealistic age," the author makes it clear that, as a knight-errant, he lacks the purity of motive which spurred Don Quixote and the equivalent of a Sancho Panza. Instead, he has only his most unfaithful dog, Hudley, as his "Rozinante though without saddle or snaffle."

Part Two opens with an image of Warlock setting north on his first mission, completely undaunted despite the fact that he is en route to walk a two-thousand-acre area in the Upper Peninsula in search of lumber poachers. While he has the appropriate sense of adventure for the mission he undertakes, his idealism repeatedly blinds him to clues that should have been obvious to the most amateur sleuth. During the third part of the novel, Warlock abruptly discovers that reality is far more evanescent than even the most fleeting of dreams. Sent to Florida to "get the goods" on Rabun's estranged wife and his ostensibly homosexual son, who appear to be cheating Rabun out of millions of dollars, and on a society dame who has filed a seemingly outrageous suit against Rabun for injuries incurred when one of his health spa machines went wild, Warlock finds himself in a veritable house of mirrors.

The events which transpire during his Florida sally are unexpected and outrageously comedic. Again, Harrison relies on "harmless" humor and evokes compassion for the hapless hero. As a result of Warlock's adventures, Harrison abruptly turns the tables and destroys his preconceptions by unmasking Rabun as a perverted swindler and forcing Warlock to the realization that he has been "played for the fool" by almost everyone, including the charmed Diana.

After recovering a modicum of equilibrium, Warlock takes the offensive; reading only children's books "to keep his mind cruel and simple," he launches a counterattack which is simultaneously programmatic and impulsive, the former aspects resulting from the work of his father and the latter from Warlock's own primal energies. There is a good deal of mock-heroics on Warlock's part, but in the end, Rabun is brought to justice and Warlock and Diana are reunited. Like his spiritual heir who returns to La Mancha after having been bested by the Knight of the White Moon, Warlock rejects a job offer to track down a Moony and returns to his pursuit of Pan.

While *Warlock* is not a "representative" novel, it contains many of the elements which unify Harrison's oeuvre. Warlock, like Swanson in *Wolf* and Joseph in *Farmer*, is a romantic and a dreamer; he is a man ruled by elemental desires, who repeatedly becomes embroiled in ill-conceived liaisons and who "belongs" in northern Michigan despite the fact that he has a habit of getting lost in the woods. All of Harrison's central characters seem to have a "capsulated longing for a pre-Adamic earth" and a nostalgia for the unsullied woodlands of their childhoods.

With the publication of *Sundog*, Harrison returns to his technique of employing the almost all too present narrator. The novel hopscotches between revealing the life of Robert Corvus Strang and chronicling the misadventures of the narrator, who bears a strong resemblance to the persona Harrison has created in his earlier works.

The narrator meets Strang during what he describes as a "long voyage back toward Earth," a voyage that would put him in touch with the quintessential American. Strang pursued the American Dream only to be crippled in a fall down a three-hundred-foot dam. His experiences, no less than his persistent refusal to accept defeat, make Strang worth knowing. He is, as Harrison describes him, "a man totally free of the bondage of the appropriate."

It becomes clear that Strang and the narrator are kindred spirits—two sides of a single being. Both have more than average appreciation and respect for the forces of nature, even if the narrator is far less willing to plunge heart, soul, and body into its incomprehensible eddy. Both have unbounded passions and lusts, even if the narrator seems less in control of his anima or animus than Strang and more prone to succumb to melancholy, confusion, and despair. Both harbor a deep need to make sense of their own biographies and to plumb the depths of forgotten events that have unmistakably marked their personalities and approaches toward life. The hint of a biographical connection only strengthens their correspondences.

Robert Corvus Strang, as the reader comes to know him, is a man who has been involved on an international scale, building bridges, dams, and irrigation systems since his debut involvement in the construction of the Mackinac Bridge. This despite the fact that he contracted epilepsy after he was struck by lightning at the age of seven. His has been a life influenced by the polar personalities of his father, who traveled the revival circuit, and his older brother, Karl, who viewed truth as largely situational. His understanding of mechanical and electrical principles is balanced by his understanding of people, most of whom suffer, in his estimation, "because they live without energy" and can accomplish nothing. Strang, on the other hand, even as he attempts to recover from the side effects of a local remedy for his epilepsy, lives with great energy and maintains his commitment to regain his health and resume his career as a contractor on an upcoming project in New Guinea.

His self-imposed cure requires him to regress to a preadolescent state so as to "repattern his brain and body," the physical corollary to what the narrator asks him to do on a more personal and emotional level. At the novel's conclusion, Strang's attempts to begin again can be seen both as a therapeutic renewal process and as an exorcism through which he conquers the artificial barriers imposed by both modern medicine and those who profess to care for him.

Among the personal dramas of Strang's early life and his current battles, Harrison interweaves a sense of wonder that has served as a leitmotif in each of his earlier works, again claiming the Upper Peninsula as his own. Against this setting, Harrison offers counterpoints of urban violence, corporate greed and venality, and the unbridled insensitivity and martyrdom of the missionaries.

Harrison's ambiguous denouement only serves to underline his conviction that life resembled a "crèchelike tableau, a series of three-dimensional photographs of the dominant scenes, the bitterest griefs and the accomplishments." Harrison captures these images in his portrayal of Strang, whose life is keynoted by "love, work, and death. . . . held together by wholeness, harmony and radiance."

Despite its multiple plot lines, *Dalva* is also held together by a wholeness and a humanitarian spirit. The novel, in some ways, is Harrison's most ambitious undertaking. It is ambitious not only because it seeks to communicate a multigenerational family history but also because two-thirds of the novel is told from a woman's perspective.

Harrison's use of Dalva as the primary narrator, no less than his use of Clare as the major force in *The Woman Lit by Fireflies*, demonstrates his capacity to transcend the masculine point of view and enter into a world that, according to the majority of critics, he has never even conceptualized. Dalva, like her mother Naomi, emerges as a woman capable of acting and reacting with an equal amount of certitude.

From the beginning it is clear that, despite caprice and mistreatment, Dalva is not about to "accept life as a brutal approximation." Having lost her only child to adoption, and Duane, the only man she ever loved, to circumstances (and later death), Dalva is caught amid conflicting emotions—knowing what she has to do to earn her own freedom but fearing the consequences and the pain she could cause others. She is also mired in a family matrix that defies easy explanation.

Harrison structures *Dalva* as a three-part novel, centering the first book on Dalva's longings and aspirations, the second on Michael's misbegotten attempts at scholarship, and the third on the events leading up to Dalva's eventual reintegration of the various aspects of her biography. While each of the books has a completeness on a superficial level, the three are ineluctably associated with Dalva's grandfather and his allegiance to the American Indians.

Grandfather's journals allow the reader to comprehend a period of history that has long been whitewashed in history textbooks, and his sage advice allows Naomi, Dalva, Rachael, and others to make sense out of the tragedies that pepper their lives. His attitude is one born of pragmatism and necessity; having seen the less seemly side of American culture, he fully understands that "each of us must live with a full measure of loneliness that is inescapable and we must not destroy ourselves or our passion to escape this aloneness." It was this same uncanny understanding of the human condition that allowed Grandfather to coexist with the Sioux, who found his ethic toward the land and his rapport with people akin to their own.

The ongoing vulnerability of the Indians is a theme that dominates *Brown Dog*, the first of the three novellas that constitute *The Woman Lit by Fireflies*. Harrison's tone, however, is distinctly different. Rather than delving into the historical record, Harrison highlights the insensitivity of modern Americans to Indian traditions and culture and lampoons a legal system that defends the denigrators of history. While his sympathies remain the same as in his earlier works, the approach he takes is more reminiscent of *Warlock* than of *Dalva*.

Because of the seriocomic tone of the work, the book is dominated by characters (both living and dead) who are not entirely believable and who serve, instead, to buttress an assault against the materialism and insensitivity of the modern world. That Harrison casts his story through the filtered lens of Shelly, an aspiring anthropology graduate student, tips his hand from almost the first page of the book. While it is clearly apparent that Brown Dog may well need an editor, Shelly serves as a deflector rather than an editor.

Brown Dog, as a typical Harrison protagonist, is a man trying to cope with middle age. When he finds a three-hundred-pound Indian chief at the bottom of Lake Superior, he responds with the same degree of maturity that destined Warlock to his misadventures. Like Warlock, he stumbles through life, but unlike Warlock, he lacks an intelligent counterpart. Instead, Brown Dog is teamed with the female equivalent of Dalva's Michael. Shelly is opportunistic and insensitive to the values that make certain areas off-limits to outsiders. She is not unlike Brown Dog, however, as both are comic characters obviously unprepared to deal with the modern world. What she has over Brown Dog is that she comes from a wealthy family and can generally extract the results that she desires.

The ability to buy oneself out of trouble is also a theme which dominates *Sunset Limited*, the second novella in *The Woman Lit by Fireflies*. *Sunset Limited*, unlike "Brown Dog," reads as a parable in which one is forced to reconsider the parable of the camel and the eye of the needle. It is an abbreviated retrospective akin to Thomas Pynchon's *Vineland* (1989), in which the reader is reacquainted with 1960's radicals and forced to deal with the ways in which their pasts have shaped their presents. Gwen, who seems like an unlikely revolutionary, is teamed with two individuals who have clearly abandoned any insurrectionary thoughts and another who has merely retreated from the fray. That their quest is to gain the freedom of a tired gadfly of a revolutionary who has been hanging on long after his time is both relevant and beside the point. Harrison rather heavy-handedly points out in the final chapter that this is a fable, and as in most fables, there is a moral that has to do with basic values and the risks of renouncing those values at the expense of the immediate community. Hence, once Billy confesses to his past complicity with the authorities, it comes as no surprise that if a life must be spared, it will be his. Riches, in the elemental world in which Harrison dwells, guarantee very little.

As if to reinforce this point, but from a very different perspective, Harrison closes his set of novellas with *The Woman Lit by Fireflies*, which leaves the reader with no illusions about the protections offered by money. *The Woman Lit by Fireflies* may silence those critics who cannot see Harrison as a universal novelist. His appreciation for the lot of women—their failed expectations, existential angst, and lack of challenge—comes through quite clearly. Clare is a woman wearied from "trying to hold the world together, tired of being the living glue for herself, as if she let go, great pieces of her life would shatter and fall off in a mockery of the apocalypse."

Clare is not an extraordinary character, yet she has the courage to abandon a marriage that has betrayed her expectations decades before. The impetuous escape, half-consciously orchestrated by Clare, constitutes a psychic rebirth, a coming to terms with her childhood, adulthood, and future. In relinquishing the creature comforts to which she had always been accustomed, she finds new sources of strength as she conquers the dangers of finding shelter, water, and mental balance in a world that is dominated by elemental urges and necessities.

Clare is not renouncing money or creature comforts, although along the way she does prove that she can live without them; instead, she is renouncing the predatory ethic of dominance. As she says at one point, "I want to evoke life and [Donald] wants to dominate it."

Herein lies the heart of Harrison's fiction. He is willing to tackle topics considered too pedestrian for other artists. He is willing to experiment and risk the wrath of his critics. While in terms of his allusions he is very much an artist's artist, he is also very much a people's artist—willing to confront the dilemmas of aging that confront us all and make us look ridiculous on more than one occasion. More important, Harrison is capable of conveying a sense of loss and dispossession as it relates to the wilderness. What saves this sense from overwhelming his writing is his capacity for wonder and his ability to capture the mystery resident in the land and to imagine in life legendary figures whose exploits make life bearable. If one accepts Waldo Frank's definition of a mystic as being one "who *knows* by immediate experience the organic continuity between himself and the cosmos," then Harrison is a mystic. He is a superlative storyteller who is attuned to the rhythms of the earth and a poet whose lyrical voice can be heard on every page.

C. Lynn Munro

Other major works

POETRY: *Plain Song*, 1965; *Locations*, 1968; *Outlyer and Ghazals*, 1971; *Letters to Yesenin*, 1973; *Returning to Earth*, 1977; *Selected and New Poems: 1961-1981*, 1982; *The Theory and Practice of Rivers: Poems*, 1986.

Bibliography
Bourjaily, Vance. "Three Novellas: Violent Means." *The New York Times Book Review* (June 17, 1979): 14. With an understanding of the modus operandi needed for a successful novella, Bourjaily evaluates Harrison's

craftsmanship in each of the three novellas included in *Legends of the Fall*. Most useful for the points that are raised and are equally pertinent to Harrison's later collection of novellas *The Woman Lit by Fireflies*.

Gilligan, Thomas Mahler. "Myth and Reality in Jim Harrison's *Warlock*." *Critique* 25 (Spring, 1984): 147-153. The range of concerns Harrison explores and the methods he employs to deal with them economically are captured in this insightful review. Comparing Harrison to Kurt Vonnegut, among others, Gilligan comes to terms with Harrison's comic use of mythology, mock-heroics, and deflation to make Warlock a clumsy yet likable character. Though his focus is exclusively on *Warlock*, many of his conclusions apply to Harrison's other works.

Harrison, Jim. "From the *Dalva* Notebooks: 1985-1987." *Antaeus* 61 (Autumn, 1988): 208-214.

_____. "Poetry as Survival." *Antaeus* 64 (Spring/Autumn, 1990): 370-380. These articles can be considered companion pieces. The first sheds insight into both *Dalva* and *The Woman Lit by Fireflies*, and the latter does much to explain Harrison's affinity with the poetic process and American Indian art. Taken together, the two pieces remind the reader that Harrison remains a reflective critic and commentator, attuned to the forces of the late twentieth century.

_____. "An Interview with Jim Harrison." Interview by Kay Bonetti. *Missouri Review* 8, no. 3 (1985): 63-86. In this wide-ranging interview, Harrison discusses his impetus for writing, the writers who have influenced him, his view of art, and his sources for ideas. He explains that building sentences and plausible explanations constitutes his defense against the outside world.

Roberson, William H. "Macho Mistake: The Misrepresentation of Jim Harrison's Fiction." *Critique* 29 (Summer, 1988): 233-244. Roberson directly confronts Harrison's reputation as a "macho" fiction writer, analyzing and debunking critics' claims with pithy analyses of Harrison's first six novels. He acknowledges that figures such as Tibey in *Revenge* and Tristan in *Legends of the Fall* support the "myopic critical perception of [Harrison's] fiction" but delves deeper to unearth the "angst of the middle-aged American male" struggling to come to terms with both himself and his surroundings—subjects that have long been Harrison's forte.

Siegel, Eric. "A New Voice from the North Country." *Detroit Magazine* (April 16, 1972): 19-20. A good article for those who want a sense of Harrison, the person, replete with family obligations and biographical scars. Also depicts Harrison's writing regimen and his various therapeutic diversions.

L. P. HARTLEY

Born: Whittlesea, England; December 30, 1895
Died: London, England; December 13, 1972

Principal long fiction

Simonetta Perkins, 1925; *The Shrimp and the Anemone*, 1944; *The Sixth Heaven*, 1946; *Eustace and Hilda*, 1947; *The Boat*, 1949; *My Fellow Devils*, 1951; *The Go-Between*, 1953; *A Perfect Woman*, 1955; *The Hireling*, 1957; *Facial Justice*, 1960; *The Brickfield*, 1964; *The Betrayal*, 1966; *Poor Clare*, 1968;, *The Love-Adept*, 1969; *My Sisters' Keeper*, 1970; *The Harness Room*, 1971; *The Collections*, 1972; *The Will and the Way*, 1973.

Other literary forms

L. P. Hartley published, in addition to eighteen novels, six collections of short stories, *Night Fears* (1924), *The Killing Bottle* (1932), *The Traveling Grave* (1948), *The White Wand* (1954), *Two for the River* (1961), and *Mrs. Carteret Receives* (1971). Reprinted in *The Complete Short Stories of L. P. Hartley* (1973), with the exception of ten apprentice pieces from *Night Fears*, the stories reveal Hartley's reliance on the Gothic mode. At their least effective, they are workmanlike tales utilizing conventional supernatural machinery. At their best, however, they exhibit a spare symbolic technique used to explore individual human personalities and to analyze the nature of moral evil. The best of Hartley's ghost and horror stories include "A Visitor from Down Under," "Feet Foremost," and "W. S.," the last dealing with an author murdered by a character of his own creation. "Up the Garden Path," "The Pampas Clump," and "The Pylon" reveal a more realistic interest in human psychology, and they deal more directly with the theme central to Hartley's major fiction: the acquisition, on the part of an innocent, even morally naïve, protagonist, of an awareness of the existence of evil.

A frequent lecturer, and a reviewer for such periodicals as *The Observer*, *Saturday Review*, and *Time and Tide* from the early 1920's to the middle 1940's, Hartley published a volume of essays entitled *The Novelist's Responsibility: Lectures and Essays* (1967), in which he deplored the twentieth century devaluation of a sense of individual moral responsibility. These essays explain Hartley's fictional preoccupation with identity, moral values, and spiritual insight. His choice of subjects, particularly the works of Jane Austen, Emily Brontë, Nathaniel Hawthorne, and Henry James, suggests the origins of the realistic-symbolic technique he employs in both his short stories and his novels.

Achievements

While Hartley's novels from *Simonetta Perkins* to *Facial Justice* were published in the United States, they did not enjoy the popularity there which they earned in England. *The Go-Between*, for example, has been in print in England ever since its publication in 1953, and the *Eustace and Hilda* trilogy— comprising *The Shrimp and the Anemone*, *The Sixth Heaven*, and *Eustace and Hilda*—was given a radio dramatization by the British Broadcasting Corporation. In the course of a literary career of roughly fifty years, Hartley came to be a noted public figure, and his work received favorable attention from Lord David Cecil, Walter Allen, and John Atkins. Only in the United States, however, did his novels receive detailed critical attention. The three full-length studies of his fiction—Peter Bien's *L. P. Hartley* (1963), Anne Mulkeen's *Wild Thyme, Winter Lightning: The Symbolic Novels of L. P. Hartley* (1974), and Edward T. Jones's *L. P. Hartley* (1978)—are all American, as are the notable treatments of Hartley's work by James Hall and Harvey Curtis Webster.

Biography

Born on December 30, 1895, near Whittlesea in Cambridgeshire, Leslie Poles Hartley was named for Sir Leslie Stephen, the father of Virginia Woolf and himself a noted late Victorian literary man. Hartley's mother, Mary Elizabeth Thompson, according to Edward T. Jones, whose book on the novelist contains the most complete biographical account, was the daughter of a farmer named William James Thompson of Crawford House, Crowland, Lincolnshire. His father, H. B. Hartley, was a solicitor, justice of the peace, and later director of the successful brickworks founded by the novelist's paternal grandfather. This information figures as part of the background to Hartley's *The Brickfield* and *The Betrayal.* [1]

Hartley was the second of his parents' three children; he had an older sister, Enid, and a younger, Annie Norah. None of the three ever married. Reared at Fletton Tower, near Peterborough, Hartley was educated at Harrow and Balliol College, Oxford, his stay at the latter interrupted by military service as a second lieutenant in the Norfolk Regiment during World War I. He was discharged for medical reasons and did not see action in France. In Oxford after the war, Hartley came into contact with a slightly younger generation of men, among them the future novelists Anthony Powell, Graham Greene, and Evelyn Waugh. His closest literary friend at this period, however, may have been Lord David Cecil. After leaving Balliol with a Second Honours Degree in 1921, Hartley worked as a reviewer for various periodicals, wrote the stories later collected in *Night Fears* and *The Killing Bottle*, and cultivated friendships with members of both Bohemian Bloomsbury and British society. His novella *Simonetta Perkins*, a Jamesian story of a young American woman's inconclusive passion for a Venetian gondolier, was published in 1925.

Hartley made many trips to Venice. From 1933 to 1939, he spent part of each summer and fall there, and he drew on this experience for parts of

Eustace and Hilda, *The Boat*, and *My Fellow Devils*. Returning to England just before the start of World War II, Hartley started work on the series of novels which earned for him a place in the British literary establishment. Given the James Tait Black Memorial Prize for *Eustace and Hilda* in 1947 and the Heinemann Foundation Prize for *The Go-Between* in 1953, he served as head of the British Association of Poets, Playwrights, Editors, Essayists, and Novelists (PEN) and on the management committee of the Society of Authors. In 1956, he was created a Commander of the British Empire by Queen Elizabeth II. In his later years, Hartley gave frequent talks, most notably the Clark Lectures delivered at Trinity College, Cambridge, in 1964. Joseph Losey won the Grand Prize at Cannes, France, in 1971 for a film version of *The Go-Between*, for which Harold Pinter wrote the script, and in 1973, Alan Bridges's film of *The Hireling*, from a script by Wolf Mankowitz, won the same prize. Hartley died in London on December 13, 1972.

Analysis

Indebted to Bloomsbury, as shown by a concern with personal conduct and a highly impressionistic style, L. P. Hartley betrays affinities with D. H. Lawrence, Aldous Huxley, and George Orwell in a more fundamental concern with larger social and moral issues. His best books argue for the existence of a spiritual dimension to life and demonstrate that recognition of its motive force, even union of oneself with its will, is a moral imperative. In this emphasis on connection, his novels recall those of E. M. Forster, but unlike his predecessor, Hartley insists that the nature of the motive force is supernatural, even traditionally Christian. In his most successful books, Hartley draws upon elements of both novel and romance, as Richard Chase defines them in *The American Novel and Its Tradition* (1957), and the uniqueness of the resulting hybridization precludes comparisons with the work of most of his contemporaries.

Hartley's moral vision, revealed by the gradual integration of realism and symbolism in his novels, is the most striking characteristic of his long fiction. In a book such as *The Go-Between*, he shows that all men are subject to the power of love, even when they deny it, and that achievement of insight into love's capabilities is a prerequisite to achieving moral responsibility. This pattern of growth at the center of Hartley's novels is conventionally Christian in its outlines. The protagonist of each book, beginning with Eustace Cherrington in the *Eustace and Hilda* trilogy, accepts his status as a "sinner" and experiences, if only briefly and incompletely, a semimystical transcendence of his fallen state. The epiphanic technique Hartley develops in the trilogy to objectify these moments of insight recurs in various forms in all of his novels, coming in time to be embodied not in symbolism but in the pattern of action in which he casts his plots. Without suggesting that Hartley's fiction is about theology, it is clear that his concern with the subject of morality cannot avoid having religious overtones. Like Nathaniel Hawthorne, he traces the process of spiritual growth in innocent, morally self-assured, and thereby flawed personalities who experience temptation, even commit sins, and eventually attain spiritual kinship with their fellow men. These encounters, in a book such as *Facial Justice*, occur in settings symbolic of traditional religious values, and so while Hartley's novels may be read from psychoanalytic or mythic points of view, they are more fully comprehended from a metaphysical vantage point.

There is a thematic unity to all of Hartley's longer fiction, but after 1960, there is a marked decline in its technical complexity. In one sense, having worked out his thematic viewpoint in the process of fusing realism and symbolism in his earlier books, Hartley no longer feels the need to dramatize the encounter of good and evil and to set it convincingly in a realistic world. His last novels are fables, and in *The Harness Room*, the most successful of them, the lack of realism intensifies his treatment of the psychological and sexual involvement of an adolescent boy and his father's slightly older chauffeur. This book brings Hartley's oeuvre full circle, back to the story of the American spinster and the Venetian gondolier he produced in *Simonetta Perkins* at the start of his career.

The three novels constituting the *Eustace and Hilda* trilogy—*The Shrimp and the Anemone*, *The Sixth Heaven*, and *Eustace and Hilda*—objectify a process of moral growth and spiritual regeneration to be found in or behind all of Hartley's subsequent fiction. The process is not unlike that which he describes, in the Clark Lectures reprinted in *The Novelist's Responsibility*, as characteristic of Hawthorne's treatment of the redeeming experience of sin in *The Marble Faun* (1860). The epiphanic moments Hartley uses to dramatize his protagonist's encounters with Christ the Redeemer reveal truths which can be read on psychological, sociological, and theological levels.

In *The Shrimp and the Anemone*, Hartley depicts the abortive rebellion of Eustace Cherrington, aged nine, against the moral and psychological authority of his thirteen-year-old sister Hilda. Set in the summers of 1905 and 1906, the novel reveals young Eustace's intimations of a spiritual reality behind the surface of life. Unable to act in terms of these insights, for they are confused with his aesthetic sense, Eustace feeds his romantic inclination to construct an internal fantasy world and refuses to see the moral necessity of action. In *The Sixth Heaven*, Hartley details Eustace's second effort to achieve his freedom from Hilda, this time by engineering a socially advantageous marriage for her with Dick Staveley, a war hero and rising young member of Parliament. This novel focuses on a visit the Cherringtons make in June, 1920, to the Staveleys, acquaintances who live near their childhood home at Anchorstone. Eustace's adult epiphanic experiences are more insistent. Less tied to his childish aestheticism, they emerge in the context of the novel as hauntingly ambiguous intimations of a moral and spiritual realm which he unconsciously seeks to avoid acknowledging. In *Eustace and Hilda*, the final novel in the trilogy, Hartley brings his protagonist face to face with Christ during the Venetian Feast of the Redeemer, the third Sunday in July, 1920. This encounter leads to Eustace's return to Anchorstone and acceptance of moral responsibility for the emotionally induced paralysis Hilda experienced at the end of her love affair with Dick Staveley. Back in his childhood home, Eustace learns the lesson of self-sacrificial love in Christ's example, and he effects a cure for Hilda by staging a mock-accident for her at the edge of Anchorstone Cliff. Because of the strain this involves, he suffers a fatal heart attack, and the novel ends. His death signals the genuineness of the moral growth and spiritual regeneration which had begun in Venice. The interpenetration of realistic narrative and symbolic subtext which occurs by the end of the *Eustace and Hilda* trilogy objectifies Hartley's vision of the world.

Hartley's equivalent of Ford Madox Ford's and Evelyn Waugh's treatments of men at war, *The Boat* presents the mock-epic struggle of Timothy Casson, a forty-nine-year-old bachelor writer, to gain permission to use his rowing shell on the fishing stream that runs through Upton-on-Swirrell. Timothy, settling back in England in 1940 after an eighteen-year stay in Italy, consciously attempts to isolate himself from the effects of the war in progress in the larger world. He devotes himself to collecting china, to cultivating friends, to raising a dog, and to forcing the village magnates to allow him to row on the Swirrell. In the process, Timothy violates his own self-interest, as well as that of his nation and his class, but he is not the tragicomic figure that Eustace Cherrington becomes in the trilogy. In Hartley's hands, Timothy achieves only a degree of the self-awareness that Eustace does, and this enables the novelist to label him the "common sinner" that all men are, a figure both sinned against and sinning.

Timothy's desire to take his boat out on the river is an assertion of individuality which polarizes the community. His attachment to his boat becomes a measure of his moral and political confusion, for Timothy is torn between the influences of Vera Cross, a Communist secret agent sent to Upton-on-Swirrell to organize unrest among the masses, and Volumnia Purbright, the wife of the Anglican Vicar and an unconventional, perhaps mystical, Christian. The emblematic names suggest the comic possibilities Hartley exploits in his treatment of the two, but *The Boat* is a serious novel. Vera represents a social disharmony resultant upon the advocacy of ideology, while Volumnia reflects both social harmony and personal tranquillity resulting from sacrifice of self. Indeed, when Timothy persists in his protest against the prohibition against rowing and sets forth on the flooded Swirrell with two children and his dog as passengers, Volumnia confronts Vera on the river bank. Vera attacks the Vicar's wife, and the two women tumble into the water. When Vera drowns in the Devil's Staircase, Volumnia blames herself for the younger woman's death and subsequently dies from exposure and pneumonia. When at the end of *The Boat* Timothy, who has had to be rescued from the river when his boat capsizes in the flooded stream, dreams he receives a telephone call from Volumnia inviting him to tea, he hears Vera's voice as well as Volumnia's, and the two women tell him that they are inseparable, as are the moral and ethical positions they represent.

Near the end of the novel, Timothy prepares to leave Upton-on-Swirrell in the company of two old friends, Esther Morwen and Tyrone MacAdam. The two discuss the prospects for Timothy's acceptance of himself as an ordinary human being. At the time of the boating accident, he had managed to rescue one of the children with him, but he needed the fortuitous help of others to rescue the second child and to reach safety himself. Timothy is clearly partially responsible for the deaths of Vera Cross and Volumnia Purbright, and the "true cross" he must bear is an acceptance of moral complexity. Whether he will achieve this insight is an open question at the end of *The Boat*, and Hartley's refusal to make the book a neat statement reinforces its thematic point.

Hartley's *The Go-Between*, arguably his finest novel, is the only one with a first-person narrator as protagonist. Leo Colston, like the focal characters of the *Eustace and Hilda* trilogy and *The Boat*, frees himself from psychological constraints and achieves a measure of moral insight. Indeed, Leo's story amounts to a rite of passage conforming to the pattern of initiation characteristic of the *Bildungsroman*. More significantly, *The Go-Between* is a study of England on the verge of its second Elizabethan Age, and the patterns of imagery which Hartley uses to reveal the personality of Leo suggest indirectly that the Age of Aquarius will be a golden one.

These linguistic patterns, introduced into the novel by Leo himself, derive from the signs of the zodiac. On the one hand, they are a pattern manufactured by Leo as a schoolboy and utilized to explain his conviction that the start of the twentieth century, which he dates incorrectly as January 1, 1900, is the dawn of a second Golden Age. On the other hand, the zodiac motifs, as associated with Leo and other characters in the novel, underscore Hartley's thematic insistence on the power of self-sacrificial love to redeem both individual and society from error. At the start of the novel in 1951 or 1952, Leo is an elderly man engaged in sorting through the accumulated memorabilia of a lifetime. Coming upon his diary for the year 1900, inside the cover of which are printed the zodiac signs, he recalls his experiences at Southdown Hill School and his vacation visit to a schoolmate, Marcus Maudsley. In the body of the novel, the account of that nineteen-day visit to Brandham Hall, the narrative voice is split between that of the thirteen-year-old Leo of 1900 and that of the aged man with which the book begins. Used by Marcus' sister Marian to carry messages to her lover, the tenant farmer Ted Burgess, Leo finds himself faced with the dubious morality of his actions when Marcus tells him that Marian is to marry Viscount Trimingham, the owner of Brandham

Hall and a scarred veteran of the Boer War.

In Leo's mind, Marian is the Virgin of the zodiac, Trimingham the Sagittarian archer, and Burgess the Aquarian water-carrier. Determined to break the bond between Marian and Ted and to restore her to Viscount Trimingham, Leo resorts to the schoolboy magic with which he had handled bullies at school. He plans a spell involving the sacrifice of an *atropa belladonna* or deadly nightshade growing in a deserted outbuilding, but the ritual goes awry and he finds himself flat on his back with the plant on top of him. The next day, his thirteenth birthday, Leo is forced to lead Marian's mother to the spot where the girl meets her lover, and they discover the pair engaged in sexual intercourse. For Leo, whose adult sexuality has just begun to develop, this is a significant shock, and he feels that he has been defeated by the beautiful but deadly lady, both the deadly nightshade and Marian herself.

In the epilogue to *The Go-Between*, the elderly Leo Colston returns to Norfolk to find out the consequences of the mutual betrayal. Encountering Marian, now the dowager Lady Trimingham, once more, he undertakes again to be a messenger. This time he goes to her grandson Edward in an effort to reconcile him to the events of the fateful year 1900, to the fact that his father was really the son of Ted Burgess. This action on Leo's part embodies the theme of all of Hartley's fiction: the only evil in life is an unloving heart. At the end of his return journey to Brandham Hall, Leo Colston is a more vital man and a more compassionate one. Having faced the evil both inside and outside himself, he is open to love, and the Age of Aquarius can begin. That it will also be the age of Elizabeth II, given the political and sociological implications of the central action, gives Hartley's *The Go-Between* its particular thematic rightness.

Robert C. Petersen

Other major works

SHORT FICTION: *Night Fears*, 1924; *The Killing Bottle*, 1932; *The Traveling Grave*, 1948; *The White Wand*, 1954; *Two for the River*, 1961; *Mrs. Carteret Receives*, 1971; *The Complete Short Stories of L. P. Hartley*, 1973.

NONFICTION: *The Novelist's Responsibility: Lectures and Essays*, 1967.

Bibliography

Bien, Peter. *L. P. Hartley.* University Park: Pennsylvania University Press, 1963. The first book on Hartley's fiction, important for its Freudian analysis of his novels, its identification of his indebtedness to Nathaniel Hawthorne, Henry James, and Emily Brontë, and its examination of Hartley's literary criticism. At its best when discussing the novels about the transition from adolescence to adulthood. Includes a brief bibliography.

Bloomfield, Paul. *L. P. Hartley.* London: Longmans, Green, 1962. An early short monograph by a personal friend of Hartley, coupled with one on Anthony Powell by Bernard Bergonzi. Focuses on character analysis and thematic concerns, providing a brief discussion of Hartley's novels. Laudatory, perceptive, and very well written.

Hall, James. *The Tragic Comedians: Seven Modern British Novelists.* Bloomington: Indiana University Press, 1963. Claims that the Hartley protagonist possesses an inadequate emotional pattern that leads inevitably to failure. This neurotic behavior is discussed in his major fiction: *The Boat, Eustace and Hilda, My Fellow Devils,* and *The Hireling.* In these novels Hartley demonstrates that confidence is accompanied by a contradictory desire to fail.

Jones, Edward T. *L. P. Hartley.* Boston: Twayne, 1978. Provides an excellent analysis of Hartley's literary work, particularly of his novels, which are conveniently grouped. Also contains a chronology, a biographical introductory chapter, a discussion of Hartley's literary criticism, and an excellent annotated bibliography. Of special interest are Jones's definition of the "Hartleian novel" and his discussion of Hartley's short fiction.

Mulkeen, Anne. *Wild Thyme, Winter Lightning: The Symbolic Novels of L. P. Hartley.* Detroit: Wayne State University Press, 1974. Focuses on Hartley's fiction until 1968, stressing the Hawthornian romance elements in his early novels. Particularly concerned with his adaptations of the romance and how his characters are at once themselves and archetypes or symbols. An intensive list of helpful secondary sources is provided.

Webster, Harvey Curtis. *After the Trauma: Representative British Novelists Since 1920.* Lexington: University Press of Kentucky, 1970. The chapter on Hartley, entitled "Diffident Christian," concerns his protagonists' struggles to distinguish between God's orders and society's demands. Discusses *Facial Justice, Eustace and Hilda, The Boat,* and *The Go-Between* extensively, concluding that Hartley merits more attention than he has been given.

JOHN HAWKES

Born: Stamford, Connecticut; August 17, 1925

Principal long fiction

The Cannibal, 1949; *Charivari*, 1950; *The Beetle Leg*, 1951; *The Goose on the Grave*, 1953 (includes *The Owl*); *The Lime Twig*, 1961; *Second Skin*, 1964; *The Blood Oranges*, 1971; *Death, Sleep & the Traveler*, 1974; *Travesty*, 1976; *The Passion Artist*, 1979; *Virginie: Her Two Lives*, 1982; *Adventures in the Alaskan Skin Trade*, 1985; *Whistlejacket*, 1988.

Other literary forms

In addition to his novels, John Hawkes has published a collection of four plays (*The Innocent Party: Four Short Plays*, 1966), some poetry (*Fiasco Hall*, 1943—privately printed), volumes of short fiction, and many fragments taken from his longer works and published separately, often while still in progress.

Hawkes has given a number of highly informative interviews, not only about past works but also concerning those in progress. His "official" bibliographer, Carol A. Hryciw, has mentioned most of the early interviews in her *John Hawkes: An Annotated Bibliography* (1977); other notable conversations may be found in Anthony C. Santore's and Michael Pocalykov's *A John Hawkes Symposium: Design & Debris* (1977). Important dialogues were also conducted with Thomas LeClair (*The New Republic*, November 10, 1979) and with John Barth (*The New York Times Book Review*, April 1, 1979).

Achievements

Hawkes's lack of a wide readership has always been counterbalanced by a literate and highly vocal following among readers who are professionally interested in contemporary fiction. In fact, perhaps his most accessible and widely read work, *The Blood Oranges*, winner of Le Prix du Meilleur Livre Étranger (France, 1973), is a novel primarily read by college students and professors. Although he belongs to no recognizable school of fiction, many think Hawkes is "feasibly our best writer" of the late twentieth century, as the novelist Thomas McGuane put it. A ruthless poeticizer of fictional terror and aesthetic shock, Hawkes is both a satirist in the tradition of Franz Kafka, Flannery O'Connor, and Nathanael West and an explorer of the interior life in the tradition of Joseph Conrad. His achievement was recognized in 1986 with the awarding of the Prix Medicis Étranger (Paris).

Biography

Born in Stamford, Connecticut, reared in New York City and in Juneau, Alaska, John Clendennin Burne Hawkes, Jr., went to Harvard for his higher education, which was interrupted when World War II broke out. He then joined the American Field Service, driving an ambulance in Italy as Ernest Hemingway and several other American writers did in World War I. After service in Italy, Belgium, and Germany, Hawkes returned to Harvard, took Albert J. Guerard's creative writing class, and stunned classmates and teacher alike with his first major work, *Charivari*, a novel written while Hawkes and his wife were in Montana; *The Cannibal* followed shortly thereafter. In his own words, Hawkes began life in the late summer or early fall of 1947 when he "married Sophie, went back to Harvard, met Albert Guerard, and began to write, and through Albert . . . [met] James Laughlin, who became my publisher. So I had a wife, a teacher, and a publisher—all at the age of 22." Hawkes was graduated in 1949 with an A.B. from Harvard, where he later held various jobs, including assisting the production manager of Harvard University Press and lecturing in creative writing. In the late 1950's, Hawkes moved to Brown University, eventually becoming a full professor of English. He has held a number of visiting professorships and lectureships and has lived in Providence, Rhode Island, and in a variety of exotic places in the Caribbean, Greece, and France. He and his wife, formerly Sophie Goode Tazewell, have four children.

Even though many of his works have a nightmarish, violently hallucinatory quality about them, Hawkes himself is hardly an advocate of ugliness in real life. As he said to Thomas LeClair (*The New Republic*, November 10, 1979), "I deplore violence. I want to lead a safe, ordinary life with my wife and children and my friends and students. But ugliness is as essential to fiction as it is to the dream."

Hawkes retired from university teaching in 1988 but continued to make his home in Providence.

Analysis

Essentially a lyric poet operating as a fellow traveler in fiction, John Hawkes writes novels that are finely honed and superbly crafted, whose meaning and coherence arise largely from recurring patterns of imagery, autotelic thematic concerns, and highly unusual and largely unreliable narrative voices. Although the basic unit in the triad of the 1970's (*The Blood Oranges*, *Death, Sleep & the Traveler*, and *Travesty*) was the relatively short scene arranged in a more or less nonsequential format, Hawkes's novels *The Passion Artist* and *Virginie* represent a return to more linear scenic development, albeit still employing nonsequential flashbacks. Indeed, Hawkes told John Barth in 1979 that he no longer subscribed to his earlier, oft-quoted statement that "plot, character, setting, and theme" are the "true enemies" of his fiction, a remark made, he said, when he was very young. Rather, Hawkes's later work combines these linear patterns of development with comically grotesque narrators whose innocence in the face of a horrifying universe only magnifies the tension associated with that horror and with a mode of exposition that relies less heavily on unusual metaphoric connections and more on directed statement; in fact, Hawkes at times quite explicitly and directly tells readers what they are to understand. Nevertheless, even these directed statements are not ordinary referrals to the real world but are, rather, references one can only understand by looking forward or back to something else in Hawkes's mental Yoknapatawpha County.

By creating such unusual and self-contained fictional worlds, Hawkes draws the reader into some rather extraordinary literary experiences: ordinary fragments of conversation refer to highly stylized portrayals of bizarre activities and images of reality that take on nightmarish, hallucinogenic qualities. Explicit literary allusions, when followed up, only point to their own idiosyncratic employment. Narrators tell stories that, from a realistic perspective, could not possibly be told. For example, if there *is* a car crash in *Travesty*, who tells Papa's story? Similarly, how does one know Virginie's impossible story if she, herself, is an impossible child? The genius of Hawkes's writing is that all the possibilities—and perhaps none of them—may be true. One opens each new novel with the expectation of joining the author in creating a fictional world unlike any before known. Straining to make even elementary sense of what is being read, the "ideal" reader finds himself forced to discard most of the more familiar relationships between fictional and real worlds.

As Hawkes himself has reiterated several times, his major themes and interests include the imagination, consciousness, and the nature of women. In the later 1970's and early 1980's, he started discounting—perhaps better stated, demystifying—his interest in women as a crucial subject. For Hawkes, "we live by our imaginations and a sense of strangeness," imaginations which are always "trying to create something from nothing." In addition, paradox is "the second word, after imagination that's most important to [Hawkes], and . . . the word, dignity" (*Imagination on Trial*, 1981). Add to these preoccupations an obsession "with such things as horses, dogs, birds, sexual destructiveness, lyricisms, children." All the children in Hawkes's fictions are "maimed, injured, harmed, killed, punished in one way or another because [they] . . . represent the writer himself." Although these sufferings by children and animals may seem cruel, such cruelty "helps to produce a lot of the power of the language."

This cruelty and power, coupled with Hawkes's insistence on the separation of author and narrator, allow him to organize his prose objectively, obtaining the greatest possible tonal dissonance for superb aesthetic effects. Such detachment has led critics to question Hawkes's apparent lack of ethical responsibility. These questions, confusing mimetic and aesthetic ends, are, perhaps, inevitable about someone who says, "I want fiction always to situate us in the psychic and literal spot where life is most difficult, most dangerous, most beautiful."

Hawkes's best-known early work is *The Cannibal*, a novel that, as Albert Guerard has pointed out, tiptoes on a fine line between the creation of a new universe and the fantastical exploration of the present one. The war-ravaged, degenerating town of Spitzen-on-the-Dein becomes the allegorical micro-cosmic version of Germany, pre- and postwar, during the twentieth century. Although Parts I and II focus on the events of 1945 and following, and Part II centers on the militaristic Germany prior to the outbreak of war, the thrust of the novel points toward a time in the future when Teutonic Germany will, for the third time in this century, rise again from the ashes of total defeat. By extension, such a renewal of nationalistic fervor makes a stable, peaceful world all but impossible.

Zizendorf, the narrator of Parts I and III, wants to restore order to the German town (and, by analogy, to the nation). He is convinced that the first step involves killing the allied representative, the overseer on motorcycle who patrols one-third of the occupied country. Part II details, in both comple-mentary and contrapuntal imagery to the first and last section of the novel, the love affair and subsequent marriage of Madame Stella Snow and her husband, Ernst, which occurs prior to and during World War I. The imagery patterns in all three sections demonstrate how Germany's martial atmosphere made a century of warfare virtually inevitable as the casual, surrealistic horror of life in Spitzen-on-the-Dein suffuses everything, even the newspaper which is called, comically, the "Crooked Zeitung."

Stella's sister, Jutta, for example, an innocent girl during World War I, marries and bears two children between the wars, and, after her husband is captured in Russia, she must turn to prostitution to stay alive. One child, a girl, barely tolerated by Zizendorf, sees in the war-torn town a kind of beauty in the fires. Another child, a boy, is chased throughout the novel by a mad Duke, who eventually kills, fillets, and cooks the "small fox" in what has to be Hawkes's masterpiece of sustained metaphoric terror. The Duke's arrog-ance and bearing impresses Zizendorf, who thinks of staffing the offices of the new nation with his friends and acquaintances; indeed, thinks Zizendorf, the mad Duke "would perhaps make a good Chancellor."

By the end of the novel, the overseer has been killed, the people are informed that once again Germany is "free," and Zizendorf gives one of his first orders to Jutta's child, whom the Commander believes "will have to go" eventually. As many of the citizens of Spitzen-on-the-Dein line up to return to the insane asylum, the girl does "as she was told."

Mere plot summary, however, captures little of the essence of Hawkes's novel; only the experience of reading can fully impart the flavor of the work. In the chase of Jutta's boy by the mad Duke, for example, the reader first feels puzzled; he marvels how Hawkes has so easily and so well employed the metaphor of the fox hunt yet is vaguely unsettled by the juxtaposition of the hunt and the impact of the novel's title. When Stella's son comes upon them accidentally, one first tends to anticipate some sort of sexual child abuse signified through the chasing of the fox. Most readers, lulled by the son's "uncommon pleasure in the visit of the Duke," are stunned when they realize just how literal the fox hunt has been, as the Duke cuts, slices, and finally skins his little "furry animal."

The objectivity and the detachment of the narrative surrounding the boy's dismemberment and the boy's role at the Duke's dinner party combine forcefully to demonstrate how skillfully Hawkes is able to write about the most horrible scenes, employing an almost schizophrenic split between description and valuation, between perception and cognition. This ability gives the average reader an experience in what Hawkes calls "true fictive sympathy."

The problems of consciousness, ethics, the imagination, and sexual love get extensive and unusual treatment in *The Blood Oranges*, a novel set in the mythical kingdom of Illyria, where Cyril and Fiona, a couple who practice sexual extension and multiplicity, meet a second couple, Hugh and Catherine (and their three children), the former a puritanical voyeuristic photographer, the latter a housewife seeking adventure. As Cyril and Fiona encourage Hugh and Catherine to join them in their tapestry of love, momentary acquiescence becomes wholehearted acceptance by Catherine; Hugh, unfortunately, cannot purge himself of his former demons and accidentally hangs himself.

For the initial reviewers, the most important question in *The Blood Oranges* seemed to be an ethical one. Many equated the central character Cyril "with a studied, self-conscious, and all-pervading aestheticism" that can coldly watch the perpetration of the "greatest of evils," that of a person's apparent suicide. Following this understanding of the plot, critics would then go on to picture Cyril as a latter-day Oscar Wilde, a moral monster whose creator was guilty of either a bankrupt moral vision or a "self-conscious artificiality" so brittle and corrupt that "people have stopped mattering." Later, as the novel went past its sixth printing, various readers came to understand that its lyrical qualities made any naïvely realistic reading of the novel distorted. The reader is not supposed to see the characters as *only* separate individuals. Instead, in almost Dickensian fashion, the reader must understand that each character represents only part of the issues being raised.

Indeed, *The Blood Oranges* is a wonderfully lyrical and highly moral work of fiction that was influenced not only by William Shakespeare's *Twelfth Night* (1599-1600) and Ford Madox Ford's *The Good Soldier* (1915), but also by selected Platonic dialogues, the Bible, John Milton, Wallace Stevens, and medieval flower symbology. Hawkes's intention seems to be the creation of a new moral order to take the place of Western sexual mores associated with a dying Christian symbolic and ethical tradition. This transposition is done by arranging the story into forty-two nonsequential scenes and scenic fragments arranged imagistically and thematically. Since all of the information comes filtered through Cyril's unusually self-confident voice, the reader must be extremely careful not to make predictions about the "unreality" found in the fictional world without also checking for symbolic patterns, comic utterances, and unusual tonal qualities. Hawkes's vision is so complex, so paradoxical, that to understand any of his fictional patterns, one must be prepared to watch each of them resonate throughout the whole.

As one pieces together the chronology of *The Blood Oranges*, one begins to see that single, apparently simple scenes contain many of the novel's major thematic and character contrasts, contrasts that only later become clear, thus beginning the process of analysis, not ending it. The first major scene starts in a "little medieval church of cold passion" where Cyril and Fiona note that "the little motheaten dress of the infant in Mary's arms," the "thicklettered unreadable injunctions against frivolity and sex," the "effluvium of devotion," and the "comic miracle" of a life-sized wooden arm are all enclosed by a "sagging and worm-eaten church door." These images form the first set of oppositions: Christianity as an ethically and aesthetically decaying force. The opposite of the rotting chapel is the composite of Fiona/Cyril, whose sexual and emotional life-style counterpoints the images just seen.

As an unusual sort of narrator, Cyril arouses the reader's interest in questioning his value choices, his assessment of other people, and, most important, his ability to characterize himself accurately. In contrast to his unblushing references to his "diligent but unemotional study of sex literature," his living "a life without pain," his role as "a steady, methodical, undesigning lover," Cyril states uncategorically that he is "a man of feeling." Intellectual Cyril and spontaneous Fiona meet Catherine and Hugh in the chapel, a scene that adumbrates the oppositions: the decaying church, the sex-singing couple, and the curious relationships they all share.

After all four meet, one notices that Hugh, with a face like "Saint Peter in stone," has numerous imagistic connections with the church: black clothing and a missing arm that Cyril thinks corresponds to the one over the pulpit. By contrast, the imagistic opposition points obviously to Cyril as exemplar of a joyous sensuality, an aesthetic delight in color, harmony, and sexual extension, and, most important, to an almost religious desire to fertilize the sterility associated with Hugh, the Church, and sexual monogamy. The latter all reflect blackness, decay, repression, and ultimately death. Nevertheless, such pictorial polarities only represent part of Hawkes's master plan, because Cyril, although perceiving himself as gold while Hugh is black, will not be "unduly critical of Hugh."

As the story progresses nonsequentially, the reader senses that not only do Hugh/Cyril form both a set of polarities and of complementarities, but Fiona/Catherine, Christ/Goat-faced man, and sex-singing/child rearing do as well. Neither is complete nor well defined without the opposition/attraction of the other. For example, however seriously the pompous Cyril tries to interest himself in "the possibilities of sex in the domestic landscape," he can never, psychologically speaking, become a parent; Fiona and he are fated only to one cycle. As negative an example as Hugh is, he has created new life with Catherine and will perpetuate the possibility of other beings who may adopt Cyril's values. For Hawkes, the new Jerusalem must be based realistically on the whole of life. Children, family, all life must test the validity of sex-singing and a new moral order.

This type of character dualism is typical of Hawkes's narrators and so becomes a tool with which to read his later novels. One must listen to Cyril, or to Allert (*Death, Sleep & the Traveler*), or Papa (*Travesty*), or Konrad Vost (*The Passion Artist*), or Virginie (*Virginie*) with an ear for self-delusions, mental mistakes, and misleading self-justifications. Only as the reader understands Hawkes's narrative playfulness will he be able to feel the complications arising from the author's paradoxical and fictive imagination.

In *Travesty*, Papa is mad and tears down a country road in Southern France at "one hundred and forty-nine kilometers per hour . . . in the darkest quarter of the night," hell-bent on killing himself, his daughter, Chantal, and his daughter's lover, Henri (a poet who also happens to be Papa's best friend and the lover of Honorine, Papa's wife). As the car races toward death, the three of them have an hour and forty minutes to discuss why Papa is going to kill them. The only narrative voice, however, is Papa's, a kind of novelistic dramatic monologue sounding like many of Hawkes's other narrators: a voice frighteningly rational, and chillingly single-minded.

As they race along, Papa's calm refutation of Henri's terrified yet suffocating theorizing mesmerizes the reader into what Hawkes has earlier called an intense kind of novelistic sympathy. Readers find themselves shocked yet almost swayed by Papa's self-assurance. He will take them to their "destination"—"Perhaps 'murder' is the proper word, though it offends [his] ear"—not out of cosmic dread, or of hatred for Henri, or jealousy over Honorine or Chantal, and certainly not out of disgust with life. Papa says he wants, above all else, the "purity," the "clarity," the "ecstasy" of an accident in which "invention quite defies interpretation," a matter of "design and debris." Thus, Papa intends to commit the "final and irrevocable act" he so feared in childhood, an act which will elicit this purity, clarity, and perhaps even a "moment of genuine response from Henri." Their death, says Papa, will be "an ironic triumph," signifying "the power to invent the very world we are quitting."

It is through this last statement that Hawkes's larger purposes become clearer; and a formative event in Papa's youth—the "travesty" concerning a car, an elderly poet, and a young girl—points the reader to a greater understanding of the conversation between Papa and Henri. The latter, by ultimately agreeing with Papa's contention that "imagined life is more exhilarating than remembered [real] life," misses his chance to see the light of life and is doomed to die.

Henri and Papa, locked together "like two dancers at arm's length," share mistress, wife, daughter, and near metaphysical bond as well. To read them as if they were merely realistic characters has lead some critics to condemn the seemingly moral emptiness of Hawkes's narrators and the author's refusal to provide even minor external clues with which to judge the ethical validity of the storytellers. A realistic reading of *Travesty*, however, may miss half of Hawkes's intentions. It has been argued that no one else but Papa is in the car, that readers are hearing Papa talking only to himself.

Another and more inclusive reading of *Travesty*, one in keeping with Hawkes's artistic intentions and concerns for artists creating art, discounts the stress on arguable realism and focuses instead on the novel as an allegorical playing with Friedrich Nietzsche's fundamental question for the modern world: Suicide or not? If not, philosophy and life continue. If so, then dying with grace and imagination, creating design out of debris, forming debris in order to make possible new design, may be all the control postmodern man has left over his brief life. With this idea in mind, Papa, the other "characters," and the impossible narrative voice all recede into the background, and readers are left with a brilliant but somewhat brittle art object: a work in which the realism is muted, the artifice very obvious, a work which points both to and away from a deadly world made somewhat livable by the imposition of great art between man and the void.

Moving from the allegories of *Travesty* to the unusual "realism" of *The Passion Artist*, the informed reader can only marvel at the maturity of style and vision Hawkes displays. Although the novel is suffused with influences from Franz Kafka and especially from Rainer Maria Rilke, his voice is still very much his own as he digs deeper into the human condition. Unlike earlier Hawkes protagonists, Konrad Vost is depicted through the filtered yet illuminating light of both his childhood and his mother's. It is a light everyone eventually must face, implies Hawkes, since no one escapes the dragons of childhood.

The Passion Artist concerns the last several days in the life of Konrad Vost, a modern-day Malvolio. Vost spends much of his free time in the café La Violaine (a French portmanteau word, combining the concepts of rape and filth in a beautiful sounding word—a typical Hawkesian trope), situated across the street from the prison of the same name, waiting for his imprisoned mother, who had murdered his father when Konrad was a small boy. Father burned to death, notorious mother imprisoned for life, young Konrad is sent to a bizarre foster home, the dumping ground for his village's orphans and human refuse, presided over by Anna Kossowski, an older drunken woman with a large body and perverted sexual habits. After his graphic and yet highly lyrical sexual initiation with a horse also named Anna Kossowski and a young but not so innocent girl named Kristol, Konrad runs away, having suffered through those life events which will shape the revolting human encountered at the opening of the novel.

Learning about Konrad's youth in sensuous flashback, the reader opens the novel to Konrad as an adult in his fifties, a psychic cripple unable to finish grieving for his wife, dead for more than five years, unable and/or unwilling to recognize that his teenage daughter, like a jinni in a bottle, has escaped his care and become a prostitute. Konrad remains unrequited in his love for his mother, who, in the prison across from La Violaine café, has never written or spoken to him since the murder. After a brief encounter with a child prostitute, who is both friend of and psychic double for his daughter, Konrad Vost volunteers to help put down a prison revolt. Rendered unconscious during the battle for control of the prison, Konrad's unconscious takes command as he dreams of women who describe his personality flaws. Awakening, he believes that his right hand has been axed off, replaced by a silver one encased in a black glove, and vows to conduct a personal search for the escapees. This silver hand is an important image: as a child, Konrad was called "the little trumpeter of the silver hands."

During the search, Konrad frightens an old woman to death and betrays another, a slim young child-woman whom he spies upon, bathing. Konrad, looking for shelter, is seized by two older escapees from La Violaine and is put in the prison, a place where he knew he had wanted to be all along. There, he encounters his mother and a tall, handsome woman with red hair who seduces him and finally shows him a "willed erotic union" and the possibilities of mature sexual expression. Hawkes, however, unwilling to end the novel happily, has Konrad Vost die at the hands of a La Violaine café habitué, possibly the father of a girl Konrad had beaten earlier.

The plot of this novel is detailed in order to show how it represents the skeleton, the outer shell of a highly elaborate work of art. In *The Passion Artist*, Hawkes returns both stylistically and imagistically to the bleak, rotting, rust-filled world of *The Cannibal* and *The Owl*. For example, Konrad Vost thinks of himself as some "military personage" walking "with feigned complacency down a broad avenue awash with urine." La Violaine, the place where his mother is imprisoned, is enclosed by "high narrow rusted gates" and sits in the middle of a city which was "the very domain of the human psyche." As with the earlier novels, the imagistic and metaphoric patterns become the reality of *The Passion Artist*. When the reader looks for a focus, a place with which to begin interpretation, he must pay close attention to the repeated visualizations toward which Hawkes continually draws the readers' attention.

In the novel, for example, a pattern of flower references and women is established, and the reader soon realizes the importance of the relationships between Konrad's mental state and the descriptions of landscapes and flowers. To solidify this innocent impression, Hawkes says explicitly, during Konrad's hunt through the swamps, that his inner landscape "had become externalized." There, in the marshes, plants fester "in sockets of ice," reminding the reader that when Konrad's father was killed, the "flowers on the porcelain stove were frozen."

The flower references all point toward an understanding of Konrad's sexuality as locked in cold storage, decaying, unable to flower. Anna Kossowski, wearing a birthmark, a "brown toadstool" on her cheek, and in part responsible for Konrad's problems, becomes a variation of the same basic pattern. Hawkes vividly demonstrates the possibilities of change in Konrad's life by giving the tall, handsome woman with red hair who loves and seduces him at the end of the novel the same image as the prostitute: she too wears a brown rose. With her, however, Konrad Vost learns, after all he has gone through, "the transports of that singular experience which makes every man an artist," a passion artist. In this way, Hawkes uses visual images in place of didactic narrative statement, but he does it so well that information is communicated through an almost completely aesthetic transmission.

Like so many of Hawkes's other narrators, Konrad Vost must never be confused with the author. In the instance of *The Passion Artist*, Konrad Vost's understanding of the world is so clouded, so distorted with his own neuroses, that Hawkes is able to frighten the reader more with what Konrad does not see and feel than he could with a more reasonable or observant narrator. The mental double talk, for example, which so far reflects Konrad's apathetic feelings about killing an old woman, serves only to confirm how despicable a character he really is; and yet, Konrad still remains understandable and even sympathetic to the reader. This attitude is as it should be, as Hawkes has arranged it: readers can sympathize with both victim and victimizer; they can be both murdered and murderer. The simple oppositions Hawkes labors to draw convincingly finally become united in the minds of the readers in what Hawkes has termed "true fictive sympathy."

Thus, Hawkes's wonderfully imaginative, self-contained worlds, his lyrically passionate prose style, his rare ability to make the reader know and understand both victim and victimizer are some of the qualities that make reading the longer fictions of John Hawkes one of the most rewarding aesthetic experiences to be found in contemporary American fiction.

John V. Knapp

Other major works

SHORT FICTION: *Lunar Landscapes*, 1969; *Innocence in Extremis*, 1985.
PLAY: *The Innocent Party: Four Short Plays*, 1966.
POETRY: *Fiasco Hall*, 1943.
MISCELLANEOUS: *Humors of Blood and Skin: A John Hawkes Reader*, 1984.

Bibliography

Berry, Eliot. *A Poetry of Force and Darkness: The Fiction of John Hawkes*.

San Bernardino, Calif.: Borgo Press, 1979. Discusses the imaginative art of Hawkes's writing in the context of the romantic novel, likening it to poetry with its rich language and depth. Compares Hawkes to both William Faulkner and Nathaniel Hawthorne.

Bradbury, Malcolm. *The Modern American Novel*. Oxford, England: Oxford University Press, 1983. Bradbury places Hawkes in the genre of postmodernism, citing him as a powerfully compelling writer of the "imaginative grotesque" who draws on the tradition of the American Gothic. Discusses his novels up to and including *The Passion Artist*, noting his increased clarity of technique and greater complexity.

Busch, Frederick. *Hawkes: A Guide to His Fictions*. Syracuse, N.Y.: Syracuse University Press, 1973. Valuable when examining the intricacies of the plots in Hawkes's fiction, but less so when discussing stylistic and thematic concerns. Analyzes image patterns in his novels through *The Blood Oranges*, with a helpful discussion on his use of animal imagery.

Greiner, Donald J. *Comic Terror: The Novels of John Hawkes*. Memphis, Tenn.: Memphis State University Press, 1978. Greiner cites Hawkes as one of the few "truly gifted writers of the so-called black humor movement" since 1950. Notes that Hawkes's main concern is to disrupt conventional forms of fiction while constructing controlled imaginative visions. Discusses his later works (*The Blood Oranges*, *Death*, *Sleep & the Traveler*, and *Travesty*) and shows how they have modified earlier works. Includes a checklist of primary and secondary sources. An important contribution to criticism on Hawkes.

Kuehl, John. *John Hawkes and the Craft of Conflict*. New Brunswick, N.J.: Rutgers University Press, 1975. Treats the relationship between Hawkes's central themes and his craft, simultaneously tracing the evolution of both. Explores the Eros/Thanatos conflict in his work and is therefore useful to the Hawkes specialist. Also includes an interview with Hawkes.

O'Donnell, Patrick. *John Hawkes*. Boston: Twayne, 1982. A good introduction for the beginning reader of Hawkes, this study provides thorough readings of his works and some biographical information of interest. The purpose of this study is to explain to the general reader the difficulties of Hawkes's fiction and to explore the probing clarity of his imagination. Includes a useful selected bibliography.

NATHANIEL HAWTHORNE

Born: Salem, Massachusetts; July 4, 1804
Died: Plymouth, New Hampshire; May 19, 1864

Principal long fiction

Fanshawe: A Tale, 1828; *The Scarlet Letter*, 1850; *The House of the Seven Gables*, 1851; *The Blithedale Romance*, 1852; *The Marble Faun*, 1860; *Septimius Felton*, 1872 (fragment); *The Dolliver Romance*, 1876 (fragment); *The Ancestral Footstep*, 1883 (fragment); *Doctor Grimshawe's Secret*, 1883 (fragment).

Other literary forms

Many of Nathaniel Hawthorne's short stories were originally published anonymously in such magazines as the *Token* and the *New England Magazine* between 1830 and 1837. Several collections appeared during his lifetime, including *Twice-Told Tales* (1837; expanded, 1842), *Mosses from an Old Manse* (1846, 1854) and *The Snow-Image and Other Twice-Told Tales* (1851). Houghton Mifflin published the complete works in the Riverside edition (1850-1882) and the Old Manse edition (1900). Hawthorne also wrote stories for children, collected in *Grandfather's Chair* (1841), *Biographical Stories for Children* (1842), *True Stories from History and Biography* (1851), *A Wonder-Book for Boys and Girls* (1852), and *Tanglewood Tales for Boys and Girls* (1853). With the help of his sister Elizabeth, he edited the *American Magazine of Useful and Entertaining Knowledge* (1836) and *Peter Parley's Universal History* (1837) and, as a favor to Franklin Pierce, wrote a biography for the presidential campaign. His last completed work was *Our Old Home* (1863), a series of essays about his sojourn in England. At the time of his death, he left four unfinished fragments: *Septimius Felton* (1872), *The Dolliver Romance* (1876), *The Ancestral Footstep* (1883), and *Doctor Grimshawe's Secret* (1883).

Achievements

Few other American authors, with the possible exception of Henry James, have engaged in so deliberate a literary apprenticeship as Hawthorne. After an initial period of anonymity during his so-called "solitary years" from 1825 to 1837, he achieved an unfaltering reputation as an author of short stories, romances, essays, and children's books. He is remembered not only for furthering the development of the short-story form, but also for distinguishing between the novel and the romance. The prefaces to his long works elucidate his theory of the "neutral ground"—the junction between the actual and the imaginary—where romance takes place. He is noted for his masterful exploration of the psychology of guilt and sin; his study of the Puritan heritage contributed to the emerging sense of historicity which characterized the American Renaissance of the mid-nineteenth century. Hawthorne is unrivaled as an allegorist, especially as one whose character typologies and symbols achieve universality through their psychological validity. While he has been faulted for sentimentality, lapses into archaic diction, and Gothicism, Hawthorne's works continue to evoke the "truth of the human heart" that is the key to their continuing appeal.

Biography

Nathaniel Hawthorne was born in Salem, Massachusetts, on July 4, 1804. On his father's side, Hawthorne was descended from William Hathorne, who settled in Massachusetts in 1630 and whose son John was one of the judges in the 1692 Salem witchcraft trials. Hawthorne's father, a sea captain, married Elizabeth Clarke Manning in 1801. Mrs. Hathorne's English ancestors emigrated to the New World in 1679; her brother Robert, a successful businessman, assumed responsibility for her affairs after Captain Hathorne died of yellow fever in Surinam in 1808.

After his father's death, Hawthorne, his two sisters Elizabeth Manning and Maria Louisa, and his mother moved into the populous Manning household, a move that on the one hand estranged him from his Hathorne relatives and on the other provided him with an attentive family life, albeit an adult one, for the eight aunts and uncles living there were unmarried at that time. Perhaps the adult company accounted in part for his literary tastes, as did his less than regular education. Although he attended a school taught by Joseph Emerson Worcester, a renowned philologist of the time, Hawthorne led a sedentary existence for almost three years after being lamed at the age of nine. During his enforced inactivity, he spent long afternoons reading Edmund Spenser, John Bunyan, and William Shakespeare, his favorite authors.

When Hawthorne was twelve, his mother moved the family temporarily to Raymond, Maine, where the Mannings owned a tract of land. The outdoor activity occasioned by nearby Lake Sebago and the surrounding forest land proved beneficial to Hawthorne; quickly recovering his health, he became an able marksman and fisherman. During these years, interrupted by schooling with the Reverend Caleb Bradley, a stern man not to Hawthorne's liking, Hawthorne accumulated Wordsworthian memories of the wilderness and of village life that were to be evoked in his fiction. Recalled to Salem, he began in 1820 to be tutored for college by the lawyer Benjamin Lynde Oliver, working, in the meantime, as a bookkeeper for his Uncle Robert, an occupation that foreshadowed his later business ventures. He continued his reading, including such authors as Henry Fielding, Sir Walter Scott, William Godwin, "Monk" Lewis, and James Hogg, and produced a family newspaper, *The Spectator*, characterized by humorous notices and essays and parodies of sentimental verse. The first member of his family to attend college, he was sent to Bowdoin, where he was graduated eighteenth in a class of thirty-eight. Known for his quietness and gentle humor, he disliked declamations, was negligent in many academic requirements, and, indeed, was fined for playing cards. His fellow students at Bowdoin included Henry Wadsworth Longfellow and Franklin Pierce, who later was elected President of the United States.

Hawthorne had determined early on a career in letters. Returning to Salem upon graduation, he began a self-imposed apprenticeship, the so-called "solitary years." During this time, Hawthorne privately published *Fanshawe*, a work that he so thoroughly repudiated that his wife, Sophia, knew nothing of it; he published many short stories anonymously and unsuccessfully attempted to interest publishers in such collections as *Seven Tales of My Native Land*, *Provincial Tales*, and *The Storyteller*. As a means of support he edited the *American Magazine of Useful and Entertaining Knowledge* and compiled *Peter Parley's Universal History*. Not until the publication of *Twice-Told Tales* under the secret financial sponsorship of his friend Horatio Bridge did Hawthorne's name become publicly known. The label "solitary years" is somewhat of a misnomer, for, as his journals indicate, Hawthorne visited with friends, went for long walks and journeys, and, most important, met Sophia Peabody, the daughter of Dr. Nathaniel Peabody. For Hawthorne, Sophia was the key by which he was released from "a life of shadows" to the "truth of the human heart." Four years passed, however, before they could marry—four years in which Hawthorne became measurer in the Boston Custom House, which he called a "grievous thraldom," and then, although not sympathetic to the burgeoning transcendental movement, joined the utopian community Brook Farm (April, 1841), investing one thousand dollars in an attempt to establish a home for himself and Sophia.

After little more than six months, Hawthorne gave up the communal venture and, settling in the Old Manse at Concord, married Sophia on July 19, 1842. His financial difficulties were exacerbated by the birth of Una in 1844; finally, in 1846, when his son Julian was born and *Mosses from an Old Manse* was published, he was appointed Surveyor of the Salem Custom House, a post he held from 1846 to 1849, when a political upset cost him his job. With more time to write and with the pressure to support a growing family, Hawthorne began a period of intense literary activity; his friendship with Herman Melville dates from that time. *The Scarlet Letter*, whose ending sent Sophia to bed with a grievous headache, was finished in February, 1850. *The House of the Seven Gables* appeared in 1851, the year Hawthorne's daughter Rose was born; by the end of the next year, Hawthorne had completed *The Blithedale Romance*, two volumes of children's tales, *The Life of Franklin Pierce*, and a collection of stories, *The Snow-Image and Other Twice-Told Tales*.

From 1853 to 1857, Hawthorne served as United States Consul at Liverpool, England, a political appointment under President Pierce. After four years of involvement with the personal and financial problems of stranded Americans,

Hawthorne resigned and lived in Rome and Florence from 1857 to 1858, where he acquired ideas for his last romance, *The Marble Faun*. After returning with his family to the United States, Hawthorne worked on four unfinished romances, *Doctor Grimshawe's Secret, Septimius Felton, The Dolliver Romance*, and *The Ancestral Footstep*, in which two themes are dominant: the search for immortality and the American attempt to establish title to English ancestry. His carefully considered essays on the paucity of American tradition, the depth of British heritage, and the contrast between democracy and entrenched class systems were first published in *The Atlantic* and then collected as *Our Old Home*. After a lingering illness, he died at Plymouth, New Hampshire, on May 19, 1864, during a trip with Franklin Pierce. He was buried at Sleepy Hollow Cemetery in Concord, Massachusetts.

Analysis

Central to Nathaniel Hawthorne's romances is his idea of a "neutral territory," described in the Custom House sketch that precedes *The Scarlet Letter* as a place "somewhere between the real world and fairy-land, where the Actual and the Imaginary may meet, and each imbue itself with the nature of the other." A romance, according to Hawthorne, is different from the novel, which maintains a "minute fidelity . . . to the probable and ordinary course of man's experience." In the neutral territory of romance, however, the author may make use of the "marvellous" to heighten atmospheric effects, if he also presents "the truth of the human heart." As long as the writer of romance creates characters whose virtues, vices, and sensibilities are distinctly human, he may place them in an environment that is out of the ordinary— or, that is, in fact, allegorical. Thus, for example, while certain elements— the stigma of the scarlet letter, or Donatello's faun ears—are fantastical in conception, they represent a moral stance that is true to nature. Dimmesdale's guilt at concealing his adultery with Hester Prynne is, indeed, as destructive as the wound on his breast, and Donatello's pagan nature is expressed in the shape of his ears.

A number of recurring thematic patterns and character types appear in Hawthorne's novels and tales, as Randall Stewart suggests in the Introduction to *The American Notebooks by Nathaniel Hawthorne*. These repetitions show Hawthorne's emphasis on the effects of events on the human heart rather than on the events themselves. One common motif is concern for the past, or, as Hawthorne says in the Preface to *The House of the Seven Gables*, his "attempt to connect a bygone time with the very present that is flitting away from us." Hawthorne's interest in the Puritan past was perhaps sparked by his "discovery," as a teenager, of his Hathorne connections; it was certainly influenced by his belief that progress was impeded by inheritance, that "the wrong-doing of one generation lives into the successive ones, and . . . becomes a pure and uncontrollable mischief." For Hawthorne, then, the past must be reckoned with, and then put aside; the eventual decay of aristocratic families is not only inevitable, but desirable.

Hawthorne's understanding of tradition is illustrated in many of his works. In *The Scarlet Letter*, for example, he explores the effect of traditional Puritan social and theological expectations on three kinds of sinners: the adultress (Hester), the hypocrite (Dimmesdale), and the avenger (Chillingworth), only to demonstrate that the punishment they inflict on themselves far outweighs the public castigation. Hester, in fact, inverts the rigidified Puritan system, represented by the scarlet letter, whose meaning she changes from "adultress" to "able." Probably the most specific treatment of the theme, however, is found in *The House of the Seven Gables*, in which the Pyncheon family house and fortune have imprisoned both Hepzibah and Clifford, one in apathy and one in insanity; only Phoebe, the country cousin who cares little for wealth, can lighten the burden, not only for her relatives, but also for Holgrave, a descendent of the Maules who invoked the original curse. In *The Marble Faun*, Hawthorne goes to Italy for his "sense of the past," although Hilda and Kenyon are both Americans. The past in this novel is represented not only in the setting, but also in Donatello's pagan nature; at the end, both Miriam and the faun figure engage in a purgatorial expiation of the past.

Another recurring theme is that of isolation. Certainly Hawthorne himself felt distanced from normal social converse by his authorial calling. The first-hand descriptions of Hawthorne extant today present him more as an observer than as a participant, a stance over which he himself agonized. In writing to Longfellow about his apprenticeship years, he complained that he was "carried apart from the main current of life" and that "there is no fate in this world so horrible as to have no share in either its joys or sorrows. For the last ten years, I have not lived, but only dreamed about living." For Hawthorne, Sophia was his salvation, his link to human companionship. Perhaps that is why he wrote so evocatively of Hester Prynne's isolation; indeed, Hester's difficult task of rearing the elfin child Pearl without help from Dimmesdale is the obverse of Hawthorne's own happy domestic situation. Almost every character that Hawthorne created experiences some sense of isolation, sometimes from a consciousness of sin, sometimes from innocence itself, or sometimes from a deliberate attempt to remain aloof.

According to Hawthorne, this kind of isolation, most intense when it is self-imposed, frequently comes from a consciousness of sin or from what he calls the "violation of the sanctity of the human heart." For Hawthorne, the "unpardonable sin" is just such a violation, in which one individual becomes subjected to another's intellectual or scientific (rather than emotional) interest. Chillingworth is a good example; as Hester's unacknowledged husband, he lives with Dimmesdale, deliberately intensifying the minister's hidden guilt. In *The Blithedale Romance*, Coverdale's voyeurism (and certainly his name) suggests this kind of violation, as does Westervelt's manipulation of Priscilla and Hollingsworth's of Zenobia. Certainly, Clifford's isolation in insanity is the fault of Judge Pyncheon. There is also the implication that the mysterious model who haunts Miriam in *The Marble Faun* has committed the same sin, thereby isolating both of them. One of the few characters to refuse such violation is Holgrave, who, in *The House of the Seven Gables*, forbears to use his mesmeric powers on Phoebe.

Such a set of recurring themes is bolstered by a pervasive character typology. While literary works such as those by Edmund Spenser, John Milton, William Shakespeare, and John Bunyan, form the historical context for many of Hawthorne's characters, many are further developments of his own early character types. *Fanshawe*, for example, introduced the pale, idealistic scholarly hero more fully developed in Dimmesdale. Others, personifications of abstract qualities, seem motivated by purely evil ends. Westervelt is one type; sophisticated and learned in mesmerism, he takes as his victim the innocent Priscilla. Chillingworth, whose literary ancestry can probably be traced to Miltonic devil-figures, is old and bent, but possesses a compelling intellect that belies his lack of physical strength. Finally, the worldly Judge Pyncheon manifests a practical, unimaginative streak that connects him to Peter Hovenden of "The Artist of the Beautiful." As for Hawthorne's heroines, Hilda and Phoebe embody the domesticity that Hawthorne admired in Sophia; Priscilla, like Alice Pyncheon before her, is frail and easily subjugated; and Hester, Zenobia, and Miriam exhibit an oriental beauty and intellectual pride.

Three years after Hawthorne was graduated from Bowdoin College, he anonymously published the apprenticeship novel *Fanshawe* at his own expense. While he almost immediately repudiated the work, it remains not only a revealing biographical statement, but also a testing ground for themes and characters that he later developed with great success.

"No man can be a poet and a bookkeeper at the same time." Hawthorne complained in a letter he wrote while engaged in his Uncle Robert's stagecoach business before college. Just such a dichotomy is illustrated in *Fanshawe*, in which the pale scholar fails to rejoin the course of ordinary life and, in effect, consigns himself to death, while the active individual Edward Walcott wins the heroine, Ellen Langton, and so becomes, to use Hawthorne's later words, part of "The magnetic chain of humanity." To be sure, Fanshawe is an overdrawn figure, owing, as Arlin Turner points out, something to Gorham Deane, a Bowdoin schoolmate, and much to Charles Maturin's Gothic novel, *Melmoth the Wanderer* (1820), from which Ellen's guardian, Dr. Melmoth, takes his name. In repudiating the book, however, Hawthorne is less repudiating the Gothic form than he is an early, faulty conception of a writer's life. Certainly, Hawthorne recognized the tension between the intellectual and the practical lives, as his letters and journals suggest, especially when he was at the Boston and Salem Custom Houses and at the Consulate in Liverpool. Moreover, as Frederick Crews notes, Fanshawe and Walcott are "complimentary sides," together fulfilling Hawthorne's twin desire for "self-abnegation" and "heroism and amorous success." Nevertheless, as the pattern of his own life makes clear, Hawthorne did not retire (as did Fanshawe) to an early grave after the solitary apprenticeship years; rather, he married Sophia Peabody (fictionally prefigured in Ellen Langton) and, in becoming involved in the ordinary affairs of life, merged the figures of Fanshawe and Walcott.

The plot of the novel—the abduction of Ellen by the villainous Butler—introduces Hawthorne's later exploration of the misuse of power, while the configuration of characters foreshadows not only the scholar figure, but also two other types: the dark villain, whose sexual motivation remains ambiguous, and the innocent, domestic young heroine, later developed as Phoebe and Hilda. That Fanshawe should rescue Ellen, appearing like Milton's Raphael over the thickly wooded valley where Butler has secluded her, suggests that he is able to enter the world of action; but that he should refuse her offer of marriage, saying, "I have no way to prove that I deserve your generosity, but by refusing to take advantage of it," is uncharacteristic in comparison with Hawthorne's later heroes such as Holgrave and Kenyon. It may be that after his marriage to Sophia, Hawthorne could not conceive of a triangle existing when two "soul mates" had found each other, for in similar character configurations in *The House of the Seven Gables* and *The Marble Faun*, both Holgrave and Kenyon have no rivals to fear for Phoebe and Hilda.

In setting, however, *Fanshawe* is a precursor to the later novels, as well as an unformulated precedent for Hawthorne's famous definition of romance. Probably begun while Hawthorne was enrolled at Bowdoin, the novel has as its setting Harley College, a picturesque, secluded institution. Formal classroom tutoring is not the novel's central interest, however, just as it was not in Hawthorne's own life; nor is the novel completely a *roman à clef* in which actual people and places are thinly disguised. Rather, as is the case in the later novels in which Salem itself, Brook Farm, and Rome are the existing actualities on which Hawthorne draws, so in *Fanshawe* the setting is an excuse for the psychological action. To be sure, the later, sophisticated, symbolic effects are missing, and the interpenetration of the actual by the imaginary is not as successful as in, for instance, *The Scarlet Letter*; nevertheless, although what later becomes marvelous is here simply melodramatic, the imagination plays a large, if unformulated, role in the novel's success.

Begun as a tale and completed shortly after Hawthorne's dismissal from the Salem Surveyorship, *The Scarlet Letter* is prefaced by an essay entitled "The Custom House" in which Hawthorne not only gives an imaginative account of his business experience, but also presents a theory of composition. The essay is thus a distillation of the practical and the imaginative. It includes scant praise for the unimaginative William Lee, the antediluvian permanent inspector whose commonplace attitude typified for Hawthorne the Customs operation. In writing, however, Hawthorne exorcised his spleen at his political dismissal which, coupled with charges of malfeasance, was instigated by the Whigs who wanted him replaced; as Arlin Turner comments, "The decapitated surveyor, in becoming a character in a semifictional account, had all but ceased to be Hawthorne." The writer, in short, had made fiction out of his business experiences. He also had speculated about the preconceptions necessary for the creator of romances; such a man, he decided, must be able to perceive the "neutral territory" where the "actual" and the "imaginary" meet. The result of that perception was *The Scarlet Letter*.

In the prefatory essay to the book, Hawthorne establishes the literalism of the scarlet letter, which, he says, he has in his possession as an old, faded, tattered remnant of the past. Just as Hawthorne is said by Terence Martin to contemplate the letter, thus generating the novel, so the reader is forced to direct his attention to the primary symbol, not simply of Hester's adultery or of her ability, but of the way in which the restrictions of the Puritan forebears are transcended by the warmth of the human heart. Through this symbol, then, and through its living counterpart, Pearl, the daughter of Hester and Dimmesdale, Hawthorne examines the isolating effects of a sense of sin, using as his psychological setting the Puritan ethos.

With Hester's first public appearance with the infant Pearl and the heavily embroidered scarlet letter on her breast, the child—Hester's "torment" and her "joy"—and the letter become identified. Hester's guilt is a public one; Dimmesdale's is not. To admit to his share in the adultery is to relinquish his standing as the minister of the community, and so, initially too weak to commit himself, he pleads with Hester to confess her partner in the sin. She does not do so, nor does she admit that Chillingworth, the doctor who pursues Dimmesdale, is her husband. Three solitary people, then, are inexorably bound together by the results of the sin, but are unable to communicate with one another.

The Puritan intention of bringing the sinner into submission has the opposite effect upon Hester, who, with a pride akin to humility, tenaciously makes a way for herself in the community. As an angel of mercy to the suffering, the sick, and the heavy of heart, she becomes a living model of charity which the townspeople, rigidly enmeshed in their Puritan theology, are unable to emulate. In addition, she exercises a talent for fine embroidery, so that even the bride has her clothing embellished with the sinner's finery. Hester's ostracization hardens her pride until, as she says to Dimmesdale in the forest, their act has a "consecration of its own." The adultery, in short, achieves a validation quite outside the letter of the Puritan law, and Hester finds no reason not to suggest that Dimmesdale run away with her in a repetition of the temptation and the original sin.

In the meantime, Dimmesdale has not had the relief of Hester's public confession. As veiled confessions, his sermons take on an ever growing intensity and apparent sincerity, gaining many converts to the church. Under Chillingsworth's scrutiny, however, Dimmesdale's concealed guilt creates a physical manifestation, a scarlet letter inscribed in his flesh. While Hester's letter has yet to work its way inward to repentance, Dimmesdale's is slowly working its way outward. Chillingworth himself, initially a scholar, becomes dedicated to the cause of intensifying the minister's sufferings. Although Chillingworth eventually takes partial responsibility for Hester's sin, admitting that as a scholarly recluse he should not have taken a young wife, he inexorably causes his own spiritual death. He joins a line of scientist-experimenters who deprave their victims of intellectual curiosity, violating "the truth of the human heart," and severing themselves from "the magnetic chain of humanity." He becomes, as Harry Levin notes, the lowest in the hierarchy of sinners, for while Hester and Dimmesdale have at least joined in passion, Chillingworth is isolated in pride.

As Terence Martin suggests, the scaffold scenes are central to the work. For Dimmesdale, public abnegation is the key: standing as a penitent on the scaffold at midnight is insufficient, for his act is illuminated only by the light of a great comet. His decision to elope with Hester is also insufficient to remove his guilt; what he considers to be the beginning of a "new life" is a reenactment of the original deed. In the end, the scaffold proves the only real escape from the torments devised by Chillingworth, for in facing the community with Hester and Pearl, the minister faces himself and removes the concealment that is a great part of his guilt. His "new life" is, in fact, death, and he offers no hope to Hester that they will meet again, for to do so would be to succumb to temptation again. Only Pearl, who marries a lord, leaves the community permanently; as the innocent victim, she in effect returns to her mother's home to expiate her mother's sin.

Like Fanshawe, then, Dimmesdale causes his own demise, but he is provided with motivation. In Pearl, Hawthorne was influenced perhaps by the antics of Una, his first child, but even her name, which is reminiscent of the medieval Pearl-Poet's "pearl of great price"—his soul—indicates that she is emblematic. Likewise, the minister's name is indicative of the valley of the shadow of death, just as Chillingworth's suggests his cold nature. The successful meshing of the literal and allegorical levels in this tale of the effects of concealed sin and the universality of its theme, continue to lend interest to the work.

As Hawthorne notes in his Preface to *The House of the Seven Gables*, he intends to show the mischief that the past does when it lives into the present, particularly when coupled with the question of an inheritance. Hawthorne's mood is similar to that of Henry David Thoreau when, in *Walden* (1854), he makes his famous plea to "simplify," evoking the image of Everyman traveling on the road of life, carrying his onerous possessions on his back. The family curse that haunts Hepzibah and Clifford Pyncheon, the hidden property deed, and even Hepzibah's dreams of an unexpected inheritance are so centered on the past that the characters are unable to function in the present. In fact, says Hawthorne, far more worrisome than the missing inheritance is the "moral disease" that is passed from one generation to the next.

This "moral disease" results from the greed of the family progenitor, Colonel Pyncheon, who coveted the small tract of land owned by one Matthew Maule. Maule's curse—"God will give him blood to drink"—comes true on the day the new Pyncheon mansion, built on the site of Maule's hut, is to be consecrated. The Colonel dies, presumably from apoplexy but possibly from foul play, and from that day, Hawthorne says, a throwback to the Colonel appears in each generation—a calculating, practical man, who, as the inheritor, commits again "the great guilt of his ancestor" in not making restoration to the Maule descendants. Clifford, falsely imprisoned for the murder of his uncle Jaffrey Pyncheon, the one Pyncheon willing to make restitution, is persecuted after his release by Judge Pyncheon, another of Jaffrey's nephews and Jaffrey's real murderer, for his presumed knowledge of the hiding place of the Indian deed giving title to their uncle's property.

In contrast to these forces from the past, Hawthorne poses Phoebe, a Pyncheon country cousin with no pretensions to wealth but with a large fund of domesticity and a warm heart. Almost certainly modeled on Sophia, Phoebe, like Hilda in *The Marble Faun*, possesses an unexpected power, a "homely witchcraft." Symbolically, as Crews suggests, she neutralizes the morbidity in the Pyncheon household and eventually stands as an "ideal parent" to Hepzibah and Clifford. Indeed, Phoebe brings her enfeebled relatives into the circle of humanity.

If Phoebe represents the living present, Holgrave, the daguerreotypist and descendant of the Maules, represents the future. Like Clifford, however, who is saved by his imprisonment from an aesthetic version of the unpardonable sin, Holgrave runs the risk of becoming merely a cold-blooded observer. Like Hawthorne, Holgrave is a writer, boarding at the House of the Seven Gables to observe the drama created as the past spills into the present and turning Pyncheon history into fiction. He is, nevertheless, a reformer. In an echo of Hawthorne's Preface, he would have buildings made of impermanent materials, ready to be built anew with each generation; likewise, he would merge old family lines into the stream of humanity. While Holgrave's progressive views become mitigated once he marries Phoebe, he is rescued from becoming a Chillingworth by his integrity, his conscience, and his reverence for the human soul. Although he unintentionally hypnotizes Phoebe by reading her his story of Matthew Maule's mesmerism of Alice Pyncheon, he eschews his power, thereby not only saving himself and her from a Dimmesdale/Chillingworth relationship, but also breaking the chain of vengeance which was in his power to perpetuate. The chain of past circumstances is also broken by the death of Judge Pyncheon, who, unlike Holgrave, intended to exercise his psychological power to force Clifford to reveal where the Indian deed is hidden. Stricken by apoplexy (or Maule's curse), however, the Judge is left in solitary possession of the house as Clifford and Hepzibah flee in fear.

Holgrave's integrity and death itself thus prevent a reenactment of the original drama of power and subjection that initiated the curse. As Holgrave learns, the Judge himself murdered his bachelor uncle and destroyed a will that gave the inheritance to Clifford. Although exonerated, Clifford's intellect cannot be recalled to its former state, and so he remains a testimonial to the adverse effects of "violation of the human heart."

During Hepzibah and Clifford's flight from the scene of the Judge's death, Phoebe, representing the present, and Holgrave, the future, pledge their troth, joining the Pyncheon and Maule families. Hawthorne's happy ending, although deliberately prepared, surprised many of his critics, who objected that Holgrave's decision to "plant" a family and to build a stone house were motivated only by the dictates of the plot. F. D. Matthiessen, for example, suggests that Hawthorne's democratic streak blinded him to the implication that Holgrave was simply setting up a new dynasty. On the other hand, for Martin, the decision is foreshadowed; Holgrave's is a compromise position in which he maintains the importance of the structure of society while suggesting that the content be changed, just as a stone house might be redecorated according to its owners' tastes. In marrying Holgrave, Phoebe incorporates Pyncheon blood with the "mass of the people," for the original Maule was a poor man and his son a carpenter.

The only one of Hawthorne's romances to be told by a first-person narrator, *The Blithedale Romance* is grounded in Hawthorne's abortive attempt to join the utopian Brook Farm. Like Hawthorne, Miles Coverdale notes the disjunction between a life of labor and a life of poetry; like Hawthorne, he never wholeheartedly participates in the community. In fact, to Crews, the work displays "an inner coherence of self-debate." Coverdale is the isolated man viewed from inside; as a self-conscious observer, he is the most Jamesian of all of Hawthorne's characters. As Martin notes, Hawthorne sacrifices certain aesthetic advantages in allowing Coverdale to tell his own story. Although his name is as evocative as, for example, Chillingworth's, Coverdale loses symbolic intensity because many of his explanations—his noting, for example, that his illness upon arriving at Blithedale is a purgatory preparing him for a new life—sound like figments of an untrustworthy narrator's imagination.

As in his other romances, Hawthorne begins with a preface. While he points out the realistic grounding of the romance, he maintains that the characters are entirely imaginary. He complains that since no convention yet exists for the American romance, the writer must suffer his characters to be compared to real models; hence, says Hawthorne, he has created the Blithedale scenario as a theatrical device to separate the reader from the ordinary course of events (just as the Gothic writer did with his medieval trappings). In effect, Coverdale, isolated as he is, serves as the medium who moves between two worlds.

Coverdale's destructive egocentricism is evident throughout the work. His unwillingness to grant a favor to Old Moodie loses him an early acquaintanceship with Priscilla; he cements his position as an outsider by belittling Priscilla and by spying on Zenobia; finally, seeing the intimacy that develops between Priscilla and Hollingsworth after Zenobia's suicide, he retires to enjoy his self-pity. As a minor poet, an urban man who enjoys his cigars and fireplace, he is out of place in the utopian venture; in fact, after his purgatorial illness, he wakes up to death-in-life rather than to reinvigoration. As he moves from Blithedale to the city and back again, his most active participation in the events is his searching for Zenobia's body.

Zenobia herself harks back to Hester, another in the line of Hawthorne's exotic, intellectual women. Like Miriam in *The Marble Faun*, Zenobia has a mysterious past to conceal. She is dogged by Westervelt, her urbane companion whose mesmeric powers become evident in his attempted despoilation of Priscilla. Coverdale imagines her as an orator or an actress; indeed, she is a female reformer whose free and unexpected rhetoric seems to bypass convention. Priscilla, on the other hand, is a frail version of Phoebe and Hilda; she is pliant, domestic, and biddable—hence her susceptibility to Westervelt's powers and her brief tenure as the Veiled Lady. Like Zenobia (whose sister she is revealed to be), she believes in Hollingworth's reformism, but less as a helpmate than as a supporter. In coming to Blithedale, Priscilla really does find the life that is denied to Coverdale, but in falling in love with Hollingsworth, she finds spiritual death.

Hollingsworth is related to Hawthorne's scientist figures. With Holgrave he wants to change society, but his special interest is in criminal reformation. It is Zenobia who, at the end of the novel, realizes that Hollingsworth has identified himself so closely with his plan that he has *become* the plan. Hollingsworth encourages Zenobia's interest in him because of her wealth; he spurns Coverdale's friendship because Coverdale objects to devoting himself entirely to the monomaniacal plan. It is, however, Hollingsworth who rescues Priscilla from Westervelt, exercising the power of affection to break mesmerism, but with him Priscilla simply enters a different kind of subjection.

Indeed, all of the main characters suffer real or metaphorical death at the end of the book. Westervelt, like Chillingworth, is frustrated at his victim's escape; Zenobia's suicide has removed her from his power, Priscilla becomes a handmaiden to the ruined ideal of what Hollingsworth might have been, and Hollingsworth becomes a penitent, reforming himself—the criminal responsible for Zenobia's death. Even Coverdale relinquishes a life of feeling; his final secret, that he loves Priscilla, seems only to be fantasizing on the part of the poet who was a master of missed opportunities and who was more comfortable observing his own reactions to a lost love than in pursuing her actively himself.

In *The Marble Faun*, the product of a sojourn in Rome, Hawthorne seems to have reversed a progressively narrowing treatment of the effect of the past. In *The Scarlet Letter*, he deals with Puritan theology; in *The House of the Seven Gables*, a family curse; and in *The Blithedale Romance*, the effects of Coverdale's self-created past. In his last completed work, however, he takes the past of all Rome; in short, he copes with a length of time and complexity of events unusual in his writing experience. Hawthorne's reaction to Rome, complicated by his daughter Una's illness, was mixed. While he objected to the poverty, the dirt, and the paradoxical sensuality and spirituality of Rome, he never, as he put it, felt the city "pulling at his heartstrings" as if it were home.

Italy would seem to present to Hawthorne not only the depth of the past he deemed necessary for the flourishing of romance, but also a neutral territory, this time completely divorced from his readers' experience. It can be said, however, that while *The Marble Faun* is Hawthorne's attempt to come to terms with the immense variety of the Italian scene, he was not completely successful. In his Preface, he once again declares that the story is to be "fanciful" and is to convey a "thoughtful moral" rather than present a novelistic, realistic picture of Italian customs. He inveighs against the "commonplace prosperity" and lack of "antiquity" in the American scene, a lack which satisfies the kind of reforming zeal pictured in Holgrave but mitigates against the writer of romance.

Hawthorne broadens his canvas in another way as well; instead of presenting one or two main characters, he gives the reader four: Donatello, presumably the living twin of the sculptor Praxitiles' marble faun; Miriam Schaeffer, the mysterious half-Italian painter pursued by the ill-fated Brother Antonio; Kenyon, the American sculptor; and Hilda, the New England copyist. Donatello's double is not found elsewhere in the romances; in fact, he seems to be a male version of both Phoebe and Hilda. Unlike the two women, however, he comes in actual contact with evil and thereby loses his innocence, whereas Hilda's and Phoebe's experiences are vicarious. Perhaps the nearest comparison is Dimmesdale, but the minister is portrayed after he chooses to hide his guilt, not before he has sinned. In Donatello's case, Hawthorne examines the idea of the fortunate fall, demonstrating that Donatello grows in moral understanding after he murders the model, a movement that seems to validate Miriam's secular interpretation of the fall as necessary to the development of a soul more than it validates Hilda's instinctive repudiation of the idea. For some critics, such as Hyatt Waggoner and Richard Fogle, the *felix culpa* or fortunate fall is indeed the theme of *The Marble Faun*; Crews, however, emphasizes Hawthorne's unwillingness to confront the question, noting that Kenyon is made to accept Hilda's repudiation without question. In the final analysis, Hawthorne does indeed seem reluctant to examine the ramifications of the theme.

Like Zenobia and Hester, Miriam is presented as a large-spirited, speculative woman whose talents are dimmed by a secret past, symbolized by the
blood-red jewel she wears. Supposedly, Miriam, (unlike Hester) has run away
from a marriage with a much older man, but, Hawthorne suggests, her family
lineage reveals criminal tendencies. She is followed by Brother Antonio, a
wandering devil-figure whom she meets in the catacomb of St. Calixtus and
whom she employs as a model. The crime that links Miriam to Donatello is
not, in this case, adultery, but rather murder. Donatello, who accompanies
Miriam everywhere, throws the model from the Tarpeian Rock, the traditional
death-place for traitors, saying later that he did what Miriam's eyes asked
him to do. Linked in the crime and initially feeling part of the accumulated
crimes of centuries, they become alienated from each other and must come
separately to an understanding of their own responsibility to other human
beings. During this time, Donatello retires to Monte Beni, the family seat,
to meditate, and Miriam follows him, disguised.

Just as Miriam and Donatello are linked by their complicity, Kenyon and
Hilda are linked by a certain hesitation to share in the other pair's secrets,
thereby achieving an isolation that Hawthorne might earlier have seen as a
breaking of the magnetic chain of humanity. Unnoticed as she observes the
murder, Hilda nevertheless becomes a vicarious participant. She rejects Miriam's friendship, maintaining that she has been given an unspotted garment
of virtue and must keep it pristine, but she does agree to deliver a packet of
Miriam's letters to the Palazzo Cenci. For his part, Kenyon compensates for
his earlier coldness to Miriam by effecting a reconciliation between her and
Donatello. Visiting Monte Beni, he is struck by Donatello's air of sadness
and maturity and believes that the pagan "faun," whose power to talk to
animals was legendary, has come to an understanding of good and evil and
has thereby escaped the possibility of a sensual old age to which the throwback
Monte Beni eventually succumbs. Kenyon encourages his friend to work out
his penitence in the sphere of human action and reunites him with Miriam
under the statue of Pope Julius III in Perugia.

In the meantime, Hilda, suffering the pains of guilt for the murder as if
she were the perpetrator, paradoxically gains comfort from confession in St.
Peter's. Once she goes to the Palazzo Cenci to deliver Miriam's letters, however, she is incarcerated as a hostage for Miriam. Her disappearance is the
novel's analogue to Donatello's self-imposed isolation; her experience in the
convent, where she is detained, convinces her of her need for Kenyon. In
searching for Hilda, Kenyon undergoes his own purgation, meeting the
changed Donatello and Miriam in the Compagna and learning about Miriam's
past. On Miriam's advice, he repairs to the Courso in the height of the carnival;
it is there that he is reunited with Hilda. Her freedom means the end of
Miriam and Donatello's days together, for Donatello is imprisoned for the
murder of Brother Antonio.

As did Sophia for Hawthorne, Hilda becomes Kenyon's guide to "home"; she is Hawthorne's last full-length evocation of the New England girl on whose moral guidance he wished to rely.

Patricia Marks

Other major works

SHORT FICTION: *Twice-Told Tales*, 1837, expanded 1842; *Mosses from an Old Manse*, 1846; *The Snow-Image and Other Twice-Told Tales*, 1851.

NONFICTION: *Life of Franklin Pierce*, 1852; *Our Old Home*, 1863.

CHILDREN'S LITERATURE: *Grandfather's Chair*, 1841; *Biographical Stories for Children*, 1842; *True Stories from History and Biography*, 1851; *A Wonder-Book for Boys and Girls*, 1852; *Tanglewood Tales for Boys and Girls*, 1853.

EDITED TEXT: *Peter Parley's Universal History*, 1837.

MISCELLANEOUS: *Complete Works*, 1850-1882 (13 volumes); *The Complete Writings of Nathaniel Hawthorne*, 1900 (22 volumes).

Bibliography

Baym, Nina. *The Shape of Hawthorne's Career.* Ithaca, N.Y.: Cornell University Press, 1977. This mid-sized book presents a readable and challenging portrait of Hawthorne as an artist in touch with the demands of his readers and his society. Identifies three distinctive phases in Hawthorne's artistic development and successfully brings feminist sensitivities to the discussion of his work.

Bloom, Harold, ed. *Nathaniel Hawthorne.* New York: Chelsea House, 1986. This collection of fourteen concise essays by different contemporary critics is introduced by Bloom and presents a useful overview of topical critical methods and issues as relating to Hawthorne's work. A chronology and rich bibliography make this collection valuable for a reader interested in a contemporary discussion of Hawthorne's art.

Colacurcio, Michael J. *The Province of Piety: Moral History in Hawthorne's Early Tales.* Cambridge, Mass.: Harvard University Press, 1984. The definitive modern guide to Hawthorne's early works, this voluminous book offers a thorough and exhaustive discussion of the tales covered; individual chapters read well on their own. Colacurcio's scholarship is outstanding, his style gripping, and his critical observations compelling, with their insistence on the importance of history for Hawthorne's fiction. Notes and an index are included.

Crews, Frederick C. *The Sins of the Fathers: Hawthorne's Psychological Themes.* New York: Oxford University Press, 1966. Rejects earlier, religiously oriented criticism of Hawthorne's work and proceeds along the lines of a psychoanalytical study, but avoiding distracting jargon. Hawthorne's innovative creation of psychologically motivated characters bestows some validity on Crews's ideas, yet his insistence on the dark obsessions of the author is not undisputed.

Mellow, James R. *Nathaniel Hawthorne in His Times.* Boston: Houghton Mifflin, 1980. A vivid and enjoyable full-length biography presenting the author in historical context without losing sight of his artistic development and achievement. Forty-two illustrations help visualize the world of Hawthorne's New England community and his travels, friends, and intellectual companions. A bibliography, notes, and an index make the book even more accessible.

Newman, Lea Bertani Vozar. *A Reader's Guide to the Short Stories of Nathaniel Hawthorne.* Boston: G. K. Hall, 1979. For each of the fifty-four tales discussed, provides a "Publication History," "Circumstances of Composition, Sources, and Influences," "Relationship with Other Hawthorne Works," and "Interpretation and Criticism." Extremely valuable to a reader interested in detailed information about a particular tale; the bibliography is nicely specific as well.

Stoehr, Taylor. *Hawthorne's Mad Scientists.* Hamden, Conn.: Archon Books, 1978. This lucid and concise discussion of the science and pseudoscience of Hawthorne's age shows how these respective ideas were handled by him. Distinguishes two kinds of Hawthornian scientist: the utopian idealist, who functions much like an early social scientist, and the gothic "pseudoscientist," who is given evil ambitions and uncanny powers.

JOSEPH HELLER

Born: Brooklyn, New York; May 1, 1923

Principal long fiction
Catch-22, 1961; *Something Happened*, 1974; *Good as Gold*, 1979; *God Knows*, 1984; *Picture This*, 1988.

Other literary forms
Joseph Heller has often stated that novels are the only kind of fiction he really wishes to write. His first published piece, however, was a short story in *Story Magazine* (1945), and in the late 1940's, he placed several other stories with *Esquire* and *The Atlantic*. Heller's enthusiasm for the theater accounts for the topic of his master's thesis at Columbia University, "The Pulitzer Prize Plays: 1917-1935," and he has since written three plays, all of which deal directly or indirectly with the material he used in *Catch-22*. *We Bombed in New Haven*, a two-act play, was first produced by the Yale School of Drama Repertory Theater in 1967. It later reached Broadway and was published in 1968. *Catch-22: A Dramatization* (1971) was first produced at the John Drew Theater in East Hampton, Long Island, where Heller spends his summers. *Clevinger's Trial*, a dramatization of Chapter 8 of *Catch-22*, was produced in London in 1974. Only *We Bombed in New Haven* enjoyed a modicum of critical and commercial success. Heller has also contributed to a number of motion-picture and television scripts, the best-known of which is *Sex and the Single Girl* (Warner Bros., 1964), for which he received his only screen credit.

Achievements
Heller's reputation rests largely on his first novel, *Catch-22*, the publication of which vaulted Heller into the front ranks of postwar American novelists. Critics have hailed it as "the great representative document of our era" and "probably the finest novel published since World War II." The phrase "Catch-22" quickly entered the American lexicon; eight million copies of the novel have been printed; and it has been translated into more than a dozen languages. In 1970, Mike Nichols' movie adaptation of Heller's tale sparked renewed interest in the novel itself and launched it onto the best-seller lists.

Catch-22 was one of the most widely read and discussed novels of the 1960's and early 1970's; its blend of humor and horror struck a responsive chord, particularly with the young, during the upheavals of the Vietnam era. The critic Josh Greenfield, writing in 1968, claimed that it had "all but become the chapbook of the sixties." Within the context of Vietnam, the novel seemed to be less about World War II than about that Asian war over which America was so furiously divided. *Catch-22*, then, remains the classic fictional statement of the antiwar sentiments of its time; indeed, one student of twentieth century American war literature has suggested that "*Catch-22* has probably contributed more than any other work to the literary apprehension of war during the last two decades."

Although some have compared *Catch-22* to Norman Mailer's *The Naked and the Dead* (1948), James Jones's *The Thin Red Line* (1962), and other essentially naturalistic war tales written by Heller's contemporaries, its conception of war in basically absurdist terms and its crazy-quilt structure suggest affinities rather with such works as Kurt Vonnegut's *Slaughterhouse-Five* (1969). Although he objects to the term and prefers to characterize his novels as "burlesques," Heller's fiction is frequently described as "black comedy." In the tradition of Nathanael West, Günter Grass, Ralph Ellison, and Thomas Pynchon, Heller stretches reality to the point of distortion.

In all three of his novels, as well as in his plays, Heller displays a world view which shares much with twentieth century existentialist thought: the world is meaningless, it simply exists; man by his very nature seeks meaning; the relationship between man and his world is thus absurd; when a man recognizes these facts, he experiences what Jean-Paul Sartre termed the "nausea" of modern existence. In all of his work, Heller argues for "massive resistance" to routine, regimentation, and authority in whatever form. He affirms, no matter how much that affirmation may be qualified by pain and defeat, the sanctity of the individual. He writes not so much about the life of a soldier (as in *Catch-22*), the life of a businessman (as in *Something Happened*), or the life of a would-be politician (as in *Good as Gold*), as about the threats posed to individual identity by the institutions of modern life.

Biography

Joseph Heller was born in Brooklyn, New York, on May 1, 1923, the son of Russian-Jewish immigrants only recently arrived in America. His mother then barely spoke English; his father drove a delivery truck for a bakery until, when Heller was only five, he died unexpectedly during a routine ulcer operation. The denial of this death in particular and the bare fact of mortality in general were to color Heller's later life and work. The youngest of three children, Heller spent his boyhood in the Coney Island section of Brooklyn, an enclave of lower- and middle-class Jewish families, in the shadow of the famed amusement park. Both his family and his teachers recognized Heller as a bright but bored student; he tinkered with writing short stories while still in high school.

In 1942, at the age of nineteen, Heller joined the Army Air Corps. He spent one of the war years flying sixty missions as a wing bombadier in a squadron of B-25's stationed on Corsica. This proved to be the crucial year of his life; it provided him with the materials, and the bitterly sardonic attitude, out of which he forged his major work—*Catch-22*—as well as his three plays.

Moreover, his sixty missions, many of them brutal and bloody (including the series of raids on Bologna which form the core of *Catch-22*), profoundly affected the attitude toward death which informs all of his work.

Demobilized in 1945, having achieved the rank of first lieutenant, Heller married fellow Brooklynite Shirley Held, with whom he has had two children. Heller spent the next seven years within academe. Under the G.I. Bill, he attended college, first at the University of Southern California and then at New York University, where he received his B.A. in 1948. Heller then traveled uptown to take a master's degree at Columbia University before receiving one of the first Fulbright scholarships to study at Oxford. He returned to the United States to teach English at Pennsylvania State University between 1950 and 1952.

During the remainder of the 1950's, Heller was employed in the advertising departments of *Time*, *Look*, and *McCall's* magazines successively. In 1954, he began writing, at night and during odd hours, the manuscript that would be published eight years later as *Catch-22*. Almost forty when *Catch-22* finally appeared, Heller ironically referred to himself as an "aging prodigy."

Heller abandoned his successful advertising career during the 1960's and returned to teaching. His position as Distinguished Professor of English at the City University of New York afforded him both the salary to support his family and the free time to devote to his writing. In these years, he began work on a second novel, wrote several motion-picture and television scripts (usually adaptations of the work of others and often using a pseudonym), and completed his first play, *We Bombed in New Haven*.

Something Happened, Heller's second novel, took thirteen years to complete before appearing in 1974. Never fully at ease with academic life, Heller resigned his chair at CUNY in 1975, and in 1979 published his third novel, *Good as Gold*. Although he has occasionally lectured on the college circuit and has served as writer-in-residence at both Yale University and the University of Pennsylvania, Heller is basically a reclusive writer, uncomfortable at literary gatherings and suspicious of the trappings of literary success. His life and work seem guided by Ralph Waldo Emerson's dictum that "a foolish consistency is the hobgoblin of little minds."

In December, 1981, Heller was diagnosed as a victim of Guillain Barré syndrome, a sometimes fatal condition involving progressive paralysis. He was hospitalized for several months but eventually recovered. The experience resulted in a book, *No Laughing Matter* (1986), written with his friend Speed Vogel, describing Heller's condition and its resolution; the illness also led to his second marriage, to one of his nurses, Valerie Humphries, in 1987.

God Knows returns to the irreverence and defiance of logic which characterized *Catch-22*. Its narrator, the biblical King David, speaks in modern jargon and in his extended version of his life and career displays knowledge of events long after his own time. *Picture This* is a protracted meditation on the ironies of history and of human life, focusing on the Netherlands of Rembrandt's time and the Athens of Aristotle. Heller has continued to live in New York City and East Hampton, Long Island.

Analysis

At first glance, Joseph Heller's novels seem quite dissimilar. Heller's manipulation of time and point of view in *Catch-22* is dizzying; it is a hilariously macabre, almost surreal novel. *Something Happened*, on the other hand, is a far more muted book composed of the slow-moving, pessimistic broodings of an American business executive. *Good as Gold* is part remembrance of family life in the impoverished sections of Coney Island, and part savage satire of contemporary American political life. Throughout Heller's work, however, all his characters are obsessed with death and passionately searching for some means to deny, or at least stay, their mortality. Heller's characters, like those of Saul Bellow, cry out to assert their individuality, their sense of self, which seems threatened from all sides. Yossarian, for example, in *Catch-22*, finds the world in conspiracy to blow him out of the sky. The worlds of *Catch-22*, *Something Happened*, and *Good as Gold* are not so much chaotic as absurdly and illogically routinized. In such an absurd world of callous cruelty, unalloyed ambition, and blithe disregard for human life, Heller maintains, the individual has the right to seek his own survival by any means possible.

While *Catch-22*'s most obvious features are its antiwar theme and its wild, often madhouse humor, the novel itself is exceedingly complex in both meaning and form. In brief, the plot concerns a squadron of American airmen stationed on the fictional Mediterranean island of Pianosa during World War II. More specifically, it concerns the futile attempts of Captain John Yossarian, a Syrian-American bombadier, to be removed from flying status. Every time he approaches the number of missions necessary to complete a tour of duty, his ambitious commanding officers increase it. Yossarian tries a number of ploys to avoid combat. He malingers, feigns illness, and even poisons the squadron's food with laundry soap to abort one mission. Later, after the gunner Snowden dies in his arms during one particularly lethal mission, Yossarian refuses to fly again, goes naked, and takes to walking backward on the base, all in an attempt to have himself declared insane.

Yossarian is motivated by only one thing—the determination to stay alive. He sees his life threatened not only by the Germans who try to shoot him out of the sky but also by his superior officers, who seem just as intent to kill him off. "The enemy," he concludes at one point, "is anybody who's going to get you killed, no matter which side he's on." When Yossarian attempts to convince the camp's medical officer that his fear of death has driven him over the brink and thus made him unfit to fly, he first learns of the "catch" which will force him to keep flying: "There was only one catch and that was

Catch-22, which specified that a concern for one's own safety in the face of dangers that were real and immediate was the process of a rational mind." As Doc Daneeka tells Yossarian, "Anyone who wants to get out of combat duty isn't really crazy."

Most of the large cast of characters surrounding Yossarian are, by any "reasonable" standard, quite mad. They include Colonel Cathcart, who keeps raising the number of missions his troops are required to fly not for the sake of the war effort but for his own personal glory; Major Major Major, who forges Washington Irving's name to official documents and who is pathologically terrified of command; and Milo Minderbinder, the mess officer, a black marketeer who bombs his own base under contract with the Germans. These supporting characters most often fall into one of four categories. The ranking officers—Cathcart, Dreedle, Korn, Black, Cargill, and Scheisskopf—appear more concerned with promotion, neat bombing patterns, and their own petty jealousies than with the war itself or the welfare of their men. A second group, including Doc Daneeka, Minderbinder, and Wintergreen, are also concerned with pursuing the main chance. They are predatory, but also extremely comic and very much self-aware. Another group, including Nately, Chief Halfoat, McWatt, Hungry Joe, and Chaplain Tappman, are (like Yossarian himself) outsiders, good men caught within a malevolent system. The dead—Mudd, Snowden, Kraft, and "the soldier in white"—constitute a final group, one which is always present, at least in the background.

It is the military system—which promulgates such absurdly tautological rules as "Catch-22"—that is Yossarian's real enemy. He and the other "good" men of the squadron live in a world that is irrational and inexplicable. As the company's warrant officer explains, "There just doesn't seem to be any logic to their system of rewards and punishments. . . . They have the right to do anything we can't stop them from doing."

As the novel progresses, the victims, increasingly aware of the menace posed by this system, carry their gestures of rebellion to the point of open defiance. Yossarian is the most blatant in this regard: he moans loudly during the briefing for the Avignon mission; he insists that there is a dead man in his tent; he goes naked during the Avignon mission itself and then again during the medal ceremony afterward; he halts the Bologna raid by putting soap in the squadron's food and by moving the bomb-line; he requests that he be grounded and eventually refuses to fly. Finally, he deserts, hoping to reach sanctuary in neutral Sweden.

In the world of *Catch-22*, then, the reader is forced to question the very nature of sanity. Sanity is commonly defined as the ability to live within society and to act appropriately according to its rules. If those rules—such as Catch-22—are patently false, however, then adhering to them is in truth an act of insanity, for the end result may be death or the loss of freedom. The world of *Catch-22* is, to Yossarian, a spurious culture, as anthropologists would call it, one which does not meet the basic needs of its members—above all, the need to survive. Authority, duty, and patriotism are all called into question, and Heller demonstrates that when those in authority lack intelligence or respect for life, as is the case with Yossarian's commanding officers, obeying authority can only be self-defeating. Heller thus argues that in an absurd universe, the individual has the right to seek his own survival; he argues that life itself is infinitely more precious than any cause, however just. When Yossarian decides that he has done his part to defeat the Nazis (and after all, he has flown many more missions than most other airmen), his principal duty is to save himself. Yossarian's desertion, then, is a life-affirming act. As one critic noted, *Catch-22* "speaks solidly to those who are disaffected, discontented, and disaffiliated, and yet who want to react to life positively. With its occasional affirmations couched in terms of pain and cynical laughter, it makes nihilism seem natural, ordinary, even appealing." Thus the surface farce of *Catch-22*, when peeled away, reveals a purpose which is literally deadly serious.

If the basic plot of *Catch-22* is fairly simple, its narrative technique and structure most certainly are not. The novel appears to be a chronological jumble, flashing forward and backward from the central event—the death of Snowden—which marks Yossarian's final realization of the mortal threat posed by Catch-22. Time in the novel exists not as clock-time but rather as psychological time, and within Yossarian's stream-of-consciousness narrative, events in the present intermingle with cumulative repetitions and gradual clarifications of past actions. For example, in Chapter 4, the bare facts of Snowden's death are revealed, that he was killed over Avignon when Dobbs, his copilot, went berserk and grabbed the plane's controls at a crucial moment. Yossarian returns to this incident throughout the novel, but it is not until the penulitimate chapter that he reconstructs the story in full. In this fashion, Heller seeks to capture the real ways in which people apprehend the world, incompletely and in fragments.

Catch-22 is intricately structured despite its seeming shapelessness. Until Chapter 19, almost everything is told in retrospect while Yossarian is in the hospital; Chapter 19 itself begins the movement forward in time leading to Yossarian's desertion. The gradual unfolding of the details of Snowden's death provides another organizing device. Such structural devices as parallelism, doubling, and—most important—repetition, force the reader to share Yossarian's perpetual sense of *déjà vu*, the illusion of having previously experienced something actually being encountered for the first time. The ultimate effect of such devices is to reinforce the novel's main themes: Yossarian is trapped in a static world, a world in which nothing seems to change and in which events seem to keep repeating themselves. He does not move *through* his experiences, but rather seems condemned to a treadmill existence. The only way to resist this world is to escape it, to desert.

Heller himself once revealed that he considered Bob Slocum, the protagonist-narrator of his second novel, *Something Happened*, to be "the antithesis of Yossarian—twenty years later." Indeed, the scene shifts dramatically from the dusty, littered airfields of Pianosa to the green, well-kept lawns of suburban Connecticut. In *Something Happened*, Heller details— some say monotonously details—the inner life of an outwardly successful man and, in doing so, seeks to expose the bankruptcy of contemporary middle-class American culture.

Slocum works as a middle-level marketing research manager in a large company. He is middle-aged, married, and the father of three children. Although he is by all appearances successful, Slocum's extended monologue of memories, self-analysis, and carpings at the world reveal that he is anything but happy: "I keep my own counsel and drift speechlessly with my crowd. I float. I float like algae in a colony of green scum, while my wife and I grow old." He sees his life as a series of humiliating failures of nerve, of unfulfilled expectations and missed opportunities. Slocum harks back repeatedly and with regret to his adolescent yearnings for an office girl—later a suicide— with whom he had worked shortly after finishing high school. He now wishes in vain that he could desire someone or something as desperately as he once desired her.

Slocum despises his present job and mistrusts his associates, yet politics shamelessly for promotion; he feels bound to his family, yet commits numerous adulteries. He is hopelessly at odds with himself and his life. For example, he loves his family in a temporizing kind of way, but he also fears that he has made them all unhappy. His wife, bored and restless, feels isolated in the suburbs and turns to alcohol. His sixteen-year-old daughter is sullen and promiscuous. One son is hopelessly brain-damaged and an insufferable burden to Slocum; the other, Slocum seems truly to want to love, but he cannot help browbeating him. The novel reaches its bleak climax when this latter son is hit by a car and lies bleeding in the street. Slocum cradles the boy in his arms and, at the moment when he feels he can express his love, inadvertently smothers him.

There is no real resolution in *Something Happened*. At novel's end, Slocum has not changed or learned anything of importance. Unlike Yossarian, who is threatened from without, Slocum is his own worst enemy. His sense of alienation, of loss, of failure, are unrelieved.

Critical opinion of *Something Happened* has been mixed. Those who admire the novel most often praise its exact and mercilessly honest replication of the banality and vacuousness of everyday life among the American middle-classes, and they argue that Heller, as in *Catch-22*, nicely fuses form and meaning. Others find the novel irritatingly tedious and pessimistic and consider the character of Slocum seriously flawed, unlikable, and unheroic by any standard. Many reviewers could not resist quipping that a more appropriate title for

Heller's novel would be *Nothing Happens*.

Heller's third novel, *Good as Gold*, savagely satirizes the aspirations of the Jewish intellectual community in America. The comic dimension of *Catch-22*, so absent from *Something Happened*, returns. Bruce Gold is a forty-eight-year-old Brooklyn-born English professor who desperately wants to make— or at least have—money. Like Bob Slocum, Gold has problems with his family, which, he knows, considers him a failure because he is not rich. Much of the novel takes place within the Gold family itself, which Gold finds oppressive, if at times amusingly so.

Gold is in most ways a fool—albeit a cynical one—a hypocrite, and a congenital social climber. He is a 1970's version of Budd Schulberg's Sammy Glick. One evidence of this is his engagement to a wealthy WASP socialite with political connections. Gold himself harbors political ambitions. He hungers to replace his alter-ego and arch-nemesis Henry Kissinger as Secretary of State, and hopes that his fiancée's tycoon-father will help him in his quest for political power. Heller savages both Gold and Kissinger, and for precisely the same reason: they represent to him those in the Jewish community who want to escape their heritage while at the same time exploiting it (to further his financial, academic, and political fortunes, Gold wants to write a "big" book about the Jewish experience in America, about which he knows next to nothing).

Gold understands his own hypocrisy but promptly dismisses it. Yet, when Gold is eventually offered Kissinger's former cabinet position, he experiences a change of heart. Prompted by the death of his older brother, Gold refuses the post and returns to New York and his family. Like Yossarian, Gold is able to restore his own integrity by deserting.

Heller's work has been compared to that of artists as varied as Eugène Ionesco and the Marx Brothers; *Good as Gold* lies closer to the latter than to the former. Until his decision to renounce his political ambitions, Gold is very much the comic intellectual, pathetically incapable of coping with the difficulties in which he finds himself. The humor of *Good as Gold* is painted with the broadest brush of Heller's career, but its target is his familiar one: the means by which institutions in the modern world coerce the individual, and the way in which individuals—such as Slocum and, until his turnabout, Gold—become coconspirators in their own demise.

God Knows is Heller's rewriting of a major element of the Old Testament, the story of David. As in all of his fiction, Heller focuses here on the human insistence on repeating earlier mistakes and on the ironies of life. His David is a prototypical wise guy, looking back over his life from his death bed; his language veers from that of the King James version of the Bible to twentieth century slang as he presents his side of various stories, from his encounter with Goliath to his problems with King Saul to his troubles with his children and his various wives.

His first wife, Saul's daughter Michal, was a shrew to whom he refers as the first Jewish American Princess. He misses Abigail, his second wife, the only one who loved him completely; she has been dead for many years. Bathsheba, the great passion of his life, has turned into an overweight nag, bored with sex and interested only in trying to convince David to name their son, Solomon, as his successor. Solomon, in David's eyes, is an idiot, a humorless man with no original thoughts who writes down everything his father says and later pretends that they are his ideas. The old king's only solace is the young virgin Abishag the Shunnamite, who waits on him and worships him.

David complains about his present state, remembers his days of glory, and rationalizes his deeds, avoiding responsibility for any evil that has befallen others but claiming credit for benefits. His knowledge is modern. He maintains, for example, that Michelangelo's famous statue of him is a nice piece of work but it is not "him." His language is laden with quotations from William Shakespeare, Robert Browning, T. S. Eliot, and many others, and he seems to have direct knowledge of most of ancient and modern history.

God Knows is Heller's most engaging fiction since *Catch-22*. Suspense is maintained by David's reluctance to name Solomon as his successor, as he must do, and by the question of whether he will ever hear the voice of God, which he desperately wants. Heller's David is not an admirable man, but he is a fascinating one and an interesting commentator not only on his own life but on human frailty and ambition as well. He is cynical, his faith in God and man having left him years before, but even as he complains about the pains of old age, his memory keeps reminding him of the enjoyments of the life he has led.

Picture This is neither conventional fiction nor history, but a kind of extended meditation on human weakness. Its inspiration is the famous painting, *Aristotle Contemplating the Bust of Homer*, by the Dutch painter Rembrandt van Rijn. Heller presents many historical facts, chiefly about the Greece of the time of Aristotle, Plato, and Socrates, as well as the Netherlands of the time of Rembrandt, and he draws frequent parallels between events of those periods and those of the modern age. In discussing the Athenian wars, for example, he makes clear his conviction that the motivations, the mistakes, and the stupidities are parallel to those made by the United States in the years since World War II.

Picture This contains much authentic information, most of which is intended to demonstrate human greed and weakness. Heller seems to be fascinated by the financial aspects of Rembrandt's life, in which great success was frittered away and in which a life of luxury ended with enormous debts; he also writes at length about Rembrandt's marriage and his mistresses. In writing about Greece in the Golden Age, he focuses on the failings of government. The great leader Pericles, in his view, led Athens into self-destructive wars. Pericles was personally noble, but he did his city no good. The tyrant

Creon was even worse. Much of what Plato wrote about he could not have observed.

Unlike either *Catch-22* or *God Knows*, *Picture This* fails to provide a leavening of irreverent humor to lighten Heller's dark view of human existence. The only fictional elements in the book are imaginary dialogues between some of the historical figures and the fantasy that Aristotle exists in the painting of him and can observe Rembrandt and his labors; these imaginary flights are only occasionally humorous. Otherwise, the irony in *Picture This* is unrelenting and bitter.

Richard A. Fine

Other major works
PLAYS: *We Bombed in New Haven*, 1968; *Catch-22: A Dramatization*, 1971; *Clevinger's Trial*, 1973.
NONFICTION: *No Laughing Matter*, 1986 (with Speed Vogel).

Bibliography

Aldridge, John W. *The American Novel and the Way We Live Now*. New York: Oxford University Press, 1983. Aldridge's overview of American fiction since World War II gives Heller's work high marks, praising his skeptical view of modern society and the imaginative qualities of his novels.

Klinkowitz, Jerome. *The American 1960's: Imaginative Acts in a Decade of Change*. Ames: Iowa State University Press, 1990. This analysis of recent American fiction in political terms suggests that Heller's *Catch-22* introduces a distinctively new kind of politics, that of withdrawal from impossible situations, and that in this sense the novel is one of the truly original works of its time.

LeClair, Thomas. "Joseph Heller, *Something Happened*, and the Art of Excess." *Studies in American Fiction* 9 (Autumn, 1981): 245-260. This essay focuses on Heller's second novel, defending its repetitive quality as a stylistic device, necessary to the portrayal of the dullness and mediocrity of the life of its protagonist and the other characters.

Martine, James J., ed. *American Novelists*. Detroit, Mich.: Gale Research, 1986. This extended bibliography includes Heller's work and the criticism devoted to him.

Merrill, Robert. "The Structure and Meaning of *Catch-22*." *Studies in American Fiction* 14 (Autumn, 1986): 139-152. This offers the most detailed outline of the careful structure which underlies the apparently chaotic movement of Heller's first novel and the ways in which the novel's meaning depends on that structure.

Plimpton, George, ed. *Writers at Work*. Vol 5. New York: Penguin Books, 1981. An extended and informative interview with Heller dealing with his own conception of what his fiction is about.

ERNEST HEMINGWAY

Born: Oak Park, Illinois; July 21, 1899
Died: Ketchum, Idaho; July 2, 1961

Principal long fiction

The Sun Also Rises, 1926; *The Torrents of Spring*, 1926; *A Farewell to Arms*, 1929; *To Have and Have Not*, 1937; *For Whom the Bell Tolls*, 1940; *Across the River and into the Trees*, 1950; *The Old Man and the Sea*, 1952; *Islands in the Stream*, 1970; *The Garden of Eden*, 1986.

Other literary forms

Ernest Hemingway will be best remembered for his novels and short stories, though critical debate rages over whether his literary reputation rests more firmly on the former or the latter. In his own time, he was known to popular reading audiences for his newspaper dispatches and for his essays in popular magazines. He wrote, in addition, a treatise on bullfighting (*Death in the Afternoon*, 1932) which is still considered the most authoritative treatment of the subject in English; an account of big-game hunting (*Green Hills of Africa*, 1935); two plays (*The Fifth Column*, 1938, and *Today Is Friday*, 1926); and reminiscences of his experiences in Paris during the 1920's (*A Moveable Feast*, 1964).

Achievements

There is little question that Hemingway will be remembered as one of the outstanding prose stylists in American literary history, and it was for his contributions in this area that he was awarded the Nobel Prize in Literature in 1954, two years after the publication of *The Old Man and the Sea*. The general reader has often been more intrigued by Hemingway's exploits— hunting, fishing, and living dangerously—than in his virtues as an artist. Ironically, he is often thought of now primarily as the chronicler of the "lost generation" of the 1920's, a phrase which he heard from Gertrude Stein and incorporated into *The Sun Also Rises* as one of its epigraphs. The Hemingway "code," which originated as a prescription for living in the post-World War I decade, has become a catch phrase for academicians and general readers alike.

Biography

Ernest Miller Hemingway was the first son of an Oak Park, Illinois, physician, Clarence Edmonds Hemingway, and Grace Hemingway, a Christian Scientist. As a student in the Oak Park public schools, Hemingway received his first journalistic experience writing for *The Trapeze*, a student newspaper. After serving as a reporter for the Kansas City *Star* for less than a year, he enlisted as an ambulance driver for the American Red Cross and was sent in 1918 to serve on the Italian front. He received a leg wound which required that he be sent to an American hospital in Milan, and there he met and fell in love with Agnes Von Kurowski, who provided the basis for his characterization of Catherine Barkley in *A Farewell to Arms*. Hemingway was married in 1921 to Hadley Richardson. They moved to the Left Bank of Paris, lived on her income from a trust fund, and became friends of Gertrude Stein and other Left Bank literary figures. The Paris years provided Hemingway with material for the autobiographical sketches collected after his death in *A Moveable Feast*. Also in the Paris years, he met the people who would become the major characters in his *roman à clef*, *The Sun Also Rises*. Hemingway dedicated the novel to Hadley, divorced her (in retrospect, one of the saddest experiences in his life), and married Pauline Pfeiffer in 1927. During the 1930's, Hemingway became attached to the Loyalist cause in Spain, and during the years of the Spanish Civil War, he traveled to that country several times as a war correspondent. His feelings about that war are recorded in *For Whom the Bell Tolls*, which was an enormous popular success. In 1940, he divorced Pauline and married the independent, free-spirited Martha Gellhorn, whom he divorced in 1945, marrying in that same year Mary Welsh, his fourth wife. The 1952 publication of *The Old Man and the Sea* is usually regarded as evidence that the writing slump, which Hemingway had suffered for nearly a decade, was ended. The last years of his life were marked by medical problems, resulting to a great extent from injuries which he had sustained in accidents and from years of heavy drinking. In 1961, after being released from the Mayo Clinic, Hemingway returned with his wife Mary to their home in Ketchum, Idaho. He died there on July 2, 1961, of a self-inflicted shotgun wound.

Analysis

"All stories, if continued far enough, end in death, and he is no true story teller who would keep that from you," Ernest Hemingway wrote in *Death in the Afternoon*. He might have added that most of his own stories and novels, if traced back far enough, also begin in death. In *The Sun Also Rises*, death from World War I shadows the actions of most of the main characters; specifically, death has robbed Brett Ashley of the man she loved before she met Jake, and that fact, though only alluded to in the novel, largely accounts for her membership in the lost generation. *A Farewell to Arms* begins and ends with death: Catherine Barkley's fiancé was killed before the main events of the novel begin; and her own death at the end will profoundly influence the rest of Frederic Henry's life. The Caporetta retreat scenes, often referred to as the "death chapters" of *A Farewell to Arms*, prompt Frederic Henry to give up the death of war for what he believes to be the life of love. In *For Whom the Bell Tolls*, death is nearby in every scene, a fact suggested first by the image of the bell in the novel's title and epigraph, the bell whose tolling is a death knell. Perhaps most important in *For Whom the Bell Tolls*, Robert Jordan's choice to die as he does comes from his reflections on the heroic death of his grandfather compared with what he sees as the cowardly suicide of his father. Finally, Santiago's memories of his dead wife in *The Old Man and the Sea* play in and out of his mind as he confronts the possibility of his own death in his struggle against the great marlin and the sea.

Indeed, in Hemingway's work, as Nelson Algren observes, it seems "as though a man must earn his death before he could win his life." Yet it would be a mistake to allow what may appear to be Hemingway's preoccupation— or, to some, obsession—with death to obscure the fact that he is, above all, concerned in his fiction with the quality of individual life, even though it must be granted that the quality and intensity of his characters' lives seem to increase in direct proportion to their awareness of the reality of death.

There is a danger, however, in making so general an observation as this. Hemingway's attitudes about life, about living it well and living it courageously in the face of death, changed in the course of his most productive years as a writer, those years between 1926 and 1952, which were marked by the creation of his three best novels, and the Nobel Prize-winning novella *The Old Man and the Sea*. During this period, Hemingway shifted away from what many consider the hedonistic value system of Jake, Brett, Frederic, and Catherine, a system often equated with the Hemingway code, to a concern with the collective, almost spiritual value of human life reflected in the actions of Robert Jordan and Santiago. If the constant in Hemingway's works, then, is the fact that "all stories, if continued far enough, end in death," the variable is his subtly changing attitude toward the implications of this fact, no better gauge of which can be found than in the ways his characters choose to live their lives in his major novels.

The best prologue to Hemingway's novels is a long short story, "Big Two-Hearted River," which has been described as a work in which "nothing happens." By the standards of the traditional, heavily plotted story, very little does happen in "Big Two-Hearted River," but the main reason for this is that so much has happened before the story opens that Nick, Hemingway's autobiographical persona, has been rendered incapable of the kind of action one usually associates with an adventure story. Death has occurred: not literal human death, but the death of the land, and with it the death of Nick's old values. It has been brought about by the burning of once-lush vegetation that covered the soil and surrounded the water of Nick's boyhood hunting and fishing territory. Presented with this scene, Nick must find a way of living in the presence of it, which he does by granting supremacy to his senses, the only guides he can trust. He earns the right to eat his food by carrying the heavy backpack containing it to his campsite; after working with his own hands to provide shelter, he can savor the cooking and eating of the food.

He can then catch grasshoppers, which have adapted to the burning of the woods by becoming brown, and use them as natural bait for fishing. Then he can catch fish, clean them, eat them, and return their inedible parts to the earth to help restore its fertility.

It is appropriate that "nothing happens" in this prologue to Hemingway's novels because the dilemma of his main characters is that "nothing" is going to happen unless a modern Perceval removes the plagues of the people and restores fertility to the land. The task for Hemingway's characters, particularly those in his early works, is to establish a code by which they can live in the meantime. Nick, like T. S. Eliot's Fisher King, who sits with his back to an arid plain at the end of *The Waste Land* (1922), is shoring up fragments against his ruins: he is developing a personal system that will enable him to cope with life in the presence of a burned out, infertile land. Also, like Eliot and many other lost-generation writers, Hemingway suggests that the actual wasteland is a metaphor for the spiritual and psychological impotence of modern man, since the state of the land simply mirrors the condition of postwar man's psyche. Like the grasshoppers in "Big Two-Hearted River," who have changed color to adapt outwardly to the changing of the land, Nick must adjust internally to the altered condition of his psyche, whose illusions have been destroyed by the war, just as the land has been destroyed by fire.

An understanding of the principles set forth in "Big Two-Hearted River" is perhaps essential to an understanding of the life-in-death/death-in-life philosophy that Hemingway presents in his major novels, particularly in *The Sun Also Rises* and *A Farewell to Arms*. Bringing these principles in advance to *The Sun Also Rises* enables a reader to see the mythical substructure that lies beneath the apparent simplicity of the story line. On the face of it, *The Sun Also Rises* tells the story of Jake Barnes, whose war wound has left him physically incapable of making love, though it has done so without robbing him of sexual desire. Jake has the misfortune to fall in love with the beautiful and, for practical purposes, nymphomaniac Lady Brett Ashley, who loves Jake but must nevertheless make love to other men. Among these men is Robert Cohn, a hopeless romantic who, alone in the novel, believes in the concept of chivalric love. Hemingway explores the frustration of the doomed love affair between Jake and Brett as they wander from Paris and its moral invalids to Pamplona, where Jake and his lost-generation friends participate in the fiesta. Jake is the only one of the group to have become an *aficionado*, one who is passionate about bullfighting. In the end, though, he betrays his *aficion* by introducing Brett to Pedro Romero, one of the few remaining bullfighters who is true to the spirit of the sport—one who fights honestly and faces death with grace—and this Jake does with full knowledge that Brett will seduce Romero, perhaps corrupting his innocence by infecting him with the jaded philosophy that makes her "lost." Predictably, she does seduce Romero, but less predictably lets him go, refusing to be "one of these bitches that ruins children." Finally, she and Jake are left where they started, she unrealistically musing that "we could have had such a damned good time together"—presumably if he had not been wounded—and he, perhaps a little wiser, responding, "Yes. . . . Isn't it pretty to think so."

Few will miss the sense of aimless wandering from country to country and bottle to bottle in *The Sun Also Rises*. The reader who approaches Jake's condition as a logical extension, symbolically rendered, of Nick's situation in "Big Two-Hearted River," however, will more fully appreciate Hemingway's design and purpose in the novel. As is the case in "Big Two-Hearted River," the death with which *The Sun Also Rises* begins and ends is less a physical death than it is living or walking death, which, granted, is most acute in Jake's case, but which afflicts all of the characters in the novel. They must establish rules for playing a kind of spiritual solitaire, and Jake is the character in the novel who most articulately expresses these rules, perhaps because he is the one who most needs them. "Enjoying living," he says, "was learning to get your money's worth and knowing when you had it." In a literal sense, Jake refers here to the practice of getting what one pays for with actual money, but in another sense, he is talking more abstractly about other kinds of economy—the economy of motion in a good bullfight, for example.

To see how thoroughly Hemingway weaves this idea of economy into the fabric of the novel, one needs only to look at his seemingly offhand joke about writing telegrams. On closer examination, the joke yields a valuable clue for understanding the Hemingway code. When Jake and Bill, his best friend, are fishing in Burguete, they receive a telegram from Cohn, addressed simply, "Barnes, Burguete": "Vengo Jueves Cohn" [I come Thursday]. "What a lousy telegram!" Jake responds. "He could send ten words for the same price." Cohn thinks that he is being clever by writing in Spanish and saving a word, an assumption as naïve as the one that leads him to shorten the name and address to "Barnes, Burguete." The address was free, and Cohn could have included full name and address, thus increasing the probability that Jake would get the message. As a response to Cohn's telegram, Jake and Bill send one equally wasteful: "Arriving to-night." The point is that the price of the telegram includes a laugh at Cohn's expense, and they are willing to pay for it.

After the Burguete scene, there is no direct discussion of the price of telegrams, but through this scene, Hemingway gives a key for understanding how each character measures up to the standards of the code. Ironically, Bill, with whom Jake has laughed over Cohn's extravagance and whom Jake admires, is as uneconomical as Cohn. From Budapest, he wires Jake, "Back on Monday"; his card from Budapest says, "Jake, Budapest is wonderful." Bill's wastefulness, however, is calculated, and he is quite conscious of his value-system. In his attempt to talk Jake into buying a stuffed dog, Bill indicates that, to him, things are equally valueless: whatever one buys, in essence, will be dead and stuffed. He is a conscious spendthrift who has no intention of conserving emotions or money. He ignores the fact that letters, cards, and telegrams are designed to accommodate messages of different lengths and that one should choose the most appropriate (conservative) form of communication available. At first, it seems strange that Jake can accept as a true friend one whose value-system is so different from his, but just as Frederic Henry in *A Farewell to Arms* will accept the priest, whose code is different, so can Jake accept Bill. Both the priest and Bill are conscious of their value-systems. Thus, if Bill's extravagance appears to link him with the wasteful Cohn, the similarity is a superficial one. Like Jake—and unlike Cohn, who still believes in the chivalric code—he has merely chosen extravagance as a way of coping, knowing that whatever he gets will be the equivalent of a stuffed dog. Morally, Bill is less akin to Cohn than he is to Rinaldi in *A Farewell to Arms*, who continues his indiscriminate lovemaking, even though he knows it may result in syphilis. Just as Frederic Henry remains true to Rinaldi, so Jake remains true to Bill.

Standing midway between Bill and Cohn is Brett's fiancé Michael, whose values, in terms of the code, are sloppy. Like Cohn, Mike sends bad telegrams and letters. His one telegram in the novel is four words long: "Stopped night San Sebastian." His letters are in clipped telegraphese, filled with abbreviations such as "We got here Friday, Brett passed out on the train, so brought her here for 3 days rest with old friends of ours." Michael could have gotten more for his money in the telegram by using the ten allotted words, just as he could have sent a letter without abbreviations for the same price. The telegram and the letter suggest that although he is conscious of the *principle* of economy, he simply has no idea how to be economical. Thus, when Brett says of Michael that "He writes a good letter," there is an irony in her comment which Jake acknowledges: "I know. . . . He wrote me from San Sebastian." In juxtaposing the telegram and the letter, Hemingway shows Michael to be a man without a code, a man who, when asked how he became bankrupt, responds, "Gradually and then suddenly," which is precisely how he is becoming emotionally bankrupt. He sees it coming, but he has no code that will help him deal directly with his "lostness."

Unlike Cohn, Bill, and Mike, both Brett and Jake send ten-word telegrams, thus presumably getting their money's worth. When Brett, in the last chapters of the novel, needs Jake, she wires him: "COULD YOU COME HOTEL MONTANA MADRID AM RATHER IN TROUBLE BRETT"—ten words followed by the signature. This telegram, which had been forwarded from Paris, is immediately followed by another one identical to it, forwarded from Pamplona. In turn, Jake responds with a telegram which also consists of ten words and the signature: "LADY ASHLEY HOTEL MONTANA MADRID ARRIVING SUD EXPRESS TOMORROW LOVE JAKE." Interestingly, he includes the address in the body of the telegram in order to obtain the ten-word limit. The sending of ten-word telegrams indicates that Jake and Brett are bonded by their adherence to the code; since they alone send such telegrams, the reader must see them as members of an exclusive society.

Yet ironically, to Jake and Brett, the code has become a formalized ritual, something superimposed over their emptiness. They have not learned to apply the code to every aspect of their lives, the most striking example of which is Brett's ten-word (excluding the signature) postcard at the beginning of Chapter Eight: "Darling. Very quiet and healthy. Love to all the chaps. Brett." The postcard has no word limit, except that dictated by the size of one's handwriting. Brett, however, in the absence of clearly labeled values, must fall back on the only form she knows: in this case, that of the ten-word telegram, which is here an empty form, a ritual detached from its meaningful context.

Jake and Brett, then, come back full circle to their initial frustration and mark time with rituals to which they cling for not-so-dear life, looking in the meantime for physical pleasures that will get them through the night. Yet if this seems a low yield for their efforts, one should remember that Hemingway makes no pretense in *The Sun Also Rises* of finding a cure for "lostness." In fact, he heightens the sense of it in his juxtaposition of two epigraphs of the novel: "You are all a lost generation" from Gertrude Stein, and the long quotation from Ecclesiastes that begins "One generation passeth away, and another generation cometh; but the earth abideth forever. . . . The sun also ariseth, and the sun goeth down. . . . " As Hemingway maintained, the hero of *The Sun Also Rises* is the abiding earth; the best one can hope for while living on that earth, isolated from one's fellowman and cut off from the procreative cycle, is a survival manual. Finally, that is what *The Sun Also Rises* is, and this is the prescription that it offers: one must accept the presence of death in life and face it stoically, one must learn to exhibit grace under pressure, and one must learn to get his money's worth. In skeleton form, this is the foundation of the Hemingway code—the part of it, at least, that remains constant through all of his novels.

Many of the conditions that necessitated the forming of a code for Jake and Brett in *The Sun Also Rises* are still present in *A Farewell to Arms*, and there are obvious similarities between the two novels. Like Jake, Frederic Henry is wounded in the war and falls in love with a woman, Catherine Barkley, whose first love, like Brett's, has been killed before the main events of the novel begin. Yet there has been a subtle change from *The Sun Also Rises* to *A Farewell to Arms* in Hemingway's perception of the human dilemma. The most revealing hint of this change is in the nature of the wound that Frederic receives while serving as an ambulance driver on the Italian front. Unlike Jake's phallic wound, Frederic's is a less debilitating leg wound, and, ironically, it is the thing which brings him closer to Catherine, an English nurse who treats him in the field hospital in Milan. Though their relationship begins as a casual one, viewed from the beginning by Frederic as a "chess game" whose object is sexual gratification, it evolves in the course of Catherine's nursing him into a love that is both spiritual and physical. Catherine's pregnancy affirms at least a partial healing of the maimed fisher king and the restoration of fertility to the wasteland that appeared in *The Sun Also Rises*.

With this improved condition, however, come new problems, and with them a need to amend the code practiced by Jake and Brett. Frederic's dilemma at the beginning of the novel, how to find meaning in life when he is surrounded by death, contains clear-cut alternatives: he can seek physical pleasure in the bawdy houses frequented by his fellow soldiers, including his best friend Rinaldi, or he can search for meaning through the religion practiced by the priest from the Abruzzi; he can do either while fulfilling his obligation to the war effort. His choices, simple ones at first, become limited by forces beyond his control. First, he must discard the possibility of religion, because he cannot believe in it; then, he must reject the life of the bawdy houses, both because it is not fulfilling and because it often brings syphilis. These are choices which even a code novice such as Frederic Henry can make, but his next decision is more difficult. Knowing that Catherine is pregnant and knowing that he loves her, how can he continue to fight, even for a cause to which he feels duty bound? Catherine, who had earlier lost her fiancé to the war and who had refused to give herself to him completely because of her sense of duty to the abstract virtue of premarital sexual purity, has prepared Frederic for his decision, one forecast by the title *A Farewell to Arms*. Frederic's choice is made easier by the disordered and chaotic scenes that he witnesses during the Caporetta retreat, among them the shooting of his fellow officers by carabinieri. Partly because Catherine has initiated him into the life of love, then, and partly because he needs to escape his own death, Frederic deserts the Italian army in one of the most celebrated baptismal rites in American literature: he dives into the Tagliamento River and washes away his anger "with any obligation," making what he terms a separate peace.

If Hemingway were a different kind of storyteller, the reader could anticipate that Frederic and Catherine would regain paradise, have their child, and live happily ever after. In fact, however, no sooner have they escaped the life-in-death of war in Italy to the neutrality of Switzerland, where the reader could logically expect in a fifth and final chapter of the novel a brief, pleasant postscript, than does the double edge hidden in the title become clear. Catherine has foreseen it all along in her visions of the rain, often a symbol of life but in *A Farewell to Arms* a symbol of death: "Sometimes I see me dead in it," she says. The arms to which Frederic must finally say farewell are those of Catherine, who dies in childbirth. "And this," Frederic observes, "is the price you paid for sleeping together. . . . This was what people get for loving each other."

Some will take this ending and Frederic Henry's observations about love at face value and accuse Hemingway of stacking the odds against Frederic and Catherine, maintaining finally that Hemingway provides a legitimate exit from the wasteland with a code that could work and then barricades it capriciously. There is, however, ample warning. From the beginning of the novel, Hemingway establishes Catherine as one who knows well the dangers of loving, and from the time of her meeting with Frederic, she balances them against the emptiness of not loving. In most ways, Catherine is a model of the code hero/heroine established in *The Sun Also Rises*: she stoically accepts life's difficulties, as evidenced by her acceptance of her fiancé's death; and she exhibits grace under pressure, as shown in her calm acceptance of her own death. In giving herself to Frederic, she adds a dimension to the code by breaking through the isolation and separateness felt by Jake and Brett; finally, even though she does not complete the re-creative cycle by giving birth to a child conceived in love, she at least brings the possibility within reach. The reader must decide whether Frederic will internalize the lessons he has learned through Catherine's life and allow his own initiation into the code, which now contains the possibility of loving, to be accomplished.

There are some tenets of Hemingway's philosophy through the publication of *A Farewell to Arms* about which one is safe in generalizing. The most obvious and most important of these is his belief that the only things in life that one can know about with certainty are those things that can be verified through the senses, as Jake can confirm that he has had good food or good wine and as Frederic can verify that being next to Catherine feels good. Hemingway refuses to judge this belief in the primacy of the senses as moral or immoral, and Jake articulates this refusal with mock uncertainty during a late-night Pamplona monologue on values: "That was morality; things that made you disgusted after. No, that must be immorality." The point is that in referring observations about life to the senses, one relieves himself of the need to think about abstractions such as love and honor, abstractions that the main characters in the first two novels carefully avoid. Frederic, for example, is "always embarrassed by the words sacred, glorious, and sacrifice and the expression in vain." With such a perspective, the value of life can be rather accurately measured and described in empirical terms. Similarly, death in such a system can be described even more easily, since there is nothing in death to perceive or measure, an idea vividly rendered in Frederic's remarks about his farewell to Catherine: "It was like saying good-by to a statue."

In looking back on Catherine's death, Frederic or the reader may conclude that it had sacrificial value, but until the 1930's, Hemingway was reluctant in his novels to identify death with an abstract virtue such as sacrifice or to write about the value of an individual life in a collective sense. By 1937, however, and the publication of what most critics regard as his weakest novel, *To Have and Have Not*, Hemingway's attitudes toward life and death had changed. Harry Morgan, the "have not" spokesman of the novel, finally with much effort is able to mutter at the end, "One man alone ain't got . . . no chance." After saying this he reflects that "it had taken him a long time to get it out and it had taken him all his life to learn it." The major works to come after *To Have and Have Not*, namely, *For Whom the Bell Tolls* and *The Old Man and the Sea*, amplify Morgan's view and show Hemingway's code characters moving toward a belief in the collective values of their own lives.

The epigraph of *For Whom the Bell Tolls*, which was taken from a John Donne sermon and which gives the novel its title, points clearly to Hemingway's reevaluation of the role of death in life: "No man is an *Iland*, intire of it selfe; every man is a peece of the *Continent*, a part of the *maine*. . . . And therefore never send to know for whom the bell tolls; It tolls for thee." Regardless of the route by which Hemingway came to exchange the "separate peace" idea of *The Sun Also Rises* and *A Farewell to Arms* for the "part of the *maine*" philosophy embraced by Robert Jordan in *For Whom the Bell Tolls*, one can be sure that much of the impetus for his changing came from his strong feelings about Spain's internal strife, particularly as this strife became an all-out conflict during the Spanish Civil War (1936-1939). This war provides the backdrop for the events of *For Whom the Bell Tolls*, and the novel's main character, like Hemingway, is a passionate supporter of the Loyalist cause. The thing that one immediately notices about Jordan is that he is an idealist, which sets him apart from Jake and Frederic. Also, unlike Jake, who wanders randomly throughout Europe, and unlike Frederic, whose reasons for being in Italy to participate in the war are never clearly defined, Jordan has come to the Sierra de Guadaramas with the specific purpose of blowing up a bridge that would be used to transport ammunition in attacks against the Loyalists. Thrown in with the Loyalist guerrillas of Pablo's band at the beginning of the novel, Jordan is confronted with the near-impossible task of accomplishing the demolition in three days, a task whose difficulty is compounded by Pablo's resistance to the idea and, finally, by increased Fascist activity near the bridge.

Potentially even more threatening to Jordan's mission is his meeting and falling in love with the beautiful and simple Maria, who is in the protection of Pablo's band after having been raped by the Falangists who killed her parents. Again, however, Jordan is not Frederic Henry, which is to say that he has no intention of declaring a separate peace and leaving his duty behind in pursuit of love. He sees no conflict between the two, and to the degree that Hemingway presents him as the rare individual who fulfills his obligations without losing his ability to love, Jordan represents a new version of the code hero: the whole man who respects himself, cares for others, and believes in the cause of individual freedom. Circumstances, though, conspire against Jordan. Seeing that his mission stands little hope of success and that the offensive planned by General Golz is doomed to failure by the presence of more and more Fascists, he attempts to get word through to Golz, but the message arrives too late. Although he manages successfully to demolish the bridge and almost escapes with Maria, his wounded horse falls, rolls over, and crushes Jordan's leg. He remains at the end of the novel in extreme pain, urging the others not to stay and be killed with him, and waiting to shoot the first Fascist officer who comes into range, thus giving Maria and Pablo's group more time to escape.

Jordan is perhaps Hemingway's most ambitious creation, just as *For Whom the Bell Tolls* is his most elaborately conceived novel. Its various strands reflect not only what had become the standard Hemingway subjects of personal death, love, and war, but also his growing concern with the broader social implications of individual action. Jordan's consideration of his mission in Spain clearly demonstrates this: "I have fought for what I believe in for a year now," he says. "If we win here we will win everywhere. . . . " How well Hemingway has woven together these strands remains a matter of critical debate, but individually the parts are brilliant in conception. One example of the many layers of meaning contained in the novel is the Civil War framework, which leads the reader not only to see the conflict of social forces in Spain but also to understand that its analogue is the "civil war" in Jordan's spirit: the reader is reminded periodically of the noble death of Jordan's grandfather in the American Civil War, compared to the "separate peace" suicide of Jordan's father. Jordan debates these alternatives until the last scene, when he decides to opt for an honorable death which gives others a chance to live. This, Hemingway seems finally to say, gives Jordan's life transcendent value.

F. Scott Fitzgerald theorized early in his friendship with Hemingway that Hemingway would need a new wife for each "big book." As Scott Donaldson observes, the "theory worked well for his [Hemingway's] first three wives (Hadley: *The Sun Also Rises*; Pauline: *A Farewell to Arms*; Martha: *For Whom the Bell Tolls*), but breaks down in Mary's case" because *The Old Man and the Sea* does not qualify as a "big book." It does qualify, however, as a major epilogue to the "big books," much as "Big Two-Hearted River" qualifies as their prologue. In the prologue, Hemingway outlines the dilemma of modern man and establishes the task with which he is confronted in a literal and figurative wasteland. For Nick in the story, Hemingway posits a swamp, which Nick may fish "tomorrow" and which is a symbolic representation of life with all its complexities, including male-female relationships. In the "big books," Hemingway leads the reader through the wasteland, showing first, in *The Sun Also Rises*, the risk of personal isolation and despair in a life cut off from the regenerative cycles of nature. In *A Farewell to Arms*, he dramatizes the vulnerability of the individual even in a life where there is love; and finally, in *For Whom the Bell Tolls*, he presents a "whole man" who recognizes the value of individual sacrifice for the survival of the human race. In the epilogue, *The Old Man and the Sea*, Hemingway carries this principle to its final step and issues, through Santiago, his definitive statement about the role of life in death.

It is no surprise that *The Old Man and the Sea* takes the form of a parable and that its old man takes the form of the archetypal wise man or savior common to most cultures, mythologies, and religions. While others who surround Santiago depend on gadgets to catch their fish, Santiago relies only on his own endurance and courage. He goes eighty-four days before hooking the marlin, against whose strength he will pit his own for nearly two full days, until he is finally able to bring him to the boat and secure him there for the journey from the Gulf Stream. Numerous critics have noted the similarities between Santiago and Christ. Santiago goes farther out than most men, symbolically taking on a burden for mankind that most men could not or would not take on for themselves. When Santiago returns to land from his ordeal, secures his boat, and heads toward his shack, Hemingway describes his journey explicitly in terms of Christ's ascent to Calvary: "He started to climb again and at the top he fell and lay for some time with the mast across his shoulder." Moreover, Santiago talks with the boy Manolin about those who do not believe in him or his ways in terms that are unmistakably religious: of the boy's father, who does not want his son to be with the old man, Santiago remarks, "He hasn't much faith." In all of this, Hemingway is leading the reader to see that some, in going out "too far," risk their lives in order to transmit to others the idea that "A man can be destroyed but not defeated." Finally, it is of little importance that sharks have reduced Santiago's great fish to a skeleton by the time he has reached land because the human spirit which has been tested in his battle with the fish has in the end prevailed; those who are genuinely interested in that spirit are rarely concerned with ocular proof of its existence. Santiago's legacy, which must stand as Hemingway's last major word on the human condition, will go to Manolin and the reader, since, as the old man tells him, "I know you did not leave me because you doubted"; he did not doubt that man's spirit can prevail.

Hemingway, then, traveled a great distance from the nihilistic philosophy and hedonistic code of *The Sun Also Rises* to the affirmative view of mankind expressed in *The Old Man and the Sea*. His four major works, if read chronologically, lead the reader on an odyssey through the seasonal cycle of the human spirit. "All stories, if continued far enough, end in death," and Hemingway never stops reminding the reader of that fact. He does add to it, though, in his later work, the hope of rebirth that waits at the end of the journey, a hope for which nature has historically provided the model. The reader of Hemingway's work may find the idea of metaphorical rebirth less a solace for the individual facing literal death than Hemingway seems to suggest it can be. Few, however, will leave Hemingway's work—"his shelf of some of the finest prose by an American in this century"—without feeling that he, at least, speaks in the end with the authority of one who has earned, in Carlos Baker's words "the proud, quiet knowledge of having fought the fight, of having lasted it out, of having done a great thing to the bitter end of human strength."

Bryant Mangum

Other major works

SHORT FICTION: *Three Stories and Ten Poems*, 1923; *In Our Time*, 1924, 1925; *Men Without Women*, 1927; *Winner Take Nothing*, 1933; *The Fifth Column and the First Forty-nine Stories*, 1938; *The Snows of Kilimanjaro and Other Stories*, 1961; *The Nick Adams Stories*, 1972.

PLAYS: *Today Is Friday*, 1926; *The Fifth Column*, 1938.

NONFICTION: *Death in the Afternoon*, 1932; *Green Hills of Africa*, 1935; *A Moveable Feast*, 1964; *By-Line: Ernest Hemingway, Selected Articles and Dispatches of Four Decades*, 1967; *Ernest Hemingway: Selected Letters, 1917-1961*, 1981; *The Dangerous Summer*, 1985; *Dateline, Toronto: The Complete "Toronto Star" Dispatches, 1920-1924*, 1985.

Bibliography

Benson, J. J. "The Life as Fiction and the Fiction as Life." *American Literature* 61 (October, 1989): 345-358. One of relatively few critical articles on Hemingway to appear in the 1980's, addressing his creation of self through fiction.

Bloom, Harold, ed. *Ernest Hemingway: Modern Critical Views*. New York: Chelsea House, 1985. After an introduction that considers Hemingway in relation to recent criticism and to earlier American writers, includes articles by a variety of critics who treat topics such as Hemingway's style, unifying devices, and visual techniques.

Brenner, Gerry. *Concealments in Hemingway's Works*. Columbus: Ohio State University Press, 1983. Draws on psychoanalytic theory, thoroughly treating the relationships of Hemingway's characters to the father figure and the "concealment" of feelings.

Donaldson, Scott. *By Force of Will: The Life and Art of Ernest Hemingway*. New York: Viking Press, 1977. A thematic approach to Hemingway's life and works, addressing his concerns with topics such as politics, sports, friendship, art, war, and death in a lengthy critical biography. Forty-two pages of notes cite major scholars on Hemingway.

Harper, Michael. "Men Without Politics? Hemingway's Social Consciousness." *New Orleans Review* 12 (Spring, 1985): 15-26. Treats Hemingway's use of ideology to create seemingly "apolitical" male characters.

Love, Glen A. "Hemingway's Indian Virtues: An Ecological Reconsideration." *Western American Literature* 22, no. 4 (1987): 201-223. This important study explores Hemingway's relationship to primitivism and to nature.

Noble, Donald R. *Hemingway: A Revaluation*. Troy, N.Y.: Whitson, 1983. A renewal of Hemingway scholarship that focuses on the author's treatment of travel and the influence of Joseph Conrad on his fiction.

JOHN HERSEY

Born: Tientsin, China; June 17, 1914

Principal long fiction

A Bell for Adano, 1944; *The Wall*, 1950; *The Marmot Drive*, 1953; *A Single Pebble*, 1956; *The War Lover*, 1959; *The Child Buyer*, 1960; *White Lotus*, 1965; *Too Far to Walk*, 1966; *Under the Eye of the Storm*, 1967; *The Conspiracy*, 1972; *My Petition for More Space*, 1974; *The Walnut Door*, 1977; *The Call*, 1985; *Antonietta*, 1991.

Other literary forms

John Hersey is as well-known for his nonfiction as he is for his novels. As a young journalist in World War II, Hersey wrote for *Time* and *Life*, interviewing such figures as Japan's Foreign Minister Matsuoka, Ambassador Joseph Grew, and Generalissimo Chiang Kai-shek. His first book, *Men on Bataan* (1942), was written in New York from files and clippings; his second, *Into the Valley: A Skirmish of the Marines* (1943), from his own experiences. *Hiroshima* (1946), generally considered to be his most important book, was based on a series of interviews. After *Hiroshima*, he concentrated on writing novels for twenty years, though he often employed the techniques of interviewing and research to establish a factual basis for his novels. *Here to Stay: Studies in Human Tenacity* (1962) reprinted *Hiroshima* and a number of other interviews with people who had survived similar horrors, such as the Warsaw Ghetto. *The Algiers Motel Incident* (1968) was based on research and interviews concerning the Detroit police killing of three blacks during a period of riots. *Letter to the Alumni* (1970) was a portrait of Yale University during May Day demonstrations, and *The President* (1975) followed President Gerald R. Ford on a typical day. *Life Sketches* (1989) is a book of autobiographical pieces. Hersey has published one collection of short stories, *Fling and Other Stories* (1990). *Blues* (1987), also classified as short fiction, is an idiosyncratic book about bluefishing, cast in the form of a dialogue between a fisherman and a curious stranger and interspersed with poems by Elizabeth Bishop, James Merrill, and others. Hersey has also edited *The Writer's Craft* (1974), an anthology of famous writers' comments on the aesthetics and techniques of literary creation.

Achievements

Hersey's primary achievement is his mastery of the "nonfiction novel." Although all of the particular techniques of the "nonfiction novel" have been used for centuries, Hersey can be said to have anticipated the form as it was practiced during the 1960's and 1970's, the era of the New Journalism and of such novels as Gore Vidal's *Burr* (1973) and E. L. Doctorow's *Ragtime* (1975), to cite only two examples. At the beginning of his career as a writer, Hersey was a reporter and based his books on events and people he had observed. Rather than merely recounting his experiences, Hersey molded characters and events to fit a novelistic form, basing, for example, *A Bell for Adano* on what he observed of the American military government at Licata, Sicily. This attention to realistic detail and psychological insight characterizes his best writing and enriches his more imaginative novels, such as *White Lotus*, although these novels were not nearly as well received. Hersey's humanistic perspective is also an important trait of his works and provides a sense of values which is lacking in much contemporary fiction.

Biography

John Richard Hersey was born in Tientsin, China, on June 17, 1914, to Roscoe and Grace Baird Hersey. His father, a Young Men's Christian Association (Y.M.C.A.) secretary, and his mother, a missionary, took him on a trip around the world when he was three years old, but most of the first decade of his life was spent in the missionary compound, where, although isolated to an extent from the community, he learned to speak Chinese before he spoke English. From the time he learned to read and write, he amused himself by playing reporter and writing his family news and daily events at the British Grammar School and the American School in Tientsin. Despite his early life abroad, Hersey considers his life there "no more exciting than the average child's."

In 1924, Hersey, who knew of the United States only from secondhand accounts and what could be gleaned from books and magazines, was enrolled in the Briarcliff Manor public schools in New York. Three years later, he entered the Hotchkiss School in Lakeville, Connecticut, and was graduated in 1932. After receiving his B.A. from Yale in 1936, he went on to study eighteenth century English literature on a Mellon Scholarship at Clare College, Cambridge. During this time, he became determined to be a reporter for *Time*, because it seemed "the liveliest enterprise of its type." While waiting for an opening, he became the secretary and driver of Sinclair Lewis in the summer of 1937, the same summer that the Japanese invaded Manchuria. Born in China, Hersey was a natural choice for covering the Sino-Japanese War, and he served as a staff member for *Time* from the fall of 1937 until he was assigned to the Chungking bureau under Theodore White in 1939, where he began the itinerant life he would lead throughout the war.

An enthusiastic, courageous reporter, Hersey often found himself in mortal danger as he covered the war in the South Pacific in 1942, the Sicilian invasion and Mediterranean theater in 1943, and Moscow between 1944 and 1945. Twice, he went down in planes; once he crashed into the Pacific, nearly losing the notes he had taken on Guadalcanal. He was treading water when his notebooks from the sunken plane surfaced only a few feet in front of him. Among other stories which he covered was the first account of PT 109 and its young lieutenant, John F. Kennedy, an account that Kennedy would later use in his campaign for Congress. During one trip to the United States from Asia, he married Frances Ann Cannon on April 27, 1940. They had four children (Martin, John, Ann, and Baird) before being divorced in 1958, when he married Barbara Day Addams Kaufman, with whom he had a daughter, Brook.

In 1942, Hersey published his first book, *Men on Bataan*, basically a morale-builder for an America that had suffered serious setbacks at Pearl Harbor and in the Philippines. Hersey wrote the book only a month after the fall of Corregidor, when most of the men who had actually been on Bataan were imprisoned or assigned to new posts in the Pacific. In New York, he combined *Time-Life* files, letters to the servicemen's families, and a few interviews with reporters and other witnesses to write the book, which had a generally favorable if not overenthusiastic reception. In 1943, he published *Into the Valley*, based on his own experiences with the Marines at the Matanikau River on Guadalcanal. With his experience in actual combat, *Into the Valley* had a substantially different tone from that of *Men on Bataan*, which often tended to jingoism. The extent of Hersey's closeness to combat can be measured by his receiving a letter of commendation from the Secretary of the Navy for his work removing wounded during the fighting.

A Bell for Adano, the first book Hersey published as fiction, followed in 1944, based on his observations of the American military governance of Licato, Sicily. The novel was later turned into a Broadway play and a motion picture. Hersey missed much of the praise because of his continuing assignments as a journalist. During the last year of the war, he observed the evidence of Nazi atrocities in Warsaw and Tallinn which would later lead to his novel, *The Wall*. Just as V-E Day occurred, Hersey was awarded the Pulitzer Prize for *A Bell for Adano* and emerged from World War II as an extremely successful writer.

During the rest of 1945 and 1946, Hersey was assigned to China and Japan, where he wrote for *Life* and *The New Yorker* and gathered material for what would be his most famous book, *Hiroshima*, the carefully understated story of six people who were in the city when the first atomic bomb was dropped. The editor of *The New Yorker*, William Shawn, had intended to run *Hiroshima* as a three-part article; he later changed his mind, however, and decided to print the entire text alone. Nothing else would share the issue with *Hiroshima* except advertising. This dramatic step was kept a secret from the regular staff as Shawn and Hersey sequestered themselves in the office from ten A.M. to two P.M., Hersey rewriting while the text was fed to a harried makeup man.

Hiroshima became a phenomenon. The Book-of-the-Month Club distributed free copies to its members. It was read aloud in four hour-long radio programs. Albert Einstein ordered a thousand copies, Bernard Baruch was said to have ordered five hundred, and the Mayor of Princeton sought three thousand reprints. The Belgian Chamber of Commerce ordered five hundred copies to distribute to officials in Brussels. Three London newspapers requested serial rights. *Hiroshima*, with its concentration on ordinary people trying to cope with the horror of the first atomic blast, made Hersey known worldwide, except in Japan, where the book was banned by the American military government. Hersey donated many of his proceeds from the book to the American Red Cross. Nearly twenty years later, in 1965, when Hersey was invited to the White House Festival of the Arts by President Lyndon Johnson, *Hiroshima* was still considered Hersey's most profound work; he read sections of it at the White House gathering in a dramatic protest against the escalation of the war in Vietnam.

The year following *Hiroshima*, Hersey became one of the founders, writers, and editors of *'47—The Magazine of the Year*. It only survived one issue. Hersey became increasingly involved in politics, an involvement that would continue throughout his career. He vigorously supported the United Nations and became a member of such organizations as the Author's League. During the 1950's, he became a speechwriter for Adlai Stevenson and actively campaigned for his election by serving as chairman of Connecticut Volunteers for Stevenson. Long before Watergate made it fashionable to question the roles of the FBI and CIA, Hersey was a member of the Committee to End Government Secrecy. He also became interested in education, becoming a member of various educational committees and study groups, including the Westport, Connecticut, Board of Education.

Writing *The Wall* left Hersey little time for journalism in the late 1940's, though he published a few items such as a profile of Harry S Truman in *The New Yorker*. After extensive research, Hersey published *The Wall* in 1950, repeating the success of *A Bell for Adano* by winning such awards as the Anisfield-Wolf Award, the Daroff Memorial Fiction Award of the Jewish Book Council of America, and the Sidney Hillman Foundation Award. *The Wall*, like *A Bell for Adano*, was later dramatized and then made into a motion picture.

In the early 1950's, Hersey was one of America's most famous writers and was placed in the awkward position of trying to write up to the increasingly higher level expected of him. He began to rely more heavily on his imagination, which tended toward allegorical situations. *The Marmot Drive*, set in Tunxis, a rural New England town, made a political allegory of the town's attempt to rid itself of a threatening colony of woodchucks. A number of Hersey's later books, including *The Child Buyer*, *White Lotus*, *Too Far to Walk*, *Under the Eye of the Storm*, *The Conspiracy*, *My Petition for More Space*, and *The Walnut Door*, have been criticized for their reliance on an underlying allegory or parable to support the plot.

Since the 1950's, Hersey has been associated with Yale University, with Berkeley College from 1950 to 1965 as a nonteaching fellow, and with Pierson College from 1965 to 1970, as master. In the later position, Hersey served as a counselor, confidant, resident administrator, social director, and intellectual mentor for the students, among whom was his son John, Jr. His closeness to the students allowed him the perceptions he revealed in *Letter to the Alumni*, which was a factual description of the May Day demonstrations of 1969, when Yalies supported the Black Panthers.

Hersey continues to live in Connecticut, involving himself in political issues of the day, especially those directly affecting writers. Although he is not a recluse, Hersey generally avoids media attention, only occasionally speaking in public and granting interviews.

Analysis

Critics have generally agreed that John Hersey's greatest strengths as a novelist derive from two sources: the observational skills he developed as a journalist, and his belief in the importance of individual human beings in difficult situations. Reviewers throughout his career have praised his attention to realistic detail, which rivals that of William Dean Howells. Hersey gets very close to the realistic details of the lives of his characters, so that in his most successful works (both fiction and nonfiction), the reader gets a strong sense of "being there."

When Hersey recaptured his memories of China in the novel *A Single Pebble*, in 1956, he was praised for his acute observations and simple handling of realistic detail, as he would be for nonfictional works such as *Here to Stay*, *The Algiers Motel Incident*, *Letter to the Alumni*, and *The President*. Throughout his career, however, Hersey has insisted that he mentally separates and sees a clear difference between the way he writes fiction and the way he writes nonfiction. He sees the fiction as his chance to make more profound statements of lasting value—tending to push the works into the allegorical realm—although, ironically, most critics have seen his most profound themes in his more journalistic works, whether fiction or nonfiction, such as *Hiroshima*, *The Wall*, and *A Single Pebble*.

Sometimes, however, Hersey has been criticized for having insufficently explored his characters in the apparent belief that documentary evidence sufficiently explains them. He has also been charged with cluttering his narratives with excessive detail. Although *A Single Pebble* was generally positively received, one of the criticisms leveled at it was its heavy use of nautical terms that the main character would readily understand but that are confusing to most readers. A similar criticism was leveled at *The War Lover* by a reviewer who asked if Hersey's accounts of twenty-three bombing raids, heavily laden with hour-by-hour details, were really necessary to develop his theme.

Ironically, in his 1949 essay for *The Atlantic*, "The Novel of Contemporary

History," Hersey presented an aesthetic which established the primacy of character over realistic detail. "Palpable facts," he wrote, "are mortal. . . . The things we remember . . . are emotions and impressions and illusions and images and characters: the elements of fiction." He went on to argue that the aim of the novelist of contemporary history was not to illuminate events, but to illuminate the human beings caught up in the events. This concern with the individual gives Hersey great sensitivity to suffering, a sympathy that combined with his liberal political views, makes his thematic intentions manifest in nearly all of his works, leading to the accusation that Hersey is too allegorical, too moralistic, and too "meaningful" to be taken seriously as a creative artist. Although some critics hoped he would reverse the general trend of antimoralism and experimentalism in the postmodern fiction of the 1950's and 1960's, the more Hersey tried to escape the reportorial style, the less critically successful his novels became, though they continued to sell well.

The genesis of Hersey's first novel, *A Bell for Adano*, was a journalistic assignment in wartime Italy. During the Sicilian campaign, he visited the seaport of Licata, where he observed the workings of the American Military Government and filed a story for *Life* entitled "AMGOT at Work," which was printed on August 23, 1943, along with photographs. The article described a typical day in the life of an anonymous Italo-American major from New York as he tried to cope with the problems of governing the newly liberated town. Obviously impressed by the major's common sense, fairness, and accessibility to the natives, Hersey wrote *A Bell for Adano*, based upon the article, within six weeks of the *Life* publication.

A comparison of the article with the book provides an interesting insight into Hersey's work methods in those days. He retained every person in the article and expanded several of the problems. The major became Major Victor Joppolo; Licata became Adano. The central problem of the novel is Joppolo's attempt to find a bell to replace the seven-hundred-year-old bell melted down for bullets by the Nazis. Introducing the unsympathetic character of General Marvin, Hersey was clearly making reference to General George Patton, who was known among reporters for his having slapped two shell-shocked soldiers. Because Joppolo disobeys Marvin's orders, he is reassigned to North Africa after getting Adano its bell. Hersey also invented a romantic interest for Joppolo, an invention that later led to a lawsuit by the original major.

With the exception of *Hiroshima*, *A Bell for Adano* is Hersey's most widely read book. Published by Alfred A. Knopf in early 1944, it was a huge success, mostly because of its representation of the ordinary American as good-hearted, sentimental, and rigorously fair. The book reminded the reader that the war was a struggle to preserve democracy, that government was only as good as the men who govern, and that Americans were better than Fascists. Despite all the praise, Hersey understood the effect the political situation of the time was having on the evaluation of his work. In 1944, he was in the Soviet Union and wrote an article on the role of Soviet writers in the war effort, saying "Not a word is written which is not a weapon." One sees, perhaps, in Hersey's ambivalent feelings about his instantaneous success, a motivation for his continual effort to increase the literary merit of his fiction, an effort which, in the estimate of many readers, worked against his best qualities.

Not all reviewers joined the chorus of praise for Hersey's first novel. Malcolm Cowley said that *A Bell for Adano* should be read as a tract and should not be expected to meet the criteria for a novel as well. Diana Trilling ascribed the book's success to its "folk-idealisms and popular assumptions" that surfaced because of the speed of its composition; she saw "very little writing talent" in the novel. These criticisms, though not entirely without justification, did not diminish Hersey's instant reputation as an important novelist.

Shortly after his assignment to Moscow by *Time-Life* in 1945, Hersey and several other reporters were given a tour of the Eastern Front by the Red Army. He saw the ruins of the Warsaw Ghetto, interviewed the survivors of the Lodz Ghetto, and saw signs of the atrocities at Tallinn and Rodogoscz. He knew immediately that he would have to write a novel on what he had seen, though his interviews with survivors of Auschwitz convinced him he could never write about the death camps themselves. Later, he wrote, his time spent in Hiroshima "lent urgency to what had been a vague idea." Another possible source of inspiration for *The Wall* may have come from Hersey's childhood friendship with Israel Epstein, who first interested Hersey in the history of the Jews and later became a staunch supporter of the Chinese revolution, editing the English-language magazine *China Reconstructs*.

He went to the survivors in Eastern Europe and discovered a wealth of diaries, medical records, and other documentary evidence, most of which was untranslated from the original Polish and Yiddish. He hired Mendel Norbermann and L. Danziger to translate directly from the text onto a wire recorder and did further research himself, reading *The Black Book of Polish Jewry* (1943), the works of Sholom Aleichem, the Old Testament, and the Orthodox prayer book, among other sources. Immersed in the moving experience of listening to the tapes, he began writing and soon found the number of characters, themes, and action had grown far too complicated. Four-fifths of his way through the novel, he scrapped what he had written to retell the story through the point of view of Noach Levinson, chronicler of life in the ghetto from November, 1939, to May, 1943, when the last of the buildings was leveled.

Hersey has observed that "Fiction is not afraid of complexity as journalism is. Fiction can deal with confusion." In *The Wall*, Hersey confronted a multiplicity of emotions, attitudes, customs, and events beyond a journalist's interest. The novel derives its power from this confrontation with the ragged edges of reality, and a number of critics consider it to be Hersey's greatest work. Although many reviewers expressed reservations about the length of the book and its numerous characters, most praised Hersey's compassion and argued that the strong feelings which emerged from the sustained reading of it more than made up for the technical faults of the book. Leslie Fiedler, however, said that *The Wall* lacked the strength of inner truth, depending too heavily on statistical, objective material, and he particularly criticized Hersey's themes as being unconvincing.

Although Hersey argued in *The Atlantic* that fiction allowed the writer to deal with confusion and complexity, most of his novels since *The Wall* have been criticized for their overly simplistic, message-bearing, allegorical intent. Hersey's works have continued to sell very well, but he has not earned the esteem of literary critics. Some critics, such as Thomas McDonnell, see Hersey as offering an alternative to the sterility and existential nihilism which, in their estimation, have taken over the novel, but most critics have considered Hersey's work to be without sufficient technical expertise. Some defenders of his work, however, compare it to that of John Dos Passos and argue that his humanistic themes are too valuable to ignore.

J. Madison Davis

Other major works

SHORT FICTION: *Blues*, 1987; *Fling and Other Stories*, 1990.

NONFICTION: *Men on Bataan*, 1942; *Into the Valley: A Skirmish of the Marines*, 1943; *Hiroshima*, 1946; *Here to Stay: Studies in Human Tenacity*, 1962; *The Algiers Motel Incident*, 1968; *Letter to the Alumni*, 1970; *Ralph Ellison: A Collection of Critical Essays*, 1974 (edited); *The Writer's Craft*, 1974 (edited); *The President*, 1975; *Aspects of the Presidency: Truman and Ford in Office*, 1980; *Life Sketches*, 1989.

Bibliography

Fiedler, Leslie. "No! in Thunder." In *The Novel: Modern Essays in Criticism*, edited by Robert Murray Davis. Englewood Cliffs, N.J.: Prentice-Hall, 1969. In discussing authors from his point of view that "art is essentially a moral activity," the controversial Fiedler accuses Hersey of being the author of "The Sentimental Liberal Protest Novel" who fights for "slots on the lists of best sellers" with his "ersatz morality." The essay makes for lively reading at best.

Huse, Nancy L. *The Survival Tales of John Hersey*. New York: Whitston, 1983. An eminently readable and informed study on Hersey which is useful in understanding the scope and development of Hersey as a writer. Explores the relationship between art and moral or political intentions. Includes extensive notes and a bibliography.

Sanders, David. "John Hersey." In *Contemporary Novelists*, edited by James Vinson. New York: St. Martin's Press, 1982. Covers Hersey's work from wartime journalist to novelist. Cites *The Wall* as his greatest novel and considers him the "least biographical of authors." A rather dense study but helpful in quickly establishing themes in Hersey's writings. A chronology and a bibliography are provided.

_____. *John Hersey.* New York: Twayne, 1967. A book-length study on Hersey in which his novels up to and including *White Lotus* are discussed. The same density of style persists as in Sanders' piece in *Contemporary Novelists*; however, the thoroughly researched material and background information puts Hersey's work in context. Contains a selected bibliography.

_____. "John Hersey: War Correspondent into Novelist." In *New Voices in American Studies*, edited by Ray B. Browne, Donald M. Winkelman, and Allen Hayman. West Lafayette, Ind.: Purdue University Press, 1966. A well-known scholar on Hersey, Sanders defends him and insists that he should not be dismissed because of his popularity. Traces Hersey's origins as a war correspondent and the writings that emerged from these experiences. Finally, Sanders settles the dispute as to whether Hersey is a novelist and hails him as a "writer."

JAMAKE HIGHWATER

Born: Glacier County, Montana; February 14, 1942

Principal long fiction
Anpao: An American Indian Odyssey, 1977; *Journey to the Sky*, 1978; *The Sun, He Dies*, 1980; *Legend Days*, 1984; *The Ceremony of Innocence*, 1985; *Eyes of Darkness*, 1985; *I Wear the Morning Star*, 1986.

Other literary forms
Published under the name of J. Marks, the early works of Jamake (juh-MAH-kuh) Highwater include *Rock and Other Four Letter Words* (1968) and *Mick Jagger: The Singer, Not the Song* (1973), books that show the author's interest in the culture of rock music. *Moonsong Lullaby* (1981), relating the importance of the moon in Indian culture, is a tale for young children. Highwater has also published books on Indian painting, Indian artists, and Indian history through art as well as on Indian dance and other Indian ceremonies. Other book-length publications include five editions of *Europe Under Twenty-five: A Young Person's Guide* (1971) and *Indian America: A Cultural and Travel Guide* (1975). This latter book, the first Fodor guide on American Indians, is important not only as a guide for tourists, but also as a study of the history and culture of the American Indian. Highwater has also written short fiction and magazine articles as well as scripts for television shows.

Achievements
Highwater, a young author described by Edward K. Thompson of *Smithsonian Magazine* as "A brilliant and authoritative representative of the Native Americans," already has become recognized for many different talents. The late John Gardner said of Highwater that "he is one of the purest writers at work—a clean, clear voice." In addition to writing books and articles, the energetic Highwater has hosted, written, and narrated *Songs of the Thunderbird* (1979) for the Public Broadcasting System. In the field of music, Highwater's interests are diverse: rock, Indian, and classical; he is a contributing editor of *Stereo Review* and classical music editor of the *Soho Weekly News*.

Highwater has been called "A writer of exceptional vision and power" by Anaïs Nin, and "a young man of impressive literary and artistic accomplishments, ideally suited to be a spokesperson for Native Americans" by Weston LaBarre, Professor of Anthropology Emeritus at Duke University. Recognized as an authority in the arts, Highwater is a consultant to the New York State Council on the Arts, and at one time he served on the Art Task Panel of the President's Commission on Mental Health. He has also been named an Honorary Citizen of Oklahoma.

Among the many honors that Highwater has received, one of the most important was awarded at the Blackfeet Reserve in Alberta, Canada, when Ed Calf Robe, elder of the Blood Reserve of Blackfeet Indians, gave Highwater the name of Piitai Sahkomaapii, which means Eagle Son. This honor, the highest that a tribe can bestow on one of its members, was given because "he soars highest and catches many truths which he carries to many lands."

Biography

Jamake Highwater was born in Glacier County, Montana, on February 14, 1942. His mother, Amana Bonneville, was of the Blackfeet nation and his father, Jamie, was of the Cherokee nation (Eastern band). His early years were spent on the Blackfeet Indian Reservation in Montana and in Alberta, Canada, where the Blackfeet people held their summer encampments. A very important influence on his life was his teacher, Alta Black, who gave the eight-year-old Highwater a secondhand typewriter with the advice that he should learn to use it because he would become a writer. She also tutored him prior to his entrance into college at age thirteen.

At the age of eight, Highwater went to Hollywood with his father, a founding member of the American Indian Rodeo Association and a stunt man in Western films. After his father was killed in an automobile accident, Highwater lived in an orphanage until his mother remarried. His stepfather, Alexander Marks, a white man, adopted him. Highwater later used the pen name J. Marks-Highwater, combining the names of his stepfather and his father. Highwater's mother was a strong but bitter woman—bitter because her parents had starved to death during the Depression and because her older son Jaime (nicknamed Reno) was killed in 1953, fighting for America in the Korean War.

Highwater holds degrees in music, comparative literature, and cultural anthropology. When he was awarded the Ph.D. at age twenty, there were only about forty Indians who held doctorates.

Highwater's life, after his mother remarried, was clearly a blend of two cultures. Today, both cultures are a part of his life. Highwater lives in the Soho section of Manhattan and maintains residences in Montana, in Turkey, and in Switzerland. Although very much a world traveler and a man of the twentieth century, Highwater is loyal to his Indian heritage; he returns to Montana to renew his links to his past because, as he says, he is "a traditional Northern Plains Indian." Like many Native Americans, he wants his son to know and honor his Indian heritage. Although not enrolled in the Blackfeet nation, Highwater maintains close ties with the Blackfeet people, as is evident from the award they have accorded him, naming him Piitai Sahkomaapii, the Eagle Son.

Analysis

The truths that the Eagle Son of the Blackfeet nation has conveyed are integral to his works of fiction: *Anpao, Journey to the Sky, The Sun, He Dies, Legend Days, The Ceremony of Innocence, Eyes of Darkness,* and *I Wear the Morning Star.* In his fiction as well as in his nonfiction, Highwater attempts to build cultural bridges by conveying basic Indian beliefs and presuppositions. When Highwater, who insists that he lives in two worlds or two Americas, emphasizes the differences between contemporary American values and those of his heritage, he stresses that there is more than one reality. One is not necessarily more valid than the other; instead, each reality has its own truths. By conveying the truths in various Indian cultures, Highwater attempts to foster the understanding which must precede peaceful coexistence. Highwater believes that if the two cultures can coexist in one man, they can coexist in the larger space of the world.

Anpao, a Newbery Honor book in 1978, has perhaps received less attention than it deserves because of this honor. Recognition as an outstanding book for children suggests to some critics that a book is intended only for a young audience. Like Mark Twain's *The Adventures of Huckleberry Finn* (1884), however, *Anpao* should be read by persons of all ages. As an odyssey of the American Indian, *Anpao* is a compilation of legends, the oral history of Indian tribes. Highwater chooses a number of versions from recorded accounts of these legends, giving full credit to his sources, but the hero, Anpao, is his own creation.

The novel begins with Anpao's falling in love with the beautiful Ko-ko-mik-e-is, who agrees to marry him if he will journey to the Sun and get the Sun's permission for her to marry. The quest begins; Anpao, also called Scarface, sets forth. On his journey, he learns that Anpao means "the Dawn" and that his father is the Sun. Anpao's mother was a human who went to the World-Above-the-World without dying. After the birth of her son, Anpao, she becomes homesick and attempts an escape with her son, but manages to get only part way to the earth because the rope that she has woven from sinew is not long enough. When the Sun is taunted by his jealous first wife, the Moon, he becomes angry. He follows the footsteps of his human wife to a hole in the sky. Seeing her dangling just above the trees on earth, he makes a hoop from the branch of a willow tree and orders the hoop to kill the woman but to spare the child. The Sun is not quick enough to snatch the rope when the root which holds the rope in the World-Above-the-World sags because of pity for the dead mother of Anpao. When the child falls onto the dead body of his mother, blood from her body causes a scar to appear on his face. The child, Anpao, lives on the earth, and his journey toward the Sun involves the learning of basic truths of Indian culture. The legends that he learns on his travels are primarily learned through traditional storytelling, a mode of teaching used not only by Indians but also by ancient Greeks and Romans.

Like Homer in the *Iliad* and the *Odyssey* (both c. 800 B.C.), Highwater states his theme in the short opening chapter and then moves, again like Homer, *in medias res*. Anpao and his twin brother (created when Anpao disobeyed the warning of the Spider Woman, with whom he lived, not to throw his hoop into the air) are poor youths who arrive in the village where the beautiful young girl Ko-ko-mik-e-is lives. After Anpao sets forth on his journey to the Sun, he meets an old woman who tells him the story of the beginning of the world, of the death of the creator Napi, and of his own birth. Then the creation of Oapna, the contrary twin brother of Anpao, is accounted for, and his death is also told. The Clown/Contrary is a familiar figure in Indian legends.

In another typical Indian legend, Anpao meets with a sorceress, a meeting which invites comparison with Odysseus' meeting with Circe. One of the most important obstacles that Anpao has to overcome is the intense dislike of the Moon, who, as the first wife of the Sun, despises the child born to the human responsible for the Sun's misalliance. Anpao, however, earns the love of the Moon when he saves her son, Morning Star, from death; thus, Anpao becomes the first person to have the power of the Sun, Moon, and Earth.

As a result of his journey to the Sun, Anpao has the ugly scar removed from his face, thus enabling him to prove to Ko-ko-mik-e-is that he did indeed make the journey. The marriage of Anpao (the Dawn and the son of the Sun) and Ko-ko-mik-e-is (Night-red-light, which is related to the Moon) takes place, and Anpao begs the people of Ko-ko-mik-e-is' village to follow the couple as they leave to escape the death, sickness, and greed which are coming to their world. The people will not follow; instead they laugh at Anpao. (This action suggests the lack of unity among Indians, a lack that may have been crucial to the course of Indian history.) Undaunted, Anpao, taking his beautiful bride with him, goes to the village beneath the water. Ko-ko-mik-e-is is assured by Anpao that what is happening will not be the end, because they and their people are the rivers, the land, the prairies, the rocks—all of nature. This unity with nature is fundamental to Indian culture.

Most of the legends in *Anpao* belong to times long ago, but Highwater has also included some more modern tales which tell of the arrival of the white man with his horses, weapons, and disease. The legends selected by Highwater are, as the widely acclaimed Indian writer N. Scott Momaday says, "truly reflective of the oral tradition and rich heritage of Native American storytelling." The legends, old and new, are the cornerstone of Indian culture.

After writing *Anpao*, essentially a mythical journey, Highwater turned to recorded events for material for his next novel, *Journey to the Sky*. This journey is a chronological account of the actual explorations of two white men, John Lloyd Stephens, a New York attorney, and Frederick Catherwood, a British artist and architect, who began their first trip in search of the lost cities of the Mayan kingdom in October, 1839. Although these men made two extended trips to the kingdom of the Mayan peoples, Highwater confines his tale to the first exploration, which ended late in July, 1840.

Journey to the Sky is a suspense-filled adventure story which displays Highwater's talents as a writer more effectively than does his first novel. Although the narrative is interrupted from time to time by Highwater's accounts of more recent findings, the suspense and excitement of the journey are sustained throughout the novel. Particularly impressive is Highwater's narrative skill in selecting highlights from the historical account of the Stephens-Catherwood expedition (John Stephens did the writing, while Frederick Catherwood provided illustrations). Like a number of recent novels as diverse as E. L. Doctorow's *Ragtime* (1975) and Aleksandr Solzhenitsyn's *Lenin in Zurich* (1976), *Journey to the Sky* is a new kind of historical fiction.

Having been appointed by President Martin Van Buren as United States diplomatic agent to the Central American Confederacy, Stephens fulfills his public duties as a diplomat, but the secret purpose of the trip is the search for ruins. He meets with leaders of various colonies in Central America, paying courtesy calls and extending greetings from the American government. Although Stephens finds the performance of his official duties pleasurable, he is in a hurry to begin explorations.

Early in the trip, while in Belize, the two explores hire a young cutthroat, Augustin, as their servant. Although they seriously doubt that he will serve them well, by the end of the journey, they realize the rightness of their choice, because he proves to be a loyal and valuable servant and friend. They also hire men to help transport their belongings, which include tools, food (including live chickens), and clothing. From time to time, and for differing reasons, new employees have to be found.

The trip over Mico Mountain is extremely hazardous because of the jungle, the rocks, the mud, and the gullies. The rough terrain is only one of many natural hazards that they encounter during their explorations in Central America. Insects, climate, earthquakes, and malaria are some of the other forces of nature that they encounter. In addition, they meet such varied characters as the double-dealing Colonel Archibald MacDonald, superintendent of the English colonies in Central America; the petty tyrant Don Gregorio in Copan; good and bad padres; and hospitable and inhospitable people. The explorers are imprisoned, threatened with murder, and surrounded by an active rebellion in Central America.

Highwater captures the enthusiasm of Stephens and Catherwood as they discover the "lost city" just outside Copan. They are the first white men to see these tumbling pyramids and idols, evidence of the religion of the Mayas. Stephens and two helpers begin removing the foliage from rock piles that the people of Copan have been ignoring as piles of rubbish, and Catherwood sets to work documenting their discovery by making drawings of each of the fallen figures. To Stephens, this desolate city with its many magnificent works of art is evidence that the Mayas were master craftsmen.

Having located and documented the ruins at Copan, Stephens and Catherwood move to other sites, where they find further evidence of the Mayan culture. Even illness cannot deter them. From one site to another, the explorers continue their amazing trip. Although warned not to go to Palenque because of the danger to white men as a result of political upheaval, they go. There they find ruins that are quite different from those in Copan. After documenting the Palenque ruins, they go to Uxmal. Many times during the journey in Central America, the New York attorney and the British artist are warned about the hostile Indians, yet the Indians are often more hospitable than the white people they encounter. Stephens and Catherwood's discoveries of a Mayan civilization which rose and fell prior to the Spanish invasion corroborate a basic thesis of Highwater's—that the Indian culture, although different from that of the white man, is nevertheless meaningful and remarkable.

In *The Sun, He Dies*, Highwater once again turned to recorded history for a firm base. The overthrow of Montezuma II, ruler of the Aztec nation, by the Spaniard Hernando Cortés with a small contingent of men has perplexed historians, who sometimes credit Cortés with an unusual amount of tactical knowledge and ability. Highwater, on the other hand, looks carefully at the character of Montezuma and the religious beliefs of this powerful man and concludes that these elements were the basic causes of his downfall.

Although the downfall of Montezuma is the backdrop for *The Sun, He Dies*, the novel is also an initiation story, a history of an important Aztec ruler, a history of the Aztec people, and an immersion into Indian culture; Highwater has tightened the structure of the novel by creating a narrator, Nanautzin, to tell the story: this narrative voice unifies the episodic material drawn from the oral traditions of Indian peoples.

Beginning with "Call me Nanautzin," echoing the opening sentence of Herman Melville's *Moby Dick* (1851), *The Sun, He Dies* develops in chronological order. In the epic tradition, Nanautzin, the outcast woodcutter, despised by his people, announces his intention to sing of the great Aztec nation. Like Ishmael in *Moby Dick*, he alone is left to tell the story of all that happened.

Nanautzin briefly tells of his early life in his native village, where he is taunted by the children, cast away by his father, and loved by his mother. The ugly scars that signal the beginning of the unhappy life of the narrator are created by his fall, as a small child, into a cooking fire. The resultant deformities cause his father to abandon him and the villagers to name him the Ugly One. Unlike Oedipus, Nanautzin is not physically cast away; he is given an ax, called a woodcutter, and forgotten. He grows up lonely and friendless.

Nanautzin goes to Tenochtitlan for the installation of Montezuma II as the

Great Speaker, even though the people of his village, Tlaxcala, loathe the lord of the greatest city in Mexico. Although Nanautzin feels honor for this great man, the trip does nothing to win for him honor or friends among his people. Because of his physical appearance, he remains the Ugly One, despised and rejected.

Eventually, Nanautzin wanders into a marvelous forest, where, although he knows he should not, he begins to chop firewood. Soon a man appears and questions him, demanding to know why he is cutting wood in the forest. The young man blurts out that, since Montezuma has become ruler, the people of Tlaxcala have not been permitted to cut dead wood wherever they wish and life has become very difficult for his people. Instead of being punished on the spot, Nanautzin is ordered to appear at the Palace of Tenochtitlan on the following day.

Fearing for his life, yet obedient, Nanautzin goes to the palace, where he discovers that the stranger he met in the forest is the Great Speaker himself. Instead of receiving punishment for his honest reply to Montezuma on the preceding day, Nanautzin is transformed into the Chief Orator because of his honesty. Then he is taken to the ruins at Tula, the once great city of the ancient Toltecs, where he, along with young boys, is taught by the priests and where he learns that here the greatest of all men once lived. This experience at Tula is both an initiation and a religious experience.

After his experience at Tula, Nanautzin becomes the confidant of Montezuma, who tells him the many legends of his people. Montezuma also confides that, according to his horoscope, his life is balanced between the war god, Huitzilopochtli, who fills the body of Montezuma with power, and the gentle god, Quetzalcoatl, who fills Montezuma's body with love. The Toltecs were the wise people created by the gentle Quetzalcoatl, who, like the Norse god Odin, was a benefactor to his people. Evil men loathed Quetzalcoatl, the tall, noble, holy white god who would not permit his people to be sacrificed. The evil men managed to trick this loving god with a mirror; drunk with pulque, Quetzalcoatl, who had seen his body in the mirror, became passionate and slept with a forbidden priestess. Evil came into the land and Quetzalcoatl went into exile in the land of Yucatan, but promised to return in the year One Reed, at which time he would recapture his throne and bring peace forevermore. Montezuma believes that Quetzalcoatl will return.

Although believing in the return of Quetzalcoatl, Montezuma also believes the horoscope, thus making him susceptible to doubt about himself. Is he one of the evil ones who destroyed this great god or one of the faithful who follow him? On the one hand, he demands tributes and sacrifices from the people, ruling much of the time by force, thus acceding to Huitzilopochtli and alienating many of the tribes. On the other hand, he honors the gentle Quetzalcoatl and longs for his return.

During his early years as Chief Orator, Nanautzin learns the beliefs of this mighty leader and the history of the people. He recognizes the goodness in the Great Speaker of Tenochtitlan. Even though Montezuma appears to be a ruthless ruler, he has been kind to Nanautzin, he admires honesty, and he has great faith in the prediction that Quetzalcoatl will return. Montezuma's faith in the promise of this great and good god indicates the Aztec ruler's devotion to his religion.

From the favorable signs that appear in the year One Reed, Montezuma draws great confidence, but a time comes when the signs change. Montezuma is no longer the almost divine figure that Nanautzin has observed. Instead, the Great Speaker can no longer make up his own mind, which has become so divided that one part is contrary to the other part. Montezuma, like Ahab in *Moby Dick*, becomes a man obsessed. When he learns of the white men who have arrived at Chalco, the Great Speaker concludes that Quetzalcoatl's prediction is about to come true. Although the priests, the soothsayers, the noblemen, and the warriors warn Montezuma that these mysterious men are not Quetzalcoatl and his court, the Great Speaker is not to be shaken in his belief. Because Montezuma has alienated many of the neighboring tribes, he is hated; it is, therefore, easy for these white men (Cortés and his troops) to enlist the aid of the alienated tribes, including the people of Tlazcala, in the march against Tenochtitlan.

Instead of trying to defend his city, Montezuma makes offerings to Cortés, whom he believes to be the gentle god Quetzalcoatl. It becomes an easy matter for Cortés to enter the realm of Montezuma and then, with the help of the alienated tribes, wreak havoc not only on the Great Speaker but also on the people of Tenochtitlan.

The narrative structure of *The Sun, He Dies* is strong, and the development of the character of Montezuma makes believable the Indian version that the Great Speaker of Tenochtitlan falls, not because of the tactical superiority of Cortés, but because of Montezuma's religious beliefs and obsessions. In addition to the recounting of history, the novel is a collection of tales that are an integral part of the beliefs of the Aztec nation. The Ugly One who becomes the Chief Orator for Montezuma II, although he comes full circle from being a lonely figure in Tlaxcala to being the figure left alone, is far wiser than the ignorant woodcutter Nanautzin who wanders into the forest owned by the Great Speaker. Nevertheless, the once powerful Aztec nation is destroyed and Nanautzin can only sing of what has been.

"What has been" is pertinent to each of Highwater's novels. Based on oral and recorded history, *Anpao*, *Journey to the Sky*, and *The Sun, He Dies*, for example, convey truths of three important Indian cultures. The Indian respect for and allegiance to the forces of nature have determined their actions, just as the basic beliefs of a people have always influenced their history. The significance of religion in the fall of Montezuma, in the ruins of Yucatan, and in the lives of Native Americans adds another dimension to recorded history.

Using his knowledge of Native American myth and techniques of storytelling, Highwater applied his enthusiasm for the retelling of history to his own unique background in his recent trilogy, collectively referred to as *The Ghost Horse Cycle*. In the first book, *Legend Days*, the story begins as a mythic chronicle of the character Amana, a young girl of the Blood tribe of the northern plains, who lived in the late nineteenth century. Her people have contracted smallpox from the white traders, and are dying in record numbers. Her sister, SoodaWa, sends Amana away; and in a strange, dreamlike sequence, Amana is captured by the evil owls, rescued by the kindly foxes, and protected from harm by sleeping in a cave for a year. During that time, she receives a vision in which she becomes a man, a warrior, and hunts with other men. She is given a set of warrior's clothes by her spirit helper, which she must never reveal until the proper time. She returns to her village only to find two old women left, all the rest having died or fled.

Eventually Amana is reunited with her sister SoodaWa and her sister's husband Far Away Son, who have been living with Big Belly, a chief of the Gros Ventres tribe. Amana marries Far Away Son, as is the custom among the Bloods—orphaned girls marry their sister's husbands. She tries to be a good wife, but secretly her vision makes her long to be a warrior. The story rehearses the agonizing plight of the northern plains tribes as the extensive hunting of buffalo dwindled the supply of food, disease ravaged the population, and the white man's influence, such as whiskey, paralyzed Indian culture.

Legend Days—being a book written as a myth and centered in recorded history—reads very much like other Highwater narratives, but *The Ghost Horse Cycle* is more personal than most Highwater stories. Continuing with *Eyes of Darkness* and then with *I Wear the Morning Star*, it becomes evident that the myth only begins the story. Amana eventually weds a French trader named Jean-Pierre Bonneville and has a daughter, Jemina Bonneville, who in turn weds Jamie Ghost Horse, a Native American working as a Hollywood stuntman. They have two children, Reno and Sitko. The focus of the novels turns from the rather hazy myth of *Legend Days* to the very concrete story of one family's efforts to survive the onslaught of the modern world in their lives. *Eyes of Darkness* chronicles the marriage of Amana and Jean-Pierre, as well as Amana's introduction into white society, a transition that for her was never really successful. Her daughter Jemina's stormy marriage to Jamie Ghost Horse reveals the problem of Native Americans confronting newly acquired economic realities, newly acquired social problems, such as alcoholism, and newly acquired stigmas, such as discrimination and racism.

I Wear the Morning Star focuses on Jemina's two children, Reno, who seeks to deny his Indian heritage, and Sitko, who listens attentively to his grandmother's stories and longs for the old ways. Forced because of circumstance and poverty, Jemina places the boys in an orphanage until she remarries a white man named Alexander Miller, and the boys return to her household only to aggravate further the number of underlying problems each is having. For the grandchildren of Amana, life has become too complex; they live in a world that is neither Indian nor completely white, not knowing whether to follow the ways of the whites or to listen to the compelling stories of the grandmother. The need to adopt the customs and the practices of the whites is apparent, but Sitko especially learns that Grandmother Amana offers something that the whites cannot. He says that "from Grandmother Amana I learned how to dream myself into existence." Sitko becomes an artist and begins to explore his heritage through his art.

The Ghost Horse Cycle is autobiographical in that Sitko's life parallels much of Highwater's. The author's mother, Amana, was a Blackfeet Indian, his father, Jaime, a Cherokee who did stunts for various Hollywood films. After an automobile accident took his father's life, Jamake and his brother Reno lived in an orphanage until his mother married a white man. The confusion exhibited by Sitko in the story parallels Jamake's early experience, and his redemption through art is especially poignant. Yet the story of Amana and her descendants emphasizes certain truths for all Native Americans and reveals, in a very personal way, the predicament of Native American culture's inevitable clash with white culture.

In fictionalizing Indian lore and Indian experience, Highwater explores mythic elements of the Indian experience as Homer did for the Greeks, and Melville and William Faulkner did for segments of American culture. From Highwater's exploration of mythic elements, Indian realities emerge. Dr. Logan Wright of the University of Oklahoma says that Highwater "profoundly influences our thinking and . . . possesses the courage to risk changing lives. He is clearly one of the most creative minds now before us."

Virginia A. Duck

Other major works

NONFICTION: *Rock and Other Four Letter Words*, 1968 (as J. Marks); *Europe under Twenty-five: A Young Person's Guide*, 1971; *Mick Jagger: The Singer, Not the Song*, 1973 (as J. Marks); *Indian America: A Cultural and Travel Guide*, 1975; *Fodor's Indian America*, 1975; *Song from the Earth: American Indian Painting*, 1976; *Ritual of the Wind: North American Indian Dances and Music*, 1977; *Many Smokes, Many Moons: A Chronology of American Indian History Through Indian Art*, 1978; *Dance: Rituals of Experience*, 1978; *The Sweet Grass Lives On: Fifty Contemporary North American Indian Artists*, 1980; *The Primal Mind: Vision and Reality in Indian America*, 1981; *Arts of the Indian Americas: Leaves from the Sacred Tree*, 1983; *Native Land: Sagas of the Indian Americas*, 1986; *Shadow Show: An Autobiographical Insinuation*, 1986.

ANTHOLOGY: *Words in the Blood: Contemporary Indian Literature of North and South America*, 1984.

CHILDREN'S LITERATURE: *Moonsong Lullaby*, 1981.

Bibliography

Adams, Phoebe-Lou. "Review of *Song of the Earth*." *The Atlantic* 240 (March, 1977): 117. Adams' short review of the Indian paintings and the commentary that accompanies them is somewhat condescending toward what she terms the various "schools" of Indian art which have emerged in recent times. She mentions several remarks by Buckbear Bosin in the work which indicate a reluctance on the part of Indian artists to acknowledge white culture, an element of Indian art that Adams finds less than realistic.

Katz, Jane, ed. *This Song Remembers: Self-Portraits of Native Americans in the Arts*. Boston: Houghton Mifflin, 1980. Katz's work is comprehensive, including essays from many different Indian artists who are active in the visual arts, poetry, literature, and dance. Highwater's self-portrait centers on the importance of myth and Indian culture on his life and art.

EDWARD HOAGLAND

Born: New York, New York; December 21, 1932

Principal long fiction

Cat Man, 1956; *The Circle Home*, 1960; *The Peacock's Tail*, 1965; *Seven Rivers West*, 1986.

Other literary forms

Edward Hoagland is known primarily not for his novels but for his essays and travel books. As an essayist and reviewer, he has been published in such periodicals as *Harper's*, *The Village Voice*, *Sports Illustrated*, *Commentary*, and *The Atlantic*; several anthologies of his essays are now in print. His travel narratives include *Notes from the Century Before: A Journal from British Columbia* (1969) and *African Calliope: A Journey to the Sudan* (1979). During the 1960's he also wrote short stories, which appeared in publications such as *Esquire*, *The New Yorker*, *New American Review*, and *The Paris Review*; three of his short stories have been republished in *City Tales* (1986). In addition, he has contributed nature editorials to *The New York Times* since 1979.

Achievements

With the publication of his first novel, *Cat Man*, in 1956, Hoagland received much favorable attention from the critics. The book won for Hoagland a Houghton Mifflin Literary Fellowship, and critics saw in him the makings of a first-rate novelist. They particularly praised his ability to capture a milieu—in this case, the seamy world of circus roustabouts, a world he presents with knowledgeable and detailed frankness. His second novel, *The Circle Home*, confirmed his potential. Once again, he succeeded in vividly re-creating a colorful environment, the sweaty world of a boxing gymnasium. He received several honors during this period as well, including a Longview Foundation Award in 1961, an American Academy of Arts and Letters Traveling Fellowship in 1964, and a Guggenheim Fellowship in 1964.

With the publication of *The Peacock's Tail*, however, Hoagland's career suffered a setback. In both the critics' and his own opinion, this book was a failure, and Hoagland, whose novels had never won for him a wide audience, turned away from long fiction. For the next twenty years, he worked primarily in nonfiction, producing essays and travel narratives to considerable acclaim, but in 1986, he made a triumphal return to the novel. *Seven Rivers West* was well received, combining as it does Hoagland's ability to re-create a sense of place—here, the North American wilderness—with his impressive knowledge of the natural world.

Biography

Edward Hoagland was born on December 21, 1932, in New York City. His father was a financial lawyer whose employers included Standard Oil of New Jersey and the United States defense and state departments. When he was eight, his family moved to New Canaan, Connecticut, a fashionable community of country estates and exclusive clubs. He was sent off to boarding school at Deerfield Academy, where, because of his bookishness, he was assigned to a special corridor known as the Zoo, which was reserved for those whom the school deemed incorrigible misfits. Hoagland did have great difficulty fitting in as a child. In large part this was because of his stutter. Understandably, he shunned potentially embarrassing social situations, developing a love of solitude and wildlife instead. Indeed, from the age of ten onward, he became very close to nature and kept a variety of pets ranging from dogs to alligators.

He went to Harvard, where he was strongly drawn to writing, a medium in which he could speak unhampered by his stutter. He studied literature under such notables as Alfred Kazin, Archibald MacLeish, and John Berryman; encouraged by his professors, he set to work on his first novel. In his spare time he read Socialist publications and attended meetings of a Trotskyite cell in the theater district of Boston. He was graduated from Harvard cum laude in 1954 with his first novel already accepted by Houghton Mifflin.

Hoagland had to put his literary career on hold, however, when he was drafted. He served in the army from 1955 to 1957, working in the medical laboratory and looking after the morgue at Valley Forge Army Hospital in Pennsylvania. Following his discharge, Hoagland returned to New York City. Financially, times were very difficult. His father, who disapproved of his decision to become a writer, had cut him off. In fact, his father was so opposed to his son's career that he wrote to Houghton Mifflin's lawyer to try to stop publication of his first novel. Hoagland's annual income over the next fifteen years averaged three thousand dollars.

In 1960, his second novel was published and he married Amy Ferrara, from whom he was divorced in 1964. At about this time he also became active politically, marching in civil rights and peace demonstrations and mailing his draft card to President Lyndon Johnson. To supplement his income, he began accepting academic posts as well, teaching at such schools as Rutgers, Sarah Lawrence, the University of Iowa, and Columbia. In 1968, he married Marion Magid, the managing editor of *Commentary*, with whom he has a daughter, Molly. He and his family make their home in West Greenwich Village, but for five months of every year Hoagland lives in an eight-room farmhouse on one hundred acres of woodland near Barton, Vermont.

Analysis

Edward Hoagland's novels are marked by a keen eye for detail and a remarkable sense of place. They masterfully re-create unusual and often male-dominated environments, such as that of the circus or a boxing gymnasium. His protagonists tend to be isolated and lonely men, cut off through their own actions from those they love, men who generally have failed in their relationships with women. They are misfits, drifters, or dreamers, and the novels are often organized around their journeys, which may be merely flight, as in *The Circle Home*, or a clearly focused quest, as in *Seven Rivers West*. Because of this episodic structure, the books have a looseness that can approach the discursive at times, with flashbacks and digressions slowing the pace.

Many of these traits are already apparent in Hoagland's first work, *Cat Man*. Drawn from his own experience working in a circus, *Cat Man* offers a graphic and harrowing portrayal of the life of the low-paid circus roust-abouts, most of whom are derelicts or social outcasts. With his usual attraction to the eccentric and offbeat, Hoagland creates a human menagerie, a gallery of grotesques such as Dogwash, who will not touch water and cleans himself by wiping his whole body as hard as he can with paper. The novel presents a brutal world in which violence threatens constantly from both the workers and the animals. In fact, the book begins with an attempted murder and ends with a lion attack. It is also a world of rampant racism, a world in which the insane are to be laughed at and women sexually used and abandoned. As sordid and disturbing as all this is, Hoagland conveys it with remarkable vividness and attention to detail. Indeed, it is the searing portrayal of this world that is the novel's great strength.

Fiddler, the main character, is a classic Hoagland protagonist. A youth who has been with the circus only seven weeks, he has been cut off from his family by his alcoholism and is very much an alienated man. Suffering from low self-esteem, he develops a foolhardy and almost obsessive fascination with the beauty and grace of his charges, the lions and tigers that it is his job, as a cat man, to tend. Hoagland's own interest in and knowledge of animals is quite evident, as he endows the cats with as much individuality as the humans. Yet while Hoagland is clearly as fascinated as Fiddler with the animals, he never sentimentalizes them. The cats may be magnificent but they can also be uncaring and deadly, a lesson that Fiddler finally and fatally learns.

Also typical of Hoagland's novels is the fact that *Cat Man* has a loose structure. Ostensibly, it is the story of one tragic day in Council Bluffs, but interspersed throughout the narrative are the events of other days in other places as Fiddler travels cross-country with the circus. Many of these episodes could stand on their own as quite good short stories, but inserted as they are within the novel's main narrative they interrupt the momentum and slow the book's flow.

Hoagland's second novel, *The Circle Home*, once again features a main character who is a lonely misfit. In this work, the protagonist is an over-the-hill boxer who rightly fears that he is doomed to become a derelict like his father. Again, too, he is a man who, through his own actions, is alienated from his family. Denny Kelly, though, is a less sympathetic figure than Fiddler. He has been so abusive toward his wife, Patsy, that she has repeatedly thrown him out. In fact, Denny seems incapable of committing himself to another person and simply takes advantage of women such as his wife or Margaret, an older woman whom he exploits for whatever material and sexual comforts she can supply.

Essentially, Denny is an immature child (indeed, he is strongly attracted to children), with all the selfishness and irresponsibility that that implies. Moreover, he avoids serious introspection whenever possible and actively fights any inclination toward thought by drowning himself in sensual pleasures. If Hoagland presents animals with considerable understanding in *Cat Man*, in *The Circle Home* he focuses on an individual who exists on little more than an animal level. Denny is a man who is incapable of expressing his feelings or organizing his life, who responds simply to the need for food, shelter, and sex.

If Fiddler clung to the cats in an attempt to give his life meaning, the one element in Denny's life that gives him a sense of achievement is boxing. The novel examines his fate once that is lost to him. Completely demoralized by being brutally beaten in a training bout, Denny abandons the ring and takes to the road, drifting closer and closer to his feared future as a derelict. While the ending of *Cat Man* was utterly bleak, *The Circle Home* offers some hope: In hitting rock bottom, Denny gains some degree of self-awareness. Although his future is far from certain, Denny does at least attempt to overcome his irresponsibility and selfishness as he tries to reconcile with his wife. He has made "the circle home," returning via a long and circuitous route of self-discovery.

Critics were generally enthusiastic about *The Circle Home*, praising in particular its convincing portrayal of the grimy world of the Better Champions' Gym. If *Cat Man* showed Hoagland's detailed knowledge of the circus, this novel shows his thorough familiarity with boxing, as he digresses on such subjects as types of fighters and gym equipment. The book's structure, however, is again quite loose, with repeated shifts in time and place and the use of an episodic journey as an organizing principle.

In Hoagland's third novel, however, the problems are more than simply structural. Regarded by the critics as his weakest piece of long fiction, *The Peacock's Tail* is the rambling story of Ben Pringle, a prejudiced and maladjusted WASP who has taken up residence in a seedy New York City hotel. As usual, Hoagland's main character is a misfit isolated from those he loves. Like Denny, Ben has difficulty maintaining a lasting relationship with a woman and has just been rejected by his lover, an experience that has left him with a badly damaged ego. Indeed, like the earlier protagonists, Ben in his troubled state needs stability and support. While Fiddler clung to his cats and Denny to boxing to retain some sense of pride and avoid a total collapse, Ben turns to children, becoming a storyteller and pied piper to the hordes of youngsters who inhabit his hotel.

If Denny was attracted to children, who mirrored his own arrested development, Ben seems to turn to them out of an inability to deal with adults, using their approval to boost his crumbling sense of self-worth. Powerless and out of control with his peers, he derives a sense of power and control from the adulation of the young. Hoagland apparently intends for the reader to believe that Ben finds happiness and fulfillment leading hundreds of children through the streets of New York to the strains of his newly acquired harmonica. Yet Ben's newfound role as pied piper seems less a solution to his problems than a frenzied attempt to escape them.

Once one doubts the validity of Ben's solution, however, one is also forced to question the reality of the novel's setting. While the faithful depiction of milieu was the great strength of Hoagland's earlier novels, *The Peacock's Tail* takes place in an Upper West Side welfare hotel, which is presented as if it were one large amusement park. The hotel is inhabited by vibrant, lusty blacks and Hispanics who exude an earthiness and enthusiasm that is apparently meant to balance Ben's Waspish reserve and alienation. The earlier novels portrayed their environments with a hard-edged and knowledgeable use of detail. Here the portrait is sentimentalized, a musical-comedy version of a welfare hotel.

This artistic and critical failure represented a setback for Hoagland's promising novelistic career, and he followed it with a twenty-year hiatus from long fiction. With his fourth novel, however, Hoagland fully redeemed himself. *Seven Rivers West* is an entertaining and dazzlingly inventive tale. Set in the North American West of the 1880's, it features the most likable incarnation of the Hoagland protagonist: Cecil Roop. Another man isolated from his loved ones, he, like Denny, has abandoned his family and is now on a journey. Yet while Denny drifted aimlessly, Cecil is on a quest: He wants to capture a grizzly bear. At least, that is his goal until he learns of the existence of Bigfoot, which then becomes his obsession. Like Fiddler's obsession with cats, however, Cecil's fascination with this mysterious creature ultimately proves tragic.

If this sounds like a tall tale, Hoagland grounds it in an utterly convincing reality, presented with documentary exactness. In fact, the novel includes a wealth of information about nature. Yet this information emerges spontaneously as the characters seek to understand their magnificent and overwhelming environment; the pace never slows as the book vigorously follows the characters' picaresque and perilous journey. Moreover, the novel includes Hoagland's most colorful assortment of eccentrics, ranging from Cecil's companion who specializes in jumping forty feet into a tub of water to a trader celebrated for his prowess in bladder-voiding competitions.

Probably the book's greatest achievement, however, as in Hoagland's first two novels, is its stunning and detailed sense of place. The unsentimental portrayal of the unspoiled West is at times rhapsodic as Hoagland presents a world that can chill with its beauty. Hoagland depicts not only the full glory but also the full fury of nature. He offers the reader a world that is as casually violent as that of *Cat Man*, a world where creatures can almost without warning be swept away in torrents or mauled by savage beasts. With its energy, its imaginativeness, and its sheer grandeur, *Seven Rivers West* is Hoagland at his best.

Hoagland's novels, published over a period of thirty years, have a number of traits in common. One is their focus on and sympathy for the downcast and outcast, for the social misfit who finds himself alone as he journeys through a hostile and dangerous world in which his mere survival is tenuous. Isolation is a constant theme, with the protagonists having great difficulty maintaining relationships with women. Yet as harsh and as lonely as these environments are, Hoagland's ability to describe them with honesty and fidelity gives his books a vividness and immediacy that leaves a lasting impact.

Charles Trainor

Other major works

SHORT FICTION: *City Tales*, 1986.

NONFICTION: *Notes from the Century Before: A Journal from British Columbia*, 1969; *The Courage of Turtles: Fifteen Essays About Compassion, Pain, and Love*, 1970; *Walking the Dead Diamond River*, 1973; *The Moose on the Wall: Field Notes from the Vermont Wilderness*, 1974; *Red Wolves and Black Bears*, 1976; *African Calliope: A Journey to the Sudan*, 1979; *The Tugman's Passage*, 1982.

ANTHOLOGIES: *The Edward Hoagland Reader*, 1979; *Heart's Desire*, 1988.

Bibliography

Hall, Donald. "Hoagland Was There." Review of *The Edward Hoagland Reader* and *African Calliope*, by Edward Hoagland. *National Review* 32 (May 30, 1980): 669-670. Refuses to call *African Calliope* a travel book, describing it as a fact-piece like the work of John McPhee. Hoagland is basically an autobiographer who writes of himself even when he seems to be writing about the world at large; however, he has the ability to make readers feel that they are there in the scene described. In his style of enthusiasm for daily existence, Hoagland creates exciting experiences of improvisation and speculation.

Hicks, Granville. "The Many Faces of Failure." *Saturday Review* 48 (August

14, 1965): 21-22. Many novels seem to consider adjustment to society disgraceful and misfits both admirable and pathetic. Hoagland wrote of misfits in *Cat Man* and *The Circle Home* and approaches the same subject, though differently, in *The Peacock's Tail*. The hero in this novel is from a more proper background than the circus of the *Cat Man* or the boxing world of *The Circle Home*, but his experience of unemployed drifting is in the end not very substantial. Hoagland creates splendid scenes for the novel, but the narrative is not a significant experience.

Johnson, Ronald L. Review of *Seven Rivers West*, by Edward Hoagland. *Western American Literature* 22 (November, 1987): 227-228. *Seven Rivers West*, a fictional tale after several nonfiction books, reads like a travel guide through the Canadian Rockies in 1887. It is lavish in its physical detail, with a loving response to mountain landscapes and the animals inhabiting them. Its most impressive feature is this response—which, consequently, renders the narrative about the meeting with Bigfoot less than memorable. On the other hand, the episodes of crossing a flooded river and meeting Indians are exciting and provide much good-humored entertainment.

Mills, Nicolaus. "A Rural Life Style." *The Yale Review* 60 (June, 1971): 609-613. Looks at *The Courage of Turtles* as an expression of the rural movement in American writing. Compares Hoagland's book with those by Raymond Mungo and Helen and Scott Nearing, deciding that the city is essential to Hoagland's view of the country, providing distance and allowing him to see the comic weaknesses as well as the sober virtues of country life. He notices what others miss about rural life: that it can be uncomfortable, angry, and in need of political organization. He also shows that it is ironically inaccessible to the very people who need it the most—those who have had to move from the country to the city because they could not afford their rural life-style.

Sagalyn, Raphael. Review of *The Edward Hoagland Reader* and *African Calliope*, by Edward Hoagland. *The New Republic* 181 (December 19, 1979): 30-31. Claims that Hoagland has become a master of the personal essay because he has not been writing much fiction. Praises Hoagland's style and argues that he deserves a wider audience. Hoagland likes to create heroes in his short prose and stories such as Sugar Hart in "Heart's Desire" or Henri Le Mothe in the story by that name. *African Calliope* is described as an apparently disjointed travel book which becomes clearer as its people come alive and discoveries are made while journeying through the Sudan.

Updike, John. "Back to Nature." *The New Yorker* 63 (March 30, 1987): 120-124. Compares Hoagland with Elizabeth Marshall, also of the Harvard-Radcliffe class of 1954, as writers seeking rapport with animals in faraway places, writing with a refreshing sense of wonder at life in the outdoors. The focus is on *Seven Rivers West*, which Updike praises for its detailed information about frontier life. While there is much visual material, there is less sound and feeling in the novel, and the heroes' motives are not as exciting as those of the hero in *Cat Man*. In the pursuit of Bigfoot, Updike finds an invitation to compare it with the quest for Moby Dick, and pronounces Hoagland significant in the company of the American nineteenth century Transcendentalists.

——————. "Journeyers." *The New Yorker* 56 (March 10, 1980): 150-159. *The Edward Hoagland Reader* is examined in the context of its preceding novel, *Cat Man*, and compared with other travel books of the time. Hoagland is interested in lonely places and remote terrains but can find them in the back corners of New York City as well as in the deserts of Africa. Hoagland like Henry David Thoreau, wrote in a modest tone with a cosmic perspective; however, Hoagland sometimes forgets to be entertaining, as when he expresses the grimness of life while describing his own self-testing in *African Calliope*, a work which does not provide clarity or the comfort of understanding the journey's meaning.

PAUL HORGAN

Born: Buffalo, New York; August 1, 1903

Principal long fiction

The Fault of Angels, 1933; *No Quarter Given*, 1935; *Main Line West*, 1936; *A Lamp on the Plains*, 1937; *Far from Cibola*, 1938; *The Habit of Empire*, 1938; *The Common Heart*, 1942; *The Devil in the Desert: A Legend of Life and Death in the Rio Grande*, 1952; *The Saintmaker's Christmas Eve*, 1955; *Give Me Possession*, 1957; *A Distant Trumpet*, 1960; *Mountain Standard Time*, 1962 (includes *Main Line West*, *Far from Cibola*, and *The Common Heart*); *Things as They Are*, 1964; *Memories of the Future*, 1966; *Everything to Live For*, 1968; *Whitewater*, 1970; *The Thin Mountain Air*, 1977; *Mexico Bay*, 1982.

Other literary forms

Throughout his long and meritorious career, Paul Horgan has been known as widely for his short fiction and nonfiction as for his novels. Most of his short fiction is found in three collections, but the best of his stories appear in *The Peach Stone: Stories from Four Decades* (1967). Like his fiction, Horgan's histories and biographies revolve around events and people of the American Southwest. His most prestigious history is *Great River: The Rio Grande in North American History* (1954), but *The Centuries of Santa Fe* (1956) and *Conquistadors in North American History* (1963) are also important works. His biographies, most notably *Lamy of Santa Fé: His Life and Times* (1975) and *Josiah Gregg and His Visions of the Early West* (1979), vividly chronicle the struggle of individuals and the clash of Spanish and Indian cultures on the Southwestern frontier. Horgan's work in drama includes the play *Yours, A. Lincoln* (1942) and the libretto to *A Tree on the Plains: A Music Play for Americans* (1943), an American folk opera with music by Ernst Bacon. His *Approaches to Writing* (1973) is composed of three long essays explaining his craft. Horgan's novel *A Distant Trumpet* was filmed in 1964; *Things as They Are* was filmed in 1970.

Achievements

As a novelist as well as a distinguished writer of nonfiction, Horgan has devoted his career to the American Southwest. Although he is regarded as a regionalist, some critics have rightly pointed out that he uses regional figures and settings essentially as vehicles for universal themes, much as William Faulkner used regional materials. Horgan's work should not be identified with the popular, formulaic Western writing of such authors as Zane Grey, Louis L'Amour, and Max Brand; rather, he should be seen as a significant figure in the tradition of literary Western fiction that has attracted the attention of critics and readers since the early 1960's.

Recognition for his writing has come in many forms. He won seventy-five hundred dollars in the Harper Prize Novel Contest for *The Fault of Angels* in 1933. He has been awarded two Guggenheim Fellowships (one in 1945, the other in 1958) to work on his nonfiction. For *Great River*, Horgan won the Pulitzer Prize in History and the Bancroft Prize of Columbia University. In 1957, the Campion Award for eminent service to Catholic letters was presented to him. The Western Literature Association paid tribute to Horgan with its distinguished Achievement Award (1973), and the Western Writers of America cited him with their Silver Spur Award (1976). He has twice been honored by the Texas Institute of Letters (in 1954 and in 1971).

Just as important as these awards, and an indication of the wide range of his interests and abilities, are the ways in which he has served his community and country. Horgan served as president of the board of the Santa Fe Opera (1958-1962) and the Roswell Museum (1946-1952). He became director of the Wesleyan Center for Advanced Studies in 1962 and remained so until 1967. President Lyndon B. Johnson made Horgan one of his first appointees to the Council of the National Endowment for the Humanities. In addition to being visiting scholar and writer-in-residence at a number of colleges and universities, Horgan has served on the board of the Aspen Institute and the Book-of-the-Month Club. Although some of his novels have sold in the millions and despite his long career, Horgan is not as well known as many of his contemporaries. Those who are familiar with his work, however, see him as a prescient figure, a writer whose concern with the complex, multicultural history of the Southwest anticipated the challenging revisionism of the 1970's and the 1980's, when scholars and fiction writers alike offered a new, critical look at the West.

Biography

Paul Horgan was born in Buffalo, New York, on August 1, 1903. He moved to Albuquerque, New Mexico, with his parents in 1915, and attended the New Mexico Military Institute in Roswell until 1921, when he left to be at home when his father was dying. After working for a year at the Albuquerque *Morning Journal*, he moved to the East in 1923 to study at the Eastman School of Music in Rochester, New York. He returned to Roswell in 1926 and accepted the job of librarian at the New Mexico Military Institute. He remained in Roswell until 1942 and wrote his first five novels. Horgan spent World War II in Washington as chief of the Army Information Branch of the Information and Education Division of the War Department, where he supervised all the information that was sent to American troops all over the world. Horgan returned to New Mexico after the war and worked on his nonfiction, but after 1960 he became associated with Wesleyan University in different capacities, living and writing on the Wesleyan campus.

Analysis

Paul Horgan's fiction is dominated on one level by a skillful, aesthetic evocation of Southwestern landscape and climate and a sensitive delineation of character. His novels are exceptionally well written, with sharp detail and imagery often matched by a lyrical tone perfectly suited to the basic goodness of his protagonists. Yet to dwell on this strong sense of place is to miss a basic theme in his works and to misjudge the appeal of his writing. The strength of Horgan's fiction lies in the reader's immediate and sympathetic identification with the protagonists. Curiosity is perhaps man's most distinguishing feature. This is true not only in an academic sense but in a personal way as well: To varying degrees, people take an interest in their ancestry and family histories. They want to know who they are and whence they come. It is both a peculiarity and a trademark of Horgan's fiction that this kind of knowing is its constant concern. The dramatic center in Horgan's books revolves around people learning the truth about themselves and their lives.

Horgan employs two main narrative strategies to accomplish his end. In books such as *Far from Cibola* and *A Distant Trumpet*, individuals must deal with an unexpected event upsetting the routine of everyday life and, as a result, are challenged to define their own lives more clearly. On the other hand, in novels such as *Things as They Are* and *Whitewater*, his protagonists conduct a more conscious search for an understanding of who they are and make a deliberate attempt to come to terms with their own pasts.

Often in Horgan's fiction, discovering the truth about oneself occurs after some startling event disrupts the ordinary flow of life. Such is the case in *Far from Cibola*, which many critics regard as Horgan's best novel. This short work, set in and around a small town in New Mexico during the early years of the Great Depression, records what happens to a dozen of the local inhabitants during a day in which they are all briefly brought together as part of a large crowd protesting economic conditions. After the crowd threatens to turn into an unruly mob, the sheriff fires a warning shot above their heads into some trees and accidentally kills a teenager who had climbed up the tree to watch the excitement. The crowd disperses after the gunfire, and the remaining chapters describe what happens to the dozen characters the rest of the day. Although these figures span a broad band of the socioeconomic spectrum of the New Mexican (and American) landscape of the 1930's, *Far from Cibola* is not simply another proletarian novel of that decade. Economic problems and hardships are uppermost in the mind of almost everyone in the story, but the fate of each character hinges on his or her ability to recognize and accept reality as it suddenly appears.

The opening chapter provides a good example of what happens to all the characters in the novel. It begins with serene, pastoral images: Mountains are shimmering in the morning haze, and smoke from breakfast fires rises straight into the clear April sky. In Ellen Rood's kitchen, there is a springlike feeling of peace and well-being. As she lays wood for her own stove, Ellen listens to the sounds of her two small children out in the farmyard. Her son Donald is chopping at some wood with an ax that is too big for his hands, and her daughter Lena is washing her face from a tin dish sitting on the edge of the well. Without warning, however, smoke rolls back into her eyes and sparks sting her arms when Ellen attempts to start the fire. At about the same time, Ellen realizes that her children are strangely quiet. When she investigates, she discovers a huge rattlesnake nearby; she quickly hacks it to death before it can harm her children. There are many scenes such as this one in *Far from Cibola*, in which people suddenly have an idyllic world overturned by a more sober, often harsher reality. How they react is a good measure of their character. Not everyone can prevail as Ellen does.

The incident in the courthouse provides a social context for what happens to the novel's individuals. Until the crowd becomes violent, everything is fairly calm and orderly. There may be hunger and economic desperation in the community, but people have not yet fully faced the fact that there are no hidden food supplies and the government cannot help them. The killing underscores this bleak reality, and society as a whole must deal with this truth, as Ellen had to face the rattlesnake outside her kitchen door.

A Distant Trumpet, written more than two decades later, shows thematic concerns similar to those of *Far from Cibola*, but Horgan achieves this in a slightly different manner. The novel's primary setting is Fort Delivery, a frontier outpost near the Mexican border in the Arizona Territory during the late 1880's. Although there are a number of characters, the story centers on a young army lieutenant named Matthew Hazard and an Apache scout called Joe Dummy. Deftly and incisively, Horgan dramatizes Hazard's and Joe Dummy's roles in helping to make peace with a rebellious band of Indians who had escaped into Mexico, and the novel ends with Hazard, bitter and disillusioned, resigning from the army when Joe Dummy is treated no better than the Indians he helped to defeat.

Rather than using startling and often violent images, as in *Far from Cibola*, Horgan makes extensive use of flashbacks to the Civil War period and earlier as a useful device for pulling down and digging out illusion and sham and seeing the truth clearly. That Matthew Hazard is Horgan's vehicle for showing the necessity not only of recognizing but also of maintaining self-knowledge is brought out in a very short section titled "Scenes from Early Times." Consisting of a series of short questions and answers between Hazard and an unknown person, the conversation reveals the earliest and most important knowledge Matthew can recall: that he was his father's child. Indeed, it is no accident that this book often reads like a biography. To be one's father's child in *A Distant Trumpet* means being able to acknowledge the less well-known aspects of self as well as the more openly accepted parts. Tragedy occurs when individuals cannot or will not see that darker side.

One of the more striking scenes in the novel occurs when Matthew, on his way to Fort Delivery for the first time, meets White Horn. Sergeant Blickner, who has come to take Matthew to the fort, refuses to take an Indian along in his wagon, and Matthew must give him a direct order to do so. Even after this, Blickner baits White Horn on the way back and calls him "Joe Dummy," a nickname picked up later by soldiers at the fort. In previous sections, however, White Horn's courageous and often heroic life has been described at length, so that he has become an individual to the reader. Thus, readers share the narrator's feeling of outrage and indignation that no one at the fort can see Joe Dummy as anything but another "grimy" Indian. Horgan laments bitterly the failure of these people to see clearly and suggests that they will be lost until they somehow discover the truth about themselves and their social structure. In this sense, Fort Delivery becomes an ironic name for an individual's self-imprisonment. Horgan's flashbacks in *A Distant Trumpet* force his readers to look beyond appearance and not accept the false and commonplace, in much the same way the rattlesnake and courthouse incident in *Far from Cibola* made people confront the unpleasant realities in their lives. *A Distant Trumpet* poignantly reveals what happens when individuals (and society) are unable to see worlds other than their own.

In *Things as They Are*, perhaps the most autobiographical of all of his works, Horgan approaches the question of knowing oneself more directly. The novel is narrated by Richard, an adult writer who recounts certain events in his early childhood to help him understand the way he is now. Horgan continues Richard's story in two later novels: *Everything to Live For* and *The Thin Mountain Air*. *Things As They Are*, then, is a *Bildungsroman*, a story of growth and awakening, and through this format, Richard articulates his need to understand himself and others more clearly.

Like most stories about growing up, the boy Richard undergoes a variety of experiences that the adult Richard must now interpret if he is to make some sense of his life. Although he describes a close family life and happy summer trips to the mountains, Richard also discloses certain important conflicts and tensions for the young boy: an uncle who commits suicide, an autocratic grandfather, a well-meaning but overly protective mother, a father who is not quite strong enough. The novel's structure in its simplest terms is a delicate balancing act between Richard's honestly depicting these family tensions and then explaining both what they meant to him and how they resulted in his seeing things as they are.

Things as They Are may be regarded as a prelude to *Whitewater*, which is also about a young man, Phillipson Durham, growing up. Set in the West Texas town of Belvedere during the years 1948-1949, the novel describes what happens to Phillipson and two high school classmates (Billy Breedlove and Marilee Underwood) during his senior year. Within this framework, the novel is essentially one long flashback by a much older Phillipson, who has written it, as the last chapter makes clear, for much the same reason Richard told his story in *Things as They Are*. Phillipson is probing for clues in his past that will allow him to understand the events of his senior year and what has happened to him since. Phillipson's search is less successful than Richard's and his conclusions more tentative.

Phillipson's quest for self-knowledge is marked by three central images in the novel: Lake Whitewater, Victoria Cochran's house, and the town's water tower. Lake Whitewater is a large, man-made lake formed when Whitewater Dam went into operation. What intrigues Phillipson is that deep under the lake's surface lies an abandoned town complete with houses, yards, and streetlamps. Billy informs Phillipson that when the lake is calm, the town can still be seen. The lake and submerged town thus become a metaphor for Phillipson's own lost knowledge about himself. Like the town, his past is still there, waiting to be viewed and understood if only he can see it clearly. Linked with this image is Crystal Wells, the home of Victoria Cochran, an elderly widow who befriends Phillipson and becomes his mentor. At Crystal Wells, Phillipson escapes the dreary provincialism of Belvedere and explores his own ideas and beliefs. It becomes an intellectual oasis where he can begin to define his own life. Opposed to this image is that of Belvedere's water tower, which Horgan unmistakably identifies with unthinking and impulsive behavior. Caught up in the excitement of springtime and the end of his senior year, Billy Breedlove climbs to the top of the tower to paint the words "Beat Orpha City" on its side. He loses his footing, however, and falls ninety feet to the ground below. Billy's death and Marilee's subsequent suicide are warnings to Phillipson that impulse and feeling by themselves threaten understanding and growth. Phillipson overcomes his grief at Crystal Wells and recognizes that his own education is only beginning. As the last section of *Whitewater* suggests, however, Phillipson years later is still growing, still trying to understand those events and himself, quite aware that there are things that he cannot and perhaps will never know completely. Nevertheless, as Richard does in *Things as They Are*, Phillipson focuses on maintaining moments of wakeful insight.

Horgan's novels are best understood by recognizing that his protagonists are driven by a need to know themselves and their pasts. Given this theme, Horgan uses two main narrative techniques. On the one hand, as in *Far from Cibola* and *A Distant Trumpet*, his characters are confronted with events suddenly disrupting their lives and their normal sense of things. In novels such as *Things as They Are* and *Whitewater*, however, his protagonists deliberately set about exploring their pasts to learn about themselves. Horgan's message is the same with either method: The truth about oneself must be pursued, no matter what the cost. Anything else is escapism, a kind of vicarious participation in life.

Terry L. Hansen

Other major works

SHORT FICTION: *The Return of the Weed*, 1936; *Figures in a Landscape*, 1940; *The Peach Stone: Stories from Four Decades*, 1967.

PLAYS: *Yours, A. Lincoln*, 1942; *A Tree on the Plains: A Music Play for Americans*, 1943 (libretto, music by Ernst Bacon).

POETRY: *Lamb of God*, 1927; *Songs After Lincoln*, 1965; *The Clerihews of Paul Horgan*, 1985.

NONFICTION: *New Mexico's Own Chronicle*, 1937 (with Maurice G. Fulton); *Great River: The Rio Grande in North American History*, 1954; *The Centuries of Santa Fe*, 1956; *Rome Eternal*, 1959; *A Citizen of New Salem*, 1961; *Conquistadors in North American History*, 1963; *Peter Hurd: A Portrait Sketch from Life*, 1965; *The Heroic Triad: Essays in the Social Energies of Three Southwestern Cultures*, 1970; *Encounters with Stravinsky: A Personal Record*, 1972; *Approaches to Writing*, 1973; *Lamy of Santa Fé: His Life and Times*, 1975; *Josiah Gregg and His Visions of the Early West*, 1979; *A Writer's Eye*, 1988; *A Certain Climate: Essays on History, Arts, and Letters*, 1988.

CHILDREN'S LITERATURE: *Men of Arms*, 1931.

Bibliography

Erisman, Fred. "Western Regional Writers and the Uses of Place." *Journal of the West* 19 (1980): 36-44. Reprinted in *The American Literary West*, edited by Richard W. Etulain. Manhattan, Kans.: Sunflower University Press, 1980. Placing Horgan in the company of Willa Cather, John Steinbeck, and John Graves, this article presents Horgan's writings as among those which meet the challenge of Ralph Waldo Emerson for artists to use the most American of materials, the experience of the West. These writers make strong use of the visual sense of specific place but transcend the limitations of local-color writers by putting the subjectivity of human experience at the center of their visions, making place secondary. All pursue themes of human individuality developed through nature, and Horgan shows this development in the context of Indian and Spanish cultures.

Gish, Robert. "Paul Horgan." *A Literary History of the American West*. Fort Worth: Texas Christian University Press, 1987. Horgan receives a chapter in this important book of literary scholarship which assesses his place in American literary history as attached to the materials of Southwest regionalism, but often lifted above their limitations by his skill. His life took him from East to West, providing him with a personal model for understanding the settlement of the Southwest, and his experience in a New Mexico military academy was also an important influence. His writings are listed chronologically as to his life experiences, and a few are singled out for commentary as examples of his style, subjects, and themes. Contains a selected bibliography of primary and secondary sources.

_____. *Paul Horgan*. Boston: Twayne, 1983. Horgan's writing is not merely regionalist, but moves from East to West and back again. Chapter Two surveys his novels with chronological sections paraphrasing the plots for each, dividing them into those written before World War II and those after. Chapter Three is pressed to cover the great amount of shorter fiction, novellas and short stories obscurely published in magazines such as *Ladies' Home Journal* in the 1930's, classifying them regionally, with subdivisions for historical and present settings, as Southwest, Far West, or Northeast. Chapter 4 presents Horgan as a humanist historian in the biographical mode in *Great River* and *Lamy of Santa Fé* and the last chapter analyzes his essays and speeches for humanist aesthetic principles. Includes a chronology, notes and references, a selected, annotated bibliography, and an index.

Kraft, James. "No Quarter Given: An Essay on Paul Horgan." *Southwestern Historical Quarterly* 80 (July, 1976): 1-32. Represents the pattern of Horgan's life movements as a special twentieth century American phenomenon—the possibility for a creative life in the United States. He studied American Indians of the Southwest in preparation for writing *Great River*, from which he took material for *The Heroic Triad*, an excellent source for studying the three cultures of the Southwest: Indian, Spanish, and Roman Catholic. Horgan is an artist, both a writer and a painter, but also a public servant without fear of the tragic or the brutal in life. His work and his life are affirmed through the creative process.

Pilkington, William T. "Paul Horgan." In *My Blood's Country: Studies in Southwestern Literature*. Fort Worth: Texas Christian University Press, 1973. Although Horgan has been a prolific writer in a variety of forms, his best work reveals an understanding of human desires and disappointments as expressed in the concrete details of lived experience. Besides Christian values, his writing expresses features of Ralph Waldo Emerson's transcendental philosophy. Analyzes many of Horgan's books, beginning with *The Fault of Angels* and ending with *A Distant Trumpet*. Horgan's stylistic faults are outweighed by his skill in presenting believable human beings as characters with vitality.

WILLIAM DEAN HOWELLS

Born: Martin's Ferry, Ohio; March 1, 1837
Died: New York, New York; May 11, 1920

Principal long fiction

Their Wedding Journey, 1872; *A Chance Acquaintance*, 1873; *A Foregone Conclusion*, 1875; *The Lady of Aroostook*, 1879; *The Undiscovered Country*, 1880; *Doctor Breen's Practice*, 1881; *A Modern Instance*, 1882; *A Woman's Reason*, 1883; *The Rise of Silas Lapham*, 1885; *Indian Summer*, 1886; *The Minister's Charge: Or, The Apprenticeship of Lemuel Barker*, 1887; *April Hopes*, 1888; *Annie Kilburn*, 1889; *A Hazard of New Fortunes*, 1890; *The Shadow of a Dream*, 1890; *The Quality of Mercy*, 1892; *An Imperative Duty*, 1892; *The World of Chance*, 1893; *The Coast of Bohemia*, 1893; *A Traveler from Altruria*, 1894; *The Day of Their Wedding*, 1896; *A Parting and a Meeting*, 1896; *An Open-Eyed Conspiracy: An Idyl of Saratoga*, 1897; *The Landlord at Lion's Head*, 1897; *The Story of a Play*, 1898; *Ragged Lady*, 1899; *Their Silver Wedding Journey*, 1899; *The Kentons*, 1902; *Letters Home*, 1903; *The Son of Royal Langbirth*, 1904; *Miss Bellard's Inspiration*, 1905; *Through the Eye of the Needle*, 1907; *Fennel and Rue*, 1908; *New Leaf Mills*, 1913; *The Leatherwood God*, 1916; *The Vacation of the Kelwyns*, 1920; *Mrs. Farrell*, 1921.

Other literary forms

William Dean Howells was unquestionably one of the most versatile and productive writers of the nineteenth century. In addition to approximately forty novels, Howells produced several volumes of short fiction, among them *A Fearful Responsibility and Other Stories* (1881) and *Christmas Every Day and Other Stories Told for Children* (1893). He also wrote more than thirty dramas, including *The Parlor Car* (1876), *The Mouse-Trap and Other Farces* (1889), and *Parting Friends* (1911), which generally were designed to be read aloud rather than performed. In addition, one of Howells' earliest and most enduring passions was the writing of poetry. His first published collection was *Poems of Two Friends* (1860); nearly fifty years later, he published *The Mother and the Father* (1909). The genre which first brought him to public attention was travel literature, including *Venetian Life* (1866) and *Italian Journeys* (1867); other volumes continued to appear throughout his career. Howells also continues to be renowned as a perceptive critic and literary historian. Currently of literary value are *Criticism and Fiction* (1891), *My Literary Passions* (1895), *Literature and Life* (1902), and *My Mark Twain* (1910). In addition, a substantial number of Howells' critical essays appeared in *Harper's* magazine from 1886 to 1892, and between 1900 until his death in 1920. Finally, Howells wrote biographies such as *Lives and Speeches of Abraham Lincoln and Han-*

nibal Hamlin (1860), as well as several autobiographical works, including *My Year in a Log Cabin* (1893) and *Years of My Youth* (1916).

Achievements

Howells is remembered today as an important early exponent of realism in fiction. Reacting against the highly "sentimental' novels of his day, Howells—both in his own fiction and in his criticism—advocated less reliance on love-oriented stories with formulaic plots and characters, and more interest in emphasizing real people, situations, and behavior. This is not to say that Howells shared the naturalists' interest in sex, low-life, and violence, for in fact he was quite reserved in his dealings with these darker aspects of life. He did, however, acknowledge their existence, and in so doing paved the way for Theodore Dreiser, Stephen Crane, and the modern realistic novel. Inspired by his reading of European literature (notably Leo Tolstoy), Howells also argued that fiction could be a tool for social reform. Finally, in his influential positions at *The Atlantic* and *Harper's*, Howells was able to offer help and encouragement to rising young American authors, including Crane and Henry James.

Howells' later years were full of recognition: he received an honorary Litt. D. from Yale (1901), as well as from Oxford (1904) and Columbia (1905); he received the L.H.D. from Princeton in 1912. He was elected first president of the American Academy of Arts and Letters in 1908, and seven years later received the Academy's gold medal for fiction.

Biography

Although early in his career he was accepted into the charmed literary circles of Boston and New York, William Dean Howells was born and reared in the Midwest, and he never fully lost touch with his Midwestern background. He was born on March 1, 1837, in Martin's Ferry (then Martinsville), Ohio, the second of eight children. His early life was singularly unstable: because his father was something of a political radical whose principles jeopardized the prosperity of every newspaper with which he was associated, the family was periodically compelled to move away from one conservative Ohio village after another. Despite such instability, Howells found the variety of experiences enriching and was able to make the most of the spotty formal education he received. His exposure to the written word came at an early age: when Howells was only three, his father moved the little family to Hamilton, Ohio, where he had acquired a local newspaper, the *Intelligencer*; by the age of six, the precocious William was setting type in his father's printing office, and not long after that he began to compose poems and brief sketches. In 1850, the family made one of their more fortunate moves by establishing themselves in a one-room log cabin in the utopian community at Eureka Mills near Xenia, Ohio. It was a welcome interlude in the family's struggle to find a political, economic, and social niche which would satisfy the father, and Howells would remember it fondly much later in *My Year in a Log Cabin*. The next move was to Columbus, where young Howells acquired a position as a compositor on the *Ohio State Journal*. Already beginning to diversify his literary endeavors, the fourteen-year-old Howells was also writing poetry in the manner of Alexander Pope.

In 1852, Howells' father bought a share in the Ashtabula *Sentinel* and moved it to Jefferson, Ohio. For once, his principles did not clash with those of the community: the little newspaper was a success, and it was to remain in the Howells family for forty years. While living in Jefferson, a community composed largely of well-educated transplanted New Englanders, the teenaged Howells embarked on a plan of intensive self-education which included studies of Pope, Oliver Goldsmith, Oliver Wendell Holmes, Edgar Allan Poe, and Heinrich Heine. As much as this program compromised his social life, Howells derived enormous intellectual benefits from it, and several of the townspeople of Jefferson even offered to help finance a Harvard education for this gifted lad; his father declined the offer, however, and Howells remained at Jefferson, publishing his stories pseudonymously beginning in 1853.

As his father gradually rose in Ohio state politics (he was elected clerk of the House of Representatives in 1855), Howells rose with him, and in 1857 he was offered a permanent position as a correspondent on the Cincinnati *Gazette*. Howells, not yet twenty years old, was too emotionally dependent upon his family and too much of a hypochondriac to stay more than a few weeks at the *Gazette*, but when in the following year he received another opportunity in journalism, this time from the *Ohio State Journal*, he was able to accept the offer from his previous employer and to succeed. In addition to his duties as a reporter and editor, Howells found time to write sketches and verse, and some of his writings appeared in *The Atlantic*, the prestigious Boston-based journal of which he was to become editor-in-chief many years later.

The year 1860 was the most significant one of his life: he met Elinor Mead of Brattleboro, Vermont, whom he would marry two years later in Paris; he published his first book, *Poems of Two Friends*, coauthored with John J. Piatt; and—at the urging of the volume's Cincinnati publisher, Frank Foster—Howells prepared a campaign biography of Abraham Lincoln. Although assembled out of information Howells had gleaned from printed sources rather than from Lincoln himself, and written in only a few weeks, the book proved to be a moving and inspiring account of his fellow Midwesterner. With its royalties, the resourceful and ambitious Howells financed a trip to America's two literary meccas, Boston and New York, where he arranged to meet some of the most important writers and editors of the day, and he returned to Ohio confirmed in his desire to pursue a career in literature.

Following the outbreak of the Civil War, Howells—temperamentally ill-suited to army life—decided to seek a foreign diplomatic post. Cashing in on the success of his popular Lincoln biography, the twenty-four-year-old Howells managed to be appointed as the United States Consul at Venice, a pleasant and remunerative position he held for four years. Howells was able to draw on his Italian experiences in a series of travel essays which were collected in book form as *Venetian Life* and *Italian Journeys*. When he returned to the United States in the summer of 1865, he was sufficiently established as a writer to be able to embark on a free-lance writing career in New York. After a brief stint at the newly founded *The Nation*, Howells was lured to Boston and a subeditorship at *The Atlantic* under James T. Fields; after five years he became editor-in-chief (1871-1881). By the age of thirty, Howells was already a prominent member of Boston's literati. He received an honorary M. A. from Harvard in 1867, and was forging friendships with such literary figures as Henry James (whom he met in 1866) and Samuel Clemens, destined to become a lifelong friend.

At about that time (the late 1860's) Howells came to accept the fact that there was no market for his poetry; so, while he continued to write travel literature, he began to prepare descriptive sketches which would evolve rapidly into the literary form to which he was particularly well-suited: the novel. The first product of this transitional period was *Their Wedding Journey*, which was serialized in *The Atlantic* in 1871 and published in book form in 1872. *Their Wedding Journey*, which manages to straddle both travel literature and fiction, features Basil and Isabel March (based upon William and Elinor Howells), characters who would recur throughout Howells' fiction, most notably in *A Hazard of New Fortunes*. After *Their Wedding Journey*, Howells produced novels with almost machinelike speed and regularity. *A Chance Acquaintance* is a psychological romance which served to demythologize the idea of the "proper Bostonian" that Howells had so admired in his youth; *A Foregone Conclusion*, in which a young American girl clashes with traditional European society, anticipates James's *Daisy Miller* by three years; two "international novels" which contrast American and Italian values and life-styles are *The Lady of Aroostook* and *A Fearful Responsibility and Other Stories*; *The Undiscovered Country* probes spiritualism and the Shakers; *Doctor Breen's Practice* is the social and psychological study of a woman physician.

In 1881, Howells found himself caught in the dissolution of his publisher's partnership, Osgood and Houghton, so he left *The Atlantic* and began to serialize stories in the *Century* magazine. During this period, Howells began to focus increasingly on ethical problems, and in the 1880's he produced in rapid succession the novels which are generally held to be his greatest achievements in fiction. In 1882, *A Modern Instance* appeared, the so-called "divorce novel" which is now regarded as Howells' first major work in long fiction. During its composition, he suffered a breakdown, in part the result of the worsening health of his daughter Winny, who would die only a few years later at the age of twenty-six. An extended trip to Italy proved disappointing, but it enabled Howells to recover sufficiently to write another major novel, *The Rise of Silas Lapham*, followed immediately by the book he enjoyed writing most, *Indian Summer*. As a comedy of manners set in Italy, *Indian Summer* was both a reversion to Howells' earliest fictional style and subject matter, as well as a welcome change from the intense social realism which characterized his fiction in the 1880's.

By that time, Howells was living permanently in New York and was a member of the editorial staff of *Harper's*. In January, 1886, he began a regular feature in *Harper's* called the "Editor's Study," which continued until 1892 and served as the organ through which he campaigned for realism and a greater social consciousness in fiction. Howells had in fact so reoriented himself away from Boston, the cynosure of his youth, that he turned down a professorship at Harvard and wrote his first novel set in New York, *A Hazard of New Fortunes*, regarded as one of his finest works. Howells' novels in the 1890's were even more insistently illustrative of his strong social consciousness than those of the previous decade. *The Quality of Mercy* is the study of a crime (embezzlement) which is to be blamed less on the individual who committed it than on the society which created him; *An Imperative Duty* deals with miscegenation; *A Traveler from Altruria* and its belated sequel, *Through the Eye of the Needle*, were written within the literary tradition of the utopian novel. Late in his career, Howells tended to resurrect and rework earlier material (the March family of *Their Wedding Journey*, Howells' earliest novel, reappeared in *Their Silver Wedding Journey*); one of his finest character studies is that of Jeff Durgin in the late novel *The Landlord at Lion's Head*, the only work by Howells which clearly shows the influence of naturalism.

After a lecture tour through the West, Howells, in 1900, began to write a regular column, the "The Editor's Easy Chair," for *Harper's*, and continued to do so until his death in 1920. His last major works were *My Mark Twain*, an appreciative account of his friend published in 1910 (the year of the deaths of Samuel Clemens and Mrs. Howells), and the posthumous *The Vacation of the Kelwyns*, published in 1920. Howells died in New York City on May 11, 1920, still productive until his death; although he realized that his creative powers had long since dimmed, he nevertheless had managed to maintain over much of his extraordinary life his well-deserved position as the "Dean of American Letters."

Analysis

Throughout his career as a fiction-writer, William Dean Howells worked against the sentimentality and idealization which pervaded popular American literature in the nineteenth century. He pleaded for characters, situations, behavior, values, settings, and even speech patterns which were true to life. While twentieth century readers have come to take such elements for granted, the fact remains that in Howells' day he was regarded as something of a literary radical. One indication of his radicalism was his preference for character over plot in his fiction: he was far less interested in telling a good story (albeit his stories are good) than in presenting flesh-and-blood characters who think, feel, make mistakes, and are products of genetic, social, and economic conditions—in other words, who are as imperfect (and as interesting) as real people. Howells did not indulge in meticulous psychological analyses of his characters, as did his friend Henry James, and his plots tend to be far more linear and straightforward than are the convoluted and carefully patterned ones of James. Nevertheless, he was an innovative and influential writer who changed the quality of American fiction.

A hallmark of Howells' advocacy of realism was his interest in topics which were taboo in Victorian times. Such a topic was divorce, which in the nineteenth century was still regarded by much of society as scandalous and shameful, and which Howells utilized as the resolution of his first major novel, *A Modern Instance*. This was not a "divorce novel" per se, as was maintained by several of Howells' shocked contemporaries, but in an era when "they married and lived happily ever after" was a fictional norm, the divorce of Bartley and Marcia Hubbard was quite unpalatable. Given the situation of the characters, however, the breakup was inevitable—in a word, "realistic." As William M. Gibson explains in his excellent introduction to the Riverside edition of *A Modern Instance* (1957), the story apparently germinated when Howells saw an impressive performance of *Medea* in Boston in the spring of 1875, and in fact the working title of the novel was *The New Medea*. The novel's genesis and working title are significant, for the story's female protagonist harbors a passion which is both overpowering and destructive.

Marcia Gaylord, the only child of Squire Gaylord and his self-effacing wife Miranda, grows up in Equity, Maine, in an era when the state's once-impressive commercial prominence has all but decayed. Her domineering but indulgent father and her ineffectual mother have failed to mold Marcia's personality in a positive way, and this lack of a strong character, interacting with an environment caught in economic, cultural, political, and spiritual decline, compels Marcia to leave Equity while rendering her utterly unequipped to deal with the outside world. Not surprisingly, she becomes enamored of the first attractive young man to happen her way: Bartley Hubbard, editor of the newspaper of Equity. Superficially, Hubbard has all the earmarks of the hero of a romantic novel: orphaned young, he is intelligent enough to have succeeded at a country college, and with his education, charm, and diligence, he seems well on his way to a career in law. There, however, the Lincolnesque qualities end. Ambitious, manipulative, shrewd, unscrupulous, and self-centered, Bartley is the worst possible husband for the shallow Marcia, and after a courtship rife with spats, jealousy, and misunderstandings (even the short-lived engagement is the result of misinterpreted behavior), the ill-matched pair elope and settle in Boston.

The remainder of the novel is an analysis of the characters of Marcia and Bartley as they are revealed by the social, professional, and economic pressures of Boston, and a concomitant study of the deterioration of their marriage. Marcia is motivated by her sexual passion for Bartley and her deep emotional attachment to her father—an attachment so intense that she names her daughter after him and attempts to force Bartley into following in his footsteps as a lawyer. Locked into the roles of wife and daughter, Marcia has no separate identity, no concrete values, no sense of purpose. As Marcia struggles with her disordered personality, Bartley's becomes only too clear: his success as a newspaperman is the direct result of his being both shrewd in his estimation of the low level of popular taste, and unscrupulous in finding material and assuming (or disavowing) responsibility for it.

Bartley's foil is a native Bostonian and former classmate, Ben Halleck. A wealthy man without being spoiled, a trained attorney too moralistic to practice law, and a good judge of character who refuses to use that talent for ignoble ends, Halleck is all that Bartley Hubbard could have been under more favorable circumstances. Even so, Ben does not fit into the world of nineteenth century America: as is graphically symbolized by his being crippled, Ben cannot find a satisfying occupation, a meaningful religion, or a warm relationship with a woman. In fact, it is Howells' trenchant indictment of the social, economic, and spiritual problems of nineteenth century America that not a single character in *A Modern Instance* is psychically whole. To further compound his difficulties, Ben loves Marcia, having adored her for years after noticing her from afar as a school girl in Maine. In his efforts to aid her by lending money to Bartley and pressuring her to stand by her husband, Ben unwittingly contributes to Bartley's abandonment of Marcia, to her resultant emotional crisis, and to the devastating divorce in Indiana.

Carefully avoiding the traditional happy ending, Howells completes his story with a scene of human wreckage: Bartley, unscrupulous newspaperman to the end, is shot to death by a disgruntled reader in Arizona; Squire Gaylord, emotionally destroyed by defending his daughter in the divorce suit, dies a broken man; Ben, unsuccessful as a schoolteacher in Uruguay, flees to backwoods Maine to preach; and Marcia returns to the narrow world of Equity, her beauty and spirit long vanished. Interesting, complex, and bitter, *A Modern Instance* so strained Howells' emotional and physical well-being that he suffered a breakdown while writing it. The "falling off" of energy and style in the second part of the novel which so many commentators have noticed may be attributed to the breakdown, as well as to the related stress engendered by the serious psychosomatic illness of his beloved daughter Winny; it should be borne in mind, however, that the novel's singularly unhappy ending cannot be attributed to either crisis. The book's conclusion, planned from the story's inception, was itself meant to be a commentary on a nation buffeted by spiritual, social, and economic change.

On a level with *A Modern Instance* is Howells' best-known novel, *The Rise of Silas Lapham*. Serialized in the *Century* magazine from November, 1884, to August, 1885, and published in book form in the late summer of 1885, *The Rise of Silas Lapham* takes a realistic look at the upheavals in late nineteenth century America by focusing on the archetypal self-made man. Colonel Silas Lapham of Lumberville, Vermont, has made a fortune in the paint business by virtue of hard work, honest dealings, and the help and guidance of a good woman, his wife, Persis. The sentimental portrait of the self-made American captain of industry is significantly compromised, however, by the fact that Lapham owes much of his success to simple luck (his father accidentally found a superb paint mine on his farm) and to an early partner's capital (Rogers, a shadowy and rather demonic figure whom Lapham "squeezed out" once his paint business began to thrive). Even more compromising is the fact that Lapham's great wealth and success cannot compensate for his personality and background: boastful, oafish (his hands are "hairy fists"), and devoid of any aesthetic sensibility, Lapham seeks to buy his way into proper Boston society by building a fabulous mansion on the Back Bay and encouraging a romance between his daughter and Tom Corey, a Harvard graduate with "old" Boston money.

The Coreys are, in fact, foils of the Laphams: Tom's father, Bromfield Corey, is also indirectly associated with paint (he has a talent for portraiture), but having inherited substantial wealth, he has never worked, preferring instead to live off the labors of his ancestors. Ultimately, neither man is acceptable to Howells: Lapham, for all his substantial new wealth, is vulgar and ambitious; Bromfield Corey, for all his old money and polish, is lethargic and ineffectual. The wives do not fare much better. Persis Lapham is burdened with a Puritan reserve which at vital moments renders her incapable of giving her husband emotional support, and Anna Corey, despite her fine manners, is stuffy and judgmental.

The most admirable characters in the novel are two of the five children. Penelope Lapham is a quick-witted, plain girl with a passion for reading George Eliot, while Tom Corey is an educated, enterprising young man who sincerely wants an active business career. Although clearly Pen and Tom are ideally suited to each other, their relationship almost fails to materialize because virtually everyone in the novel—and the reader as well—naturally assumes Tom to be attracted to young Irene Lapham, who is strikingly pretty, beautifully attired, and considerably less intellectually endowed than her sister. In his campaign for realism in literature, Howells intentionally blurs the distinctions between the world of reality (where people like Pen and Tom fall in love) and the world of sentiment (where beautiful, empty-headed Irene is the ideal girl). The blurring is so complete that the Laphams, brainwashed by the romanticized standards of nineteenth century American life, almost deliberately scuttle Pen's relationship with Tom simply because pretty Irene had a crush on him first. The level-headed Reverend Sewell, with his realistic belief in the "economy of pain," is needed to convince the parties involved that they were acting out of "the shallowest sentimentality" rather than common sense in promoting Irene's match with Tom.

As part of his questioning of nineteenth century sentimentality, Howells specifically attacks one of its most graphic manifestations, the self-made man. In the heyday of the Horatio Alger stories, Howells presents a protagonist who to many Americans was the ultimate role model: a Vermont farm lad who became a Boston millionaire. Howells undermining of Lapham is, however, so meticulous and so complete—he even opens the novel with Lapham being interviewed by sardonic Bartley Hubbard (of *A Modern Instance*) for the "Solid Men of Boston" series in a local pulp newspaper—that the reader is left uncertain whether to admire Lapham for his sound character and business achievements, or to laugh at him for his personality flaws and social blunders. This uncertainty is attributable to the unclear tone of the novel, as George Arms points out in his excellent introduction to *The Rise of Silas Lapham* (1949). The tone is, in fact, a major flaw in the novel, as are some episodes of dubious worth (such as the ostensible affair between Lapham and his typist) and Howells' disinclination to develop some potentially vital characters (such as Tom Corey's uncle and Lapham's financial adviser, James Bellingham). A more fundamental problem is Howells' refusal to face squarely the matter of morality: he never fully resolves the complex relationship between Lapham and his ex-partner Rogers, a relationship which raises such questions as whether good intentions can serve evil ends, and to what extent one has moral obligations toward business associates, friends, and even strangers.

Not surprisingly, the end of the novel is less than satisfying: Tom Corey marries Pen Lapham and moves to Mexico, where presumably the disparity in their backgrounds will be less glaring; the financially ruined Laphams return to the old Vermont farm, where ostensibly they are far happier than they were as wealthy Bostonians; and pretty young Irene is enduring spinsterhood. Despite these problems and an overreliance on dialogue (at times the novel reads like a play), *The Rise of Silas Lapham* is indeed, as Arms remarks, "a work of competence and illumination" which rightly deserves its status as an outstanding example of late nineteenth century realistic fiction.

Nearly half a dozen years after *The Rise of Silas Lapham*, Howells published the novel which he personally felt to be his best and "most vital" book: *A Hazard of New Fortunes*. A long novel (well over five hundred pages), it features a rather unwieldy number of characters who all know one another professionally or socially (indeed, the "it's a small world" motif is rather strained at times); who possess widely varying degrees of social consciousness; and who come from a number of geographical, economic, and intellectual backgrounds. This cross section of humanity resides in New York City, and the interaction among the remarkably diverse characters occurs as a result of three catalysts: a new magazine entitled *Every Other Week*; a boardinghouse run by the Leightons; and a period of labor unrest among the city's streetcar workers.

The magazine subplot nicely illustrates Howells' extraordinary ability to interweave characters, plot, and themes around a controlling element. *Every Other Week* is a new magazine to be published under the general editorship of one Fulkerson. As its literary editor, he hires Basil March, a transplanted middle-class Indianian who has left his position as an insurance agent in Boston to begin a new life at fifty in New York; as its art editor, there is young Angus Beaton, a shallow ladies' man and dilettante who cannot escape his humble background in Syracuse; the translator is Berthold Lindau, an elderly, well-read German who had befriended March as a boy and lost a hand in the Civil War; and the financial "angel" of the magazine is Jacob Dryfoos, an uncultured Midwestern farmer who has made a fortune through the natural gas wells on his land, and who forces his Christlike son, Conrad, to handle the financial aspects of the magazine as a way of learning about business. The magazine's cover artist is Alma Leighton, a feminist whom Beaton loves, and a frequent contributor of articles is Colonel Woodburn, a ruined Virginian who boards with the Leightons and whose daughter marries Fulkerson.

Each individual associated with *Every Other Week* perceives the magazine in a different light; each is attracted to it (or repulsed by it) for a different reason. As *Every Other Week* becomes a success, Howells allows it to drift out of the focus of the novel, leaving the reader to observe the interactions (usually clashes) of the various characters' personalities, interests, and motives. Lindau, whose social consciousness calls for unions and socialism, is in essential agreement with Conrad Dryfoos, although the latter disdains the German's advocacy of violence; both men clash with Jacob Dryfoos, who, no longer in touch with the earthy Indiana life-style of his early years, believes that pro-union workers should be shot. The artist Beaton—who loves the feline quality of Conrad's sister Christine as much as he loves the independence of Alma Leighton and the goodness of socialite worker Margaret Vance—does not care about economic and social matters one way or another, while Colonel Woodburn advocates slavery.

The character whose attitudes most closely parallel those of Howells himself is Basil March, whose social consciousness grows in the course of the novel as he witnesses the poverty of the New York slums, the senseless deaths of Lindau and Conrad, and the pathetic, belated efforts of Jacob Dryfoos to correct his mistakes through the lavish spending of money. In many respects, March is a projection of Howells' attitudes and experiences, and his tendency at the end of the novel to make speeches to his wife about labor, religion, and injustice is a reflection of Howells' reading of Tolstoy. Even so, it would be incorrect to perceive March as the story's main character. That distinction most properly belongs to Jacob Dryfoos, a sort of Pennsylvania Dutch version of Silas Lapham whose values, home, life-style, and attitude have been undermined forever by the finding of gas deposits on his farm.

Although much of Howells' fiction deals with social and personal upheaval in late nineteenth century America, nowhere is it more poignantly depicted than in *A Hazard of New Fortunes*. In the light of this poignancy, it is to Howells' credit that the novel does not turn into a cold social tract: the characters are flesh-and-blood rather than caricatures. The novel contains considerable humor, most notably in the early chapters dealing with the Marches house-hunting in New York. There is also a surprising emphasis on feminism and a concomitant questioning of marriage and the false behavioral ideals propagated by sentimental fiction. In addition, Howells provides psychological probing (particularly in the form of fantasizing) such as one would expect of James more readily than Howells, and above all there is the aforementioned interweaving of characters, incidents, and themes.

Of Howells' approximately forty novels written during his long career, at least half a dozen—including *A Modern Instance*, *The Rise of Silas Lapham*, and *A Hazard of New Fortunes*—have endured, a testament not only to their brilliant, realistic evocation of life in late nineteenth century America, but also to the distinctive skills, interests, and sensibility of the Dean of American Letters.

Alice Hall Petry

Other major works

SHORT FICTION: *A Fearful Responsibility and Other Stories*, 1881; *Christmas Every Day and Other Stories Told for Children*, 1893; *Mrs. Farrell*, 1921.

PLAYS: *The Parlor Car*, 1876; *A Counterfeit Presentment*, 1877; *Out of the Question*, 1877; *The Register*, 1884; *A Sea-Change*, 1888; *The Albany Depot*, 1892; *A Letter of Introduction*, 1892; *The Unexpected Guests*, 1893; *A Previous Engagement*, 1897; *The Mouse-Trap and Other Farces*, 1899; *Room Forty-five*, 1900; *The Smoking Car*, 1900; *An Indian Giver*, 1900; *Parting Friends*, 1911; *The Complete Plays of W. D. Howells*, 1960 (Walter J. Meserve, editor).

POETRY: *Poems of Two Friends*, 1860 (with John J. Piatt); *Poems*, 1873; *Samson*, 1874; *Priscilla: A Comedy*, 1882; *A Sea Change: Or, Love's Stowaway*, 1884; *Poems*, 1886; *Stops of Various Quills*, 1895; *The Mother and the Father*, 1909.

NONFICTION: *Lives and Speeches of Abraham Lincoln and Hannibal Hamlin*, 1860; *Venetian Life*, 1866; *Italian Journeys*, 1867; *The Undiscovered Country*, 1880; *Tuscan Cities*, 1885; *Modern Italian Poets*, 1887; *A Boy's Town*, 1890; *Criticism and Fiction*, 1891; *My Year in a Log Cabin*, 1893; *My Literary Passions*, 1895; *Impressions and Experiences*, 1896; *Stories of Ohio*, 1897;

Literary Friends and Acquaintances, 1900; *Heroines of Fiction*, 1901; *Literature and Life*, 1902; *Letters Home*, 1903; *London Films*, 1905; *Certain Delightful English Towns*, 1906; *Roman Holidays*, 1908; *Seven English Cities*, 1909; *Imaginary Interviews*, 1910; *My Mark Twain*, 1910; *Familiar Spanish Travels*, 1913; *New Leaf Mills*, 1913; *Years of My Youth*, 1916; *Eighty Years and After*, 1921; *The Life and Letters of William Dean Howells*, 1928.

Bibliography

Cady, Edwin H., and Norma W. Cady. *Critical Essays on W. D. Howells, 1866-1920*. Boston: G. K. Hall, 1983. Gathers together important criticism on Howells, both reprints and original essays. Includes reviews by contemporaries such as Henry James, George Bernard Shaw, and Mark Twain, as well as commentaries by modern critics, such as Van Wyck Brooks, H. L. Mencken, and Wilson Follett. Contains essays by advocates and detractors of Howells.

Crowley, John W. *The Masks of Fiction: Essays on W. D. Howells.* Amherst: University of Massachusetts Press, 1989. The introduction addresses the debate among writers about Howells' contribution to American literature. The main thrust of the study, however, is the examination of Howells' unconscious in his writings, incorporating both the "probing psychologism of the 1890s" and his later light fiction with its deeper psychic integration. Explores in particular the Oedipus complex in the light of the relationship between father and son. Crowley sees his study on Howells as revisionist, not revivalist, in spirit. An important contribution to critical studies on Howells which is also useful for its extensive notes.

Eble, Kenneth E. *William Dean Howells.* 2d ed. Boston: Twayne, 1982. Contains a commentary on Howells' early life, his development as a novelist, and the later years. The chapter entitled "Fiction and Fact of the Nineties" gives valuable perspective on Howells' novels during this decade—a prolific period in his writing—including his autobiographical works.

Escholtz, Paula A., ed. *Critics on William Dean Howells.* Miami: University of Miami Press, 1975. An accessible introduction to Howells as both author and critic, with critical essays on his major novels. The volume is designed to show how Howells' reputation has fared since the 1860's. Includes a selected bibliography.

Lynn, Kenneth S. *William Dean Howells: An American Life.* New York: Harcourt Brace Jovanovich, 1970. A highly regarded study for its blending of biographical scholarship and criticism of Howells' works.

Wagenknecht, Edward. *William Dean Howells: The Friendly Eye.* New York: Oxford University Press, 1969. A notable study because it is written out of admiration for Howells and interest in his work. Contains extracts from Howells' novels, as well as from a few selected poems.

W. H. HUDSON

Born: Quilmes, Argentina; August 4, 1841
Died: London, England; August 18, 1922

Principal long fiction

The Purple Land, 1885 (originally published as *The Purple Land That England Lost*); *A Crystal Age*, 1887; *Fan: The Story of a Young Girl's Life*, 1892 (as Henry Harford); *El Ombú*, 1902 (reissued as *South American Sketches*, 1909, published in the United States as *Tales of the Pampas*, 1916); *Green Mansions*, 1904; *A Little Boy Lost*, 1905.

Other literary forms

W. H. Hudson was most prolific as an essayist; most of his essays record his observations as a field naturalist. He was particularly fascinated by bird life; between 1888 and 1889 he compiled and published, with the aid of Professor Sclater, *Argentine Ornithology* which was later revised as *Birds of La Plata* (1920). He followed this with a book entitled *British Birds* (1895). More general reflections on nature can be found in such of his books as *Idle Days in Patagonia* (1893) and *Nature in Downland* (1900). Although Hudson was primarily an observer and not a theorist, his last book of this type, *A Hind in Richmond Park* (1922), is a much more philosophical work, occasionally tending to the mystical, discussing the nature of sensory experience in animals and man and linking this analysis to aesthetic theory and the "spiritualizing" of man. He also wrote an autobiography, *Far Away and Long Ago* (1918), a lyrical work recalling his childhood in South America; it deals only with his early life and refers to no incidents after 1859.

Achievements

Hudson is almost a forgotten writer today, remembered primarily for *Green Mansions*. He was equally unappreciated for most of his own lifetime—he lived in poverty, and was virtually ignored by the literary public until *Green Mansions* became a best-seller in America, by which time he was well into his sixties. He seems to have had mixed feelings about this late success—it is significant that he refrained from writing any further romances, though his juvenile novel *A Little Boy Lost* appeared the following year. Hudson wanted to be known as a naturalist, and he considered his essays on nature to be his most important works. These books did, indeed, attract a small coterie of admirers, and for a few years before and immediately after his death they received due attention. He is commemorated by a bird sanctuary in Hyde Park, where there is a Jacob Epstein statue representing Rima, the enigmatic nature-spirit from *Green Mansions*. In 1924, J. M. Dent and Sons reissued his complete works in twenty-four volumes and his friend Morley Roberts published an appreciative memoir of him.

Hudson's nonfiction is generally more interesting and more valuable than his fiction. His essays on nature provide an unusual combination of patient and scrupulous observation with occasional speculative rhapsodies of a metaphysical character. In his visionary moments, Hudson held a view of the living world akin to that of Henri Bergson, author of *Creative Evolution* (1907), but this aspect of his work is of historical and psychological interest only. His careful and minute observations are of more enduring value, especially when he turned his attention—as he often did—from birds to men. His accounts of human life from the detached viewpoint of the field naturalist are always fascinating, and his documentation of the life of a small rural village in *A Shepherd's Life* (1910) is a rare glimpse of a world which has passed almost without record.

Hudson's fiction is interesting, and enjoys what reputation it has, because of its combination of the same contrasting traits that are to be found in his nonfiction: his descriptions of the natural world in his South American romances are delicate and scrupulous, and the same is true of his observations of the life of the inhabitants of the Banda Oriental in *The Purple Land* or the savages in *Green Mansions*. At the same time, though, the best of these stories has an imaginative component so ambitious that it permits the reader to see the world—and other possible and impossible worlds too—through new eyes. There is a sense in which his visions of a quasisupernatural ecological harmony fit in better with ideas that are current today than they did with the *Zeitgeist* of Hudson's own age, and it is therefore surprising that his work does not get more attention. It is possible that he is ripe for rediscovery, and that a new assessment of his achievement may yet be made.

Biography

William Henry Hudson was born on August 4, 1841, on an *estancia* about ten miles outside Buenos Aires. His parents were both American, but he had British grandparents on both sides of the family. His parents seem to have been very devoted to their children, and Hudson apparently enjoyed an idyllic childhood on the pampas; his memories of it recorded in *Far Away and Long Ago* were fond in the extreme. During his adolescence, however, he developed solitary tendencies, drifting away from the company of his siblings. During these years, he gave himself over to the patient and lonely study of nature.

Very little is known of his later years in South America; his autobiography has nothing to say of his life after reaching adolescence, and Morley Roberts, who wrote a book about Hudson's later life, did not meet him until 1880. By the time that Hudson came to England in 1869, his parents were dead and the family had dispersed. Apparently, he had spent a good deal of the previous few years wandering aimlessly in South America; it is tempting to associate certain incidents described in *The Purple Land* with experiences he may have had during these years, but to do so would be mere conjecture.

Hudson's early days in England are also undocumented. He apparently had various odd jobs, including researching genealogies for Americans, but did not settle down or make much of a living. In 1876, he met and married Emily Wingrave, who was some twenty years older than he. While he wrote, she gave singing lessons, but neither activity brought in much money and the two had to run a boardinghouse in Bayswater for some years. Even after the publication of *The Purple Land* (which was received with indifference), they were close to desperation, but Emily inherited a large house in Bayswater which they turned into flats, retaining two rooms for themselves and living off the rents from the remainder. Though Hudson frequently went on long excursions into the country, and in later life took to wintering in Penzance, the couple stayed in Bayswater until their deaths, Emily's in 1921 and Hudson's in 1922. Hudson was naturalized in 1900, by which time he was just beginning to attract favorable attention through his essays. Sir Edward Grey procured for him a state pension in 1901, a few years before the commercial success of *Green Mansions* freed him from financial worry.

Hudson's acquaintances seem to have formed very different impressions of him. Robert Hamilton quotes summaries of his character offered by half a dozen different people which are anything but unanimous—some are flatly contradictory. If an overall impression can be gained, it is that he was usually friendly and courteous but rather reserved. More than one acquaintance suspected that he was secretly lonely and unhappy, and women seem to have formed a distinctly poorer opinion of him than men, suggesting that he was uneasy in their company. The autobiography which ceases so early in his life may provide the best insight into his character, as much by what it omits as by what it says. Hudson seems to have emerged from childhood reluctantly and with great regret; he apparently never tried particularly hard to adapt himself to the adult world, where he always felt himself to be an outsider. Although he did not marry until he was in his mid-thirties, the woman he selected as a wife probably served as a mother-substitute whose age precluded any possibility of parenthood. These details are highly significant in the consideration of his novels, especially *A Crystal Age*.

Analysis

The majority of W. H. Hudson's fictions are categorized as "South American romances"—at one time a collection was issued under that title. Included under this label are the novels *The Purple Land* and *Green Mansions* and various shorter pieces from Hudson's short-story collection *El Ombú* (1902); the most important of these shorter pieces are the novellas "El Ombú" and "Marta Riquelme." All of these works make constructive use of the author's autobiographical background.

The Purple Land is a documentary novel containing no plot, an imaginary travelogue set in the Banda Oriental (now Uruguay). Its protagonist, Richard Lamb, has been forced to flee to Montevideo after eloping with the daughter of a powerful Argentinean family. The story concerns Lamb's wanderings in connection with an abortive attempt to find a job managing an inland plantation. At one point, he becomes entangled in the affairs of the rebel general Santa Coloma and fights with him in an ill-fated revolution. He also attracts the attention of several women, including two very beautiful girls who mistake him for a single man and are bitterly disappointed when he informs them belatedly of his unavailability. One of these women, however, he rescues from an awkward predicament and smuggles her back to Argentina in spite of the risk to himself (the reader has already been told in the first chapter that these wanderings preceded a long spell in jail, an event that was instigated by his vengeful father-in-law and broke his wife's heart).

The attractive features of this novel are the local color and the attention to anthropological detail. It offers a convincing picture of the life of the country, and one can easily believe that some of the episodes are based on experience, and that Hudson actually heard some of the tall stories that are told to Lamb by Santa Coloma's rebel gauchos. The amorous encounters, however, fail to convince, and there is a certain perversity in hearing the protagonist's overheated expressions of devotion to a wife from whom he is willingly separated, and whom he is destined to lose. In contrast to the bleak note on which the novel begins and ends, the protestations of love are melodramatic.

There is no trace of this fault in the two novellas set in the same region. "El Ombú" is a chronicle of unremitting cruelty and misfortune, detailing the sufferings of a family through the memories of an old man who loves to sit and reminisce in the shadow of an Ombú tree. "Marta Riquelme," which Hudson thought the best of his stories, is even more ruthless, and makes use of a legend connected with a species of bird called the Kakué fowl, into which men and women who experience unendurable suffering were said to change. The story is narrated by a Jesuit priest, who describes the tragic career of Marta, captured by Indians, robbed of her child, and so mutilated that when she returns to her own people they will not accept her and drive her out to find her fate.

These stories were called "romances" because their subject matter was exotic to an English audience; in fact, however, they are examples of determined narrative realism (unless one accepts the Jesuit priest's dubious allegation that Marta Riquelme really does turn into a Kakué fowl). They present a very different view of life in South America than does *The Purple Land*, a book which glosses over the plight of the common people and the cruelties visited upon them. They bear witness to the fact that Hudson, once emerged from the cocoon of his ideal childhood and initiated into the ways of the world, was deeply affected by what he discovered. He carried away from

South America much fonder memories of the birds than of the people, the grotesqueness of whose lives appalled him even though he tried with all his might to sympathize with them.

In between *The Purple Land* and "El Ombú," Hudson wrote two other novels. One, the pseudonymous *Fan*, appears to have been an attempt to write a conventional three-decker novel of domestic life. The book has little to recommend it, being an entirely artificial product with little of Hudson in it, appearing when the day of the three-decker was already past. The other novel, *A Crystal Age*, also appeared without Hudson's name on it, being issued anonymously, but Hudson acknowledged authorship when it was reprinted in the wake of *Green Mansions*' success.

A Crystal Age is a difficult work to classify: it is a vision of an earthly paradise, but it is arcadian rather than utopian in character and is by no means polemical. It carries no political message and might best be regarded as a fatalist parable lamenting the imperfections of nineteenth century man.

The narrator of the story tells the reader nothing about himself except that he is an Englishman named Smith. He is precipitated into a distant future where men live in perfect ecological harmony with their environment. Each community is a single family, based in a House which is organized around its Mother. The Mother of the House which takes Smith in is secluded because of illness, and it is some time before he realizes that she is an actual person rather than an imaginary goddess. When he repairs the most damaging of his many breaches of etiquette by making himself known to her, she treats him harshly but later forgives him and awards him a special place in her affections.

Smith never fully understands this peculiar world. He is passionately in love with a daughter of the House, Yoletta, whom he believes to be about seventeen years of age. Even when she tells him how old she really is, he cannot see the truth: that these people are so long-lived, and live so free from danger, that their reproductive rate has to be very slow. The Mother is revered because she really is *the* mother of the household: the only reproductive individual. When Smith tries desperately to woo Yoletta, she genuinely cannot understand him. Nor can Smith see, though the reader can, that the Mother holds him in special esteem because she plans to be followed in her role by Yoletta, and is grooming him for the role of the Father. He remains lost in an anguish of uncertainty until he finds a bottle whose label promises a cure for misery. He immediately believes that it is the means by which his hosts suppress their sexual feelings, and drinks to drown his own passion. He discovers too late that it is actually the means by which those in mortal agony achieve a merciful release.

In a sense, the world of *A Crystal Age* is the opposite of the world described in "El Ombú": it is a heaven constructed by reacting against the hellish aspects of the life of the South American peasantry. It is a world where man and nature peacefully coexist and where human society enjoys the harmonious organization of the beehive without the loss of individual identity that has made the beehive a horrific stereotype in stories of hypothetical societies. Nevertheless, *A Crystal Age* is just as misanthropic as "El Ombú," in that Smith—the book's Everyman figure—is mercilessly pilloried for being too brutal and stupid to adapt himself to the perfect world.

In view of Hudson's personal history, it is difficult to doubt that the matricentric of the imaginary society, and Smith's own peculiar relationship with the Mother, are of some psychological significance. The same seems to be true of *A Little Boy Lost*, whose protagonist, Martin, runs away from home to follow a mirage. When he becomes homesick, it is not to his real parents that he returns (there has been a quaintly unconvincing suggestion earlier that his real father was a bird—a martin) but to a surrogate mother called the Lady of the Hills. She smothers him with affection but he eventually leaves her, too, attracted to the distant seashore beyond the reach of her powers. When he falls into danger there, he longs for this surrogate mother rather than the real one, but there is no going back of any kind; in the end, he is picked up by a ship which seems to be sailing to the England which his parents left before he was born. Some of Martin's other adventures—especially his encounter with savage Indians—recall elements in Hudson's other works, and it is a rather baleful world from which the Lady of the Hills temporarily rescues him. If all of this could be analyzed in the light of a more detailed knowledge of Hudson's thoughts and feelings, it might well turn out to reveal some interesting symbolic patterns.

Hudson's idea of perfection, which is displayed as a whole world in *A Crystal Age*, is embodied in *Green Mansions* in a single person. In a sense, *Green Mansions* is *A Crystal Age* in reverse: it features a visitor from the imaginary world of ecological harmony cast adrift in the familiar world. Rima, the delicate refugee, can no more survive here than Smith could in the Mother's House: she is brutally murdered by savages who believe that she is an evil spirit ruining their hunting.

The story is told by a placid and gentle old man named Mr. Abel, recalling his youth when he was forced to flee from his native Venezuela because of his complicity in an abortive coup. After wandering for some time, the young Abel rests for a while in an Indian village somewhere in the remoter regions of the Orinoco basin. In a forested area nearby, which the Indians are reluctant to enter, he hears a voice which seems to be part bird-song and part human, and eventually discovers Rima, a tiny and somewhat ethereal girl who can communicate with birds and animals. She lives there with her adopted grandfather, Nuflo, and takes Abel in after he is bitten by a snake.

Rima is desperate to return to her half-forgotten place of origin, but Nuflo will not take her. Abel mentions a mountain chain called Riolama, and she recognizes the name, insisting that they go there. The journey is fruitless—the remote valley where Rima's people lived has been destroyed, and Abel realizes that her mother must have been the last survivor of the catastrophe. Rima decides to settle in her forest haven with Abel, but even this scheme is thwarted by the Indians, who have reclaimed the wood during Rima's absence and who destroy her by trapping her in the branches of a solitary tree and burning it. Abel, sick and hallucinating, sets off on a phantasmagoric trip through the rain forest, back to civilization. On the way, imagined encounters with Rima's ghost instill in him the capacity to rebuild his life; he becomes convinced that he can be reunited with her after death if he accepts his situation and learns patience.

Green Mansions is a magnificently lush tragedy, and it is not difficult to understand why it captured the public imagination—at least in America— firmly enough to become established as a kind of classic. The passionate yearning which drives Abel is something with which almost everyone can identify: the yearning for an imaginary golden age of love and tranquillity which somehow seems to be located equally in the personal and prehistoric past. What Abel is chasing is a fantasy that cannot be brought down to earth, and he is bound to fail, but in his failing there is a kind of disappointment which is common to all people.

Hudson's version of this particular myth is remarkable in two ways. First of all, he was able to exploit, as he had in *The Purple Land*, "El Ombú," and "Marta Riquelme," a realism which seemed to his readers to be romanticism. This encompasses both his descriptions of the various landscapes of the story (especially the forests of Abel's last delirious journey) and his description of the way of life of the savage Indians. These are no Rousseaesque examples of a wild nobility, but brutish individuals who are no better integrated into their environment than Abel is. (Indeed, Abel is the wiser, for he at least can appreciate, thanks to his intellect and imagination, the *possibility* of living in harmony with nature.) Second, the novel is remarkable for its characterization of the bird-girl Rima. Although not particularly convincing as a character, she is so close to the author's personal notion of perfection that his regard for her infects the novel and gives her the same status in the reader's eyes as she has in Abel's.

Again, one is tempted to look below the surface of *Green Mansions* for some psychological significance that will cast light on Hudson's enigmatic personality. It is easy enough to connect Rima with the Lady of the Hills, and to observe that, in common with all the other desirable women in Hudson's fiction, she has an essential inaccessibility. Monica, Mercedes, and Demetria in *The Purple Land* are all unavailable to the hero because he is married; Yoletta in *A Crystal Age* is forbidden to Smith by social convention and cannot respond to his passion because she has no sexuality of her own; Rima is a member of a different race, more nature-spirit than human, and though there seems no obvious reason why, it is always clear that she and Abel can never be united. One "explanation" for the dearth of successful amatory ventures in Hudson's work might be found in the suggestion that all these love-objects really ought to be interpreted as mother-figures rather than suitable brides, but the truth is probably more complicated. For Hudson's male characters, all feelings of sexual attraction are—or ought to be—guilt-ridden, forbidden by taboos of which they are sometimes only half aware. The possibility that Hudson suffered from a mother fixation may help to account for this, but is hardly likely to be the whole story—especially when one remembers that the Lady of the Hills, in *A Little Boy Lost*, is specifically declared to be a substitute mother who displaces the real one in the child-hero's affections.

Why Hudson wrote no more significant fiction after 1905 is not altogether clear, especially as he had only just made a name for himself. He was well into his sixties, but his creative powers showed no sign of diminution. His three best books—*A Shepherd's Life*, *Far Away and Long Ago*, and *A Hind in Richmond Park*—were still to be written, the last when he was in his eighties. Perhaps, with the death of Rima, he laid aside his dream of a supernaturally harmonized creation—the dream which provided the imaginative fuel for *A Crystal Age* and *Green Mansions*. In *A Little Boy Lost* that same dream is displayed as a childish illusion—even on the story's own terms it is difficult to decide exactly how much takes place inside Martin's head.

The new Introduction which Hudson wrote for *A Crystal Age* when it was reissued in 1906 supports this view. This brief essay is full of disillusionment, informing the reader that romances of the future are always interesting even though none of them is really any good. Hudson disparages *A Crystal Age* for being a product of its own era, and regrets that it cannot possibly induce belief because "the ending of passion and strife is the beginning of decay." This remark echoes Hudson's ambivalent feelings about Darwinism—he was resistant to the ideas of "the struggle for existence" and "the survival of the fittest." For Hudson it was the human world, not the world of nature, that was red in tooth and claw. Despite his reluctance, though, he could not help but accept much of the Darwinian argument, and was forced thereby to acknowledge the hopelessness of his own ideals. This special disenchantment is something which lurks below the surface of almost all his work; whether or not it is the cognitive reflection of a much more personal disenchantment must remain an unanswered question.

Brian Stableford

Other major works

SHORT FICTION: *Dead Man's Plack and An Old Thorn*, 1920.

NONFICTION: *Argentine Ornithology*, 1888-1889 (with Professor Sclator); *The Naturalist in La Plata*, 1892; *Birds in a Village*, 1893; *Idle Days in Patagonia*, 1893; *British Birds*, 1895; *Nature in Downland*, 1900; *Birds and Man*,

1901; *Hampshire Days*, 1903; *The Land's End*, 1908; *Afoot in England*, 1909; *A Shepherd's Life*, 1910; *Adventures Among Birds*, 1913; *Far Away and Long Ago*, 1918; *The Book of a Naturalist*, 1919; *Birds of La Plata*, 1920; *A Traveller in Little Things*, 1921; *A Hind in Richmond Park*, 1922; *153 Letters from W. H. Hudson*, 1923 (with Edward Garnett, editor); *Men, Books, and Birds*, 1925.

Bibliography

Haymaker, Richard E. *From Pampas to Hedgerows and Downs: A Study of W. H. Hudson.* New York: Bookman Associates, 1954. Perhaps the most thorough of full-length studies to date on Hudson; a must for serious scholars of this writer.

Roberts, Morley. *W. H. Hudson: A Portrait.* New York: E. P. Dutton, 1924. A personal, intimate account of Hudson from the perspective of Roberts' long-term relationship with this writer and naturalist.

Ronner, Amy D. *W. H. Hudson: The Man, the Novelist, the Naturalist.* New York: AMS Press, 1986. A much needed recent addition to critical studies on Hudson, examining Hudson's work in relationship to his contemporaries, his emigration to England, and his development as a naturalist and writer. Concludes with an interesting account of Charles Darwin's influence on Hudson and consequently on his writing. Useful bibliography is also provided.

Shrubsall, Dennis. *W. H. Hudson: Writer and Naturalist.* Tisbury, England: Compton Press, 1978. Provides much useful background on Hudson's early years in Argentina and traces his development as a naturalist and his integrity as a writer on nature.

Tomalin, Ruth. *W. H. Hudson: A Biography.* London: Faber & Faber, 1982. A lively biography that has been thoroughly and painstakingly researched. Highly recommended for any serious study of Hudson. Contains excerpts of the letter which Hudson wrote in an attack on Charles Darwin and of Darwin's response.

ZORA NEALE HURSTON

Born: Eatonville, Florida; January 7, 1903 (?)
Died: Fort Pierce, Florida; January 28, 1960

Principal long fiction
Jonah's Gourd Vine, 1934; *Their Eyes Were Watching God*, 1937; *Moses, Man of the Mountain*, 1939; *Seraph on the Suwanee*, 1948.

Other literary forms
In addition to her four novels, Zora Neale Hurston produced two collections of folklore, *Mules and Men* (1935) and *Tell My Horse* (1938), and an auto-biography, *Dust Tracks on a Road* (1942). Hurston also published plays, short stories, and essays in anthologies and in magazines as diverse as *Opportunity*, the *Journal of Negro History*, the *Saturday Evening Post*, the *Journal of American Folklore*, and the *American Legion Magazine*. Finally, she wrote several articles and reviews for such newspapers as the *New York Herald Tribune* and the *Pittsburgh Courier*. Hurston's major works have only recently been reissued. Some of her essays and stories have also been collected and reprinted. Although the anthologies *I Love Myself When I Am Laughing . . .* (1979) and *The Sanctified Church* (1981) have helped to bring her writing back into critical focus, some of her works are still not readily available, and her numerous unpublished manuscripts can only be seen at university archives and the Library of Congress.

Achievements
Hurston was the best and most prolific black woman writer of the 1930's. All her novels were highly praised. Even so, Hurston never made more than one thousand dollars in royalties on even her most successful works, and when she died in 1960, she was penniless and forgotten. Hurston's career testifies to the difficulties of a black woman writing for a mainstream white audience whose appreciation was usually superficial and racist and for a black audience whose responses to her work were, of necessity, highly politicized.

Hurston achieved recognition at a time when, as Langston Hughes declared, "the Negro was in vogue." The Harlem Renaissance, the black literary and cultural movement of the 1920's, created an interracial audience for her stories and plays. Enthusiasm for her work extended through the 1930's, although that decade also marked the beginning of critical attacks. Hurston did not portray blacks as victims, stunted by a racist society. Such a view, she believed, implies that black life is only a defensive reaction to white racism. Black and left-wing critics, however, complained that her unwillingness to represent the oppression of blacks and her focus, instead, on an autonomous, unresentful black folk culture served to perpetuate minstrel stereotypes and thus fueled white racism. The radical, racial protest literature of Richard Wright, one of Hurston's strongest critics, became the model for black literature in the 1940's, and publishers on the lookout for protest works showed less and less interest in Hurston's manuscripts. Yet, when she did speak out against American racism and imperialism, her work was often censored. Her autobiogaphy, published in 1942, as well as a number of her stories and articles were tailored by editors to please white audiences. Caught between the attacks of black critics and the censorship of the white publishing industry, Hurston floundered, struggling through the 1940's and 1950's to find other subjects. She largely dropped out of public view in the 1950's, though she continued to publish magazine and newspaper articles.

The Afro-American and feminist political and cultural movements of the 1960's and 1970's have provided the impetus for Hurston's recent rediscovery. The publication of Robert Hemenway's excellent book, *Zora Neale Hurston: A Literary Biography* (1977) and the recent reissue of her novels, her autobiography, and her folklore collections seem at last to promise the sustained critical recognition Hurston deserves.

Biography

Zora Neale Hurston was born on January 7, probably in 1903—no birth records survive. Her family lived in the all-black Florida town of Eatonville, in an eight-room house with a five-acre garden. Her father, the Reverend John Hurston, mayor of Eatonville for three terms and moderator of the South Florida Baptist Association, wanted to temper his daughter's high spirits, but her intelligent and forceful mother, Lucy Potts Hurston, encouraged her to "jump at de sun." When Hurston was about nine, her mother died. That event and her father's rapid remarriage to a woman his daughter did not like prematurely ended Hurston's childhood. In the next few years, she lived only intermittently at home, spending some time at a school in Jacksonville and some time with relatives. Her father withdrew all financial support during this period, forcing her to commence what was to be a life-long struggle to make her own living.

When Hurston was fourteen, she took a job as a wardrobe girl to a repertory company touring the South. Hurston left the troupe in Baltimore eighteen months later and finished high school there at Morgan Academy. She went on to study part-time at Howard University in 1918, taking jobs as a manicurist, a waitress, and a maid in order to support herself. At Howard, her literary talents began to emerge. She was admitted to a campus literary club, formed by Alain Locke, a Howard professor and one of the forces behind the Harlem Renaissance. Locke brought Hurston to the attention of Charles S. Johnson, another key promoter of the Harlem Renaissance. Editor of *Opportunity: A Journal of Negro Life*, he published one of her stories and encouraged her to enter the literary contest sponsored by his magazine.

With several manuscripts but little money, Hurston moved to New York City in 1925, hoping to make a career of her writing. Her success in that year's *Opportunity* contest—she received prizes for a play and a story—won her the patronage of Fanny Hurst and a scholarship to complete her education at Barnard College. She studied anthropology there under Franz Boas, leading a seemingly schizophrenic life in the next two years as an eccentric, iconoclastic artist of the Harlem Renaissance on the one hand and a budding, scholarly social scientist on the other.

The common ground linking these seemingly disparate parts of Hurston's life was her interest in black folk culture. Beginning in 1927 and extending through the 1930's, she made several trips to collect black folklore in the South and in the Bahamas, Haiti, and Jamaica. Collecting trips were costly, however, as was the time to write up their results. Charlotte Osgood Mason, a wealthy, domineering white patron to a number of Afro-American artists, supported some of that work, as did the Association for the Study of Negro Life and History and the Guggenheim Foundation. Hurston also worked intermittently during the 1930's as a drama teacher at Bethune Cookman College in Florida and at North Carolina College, as a drama coach for the WPA Federal Theatre Project in New York, and as an editor for the Federal Writer's Project in Florida.

Mules and Men and several scholarly and popular articles on folklore were the products of Hurston's collecting trips in the late 1920's and early 1930's. In 1938, she published *Tell My Horse*, the result of trips to Haiti and Jamaica to study hoodoo. As a creative writer, Hurston devised other outlets for her folk materials. Her plays, short stories, and three of her novels, *Jonah's Gourd Vine*, *Their Eyes Were Watching God*, and *Moses, Man of the Mountain*, make use of folklore. She also presented folk materials in theatrical revues, but even though the productions were enthusiastically received, she could never generate enough backing to finance commercially successful long-term showings.

Hurston's intense interest in black folklore prevented her from sustaining either of her two marriages. She could not reconcile the competing claims of love and work. She married Herbert Sheen, a medical student, in 1927 but separated from him a few months later. They were divorced in 1931. She married Albert Price III in 1939, and they too parted less than a year later. Other romantic relationships ended for the same reason.

In the 1940's, Hurston lost her enthusiasm for writing about black folk culture. She wrote her autobiography and in 1948 published her last novel *Seraph on the Suwanee*, a work which turns away from black folk culture entirely. The last decade of her life took a downward turn. Falsely accused of committing sodomy with a young boy, Hurston, depressed, dropped out of public view. Through the 1950's, she lived in Florida, struggling for economic survival. She barely managed to support herself by writing newspaper and magazine articles, many of which expressed her increasing political conservatism, and by working as a maid, a substitute teacher, and a librarian. In 1959, she suffered a stroke. Too ill to nurse herself, she was forced to enter a welfare home. She died there on January 28, 1960.

Analysis

For much of her career, Zora Neale Hurston was dedicated to the presentation of black folk culture. She introduced readers to hoodoo, folktales, lying contests, spirituals, the blues, sermons, children's games, riddles, playing the dozens, and, in general, a highly metaphoric folk idiom. Although she represented black folk culture in several genres, Hurston was drawn to the novel form because it could convey folklore as communal behavior. Hurston knew that much of the unconscious artistry of folklore appears in the gestures and tones in which it is expressed and that it gains much of its meaning in performance. Even *Mules and Men*, the folklore collection she completed just before embarking on her first novel (although it was published after *Jonah's Gourd Vine*), "novelizes" what could have been an anthology of disconnected folk materials. By inventing a narrator who witnesses, even participates in the performance of folk traditions, she combated the inevitable distortion of an oral culture by its textual documentation.

Hurston's motives for presenting black folklore were, in part, political. She wanted to refute contemporary claims that Afro-Americans lacked a distinct culture of their own. Her novels depict the unconscious creativity of the Afro-American proletariat or folk. They represent community members participating in a highly expressive communication system which taught them to survive racial oppression and, moreover, to respect themselves and their community. At the beginning of Hurston's second novel, for example, the community's members are sitting on porches. "Mules and other brutes had occupied their skins" all day, but now it is night, work is over, and they can talk and feel "powerful and human" again: "They became lords of sounds and lesser things. They passed nations through their mouths. They sat in judgment." By showing the richness and the healthy influence of black folk culture, Hurston hoped not only to defeat racist attitudes but also to encourage racial pride among blacks. Why should Afro-Americans wish to imitate a white bourgeoisie? The "Negro lowest down" had a richer culture.

Hurston also had a psychological motive for presenting black folk culture. She drew the folk materials for her novels from the rural, Southern black life she knew as a child and subsequently recorded in folklore collecting trips in the late 1920's and 1930's. She had fond memories of her childhood in the all-black town of Eatonville, where she did not experience poverty or racism. In her autobiographical writings, she suggests that she did not even know that she was "black" until she left Eatonville. Finally, in Eatonville, she had a close relationship with and a strong advocate in her mother. In representing the rich culture of black rural Southerners, she was also evoking a happier personal past.

Although the novel's witnessing narrator provided Hurston with the means to dramatize folklore, she also needed meaningful fictional contexts for its presentation. Her novels are a series of attempts to develop such contexts. Initially, she maintained the Southern rural setting for black folk traditions. In her first novel, *Jonah's Gourd Vine*, she re-created Eatonville and neighboring Florida towns. Hurston also loosely re-created her parents' lives with the central characters, John and Lucy Pearson. Though Hurston claimed that an unhappy love affair she had had with a man she met in New York was the catalyst for her second novel, *Their Eyes Were Watching God*, the feeling rather than the details of that affair appear in the novel. The work takes the reader back to Eatonville again and to the porch-sitting storytellers Hurston knew as a child.

With her third novel, however, *Moses, Man of the Mountain*, Hurston turned in a new direction, leaving the Eatonville milieu behind. The novel retells the biblical story of Moses via the folk idiom and traditions of Southern rural blacks. Hurston leaves much of the plot of the biblical story intact— Moses does lead the Hebrews out of Egypt—but, for example, she shows Moses to be a great hoodoo doctor as well as a leader and law-giver. In effect, Hurston simulated the creative processes of folk culture, transforming the story of Moses for modern Afro-Americans just as slaves had adapted biblical stories in spirituals. Hurston may have reenacted an oral and communal process as a solitary writer, but she gave an imaginative rendering of the cultural process all the same.

Seraph on the Suwanee, Hurston's last novel, marks another dramatic shift in her writing. With this novel, however, she did not create a new context for the representation of folk culture. Rather, she turned away from the effort to present black folklore. *Seraph on the Suwanee* is set in the rural South, but its central characters are white. Hurston apparently wanted to prove that she could write about whites as well as blacks, a desire which surfaced, no doubt, in response to the criticism and disinterest her work increasingly faced in the 1940's. Yet, even when writing of upwardly mobile Southern crackers, Hurston could not entirely leave her previous mission behind. Her white characters, perhaps unintentionally, often use the black folk idiom.

Although Hurston's novels, with the exception of the last, create contexts or develop other strategies for the presentation of folklore, they are not simply showcases for folk traditions; black folk culture defines the novels' themes. The most interesting of these thematic renderings appear in Hurston's first two novels. Hurston knew that black folk culture was composed of brilliant adaptations of African culture to American life. She admired the ingenuity of these adaptations but worried about their preservation. Would a sterile, materialistic white world ultimately absorb blacks, destroying the folk culture they had developed? Her first two novels demonstrate the disturbing influence of white America on black folkways.

Jonah's Gourd Vine, Hurston's first novel, portrays the tragic experience of a black preacher caught between black cultural values and the values imposed by his white-influenced church. The novel charts the life of John Pearson, laborer, foreman, and carpenter, who discovers that he has an extraordinary talent for preaching. With his linguistic skills and his wife Lucy's wise counsel, he becomes pastor of the large church Zion Hope and ultimately moderator of a Florida Baptist convention. His sexual promiscuity, however, eventually destroys his marriage and his career.

Though his verbal skills make him a success while his promiscuity ruins him, the novel shows that both his linguistic gifts and his sexual vitality are part of the same cultural heritage. His sexual conduct is pagan and so is his preaching. In praying, according to the narrator, it was as if he "rolled his African drum up to the altar, and called his Congo Gods by Christian names." Both aspects of his cultural heritage speak through him. Indeed, they speak through all members of the Afro-American community, if most intensely through John. A key moment early in the novel, when John crosses over Big Creek, marks the symbolic beginning of his life and shows the double cultural heritage he brings to it. John heads down to the Creek, "singing a new song and stomping the beats." He makes up "some words to go with the drums of the Creek," with the animal noises in the woods, and with the hound dog's cry. He begins to think about the girls living on the other side of Big Creek: "John almost trumpeted exultantly at the new sun. He breathed lustily. He stripped and carried his clothes across, then recrossed and plunged into the swift water and breasted strongly over."

To understand why two expressions of the same heritage have such different effects on John's life, one has to turn to the community to which he belongs. Members of his congregation subscribe to differing views of the spiritual life. The view most often endorsed by the novel emerges from the folk culture. As Larry Neal, one of Hurston's best critics, explains in his introduction to the 1971 reprint of the novel, that view belongs to "a formerly enslaved communal society, non-Christian in background," which does not strictly dichotomize body and soul. The other view comes out of a white culture. It is "more rigid, being a blend of Puritan concepts and the fire-and-brimstone imagery of the white evangelical tradition." That view insists that John, as a preacher, exercise self-restraint. The cultural conflict over spirituality pervades his congregation. While the deacons, whom Hurston often portrays satirically, pressure him to stop preaching, he still has some loyal supporters among his parishioners.

White America's cultural styles and perceptions invade Pearson's community in other ways as well. By means of a kind of preaching competition, the deacons attempt to replace Pearson with the pompous Reverend Felton

Cozy, whose preaching style is white. Cozy's style, however, fails to captivate most members of the congregation. Pearson is a great preacher in the folk tradition, moving his congregation to a frenzy with "barbaric thunder-poems." By contrast, Cozy, as one of the parishioners complains, does not give a sermon; he lectures. In an essay Hurston wrote on "The Sanctified Church," she explains this reaction: "The real, singing Negro derides the Negro who adopts the white man's religious ways. . . . They say of that type of preacher, 'Why he dont preach at all. He just lectures.'"

If Pearson triumphs over Cozy, he nevertheless ultimately falls. His sexual conduct destroys his marriage and leads to an unhappy remarriage with one of his mistresses, Hattie Tyson. He is finally forced to stop preaching at Zion Hope. Divorced from Hattie, he moves to another town, where he meets and marries Sally Lovelace, a woman much like Lucy. With her support, he returns to preaching. On a visit to a friend, however, he is tempted by a young prostitute and, to his dismay, succumbs. Although he has wanted to be faithful to his new wife, he will always be a pagan preacher, spirit *and* flesh. Fleeing back to Sally, he is killed when a train strikes his car.

In its presentation of folklore and its complex representation of cultural conflict, *Jonah's Gourd Vine* is a brilliant first novel, although Hurston does not always make her argument sufficiently clear. The novel lacks a consistent point of view. Though she endorses Pearson's African heritage and ridicules representatives of white cultural views, she also creates an admirable and very sympathetic character in Lucy Pearson, who is ruined by her husband's pagan behavior. Nor did Hurston seem to know how to resolve the cultural conflict she portrayed—hence, the *deus ex machina* ending. It was not until she wrote her next novel, *Their Eyes Were Watching God*, that Hurston learned to control point of view and presented a solution to the problem of white influences on black culture.

The life of Janie Crawford, the heroine of *Their Eyes Were Watching God*, is shaped by bourgeois values—white in origin. She finds love and self-identity only by rejecting that life and becoming a wholehearted participant in black folk culture. Her grandmother directs Janie's entrance into adulthood. Born into slavery, the older woman hopes to find protection and materialistic comforts for Janie in a marriage to the property-owning Logan Killicks. Janie, who has grown up in a different generation, does not share her grandmother's values. When she finds she cannot love her husband, she runs off with Jody Stark, who is on his way to Eatonville, where he hopes to become a "big voice," an appropriate phrase for life in a community which highly values verbal ability. Jody becomes that "big voice" as mayor of the town, owner of the general store, and head of the post office. Stark lives both a bourgeois and a folk life in Eatonville. He constructs a big house—the kind white people have—but he wanders out to the porch of the general store whenever he wants to enjoy the perpetual storytelling which takes place there. Even though

Janie has demonstrated a talent for oratory, however, he will not let her join these sessions or participate in the mock funeral for a mule which has become a popular character in the townspeople's stories. "He didn't," the narrator suggest, "want her talking after such trashy people." As Janie tells a friend years later, Jody "classed me off." He does so by silencing her.

For several years, Janie has no voice in the community or in her private life. Her life begins to seem unreal: "She sat and watched the shadow of herself going about tending store and prostrating itself before Jody." One day, after Stark insults her in front of customers in the store, however, she speaks out and, playing the dozens, insults his manhood. The insult causes an irreconcilable break between them.

After Jody's death, Janie is courted by Tea Cake Woods, a laborer with little money. Though many of her neighbors disapprove of the match, Janie marries him. "Dis ain't no business proposition," she tells her friend Pheoby, "and no race after property and titles. Dis is uh love game. Ah done lived Grandma's way, now Ah mens tuh live mine." Marriage to Tea Cake lowers her social status but frees her from her submissive female role, from her shadow existence. Refusing to use her money, Tea Cake takes her down to the Everglades, where they become migrant workers. She picks beans with him in the fields, and he helps her prepare their dinners. With Tea Cake, she also enters into the folk culture of the Everglades, and that more than anything else enables her to shed her former submissive identity. Workers show up at their house every night to sing, dance, gamble, and, above all, to talk, like the folks in Eatonville on the front porch of the general store. Janie learns how to tell "big stories" from listening to the others, and she is encouraged to do so.

This happy phase of Janie's life ends tragically as she and Tea Cake attempt to escape a hurricane and the ensuing flood. Tea Cake saves Janie from drowning but, in the process, is bitten by a rabid dog. Sick and crazed, he tries to shoot Janie. She is forced to kill him in self-defense. Not everything she has gained during her relationship with Tea Cake, however, dies with him. The strong self-identity she has achieved while living in the Everglades enables her to withstand the unjust resentment of their black friends as well as her trial for murder in a white court. Most important, she is able to endure her own loss and returns to Eatonville, self-reliant and wise. Tea Cake, she knows, will live on in her thoughts and feelings—and in her words. She tells her story to her friend Pheoby—that storytelling event frames the novel— and allows Pheoby to bring it to the other members of the community. As the story enters the community's oral culture, it will influence it. Indeed, as the novel closes, Janie's story has already affected Pheoby. "Ah done growed ten feet higher from jus' listenin' tuh you," she tells Janie: "Ah ain't satisfied wid mahself no mo'."

In her novels, Hurston did not represent the oppression of blacks because she refused to view Afro-American life as impoverished. If she would not focus on white racism, however, her novels do oppose white culture. In *Their Eyes Were Watching God*, Janie does not find happiness until she gives up a life governed by white values and enters into the verbal ceremonies of black folk culture. Loving celebrations of a separate black folklife were Hurston's effective political weapon; racial pride was one of her great gifts to American literature. "Sometimes, I feel discriminated against," she once told her readers, "but it does not make me angry. It merely astonishes me. How *can* any deny themselves the pleasure of my company? It's beyond me."

Deborah Kaplan

Other major works

SHORT FICTION: *Spunk: The Selected Short Stories of Zora Neale Hurston*, 1985.

NONFICTION: *Mules and Men*, 1935; *Tell My Horse*, 1938; *Dust Tracks on a Road*, 1942; *The Sanctified Church*, 1981.

MISCELLANEOUS: *I Love Myself When I Am Laughing . . . and Then Again When I Am Looking Mean and Impressive: A Zora Neale Hurston Reader*, 1979.

Bibliography

Gates, Henry Louis, Jr. *The Signifying Monkey: A Theory of Afro-American Literary Criticism.* New York: Oxford University Press, 1988. The chapter on Hurston discusses her best-known novel, *Their Eyes Were Watching God*, as a conscious attempt to rebut the naturalistic view of blacks as "animalistic" that Gates claims she saw in Richard Wright's fiction.

Hemenway, Robert. *Zora Neale Hurston.* Urbana: University of Illinois Press, 1977. An excellent biography of Hurston which also provides much insight into her fiction. Perhaps the single best source of information about the author and her writings.

Howard, Lillie P. *Zora Neale Hurston.* Boston: Twayne, 1980. An important full-length study of Hurston's work which, nevertheless, is not as helpful as it might have been.

Johnson, Barbara. *A World of Difference.* Baltimore: The Johns Hopkins University Press, 1987. The two essays on Hurston examine how her fiction addresses the problem of the social construction of self.

Washington, Mary Helen. *Invented Lives: Narratives of Black Women, 1860-1960.* Garden City, N.Y.: Anchor Press, 1987. Includes an excellent short essay on Hurston.

Willis, Susan. *Specifying.* Madison: University of Wisconsin Press, 1987. A survey of black women's fiction. The essay on Hurston focuses on the sexual conflict in *Their Eyes Were Watching God.*

ALDOUS HUXLEY

Born: Godalming, England; July 26, 1894
Died: Los Angeles, California; November 22, 1963

Principal long fiction

Crome Yellow, 1921; *Antic Hay*, 1923; *Those Barren Leaves*, 1925; *Point Counter Point*, 1928; *Brave New World*, 1932; *Eyeless in Gaza*, 1936; *After Many a Summer Dies the Swan*, 1939; *Time Must Have a Stop*, 1944; *Ape and Essence*, 1948; *The Genius and the Goddess*, 1955; *Island*, 1962.

Other literary forms

Besides the novel, Aldous Huxley wrote in every other major literary form. He published several volumes of essays and won universal acclaim as a first-rate essayist. He also wrote poetry, plays, short stories, biographies, and travelogues.

Achievements

Huxley achieved fame as a satirical novelist and essayist in the decade following World War I. In his article, "Aldous Huxley: The Ultra-Modern Satirist," published in *The Nation* in 1926, Edwin Muir observed, "No other writer of our time has built up a serious reputation so rapidly and so surely; compared with his rise to acceptance that of Mr. Lawrence or Mr. Eliot has been gradual, almost painful." In the 1920's and the early 1930's, Huxley became so popular that the first London editions of his books were, within a decade of their publication, held at a premium by dealers and collectors. Huxley's early readers, whose sensibilities had been hardened by the war, found his wit, his iconoclasm, and his cynicism to their taste. They were also impressed by his prophetic gifts. Bertrand Russell said, "What Huxley thinks today, England thinks tomorrow." Believing that all available knowledge should be absorbed if humanity were to survive, Huxley assimilated ideas from a wide range of fields and allowed them to find their way into his novels, which came to be variously identified as "novels of ideas," "discussion novels," or "conversation novels." His increasing store of knowledge did not, however, help him overcome his pessimistic and cynical outlook on life.

Huxley's reputation as a novelist suffered a sharp decline in his later years. In *The Novel and the Modern World* (1939), David Daiches took a highly critical view of Huxley's novels, and since then, many other critics have joined him. It is often asserted that Huxley was essentially an essayist whose novels frequently turn into intellectual tracts. It has also been held that his plots lack dramatic interest and his characters are devoid of real substance. Attempts have been made in recent years, however, to rehabilitate him as an important novelist. In any case, no serious discussion of twentieth century fiction can afford to ignore Huxley's novels.

Biography

Aldous Leonard Huxley was born at Godalming, Surrey, on July 26, 1894. His father, Leonard Huxley, a biographer and historian, was the son of Thomas Henry Huxley, the great Darwinist, and his mother, Julia, was the niece of Matthew Arnold. Sir Julian Huxley, the famous biologist, was his brother. With this intellectual and literary family background, Huxley entered Eton at the age of fourteen. Owing to an attack of *keratitis punctata*, causing blindness, he had to withdraw from school within two years, an event which left a permanent mark on his character, evident in his reflective temperament and detached manner. He learned to read Braille and continued his studies under tutors. As soon as he was able to read with the help of a magnifying glass, he went to Balliol College, Oxford, where he studied English literature and philosophy.

Huxley started his career as a journalist on the editorial staff of *The Athenaeum* under J. Middleton Murry. He relinquished his journalistic career when he could support himself by his writing. By 1920, he had three volumes of verse and a collection of short stories to his credit. He had also become acquainted with a number of writers, including D. H. Lawrence. While in Italy in the 1920's, he met Lawrence again, and the two became close friends. Lawrence exercised a profound influence on Huxley, particularly in his distrust of intellect, against his faith in blood consciousness. Later, Huxley became a disciple of Gerald Heard, the pacifist, and took an active part in Heard's pacifist movement. In 1937, he moved to California, where he came into contact with the Ramakrishna Mission in Hollywood. In Hinduism and Buddhism, Huxley found the means of liberation from man's bondage to the ego, a problem which had concerned him for a long time. To see if the mystical experience could be chemically induced, Huxley took drugs in 1953, and his writings concerning hallucinogenic drugs helped to popularize their use.

Huxley married Maria Nys in 1919. After her death in 1955, he married Laura Archera in 1956. On November 22, 1963, Huxley died in Los Angeles, where his body was cremated the same day. There was no funeral, but friends in London held a memorial service the next month.

Analysis

Aldous Huxley's novels present, on the whole, a bitterly satirical and cynical picture of contemporary society. A recurring theme in his work is the egocentricity of the people of the twentieth century, their ignorance of any reality transcending the self, their loneliness and despair, and their pointless and sordid existence. Devoid of any sense of ultimate purpose, the world often appears to Huxley as a wilderness of apes, baboons, monkeys, and maggots, a veritable inferno, presided over by Belial himself. The dominant negativism in the novelist's outlook on life is pointedly and powerfully revealed by Will Farnaby, a character in his book *Island*, who is fond of saying that he will not take yes for an answer.

Though Huxley finds the present-day world largely hopeless, he reveals the possibility of redemption. Little oases of humanity, islands of decency, and atolls of liberated souls generally appear in his fictional worlds. A good number of his characters transcend their egos, achieve completeness of being, recognize the higher spiritual goals of life, and even dedicate their lives to the service of an indifferent humanity. Even Will Farnaby, who will not take yes for an answer, finally casts his lot with the islanders against the corrupt and the corrupting world. It is true that these liberated individuals are not, in Huxley's novels, a force strong enough to resist the onward march of civilization toward self-destruction, but they are, nevertheless, a testimony to the author's faith in the possibilities of sanity even in the most difficult of times. No one who agrees with Huxley's assessment of the modern world will ask for a stronger affirmation of faith in human redemption.

Huxley believed that man's redemption lies in his attainment of "wholeness" and integrity. His concept of wholeness did not, however, remain the same from the beginning to the end of his career. As he matured as a novelist, Huxley's sense of wholeness achieved greater depth and clarity. Under the influence of D. H. Lawrence, Huxley viewed wholeness in terms of the harmonious blending of all human faculties. Writing under the influence of Gerald Heard, he expanded his idea of wholeness to include a mystical awareness of the unity of man with nature. Coming under the influence of the Eastern religions, especially Hinduism and Buddhism, he gave his concept of wholeness further spiritual and metaphysical depth.

In *Crome Yellow*, his first novel, Huxley exposed the egocentricity of modern man, his inability to relate to others or recognize any reality, social or spiritual, outside himself, and the utter pointlessness of his life. Jenny Mullion, a minor character in the novel, symbolically represents the situation that prevails in the modern world by the almost impenetrable barriers of her deafness. It is difficult for anyone to carry on an intelligent conversation with her. Once early in the book, when Denis Stone, the poet, inquires if she slept well, she speaks to him, in reply, about thunderstorms. Following this ineffectual conversation, Denis reflects on the nature of Jenny Mullion.

> Parallel straight lines . . . meet only at infinity. He might talk for ever of care-charmer sleep and she of meteorology till the end of time. Did one ever establish contact with anyone? We are all parallel straight lines. Jenny was only a little more parallel than most.

Almost every character in the novel is set fast in the world that he has made for himself and cannot come out of it to establish contact with others. Henry even declaims, "How gay and delightful life would be if one could get rid of all the human contacts!" He is of the view that "the proper study of mankind is books." His history of his family, which took him twenty-five years to write and four years to print, was obviously undertaken in order to escape human contacts. If Henry is occupied with the history of Crome, Priscilla, his wife, spends her time cultivating a rather ill-defined malady, betting, horoscope reading, and studying Barbecue-Smith's books on spiritualism. Barbecue-Smith busies himself with infinity. Bodiham, the village priest, is obsessed by the Second Coming. Having read somewhere about the dangers of sexual repression, Mary Bracegirdle hunts for a lover who will provide her with an outlet for her repressed instincts. Denis constantly broods over his failure as a writer, as a lover, and as a man. Scogan, disdainful of life, people, and the arts, finds consolation only in reason and ideas and dreams about a scientifically controlled Rational State where babies are produced in test tubes and artists are sent to a lethal chamber.

Though there is a good deal of interaction among the guests at Crome, no real meeting of minds or hearts takes place among them; this failure to connect is best illustrated by the numerous hopeless love affairs described in the novel. Denis, for example, loves Anne, but his repeated attempts to convey his love for her fail. Anne, who is four years older than Denis, talks to him as if he were a child and does not know that he is courting her. Mary falls in love with Denis only to be rebuffed. Then, she makes advances to Gombauld, the painter, with no better result. Next, she pursues Ivor, the man of many gifts and talents, and is brokenhearted to learn that she means nothing to him. She is finally seen in the embrace of a young farmer of heroic proportions, and it is anybody's guess what comes of this affair. Even the relationship between Anne and Gombauld, which showed every promise of maturation into one of lasting love, meets, at the end, the same fate as the others.

Thumbing through Jenny's red notebook of cartoons, Denis suddenly becomes conscious of points of view other than his own. He learns that there are others who are "in their way as elaborate and complete as he is in his." Denis' appreciation of the world outside himself comes, however, too late in the novel. Though he would like to abandon the plan of his intended departure from Crome, particularly when he sees that it makes Anne feel wretched, he is too proud to change his mind and stay in Crome to try again with her. Thus, the characters in *Crome Yellow* remain self-absorbed, separated from one another, and hardly concerned with the ultimate ends of life. Scogan betrays himself and others when he says, "We all know that there's no ultimate point."

Antic Hay, Huxley's second novel, presents, like *Crome Yellow*, an inferno-like picture of contemporary society, dominated by egocentric characters living in total isolation from society and suffering extreme loneliness, boredom, and despair. Evidence of self-preoccupation and isolation is abundant. Gumbril Junior continually dwells on his failings and on his prospects of getting rich. He retires every now and then to his private rooms at Great Russell Street, where he enjoys his stay, away from people. Lypiatt, a painter, poet, and musician, is without a sympathetic audience. "I find myself alone, spiritually alone," he complains. Shearwater, the scientist, has no interest in anything or anyone except in the study of the regulative function of the kidneys. Mercaptan is a writer whose theme is "the pettiness, the simian limitations, the insignificance and the absurd pretentiousness of *Homo* soi-disant *Sapiens*."

The men and women in *Antic Hay*, each living in his or her private universe, are unable to establish any true and meaningful relationships with one another. Myra Viveash is cold and callous toward men who come to her and offer their love: Gumbril Junior, Lypiatt, Shearwater, and others. She contemptuously lends herself to them. Lypiatt, hopelessly in love with her, finally takes his life. Gumbril, deserted by Myra, feels revengeful; in turn, he is cruelly cynical in his treatment of Mrs. Rosie Shearwater. Because of his carelessness, he loses Emily, who might have brought some happiness and meaning into his life. Engaged in his scientific research, Shearwater completely ignores his wife, with the result that she gives herself to other men. Men and women can easily find sexual partners, which does not, however, close the distance between them: they remain as distant as ever.

On the eve of Gumbril's intended departure from London for the Continent, Gumbril and Myra taxi the entire length and breadth of the West End to meet friends and invite them to a dinner that night. Their friends are, significantly enough, engaged in one way or another and shut up in their rooms—Lypiatt writing his life for Myra; Coleman sleeping with Rosie; and Shearwater cycling in a hot box in his laboratory. Despite the lovely moon above on the summer night and the poignant sorrow in their hearts, Gumbril and Myra make no attempt to take advantage of their last ride together and come closer. Instead, they aimlessly drive from place to place.

Huxley's next novel, *Those Barren Leaves*, shows how people who might be expected to be more enlightened are as self-centered as the mass of humanity. The setting of the novel, which deals with a circle of British intellectuals in Italy, immediately and powerfully reinforces the fact of their social isolation.

Mrs. Lilian Aldwinkle, a patroness of the arts and a votary of love, wants to believe that the whole world revolves around her. As usual, she is possessive of her guests who have assembled at her newly bought palace of Cybo Malaspina in the village of Vezza in Italy, and she wants them to do as she commands. She is unable, however, to hold them completely under her control. In spite of all her efforts, she fails to win the love of Calamy, and later of Francis Chelifer; Chelifer remains unmoved even when she goes down on her knees and begs for his love. She sinks into real despair when her niece escapes her smothering possessiveness and falls in love with Lord Hovenden.

Well past her youth, Mrs. Aldwinkle finds herself left alone with nobody to blame but herself for her plight.

Miss Mary Thriplow and Francis Chelifer are both egocentric writers, cut off from the world of real human beings. Miss Thriplow is obsessed with her suffering and pain, which are mostly self-induced. Her mind is constantly busy, spinning stories on gossamer passions she experiences while moving, talking, and loving. Conscious of the unreality of the life of upper-class society, Chelifer gives up poetry and also the opportunity of receiving a fellowship at Oxford in favor of a job as editor of *The Rabbit Fanciers' Gazette* in London. The squalor, the repulsiveness, and the stupidity of modern life constitute, in Chelifer's opinion, reality. Because it is the artist's duty to live amid reality, he lives among an assorted group of eccentrics in a boardinghouse in Gog's court, which he describes as "the navel of reality." If Miss Thriplow is lost in her world of imagination and art, Chelifer is lost in "the navel of reality"— equidistant from the heart of reality.

Through the character of Calamy, Huxley suggests a way to overcome the perverse, modern world. Rich, handsome, and hedonistic, Calamy was once a part of this world, but he no longer enjoys running after women, wasting his time in futile intercourse, and pursuing pleasure. Rather, he spends his time reading, satisfying his curiosity about things, and thinking. He withdraws to a mountain retreat, hoping that his meditation will ultimately lead him into the mysteries of existence, the relationship between men, and that between man and the external world.

Calamy's withdrawal to a mountain retreat is, no doubt, an unsatisfactory solution, particularly in view of the problem of egocentricity and isolation of the individual from society raised in *Those Barren Leaves* and Huxley's two preceding novels. It may, however, be noted that Calamy's isolation is not a result of his egocentricity: he recognizes that there are spheres of reality beyond the self.

Point Counter Point, Huxley's first mature novel, is regarded by many critics as his masterpiece, a major work of twentieth century fiction. By introducing similar characters facing different situations and different characters facing a similar situation, a technique analogous to the musical device of counterpoint, Huxley presents a comprehensive and penetrating picture of the sordidness of contemporary society.

Mark Rampion, a character modeled upon D. H. Lawrence, sees the problem of modern man as one of lopsided development. Instead of achieving a harmonious development of all human faculties—reason, intellect, emotion, instinct, and body—modern man allows one faculty to develop at the expense of the others. "It's time," Rampion says, "there was a revolt in favor of life and wholeness."

Huxley makes a penetrating analysis of the failure of his characters to achieve love and understanding. Particularly acute is his analysis of Philip

Quarles, a critical self-portrait of the author. Since a childhood accident, which left him slightly lame in one leg, Philip has shunned society and has developed a reflective and intellectual temperament. As a result of his constant preoccupation with ideas, the emotional side of his character atrophies, and he is unable to love even his wife with any degree of warmth. In the ordinary daily world of human contacts, he is curiously like a foreigner, not at home with his fellows, finding it difficult or impossible to enter into communication with any but those who can speak his native intellectual language of ideas. He knows his weakness, and he tries unsuccessfully to transform a detached intellectual skepticism into a way of harmonious living. It is no wonder that his wife, Lilian, feels exasperated with his coldness and unresponsiveness and feels that she could as well love a bookcase.

Philip, however, is not as hopeless a case of lopsided development as the rest of the characters who crowd the world of *Point Counter Point*. Lord Edward Tantamount, the forty-year-old scientist, is in all but intellect a child. He is engaged in research involving the transplantation of the tail of a newt onto the stump of its amputated foreleg to find out if the tail will grow into a leg or continue incongruously to grow as a tail. He shuts himself up in his laboratory most of the day and a good part of the night, avoiding all human contact. Lady Edward, his wife, and Lucy Tantamount, his daughter, live for sexual excitement. Spandril, who prides himself on being a sensualist, actually hates women. Suffering from a sense of betrayal by his mother when she remarries, he attracts women only to torture them. Burlap wears a mask of spirituality, but he is a materialist to the core. Molly, pretty and plump, makes herself desirable to men but lacks genuine emotional interest. The novel contains an assortment of barbarians (to use the language of Rampion) of the intellect, of the body, and of the spirit, suffering from "Newton's disease," "Henry Ford's disease," "Jesus' disease," and so on—various forms of imbalance in which one human faculty is emphasized at the expense of the others.

Point Counter Point presents an extremely divided world. None of the numerous marriages, except that of the Rampions, turns out well, nor do the extramarital relationships. Both Lilian Quarles and her brother, Walter Bidlake, have problems with their spouses. Lilian plans to leave her husband, Philip Quarles, and go to Everard Webley, a political leader, who has been courting her, but the plan is terminated with Webley's murder. After leaving his wife, Walter lives with Marjorie Carling but finds her dull and unexciting within two years. Ignoring Marjorie, who is pregnant with his child, Walter begins to court Lucy Tantamount, a professional siren, who, after keeping him for a long time in a state of uncertainty, turns him away. John Bidlake, the father of Lilian and Walter, has been married three times and has had a number of love affairs. Sidney Quarles, the father of Philip, has had many secret affairs. Disharmony thus marks the marital world presented in the novel, effectively dramatized by means of parallel, contrapuntal plots.

Mark and Mary Rampion serve as a counterpoint to the gallery of barbarians and lopsided characters in the novel. Although Mary comes from an aristocratic family and Mark belongs to the working class, they do not suffer from the usual class prejudices. Transcending their origins, they have also transcended the common run of egocentric and self-divided personalities. They have achieved wholeness and integrity in personality and outlook. There is no dichotomy between what they say and what they do. Mark's art is a product of lived experience, and his concern for it is inseparable from his concern for life.

Though the dominant mood of Huxley's early novels is one of negativism and despair, the Rampions exemplify his faith in the possibility of achieving individual wholeness and loving human relationships. The Rampions may not be able to change the state of affairs in the modern world, but their presence itself is inspiring; what is more, they are, unlike Calamy of *Those Barren Leaves*, easily accessible to all those who want to meet them.

Brave New World, Huxley's best-known work, describes a centrally administered and scientifically controlled future society in A. F. 632 (A. F. standing for After Ford), around six hundred years from the present century. It is difficult to recognize the people of Huxley's future World State as human beings. Decanted from test tubes in laboratories, the population of the Brave New World comes in five standardized varieties: Alphas, Betas, Gammas, Deltas, and Epsilons. Each group is genetically conditioned to carry out different tasks. By various methods of psychological conditioning, they are trained to live in total identification with society and to shun all activities that threaten the stability of the community. The State takes full care of them, including the emotional side of their life. All their desires are satisfied; they do not want what they cannot get. With substitutes and surrogates such as the Pregnancy Substitute and the Violent Passion Surrogate, life is made happy and comfortable for everyone. Although people have nothing of which to complain, they seem to suffer pain continually. Relief from pain is, however, readily available to them in *soma*, which is distributed by the State every day.

Sentiments, ideas, and practices which liberate the human spirit find no place in Huxley's scientific utopia and are, in fact, put down as harmful to the stability of the community. Parentage, family, and home become obsolete; sex is denuded of all its mystery and significance. Small children are encouraged to indulge in erotic play so that they learn to take a strictly matter-of-fact view of sex. Men and women indulge in copulation to fill idle hours. Loyalty in sex and love is regarded as abnormal behavior. Love of nature, solitude, and meditation are looked upon as serious maladies requiring urgent medical attention. Art, science, and religion are all considered threatening. Patience, courage, self-denial, beauty, nobility, and truth become irrelevant to a society that believes in consumerism, comfort, and happiness.

Huxley shows how some people in the Brave New World, despite every care taken by the State to ensure their place in the social order, do not fall in line. Bernard Marx yearns for Lenina Crowne and wants to take her on long walks in lonely places. Helmholtz Watson's creative impulses demand poetic expression. Even Mustapha Mond, the Resident Controller of Western Europe, is somewhat regretful over his abandonment of scientific research in favor of his present position. People who stubbornly refuse to conform to the social order are removed promptly by the State to an island where they can live freely according to their wishes.

It is through the character of John, the Savage, from the Reservation, that Huxley clearly exposes the vulgarity and horror of the Brave New World. Attracted to civilization on seeing Lenina, the Savage soon comes to recoil from it. In his long conversation with Mustapha Mond, he expresses his preference for the natural world of disease, unhappiness, and death over the mechanical world of swarming indistinguishable sameness. Unable to get out of it, he retires to a lonely place where he undertakes his purification by taking mustard and warm water, doing hard labor, and resorting to self-flagellation.

In *Brave New World*, Huxley presents a world in which wholeness becomes an object of a hopeless quest. Looking back at the novel, he observed that this was the most serious defect of the story. In a Foreword written in 1946, he said that if he were to rewrite the book, he would offer the Savage a third alternative: Between the utopian and the primitive horns of his dilemma would lie the possibility of sanity—a possibility already actualized, to some extent, in a community of exiles and refugees from the Brave New World, living within the borders of the Reservation.

In *Eyeless in Gaza*, Huxley returns to the subject of egocentric modern man deeply buried in intellectual preoccupations, sensuality, ideology, and fanaticism. Sensualists abound in *Eyeless in Gaza*. The most notorious among them are Mrs. Mary Amberley and her daughter, Helen Ledwidge, both mistresses at different times to Anthony Beavis, the central character in the novel. Believing in "sharp, short, and exciting" affairs, Mary keeps changing her lovers until she gets prematurely old, spent, and poor. When nobody wants to have her any more, she takes to morphine to forget her misery. Helen marries Hugh Ledwidge but soon realizes that he is incapable of taking an interest in anything except his books. To compensate for her unhappy married life, she goes from man to man in search of emotional satisfaction. Indeed, sensuality marks the lives of most of the members of the upper-class society presented in the novel.

In addition to sensualists, various other types of single-minded characters share the world of *Eyeless in Gaza*. Brian, one of Anthony's classmates and friends, suffers from a maniacal concern for chastity, and his mother shows a great possessiveness toward him. Mark, another of Anthony's classmates, becomes a cynical revolutionary. John Beavis, Anthony's father, makes philology the sole interest of his life. There are also Communists, Fascists, Fabians, and other fanatics, all fighting for their different causes.

Anthony Beavis is estranged early in his life from men and society after the death of his mother. He grows into manhood cold and indifferent to people. He finds it a disagreeable and laborious task to establish contacts; even with his own father, he maintains a distance. He does not give himself away to his friends or to the women he loves. *Elements of Sociology*, a book Beavis is engaged in writing, assumes the highest priority in his life, and he is careful to avoid the "non-job," personal relations and emotional entanglements, which might interfere with his work's progress. As he matures, however, Beavis aspires to achieve a sense of completeness above the self: "I value completeness. I think it's one's duty to develop all one's potentialities— *all* of them." At this stage, he believes in knowledge, acquired by means of intellect rather than by Laurentian intuition. He is interested only in knowning about truth, not experiencing it like a saint: "I'm quite content with only *knowing* about the way of perfection." He thinks that experience is not worth the price, for it costs one one's liberty. Gradually, he realizes that knowledge is a means to an end, rather than an end in itself, a means to achieve freedom from the self. After being so enlightened, he feels genuine love for Helen, who remains unmoved, however, because of her past experiences with him. From Dr. Miller, the anthropologist, Beavis learns how to obliterate the self and achieve wholeness through love and selfless service. He has a mystic experience of the unity of all life and becomes a pacifist to serve mankind.

In *After Many a Summer Dies the Swan*, his first novel after his move to California, Huxley satirized the frenzied attempts made by men of the twentieth century to enrich their lives, stressing that the peace that comes with transcendence can bring an enduring joy. Huxley illustrates the vacuity of modern life through the character of Mr. Stoyte, an old California oil magnate living amid every conceivable luxury and comfort. With endless opportunities before him to make more money and enjoy life (he keeps a young mistress of twenty-two), Stoyte wants to live as long as he can. He finances Dr. Obispo's research on longevity in the hope that he will be able to benefit from the results of Dr. Obispo's experiments. He acquires the valuable Haubert Papers, relating to the history of an old English family, in order to discover the secret of the long life of the Fifth Earl, and he hires Jeremy Pordage, an English scholar, to arrange the papers. Dr. Obispo and his assistant, Pete, are basically no different from Mr. Stoyte in their outlooks. They believe that they will be rendering a great service to humanity by extending man's life, little realizing that growing up, as they conceive it, is really growing back into the kind of apelike existence represented by the life of the Fifth Earl. Jeremy Pordage has no real interest in anything except literature, and he too betrays a narrowness of outlook.

Propter exemplifies Huxley's dedicated search for more-than-personal consciousness. Retired from his university job, he spends his time helping poor migrant workers, trying to find ways of being self-reliant, and thinking about the timeless good. He argues that nothing good can be achieved at the human level, that is the level of "time and craving," the two aspects of evil. He disapproves most of what goes on in the name of patriotism, idealism, and spiritualism because he thinks that they are marks of man's greed and covetousness. One should, in his view, aim at the highest ideal: the liberation from personality, time, and craving into eternity.

Bruno Rontini, the mystic saint in *Time Must Have a Stop*, observes that only one out of every ten thousand herrings manages to break out of his carapace completely, and few of those which break out become full-sized fish. He adds that the odds against a man's spiritual maturation today are even greater. Most people remain, according to him, spiritual children.

Time Must Have a Stop presents the obstacles that Sebastian Barnack has to face before he can reach full spiritual maturation. If egocentricity and single-mindedness were the main hurdles for Philip Quarles and Anthony Beavis, Sebastian's problems are created by his weak personality, shaped by his puritanical and idealistic father. He possesses fine poetic and intellectual endowments, but he is disappointed with his own immature appearance. Even though he is aware of his superior gifts, he looks "like a child" at seventeen. Naturally, his relatives and friends take an adoptive attitude toward him and try to influence him in different ways. Eustace, his rich and self-indulgent uncle, teaches him how to live and let live and enjoy life. Mrs. Thwale helps him to overcome his shyness in a most outrageous manner. There are many others who try to mold Sebastian's destiny and prevent him from true self-realization.

Huxley offers further insights into Propter's mystical faith through the character of Bruno Rontini, under whose guidance Sebastian finally receives enlightenment. Bruno believes that there is only one corner of the universe that one can be certain of improving, and that is one's own self. He says that a man has to begin there, not outside, not on other people, for a man has to *be* good before he can *do* good. Bruno believes that only by taking the fact of eternity into account can one free one's enslaved thoughts: "And it is only by deliberately paying our attention and our primary allegiance to eternity that we can prevent time from turning our lives into a pointless or diabolic foolery." Under the guidance of Bruno, Sebastian becomes aware of a timeless and infinite presence. After his spiritual liberation, he begins to work for world peace. He thinks that one of the indispensable conditions for peace is "a shared theology." He evolves a "Minimum Working Hypothesis," to which all men of all countries and religions can subscribe.

Huxley's increasing faith in the possibility of man's liberation in this world did not, at any time, blind him to man's immense capacity for evil. *Ape and Essence* describes how man's apelike instincts bring about the destruction of the world through a nuclear World War III. New Zealand escapes the holocaust, and in A.D. 2108, about one hundred years after the war, the country's Re-Discovery Expedition to North America reaches the coast of Southern California, at a place about twenty miles west of Los Angeles, where Dr. Poole, the Chief Botanist of the party, is taken prisoner by descendants of people who survived the war. Though some Californians have survived the war, the effects of radioactivity still show in the birth of deformed babies, who are liquidated one day of the year in the name of the Purification of the Race. Men and women are allowed free sexual intercourse only two weeks a year following the Purification ceremony so that all the deformed babies that are born in the year are taken care of at one time. Women wear shirts and trousers embroidered with the word "no" on their breasts and seats, and people who indulge in sex during any other part of the year, "Hots" as they are called, are buried alive or castrated and forced to join the priesthood, unless they are able to escape into the community of "Hots" in the north. The California survivors dig up graves to relieve the dead bodies of their clothes and other valuable items, roast bread over fires fueled by books from the Public Library, and worship Belial.

Introducing the filmscript of *Ape and Essence*, Huxley suggested that present society, even under normal conditions, is not basically different from the society of the survivors depicted in the novel. Gandhi's assassination, he says, had very little impact on most people, who remained preoccupied with their own petty personal problems. Under normal conditions, this unspiritual society would grow into the kind of society represented by Dr. Poole and his team. Dr. Poole is portrayed as a middle-aged child, full of inhibitions and suppressed desires, suffering under the dominance of his puritanical mother.

Ironically, Dr. Poole experiences a sense of wholeness in the satanic post-atomic world, as he sheds his inhibitions and finds a free outlet for his suppressed desires during the sexual orgies following the Purification ceremony. Declining the invitation of the Arch Vicar to join his order, Dr. Poole escapes with Loola, the girl who has effected his awakening, into the land of the "Hots." Through the episode of Dr. Poole, Huxley suggests that self-transcendence is possible even in the worst of times.

The Genius and the Goddess describes how Rivers, brought up like Dr. Poole of *Apes and Essence* in a puritanical family, undergoes a series of disturbing experiences in the household of Henry and Katy Maartens, which apparently lead him into a spiritual awakening in the end. Rivers joins the Maartens household to assist Henry, the "genius," in his scientific research. He is shocked when Katy, the "goddess," climbs into his bed and shocked again when he sees Katy, rejuvenated by her adultery, performing her wifely devotions with all earnestness, as if nothing had happened. To his further bewilderment and shock, he discovers that he is sought by the daughter as well. The mother outwits the daughter, but Katy and Rivers face the danger of being exposed before Henry. Rivers is, however, saved from disgrace when the mother and daughter both are killed in a car accident. Rivers is an old man as he narrates the story of his progress toward awareness. Though his final awakening is not described, one can safely infer from his attitude toward his past experiences that he has risen above Katy's passion and Henry's intellect to a level outside and above time and has achieved a sense of wholeness. There is, indeed, no way of telling how grace comes.

As previously noted, Huxley creates in almost every novel an island of decency to illustrate the possibility of achieving liberation from bondàge to the ego and to time even amid the chaos of modern life. This island is generally represented by an individual or a group of individuals, or it is simply stated to be located in some remote corner of the world. In his last novel, *Island*, Huxley offers a picture of a whole society which has evolved a set of operations, such as yoga, *dhyana* (meditation), *maithuna* (yoga of love), and Zen to achieve self-transcendence and realize the Vedantic truth, *tat tvam asi*, "thou art That."

In Huxley's island of Pala, the chief concern underlying child care, education, religion, and government is to ensure among its citizens a harmonious development of all human faculties and an achievement of a sense of completeness. To save their children from crippling influences, the parents of Pala bring up one another's children on a basis of mutual exchange. In school, children are taught the important aspects of life from biology to ecology, from sex to religion. They are taken to maternity hospitals so that they can see how children are born; they are even shown how people die. No one subject or area is given exclusive importance. The credo is that "nothing short of everything will really do." When they come of age, boys and girls freely engage in sex. Suppressed feelings and emotions are given an outlet in a vigorous type of dance. An admixture of Hinduism and Buddhism is the religion of the people, but there is no orthodoxy about it. "Karuna" or compassion and an attention to "here and now," to what is happening at any given moment, are the basic tenets of their way of life. Moksha medicines are freely available to those who want to extend their awareness and get a glimpse of the Clear Light and a knowlege of the Divine Ground. As people know how to live gracefully, they also know how to die gracefully when the time for death comes. The country has followed a benevolent monarchy for one hundred years. The nation is aligned neither with the capitalist countries nor with the Communists. It is opposed to industrialization and militarization. It has rich oil resources but has refused to grant licenses to the numerous oil companies which are vying to exploit Pala. Will Farnaby, the journalist who has managed to sneak ashore the forbidden island, is so greatly impressed by the imaginative and creative Palanese way of life that he abandons the mission for which he went to the island, which was to obtain, by any means possible, a license for the South East-Asia Petroleum Company to drill for oil on the island.

Huxley fully recognizes the extreme vulnerability of the ideal of integrity and wholeness in the modern world. The state of Pala has, for example, incurred the displeasure of both the capitalist and Communist countries by its policy of nonalignment. Many big companies are resorting to bribery in an effort to get a foothold on the island. Colonel Dipa, the military dictator of the neighboring state of Randang-Lobo, has expansionist ambitions. While Pala is thus threatened by the outside world, corruption has also set in from within. Dowager Rani and Murugan, her son, disapprove of the isolationist policies of the island and want their country to march along with the rest of the world. On the day Murugan is sworn king, he invites the army from Randang-Lobo to enter the island and massacre the people who have been opposed to his progressive outlook.

Huxley's novels not only present the horrors of the modern world, but they also show ways of achieving spiritual liberation and wholeness. Huxley is among the few writers of the twentieth century who have fought a brave and relentless battle against life-destroying forces. Untiringly, he sought ways of enriching life by cleansing the doors of perception, awakening his readers to the vital spiritual side of their beings.

S. Krishnamoorthy Aithal

Other major works

SHORT FICTION: *Limbo*, 1920; *Mortal Coils*, 1922; *The Little Mexican and Other Stories*, 1924; *Two or Three Graces*, 1926; *Brief Candles*, 1930; *The Gioconda Smile*, 1938.

PLAYS: *The Discovery*, 1924; *The World of Light*, 1931; *The Gioconda Smile*, 1948.

POETRY: *The Burning Wheel*, 1916; *Jonah*, 1917; *The Defeat of Youth*, 1918; *Leda*, 1920; *Arabia Infelix*, 1929; *The Cicadas and Other Poems*, 1931.

NONFICTION: *On the Margin*, 1923; *Along the Road*, 1925; *Jesting Pilate*, 1926; *Essays New and Old*, 1926; *Proper Studies*, 1927; *Do What You Will*, 1929; *Holy Face and Other Essays*, 1929; *Vulgarity in Literature*, 1930; *Music at Night*, 1931; *Texts and Pretexts*, 1932; *Beyond the Mexique Bay*, 1934; *The Olive Tree*, 1936; *Ends and Means*, 1937; *Grey Eminence*, 1941; *The Art of Seeing*, 1942; *The Perennial Philosophy*, 1945; *Themes and Variations*, 1950; *The Devils of Loudun*, 1952; *The Doors of Perception*, 1954; *Heaven and Hell*, 1956; *Tomorrow and Tomorrow and Tomorrow*, 1956; *Adonis and the Alphabet, and Other Essays*, 1956; *Brave New World Revisited*, 1958; *Collected Essays*, 1959; *Literature and Science*, 1963.

Bibliography

Baker, Robert S. *The Dark Historic Page: Social Satire and Historicism in the Novels of Aldous Huxley, 1921-1939*. Madison: University of Wisconsin Press, 1982. Devotes separate chapters to close readings of Huxley's novels, which are analyzed in terms of the protagonist's conflict with the prevailing secular society. Claims that Huxley is concerned with dystopian dilemmas and the price to be paid for the protagonist's losing struggle against change and society. Includes an excellent bibliography.

Bowering, Peter. *Aldous Huxley: A Study of the Major Novels*. New York: Oxford University Press, 1969. Treats Huxley as a novelist of ideas and attempts to treat the fiction and nonfiction as a whole. Each of his nine novels is analyzed in a separate chapter, and in a concluding chapter the complex relationship between the novelist and the artist is discussed. Well indexed.

Firchlow, Peter. *Aldous Huxley: Satirist and Novelist*. Minneapolis: University of Minnesota Press, 1972. Although the focus is on Huxley's novels, especially *Point Counter Point* and *Brave New World*, the book does provide a biographical chapter and one on his poetry, which is ignored by most writers. One of the highlights of the book is the parallel established between Huxley's *Island* and Jonathan Swift's book 4 of *Gulliver's Travels*.

Henderson, Alexander. *Aldous Huxley*. New York: Russell & Russell, 1936. Quite helpful because of the material covered: a biography and a "psychological portrait" of Huxley, analysis of his early novels, a discussion of his literary criticism, travel books, and poetry, and a bibliography. Henderson's approach is informal and his style quite readable, and his views are important as a contemporary of Huxley.

May, Keith M. *Aldous Huxley*. New York: Barnes & Noble Books, 1972. Addresses the problem of how "novelistic" Huxley's novels are and concludes that it is language rather than structure that determines the meaning of each of his novels. The eleven novels, each of which is analyzed in a separate chapter, are divided into two chronological groups: novels of exploration and novels of certainty, with the dividing line coming between *Eyeless in Gaza* (1936) and *After Many a Summer Dies the Swan* (1939). Also contains a helpful bibliography.

Nance, Guinevera A. *Aldous Huxley*. New York: Continuum, 1988. Nance's introductory biographical chapter ("The Life Theoretic") reflects her emphasis on Huxley's novels of ideas. The novels, which are discussed at length, are divided into three chronological groups, with the utopian novels coming in the second group. Supplies a detailed chronology and a fairly extensive bibliography.

Watt, Donald, ed. *Aldous Huxley: The Critical Heritage*. London: Routledge & Kegan Paul, 1975. An invaluable chronological collection of book reviews and other short essays on Huxley's work and life. Among the literary contributors are Evelyn Waugh, E. M. Forster, William Inge, Stephen Spender, George Orwell, Thomas Wolfe, Ernest Hemingway, T. S. Eliot, and André Gide. The introduction traces the critical response to Huxley. Includes an extensive bibliography as well as information about translations and book sales.

JOHN IRVING

Born: Exeter, New Hampshire; March 2, 1942

Principal long fiction

Setting Free the Bears, 1969; *The Water-Method Man*, 1972; *The 158-Pound Marriage*, 1974; *The World According to Garp*, 1978; *The Hotel New Hampshire*, 1981; *The Cider House Rules*, 1985; *A Prayer for Owen Meany*, 1989.

Other literary forms

Unlike many contemporary fiction writers, John Irving has published very few short stories, and several of these were later incorporated into his novels. The exceptions include "Lost in New York" and "Almost in Iowa," both published in *Esquire* in 1973; "Brennbar's Rant," published in *Playboy* in 1974; and "Interior Space," written in 1974 and published in *Fiction* in 1980.

Achievements

When *The World According to Garp* became a best-seller in 1978, prompting the reissue of his three previous novels, Irving captured the attention of literary critics as well as of the popular audience. His life and works were profiled in *Time*, *Saturday Review*, and *Rolling Stone*, and his novels entered what he calls in *The World According to Garp*, "that uncanny half-light where 'serious' books glow, for a time, as also 'popular' books." Various aspects of Irving's work appeal to different audiences, making him difficult to classify as either "serious" or "popular." The sometimes ribald, occasionally grotesque humor and the explicit sexuality of the novels give them a sensational appeal, and have made Irving—and his novelist character T. S. Garp—cult heroes for the American public. On the other hand, Irving's representation of random violence in the modern world, his emphasis on love and family responsibilities, and his use of writers as major characters have prompted serious examination of his work among academic critics. *The Hotel New Hampshire* delighted Irving fans with its continuation of established motifs and themes—bears, wrestling, Vienna, children—but critics and reviewers took a cautious approach to the novel, not certain whether to place Irving in the first rank of contemporary novelists or to chide him for reiterating his themes and allowing the trivial and the clichéd to coexist with the profound. Irving's work is of uneven quality: *Setting Free the Bears*, his first novel, is in some sections overwritten and self-indulgent, and his third novel, *The 158-Pound Marriage*, is limited in scope. He has, however, proven himself a figure to be reckoned with in contemporary American fiction, in part because of his confrontation with issues that occupy the public attention. *The Cider House*

Rules deals in large part with the issue of abortion, and Irving avoids the polemic of the current debate by setting the novel in the first half of the twentieth century. *A Prayer for Owen Meany* is set against the backdrop of the Vietnam War and has a strong antiwar bias. The novel makes fresh the literary cliché of the hero as Christ figure by choosing in Owen Meany a character who seems superficially ill-suited for such heroism. The blend of contemporary issues, bizarre yet believable characters, and an old-fashioned devotion to good storytelling distinguishes Irving's novels.

Biography

John Winslow Irving was born on March 2, 1942, in Exeter, New Hampshire, to F. N. and Frances Winslow Irving. His father taught Russian history at Exeter Academy, where Irving attended prep school. At Exeter, he developed two lifelong interests, writing and wrestling, and became convinced that both required the same skills: practice and determination. Though not an outstanding student, he developed an appreciation of hard, steady work and a love of literature. Of his early apprenticeships Irving remarked in a *Rolling Stone* interview, "I was a very dull kid. But I really learned how to wrestle and I really learned how to write. I didn't have an idea in my head." After being graduated from Exeter at the age of nineteen, Irving spent a year at the University of Pittsburgh, where the wrestling competition convinced him that writing was a better career choice.

In 1962, Irving enrolled at the University of New Hampshire, where he began to work with authors Thomas Williams and John Yount, but a desire to see more of the world caused him to drop out. After an intensive summer course in German at Harvard University, he left for Vienna, where he enrolled at the Institute of European Studies. During his two years in Vienna, Irving married Shyla Leary, a painter whom he had met at Harvard, studied German, and became seriously devoted to writing. Living in an unfamiliar place sharpened his powers of observation; as he said in a 1981 *Time* interview, "you are made to notice even the trivial things—especially the trivial things." He returned to the University of New Hampshire, worked again with Thomas Williams, and was graduated cum laude in 1965. From there, with his wife and son, Colin, Irving went to the University of Iowa Writers' Workshop, where he earned an M.F.A. degree in creative writing in 1967. During his time at Iowa, Irving continued wrestling with Dan Gable, the Iowa coach who won a medal at the 1976 Munich Olympics. Encouraged by writer-in-residence Kurt Vonnegut, he also completed his first published novel, *Setting Free the Bears*, which is set in Austria.

Setting Free the Bears was well received by critics and sold well (6,228 copies) for a first novel. A projected film of the book did not materialize, and Irving moved his family back to New England. After a brief period of teaching at Windham College, he taught at Mount Holyoke College until 1972, and for 1971 to 1972 was awarded a Rockefeller Foundation grant. *The Water-Method Man*, published in 1972, did not sell as well as *Setting Free the Bears*, but Irving was invited to be a writer-in-residence at the University of Iowa from 1972 to 1975, and for 1974 to 1975 he received a fellowship from the National Endowment for the Arts. During that time, Irving published his third novel, *The 158-Pound Marriage*, which was set in Iowa City. Sales of *The 158-Pound Marriage*, which Irving considers his weakest novel, were poor, and Irving returned to New England to begin a second period of teaching at Mount Holyoke.

The turning point in Irving's career came in 1978, with the publication of *The World According to Garp*. Discouraged by the seeming reluctance of Random House to promote his novels, he moved to E. P. Dutton and the guidance of Henry Robbins, its editor-in-chief. Although Dutton promoted the novel in ways that normally disenchant the serious reviewer (bumper stickers, T-shirts), the critical reaction was good and the public reception overwhelming; combined hardback and paperback sales reached three million in the first two years. In 1982, *The World According to Garp* was made into a film, with Irving playing a bit part as a wrestling referee. The success of the novel allowed Irving to devote more of his time to writing, and in 1981 Dutton published his fifth novel, *The Hotel New Hampshire*. Although some critics expressed disappointment in the novel, it was a best seller and a Book-of-the-Month Club selection. The author of *The World According to Garp* had become a household word.

Irving's two later novels of the 1980's—*The Cider House Rules* and *A Prayer for Owen Meany*—were also best-sellers and book-club selections. Yet despite the popularity of his work, he is increasingly the subject of scholarly study; articles about and reviews of his work have been published in journals as diverse as *Novel, The Sewanee Review*, and the *Journal of the American Medical Association*.

Analysis

John Irving's fiction is distinguished by a highly personal fusion of seemingly incongruous elements. Irving's settings, actions, and characters are often bizarre and violent. The world he presents is frequently chaotic and unpredictable, full of sudden death and apparently meaningless collisions of people, values, ideologies, and objects. Among his characters are the Ellen Jamesians (*The World According to Garp*), who cut out their tongues to protest the rape and mutilation of a little girl; a blind bear-trainer named Freud (*The Hotel New Hampshire*); and a motorcyclist who locks a zoo attendant in a cage with an anteater (*Setting Free the Bears*). Characters die in excruciating ways: stung to death by thousands of bees, killed in airplane crashes, assassinated in parking lots. Irving himself has referred to *The World According to Garp* as "an X-rated soap opera." Balancing the sensational and pessimistic elements of the novels, however, is a core of humane values. Irving does not posit a violent and arbitrary world, but rather one in which violence and havoc are present in sufficient quantities to demand constant vigilance. His characters may behave strangely, but their motives are usually pure. Infidelity exists, but so does real love; children deserve protection; human kindness is paramount. Despite his characterization of *The World According to Garp* as "X-rated," Irving denies that it presents an unbelievable world: "People who think *Garp* is wildly eccentric and very bizarre are misled about the real world. I can't imagine where they've been living or what they read for news."

Irving is essentially a storyteller and often uses an omniscient narrator who feels free to interrupt the narrative. In *Setting Free the Bears*, he uses elements of the tall tale and the fairy tale, and all of his novels are characterized by broad situational comedy rather than wit. At the same time, especially in *Setting Free the Bears* and *The World According to Garp*, he writes self-conscious fiction which reflects on its own making. As Michael Priestly has commented, "Irving resembles both the Victorian novelist ('dear reader') and the 'new novelist' who writes fiction about fiction." Many issues with which his novels deal are quite contemporary: feminism, sex-change operations, political assassination. Of equal importance, however, are romantic impulses such as freeing the animals in a zoo, rescuing the afflicted, and guarding one's loved ones against harm. The tension between tradition and novelty, reverence and blasphemy, contributes to the singularity of Irving's work.

A group of common motifs and images give Irving's novels coherence as a body of work. Wrestling is the dominant sport, and is the avocation of a number of characters. Bears are set free, as indicated by the title of his first novel, to reappear in a number of guises in later books. At least one character in each novel is a writer—most notably T. S. Garp in *The World According to Garp*. There are always children to be guarded from serious injury, though not always successfully. Vienna is a frequent locale for Irving's fiction, as are Iowa and New Hampshire. These characters and motifs suggest a strong autobiographical current in Irving's fiction, and although the ingredients of his own life are transmuted by his imagination, his novels provide a rough outline of his progress from student in Vienna to graduate student in Iowa to successful novelist. Wary of readers believing that his novels are generally autobiographical, Irving has said that "people with limited imaginations find it hard to imagine that anyone else has an imagination. Therefore, they must think that everything they read in some way *happened*."

The enormous reality of Irving's characters, more than their possible identification with the author, is the central interest for his novels. Even his most bizarre characters are not caricatures; rather, they are believable people with extraordinary characteristics. Jenny Fields, Garp's mother, sets out to be impregnated by a terminally ill patient so that she will have to endure no further sexual contact, yet her action is presented as practical rather than perverse. Lilly, the youngest Berry child in *The Hotel New Hampshire*, never reaches four feet in height, but her family—and the reader—regards her not as a freak, but merely as small. Irving illustrates the diversity in the human family by presenting some of its most extreme members in his fiction, but instead of creating a circus, he urges tolerance. Violence is given the same matter-of-fact approach as are other extremes in Irving's fiction. It is present, if unwelcome, merely because it exists as a part of life. Irving is never sentimental or dramatic about motorcycle accidents, terrorists' bombs, bees which kill, or gearshifts which blind children; these are the risks of living.

The humor in Irving's novels serves both to make the bizarre and violent elements more acceptable and to reinforce the duality of his vision. No contemporary novelist better exemplifies Dorothy Parker's requisites for humor: "a disciplined eye and a wild mind." Early in his career, Irving relied heavily on slapstick comedy, such as the adventures of Siggy Javotnik in the Heitzinger Zoo in *Setting Free the Bears* and Bogus Trumper's duck hunt in *The Water-Method Man*. Increasingly, he has turned to irony and wit as major devices of humor, but all the novels have a strong element of fantasy; dreams or nightmares become reality. Comedy and tragedy are woven closely together. Irving, always sensitive to public opinion, built into *The World According to Garp* a defense against those who would accuse him of treating serious subjects too lightly. Mrs. Poole, of Findlay, Ohio, writes to T. S. Garp to accuse him of finding other people's problems funny; Garp replies that he has "nothing but sympathy for how people behave—and nothing but laughter to console them with." By insisting that life is both comically absurd and inevitably tragic, Irving espouses an acceptance of extremes. He has been described by Hugh Ruppersburg as a "stoic pessimist," a label which at this point seems appropriate, but his major contribution to the American novel is the product of imagination rather than philosophy: the creation of truly memorable people and situations which extend the reader's understanding of human existence. In the words of T. S. Garp, "a writer's job is to imagine everything so personally that the fiction is as vivid as our personal memories." At this job, Irving has succeeded admirably.

Unlike many first novels, *Setting Free the Bears* is not an autobiographical account of the author's early years. Although it is set in Austria and draws on Irving's experience there as a student, the novel is an exuberant and imaginative account of the adventures of Hannes Graff, the narrator, and his friend Siggy Javotnik as they ride a motorcycle through Austria. The middle section of the novel consists of alternating chapters of two documents written by Siggy: "The Zoo-Watch," an account of Siggy's vigil at the Heitzinger Zoo, and "The Highly Selective Autobiography of Siegfried Javotnik," which documents his family's history from the mid-1930's to the early 1960's. Siggy, who lives in the past—"I rely on pre-history for any sense and influence"—

has only one dream for the future: to free the animals from the Heitzinger Zoo. After Siggy's death from multiple bee stings, Graff accomplishes Siggy's dream and, after the ensuing chaos, rides off on his motorcycle. The novel is a youthful fantasy, full of grand adventures and characters of mythic stature: the characters have no futures and only a tenuous relationship with the present.

The basic topic of the novel is freedom. Part of Siggy's "pre-history" deals with the liberation of Austria from the Germans during World War II. In 1967, the year the frame narrative takes place, Graff frees the fairy-tale princess Gallen from her aunt's house and takes her to Vienna. Finally, Graff frees the animals from the zoo and what Siggy has assumed is their torture by the night guard, O. Schrutt. At the end of the novel, the Rare Spectacled Bears are loping across an open field to take up life in the woods, but if they survive, they will be the only ones who are free. Siggy, like the rest of his family, is dead. Gallen has sold her lovely reddish hair for money to live on while she waits for Graff to return to Vienna, and Graff is rootless and aimless on his motorcycle. In his attempt to create the perfect world denied by his ancestors by war, Siggy has become impossibly idealistic, and Graff has succumbed to his idealism, a fact he realizes at the end of the novel: "What worse awareness is there than to know there would have been a better outcome if you'd never done anything at all?" The suggestion is that freedom is best achieved by letting life run its natural course without human interference.

The nature of the novelist, however, is to interfere—that is, to impose an order on life by structuring it into novelistic form. *Setting Free the Bears* is a novel about writing. Late in his autobiography, Siggy reveals that it is more fiction than fact. Graff becomes, in a sense, Siggy's literary executor; as Graff reveals in the "P.S." at the beginning of part three, it has been his editorial decision to interleave sections of the autobiography with sections of the zoo-watch notebook. As the naïve editor-narrator, Graff does not comprehend the relationship between the two documents, though the parallels between the two types of imprisonment—war and the zoo—are apparent to the reader. Graff's attempts to impose order on Siggy's life are far more successful than Siggy's own attempts, but ultimately all that Siggy has written may be fiction— it is, of course, fiction in one sense—so Graff is left trying to order a phantom existence.

In keeping with Irving's insistence on the elusive nature of reality, the novel has a dreamlike quality. Many of the characters live fantasy lives. Graff dreams of the lovely Gallen; Siggy dreams of freeing the animals from O. Schrutt. Within Siggy's autobiography, a chicken-farmer dressed in feather-covered pie plates imagines he looks like an eagle, representing Austria's independence. Elements of fantasy, which here dominate the novel, are characteristic of Irving's later novels as well, though the line between fantasy and reality is more sharply drawn in his later work. *Setting Free the Bears* is further removed from traditional realistic fiction than any of Irving's other novels. Like "The Pension Grillparzer," T. S. Garp's first piece of fiction in *The World According to Garp*, it is a story told for the sake of telling a story. In an interview with Greil Marcus of *Rolling Stone*, Irving said, "I had no idea who the people in *Setting Free the Bears* were, or how they were going to get from A to Z." The careful plot structure of the novel suggests that at some point Irving envisioned the whole quite clearly, but the imaginative power evidenced here continued to be an important element in his fiction.

Deserving of more attention than has yet been given it, *The Water-Method Man* is Irving's most consistently comic novel. "I wanted," Irving has said, "to write a book that was absolutely comic: I wanted it to be intricate and funny and clever and I wanted it to go on and on and on." Fred "Bogus" Trumper, also known to various friends as "Bogge" and "Thump-Thump," is the narrator and main character of the novel, which is an account of his misadventures in Iowa, Austria, New York, and Maine. Bogus Trumper is a charming failure searching for meaning and order in his life. He has tried marriage to a skiing champion appropriately nicknamed "Biggie," fatherhood, a Ph.D. program in comparative literature, and filmmaking. In desperation one night, he begins to write a diary, which becomes the first-person portions of the novel. As he had in *Setting Free the Bears*, Irving alternates sections of two different pieces of writing, but in *The Water-Method Man* this device is simpler; the first-person autobiographical chapters tell of Trumper's past; the third-person narrative sections tell of his present.

The somewhat improbable metaphor for Bogus' wayward life is his penis. For years he has had problems with painful urination and orgasm; a urologist discovers that his urinary tract is "a narrow, winding road." Rejecting the alternative of surgery, Trumper chooses the "water method," which consists of flushing his system with large amounts of water. This treatment alleviates his problem rather than curing it and represents all the other unfinished business in his life. Also serving as an analogue to Trumper's life is the subject of his doctoral thesis, an Old Low Norse saga, *Akthelt and Gunnel*, which he is translating—or rather pretending to translate. His actual translation has stopped at the point where he realized the impending doom of the characters; after that, he began to invent a lusty saga with parallels to his own life. When Trumper finally achieves order and peace in his life, Irving signals the change with Trumper's corrective surgery and his completion of a faithful translation of *Akthelt and Gunnel*. He is able to come to terms with the people and events around him.

Any serious message in *The Water-Method Man*, however, is incidental to the comic dimensions of the novel. Much of the humor is ribald, though Irving's skill enables him to avoid obscenity. Several of the most memorable sequences involve equally memorable minor characters, such as Merrill Overturf, Trumper's diabetic friend who drowns while trying to find a Nazi tank he insists was sunk in the Danube, and Dante Calicchio, the New York limousine driver who takes Trumper to Maine. Though briefly sketched, these characters demonstrate Irving's ability to make the incidental character or situation come alive. The almost complete absence of violent or grotesque incidents makes *The Water-Method Man* unique in Irving's canon. Scenes such as the one in which Bogus Trumper skis into an Alpine parking lot, which in Irving's other novels would have some shocking, tragic outcome, are here handled as they are in comic strips: everyone walks away unscathed. The closest approach to serious emotional involvement comes in the scenes between Trumper and his young son, Colm. The pressured responsibilities of parenthood become a major topic in Irving's later novels, as does the relationship between life and art, here represented by Bogus Trumper's attempt to find order in writing translations (both real and fake), autobiographies, letters, and making films. The fact that Trumper is ultimately at peace with himself makes *The Water-Method Man* one of Irving's most optimistic novels.

In contrast to the boisterous comedy of *The Water-Method Man*, Irving's third novel is painfully serious. *The 158-Pound Marriage* is Irving's shortest novel to date and also the most conventional in both form and subject matter. It is the story of two couples who swap partners regularly for a period of time, an experiment which sours all the relationships involved. Irving has said that the book is about "lust and rationalization and restlessness," and it mirrors the moral floundering of the early 1970's in which it is set. Severin and Edith Winter mistakenly conceive the exchange as a means of saving their own marriage by introducing sexual variety to erase the memory of Severin's previous affair with a ballet dancer. Inevitably, the individuals become emotionally involved with their "temporary" partners, and this places both marriages in jeopardy. The first-person narrator, a novelist, considers himself a cuckold by the end of the novel (T. S. Garp's second novel in *The World According to Garp* is titled *The Second Wind of the Cuckold*), and is going to Vienna to attempt a reconciliation with his wife, Utch. Whatever the outcome of this effort, their marriage will never be the same.

Despite the significance of Irving's message about contemporary life, *The 158-Pound Marriage* is his weakest novel because he fails to take advantage of his strengths as a novelist. Instead of merging the comic and the tragic, as he does in his best work, Irving steers a course between them; as a result, the novel has a flatness rather than the peaks and valleys of emotion which Irving is capable of evoking. Only in the histories of the characters which the narrator provides at the beginning does Irving's usual inventiveness emerge. Severin and Utch have exotic yet similar backgrounds. Both were children in wartime Vienna; Severin is the son of an obscure Austrian painter and a model, and Utch is the daughter of a clever farm woman who hid Utch in the belly of a dead cow to protect her from rape at the hands of the invading Russians. Instead of being raped, the seven-year-old was christened Utchka ("calf") and virtually adopted by a Russian officer occupying Vienna. When the narrator meets Utch, she is working as a tour guide in Vienna. Edith meets Severin when she is sent by an American museum to purchase some of his father's paintings. The coincidence of the two couples' meeting and becoming intimately involved with one another years afterward lends interest to the early sections of the novel, but Irving does not manage to sustain this interest.

As the title suggests, wrestling is a major motif in *The 158-Pound Marriage*. Severin Winter is a wrestling coach as well as a professor of German, and the jargon of the sport dominates the novel as it does his speech. "Wrestling," the narrator says, "was a constant metaphor to him," and the tedious struggle of a wrestling match becomes an apt metaphor for the struggle to maintain human relationships. Were this Irving's only novel, one would have little sense of the mastery of tone and style of which he is capable; fortunately, his next two novels amply display that mastery.

By far Irving's most successful novel, *The World According to Garp* is the best example of his ability to wed the bizarre and the commonplace, the tragic and the comic. The novel deals with the extremes of human experience, embodying that dualism of vision which is Irving's greatest strength as a writer. Titled in the working draft *Lunacy and Sorrow*, it has been called "a manic, melancholic carnival of a book," and Irving manages to keep the reader poised between laughter and tears. The seriousness of *The World According to Garp* lies in its thematic concerns: the elusive nature of reality and the human need to find or impose order on existence. The "lunacy" in the novel derives from the extremes to which people will go to achieve order and meaning; the "sorrow" arises from the ultimate human inability to control destiny. The last line—"in the world according to Garp we are all terminal cases"—conveys the stoic acceptance of misfortune and disaster which Irving posits as necessary for survival, yet the lightly ironic tone of this concluding sentence also reflects the novel's utter lack of sentimentality or melodrama.

T. S. Garp, the main character, is an unlikely hero. On the one hand he is a fairly typical twentieth century man, a husband and father who worries about his children, pursues his career, jogs regularly, and has a penchant for young female baby-sitters. He loves his wife, is good to his mother, and has a few close friends. These bare facts, however, do not explain Garp, nor, Irving suggests, would such a sketch be adequate to represent most people. Garp is the son of Jenny Fields, nurse, daughter of a wealthy family, author of an autobiography, and finally sponsor of a haven for women with special needs. Garp's father, a fatally injured ball turret gunner during World War II, enters the picture only long enough to impregnate Jenny Fields. Jenny then rears the boy at the Steering School, where she is the school nurse. After Garp is graduated from Steering, mother and son go to Vienna, where Jenny writes her autobiography, *A Sexual Suspect*, and Garp writes "The Pension

Grillparzer." *A Sexual Suspect*, the beginning and end of Jenny Fields's writing career, catapults her to fame as a feminist writer and finally leads to her assassination by a reactionary gunman during a political rally. "The Pension Grillparzer" launches Garp on a career as a writer and also makes possible his marriage to Helen Holm, daughter of the wrestling coach at Steering, with whom he has two sons, Duncan and Walt. Because of his mother's fame, Garp becomes a close friend of Roberta Muldoon, a transsexual who was formerly Robert Muldoon, tight end for the Philadelphia Eagles. He also encounters the Ellen Jamesians, a radical feminist group who protest rape with self-multilation. After an automobile accident which kills Walt and blinds Duncan in one eye, Garp and Helen adopt the real Ellen James, who eventually becomes a writer. Garp himself is killed at the age of thirty-three by an Ellen Jamesian who is angered by Garp's rejection of the group's extremist practices.

Despite this grim outline, *The World According to Garp* is often humorous and occasionally wildly comic. The humor usually grows out of human foibles: Dean Bodger catching a dead pigeon as it falls from the Steering infirmary roof and mistaking it for the body of young Garp; Jenny Fields failing to recognize a well-dressed woman as a prostitute on the streets of Vienna; Garp sprinting down the streets of his neighborhood to overtake astonished speeders who endanger the lives of his children, or dressing as a woman to attend the "feminist funeral" of his mother. When the comic and tragic merge, the result is black humor in the tradition of Nathanael West. At the climax of the novel, for example, when Garp's car crashes into that of Michael Milton, Helen, in the act of performing oral sex on Milton, bites off his penis, effectively ending the affair which she has been trying to conclude, and providing an ironic counterpoint to the tonguelessness of the Ellen Jamesians.

Humor and tragedy may coexist because the nature of reality is always in question. The title of the novel suggests that the world presented in the novel may be only Garp's idiosyncratic version of reality. The short stories and the fragment of Garp's novel *The World According to Bensenhaver* are different versions of reality—those created by T. S. Garp the novelist. Ultimately, of course, the novel presents a version of the world according to John Irving. That things are not always what they seem is further evidenced in many of the novel's details. Garp's name is not really a name at all. The initials T. S. though echoing those of T. S. Eliot, do not stand for anything, and "Garp" is merely a sound made by Garp's brain-damaged father. Roberta Muldoon is occasionally uncertain whether to behave as a female or male. Jenny Fields does not set out to be a feminist, but is regarded as one by so many people that she takes up the cause. Given this confusion between reality and illusion, order is difficult to achieve. As a novelist, Garp can control only the worlds of his fiction; he cannot protect his family and friends from disaster. Garp is in many ways an old-fashioned knight attempting to deal with rapists in parks and speeding automobiles on suburban streets. Like his character Bensen-haver, who appoints himself special guardian of a family after he retires from the police force, Garp imagines himself the particular guardian of children and the enemy of rape.

Of particular interest to contemporary readers is the prominence of feminism in *The World According to Garp*. Irving's depiction of the movement is broad and essentially sympathetic, including not only its extremes, such as the Ellen Jamesians, but also the changes in social and family relationships brought about by revisions in sex roles. Jenny Fields wants to be a single parent, but artificial insemination and single-parent adoptions are not available to her in the mid-1940's. Her choice of a fatally wounded patient as the father for her child is born of pragmatism rather than feminist philosophy; only later, as she writes her autobiography, is she able to articulate the need for tolerance of those with nontraditional ways. Garp himself is a house-husband. While Helen teaches at the university, he writes at home, takes care of his sons, and cooks. He therefore must deal with public suspicion that he is an unemployed failure, and his own situation enables him to understand the plight of many women and to see the damage done to the feminist cause by extremists such as the Ellen Jamesians.

The major flaw in *The World According to Garp* is its lack of a coherent structure. The examples of Garp's own writing, though interesting and the-matically related to the rest of the novel, remain undigested lumps in the chronological narrative. In part, Irving has attempted too much by hoping to fuse the story of a writer's development with all of the other issues in the novel. In addition, he is reluctant to let go of his characters, so that the novel continues past the point of its dramatic conclusion. Chapter 19, "Life After Garp," traces all of the main characters to their inevitable ends rather than leaving the reader's imagination to envision them. Art, as the novel insists, is a way of ordering reality, but here the two become confused. There is some suggestion that Garp is a Christlike figure—his almost-virgin birth, his death at thirty-three—but the evidence is too thin to sustain a reading of the final chapter as the "lives of the disciples."

Shortly before T. S. Garp is killed in *The World According to Garp*, he has begun a new novel called *My Father's Illusions*, an apt title for *The Hotel New Hampshire*. Depending less on dreams and violence and more on the imaginative creation of real human types, the novel has a calmer, less urgent tone than *The World According to Garp*. Although themes and motifs present in Irving's earlier novels reappear in *The Hotel New Hampshire*, this novel is far less dependent on autobiography and has a more cohesive focus. Critics and reviewers expressed disappointment with the novel, one calling it "a perverse *Life With Father*, a savage situation comedy." It seems likely, how-ever, that the very absence of much of the perversity and savagery which characterized *The World According to Garp* has made it seem less vital. The tone of *The Hotel New Hampshire* is more assured, its humor more sophisticated, its presentation of life more realistic than in much of Irving's other work.

Like *The World According to Garp*, *The Hotel New Hampshire* deals with illusion and reality—specifically with one man's dreams for his family. Win Berry is a man with improbable hopes. As his son John, the narrator, says of him, "the first of my father's illusions was that bears could survive the life lived by human beings, and the second was that human beings could survive a life led in hotels." The Berry family lives in three hotels during the course of the novel, which spans the period from 1920, when Win Berry meets Mary Bates, to 1980, when the surviving Berry children are grown and have become successful at various pursuits. (Egg, the youngest, is killed in a plane crash along with his mother; Lilly, the smallest, commits suicide.) All the Berry children are marked by a childhood spent in the hotels created by their father's dreams: first a converted school in Dairy, New Hampshire; than a dubious *pension* in Vienna. Finally, Win Berry, by this time blind—as he in some ways has been all his life—returns to the Maine resort where he first met Mary Bates, shielded by his children from the knowledge that it has become a rape crisis center. The familiar Irving motifs and images are prominent in *The Hotel New Hampshire*: Win Berry's father, Iowa Bob, is a wrestling coach whose strenuous view of life contrasts sharply with his son's dreaminess; bears appear in both actual and simulated form. Near the beginning of the novel, Win Berry buys a bear named State O'Maine from a wanderer named Freud, who eventually lures Win and his family to the second Hotel New Hampshire in Vienna; there they meet Susie-the-bear, a young American who wears a bear suit as a protection against reality.

Several critics have referred to the fairy-tale quality of *The Hotel New Hampshire*, and various elements contribute to that quality: a trained bear, a dog named Sorrow who reappears in different forms, and several heroic rescues, including the Berry family's rescue of the Vienna State Opera House from terrorists who intend to bomb it. The novel partakes of the atmosphere of fantasy present in *Setting Free the Bears* and "The Pension Grillparzer"; the latter, in fact, contains the germ of this novel. Despite the premature deaths of three members of the Berry family, there is little of the bleakness or desperation of *The World According to Garp*. In part, this is the result of the narrator's point of view. John Berry, the middle child, is the keeper of the family records, and thus the one who orders their experience in writing. Though he is patient with other people's fantasies, John has few of his own, and he casts a mellow light over the experience of the family. Irving has compared him to Nick Carraway in F. Scott Fitzgerald's *The Great Gatsby* (1925), but he resembles more nearly the narrative voice in some of J. D. Salinger's work, taking the strange behavior of his family for granted and delighting in their unusual talents and proclivities. John is closest to his sister

Franny (another Salinger echo); in fact, they have a brief incestuous relationship, in part intended to ease Franny back into heterosexual relationships following her rape as a teenager.

Although the tone of *The Hotel New Hampshire* is gentler than that of *The World According to Garp*, Irving presents many of the same social problems and situations: rape (which Irving has called "the most violent assault on the body and the head that can happen simultaneously"), murder, race relations, sex roles, and the modern family. The difference between this fifth novel and those which preceded it is that Irving seems to have become reconciled to the need for illusion as a means of survival. No longer are dreams only irresponsible fantasies or terrible nightmares; they are what enable most people, in the refrain of the novel, to "keep passing the open windows" rather than taking a suicidal plunge. By treating contemporary anxieties with the traditional devices of the storyteller, Irving conveys an age-old message about the purpose of art: it can provide an illusion of order which may be more important—and is certainly more readily attained—than order itself.

John Irving's two novels following *The Hotel New Hampshire* deal more insistently with moral and ethical issues, although they also contain the bizarre characters and situations that have become hallmarks of his fiction. *The Cider House Rules* concerns, as the title suggests, the rules by which people are to conduct their lives, but just as the list of rules posted in the cider house ("Please don't smoke in bed or use candles") is consistently ignored, so Dr. Wilbur Larch, one of the novel's central characters, breaks the rules by performing abortions in rural Maine in the 1920's. As he dealt with the issue of rape in *The World According to Garp*, Irving here approaches the issue of abortion inventively: Wilbur Larch is no back-alley abortionist, but a skilled obstetrician who also runs an orphanage for the children whose mothers prefer to give birth, and he seeks to have the children adopted.

Homer Wells, the other central character, is an orphan who is never adopted, and who grows up in the orphanage absorbing the most basic lesson taught there: that one must "be of use." His final usefulness is to replace Dr. Larch when the elderly man dies, but even here he breaks the rules, for although he is a skilled obstetrician and abortionist, he has no medical degree, and so takes over the position with an assumed identity. Partly because of the precarious nature of his own existence, Homer has opposed abortion all his life, until he feels that he must perform one for a black teenager who has been raped by her father. Just as the illiterate apple pickers cannot read the rules of the orchard where Homer spends his young adulthood, Irving suggests that the rules that people should follow are those that are derived from human encounter rather than those that are arbitrarily imposed.

The apple orchard setting is part of a muted Garden of Eden theme in the novel. Homer falls in love with Candy, the daughter of the orchard's owner, and she gives birth to his child shortly before she marries another man. No one, however, is cast out of the garden; Irving instead creates another of his oddly mixed families when Homer moves in with Candy, her husband Wally, and the child, a boy named Angel. Here, too, Homer proves to have been "of use," because a serious illness during World War II prevents Wally from fathering children, and he and Candy rear Angel as their own. Despite its strong pro-abortion stance, *The Cider House Rules*, like Irving's previous fiction, evokes a special reverence for children. The children in Wilbur Larch's orphanage are cared for lovingly, Homer dotes on his son Angel, and it is the plight of the pregnant girl, Rose Rose, that converts Homer to the pro-choice position of Wilbur Larch.

As *The Cider House Rules* is set against the political and social realities of the first half of the twentieth century, *A Prayer for Owen Meany* chronicles even more directly those of the next two decades—from the escalation of the Vietnam War to the advent of heavy-metal rock music, and from the early spread of television culture to the presidency of Ronald Reagan. In its overtly religious imagery, the novel posits the need for some kind of salvation during these turbulent years. *A Prayer for Owen Meany* is more complex structurally than the straightforward storytelling of *The Cider House Rules*, features the quick juxtapositions of violence and comedy of Irving's earlier work, and is ambitious in its creation of an unlikely Christ figure.

A Prayer for Owen Meany details the friendship—from childhood in the 1950's to Owen Meany's death in the 1960's—of two boys who grow up in Gravesend, New Hampshire, at opposite ends of the social scale: Owen's reclusive family owns the local granite quarry, whereas John Wheelwright's family boasts of Mayflower origins and functions as the local gentry. Their roles are reversed and confused, however, in the course of the narrative: Owen, a diminutive boy who even as an adult is never more than five feet tall, and whose voice—rendered by Irving in capital letters—is a prepubescent squeak, becomes a Christ figure with powers over life and death, whereas John leads a rather uneventful adult life as a schoolteacher in Toronto, even remaining a virgin, as Owen does not.

Imagery and actions identifying Owen Meany with Christ begin early in the novel and accumulate rapidly to the climactic scene of his death. When he is a small child, his size and lightness seem to the other children a "miracle"; for the same reason, he is cast as the Christ child in a church Christmas pageant. Owen's father tells John that Owen's was a virgin birth—that his parents' marriage was never consummated—and Owen "plays God" to save John from being drafted during the Vietnam War by cutting off one of his fingers with a diamond wheel used to engrave granite monuments. Owen foresees the date of his own death and has a recurrent dream that he will die saving small children; the fact that both predictions are accurate lends to Owen a God-like foreknowledge.

Yet *A Prayer for Owen Meany* is far from being a solemn theological tract.

Irving's characteristically ebullient humor erupts throughout the novel in slapstick scenes, in boyish pranks, and even in the ironic contrast between Owen's small voice and the large print in which it leaps authoritatively from the page. The blending of the serious and the comic reaches its apotheosis early in the novel, when the one ball that Owen Meany ever hits in Little League baseball kills John Wheelwright's mother, Tabitha. The fact that Owen Meany is the agent of John's mother's death does not mar the boys' friendship; indeed, it brings them closer together, partly because John knows that Owen worshiped his mother (and for the rest of his life keeps her dressmaker's dummy in his bedroom as a kind of ministering angel), and partly because the event has an inevitability that foretells Owen's later powers over life and death.

A Prayer for Owen Meany is a mixture of realism and fabulism, of commentary on contemporary American culture and evocation of the magic of childhood and friendship. Religious imagery permeates but does not overwhelm the novel, which takes its tone from the narrator's somewhat self-mocking stance and his obvious delight in recalling the "miracle" of Owen Meany. The novel is indeed a "prayer" for, and to, Owen, who, in refusing to flinch from his own destiny, has given John Wheelwright the courage to face his own life with equanimity.

Nancy Walker

Bibliography

Burgess, Anthony. "A Novel of Obstetrics." *The Atlantic* 98 (July, 1985): 98-100. A review of *The Cider House Rules* in which Burgess finds the novel thematically admirable but lacking in artistry.

Carton, Evan. "The Politics of Selfhood: Bob Slocum, T. S. Garp, and Auto-American-Biography." *Novel* 20 (Fall, 1986): 41-61. Carton compares Joseph Heller's *Something Happened* (1974) and *The World According to Garp* as novels that feature male narrators who test the power of selfhood against social reality. Whereas Irving's novel presents a "reactionary" conception of the self, Heller's novel suggests a "revisionary possibility" for identity.

Davenport, Gary. "The Contemporary Novel of Sensibility." *The Sewanee Review* 94 (Fall, 1986): 672-677. Davenport examines four novels published in 1985, one of which is *The Cider House Rules*, for the ways in which they address sentimentality; he finds Irving to be today's "most conspicuous advocate of sentimental fiction."

French, Sean. "Pleasures of Plot." *The New Statesman and Society* 2 (May 12, 1989): 35-36. A very favorable review of *A Prayer for Owen Meany* in which French emphasizes Irving's abilities as a storyteller.

Haller, Scot. "John Irving's Bizarre World." *Saturday Review* 8 (September,

1981): 30-34. Based partly on an interview with Irving, Haller's article provides a brief overview of his career through the publication of *The Hotel New Hampshire*, which Haller does not believe to be as good as Irving's previous fiction.

Harter, Carol C., and James R. Thompson. *John Irving*. Boston: Twayne, 1986. Part of the Twayne United States Authors series, this clearly written study of Irving's fiction through *The Cider House Rules* emphasizes the mixture of popular and artistic appeal in the novels. The volume includes an annotated bibliography.

Kazin, Alfred. "God's Own Little Squirt." *The New York Times Book Review*, March 12, 1989, 1, 30. In his review of *A Prayer for Owen Meany*, Kazin praises Irving's humor and his abilities as a storyteller but finds the novel superficial in dealing with its central themes.

King, Stephen. "The Gospel According to John Irving." *Washington Post Book World*, March 5, 1989, 1, 14. King's review of *A Prayer for Owen Meany* is enthusiastically positive; he particularly commends Irving for the manner in which he presents miracles.

Miller, Gabriel. *John Irving*. New York: Frederick Ungar, 1982. Part of the Ungar Modern Literature series, this is a useful biographical and critical study of Irving's career through *The Hotel New Hampshire*. It includes a chronology through 1982, a 1981 interview with Irving, and a bibliography of both primary and secondary sources.

Priestley, Michael. "Structure in the Worlds of John Irving." *Critique* 23, no. 1 (1981): 82-96. Priestley analyzes the ways the novelist—and his characters—seek to impose order on their fictional worlds in Irving's first four novels.

Reisenberg, Donald E., and Morris Fishbein Fellow. "Rules." *Journal of the American Medical Association*, January 3, 1986, 97-98. This review of *The Cider House Rules* centers on the evenhanded way in which Irving approaches the abortion debate.

Ruppersburg, Hugh M. "John Irving." In *American Novelists Since World War II*. Vol. 6, 2d ser. *Dictionary of Literary Biography*, edited by James E. Kilber, Jr. Detroit, Mich.: Gale, 1980. Written after Irving had published his first four novels, the article is a biographical and critical overview of the author and his work through *The World According to Garp*.

Wymard, Eleanor B. "'A New Version of the Midas Touch': *Daniel Martin* and *The World According to Garp*." *Modern Fiction Studies* 27 (Summer, 1981): 284-286. Wymard sees similarities between Fowles's and Irving's novels: a return to old-fashioned storytelling, a celebration of the comic spirit, and compassion for their characters' struggles with the fragility of contemporary existence.

KAZUO ISHIGURO

Born: Nagasaki, Japan; November 8, 1954

Principal long fiction
A Pale View of Hills, 1982; *An Artist of the Floating World*, 1986; *The Remains of the Day*, 1989.

Other literary forms
Three of Kazuo Ishiguro's early short stories are collected in *Introduction 7: Stories by New Writers* (1981). Ishiguro has also written for literary journals and authored film scripts for television, among them *A Profile of Arthur J. Mason* (1984) and *The Gourmet* (1986).

Achievements
From the beginning, Ishiguro's carefully crafted novels, with their themes of human dignity and loyalty pledged to dubious or ambiguous causes, have found great critical acclaim; however, it was only with *The Remains of the Day*, the 1989 winner of the Booker Prize, Great Britain's most prestigious literary award, that Ishiguro became known in the United States. In Great Britain, *A Pale View of Hills* received the Winifred Holtby Award from the Royal Society of Literature; *An Artist of the Floating World* earned the Whitbread Fiction Prize as Whitbread Book of the Year 1986, another British literary distinction. All over the world, Ishiguro's skillfully imagined central characters have fascinated readers and critics with their distinctively spoken tales of lives tested by history and beliefs challenged by tragedy.

Biography
Kazuo Ishiguro was born on November 8, 1954, in the Japanese city of Nagasaki, the son of Shizuo and Shizuko (née Michida) Ishiguro. In 1960, Shizuo, an oceanographer, moved with his family to Guildford, near London, and the temporary stay became a permanent one. Immersed in British culture, and sent to what he described as a typical British school, Kazuo Ishiguro formed his vision of Japan by means of childhood memories, Japanese films of the 1950's, and the Japanese books which arrived every month at home, where the family conversed in Japanese.

After a short stint as a grouse beater for the British Queen Mother at Balmoral Castle in 1973, and employment as social worker both before and after his B.A. (with honors) in English and philosophy from the University of Kent in 1978, Ishiguro enrolled in the creative writing program at the University of East Anglia, where he earned a M.A. in 1980. Having started to write before he entered the graduate program, Ishiguro garnered immediate acclaim with his first novel, *A Pale View of Hills.* Yet he was still working part-time in a hostel for London's homeless until the rewards for *An Artist of the Floating World* allowed him to focus exclusively on his fiction and filmscripts. While working on his third novel in 1986, Kazuo Ishiguro married Lorna Anne MacDougall, a fellow social worker; when *The Remains of the Day* was published, the couple was living in an unpretentious corner of London.

As a writer, Ishiguro has rejected claims that his first two novels offer a realistic picture of his home country, which he had not seen between 1960 and 1989. Instead, he has insisted that it is a character's memory of a conflict in life that held his artistic interest.

Analysis

A common link among Kazuo Ishiguro's novels is the prominence of the first-person narrator, through whose meandering thoughts the story unfolds. The reader soon discovers, however, that these central voices are rather unreliable in their accounts of past reactions to crises. For each, there lurks in the past an experience that may invalidate their projected sense of self and destroy the vestiges of their human dignity. Yet what exactly it is that hovers in the dark as each novel opens is a mystery that unravels only slowly, and the process keeps the reader on edge until a final climactic revelation. Even then, though, pieces of the central mystery remain left to the reader to put together.

In a move that would become typical for his fiction, Ishiguro opened his first novel, *A Pale View of Hills*, with the narrator seemingly in control, living through a brief, critical moment in the present. As small events trigger a stream of personal memories, answers emerge to questions that the narrator—like all Ishiguro's central characters—refuses to discuss openly. Accordingly, the novel moves along two temporal planes after Etsuko Sheringham is visited at her home in England by Niki, her younger daughter by her second (now dead) British husband; that visit comes just after the suicide of Niki's elder, Japan-born sister, Keiko.

In a pattern that again foreshadows how later characters will interact with one another, mother and daughter communicate on a very formal, restrained level that allows neither to say what is really on her mind; instead, they hover together on the abyss opened by Keiko's death. Niki justifies her refusal to go to Keiko's funeral: for long years, before leaving the family home in the South to go away to Manchester, Keiko had locked herself up in her room, emerging only to commence bitter fights with her stepfather and half sister. It is only through Etsuko's memories, and her haunting recurring dream about a young girl, that the extent of Etsuko's pain becomes visible.

About five years after the drop of the atom bomb on her native town of Nagasaki, Etsuko was pregnant with her first child by her Japanese husband, Jiro Ogata. Living in a newly built concrete high-rise at the edge of the city just as it began to live again, she initiated a friendship with a war-widow,

Sachiko, who lived with her ten-year-old daughter, Mariko, in a riverbank cottage across a muddy wasteland.

The war years have deeply touched Mariko, who witnessed how a young mother drowned her baby and later killed herself in Tokyo. Now she fantasizes about a woman coming at night with a lantern and guiding her across the river, where hills rise above Nagasaki's port. These hills are visible to Etsuko from her apartment, and it is to them that they all go on a day of rare happiness for Mariko.

When Frank, Sachiko's American lover, whom Mariko deeply resents for his Western-style behavior—"He pisses like a pig," she says—finally seems ready to take them stateside, Sachiko goes out to drown Mariko's kittens, which cannot come along. In a stunning move characteristic of Ishiguro's love of close parallelisms, the second drowning quite clearly echoes the wartime murder of the baby; both women turn to Mariko, revealing their wet victims to the child.

Following them, Etsuko has taken up a lantern and come to the river; trying to soothe a despondent Mariko, she suddenly speaks as if she were the mother, about to leave Japan. To bring home this sudden point of ambivalent narration, Etsuko gives Niki a calendar picture taken from the hills, remarking that it was Keiko, not Mariko as related earlier, who had been "happy that day." Thus, the reader realizes that Sachiko's cruel treatment of her daughter reflects Etsuko's own fear that she may be guilty of Keiko's death because she left Japan with her second, British husband when the girl was quite small. Ishiguro ends the novel, however, with Niki's departure as Etsuko, purified by her memories, is able to wave good-bye with a smile.

While *A Pale View of Hills* centers mostly on a question of personal guilt, it also contains the story of Etsuko's first father-in-law, Seiji Ogata, a former teacher now publicly denounced by one of his former students for his imperialist leanings during World War II. This conflict of a man trying to come to terms with his past actions in a broad historical setting is made the artistic center of Ishiguro's second novel, *An Artist of the Floating World*, and is also a powerful theme for *The Remains of the Day*.

Written like a diary entry to be shared with a close friend, *An Artist of the Floating World* allows Ishiguro to develop further the subjective mind-set of his narrator, the old painter Masuji Ono, and the gradual resurfacing of suppressed memories. Like Etsuko's, however, Ono's interpretation of the past is not fully to be trusted.

Thus, the reader becomes gradually acquainted with Ono's troubled career as, in the present of the postwar period of 1948, the old man worries about marriage negotiations for his second daughter; these negotiations, he fears, may fall through because of his past acts. Starting as a fashionable artist who had taken his themes and motifs from the underworld—the Japanese term is "Floating World"—of the bohemians, artists, and geishas of his unnamed city, Ono denounced his "decadence" during the rise of imperialism in the 1930's. Rebelling against his old master, the young Ono now painted pieces in the style of "patriotic realism" preferred by the Fascists.

Success came almost immediately, but Ono's masterful pictures became powerful tools of imperial propaganda as well. To reinforce the issue of Ono's personal guilt, Ishiguro creates again a close parallel between Ono's earlier rejection by his bohemian teacher, who cruelly confiscates his pictures when Ono changes artistic directions and joins the "patriotic" cause, and Ono's own denunciation of his favorite pupil to the secret police in the 1930's. Like Ogata in *A Pale View of Hills*, Ono supports the imperialist Committee on Unpatriotic Activities—an institution that is Ishiguro's symbol for the wrongs of a system that betrayed the idealism of those who with exuberant naïveté put their talents in its service. Confronted with the consequences of his patriotism, Ono now must ask himself whether he wasted or abused his talents by serving the Devil.

Yet again, Ishiguro's resolution to Ono's crisis is marked by a disarming, gently ironic humanism. Finally ready to admit to his daughter's potential in-laws that he has, in fact, erred and been guilty, Ono's grand confession is brushed aside by the groom's family, who tell the old man that they regard his former political leanings as irrelevant to their marriage; he was never that important. His putting-in-place by the next generation of Japanese (including his daughter) is a variation on Ogata's son Jiro's refusal to finish a game of chess—symbol for a traditional fighting spirit—with his father. In the end, both old men come to accept postwar rejection and being politely put aside as instances of the eternal rebellion of the young, just as they had once rebelled. Thus, after confronting the past, Ono and Ogata win a final serenity that allows them to retreat without bitterness and to watch mirthfully as the young prepare to embark on their own lives.

As if Ishiguro considered that the punishment for these two old men had been perhaps a bit too light, even though their loss of prestige and social esteem should not be underestimated, *The Remains of the Day* undertakes to demonstrate with beautiful clarity how high the human price can be for a person who has dedicated his life to a goal that becomes tainted. Set in southern England in the summer of 1956, *The Remains of the Day* closely follows in format the structure of *An Artist of the Floating World*. This time, the first-person narrator and protagonist is Stevens, a British butler whose lifelong goal was to serve Lord Darlington; now, after the death of the lord, his mansion, complete with its prime servant, has been taken over by the American Farraday. Offered his first vacation, Stevens sets out to Cornwall to meet Mrs. Alice Benn, who as Miss Kenton had worked with him in the heyday of Darlington Hall.

Again Ishiguro envisions a masterfully developed central character whose mind the reader is allowed to enter; technically this is again done through

Stevens' diary or notes. Yet this time Ishiguro's well-matured craft and skill as a storyteller have created arguably his most fascinating character, who is at once powerful through the strength of unrelentingly upheld convictions and beautifully fragile in his total, self-effacing devotion to an unattainable ideal.

Accordingly, in the course of Stevens' travels to his final destination, his personal recollections evoke an imaginary England that is "perfect" by presenting an understated greatness that simply exists, refusing pompously to announce itself. This theme is exemplified when Stevens views the landscape of Oxfordshire, which for him, unlike the overwhelmingly grand but also gaudy natural wonders of the United States, is "great" by virtue of its unobtrusive beauty. The source of Stevens' pride, contentment, and feeling of self-worth has been that he has served at the "hub" of the society of this great island; his greatest goal always was to be perfect butler to a perfect lord. For Ishiguro, the unstated parallel of this relationship is that between samurai and shogun, a relationship dignified by mutual loyalty; his novel sets out to examine the consequences for the butler-samurai.

Insofar as Stevens' definition of a "great" butler requires the ability to maintain "a dignity in keeping with his position," Ishiguro's protagonist fulfills the requirement. In a move characteristic of Ishiguro's way of working with his main themes, Stevens' ideal is tested in a variety of ways, ranging from amusing anecdote to memories of the feats of his father William to experiences of his own. It is such an instance of "great" service that powerfully shows the full extent of the moral darkness that becomes associated with the idea, when the reader first is told how William Stevens had to serve a general whose incompetence had killed his oldest son—and gave his large tip to charity. Following in his father's steps, Stevens later flawlessly serves Lord Darlington at a crucial function while his father, whom old age saw descending in rank to that of a glorified busboy, dies in the attic and Miss Kenton— not Stevens—closes his eyes.

Another ambiguity is examined as the reader gradually learns that Lord Darlington—required by Stevens' definition to be a great man in order to bestow greatness on his butler—has fallen far short of that distinction. Moved by private pity for the defeated Germans after World War I, the lord gradually becomes an avid sympathizer with the Nazi regime in the 1930's, and his reputation is destroyed by a related political scandal, the exact nature of which is not elucidated in the novel. By 1956, Lord Darlington's name has become a badge of shame, and his former butler deliberately denies his connections with the man to whom he has devoted his life. Here, actions like Ogata's and Ono's are depicted from the point of view of those betrayed by their leaders.

If Stevens is made to suffer like the millions of citizens of the Axis nations—among them Japan—who decided to trust and follow leaders who pursued aggression and atrocities until brought down in a bitter collapse,

Ishiguro's novel constitutes a highly critical examination of the price of self-neglecting, total service. Though Darlington's betrayal is bitter, *The Remains of the Day* points out that even if Stevens had served a better lord, he would still have suffered.

The key here is the character of Miss Kenton, who was employed at Darlington Hall to share with Stevens the overseeing of its large staff. The reader knows instantly that something important is happening when Miss Kenton, freshly arrived, brings some flowers into Stevens' starkly naked pantry, a most private room reminiscent of Keiko's room in *A Pale View of Hills* and her lonely apartment in Manchester. In a fine demonstration of the novel's irony, which hinges on Stevens' tragic inability to see the world with other than the eyes of his "great" butler, Miss Kenton's constant complaints about the faults of his ailing father are revealed to spring from concern that the old man may be killing himself with work. This concern, never detected by Stevens himself, is contrasted with the uncaring view of his lord, who sees William only as a bother—an attitude Stevens also fails to detect.

Stevens' utter failure to decipher Miss Kenton's signals of affection bestows an exquisite sense of melancholy on *The Remains of the Day*. The saddest moment arrives when the two meet again in Cornwall and she finally spells out her now-impossible love for Stevens, whose heart breaks for a moment before he accepts his fate and politely helps her onto the bus to her husband. Their fate is presented in a manner that is free of easy sentimentality, and it achieves tragic status with Stevens' realization that his talents may very well have been wasted on Lord Darlington. Yet again, in a decision that echoes existential philosophy, Stevens decides to try to be a better butler to the American and improve his skill in "bantering," light irony that he hopes may bring some human warmth to Darlington Hall.

Thus, Ishiguro decides to give his most tragic character a ray of hope that may guide him as it has guided Etsuko, Ogata, and Ono, through the remains of a life that has been given over to the pursuit of a goal that led to human ruin for the pursuer. Like Etsuko, who finally confronts her lingering guilt over having uprooted her first daughter to escape a stifling marriage, and like the serene Ogata and Ono, who forgive the young for holding them responsible for their past, Stevens is able to look beyond the sadness of a life falsely sacrificed.

R. C. Lutz

Other major works
TELEPLAYS: *A Profile of Arthur J. Mason*, 1984; *The Gourmet*, 1986.

Bibliography
Bryson, Bill. "Between Two Worlds." *The New York Times Magazine*, April 29,

1990, 38. This magazine article is an excellent, well-researched portrait of the artist. By covering Ishiguro's life, art, and philosophical attitude toward his craft, and including the artist's own words, Bryson gives the reader a sense of the personal and environmental circumstances under which Ishiguro has created his art. A photograph shows Ishiguro in front of his London townhouse.

Gurewich, David. "Upstairs, Downstairs." *The New Criterion* 8 (December, 1989) 77-80. A brief but perceptive discussion of Ishiguro's *The Remains of the Day*. Gurewich's thoughtful analysis focuses on the character of Stevens and makes much of the relationship between the butler and his lord. Good critical discussion of Ishiguro's third novel, with a well-argued character analysis.

Ishiguro, Kazuo. Interview by Gregory Mason. *Contemporary Literature* 30 (Fall, 1989): 335-347. An excellent, profound, and rewarding interview. Mason asks interesting questions, and Ishiguro's answers display marked brilliance and conciseness and offer great insights into the themes and intellectual concepts of his stories. Mason's interview is one of the best guides to understanding in full Ishiguro's art.

Mason, Gregory. "Inspiring Images: The Influence of the Japanese Cinema on the Writings of Kazuo Ishiguro." *East-West Film Journal* 3 (June, 1989): 39-52. A perceptive study that argues convincingly that Ishiguro's novels share much with Japanese art films of the 1950's. There, as in Ishiguro's fiction, Mason argues, one finds a strong focus on everyday experience and an avoidance of melodrama; the plot is often unimportant in relation to the themes.

Parrinder, Patrick. "Manly Scowls." *London Review of Books* 9 (February 6, 1986): 16. A perceptive review of *An Artist of the Floating World*. Parrinder places Ishiguro's novel in the greater context of British literature and argues strongly for taking seriously Ono's confession of his guilt, not brushing it aside as irrelevant. A good introduction to the novel.

HENRY JAMES

Born: New York, New York; April 15, 1843
Died: London, England; February 28, 1916

Principal long fiction

Roderick Hudson, 1876; *The American*, 1876-1877; *The Europeans*, 1878; *Daisy Miller*, 1878; *An International Episode*, 1878-1879; *Confidence*, 1879-1880; *Washington Square*, 1880; *The Portrait of a Lady*, 1880-1881; *The Bostonians*, 1885-1886; *The Princess Casamassima*, 1885-1886; *The Reverberator*, 1888; *The Tragic Muse*, 1889-1890; *The Spoils of Poynton*, 1897; *What Maisie Knew*, 1897; *The Awkward Age*, 1897-1899; *In the Cage*, 1898; *The Turn of the Screw*, 1898; *The Sacred Fount*, 1901; *The Wings of the Dove*, 1902; *The Ambassadors*, 1903; *The Golden Bowl*, 1904; *The Outcry*, 1911; *The Ivory Tower*, 1917; *The Sense of the Past*, 1917.

Other literary forms

Fiction was assuredly where Henry James's essential talent and interest lay, and it was the form to which he devoted almost all of his literary efforts. His more than twenty novels (the count is inexact because some of his middle-length pieces, such as *The Turn of the Screw* and *Daisy Miller*, can be categorized as novellas) and roughly 112 tales attest his lifetime of dedication to this genre. Despite this clear emphasis on fiction, however, James was seduced by his desire to regain his lost popularity with the general public and his wish to attempt a kind of writing that he had studied for many years, into writing drama. For a five-year period, from 1890 to 1895, he concentrated on playwriting; during this time he wrote no novels, but continued to publish short stories. While his failure to gain a public with his plays somewhat embittered James (an emotion that has been exaggerated by some biographers; he always had loyal and appreciative readers and friends), he never lost confidence in the legitimacy of his art, and he returned to fiction with what many scholars believe to be a stronger, more ambitious inspiration, resulting in what has been called the "major phase" of his writing. It is perhaps indicative of the primacy of fiction in James's career that his most successful play was *The American* (1891), an adaptation of his earlier novel.

Unlike many creative writers, James produced an enormous volume of critical writings, chiefly literary, in which he not only studied the works of other authors (the most noteworthy are Nathaniel Hawthorne, Walt Whitman, Ralph Waldo Emerson, Ivan Turgenev, Gustave Flaubert, George Eliot, Anthony Trollope, Robert Louis Stevenson, Honoré de Balzac, and Guy de Maupassant) but also performed a detailed analysis of his own work. This latter effort appears primarily in the form of the Prefaces to the New York edition (1907-1909) of his novels and tales. Inasmuch as the New York edition occupies twenty-six volumes, these prefaces provide a considerable body of critical material which has proved to be of great value to James scholars. His often reprinted essay "The Art of Fiction" (1884) presents his general theories on the art. Aside from his literary criticism, James wrote numerous studies and critiques on other subjects, such as painting (which greatly interested him) and travel.

In recent years, James's travel sketches and books have attained critical admiration for their graceful style and penetrating insight into times that have gone and places that will never be the same. As might be expected, his studies of Italy, France, and England (the foreign countries that most intrigued him) are detailed and entertaining. More surprising is his finest work in this genre, *The American Scene* (1907), the fruit of a long visit to the United States; he toured the country extensively (partly to visit friends and places that he had not seen and others that he not been to for a long time, and partly to deliver lectures on literary topics). His account of America at the turn of the century fuses the poignance of a native's return with the distance and objectivity of a European perspective.

Achievements

James was the first American novelist to bring to the form a sense of artistic vocation comparable to Flaubert's. Except for the wide popularity of *Daisy Miller*, which appealed to audiences both in Europe and in the United States, no work of James achieved a wide readership in his lifetime. This fact, though it caused him pain, did not impel this most discriminating of writers to lower his standards in order to appeal to a mass audience. Those who did appreciate his work tended to be the better educated, more sophisticated readers, though even some of these occasionally had blind spots concerning James's novels— his brother William, for example, once wrote to James that his fiction was "bloodless." Except for the disastrous essay into drama, James adhered to his principles, always convinced that what he was doing would improve the quality of the novel and even raise the standards of conscientious readers. Events since his death have proved him right.

With the growth of courses of study in modern American literature, James began to enjoy the wide readership that was denied him during his lifetime, and since World War II, critical studies and biographical works devoted to him have proliferated in staggering numbers. This is not to say that James is without his critics. He has frequently been criticized for a lack of scope and feeling, for concentrating his formidable talents on the psychological maneuverings of the privileged few. His later style has often been judged impenetrable, grotesquely mannered—though some critics regard his late novels as the highest achievements of the novelist's art, unsurpassed before or since.

As to James's influence on the subsequent course of the novel, however, there can be no question. He refined the novelistic art, purified it, and gave it directions never thought of before his time. Four areas of emphasis have especially attracted scholars in their attempts to isolate the essential contributions to the art of fiction with which James can be credited: point of view, psychological realism, style, and the connection of moral and aesthetic values. Throughout his career, James experimented with the varieties of consciousness (the word can be found everywhere in his fiction and criticism) through which stories can be told. The completely objective point of view, in which the reader is presented solely with what anyone present would see and hear, and the first-person point of view, in which a character tells the story as he perceives it, were both traditional, and James used them frequently. As his writing became more complex and dense, though, he endeavored to relate the action more in terms of what goes on in people's minds, the most impressive example of such a "center of consciousness" being Lambert Strether in *The Ambassadors*. As Percy Lubbock noted as early as 1921, in *The Craft of Fiction*, James achieves in *The Ambassadors* a point of view remarkable for its appropriateness to the story told and astounding in its focus on Lambert Strether's consciousness, which is made possible by James's using the third-person limited point of view, but relating the hero's thoughts and feelings in a way that he himself could never manage—in short, the reader sees Strether's perceptions both from the inside and from the outside, with James gently guiding attention to the more important features of Strether's cognition. This sort of advanced work in viewpoint did two important things: it helped to prepare the way for the stream-of-consciousness novel, and it deepened the psychological realism that was to be James's chief intellectual contribution to the novel form.

Realism was in the literary air when James was starting out as a writer, but he focused his attention on fidelity to the movements of consciousness in a way that no previous writer had done. In a James novel, what is most significant is not what transpires in the plot, per se, but rather the attitudes and emotions and discoveries which unfold in the consciousnesses of the characters. Even in a work in the objective mode, such as *The Awkward Age*, which consists almost entirely of dialogue, what interests the attentive reader is the tides of feeling and realization that are implied by the speech. James appreciated the realistic aspects of the novels of Stendhal, Balzac, and Flaubert, but he resisted the naturalistic emphasis on the scientific and empirical— he believed Émile Zola to be misguided and unliterary. Indeed, James became a necessary counterfoil to this powerful literary movement in the later years of the nineteenth century.

As a stylist, James introduced the scrupulous craftsmanship of Flaubert to English-language readers. Like Flaubert, he weighed every phrase, every nuance of diction and rhythm, every comma. Indeed, for James, style was a moral imperative. Joseph Conrad, a great admirer of James (the feeling was reciprocated, but with less enthusiasm), once asserted that the American writer was "the historian of fine consciences." Certainly, no one who reads

James closely could fail to note the delicate but constant attention paid to right and wrong in the novels. What might escape detection, however, is that James evidently believed that ethics are, in somewhat intricate ways, related to aesthetics. This does not mean that all the "good" characters are beautiful and the evil ones ugly. On the contrary, in many instances, physically attractive characters such as Christina Light (*Roderick Hudson*) and Kate Croy (*The Wings of the Dove*) are sources of much wickedness (such characters are also usually very charming); while less prepossessing ones, such as Madame Grandoni (*The Princess Casamassima*) and Henrietta Stackpole (*The Portrait of a Lady*), appear to represent the forces of virtue. The true relationship between beauty and morality in James rests on his evident conviction that those elements of life which are positive and benevolent, such as freedom and personal development, have within them great beauty—and James takes considerable pains to express these qualities fully and with impressive aesthetic form. The appreciation of Fleda Vetch, in *The Spoils of Poynton*, for the beautiful appurtenances and objets d'art of the country house in the title constitutes, to some degree, a basis for the acts of renunciation and self-effacement that provide evidence of her virtue. Ever determined not to oversimplify, James offers such concatentations cautiously. This most subtle of moralists was equally understated in his presentation of beauty, revealing the ways in which it can conceal evil as well as the ways in which it can enrich life and give it greater meaning. After reading James, one cannot doubt the sincerity of his avowal, in his 1915 letter to H. G. Wells, that "It is art that *makes* life, makes interest, makes importance, for our consideration and application of these things, and I know of no substitute whatever for the force and beauty of its process."

Biography

If one wished to create for himself a background and early life that was appropriate for preparing to be an important and dedicated American novelist during the later years of the nineteenth century and the early years of the twentieth, he might very well choose just the sort of family and early experience that fate created for Henry James. The family circumstances were comfortable (his grandfather, William James, had amassed one of the three largest fortunes in New York State), and his father, Henry James, Sr., his mother, Mary Robertson Walsh James, his older brother, William, and his younger siblings, Garth Wilkinson, Robertson, and Alice, were all lively, articulate, and stimulating. It has been speculated that the very effervescence of his siblings helped to develop in Henry a tendency toward observation rather than participation, a trait that may have contributed to his decision never to marry and certainly helped to lead him to the vocation to which he devoted his life.

Another important feature of James's youth was his father's belief in the merit of unsystematic but broadly based education. The future novelist thus enjoyed the benefits of instruction by tutors as well as in excellent European institutions (made possible by a four-year stay, 1855-1858, on the Continent, in Switzerland, England, and France). Early on, the elder Henry James, an unorthodox philosopher and writer, observed that "Harry is not so fond of study, properly so-called, as of reading. He is a devourer of libraries." That this parent was not insistent on a more traditional attitude toward education is to his credit; though James was largely self-educated (his only true conventional schooling was a brief period at Harvard Law School, in 1862-1863)— resulting in some ignorances of extended areas of knowledge, such as the sciences, and in specialized concentrations, represented by his phenomenally wide reading in nineteenth century fiction but in little literature written before that era—it is generally agreed that he was one of the best-informed of the major literary men of his time.

Apart from several later trips to Europe, which finally led him to the decision to move there in 1875 and to remain there for the rest of his life (except for a number of trips to America, where he never established a home), James led, for his first thirty years, a largely domestic life in the family circle. In his early twenties he had decided to become a writer; his initial publication is thought to be an unsigned story, which appeared in 1864. This was the first of an endless stream of tales, reviews, essays, and novels (James became so proficient at French that he also translated a few works, which achieved publication); even during the period of his attempts to write plays he was turning out short pieces regularly. He was closely attached to his older brother William, a relationship that endured until William's death, in 1910, and to Alice and his cousin Mary ("Minny") Temple, whom James thought to be "the very heroine of our common scene." This charming young lady may have been the only real romantic love of James's life—it has been suggested that her death at twenty-four, in 1870, had much to do with James's resolution never to marry—and he immortalized her in Milly Theale, the ailing heroine of *The Wings of the Dove*, and perhaps in all the bright, appealing American girls who come to grief in his novels.

James was never very close to his younger brothers, a fact that has been attributed partly to his inability to serve in the army during the Civil War (because of "an obscure hurt," which was probably nothing more dramatic than a back injury—James had a painful back for all of his early manhood), in which "Wilky" and "Bob" fought, but also to the fact that he was simply temperamentally unsuited to association with these essentially unhappy men, both of whom died before him. Alice James became an invalid. The element of sadness in these three lives underlines the note of tragedy that can be found in much of James's fiction. There is no reason to doubt that, when James wrote to a friend, in 1896, "I have the imagination of disaster—and see life indeed as ferocious and sinister," he had had this grim attitude for many years, perhaps from as far back as his youth. Certainly, touches of the sinister abound in his novels.

After James's removal to Europe, the rest of his life became chiefly a matter of hard work, important friendships with literary figures (he seems to have known nearly everyone of importance in French and English belles-lettres of his time, from Stevenson to George Sand, from George Eliot to Zola—and he wrote many essays about their work), and extraordinary ranges of travel. After a year in Paris, in 1875, James decided that his art would flourish more fully in England, where he took up residence, first in London, later in Rye, Sussex. He chose this relatively remote location because, he claimed, the vigorous social life of London was draining his energy and time from writing— typically, though, it is known that he greatly enjoyed that social contact, once boasting that during a single winter he dined out 107 times. Despite the claims of some critics and biographers—most notably Van Wyck Brooks, in *The Pilgrimage of Henry James* (1925)—that James abandoned his native land to become an uncritical lover of Europe and especially of England, a careful reading of his novels reveals that he was very clear-sighted about the weaknesses and flaws in English "high" society.

Whatever one's judgment about the validity of the reasons for James's resolve to live and work in Europe, it is plain that his art was largely determined by the European experience. Abroad, James found what he believed to be lacking in America, at least for a novelist of manners interested in cultural phenomena. In his biography of Hawthorne, James listed, perhaps with tongue at least partly in check, those items that could be studied only in Europe, since they did not exist in America: "No sovereign, no court . . . no aristocracy, no church, no clergy, no army, no diplomatic service, no country gentlemen, no palaces, no castles, nor manors, nor old country-houses . . . no literature, no novels, no museums, no pictures, no political society, no sporting class." Though this list offers some hint of James's sense of humor, the works themselves are sure evidence that he was convinced that Europe provided him with indispensable materials for his novels.

James never made a great deal of money from his writing, but he always lived comfortably (he was so confident of his financial security that he turned over his share of the estate of his father, who died in 1882, to Alice). He was a generous friend, both with money and advice, to his many acquaintances and to young writers hoping to succeed. He had what some biographers call a genius for friendship, which his enormous correspondence attests. His fondness for congenial associates, particularly literary ones, did not, however, blind him to their weaknesses nor subdue his pride in his accomplishments. He once wrote home that, as to his friend Flaubert, "I think I easily—more than easily—see all round him intellectually." Such a boast may help to explain James's remarkable adherence to his absolute belief in his powers and in the rightness of his efforts. While public taste was going in one direction (downward, in his view), James's technique was headed precisely the opposite way.

This firmness has since been justified, and even in his lifetime the admiration of such respected writers as Conrad and William Dean Howells did much to console him for his lack of popularity. On James's seventieth birthday, April 15, 1913, some 270 friends presented him with a "golden bowl," and asked him to sit for a portrait by John Singer Sargent (which is now in the National Portrait Gallery, in London). More formal honors were an honorary degree from Harvard (1911) and one from Oxford (1912); perhaps the most lofty distinction was the Order of Merit, presented to James by King George V, in 1916, the year of the author's death (from heart trouble and pneumonia). This decoration was given in recognition of James's valued service to England during the opening years of World War I; James believed that the United States was dishonorable for not becoming involved.

As death approached—James wrote of it, "So here it is at last, the distinguished thing!"—he was still engaged in writing; he left two unfinished novels, *The Ivory Tower* and *The Sense of the Past*, and a number of unpublished essays and stories, all of which have since been printed. This continuation of his labors right to the end was fitting, for never before, or since, was there a man of whom it is so appropriate to say that his work *was* his life.

Analysis

Henry James's distinctive contributions to the art of the novel were developed over a long career of some fifty years. Leon Edel, possibly the most renowned and respected James scholar, has indicated that James's mature writing can be divided into three periods (with three subdivisions in the middle phase). Through the publication of *The Portrait of a Lady*, in 1881, James was chiefly interested in the now famous "international theme," the learning experiences and conflicts of Americans in Europe and Europeans in America (the former situation being by far the more frequent). This first period is represented by *Roderick Hudson*, *The American*, *Daisy Miller*, and *The Portrait of a Lady*; of these *Daisy Miller* and *The Portrait of a Lady* are probably the best examples of James's early work. The more complex second period falls into three parts. The first, roughly from 1881 through 1890, displays James's concern with social issues (not the sort of topic for which he is known), as in *The Bostonians* and *The Princess Casamassima*, the former about women's rights in the United States and the latter concerning the class struggle in England. The second of these subperiods is that during which he created plays (many of which have never been performed) and produced a variety of short stories. The final subdivision is that marked by the appearance of short and mid-length fictions dealing with the problems of artists in their relationships with society (he had already touched on this subject in *Roderick Hudson*) and of occasionally bizarre stories, such as *The Turn of the Screw* and "The Altar of the Dead," about men, women, and children who are obsessed, haunted, and perhaps insane. Some of these pieces were written during James's calamitous endeavor with drama. The final period, called "the major phase," from about 1896 till the close of his career, shows James returning to the international theme. The themes of this period are most obviously exhibited in the three large novels of his later years: *The Ambassadors* (which was written before the next novel but published after it), *The Wings of the Dove*, and *The Golden Bowl.*

During this extended development and shifting of interests and enthusiasms, James was continuously trying to refine his presentation of character, theme, and event. In his critical writing he stated that he finally recognized the value of "the *indirect* presentation of his main image" (he is here speaking of Milly Theale, in *The Wings of the Dove*, who is seen largely through the eyes of other characters and about whom the reader learns, even of her death, chiefly by report). Several critics, perhaps the most famous being F. R. Leavis, in *The Great Tradition* (1948), believe this "recognition" to be a grave error; they claim that James refined his presentation beyond clear comprehension (thus the common accusation of excessive ambiguity) and eventually beyond interest. Others—perhaps the most salient is F. W. Dupee, in *Henry James* (1951)—aver that these three late novels are James's masterpieces, works in which his study of the complexities of moral decisions reaches an elevation never attained by another author.

Two aspects of James's fiction have received little attention: not much has been written about his humor, which is usually ironic but often gentle. A fine example is his presentation of Mrs. Lavinia Penniman, the foolish aunt of Catherine Sloper in *Washington Square* and a widow "without fortune—with nothing but the memory of Mr. Penniman's flowers of speech, a certain vague aroma of which hovered about her own conversation." This romantic, meddling woman is depicted by James humorously, but with a clear indication of the harm that her interference causes. The image of her "flowers of speech" suggests another neglected style: the repetition of certain key words and images throughout his canon. Readers can easily become distracted by frequently encountered "flower" images such as the foregoing one and key words such as "figured" (as in "it figured for him"), "lucid" or "lucidly" (as in "he said it lucidly"), "idea" (as in "he had his idea of"), and a phrase such as "She took it in" to signify an understanding of a remark. Also, "theory"— in a phrase such as "She had a theory that"—reappears many times. It is, of course, not surprising that certain terms might emerge frequently in a canon as large as James's but his evident affection for particular expressions such as the foregoing ones does seem odd in a writer whose repertoire of verbal expression appears to be boundless. It would, for example, be hard to think of another writer, who, in characterizing the grim conversation of Mrs. Bowerbank, in *The Princess Casamassima*, would be able to suggest it by noting, "her outlook seemed to abound in cheerless contingencies."

All in all, though, there is little of James's subject matter and technique that has escaped the close inspection of scholarship. Possible the greatest shift of critical emphasis in James scholarship has been the increasing awareness of the moral thrust of his work. Early critics frequently charged that no consistent moral attitude was clearly expressed in his work. In more recent times, this concern has evaporated, with a realization that James was an insightful moralist who understood that general rules are of little use in dealing with complex social and personal situations. He tended to treat each novel as a sort of special problem, to be worked out by the characters. From his total production, though, two "principles" have issued: the author was a firm believer in freedom and in personal development. To become a true hero or heroine in a James novel, a character must achieve a state of self-realization (again, an acute act of consciousness is needed), must recognize the truth and face it bravely, must act freely (without emotional dependence on others), and must renounce any personal gain in order to promote the welfare of others. In this way, the person attains true personal development and achieves as much freedom as James believed the world could offer—he did not sub-scribe to the doctrine that human liberty is unlimited. The basic moral conflict in his novels is essentially between powerful, often heartless or thoughtless, oppressors, such as Gilbert Osmond in *The Portrait of a Lady* and Olive Chancellor in *The Bostonians*, and their "victims," such as Isabel Archer, in the former work, and Verena Tarrant, in the latter.

James's reputation, already high, is continuing to rise and is likely to do so for some years. The dramatizations of several of his works in the cinema (*Daisy Miller, The Europeans, Washington Square,* and *The Aspern Papers*) and television (*The Portrait of a Lady, The Ambassadors, The Turn of the Screw,* "The Author of Beltraffio," *The Spoils of Poynton,* and *The Golden Bowl*) are perhaps superficial indices of increasing acclaim, but the burgeon-ing of critical attention is not. There is no question that James belongs, in F. R. Leavis' phrase, squarely in the "great tradition" of the novel.

Daisy Miller, which established James's reputation as a leading novelist both in England and the United States, announces several of his recurring themes and motifs. The story is an uncomplicated one, from the standpoint of plot. Frederick Winterbourne, a sophisticated young American who lives in Europe, meets Daisy Miller, who is visiting Europe with her mother and younger brother; Mr. Miller is back in Schenectady, New York, presumably making enough money to allow his family to travel comfortably. The essence of the novella is the relationship which develops between the young, cos-mopolitan expatriate (a not uncommon type in James's fiction) and the pretty, naïve, and willful girl.

In *Daisy Miller* a central issue is whether Winterbourne could have pre-vented the tragedy that ends Daisy's life. As he gets to know her better and comes to like her, he becomes increasingly distressed at Daisy's refusal to heed the warnings of Mrs. Costello, his aunt, and Mrs. Walker, another

Europeanized American society matron (it is significant that the people who most condemn Daisy are not native Europeans but expatriates). Daisy stubbornly continues to consort with the gigolo Giovanelli, who is seen with her all about Rome, much to the dismay of the society people, who are scandalized by such "loose" behavior—even the Romans joke about it in a subdued fashion, which only irritates Winterbourne the more. He tries to warn Daisy that she is seen too much with Giovanelli—"Everyone thinks so"—but she refuses to take his cautions seriously: "I don't believe a word of it. They're only pretending to be shocked. They don't really care a straw what I do." This perverse attitude finally leads to Daisy's death, when she goes, against Winterbourne's urging, to the Colosseum at night (a place that, after dark, was reputed to have a miasma often fatal to foreigners) and contracts a mortal fever. When Winterbourne angrily asks Giovanelli why he took Daisy to such a dangerous place, the Italian answers, "*she*—she did what she liked."

The complexity of the moral nuances of the story is revealed when one remembers that Winterbourne, who is regarded as quite the perfect young gentleman and is welcomed in the best society, has a mistress back in Geneva. Clearly, in that "best" society what matters is not virtue (Daisy is quite guiltless of any actual wrongdoing) but the appearance of it—Winterbourne may not be virtuous, but he is discreet. The old theme of appearance versus reality thus emerges in this story, but with social implications not found in the work of other authors. To James, one of the most difficult problems for Americans trying to come to terms with Europe is that the appearance of virtue often counts for more than the reality. This problem is seen quite plainly in *The Reverberator*, written ten years later, in which an American businessman is puzzled that a French family is upset over some scandalous things said about them in a newspaper; so far as he is concerned, such things do not matter so long as they are not true.

James's realism is most evident in the close of the story. Winterbourne is remorseful over Daisy's death. He regrets that he did not try harder to understand her and correct her misconceptions. He tells his aunt, "She would have appreciated one's esteem." Then, he applies the lesson to himself: "I've lived too long in foreign parts." So far, the story has seemed to advance a moral thesis about the corruption of innocence and the valuable truths that can be learned. James closes the novella, however, on a note that proves how realistic his vision of human nature was: "Nevertheless he soon went back to live at Geneva, whence there continue to come the most contradictory accounts of his motives of sojourn: a report that he's 'studying' hard—an intimation that he's much interested in a very clever foreign lady." James had no illusions about people.

While *Daisy Miller* is told in the first person, from Winterbourne's consciousness, *The Portrait of a Lady*, a much longer and more complicated fiction, is related through the minds of a number of characters. This book is probably the most generally admired of all James's full-length novels. It carries the "international theme" to what some consider its highest level of expression, and it offers the reader one of the most impressive characters in James's work, the delightful Isabel Archer, the "lady" of the title. Again, James is psychologically realistic: while Isabel is honest, intelligent, and sensitive, she is not without fault; she does have "an unquenchable desire to think well of herself." She is an "innocent abroad" who is "affronting her destiny." This fate is to be given, first, the chance to visit Europe (offered by Mrs. Lydia Touchett, her wealthy aunt who lives in Europe) and, then, a great deal of money (provided by the will of Mr. Daniel Touchett, at the suggestion of his son Ralph, who becomes very fond of Isabel). This combination of high connections—Mr. Touchett associates with a number of prominent English families, most significantly that of Lord Warburton—opportunities for travel, and comfortable circumstances is common in James's novels.

In *The Portrait of a Lady*, James studies the relationships of the characters in great detail. When Lord Warburton proposes to Isabel, the situation is examined closely, and her rejection of him prepares for later plot developments and revelations of character. As is often the case in James, the money that Isabel inherits is both a blessing and a curse. It permits her to travel and to live almost lavishly, but it also attracts to her one of the few outright villains in James's fiction. Gilbert Osmond appears to be charming, modest, intelligent, and sensitive. He proves to be proud, arrogant, idle, and cruel. In a powerful enunciation of the international theme, Osmond courts Isabel cleverly, appealing to her sense of the artistic wonders of Europe, of which he seems to be a fine judge. He wins her hand, partly through the efforts of Madame Serena Merle, an American expatriate (as is Osmond) who, Isabel later discovers, was once Osmond's mistress (they could not marry, since neither was wealthy—the topic of marrying for money is one that James explored as thoroughly as any writer ever had and with greater insight). Mme. Merle is eager for Osmond to marry well, since they have a daughter, Pansy, whom she wishes to see well placed in the world. With James's usual subtlety and with his use of a device that again proves effective in *The Golden Bowl*, Isabel first suspects the unacknowledged intimacy between Mme. Merle and Osmond when she sees them through a window, in a room in which she is standing and he is seated—such social touches mark James's fiction repeatedly; to him, the social graces were a great deal more than simply pleasant decorations on the fringes of human intercourse.

Of course, the marriage is a failure. Osmond comes to resent Isabel, and eventually she despises him. In the famous Chapter Forty-two, Isabel examines the grim condition of her life. In an extended passage of what is clearly a precursor of the stream-of-consciousness technique, James causes Isabel to review the terrible errors she has made—"It was her deep distrust of her husband—this was what darkened her world"—and to consider how foolish her pride has made her: Ralph Touchett, among others, warned her against Osmond. Isabel's stubbornness and refusal to heed wise advice reminds one of Daisy Miller's similar folly. The plot becomes more complex when Lord Warburton directs his affections to Pansy. Naturally, Osmond is highly in favor of such a marriage, since Warburton is very rich. Isabel incurs her husband's even more intense hatred by discouraging the English peer with the simple argument that he and Pansy do not really love each other. Here, European corruption (expressed in an American expatriate, as is often the case in James's fiction) is opposed to native American innocence and emotional integrity.

The conclusion of this novel is among James's most subtle and ambiguous. Isabel returns to England to visit the deathbed of Ralph Touchett. His death has been prepared for by the announcement in the first chapter that he is in poor health. In fact, Ralph is one of James's truly virtuous characters, as is shown by his renunciation of any thought of marrying Isabel, whom he loves, because of his failing physical condition. Isabel admits to Ralph that he was right and that she committed a monumental error in marrying Osmond. Ralph, typically, blames himself for having provided her with the money that tempted Gilbert; Isabel refuses this excuse, recognizing that the mistake was her own. The puzzling aspect of the last pages of the novel is that Isabel determines to go back to Osmond as his wife. Several explanations have been offered, all of them proving the profound depth of James's penetration of human motives. The most dramatic is that Isabel's confrontation with her old lover from America, Caspar Goodwood, is so violent—he seizes her and kisses her passionately—that it frightens her (perhaps arousing an unsettling sexuality in her nature) into returning to a life that may be despicable but is safe. Another, more likely reason for the decision is that Isabel has become fond of Pansy and has promised to come back and help her to advance in life along sound and honorable lines. The most subtle reason may be that Isabel is simply too proud to admit her blunder openly to the world, which a separation would do, and prefers to live in misery rather than escape to what she would regard as shame. Whatever the true cause of her resolution (and they might all be operative), she starts back to Rome immediately. In the last passage of the book, however, Isabel's old friend and confidante, Henrietta Stackpole, suggests to Caspar that he must have patience—evidently a hint that this loyal friend of Isabel believes that she will not stay with Osmond forever.

Scholars who believe that James attained the peak of his treatment of the international theme in this novel point to the delicate illumination of Isabel's growing awareness of the sinister undertones of life and to the gallery of superb portraits of ineffectual innocence (as in Ralph, who is all good will and yet helps to ruin Isabel's life), black evil (in Mme. Merle and Osmond), and admixtures of positive and negative traits, as in Mrs. Touchett, who is essentially well-intentioned but is supremely intransigent (she does not live with the mild-mannered Mr. Touchett, and "the edges of her conduct were so very clear-cut" that they "had a knife-like effect"). Even if the reader is not quite ready to agree with the judgment of F. R. Leavis that this novel, along with *The Bostonians*, is one of "the two most brilliant novels in the language," it seems difficult to deny that *The Portrait of a Lady* is the articulate treatment of the "international theme" in American literature.

James omitted *The Bostonians* from the New York edition because it deals with purely American subjects, Americans in the United States; it has no trace of the international theme. *The Bostonians* was undervalued by critics as well as by its author, and it has taken many years for readers to recognize the novel as, in Leavis' words, "a wonderfully rich, intelligent and brilliant book." Aside from focusing on a social topic, a rare instance of this emphasis in James, *The Bostonians* also treats skillfully another subject much on his mind during this era: the problems and aberrations of obsessed, disturbed people. The conflict between the old-fashioned conservative Southerner, Basil Ransom, and his New England cousin, Olive Chancellor, makes for a novel full of tension and animation. Some of the modern interest in the book results from what has been judged a nearly lesbian relationship betwen Olive and Verena Tarrant, the attractive girl who is the source of the antagonism. As Irving Howe suggests in his Introduction to the Modern Library edition of *The Bostonians* (1956), the fact that people of James's era did not have modern terms of reference such as "lesbian" does not mean that they knew less about deviant relationships.

The social problem underlined by the novel is that of women's rights, the difficulty being, of course, that women had few of them. Today, the victories that have been won for the right of women to vote, hold office, and the like are taken for granted, but a reading of *The Bostonians* makes clear how much painful and dreary effort went into creating these advances. As usual, however, James treats the issue specifically, in terms of individual people. In discussing the book later, James said that he took too long to get the story going, provided too much background for the characters. Many current readers, however, judge the background both necessary and interesting. It is, for example, important that Ransom be presented in both a positive and negative light, in order to prepare adequately for the somewhat ambiguous resolution of the plot. As a Southerner who has come North to practice the law in a location that will provide him with opportunities not available in the war-ravaged South (it is a clever touch that James causes him to be a Civil War veteran, now living in the region populated by his recent enemies; in this way James emphasizes Basil's sense of alienation and loneliness), Ransom is both appealing—he has "a fine head and such magnificent eyes"—and repelling: "he was very long . . . and he looked a little hard and discouraging, like a column of figures."

Ransom proves very hard and discouraging. Once he meets Verena Tarrant, the daughter of a "mesmeric healer" of dubious integrity (James's depiction of this character is further evidence of his rich fund of humor), who has become by some natural inspiration, an eloquent platform speaker on behalf of the movement to extend the rights of women, the stage is set for the great contention. Olive Chancellor reluctantly allows Basil to become acquainted with Verena—by this time, the well-to-do Boston spinster has already been overwhelmed by the innocent charm of the naïve girl. Thus the battle lines are drawn early. Ransom soon realizes that Verena should be married, preferably to him, instead of wasting her life on a fruitless and, in his opinion, misguided cause. Ransom believes that the highest destiny to which a woman can aspire is "to make some honest man happy." He finds a formidable opponent in Olive, whose zeal for reform inspires her widowed sister, Mrs. Luna, who believes the whole movement to be ridiculous (since she is very interested in romantic relationships with men, particularly Ransom, for a time), to remark that "She would reform the solar system if she could get hold of it." The wit that James displays at the expense of the movement may seem to indicate that he too thinks it ridiculous, but, as usual, the author plays fair, offering a warm and sensitive picture of Miss Birdseye (a character who caused James to be much criticized in his own time, since many readers believed her to be based closely on a highly respected member of the Peabody family, of Boston—James always denied the charge), an old reformer who has been pursuing the cause for decades.

Verena and Basil meet but a handful of times before the climax of the novel, but their dialogues are artfully designed by the author to reveal that Verena, who has been welcomed into Olive's home as a permanent guest (the Boston spinster, while having no gift for oratory herself, is fully committed to Verena's promulgation of the cause—she is also deeply and possessively committed to Verena personally, having once cried passionately, "Promise me not to marry!"), is slowly becoming interested in Ransom. Finally, when he believes that he can afford to marry, a conviction that seems somewhat optimistic, since his career has advanced very slowly, and since his belief is based on the publication of only one essay on political and social philosophy, he proposes to Verena. James has not been widely accused of depending on coincidences in his plots, as Charles Dickens and Thomas Hardy, for example, have been, but a number of them do appear. In this case, Verena turns to Olive and away from Basil chiefly because Miss Birdseye, of whom she is very fond, dies shortly after the proposal.

These circumstances lead to the highly dramatic scene at the Boston Music Hall, where Verena is scheduled to address a large crowd. Ransom, learning of the planned address, arrives, manages to get backstage (to the door of the dressing room, which is guarded by a large Boston policeman, provided by the fearful and distraught Olive), and forcefully urges Verena to go away with him. She ultimately accedes to his coercion (he seizes her and almost pushes her out the door), leaving Olive weeping and desolate. James, in his customary evenhanded dealing with themes and characters, makes it clear that the marriage of Basil and Verena will certainly be anything but happy ever after. Verena is in tears when she is ushered from the theater by her lover, and in the last sentence of the book, James provides a typically ominous forecast of their future: "It is to be feared that with the union, so far from brilliant, into which she is about to enter, these were not the last she was destined to shed." Many readers find it astonishing that James could have so underrated this penetrating study of social movements and human beings torn between personal loyalties and abstract ideals. The climactic final scene is the most dramatic and lively that James ever wrote. This is, though, clearly not the end of the story. As Conrad has said, "One is never set at rest by Mr. Henry James's novels. His books end as an episode in life ends. You remain with the sense of the life still going on."

The Ambassadors, which James considered "frankly, quite the best, 'all round,' of my productions," is now generally rated as one of his masterpieces (some critics believe it to be far and away the most accomplished work of the major phase). Like many of his novels, it was based on an incident in real life. In his notebooks, James recalls being told of a visit that his old friend William Dean Howells made to Paris in his later years. According to the anecdote, told to James by Jonathan Sturges, Howells, overcome by the beauty of Paris, remarked to his youthful friend, "Oh, you are young, you are young—be glad of it: be glad of it and *live*. Live all you can: it's a mistake not to." This passage, and the rest of the speech, is almost word-for-word that made by the middle-aged Lambert Strether, the hero of *The Ambassadors*, to Little Bilham (a character thought to have been based on Sturges) in the beautiful Parisian garden of the artist Gloriani (a character carried over from *Roderick Hudson*; James sometimes became so interested in a character that he revived him for a later novel).

Strether is indeed an "ambassador." He has been given the unenviable assignment (by his formidable patroness, Mrs. Abel Newsome) of persuading her son, Chadwick Newsome, to return to his family and commercial responsibilities in Woollett, Massachusetts (probably representing Worcester, Massachusetts). The primary subject of this novel is *joie de vivre*; this quality is just what Strether finds when he arrives in Paris, where he has not been since he was a young man. It has been observed that one of the salient aspects of James's fiction is irony. Nowhere is this quality more in evidence than in *The Ambassadors*. Chad Newsome, Strether discovers, has been made a gracious gentleman by his life in Paris; Strether, charmed by the beauty and enchantment of the city, cannot in good conscience urge Chad to leave delightful Paris for dull Woollett. The irony lies in the fact that Chad is quite willing and, finally, eager to return home to make a great deal of money (the family business is very successful; it manufactures some useful article which is, typically, unidentified by James), while Strether longs to remain in Paris. Indeed, his delay in dispatching Chad home impels Mrs. Newsome to send her intimidating daughter, Mrs. Sarah Pocock, and her husband to take up the commission, since Strether has evidently failed. Thus the forces of philistinism are present, enlivening the conflict.

This conflict is chiefly in the mind of Strether, since, in this novel, James undertook to employ the third-person limited point of view to its fullest effect. As usual, the situation is not so simple as it appears. It is not merely residence in Paris that has "civilized" Chad; it has also been his mistress, Mme. Marie de Vionnet. Strether, before he knows of the intimacy between his young friend and this sophisticated and charming lady, develops an intense admiration and affection for her. Even after he learns of the liaison, accidentally seeing the two rowing on a river near an inn where they are staying, Strether is still entranced by Marie de Vionnet. When Chad decides to return home and abandon his mistress (who has been reviled, to Strether's dismay, by Mrs. Pocock, who refers to Chad's relationship with her as "hideous"), Strether recognizes her tragedy ("You are fighting for your life!") and is extremely sympathetic. He has, however, his own problems. Thanks to Mrs. Newsome's already aroused suspicions and Sarah Pocock's expected damning report, Strether sees that his comfortable position in Woollett (and possibly eventual marriage to his widowed employer) is very likely gone: "It probably *was* all at an end."

The renunciation theme, so prominent in James's novels, is perhaps more powerfully formulated at the close of this novel than in any other of his books. Despite the appeal of Paris, and the hinted offer of an agreeable marriage to Maria Gostrey, an American expatriate who had befriended Strether when he first landed in Europe, this highly moral and responsible man resolves to return to Woollett, where he believes his duty to lie. He cannot help Mme. de Vionnet. He cannot help himself. This sort of ethical resolution may seem foolish to modern readers, but it is believable in the novel, and the circumstances suggest James's belief that, in current terms, there is a price tag on everything, even happiness. The novel, then, is not only a tribute to Paris and the life of cultural elevation that it can provide but also the necessity of responsible and considerate action. James admitted that he learned a great deal from George Eliot; he shared her conviction that duty is absolute in the ethical universe. The temptation of Strether is almost overwhelming, but his New England sense of duty compels him to conquer it. It is difficult to think of another novelist, or, indeed, another novel, that illuminates so brightly the significance of conscientious moral choices.

Henry James's contributions to the evolution of the modern novel are of staggering magnitude and diversity. Perhaps his greatest contribution was best summed up by Ezra Pound shortly after James's death: "Peace comes of communication. No man of our time has so labored to create means of communication as did the late Henry James. The whole of great art is a struggle for communication."

Fred B. McEwen

Other major works

SHORT FICTION: *A Passionate Pilgrim*, 1875; *The Madonna of the Future*, 1879; *The Siege of London*, 1883; *Tales of Three Cities*, 1884; *The Author of Beltraffio*, 1885; *The Aspern Papers*, 1888; *The Lesson of the Master*, 1892; *The Real Thing*, 1893; *Terminations*, 1895; *Embarrassments*, 1896; *The Two Magics: The Turn of the Screw and Covering End*, 1898; *The Soft Side*, 1900; *The Better Sort*, 1903; *The Novels and Tales of Henry James*, 1907-1909; *The Finer Grain*, 1910; *A Landscape Painter*, 1919; *Travelling Companions*, 1919; *Master Eustace*, 1920; *Henry James: Selected Short Stories*, 1950; *Henry James: Eight Tales from the Major Phase*, 1958; *The Complete Tales of Henry James*, 1962-1965.

PLAYS: *The American*, 1891; *Guy Domville*, 1894; *Theatricals: Tenants and Disengaged*, 1894; *Theatricals, Second Series: The Album and The Reprobate*, 1895; *The Complete Plays of Henry James*, 1949.

NONFICTION: *Transatlantic Sketches*, 1875; *French Poets and Novelists*, 1878; *Hawthorne*, 1879; *Portraits of Places*, 1883; *A Little Tour in France*, 1884; *Partial Portraits*, 1888; *Essays in London*, 1893; *William Wetmore Story and His Friends*, 1903; *English Hours*, 1905; *The American Scene*, 1907; *Views and Reviews*, 1908; *Italian Hours*, 1909; *A Small Boy and Others*, 1913; *Notes of a Son and Brother*, 1914; *Notes on Novelists*, 1914; *The Middle Years*, 1917; *The Art of the Novel: Critical Prefaces*, 1934; *The Art of Criticism: Henry James on the Theory and Practice of Fiction*, 1986; *The Complete Notebooks of Henry James*, 1987.

Bibliography

Anderson, Charles R. *Person, Place, and Thing in Henry James's Novels.* Durham, N.C.: Duke University Press, 1977. In the introduction Anderson briefly surveys James's complete works, some sixty-five volumes. The body of this study deals with a selection of James's novels. Anderson salutes the "monumental achievement of this creative artist" and calls him the "father of the modern novel" because James opened up paths for it to flourish. The chapter "For Love or Money, *The Wings of the Dove*" is particularly recommended.

Bloom, Harold, ed. *Modern Critical Views: Henry James.* New York: Chelsea House, 1987. Bloom has compiled what he considers the best in criticism available on James, presented in order of their original publication. Contains much insight from knowledgeable sources on this important American novelist. Contributors include Carren Kaston, author of *Imagination and Desire in the Novels of Henry James* (New Brunswick, N.J.: Rutgers University Press, 1984), and Laurence Bedwell Holland, author of *The Expense of Vision: Essays on the Craft of Henry James* (Baltimore: The Johns Hopkins University Press, 1982).

Cargill, Oscar. *The Novels of Henry James.* New York: Macmillan, 1961. A useful study by a famous critic of James's novels who incorporates most of the outstanding scholarship on James in his commentary. The bibliographical and critical studies references are a valuable resource.

Edel, Leon. *Henry James: A Life.* Rev. ed. New York: Harper & Row, 1985. An updated and revised version of the original five-volume epic and a definitive work on James. The additions to this edition are particularly useful on the subject of James's sexuality and its relationship to his writing.

Gargano, James W. *Critical Essays on Henry James: The Early Novels.* Boston: G. K. Hall, 1987. An anthology of important criticism on James, including reviews and comments by James's contemporaries, as well as reprinted articles. An essay by Adeline R. Turner, "Miriam as the English Rachel: Gerome's Portrait of the Tragic Muse," was written specifically for this volume. A significant contribution to the criticism available on James's early novels. A second volume, on the later novels, is planned for publication.

Hutchinson, Stuart. *Henry James: An American as Modernist.* Totowa, N.J.: Barnes & Noble Books, 1982. Discusses James in an American and European context, that is creation versus re-creation. Hutchinson, a British critic, has elected to deal only with seven novels from James's prodigious output, including: *Washington Square*, *The Bostonians*, *What Maisie Knew*, *The Ambassadors*, *The Wings of the Dove*, and *The Golden Bowl*. Claims that these novels tell a significant part of the story of James.

Putt, Samuel P. *Henry James: A Reader's Guide.* Ithaca, N.Y.: Cornell University Press, 1966. A well-organized commentary on most of James's major and minor works. Although this volume attempts to make James's work accessible to the beginning reader, it is better suited to the advanced reader.

P. D. JAMES

Born: Oxford, England; August 3, 1920

Principal long fiction

Cover Her Face, 1962; *A Mind to Murder*, 1963; *Unnatural Causes*, 1967; *Shroud for a Nightingale*, 1971; *An Unsuitable Job for a Woman*, 1972; *The Black Tower*, 1975; *Death of an Expert Witness*, 1977; *Innocent Blood*, 1980; *The Skull Beneath the Skin*, 1982; *A Taste for Death*, 1986; *Devices and Desires*, 1989.

Other literary forms

Though P. D. James is known principally as a novelist, she is also a short-story writer and a playwright. The great bulk of James's work is in the form of the long narrative, but her short fiction has found a wide audience through its publication in *Ellery Queen's Mystery Magazine* and other popular periodicals. It is generally agreed that James requires the novel form to show her literary strengths to best advantage. Still, short stories such as "The Victim" reveal in microcosm the dominant theme of the long works. James's lone play, *A Private Treason*, was first produced in London on March 12, 1985.

Achievements

James's first novel, *Cover Her Face*, did not appear until 1962, at which time the author was in her early forties. Acceptance of her as a major crime novelist, however, grew very quickly. *A Mind to Murder* appeared in 1963, and with the publication of *Unnatural Causes* in 1967 came that year's prize from the Crime Writers Association. In the novels which have followed, James has shown an increasing mastery of the labyrinthine murder-and-detection plot. This mastery is the feature of her work that most appeals to one large group of her readers, while a second group of readers would single out the subtlety and psychological validity of her characterizations. Critics have often remarked that James, more than almost any other modern mystery writer, has succeeded in overcoming the limitations of the genre. In addition, she has created one of the more memorable descendants of Sherlock Holmes. Like Dorothy Sayers' Lord Peter Wimsey and Agatha Christie's Hercule Poirot, James's Adam Dalgliesh is a sleuth whose personality is more interesting than his skill in detection.

Biography

Phyllis Dorothy James was born in Oxford, England, on August 3, 1920. She was graduated from Cambridge High School for Girls in 1937. She was married to Ernest C. B. White, a medical practitioner, from August 8, 1941, until his death in 1964. She worked as a hospital administrator from 1949 to 1968 and as a civil servant in the Department of Home Affairs, London, from 1968 to 1972. From 1972 until her retirement in 1979, she was a senior civil servant in the crime department.

Analysis

P. D. James's work is solidly in the tradition of the realistic novel. Her novels are intricately plotted, as successful novels of detection must be. Through her use of extremely well delineated characters and a wealth of minute and accurate details, however, James never allows her plot to distort the other aspects of her novel. As a result of her employment, James had extensive contact with physicians, nurses, civil servants, police officials, and magistrates. She uses this experience to devise settings in the active world where men and women busily pursue their vocations. She eschews the country weekend murders of her predecessors, with their leisure-class suspects who have little more to do than chat with the amateur detective and look guilty.

A murder requires a motive, and it is her treatment of motivation that sets James's work apart from most mystery fiction. Her suspects are frequently the emotionally maimed who, nevertheless, manage to function with an apparent normality. Beneath their veneer, dark secrets fester, producing the phobias and compulsions they take such pains to disguise. James's novels seem to suggest that danger is never far away in the most mundane setting, especially the workplace. She avoids all gothic devices, choosing instead to create a growing sense of menace just below the surface of everyday life. James's murderers rarely kill for gain; they kill to avoid exposure of some sort.

The setting for *Shroud for a Nightingale* is a nursing hospital near London. The student nurses and most of the staff are in permanent residence there. In this closed society, attachments—sexual and otherwise—are formed, rivalries develop, and resentments grow. When a student nurse is murdered during a teaching demonstration, Inspector Adam Dalgliesh of Scotland Yard arrives to investigate. In the course of his investigation, Dalgliesh discovers that the murdered girl was a petty blackmailer, that a second student nurse (murdered soon after Dalgliesh's arrival) was pregnant but unmarried and had engaged in an affair with a middle-aged surgeon, that one member of the senior staff is committing adultery with a married man from the neighborhood and another is homosexually attracted to one of her charges. At the root of the murders, however, is the darkest secret of all, a terrible sin which a rather sympathetic character has been attempting both to hide and expiate for more than thirty years. The murder weapon is poison, which serves also as a metaphor for the fear and suspicion that rapidly spread through the insular world of the hospital.

Adam Dalgliesh carries a secret burden of his own. His wife and son died during childbirth. He is a sensitive and cerebral man, a poet of some reputation. These deaths have left him bereft of hope and intensely aware of the fragility of man's control over his own life. Only the rules that humankind has painstakingly fashioned over the centuries can ward off degeneration and annihilation. As a policeman, Dalgliesh enforces society's rules, giving himself a purpose for living and some brief respite from his memories. Those who commit murder contribute to the world's disorder and hasten the ultimate collapse of civilization. Dalgliesh will catch them and see that they are punished.

In *An Unsuitable Job for a Woman*, published within a year of *Shroud for a Nightingale*, James introduces her second recurring protagonist. Cordelia Gray's "unsuitable job" is that of private detective. Gray unexpectedly falls heir to a detective agency and, as a result, discovers her vocation. Again, James avoids the formularized characterization. Gender is the most obvious but least interesting difference between Dalgliesh and Gray. Dalgliesh is brooding and introspective; although the narratives in which he appears are the very antithesis of the gothic novel, there are aspects of the gothic hero in his behavior. Gray, on the other hand, is optimistic, outgoing, and good-natured, despite her unfortunate background (she was brought up in a series of foster homes). She is a truth seeker and, like William Shakespeare's Cordelia, a truth teller. Dalgliesh and Gray are alike in their cleverness and competence. Their paths occasionally cross, and a friendly rivalry exists between them.

In *Death of an Expert Witness*, James's seventh novel, Dalgliesh again probes the secrets of a small group of coworkers and their families. The setting this time is a laboratory that conducts forensic examinations. James used her nineteen years of experience as a hospital administrative assistant to render the setting of *Shroud for a Nightingale* totally convincing, and she uses her seven years of work in the crime department of the Home Office to the same effect in *Death of an Expert Witness*. In her meticulous attention to detail, James writes in the tradition of Gustave Flaubert, Leo Tolstoy, and the nineteenth century realists. Because the setting, characterizations, and incidents of a James novel are so solidly grounded in detail, it tends to be considerably longer than the ordinary murder mystery. This fact accounts for what little adverse criticism her work has received. Some critics have suggested that so profuse is the detail, the general reader may eventually grow impatient—that the pace of the narrative is too leisurely. These objections from some contemporary critics remind the reader once more of James's affinity with the novelists of the nineteenth century.

The laboratory in which the expert witness is killed serves as a focal point for an intriguing cast of characters. Ironically, the physiologist is murdered while he is examining physical evidence from another murder. The dead man leaves behind a rather vacant, superannuated father, who lived in the house with him. The principal suspect is a high-strung laboratory assistant, whom the deceased bullied and gave an unsatisfactory performance rating. The new director of the laboratory has an attractive but cruel and wanton sister, with whom he has a relationship that is at least latently incestuous. In addition, Dalgliesh investigates a lesbian couple, one of whom becomes the novel's second murder victim; a melancholy physician, who performs autopsies for the police and whose unpleasant wife has just left him; the physician's two curious children, the elder girl being very curious indeed; a middle-aged babysitter, who is a closet tippler; and a crooked cop, who is taking advantage of a love-starved young woman of the town. In spinning her complex narrative, James draws upon her intimate knowledge of police procedure, evidential requirements in the law, and criminal behavior.

The publication in 1980 of *Innocent Blood* marked a departure for James. While the novel tells a tale of murder and vengeance, it is not a detective story. Initially, the protagonist is Philippa Rose Palfrey—later, the novel develops a second center of consciousness. Philippa is eighteen, the adopted daughter of an eminent sociologist and a juvenile court magistrate. She is obsessed with her unremembered past. She is sustained by fantasies about her real parents, especially her mother, and the circumstances which forced them to give her up for adoption. Despite these romantic notions, Philippa is intelligent, resourceful, and tenacious, as well as somewhat abrasive. She takes advantage of the Children Act of 1975 to wrest her birth record from a reluctant bureaucracy.

The record shows that she was born Rose Ducton, to a clerk and a housewife in Essex. This revelation sends Philippa rushing to the dreary eastern suburb where she was born, beginning an odyssey which will eventually lead to her mother. She discovers that her fantasies cannot match the lurid realities of her past. Her father was a child molester, who murdered a young girl in an upstairs room of his house. Her mother apparently participated in the murder and was caught trying to take the body away in her car. Her father has died in prison, and her mother is still confined. Though horrified, Philippa is now even more driven to find explanations of some sort and to rehabilitate the image of her mother. She visits Mary Ducton in prison, from which she is soon to be released, and eventually takes a small flat in London, where they will live together.

In chapter 8, James introduces the second protagonist, at which time the novel becomes as much his as it is Philippa's. Norman Scase is fifty-seven and newly retired from his job as a government accounts clerk. Scase is the widowed father of the murdered girl. He retires when he learns of Mary Ducton's impending release, for all of his time will be required to stalk her so that, at the appropriate moment, he may kill her. The murder of young Julia Mavis Scase robbed her father of the same years it stole from Philippa. Philippa is desperately trying to reclaim these lost years by learning to know, forgive, and love her mother. Scase is driven to a far more desperate act.

In form, *Innocent Blood* resembles Tolstoy's *Anna Karenina* (1873-1877). Like Anna and Levin, the dual protagonists proceed through the novel along separate paths. Philippa has no knowledge of Scase's existence, and he knows her only as the constant companion of the victim he is tracking all over London. James makes the city itself a character in the novel, and as Philippa shares her London with her mother, it is fully realized in Dickensian detail. Philippa is the more appealing protagonist, but Scase is a fascinating character study: the least likely of premeditating murderers, a little man who is insignificant in everything except his *idée fixe*. James created a similar character in "The Victim," a short story appearing seven years earlier. There, a dim and diffident assistant librarian stalks and murders the man who took his beautiful young wife away from him. The novel form, however, affords James the opportunity to develop completely this unpromising material into a memorable character. As Scase lodges in cheap hotels, monitors the women's movements with binoculars, and stares up at their window through the night, the reader realizes that the little man has found a purpose which truly animates his life for the first time. He and Philippa will finally meet at the uncharacteristically melodramatic climax (the only blemish on an otherwise flawless novel).

Commander Adam Dalgliesh returns in *A Taste for Death* after an absence of nine years. He is heading a newly formed squad charged with investigating politically sensitive crimes. He is assisted by the aristocratic chief inspector John Massingham and a new recruit, Kate Miskin. Kate is bright, resourceful, and fiercely ambitious. Like Cordelia Gray, she has overcome an unpromising background: She is the illegitimate child of a mother who died shortly after her birth and a father she has never known. The title of the novel is evocative. A taste for death is evident in not only the psychopathic killer but also Dalgliesh and his subordinates, the principal murder victim himself, and, surprisingly, a shabby High Church Anglican priest, reminiscent of one of Graham Greene's failed clerics.

When Sir Paul Berowne, a Tory minister, is found murdered along with a tramp in the vestry of St. Matthew's Church in London, Dalgliesh is put in charge of the investigation. These murders seem linked to the deaths of two young women previously associated with the Berowne household. The long novel (more than 450 pages) contains the usual array of suspects, hampering the investigation with their evasions and outright lies, but in typical James fashion, each is portrayed in three dimensions. The case develops an additional psychological complication when Dalgliesh identifies with a murder victim for the first time in his career and a metaphysical complication when he discovers that Berowne recently underwent a profound religious experience in the church, one reportedly entailing stigmata. Perhaps the best examples of James's method of characterization are the elderly spinster and the ten-year-old boy of the streets who discover the bodies in chapter 1. In the hands of most other crime writers, these characters would have been mere plot devices, but James gives them a reality which reminds the reader how deeply a murder affects everyone associated with it in any way. Having begun the novel with Miss Wharton and Darren, James returns to them in the concluding chapter.

Devices and Desires possesses the usual James virtues. The story is set at and around a nuclear power plant on the coast of Norfolk in East Anglia. The geographic details are convincing (even though the author states that she has invented topography to suit her purposes), and the nuclear power industry has obviously been well researched. Although the intricate plot places heavy demands of action upon the characters, the omniscient narrator analyzes even the most minor of them in such depth that they are believable. Finally, greater and more interesting than the mystery of "who did it" is the mystery of those ideas, attitudes, and experiences which have led a human being to murder. Ultimately, every James novel is a study of the devices and desires of the human heart.

In some ways, however, the novel is a departure. The setting is a brooding, windswept northern coast, the sort of gothic background which James largely eschewed in her earlier novels. *Devices and Desires* is also more of a pot-boiler than were any of its predecessors. As the story begins, a serial killer known as the Whistler is claiming his fourth victim (he will kill again during the course of the novel). A group of terrorists is plotting an action against the Larksoken Nuclear Power Station. The intrigue is so heavy and so many people are not what they seem that at one point the following tangled situation exists: Neil Pascoe, an antinuclear activist, has been duped by Amy Camm, whom he has taken into his trailer on the headland. Amy believes that she is acting as an agent for an animal rights group, but she has been duped by Caroline Amphlett, personal secretary to the Director of Larksoken. Caroline has, in turn, been duped by the terrorists for whom she has been spying—they plot her death when she becomes useless to them. Eventually, shadowy figures turn up from MI5, Britain's intelligence agency. In this instance, so much exposition and explication is required of James's dialogue that it is not always as convincing as in the previous books.

Adam Dalgliesh shares this novel with Chief Inspector Terry Rickards. Rickards is a mirror image of Dalgliesh. He is less intelligent and imaginative, but he has the loving wife and infant child whom Dalgliesh has lost. While Dalgliesh is on the headland, settling his aunt's estate, he stumbles upon a murder (literally—he discovers the body). Hilary Robarts, the beautiful, willful, and widely disliked and feared Acting Administrative Officer of the station, is strangled, and the Whistler's method is mimicked. As usual in a James novel, the suspects comprise a small and fairly intimate group. The author has totally mastered the detective story convention whereby at some point in the novel each of the suspects will seem the most plausible murderer.

The action of *Devices and Desires* affords James the opportunity to comment upon the use and potential misuse of nuclear power, the phenomenon of terrorism, the condition of race relations in London, even the state of Christianity in contemporary Britain. Still, what James always does best is to reveal, layer by layer, the mind which has committed itself to that most irrevocable of human actions, murder.

Patrick Adcock

Other major works
PLAY: *A Private Treason*, 1985.
NONFICTION: *The Maul and the Pear Tree: The Ratcliffe Highway Murders, 1811*, 1971 (with T. A. Critchley).

Bibliography
Bakerman, Jane S. "Cordelia Gray: Apprentice and Archetype." *Clues: A Journal of Detection* 5 (Spring/Summer, 1984): 101-114. A study of *An Unsuitable Job for a Woman*, which discusses James's female detective as the heroine of a *Bildungsroman*, or apprenticeship novel. Cordelia is only twenty-two when, almost by accident, she becomes a private investigator. Her first case is her rite of passage from girlhood to maturity and professionalism.

Benstock, Bernard. "The Clinical World of P. D. James." In *Twentieth-Century Women Novelists*, edited by Thomas F. Staley. Vol. 16. Totowa, N.J.: Barnes & Noble, 1982. Benstock's essay is found on pages 104-129 of the volume. He discusses James's use of setting, her narrative technique, and the relationship between the two.

Gidez, Richard B. *P. D. James*. Boston: Twayne, 1986. An entry in Twayne's English Authors series. Chapter 1 examines James's place within the tradition of the English mystery novel. Chapters 2-10 discuss in chronological order her first nine novels. Chapter 11 is devoted to her handful of short stories, and chapter 12 summarizes her work through *The Skull Beneath the Skin*.

Hubly, Erlene. "Adam Dalgliesh: Byronic Hero." *Clues: A Journal of Detection* 3 (Fall/Winter, 1982): 40-46. The brooding Dalgliesh, aloof, often forbidding, constantly bearing the pain of a deep tragedy in his personal life, has often been likened to the heroes of nineteenth century Romantic fiction. Hubly's article treats the appropriateness of this comparison.

Porter, Dennis. "Detection and Ethics: The Case of P. D. James." In *The Sleuth and the Scholar: Origins, Evolution, and Current Trends in Detective Fiction*, edited by Barbara A. Rader and Howard G. Zettler. Westport, Conn.: Greenwood, 1988. Pages 11-18 are devoted to Porter's essay on

James, a writer for whom moral principles are an integral part of the crime and detection story. Porter concentrates upon *Death of an Expert Witness*, *An Unsuitable Job for a Woman*, and *Innocent Blood*. Robin W. Wink, who has written elsewhere on James, contributes a foreword to the book.

Siebenheller, Norma. *P. D. James*. New York: Frederick Ungar, 1981. The first four chapters discuss the eight novels, grouped by decades, that James had produced through 1980. Chapter 5 discusses the detective protagonists Adam Dalgliesh and Cordelia Gray. Chapter 6 takes up the major themes of the novels; chapter 7, the major characters other than the two detectives. The final chapter deals with the James "style," in the sense both of her craftsmanship and of her elegance.

SARAH ORNE JEWETT

Born: South Berwick, Maine; September 3, 1849
Died: South Berwick, Maine; June 24, 1909

Principal long fiction
Deephaven, 1877; *A Country Doctor*, 1884; *A Marsh Island*, 1885; *The Country of the Pointed Firs*, 1896; *The Tory Lover*, 1901.

Other literary forms
In addition to her novels, Sarah Orne Jewett wrote several collections of short stories and sketches, most of which were published initially in periodicals such as *The Atlantic*. The best known of these collections are *Old Friends and New* (1879), *Country By-Ways* (1881), *A White Heron and Other Stories* (1886), and *The King of Folly Island and Other People* (1888). Jewett also wrote a series of children's books, including *Play Days: A Book of Stories for Children* (1878), *The Story of the Normans* (1887), and *Betty Leicester: A Story for Girls* (1890). The posthumous *Verses: Printed for Her Friends* was published in 1916. Finally, Jewett was a voluminous writer of letters. Among the collections of her private correspondence are the *Letters of Sarah Orne Jewett* (1911), edited by Annie Fields and the *Sarah Orne Jewett Letters* (1956), edited by Richard Cary.

Achievements
Jewett is remembered today as perhaps the most successful of the dozens of so-called "local-color" or "regional" writers who flourished in the United States from approximately 1870 to 1900. She is especially noted for her remarkable depictions of the farmers and fishermen of Maine coastal villages at the end of the nineteenth century. Although Jewett was writing from firsthand observation (she was born and reared in Maine), she was not one of the common folk of whom she wrote. Wealthy, articulate, and well-read, Jewett was an avid traveler who moved within prominent literary circles. Her sophistication imbued her best work with a polish and a degree of cosmopolitanism which renders it both readable and timeless; as a result, Jewett's reputation has been preserved long after the names of most other regional writers have been forgotten. Jewett is also regarded as something of a technical innovator. As modern critics of fiction attempt to establish specific criteria for novels and short stories, Jewett's best work—notably her classic *The Country of the Pointed Firs*—is seen as straddling both fictional categories. As such, her work is of great interest to contemporary literary theorists.

Biography
Sarah Orne Jewett was born in South Berwick, Maine, on September 3,

1849, the second of three daughters of a country doctor. The colonial mansion in which she was born and reared had been purchased and lavishly furnished by her paternal grandfather, Theodore Furber Jewett, a sea captain turned shipowner and merchant whose fortune enabled Sarah to live in comfort and to travel and write at leisure throughout her life. Her father and maternal grandfather were both practicing physicians who early imbued Sarah with a love of science and an interest in studying human behavior, as well as a passion for literature. Her formal education was surprisingly sporadic: since she had little patience with classroom procedures and tended to be sickly, her father generally permitted Sarah to be absent from her elementary school and to accompany him on his medical rounds in the Berwick area. This proved to be an education in itself, for her father spoke to her of literature and history, the two fields which became the great interests of her life, as well as of botany and zoology. Beginning in 1861, she attended the Berwick Academy, a private school; although for awhile she considered pursuing a career in medicine, her formal education was in fact completed with her graduation from the Academy in 1865.

Under no pressure either to earn a living or to marry, Jewett went on trips to Boston, New York, and Ohio and began to write stories and sketches under various pseudonyms, including "Alice Eliot" and "Sarah O. Sweet." Her first published story, "Jenny Garrow's Lovers," was a melodrama which appeared in Boston's *The Flag of Our Union* in 1868, and the eighteen-year-old author was sufficiently encouraged by this to begin submitting children's stories and poems to such juvenile magazines as *St. Nicholas* and the *Riverside Magazine for Young People*, as well as adult stories and sketches to *The Atlantic*. Her tale "Mr. Bruce" was published in *The Atlantic* in December, 1869. The first of her Maine sketches, "The Shore House," appeared in that magazine in 1873, and a successful series of them rapidly followed. At the urging of *The Atlantic* editor William Dean Howells, she collected and revised them for publication in book form as *Deephaven*. By that time, Jewett was beginning to establish a circle of literary friends which eventually would include James Russell Lowell, John Greenleaf Whittier, Oliver Wendell Holmes, and Harriet Beecher Stowe, whose *The Pearl of Orr's Island* (1862) that Jewett had read when she was thirteen or fourteen is believed to have inspired Jewett's attempts to record Maine life.

Unquestionably the most significant of her literary relationships was that with James T. Fields of Ticknor and Fields, the Boston publishing house. When Fields died in 1881, his widow Annie established a close lifelong friendship with Jewett. The relationship inspired long visits to Annie's Boston residence at 148 Charles Street, as well as summer vacations at the Fields' cottage in Manchester-by-the-Sea. In addition, Jewett and Fields traveled extensively: in 1882, they visited England, Ireland, France, Italy, Switzerland, Belgium, and Norway, and met Alfred, Lord Tennyson, and Christina Rossetti. On other trips to Europe in 1892 and 1898, Jewett met Samuel Clemens, Rudyard Kipling, and Henry James, and in 1900 the pair traveled to Greece and Turkey.

Meanwhile, Jewett continued to write. *A Country Doctor* was published in 1884, and a visit to Florida with Fields in 1888 led to several stories with Southern settings. Jewett was strongest, however, in her fictional re-creation of Maine coastal life, as is evident from the popular and critical success of *The Country of the Pointed Firs*, published in 1896. She received an honorary Litt.D. degree from Bowdoin College in 1901, the same year she published her first (and only) historical novel, *The Tory Lover*. In 1902, an accident virtually ended her career: on her birthday, Jewett was thrown from a carriage when the horse stumbled, and she sustained serious head and spinal injuries. She never fully recovered either her physical health or her literary powers: only two brief pieces were published during the remaining few years of her life, although she was able to write letters and to encourage the literary endeavors of the young Willa Cather. In March, 1909, she had a stroke while staying at Fields' Boston home; transported to South Berwick, Jewett died on June 24 in the house where she was born.

Analysis

The proper classification of Sarah Orne Jewett's first effort at long fiction, *Deephaven*, remains problematical even after a century. In some circles it is regarded as a novel, while many literary historians regard it as a collection of short stories, a contention immediately attributable to the book's genesis. It originated as a popular series of sketches which appeared in *The Atlantic* beginning in 1873. William Dean Howells encouraged Jewett to combine the sketches and flesh them out with a suitable dramatic framework and continuity, and the result—which was entitled *Deephaven* after the composite Maine seaport in which the sketches are set—was an immediate popular success. Even if a reader were unaware of the book's origins, however, he still might be inclined to perceive it as a collection of stories, for the individual chapters—and, at times, even portions of chapters—tend to function as discrete fictional units rather than as elements subsumed within a satisfying whole. *Deephaven*'s confusing fictional status is caused in part by its young author's inexperience with revision, and as such it may be perceived as a flawed book; the fictional hybrid quality of *Deephaven*, however, ultimately became Jewett's stylistic trademark, and for many readers this blurring of the traditional distinctions between the novel and the short story is precisely the source of much of the charm and uniqueness of Jewett's work.

Regardless of whether one reacts to *Deephaven* as seriously flawed or charmingly eclectic, however, the fact remains that structurally speaking it is a sort of fictional quilt: the individual chapters retain much of their original discreteness, while the fictional framework which was constructed around them is patently an afterthought; in other words, the seams show. Jewett introduces two young ladies of Boston, Kate Lancaster and Helen Denis, who spend an extended summer vacation in Deephaven, Maine, at the home of Kate's late grandaunt, Katharine Brandon. The two women are wealthy, educated, and affectionate twenty-four-year-olds: all of this background is revealed in a flurry of exposition within the first chapter or two, and in fact one learns nothing more of the women in the course of the next 250 pages. Their sole function in the story is to react to Deephaven and to record those reactions, and although Kate and Helen fulfill this function dutifully, their characterizations suffer accordingly. One has no sense of them as flesh-and-blood humans; indeed, they disappear from the text while some salty sea captain or rugged farmer, encouraged by an occasional "Please go only on!" from Kate, recounts a bit of folklore or personal history. This narrative frame, however annoying and contrived a technique it may be, suited Jewett's interests and purposes: never skillful at portraying upper-class urbanites, she was strongest at presenting the colorful, dignified, and occasionally grim lives of common people clinging to a dying way of life in coastal Maine in the late nineteenth century. These farmers, villagers, and seafarers were a source of perennial interest to Jewett, and the rich variety of their life-styles, skills, and experiences were elements which she lovingly recorded, even as they were dying before her eyes. Ultimately, it is this impulse to record various aspects of a cross section of American life, rather than poor judgment or technical incompetence, which must be cited as the source of Jewett's distinctive fragmentary style.

That style was rapidly being crystallized in the creation of *Deephaven*. As noted, the two outsiders who react to the coastal village almost disappear from the text despite the fact that this is a first-person narration, but frankly they are not missed. The book dissolves rapidly into a series of character studies, anecdotes, events, and descriptions of the landscape or homes. Individual characters are far more memorable than the volume in toto: the reader is inclined to recall Mrs. Kew, the lighthouse keeper; the widower Jim Patton, who repairs carpets; Danny the red-shirted fisherman, whose only friend was a stray cat; the "Kentucky Giantess," a local girl turned sideshow attraction; Captain Sands, a firm believer in thought-transference and the power of dreams; and Miss Sally Chauncey, the insane survivor of a once prosperous family. Each character is painfully aware of the passing of the economic and cultural prominence of Deephaven and, concomitantly, the passing of each one's way of life; and accordingly, each (rather incredibly) recounts his or her life's high points, along with bits of folklore and anecdotes, to the two vacationing Boston ladies.

In addition to offering poignant and often penetrating studies of common folk, Jewett provides accounts of events which are symptomatic of the passing of Deephaven. These accounts include a circus full of tired performers and exhausted (or dead) animals, and a lecture on the "Elements of True Man-hood" written for young men but addressed to a town whose young men have all died or departed to find new lives in urban factories or in the West. Finally, Jewett provides extended descriptions, often of home interiors. As a symbol of the luxurious life of the past, she offers a chapter-long discussion of the house of the deceased Aunt Kate (an analysis so meticulous that it mentions the tiny spiders on the wallpaper), along with a companion study of the home of the mad Miss Sally, whose crumbling, furnitureless mansion is decorated with frames without paintings. Clearly this is not the sunny, sentimental world which is generally—and erroneously—attributed to local-color writing of the late nineteenth century. Although Jewett is often accused of avoiding the less positive aspects of life, this is certainly not the case with *Deephaven*: one finds a world of despair, poverty, unemployment, disease, alcoholism, insan-ity, and death. This is not gratuitous misery, but life as Jewett perceived it in coastal Maine.

Despite the book's rather unexpected acknowledgement of the unpleasant in life, however, it was warmly received, not only because of the limitations Jewett set for herself (she was surely no literary naturalist when compared to Émile Zola, Stephen Crane, or Jack London), but because of the two protagonists through whose eyes the reader experiences Deephaven. Early in the book, as they giggle and kiss their way through the alien environment of Deephaven, Kate and Helen generate a sentimentalized and frankly vac-uous aura which is in keeping with the book's initial focus on the superficially picturesque aspects of the town; later in the story, as Jewett progressively focuses more on the grim side of life, the two girls begin to lapse frequently into improbable dialogues. For example, it is after a poor, unemployed wid-ower dies of alcoholism that Kate reveals the lesson she's learned: "Helen, I find that I understand better and better how unsatisfactory, how purposeless and disastrous, any life must be which is not a Christian life. It is like being always in the dark, and wandering one knows not where, if one is not learning more and more what it is to have a friendship with God." Kate and Helen are ingenuous and often preachy; they offer a romanticized counterbalance to the realistic world of Deephaven. As such, the book was rendered palatable to a Victorian audience, but as a result, it appears disjointed, dated, and sentimental to modern readers. With the notable exception of *The Country of the Pointed Firs*, these unfortunate qualities tend to pervade all of Jewett's attempts to write fiction of substantial length.

Jewett's second effort at long fiction, and her one book which is most amenable to classification as a novel, is *A Country Doctor*. Unfortunately, the book is marred by technical problems. Poorly proportioned, it concen-trates so much on the childhood of its heroine, Nan Prince, that her adult activities as a determined medical student and successful physician are simply matters of unconvincing hearsay. Structurally unimaginative, it offers a dry chronological account and a glaring paucity of psychological depth: the strength of character which Nan ostensibly possesses is scarcely glimpsed as she facilely combats with laughter or thin logic the feeble attempts of acquaintances and townspeople to dissuade her from embarking on a "man's" career instead of assuming the more "natural" role of wife and homemaker. Even so, *A Country Doctor* was Jewett's favorite work and it is easy to understand why. Despite its flaws, the book is in several respects representative of her finest work; its focal character, Dr. John Leslie, is a loving portrait of Jewett's own father, Dr. Theodore Herman Jewett.

The technical problems in *A Country Doctor* are apparent from even the most cursory reading. As Jewett herself acknowledged, she was far more adept at the delineation of character than at the development of plot, but even so, the characters in *A Country Doctor* are not generally handled effectively. Four of the characters to whom the reader is initially introduced—the twins Jacob and Martin Dyer, and their wives (who coincidentally are sisters)—are interesting rural types and fascinating examples of the power of early sibling relationships, heredity, and environment in the determination of adult character and behavior. Also interesting is Grandmother Thacher, the death of whose troubled prodigal daughter Adeline leaves her with the infant Nan, and whose son John, a country lawyer, is old long before his time. Unfortunately, Jewett does not utilize the potential of these characters: the four Dyers are forgotten not long after they are introduced, Grandmother Thacher dies while Nan is still young, and the child's Uncle John is dispatched a few pages after he makes his belated appearance in the story.

Jewett clearly wished to devote her time and energy not to secondary characters, but to Dr. Leslie himself, and in fact she succeeded so well in this endeavor that she inadvertently blurred the focus of the novel. The very title *A Country Doctor* apparently was designed to do double duty, referring to both Dr. Leslie and Dr. Nan Prince, his ward after the deaths of her grandmother and uncle; in fact, however, Jewett's primary concern was the presentation of Dr. Leslie. His portrait is vivid and touching: a widower well into middle age, Leslie is a trusted, competent physician much loved in the community of Oldfields, Maine. If he possesses any character flaws or troubles, aside from occasional grief for his wife or qualms over the stress his ward will encounter as a doctor, he conceals them nicely. Even the transparently contrived visit from his ex-classmate and foil, the well-traveled surgeon Dr. Ferris, fails to convince Leslie that his life might have been more productive, happy, or exciting away from Oldfields.

Living with the obligatory salty housekeeper in an old house full of books and flowers, Dr. Leslie readily adopts the orphaned Nan and interprets her "wildness" as simply "natural" behavior—and in this respect he not only is in keeping with the autobiographical elements of the book, but also serves to express several of Jewett's own theories. For much as Dr. Leslie is Jewett's father, young Nan is Sarah herself, and their unusual fictional relationship mimics the real one. Like Dr. Leslie, Dr. Jewett permitted his daughter to be absent from school and took her with him on his rounds, educating her with his discussions of science, literature, history, and psychology. Like Nan, Sarah was far more comfortable out of doors than in a classroom, and at an early age decided to pursue a career as a physician rather than marry; although Sarah later abandoned her plans for medicine, the similarities between her own situation and the fictional one are quite pronounced.

Perhaps for this reason, the elements of the book which are least satisfying are those which are not derived from Jewett's personal experiences. The opening chapter, in which the wretched Adeline Thacher Prince decides against drowning herself and young Nan, and with her last breath returns home to die on her elderly mother's doorstep, is blatant melodrama. Nan's eventual reconciliation with her wealthy, long-lost aunt (also named Nan Prince) is a fairy-tale motif which does not even offer psychological tension to make it worthwhile. Finally, Nan's ostensible love affair with the milquetoast George Gerry utterly lacks credibility, let alone passion. In theory, the relationship has much literary potential: George is the son of Aunt Nancy Prince's former lover, much as Nan is the daughter of her once-beloved brother, and both young people desire to better themselves; but George is a dull, admittedly mercenary lawyer in equally dull Dunport, and he is so threatened by Nan's blithely setting a farmer's dislocated shoulder—George "felt weak and womanish, and somehow wished it had been he who could play the doctor"—that it is clear that the tension Jewett seeks to create between Nan's personal desire to become a physician and society's desire to make her a wife simply cannot materialize. George is a cipher; marriage is never a serious issue; and the single-mindedness with which Nan pursues her career, although obviously meant to demonstrate the strength of her character, compromises the chances for any development of her personality or the generation of interest in the plot. Indeed, the two elements which would have had extraordinary potential for the development of both character and plot—Nan's admission into medical school, and the difficulties she must overcome as a student—are simply ignored.

Part of the problem with *A Country Doctor* is that Jewett downplays plot in her desire to utilize the book as a sort of lecture platform. Much as the two girls in *Deephaven* (transparently speaking for Jewett herself) occasionally lapse into brief lectures on Christianity, the advantages of rural life, and the like, so too the characters in *A Country Doctor* embark on improbable discussions on behalf of the author. For example, in the chapter entitled "At Dr. Leslie's," one learns of Jewett's ideas about child rearing and heredity. As Dr. Leslie talks about young Nan at an incredible length with his old classmate Dr. Ferris, one finds that Nan's guardian seeks to rear her in a deliberately "natural" way. Leslie's interest in her "natural" growth is grounded in his scientific predispositon: he feels that "up to seven or eight years of age children are simply bundles of inheritances," and Nan presents a unique case for study: Grandmother Thacher was "an old fashioned country woman of the best stock," but there had been "a very bad streak on the other side" which led to Nan's mother being marginally insane, tubercular, and alcoholic. Whereas Dr. Leslie's desire to let Nan grow naturally stems from scientific curiosity, Nan's desire is eventually traced to a religious impulse: she feels it is her God-given (and hence "natural") duty to become a doctor, and indeed her final words in the story are "O God . . . I thank thee for my future."

In addition to injecting some of her ideas about child-rearing, heredity, and theology into the story, Jewett also presents her ideas about feminism ("It certainly cannot be the proper vocation of all women to bring up children, so many of them are dead failures at it; and I don't see why all girls should be thought failures who do not marry"), about the shortcomings of urban life (Nan's mother degenerates as a result of moving to Lowell to work), and about the economic deterioration of New England (the once-thriving Dunport is dying, albeit in a picturesque fashion). In short, *A Country Doctor* is typical of Jewett's work in that it shows her incapacity to sustain plot; her occasional inability to present and develop characters who are both believable and interesting; and her unfortunate tendency to preach or theorize. These difficulties were happily under control when Jewett came to write *The Country of the Pointed Firs*.

The Country of the Pointed Firs is unquestionably Jewett's masterpiece: an immediate popular and critical success, it is the only one of Jewett's five volumes of long fiction which is widely known today, and it is at the center of the perennial theoretical controversy as to how one should differentiate between a true novel and a collection of related short stories. As noted above, this situation exists with regard to *Deephaven*, but with an important difference: *Deephaven* was Jewett's first book, and so its hybrid quality is generally attributed at least in part to its author's inexperience. On the other hand, *The Country of the Pointed Firs* is clearly a more mature effort: tight in structure, consistent in tone, complex in characterization, and profound in thought, it demonstrates how two decades of writing experience had honed Jewett's judgment and technical skill. Thus, the impression that *The Country of the Pointed Firs* somehow manages to straddle the two traditionally separate fictional classifications must be regarded as intentional. Of course, *The Country of the Pointed Firs* is considerably more than a text for fictional theorists: it is a delightful book which shows Jewett at the height of her literary powers.

A comparison of *The Country of the Pointed Firs* with *Deephaven* gives some indication of the extent of those powers, for essentially *The Country of the Pointed Firs* is a masterful reworking of the earlier book. The premise is the same in both stories: a female urbanite visits a Maine coastal community for a summer and records her impressions. In *Deephaven*, the reader follows the experiences of two rather silly young women from Boston; in *The Country of the Pointed Firs*, there is only one visitor from an unspecified city, and even alone she is more than a match for Kate and Helen. A professional writer, she is by nature and training far more perceptive than the *Deephaven* girls. Well into middle age, she also has the maturity and experience to comprehend the residents of Dunnet Landing, who themselves are people who have led quite full, if not always pleasant, lives. The narrator of *The Country of the Pointed Firs* has credibility: one can believe that she enters into the world of Dunnet Landing and that people are willing to impart to her their most private and painful thoughts, whereas it is almost impossible to believe that any thinking person could be so intimate with giggly Kate and Helen. By the same token, although one knows little of the background and personal life of the narrator of *The Country of the Pointed Firs* (the reader is never told her name), one does know what goes on in her mind—her reactions, concerns, interests, misgivings—and as such she seems more like a real person than a fictional creation.

Closely aligned with this is the fact that the narrator of *The Country of the Pointed Firs* stays in focus throughout the story. Even though the book often breaks into little vignettes, character studies, or anecdotes, one never loses sight of the narrator, not only because she is the controlling consciousness who records the events at Dunnet Landing, but also because one knows how she reacts to what she sees and hears. Those reactions are not always positive: she is initially annoyed by Captain Littlepage's account of the mythical Arctic place where souls reside; she is startled (and a bit disappointed) by the modernity of Elijah Tilley's cottage; and she feels the pang of young Johnny Bowden's glance of "contemptuous surprise" as she fails to recognize a local symbol pertaining to fishing.

The narrator's revelation of her inner life is perhaps most apparent in her dealings with Mrs. Almira Todd, the owner of the house where she stays for the summer. Whereas in *Deephaven* Kate and Helen stay in a relative's mansion and bring their Boston servants to run the household for them, the narrator of *The Country of the Pointed Firs* has a close link with the community in the form of her landlady: they live, eat, visit, and occasionally work together (Mrs. Todd grows and sells medicinal herbs), a situation which enables the narrator to acquire extensive firsthand knowledge of the people and lore of Dunnet Landing. Even so, she is aware that, as a nonnative, she can never truly be admitted into the community; she feels rather out of place at Mrs. Begg's funeral and at the Bowden family reunion, and her acute awareness of her being privy to many of the more intimate or concealed aspects of the community (such as Mrs. Todd's admission that she did not love her husband), while simultaneously being denied knowledge of many others, shows her to be a more complex, perceptive, and thoughtful character than either Kate or Helen could ever be. It also shows that Jewett was able to comprehend and convey the fundamental fact that life is far less cut-and-dried, far more rich and contradictory, than was indicated in her earlier fiction. This is perhaps most evident in her treatment of Dunnet Landing itself.

Jewett goes to great lengths to emphasize the local aspects of Dunnet Landing which make it unique in time and place. She carefully records local dialect by spelling phonetically; she presents characters whose values, interests, and activities mark them as a dying breed living in an isolated area; she reveals the ways in which the region's unusual environment and situation result in so-called "peculiar people," including the woman who designed her life around the fantasy that she was the twin of Queen Victoria. While emphasizing the uniqueness of this late nineteenth century coastal Maine village, however, Jewett also emphasizes its universality: "There's all sorts o' folks in the country, same's there is in the city," declares Mrs. Todd, and it is clear that the reader is supposed to derive from *The Country of the Pointed Firs* a deeper comprehension of the universality of human nature and experience. It is significant in this regard that the reader is never told the year in which the events take place, and Jewett habitually draws analogies between the people of Dunnet Landing and those of biblical, classical, and medieval times.

Jewett's ability to strike a consistently happy balance between the universal and particular is quite remarkable, and equally remarkable is her talent for maintaining a tone which is profound without being obscure, touching without being sentimental. For once, Jewett also avoids preachiness: Captain Littlepage's discussion of the Arctic "waiting-place" inhabited by human souls does not lead into a lecture on Christian views of the afterlife nor a debate between matters of scientific fact and religious faith. Littlepage and his recital, like all the characters, anecdotes, and events of the novel, are allowed to speak for themselves, and the effect is a powerful one. Whether or not Willa Cather was justified in maintaining that *The Country of the Pointed Firs*, Nathaniel Hawthorne's *The Scarlet Letter* (1850), and Mark Twain's *The Adventures of Huckleberry Finn* (1884) were the only American books destined to have "a long, long life," it is true that *The Country of the Pointed Firs* does show Jewett in perfect control of her material and sure in her use of technique. Unquestionably, she had found the fictional milieu in which she functioned best. Given this achievement, it is all the more lamentable that in her next book Jewett deliberately abandoned the milieu.

Jewett's final attempt at long fiction proved to be her worst book. Usually classified as a historical romance or costume novel, *The Tory Lover* was transparently intended to cash in on the unprecedented and highly remunerative vogue for historical romances which characterized the American fiction market throughout the 1890's and the early years of the twentieth century; in fact, the long out-of-print book was reissued in 1975 (under the title of *Yankee Ranger*) for precisely the same reasons on the eve of the Bicentennial. *The Tory Lover* is virtually a casebook for students of the mishandling of fictional material and technique, and as such it is a perennial embarrassment to even the most devoted advocates of Jewett's work.

As usual, Jewett demonstrates her inability to handle plot, or, as she accurately lamented to Horace Scudder in 1873, "I have no dramatic talent . . . It seems to me I can furnish the theater, and show you the actors, and the scenery, and the audience, but there never is any play!" Whereas *The Country of the Pointed Firs* is strong precisely because it lacks—and in fact does not need—a plot in the usual sense of the word, *The Tory Lover* is virtually all plot, and it suffers accordingly. Although the book is set in the opening months of the American Revolution (1777), Jewett is unable to convey the excitement and tension of that most stirring era in American history. Surprisingly, little happens in this overlong story: at the urging of his girl friend Mary Hamilton, Roger Wallingford of Berwick, Maine, declares himself to be in support of the American cause; he ships out to England on the *Ranger* under Captain John Paul Jones, is captured during Jones's attempt to burn Whitehaven, and is imprisoned at Plymouth, eventually winning a full pardon thanks to the efforts of assorted English noblemen.

Although this story line is potentially rich with exciting scenes, none materializes. The transatlantic crossing is quite dull, despite Jewett's desperate efforts to render credible the novel's obligatory villain, Dickson. The disgruntled crew's unsuccessful attempt to overthrow Captain Jones, instead of being excitingly dramatized, is reduced to a comment: "There had been an attempt at mutiny on board, but the captain had quelled that, and mastered the deep-laid plot behind it." Similarly, Roger Wallingford's imprisonment, which lasts for much of the novel, is barely mentioned, and his daring and bloody escape is a matter of hearsay. Jewett's attempts to generate intrigue, mystery, or tension are no more successful. Wallingford's pardon is the result of the written request of a resident of Berwick, one Master Sullivan, but his relationship to the powerful noblemen who actually secure the pardon is never explained, and the effect generated is more annoyance than mystery. Likewise, the tension between Captain Jones and Wallingford which results from Jones's wearing Mary's ring is resolved a few pages later when Wallingford bluntly reveals the source of his ill-temper. Finally, the book's climax—the evil Dickson's admission of his role in the thwarting of Jones and the arrest of Wallingford—is not in the least surprising or convincing: quite simply, the drunken Dickson boasts of his deeds in a public house, and his fellow sailors toss him into the street. A few paragraphs later, the book abruptly ends.

Plot had never been Jewett's strong suit, but even the characterization in *The Tory Lover* is lamentable. The story's heroine, Mary Hamilton, is constantly described as "beautiful," "bright," and "charming"; but the repeated use of vague adjectives does not constitute characterization. The very little that she thinks, says, and does reveals virtually nothing about her. In this regard, she is perhaps ideally suited to her equally wooden lover, Roger Wallingford, who repeatedly is said to be "gentlemanly" and "handsome," but who in fact is not in the least missed as he languishes for much of the novel in a British prison. Even the historical figures who would be expected to have intrinsic interest, such as Benjamin Franklin and John Paul Jones, are nothing more than flaccid bundles of adjectives who are irritating in their very lifelessness. Jewett also introduces a series of dull, obligatory stock characters (Dickson as the villain, Madam Wallingford as the grande dame, Old Caesar as the loyal black servant), as well as a plethora of characters who are simply dropped a few pages after they first appear: Dr. Ezra Green, the *Ranger*'s literary surgeon; wealthy Colonel Jonathan Hamilton, Mary's allegedly dashing brother; Gideon Warren, the Berwick sailor who is reunited with Wallingford in the Plymouth prison.

Ultimately, *The Tory Lover* is a cluttered, confusing pastiche of unexciting events and lifeless characters; it is to Jewett's credit that she was able to acknowledge her inability to write historical romance. There is every indication that she agreed with Henry James's negative reaction to *The Tory Lover*: "Go back to the dear Country of the Pointed Firs, *come* back to the palpable present *intimate* that throbs responsive, and that wants, misses, needs you, God knows, and suffers woefully in your absence." Jewett's devastating buggy accident occurred before she could act on James's admonition, however, and *The Tory Lover* stands as her last, but far from best, work.

Alice Hall Petry

Other major works
SHORT FICTION: *Old Friends and New*, 1879; *Country By-Ways*, 1881; *A White Heron and Other Stories*, 1886; *The King of Folly Island and Other People*, 1888.
POETRY: *Verses: Printed for Her Friends*, 1916.
NONFICTION: *Letters of Sarah Orne Jewett*, 1911 (Annie Fields, editor); *Sarah Orne Jewett Letters*, 1956 (Richard Cary, editor).
CHILDRENS' LITERATURE: *Play Days: A Book of Stories for Children*, 1878, *The Story of the Normans*, 1887; *Betty Leicester: A Story for Girls*, 1890.

Bibliography
Cary, Richard. *Sarah Orne Jewett.* Boston: Twayne, 1962. Considered an important study because Cary maintains a balance in his approach to Jewett, appreciating her works while understanding their limitations. Contains a selected bibliography.
Donovan, Josephine. *Sarah Orne Jewett.* New York: Frederick Ungar, 1980. A useful, but somewhat limited, survey of Jewett's writings, which focuses on how many of her works concern women's issues. The final chapter is particularly useful on Jewett's critical theories. Includes a bibliography.
Magowan, Robin. *Narcissus and Orpheus: Pastoral in Sand, Fromentin, Jew-*

ett, Alain-Fournier, and Dinesen. New York: Garland, 1988. Includes one chapter on Jewett, in which Magowan defines the American pastoral and examines Jewett's works in the context on this theme. Discusses *The Country of the Pointed Firs* and *Deephaven*, comparing the former to the writings of Eugène Fromentin and Isak Dinesen.

Nagel, Gwen L. *Critical Essays on Sarah Orne Jewett.* Boston: G. K. Hall, 1984. A compilation of solid criticism on Jewett that contains nine original essays and an introduction providing a detailed bibliographic survey of Jewett scholarship. Among the original essays is a piece by Philip B. Eppard on two recently discovered Jewett stories. An important contribution to studies on Jewett, on whom there has been little contemporary criticism save for feminist scholarship.

Sherman, Sarah Way. *Sarah Orne Jewett: An American Persephone.* Hanover, N.H.: University Press of New England, 1989. A full-length, in-depth study of Jewett that attempts to go to the source of the mythic quality in her work. Sherman tells how Jewett came to terms with the culture that defined her womanhood, and sees the myth of Demeter and Persephone as a central symbol. Particular attention is given to the novel *The Country of the Pointed Firs.*

RUTH PRAWER JHABVALA

Born: Cologne, Germany; May 7, 1927

Principal long fiction

To Whom She Will, 1955 (U.S. edition, *Amrita*, 1956); *The Nature of Passion*, 1956; *Esmond in India*, 1958; *The Householder*, 1960; *Get Ready for Battle*, 1962; *A Backward Place*, 1965; *A New Dominion*, 1972 (U.S. edition, *Travelers*, 1973); *Heat and Dust*, 1975; *In Search of Love and Beauty*, 1983; *Three Continents*, 1987.

Other literary forms

Though Ruth Prawer Jhabvala is known mainly as a novelist, she is also an accomplished writer of short stories, film scripts, and essays. Among her collections of short stories are *Like Birds, Like Fishes and Other Stories* (1963), *A Stronger Climate: Nine Stories* (1968), *An Experience of India* (1972), and *How I Became a Holy Mother and Other Stories* (1976); *Out of India* (1986) is a selection of stories from these volumes. *Shakespeare Wallah* (1965; with James Ivory), *Heat and Dust* (1983), and *A Room with a View* (1986; based on E. M. Forster's novel) are her best-known film scripts.

Achievements

Jhabvala has achieved remarkable distinction, both as a novelist and as a short-story writer, among writers on modern India. She has been compared with E. M. Forster, though the historical phases and settings of the India they portray are widely different. The award of the Booker Prize for *Heat and Dust* in 1975 made her internationally famous. Placing Jhabvala in a literary-cultural tradition is difficult: Her European parentage, British education, marriage to an Indian, and—after many years in her adopted country—change of residence from India to the United States perhaps reveal a lack of belonging, a recurring "refugee" consciousness. Consequently, she is not an Indian writing in English, nor a European writing on India, but perhaps a writer of the world of letters deeply conscious of being caught up in a bizarre world. She is sensitive, intense, ironic—a detached observer and recorder of the human world. Her almost clinical accuracy and her sense of the graphic, the comic, and the ironic make her one of the finest writers on the contemporary scene.

Biography

Ruth Prawer was born in Cologne, Germany, on May 7, 1927, the daughter of Marcus and Eleonora Prawer; her family's heritage was German, Polish, and Jewish. She emigrated to England in 1939, became a British citizen in 1948, and obtained an M.A. in English from Queen Mary College,

London, in 1951. That same year, she married C. H. S. Jhabvala, an Indian architect, and went to live in India. She resided there until 1975, when she moved to New York. She has three daughters, Renana, Ava, and Feroza, who live in India. Jhabvala's friendship and collaboration with filmmakers James Ivory and Ismail Merchant, which began in the 1960's, opened a new phase of her career; her work on film scripts enriched her technique as a writer of fiction and widened her vision.

Analysis

Ruth Prawer Jhabvala's distinctive qualities as a novelist grow from her sense of social comedy. She excels in portraying incongruities of human behavior, comic situations which are rich with familial, social, and cultural implications. Marital harmony or discord, the pursuit of wealth, family togetherness and feuds, the crisis of identity and homelessness—these are among the situations that she repeatedly explores in her fiction. She writes with sympathy, economy, and wit, with sharp irony and cool detachment.

Jhabvala's fiction has emerged out of her own experience of India. "The central fact of all my work," she once told an interviewer, "is that I am a European living permanently in India. I have lived here for most of my adult life . . . . This makes me not quite an outsider either." Much later, however, in "Myself in India," she revealed a change in her attitude toward India: "However, I must admit I am no longer interested in India. What I am interested in now is myself in India . . . my survival in India."

This shift in attitude has clearly affected Jhabvala's fiction. There is a distinct Indianness in the texture and spirit of her first five novels, which are sunny, bright, social comedies offering an affirmative view of India. The later novels, darkened by dissonance and despair, reveal a change in the novelist's perspective.

Amrita inaugurates Jhabvala's first phase, in which reconciliation between two individuals (symbolic as well of a larger, social integration) is at the center of the action. Amrita, a young, romantic girl, has a love affair with Hari, her colleague in radio. Their affair is portrayed with a gentle comic touch: She tells Hari of her determination to marry him at all costs; he calls her a goddess and moans that he is unworthy of her. Jhabvala skillfully catches the color and rhythm of the Indian phraseology of love.

While this affair proceeds along expected lines, Pandit Ram Bahadur, Hari's grandfather, is planning to get his grandson married to Sushila, a pretty singer, in an arranged match. When Hari confesses to his brother-in-law that he loves Amrita, he is advised that first love is only a "game," and no one should take it seriously. Hari then is led to the bridal fire and married to Sushila. He forgets his earlier vows of love for Amrita, even the fact that he applied for a passport to go with her to England.

The forsaken maiden, Amrita, finds her hopes for a happy union revived when another man, Krishna Sengupta, writes her a letter full of love and tenderness. Enthralled after reading his six-page letter, she decks her hair with a beautiful flower, a sign of her happy reconciliation with life. Amrita shares in the sunshine of love that comes her way.

The original title of the novel, *To Whom She Will* (changed to *Amrita* for the American edition), alludes to a story in a classic collection of Indian fables, the *Panchatantra* (between 100 B.C. and A.D. 500; *The Morall Philosophie of Doni*, 1570). In the story, which centers on a maiden in love, a Hindu sage observes that marriage should be arranged for a girl at a tender age; otherwise, "she gives herself to whom she will." This ancient injunction is dramatized in the predicaments of Hari, Amrita, Sushila, and Sengupta, the four main characters. The irony lies in the fact that Amrita does not marry "whom she will." Nevertheless, the regaining of happiness is the keynote of Jhabvala's first novel of family relations and individual predicaments.

Alluding to Swami Paramananda's translation of the *Bhagavad Gītā* (c. fifth century B.C.), which Jhabvala quotes, her second novel, *The Nature of Passion*, deals with one of the three kinds of passion which are distinguished in the *Bhagavad Gītā*: that which is worldly, sensuous, pleasure-seeking. This passion, or *rajas*, rules the world of Lalaji and his tribe, who represent the rising middle class and whose debased values become the object of Jhabvala's unsparing irony. She presents a series of vignettes of the life of the affluent—such as Lalaji and the Vermas—who migrated to India after the partition and continued to prosper. Here, Jhabvala's characters are not intended to be fully rounded individuals; rather, they play their parts as embodiments of various passions.

Lalaji's role is to illustrate the contagious effects of greed and corruption. An indiscreet letter written by his older son finds its way into a government file controlled by Chandra, his second son. When Lalaji asks Chandra to remove the incriminating letter, Chandra's self-righteous wife, Kanta, objects. She soon realizes, however, that their comforts and their holidays depend upon Lalaji's tainted money, and she relents, allowing the letter to be removed. Lalaji's daughter Nimmi, too, moves from revolt to submission. Lalaji's tenderness for Nimmi is conveyed beautifully. When she cuts her hair short, Lalaji accepts this sign of modernity. Nevertheless, despite her attraction to another young man, she accepts the marriage partner chosen for her by her family.

Jhabvala's irony is cutting, but her style in this novel has an almost clinical precision, a detachment that discourages reader involvement. By concentrating on social types rather than genuinely individualized characters, she limits the appeal of the novel, which already seems badly dated.

Jhabvala's third novel, *Esmond in India*, as its title suggests, is concerned with the conflict between cultures. Esmond is an Englishman, a shallow man with a handsome face who tutors European women in Hindi language and culture and serves as a guide to visitors. He is an egotistic, aggressive colonial, and Jhabvala is relentless in her irony in sketching him, especially in a scene at the Taj Mahal where he loses his shoes. The pretentious Esmond is cut down to size and becomes a puny figure.

Esmond's relationship with his wife, Gulab, is the novel's central focus. She is a pseudoromantic Indian girl, very fond of good food. Their marriage is in ruins: Esmond feels trapped and speaks with scorn of her dull, alien mind, while she is keenly aware of his failure to care for her. Nevertheless, Gulab, as a true Hindu wife, bears Esmond's abuse, his indulgence in love affairs, until their family servant attempts to molest her. She then packs her bag and leaves Esmond.

Is Gulab a rebel or a complete conformist? In marrying Esmond, an Englishman, she surely seems to have become a rebel. Later, however, she is subservient in response to Esmond's cruelty; the servant assaults her because he knows that Esmond does not love his wife. This scts into motion her second rebellion: separation from Esmond. Gulab is a complex, memorable character.

Esmond, too, though he is drawn with sharp irony, is no mere caricature. At the heart of the novel is his overwhelming sense of a loss of identity, a crisis which grips his soul and makes him unequal to the task of facing India, that strange land.

The Householder is perhaps Jhabvala's most successful, least problematic, most organically conceived novel. A true social comedy, it is a direct, simple "impression of life." It centers on the maturation of its likable central character, Prem, a Hindi instructor in Mr. Khanna's private college. Prem is a shy, unassuming young man, in no way exceptional, yet his growth to selfhood, presented with insight and humor, makes for compelling fiction.

The title *The Householder* is derived from the Hindu concept of the four stages of a man's life; the second stage, that of a family man, is the one which the novel explores. Prem's relations with his wife, Indu, are most delicately portrayed. The scene of Prem loving Indu on the terrace in moonlight is both tender and touching. They both sense the space and the solitude and unite in deep intimacy. Prem realizes that Indu is pregnant and tenderly touches her growing belly—scenes which show Jhabvala at her best and most tender.

Prem's troubles are mainly economic—how to survive on a meager salary—and the comedy and the pathos which arise out of this distress constitute the real stuff of the novel. The indifference, the arrogance, and the insensitivity of the other characters are comically rendered, emphasizing Prem's seeming helplessness, as he struggles to survive and to assert his individuality. (A minor subplot is contributed by Western characters: Hans Loewe, a seeker after spiritual reality, and Kitty, his landlady, provide a contrast to Prem's struggle.) Nevertheless, Prem is finally able to overcome his inexperience and immaturity, attaining a tenderness, a human touch, and a balance which enable him to achieve selfhood and become a true "house-holder."

Get Ready for Battle, Jhabvala's fifth novel, resembles *The Nature of Passion*. Like that earlier novel, it pillories the selfish, acquisitive society of postindependence India. In particular, it shows how growing urbanization affects the poor, dispossessing them of their land. Like *The Nature of Passion*, *Get Ready for Battle* derives its title from the *Bhagavad Gītā*, alluding to the scene in which Lord Krishna instructs Arjuna to "get ready for battle" without fear; similarly, Jhabvala's protagonist, Sarla Devi, urges the poor to get ready for battle to protect their rights. *Get Ready for Battle* is superior to *The Nature of Passion*, however, in its portrayal of interesting and believable characters. While the characters in the later novel still represent various social groups or points of view, they are not mere types.

The central character, Sarla Devi, deeply committed to the cause of the poor, is separated from her husband, Gulzari Lal. They represent two opposite valuations of life: She leads her life according to the tenets of the *Bhagavad Gītā*, while he, acquisitive and heartless, is a worshiper of Mammon. The main action of the novel centers on her attempt to save the poor from being evicted from their squatters' colony and also to save her son from following her father's corrupt life-style. She fails in both these attempts, yet she is heroic in her failure.

Jhabvala brilliantly depicts the wasteland created by India's growing cities, which have swallowed farms and forests, at the same time destroying the value-structure of rural society. Yet *Get Ready for Battle* also includes adroitly designed domestic scenes. Kusum, Gulzari Lal's mistress, is shown with sympathy, while the relationship between two secondary characters, the married couple Vishnu and Mala, is portrayed with tenderness as well as candor. They show their disagreements (even speak of divorce), yet they are deeply in love. For them, "getting ready for battle" is a kind of game, a comic conflict, rather than a serious issue.

Jhabvala's next novel, *A Backward Place*, initiated the second phase of her career, marked by dark, despairing comedies disclosing a world out of joint. In this novel, too, Jhabvala began to focus more attention on encounters between East and West and the resulting tensions and ironies. The novel's title, which refers to a European character's condescending assessment of Delhi, suggests its pervasive irony; neither Indians nor Europeans are spared Jhabvala's scorn. While it features an appealing protagonist, the novel is too schematic, too much simply a vehicle for satire.

A Backward Place was followed by *Travelers*, a novel in the same dark mode, which presents the Western vision of contemporary India with telling irony. European girls seek a spiritual India, but the country that they actually experience is quite the opposite. Despite its satiric bite, the novel must be judged a failure: The great art of fiction seems to degenerate here into mere journalism, incapable of presenting a true vision of contemporary India.

This forgettable novel was followed by Jhabvala's most widely praised work, *Heat and Dust*, the complex plot of which traces parallels between the experiences of two Englishwomen in India: the unnamed narrator and her grandfather Douglas' first wife, Olivia. In the 1930's, Olivia came to India as Douglas' wife. Bored by her prosaic, middle-class existence, Olivia is drawn to a Muslim nawab with whom she enjoys many escapades. Invited to a picnic close to a Muslim shrine, Olivia finds the nawab irresistible. They lie by a spring in a green grove, and the nawab makes her pregnant. She then leaves Douglas, aborts her child, and finally moves to a house in the hills as the nawab's mistress.

After a gap of two generations, the narrator, who has come to India to trace Olivia's life story, passes through a similar cycle of experience. Fascinated by India, she gives herself to a lower-middle-class clerk, Inder Lal, at the same place near the shrine where Olivia lay with the nawab, and with the same result. The young narrator decides to rear the baby, though she gives up her lover; she also has a casual physical relationship with another Indian, Chid, who combines sexuality with a spiritual quest.

Heat and Dust is an extraordinary novel. Unlike many of Jhabvala's novels, it has a strong current of positive feeling beneath its surface negativism. Olivia, though she discards her baby, remains loyal to her heart's desire for the nawab, and the narrator, while not accepting her lover, wishes to rear her baby as a symbol of their love. This note of affirmation heightens the quality of human response in *Heat and Dust*, which is also notable for its fully realized characterizations.

In Search of Love and Beauty, set primarily in the United States but ranging widely elsewhere, centers on the experience of rootlessness which Jhabvala knows so well, and which is so widespread in the twentieth century. The novel is a multigenerational saga, beginning with refugees from Nazi Germany and Austria and concluding in contemporary times. The rootlessness of that first generation to be dislocated from their culture is passed on to their children and their children's children, all of whom go "in search of love and beauty."

The first generation, represented by Louise and Regi, wishes to retain its German heritage, concretely symbolized by their paintings and furniture. The second generation, represented by Marietta, is partly Americanized. The restless Marietta travels to India, falls in love with Ahmad, an Indian musician, and befriends Sujata, a courtesan, sketched with deft accuracy. The image of India is lovable, vital, and glorious, and seems almost a counterpart to Germany's ideal image. The third-generation refugees, represented by Natasha and Leo, are more affluent and still more Americanized, yet they are trapped in drug abuse, depression, and meaninglessness.

In almost all of her novels, Jhabvala assumes the role of an omniscient narrator. She stands slightly aloof from her creations, an approach which has advantages as well as disadvantages. On the one hand, she does not convey the passionate inner life of her characters, many of whom are essentially stereotypes. Even her more fully developed characters are seen largely from the outside. On the other hand, she is a consummate observer. She has a fine eye for naturalistic detail, a gift for believable dialogue, but she is also an observer at a deeper level, registering the malaise that is characteristic of the modern world: the collapse of traditional values, the incongruous blending of diverse cultures: sometimes energizing, sometimes destructive, often bizarre. Thus, her fiction, while steeped in the particular reality of India, speaks to readers throughout the world.

Vasant A. Shahane

Other major works

SHORT FICTION: *Like Birds, Like Fishes and Other Stories*, 1963; *A Stronger Climate: Nine Stories*, 1968; *An Experience of India*, 1972; *How I Became a Holy Mother and Other Stories*, 1976; *Out of India*, 1986.

SCREENPLAYS: *The Householder*, 1963; *Shakespeare Wallah*, 1965 (with James Ivory); *The Guru*, 1968; *Bombay Talkie*, 1970; *Autobiography of a Princess*, 1975 (with Ivory and John Swope); *Roseland*, 1977; *Hullabaloo Over Georgie and Bonnie's Pictures*, 1978; *The Europeans*, 1979; *Quartet*, 1981; *Heat and Dust*, 1983 (based on her novel); *The Bostonians*, 1984 (with Ivory); *A Room with a View*, 1986 (based on E. M. Forster's novel).

TELEPLAYS: *The Place of Peace*, 1975; *Jane Austen in Manhattan*, 1980.

Bibliography
Gooneratne, Yasmine. *Silence, Exile, and Cunning: The Fiction of Ruth Prawer Jhabvala*. Hyderabad, India: Orient Longman, 1983. A definitive work of Jhabvala, the title of which is taken from James Joyce's definition of a writer, with which Jhabvala concurs. Comments on the theme of loneliness and displacement that runs throughout Jhabvala's fiction as she explores the "sensibility of the Western expatriate in India." Biographical detail is interwoven with discussion of Jhabvala's fiction, including a chapter on her short stories and her writing for film. A strong critical study by an author who herself has a keen understanding of the India Jhabvala writes about.
Pritchett, V. S. "Ruth Prawer Jhabvala: Snares and Delusions." In *The Tale Bearers*. London: Chatto & Windus, 1980. Discusses Jhabvala's novel *A New Dominion*, exploring both its satirical content and the author's role as "careful truth-teller." Hails Jhabvala as a writer who knows more about India than any other novelist writing in English. A short but interesting piece that compares Jhabvala's writing to that of Anton Chekhov.

Shahane, V. A. *Ruth Prawer Jhabvala*. New Delhi: Arnold-Heinemann, 1976. The first full-length study on Jhabvala, covering her novels up to *Heat and Dust* in 1975 and three short stories, including "An Experience of India." Shahane notes that Jhabvala's literary gift lies less on her unique insider-outsider status in India as it does on her awareness of human dilemma within the constructs of society. In a style both spirited and opinionated, Shahane contributes significant criticism to the earlier work of Jhabvala.

Sucher, Laurie. *The Fiction of Ruth Prawer Jhabvala*. New York: St. Martin's Press, 1989. In discussing Jhabvala's nine novels and four books of short stories, Sucher emphasizes Jhabvala's tragic-comic explorations of female sexuality. Cites Jhabvala as a writer who deconstructs "romantic/Gothic heroism." A valuable contribution to the literary criticism on Jhabvala. Includes a useful bibliography.

Updike, John. "Louise in the New World, Alice on the Magic Molehill." Review of *In Search of Love and Beauty*, by Ruth Prawer Jhabvala. *The New Yorker* 59 (August 1, 1983): 85-90. Updike likens the novel to Marcel Proust's "great opus concerning the search for lost time" but says it falls short of Proust in the flatness of the prose. Updike claims that, in spite of this, the novel contains many vivid scenes, and that "brilliance is to be found."

CHARLES JOHNSON

Born: Evanston, Illinois; April 23, 1948

Principal long fiction

Faith and the Good Thing, 1974; *Oxherding Tale*, 1982; *Middle Passage*, 1990.

Other literary forms

Believing that a writer should be able to express himself with competence in all forms of the written word, Charles Johnson has successfully published in several genres, including more than one thousand satirical comic drawings and two books of socially relevant cartoons, *Black Humor* (1970) and *Half-Past Nation Time* (1972). Six of the eight short stories in *The Sorcerer's Apprentice* (1986) were written as psychic releases from the difficulty Johnson experienced in creating a dynamic draft of *Oxherding Tale*. Two of the eight are award winners: "Popper's Disease" (receiving the 1983 *Callaloo* Creative Writing Award) and "China" (receiving the 1984 Pushcart Prize Outstanding Writer citation).

Among Johnson's documentary drama and his screenplays are "Charlie Smith and the Fritter Tree" (aired on *Visions* in 1978), the adventure-charged story of the oldest living American who arrived on a slaver and became a Texas cowboy; *Booker* (a 1984 *Wonderworks* premiere cowritten with John Allmann), a dramatization of the young Booker T. Washington's dogged struggle to learn at a time when education was by law denied to southern black Americans; and the award-winning *Me, Myself, Maybe* (a 1982 Public Broadcasting System *Up and Coming* episode), one of the first scripts to deal with the issue of the married black woman's process of self-determination.

A literary aesthetician, Johnson has also published both articles and book reviews. *Being and Race: Black Writing Since 1970* (1988), a controversial critical analysis and winner of the 1989 Governor's Award for Literature, is the product of Johnson's twenty-year exploration into the makings of black fiction.

Achievements

Johnson has internationally propounded his belief that the process of fiction must have a vital, nonideological philosophical infrastructure. With several international editions of his novels as well as more than fifteen grants and awards and professional and public recognition of Johnson's affirmative philosophical approach to the chaotic dualities of the Western world, his profound belief in the inexhaustible capacities of humankind is unquestionable.

Johnson has been the recipient of a 1977 Rockefeller Foundation Grant, a 1979 National Endowment for the Arts Creative Writing Fellowship, and a 1988 Guggenheim fellowship. His screenplay *Booker* alone received four awards: against strong network competition, the 1985 Writers Guild Award for outstanding children's show script; the distinguished 1985-1987 Prix Jeunesse (International Youth Prize); the 1984 Black Film Maker's Festival Award; and the 1984 National Education Film Festival Award for Best Film in the social studies category. In addition, *Oxherding Tale* was given the 1983 Governor's Award for Literature, and *The Sorcerer's Apprentice* was one of the 1987 final nominees for the prestigious PEN/Faulkner Award. In 1989, Johnson was named by a University of California study as one of the ten best American short-story writers. In 1990, his *Middle Passage* was honored with a National Book Award.

Biography

In 1948, Charles Richard Johnson was born to Ruby Elizabeth (Jackson) and Benjamin Lee Johnson of Evanston, Illinois. Both parents had emigrated from the South, specifically Georgia and North Carolina. Johnson's mother, an only child (as is Johnson himself), had wanted to be a schoolteacher but could not because of her health. Instead, she fulfilled her artistic and aesthetic passions in the Johnson home. His father's education was cut short by the Depression, a time when all able-bodied males worked in the fields. Later, he worked with his brother, who was an Evanston general contractor.

Johnson describes his early years as a "benign upbringing" in a progressive *Leave It to Beaver* town of unlocked doors and around-the-clock safety. Schools had been integrated by the time Johnson became a student; therefore, he did not encounter serious racism during his childhood or adolescence. His first two short stories, "Man Beneath Rags" and "50 Cards 50" (which he also illustrated), as well as many cartoons (one award-winning), were published at Evanston Township High School, then one of the best high schools in the country. While in high school, Johnson began to work with Laurence Lariar, a cartoonist and mystery writer. In 1965, he sold his first drawing to a Chicago magazine's catalog for illustrated magic tricks. From 1965 to 1973, Johnson sold more than one thousand drawings to major magazines.

After high school graduation, Johnson had planned to attend a small art school rather than a four-year college. Nevertheless, as the first person in his extended family to attend college, he felt some obligation to fulfill his parents' hopes. This concern, combined with his art teacher's recommendation that he attend a four-year college for practical reasons, was enough to motivate Johnson to register at Southern Illinois University at Carbondale as a journalism major (with a compelling interest in philosophy). His continuing study of martial arts and, conjointly, Buddhism began in 1967. A cartoonist for the *Chicago Tribune* from 1969 to 1970, Johnson wrote and aired fifty-two fifteen-minute PBS episodes of *Charlie's Pad*, a how-to show on cartooning in 1970.

During his senior year in college, Johnson began writing novels. With his journalistic background (B.S., 1971), he saw no problem with allotting two or three months for each novel. Consequently, from 1970 to 1972, Johnson wrote six novels; three are naturalistic, while three are in the style of the Black Arts movement. Although his fourth novel was accepted for publication, Johnson withdrew it after talking with John Gardner about the implications of precipitate first publication. All six apprentice novels have been filed, unread, in a drawer. Johnson credits Gardner's tutelage on *Faith and the Good Thing* with saving him six additional years of mistakes.

In 1973, Johnson was awarded his master's degree in philosophy from Southern Illinois University with the thesis "Wilhelm Reich and the Creation of a Marxist Psychology." Following three years of doctoral work at the State University of New York at Stony Brook, Johnson began teaching at the University of Washington as well as serving as fiction editor of the *Seattle Review*. Under a 1977-1978 Rockefeller Foundation Grant, he joined the WGBH New Television Workshop as writer-in-residence. In 1982, he became a staff writer and producer for the last ten episodes of KQED's *Up and Coming* series and wrote the second season's premiere episode "Bad Business." A thirty-minute script for KCET's *Y.E.S. Inc.* aired in 1983.

From 1985 to 1987, Johnson worked on the text for *Being and Race: Black Writing Since 1970*, a project he began while guest lecturing for the University of Delaware. His 1983 draft of the first two chapters in *Middle Passage* came quickly, but Johnson worked on the novel sporadically from 1983 to 1987 before finally giving it his full attention for nine months. In addition to his continuing projects, he was a 1988 National Book Award judge and received the Lifting Up the World award and medallion presented to seventeen University of Washington faculty by Sri Chinmoy.

Since 1975, Johnson has practiced serious meditation and has studied Eastern religions. Although his upbringing was Episcopalian, he became a Buddhist in 1980. He has continued to teach at the University of Washington and to serve as fiction editor for the *Seattle Review*. In addition, his monthly reviews have been published in the *Los Angeles Times* since 1987.

Johnson was director of the University of Washington's Creative Writing Program for three years (1987-1990). On September 21, 1990, he was awarded an endowed chair, the first Pollock Professorship in Creative Writing at the University of Washington. He was to assume the lifetime position in the fall of 1991.

Johnson was married to Joan New in 1970. The couple have two children: Malik, a son born in 1975, and a daughter, Elizabeth, born in 1981. His life is chronicled in Joan Walkinshaw's PBS documentary "Spirit of Place," which has aired in Seattle.

Analysis

Because Charles Johnson believes implicitly in the power of language, he examines his writing line by line, word by word, to eliminate plot superfluities and to ensure verbal precision. (His drafts of *Oxherding Tale* totaled more than twenty-five hundred pages.) Token characterization to this author is "fundamentally immoral"; rather, he insists, a writer must expend the same energy with his fictional characters that he would in understanding and loving those in his physical world. Even further, Johnson identifies the committed writer as someone who cares enough about his work that it "is something he would do if a gun was held to his head and somebody was going to pull the trigger as soon as the last word of the last sentence of the last paragraph of the last page was finished." For Johnson, who thinks of himself as an artist rather than as an author, writing is a nonvolitional necessity.

A phenomenologist and metaphysician, Johnson constructs fictional universes that not only adhere to the Aristotelian concepts of coherence, consistency, and completeness but also elucidate integral life experiences in the universal search for personal identity. Moreover, the multiplicity of consciousness embodied by his characters seeks to strip the preconceptions from his readers so that they may "re-experience the world with unsealed vision." Consequently, the unrelenting integrity of his fictional vision resolutely reaffirms humanity's potential to live in a world without duality and in the process also reveals Johnson's own indefatigable regard for the unfathomable, moment-by-moment mystery of humankind.

Even though Johnson has dedicated himself to the evolution of "a genuinely systematic philosophical black American literature" and most frequently creates his *Lebenswelt* (world of life) within a black context, he sees the racial details as qualifiers of more universal questions. The nonlinear fictional progressions, the proliferations of synaesthetic imagery, the delicate counterbalances of comic (and cosmic) incongruities, and the philosophical underpinnings viscerally reinforced lend a Zen fluidity to the consequent shifting levels of awareness. Thus, the characters' movements toward or away from self-identity, action without ulterior motivation, and mind-body integration assume universal relevance.

Written from the fall of 1972 to the early summer of 1973 under the tutelage of John Gardner, *Faith and the Good Thing* is the metaphysical journey of eighteen-year-old Faith Cross, who believes that she is following her mother's deathbed instructions and the werewitch Swamp Woman's advice by searching the external world for the "Good Thing." This quest for the key that will release her and everyone else from servitude leads from Hatten County, Georgia, to Chicago, Illinois, and home again. Despite limitations inherent in the narrative form itself, occasional lapses in viewpoint, and infrequent verbal artifice, Johnson has created a magical novel of legendary characters and metaphysical import.

The diverse characters who people Faith's life enrich her explorations on both ordinary and extraordinary levels of existence, yet none can lead her to her Good Thing. Asthmatic, stuttering, alcoholic Isaac Maxwell insists that the real power is in money. Dr. Leon Lynch, who treats her mother, believes that the purpose of human life is death and fulfills his self-prophecy by committing suicide on Christmas Eve. Nervous Arnold Tippis, a former dentist (who lost his license because of malpractice), theater usher, and male nurse, rapes her physically and spiritually. His adaptations, like Faith's initial search, are external. Richard M. Barrett, former Princeton University professor, husband, and father, is now a homeless robber who dies on a Soldiers' Field park bench. An existentialist, he believes enough in her search to will her his blank Doomsday Book and to haunt her after his death on Friday nights at midnight until her marriage. Each character shares his path to his Good Thing with Faith, thereby allowing her to choose pieces for her own.

Faith's mystical odyssey, remembered with relish by a third-person narrator addressing his listeners "children," commits every individual to his own search and, through reflection, to the potential alteration of individual consciousness. Despite identifiable elements of naturalism, romanticism, allegory, the *Bildungsroman*, and black folktales, of far greater importance is that *Faith and the Good Thing* creates its own genre of philosophical fiction in which the metaphysical and the real are integrated into a healing totality of being.

Until her return to Swamp Woman, Faith's choices for survival thrust her upon a path of intensifying alienation from herself and from her world. Her feelings of estrangement and depersonalization escalate to an existential fragmentation during her rape and subsequent periods of prostitution, chemical abuse, and marriage. With her decision to forsake her quest for the Good Thing, to manipulate the eminently unsuitable Isaac Maxwell into marriage, and to settle for a loveless middle-class existence, Faith cripples her sense of metaphysical purpose and sees herself as one of the "dead living," an "IT," her soul severed, "still as stone."

The advent of Alpha Omega Holmes, her hometown first love, enables Faith to recover vitality, but her dependence upon others since childhood for self-definition has been consistently destructive to Faith, who has lived in the past or the future and denied her present being. Holmes continues the pattern by deserting her when she announces that she is five months pregnant with his child. Rejected by Holmes and Maxwell, Faith turns to Mrs. Beasley, her former madam, who cares for her, delivers her baby daughter, and leaves the burning candle that is responsible for the fire that kills Faith's child and critically maims Faith. Repeatedly, psychic abandonment and betrayal have been the consequences of a failure to respect her own and others' process of becoming.

Nevertheless, at the summons of Swamp Woman's white cat, Faith returns to the werewitch's holy ground. Now near death, she is finally prepared to devote her total being to the search. Accepting Swamp Woman's revelations that everyone has a path and a "truth," Faith understands that all humans are the sum of their experiences and that she, as well as they, has no beginning and no end. Thus, she has the power to exchange existence with the esoteric, iconoclastic, witty magician Swamp Woman or to become anyone she wishes, thereby personifying Barrett's premise that thinking directs being. The Good Thing is the dynamic, nonpossessive, fluid freedom of the search itself.

After *Faith and the Good Thing*, Johnson began thinking differently about the storyteller voice. He sought a means by which he could more fully and naturally embody philosophical issues within his characters. In *Oxherding Tale*, he has realized that voice, an intriguing first-person fusion of slave narrative, picaresque, and parable. In the first of two authorial intrusions, chapters 8 and 11, Johnson explains the three existing types of slave narrative. In the second, the author defines his new voice as first-person "universal," not a "narrator who falteringly interprets the world, but a narrator who *is* that world."

Yet the eight years that Johnson worked on his second novel, a novel he believes he was born to create, were fraught with frustration as he wrote and discarded draft after draft until, in 1979, he considered never writing again. Nevertheless, his passion for writing conquered the obstructions. Following a period of extended meditation, Johnson experienced a profound catharsis and eliminated the problematic static quality of the earlier drafts by refashioning the narrator-protagonist from black to mulatto and his second master from male to female.

Oxherding Tale, inspired by Eastern artist Kakukan-Shien's "Ten Oxherding Pictures," is Andrew Hawkins' rite of passage, an often-humorous, metaphysical search for self through encounters that culminate in his nondualistic understanding of himself and the world. The narrator, born to the master's wife and the master's butler as the fruit of a comic one-night adventure, sees himself as belonging to neither the fields nor the house. Although Andrew lives with his stepmother and his father (recently demoted to herder), George and Mattie Hawkins, Master Polkinghorne arranges his classical education with an eccentric Eastern scholar. An excellent student, Andrew nevertheless expresses his recognition of the dualism when he protests that he can speak in Latin more effectively than in his own dialect. As Andrew opens his mind to the learning of the ages, George Hawkins becomes progressively more paranoid and nationalistic. This delicate counterbalance is sustained throughout the novel until, at the end, the assimilated Andrew learns from Soulcatcher that his father was shot to death as an escaped slave.

At twenty, Andrew wishes to marry the Cripplegate plantation seamstress, Minty. Instead, he is sold to Flo Hatfield, a lonely woman who considers her eleven former husbands subhuman and who has the reputation of sexually using each male slave until, discarding him to the mines or through his death, she replaces him with another. Believing that he is earning the funds for his own, his family's, and Minty's manumission, Andrew cooperates. He finds himself quickly satiated, however, with the orgiastic physical pleasures Flo demands to conceal her psychic lifelessness. Thus, neither his father's intensifying spiritual separatism nor his mistress' concupiscence is a path Andrew can accept.

Andrew proceeds to seek out Reb, the Allmuseri coffinmaker in whose Buddhist voice he finds comfort, friendship, and enlightenment. Flo's opposite, Reb (neither detached nor attached) operates not from pleasure but from duty, acting without ulterior motives simply because something needs to be done. Together, the two escape Flo's sentence to her mines as well as Bannon the Soulcatcher, a bounty hunter, with Andrew posing as William Harris, a white teacher, and Reb posing as his gentleman's gentleman. When Reb decides to leave Spartanburg for Chicago because of Bannon, Andrew, emotionally attached to the daughter of the town doctor, decides that Reb's path is not appropriate for him to follow. Instead, his dharma (Eastern soul-sustaining law of conduct) is to be a homemaker married to Peggy. During their wedding ceremony, Andrew surrenders himself to his timeless vision of all that humanity has the potential to become.

The final chapter, "Moksha," like the last of Kakuan-Shien's ten pictures, reveals the absolute integration between self and universe. "Moksha" is the Hindu concept of ultimate realization, perpetual liberation beyond dualities, of self with the Great Spirit. In an illegal slave auction, the mulatto Andrew discovers and buys his dying first love, Minty. He, Peggy, and Dr. Undercliff unite to ease her transition from this world. Thus, the three move beyond self to *arete*, "doing beautifully what needs to be done," and begin the process of healing their world.

In *Oxherding Tale*, Johnson once again offers the experience of affirmation and renewal. Through the first-person universal voice of Andrew Hawkins, he constructs a tightly interwoven, well-honed portrait of actualization. Minute details, vivid visual imagery, and delicate polarities within and among the characters achieve an exacting balance between portrayal of the process and the process itself. Once again, the search does not belong solely to Johnson's characters; the search belongs to everyone who chooses to free himself of "self-inflicted segregation from the Whole."

Johnson deliberately depersonalized his third novel's working title, "Rutherford's Travels," to *Middle Passage*, a multiple literary allusion, to "emphasize the historical event rather than the character" and to enhance the novel's provocative content. Visual characteristics of Johnson's screenplay writing are sometimes evident in *Oxherding Tale*; however, in *Middle Passage*, scenic effect and synaesthetic detail purposefully dominate, with the narrative sections intended as scenic bridges. Johnson had already used members of the

Allmuseri, a mystical African tribe reputed to be the origin of the human race, in *Oxherding Tale*, as well as in two short stories, "The Sorcerer's Apprentice" and "The Education of Mingo"; yet never before had he so masterfully drawn the portrait of this compelling tribe of Zen sorcerers.

Recently manumitted Rutherford Calhoun, a landlubbing twenty-three-year-old picaro, stows away aboard the slave ship *Republic* in order to avoid a marriage forced by his prospective bride. Discovered but allowed to remain as chef's helper by the dwarflike captain, Ebenezer Falcon, the first-person universal narrator candidly records man's brutality to man during the forty-one-day voyage to Bangalang for forty captive Allmuseri and their living god. Later revealed as a duty assigned by the suicidal Falcon, Calhoun's log becomes a primary tool by which he processes his responses to his shipmates and to the ship's adventures.

Following an eerie storm in which the stars themselves shift in the heavens, the Allmuseri revolt and capture the ship less than one week after being confined in the *Republic*'s hold. Yet, this tribe believes that each individual is responsible for the creation of his own universe and that even the most minute action has eternal repercussions, echoing beyond this world. Therefore, that human death was involved in their freedom is a source of great sorrow, particularly for their leader, Ngonyama. Despite ceremonies of atonement, the *Republic* sinks, aided by a storm and the Allmuseri renegade Diamelo, who ignites a cannon pointed in the wrong direction.

Of captors and captives, only five survive until the *Juno*, a floating pleasure palace, rescues them: Rutherford Calhoun, his friend Josiah Squibb, and three Allmuseri children including Rutherford's female tribal ward, Baleka. On board *Juno* is Isadora Bailey, Rutherford's forceful fiancée, now scheduled to marry an underworld figure who profits by betraying his race. Instead, a transformed Rutherford, who understands that the way to deal effectively with dangerous people is to become even more dangerous than they, convinces the Créole gangster that marrying Isadora would not be in his best interest; now Rutherford can marry Isadora himself.

Against a backdrop of sea adventure, the poignancy of the characters' startling self-revelations becomes even more deeply moving. Falcon, the remorseless captain to whom human life has no value other than the price he can pocket, collects his treasures to fulfill his dead mother's dream. The first mate Peter Cringle, who responds from his heart to others' victimization, escapes his wealthy family's mistreatment of him by offering his body as food for the *Republic*'s last survivors. Nathaniel Meadows, who murdered his own family, is so fiercely loyal to Falcon that he conditions the ships' dogs to attack those persons he believes most likely to lead a mutiny. Conversely, Diamelo, the Allmuseri insurrectionist, is so spiritually consumed by his own anger that he blinds himself to the good of his people and destroys them. Yet Ngonyama, grieving over the loss of his tribe's metaphysical connectedness to the Whole, is able to heal Rutherford before lashing himself to the helm in propitiation for the deaths that his tribe's freedom has cost.

Rutherford, self-proclaimed liar and petty thief, finds that instead of hungering for new sensory experiences, he is finally content to experience the present with acceptance and gratitude. Faced with material choices, such as those having to do with food or bed linens, he can no longer comprehend their relevance. Instead of taking, he seeks opportunities for sharing himself without expectations and in universal love. He has taken full possession of his life. He no longer needs; he simply responds.

Middle Passage employs intricately interwoven scenes appropriate to the multiplicity of levels upon which the characters exist. The Allmuseri god, a shape-shifter, is the individual personification of the living truth most fear to face. Furthermore, the anguish of each "middle passage" is uniquely reflected internally by the character and externally by all those whom the character encounters. Recognition without preconception of humanity's magnificent complexity is a significant step toward universal communion.

Charles Johnson's innate belief in the essential goodness of humankind and his intuitive grasp of the metaphysical empower him to create living fiction with the potential to alter human consciousness. His mastery of the English language, as well as the tight word-by-word control he exercises, heightens his characters' credibility and consequently his readers' empathic sensitivity. Employing a precise awareness of human motivation, Johnson structures his writing nonlinearly to evince tantalizing pieces of the human mystery, but he withholds consummate revelation until the metaphysical world of philosophical fiction surrounding his characters is fully realized.

Kathleen Mills

Other major works

SHORT FICTION: *The Sorcerer's Apprentice*, 1986.
TELEPLAYS: *Charlie Smith and the Fritter Tree*, 1978; *Booker*, 1984.
NONFICTION: *Being and Race: Black Writing Since 1970*, 1988.
MISCELLANEOUS: *Black Humor*, 1970; *Half-Past Nation Time*, 1972.

Bibliography

Davis, Arthur P. "Novels of the New Black Renaissance, 1960-1977: A Thematic Survey." *CLA (College Language Association) Journal* 21 (June, 1978): 457-491. Davis analyzes twenty-four New Black Renaissance writers, including Johnson. The historical, thematic, and comparative contexts of this article can serve as an introduction to the major black writers of this period. The information is generally limited, however, by Davis' stated time frame and specifically limited to *Faith and the Good Thing* with regard to Johnson.

Charles Johnson 1769

Harris, Norman. "The Black University in Contemporary Afro-American Fiction." *CLA (College Language Association) Journal* 30 (September, 1986): 1-13. Harris' discussion of the aesthetic bases in the contemporary fictional universes of Toni Morrison, Johnson, and Ishmael Reed provides a contextual overview of the black movement toward nonlinear, mythical constructions in contrast to the approaches of Richard Wright's *Native Son* (1940) and Ralph Ellison's *Invisible Man* (1952).

Johnson, Charles. Interview by Nicholas O'Connell. In *At the Field's End: Interviews with Twenty Pacific Northwest Writers*. Seattle: Madrona, 1987. Presenting a superb interview in an excellent collection, O'Connell remains discreetly in the background as Johnson reveals his thoughts about the artistry and the passion inherent in the writing process, the necessary interconnectedness of philosophy and literature, and his own intrinsically caring life view. With erudition, humor, and honesty, Johnson ranges freely over such topics as the victimization of naturalism's universe, Buddhist tenets, phenomenology, and the potency of language.

_____. "Reflections on Film, Philosophy, and Fiction." Interview by Ken McCullough. *Callaloo* 1 (October, 1978): 118-128. This interview, conducted while Johnson and McCullough were editing *Charlie Smith and the Fritter Tree*, reflects their concentration upon the film as they contrast various literary art processes with an emphasis upon the screenplay and the novel. An interesting, informal, and literate profile of a writer who lives his words.

Olderman, Raymond M. "American Fiction 1974-1976: The People Who Fell to Earth." *Contemporary Literature* 19 (Autumn, 1978): 497-527. Olderman's analysis of mutual social and spiritual reverberations expressed by the major fiction writers of the mid-1970's is excellent. His comparisons and contrasts of both form and content are so well supported that the article functions as required reading for anyone interested in this period.

DIANE JOHNSON

Born: Moline, Illinois; April 28, 1934

Principal long fiction
Fair Game, 1965; *Loving Hands at Home*, 1968; *Burning*, 1971; *The Shadow Knows*, 1974; *Lying Low*, 1978; *Persian Nights*, 1987; *Health and Happiness*, 1990.

Other literary forms
The True History of the First Mrs. Meredith and Other Lesser Lives (1972; also known as *Lesser Lives*) is a biography of Mary Ellen Nicolls Meredith, the daughter of novelist and poet Thomas Love Peacock and the first wife of novelist and poet George Meredith. Diane Johnson has also written the first published biography of Dashiell Hammett, *Dashiell Hammett: A Life* (1983). *Terrorists and Novelists*, a collection of her book reviews and essays originally published in *The New York Times Book Review* and *The New York Review of Books*, appeared in 1982.

Johnson collaborated with film director Stanley Kubrick on the screenplay for *The Shining*, a motion picture released in 1980.

Achievements
Diane Johnson's novels have achieved both popularity and critical acclaim for their portrayals of insecure women grasping for a sense of identity amid chaotic surroundings. She has received the Mildred and Harold Strauss Livings Award and the Rosenthal Award from the American Academy of Arts and Letters. Her biography *The True History of the First Mrs. Meredith and Other Lesser Lives* was nominated for a National Book Award. Johnson has been a Woodrow Wilson grantee and a Guggenheim Foundation Fellow.

Biography
Born of middle-aged parents in Illinois in 1934, Diane Johnson is influenced in her writings by her orderly and stable Midwestern background. In 1953 she was married to B. Lamar Johnson, Jr.; they were later divorced. She attended Stephens College and was graduated from the University of Utah, 1957, with a B.A. in English. She received her M.A. and Ph.D (1968) from the University of California, Los Angeles, and was a member of the English faculty at the University of California, Davis, from 1968 to 1987. Johnson was married to John Frederic Murray in 1969 and lives in Berkeley, California. She has four children from her first marriage.

Analysis
In Diane Johnson's novels, the central characters are always women caught in circumstances in which they feel trapped and insecure; inevitably, the pres-

sures of contemporary life and social problems contribute to their frustrations and cause them to fight to extricate themselves. Suffering more than men from a loss of identity and dehumanization, they reach out to experiences beyond their confined lives in the hope of finding a new paradigm for surviving. Men in Johnson's novels become impediments and adversaries, for these women's difficulties and frustrations arise partly from unsatisfactory relationships with men. Her characters share a desire to be free from the wife-mother syndrome, to make choices, and to break through the complexities of relationships that keep them mired in unhappiness. Her characters are all intensely aware of the limited circumference of their lives as they are held in an emotional abyss.

The novels' settings intensify the difficulties and predicaments of the characters: for example, the unrest and impending revolution in the last days of the Shah of Iran, the decadent, atrophying Los Angeles subculture, and the social unrest of the 1960's. Although the early novels are light and satiric in tone, the subsequent works become increasingly serious as the characters are forced to reevaluate their lives and make compromises about their futures.

In *Fair Game*, Johnson's first novel, Dabney Wilhem is a creative young woman who has her own business making children's clothes and who has also written a children's book. She must grapple with the nature of woman's ultimate responsibility: marriage, children, husband, or a creative commitment. Several letters by Dabney to Mr. Trager, a famous young poet, are interspersed throughout the novel and reveal her search for an identity and her concerns.

She is acquainted with men who seek to guide her, and the narrative is told from their alternating points of view. The guru-philosopher Emerson Kado seeks to control her intellectually and to protect her creativity. A symbolic key scene is an orgy at Kado's home where, in a ritual of fertilization, real blood is thrown and he gives a speech on evil. Frightened by the event, Dabney retreats into her more ordered existence. Marcus Stein, a psychiatrist, wants to make love to her in order to free her emotions; he accuses her of not wanting to take chances and says that she is too concerned with ensuring her success. The young man to whom she is engaged, Charles Earse, wonders whether she will be a good wife and is distressed by her literary aspirations. The various emotional harnesses these men try to fit on her come to nothing when she runs off at the end with the poet.

The novel is satiric in tone; it does not have the underlying intensity that develops in Johnson's later novels, or their sense of despair. Although Dabney is searching for and exploring options in her life, she is able to assess the difficulties, make a decision, and seek her identity with confidence.

Unlike Dabney, Karen Fry in *Loving Hands at Home* is already trapped in a stultifying situation. She has no particular talent and is a middle-class housewife with two children who has married into a Mormon family only to find herself stifled by their expectations of a perfect wife-mother role for her. She finds continual frustration in trying to meet the high demands of her home-economist mother-in-law, Mrs. Fry, and to break the indifference of her husband, Garth. Karen's lopsided cake, baked for the ritual family Sunday dinner, symbolizes to Mrs. Fry her unworthiness.

Karen seeks escape in a "secret life." She applies for jobs that she has no intention of accepting—interesting, strange jobs such as fortune-telling. When she is offered a job, the approval this suggests diminishes her feeling of inadequacy. Yet whenever she breaks out of her structured life she meets with an incident that frightens her, forcing her back into the role she hates. Remembering her childhood in a small Midwestern town, she thinks of Alma, the girl nobody was permitted to play with, a member of the "shiftless poor." Alma's rebelliousness and recklessness look increasingly appealing to Karen, caught as she is in a rigid structure where domestic accomplishments represent the ideal of femininity. When she learns that Alma has died from a reaction to a drug, however, such freedom seems less appealing to Karen.

Karen becomes aware that all the Fry family togetherness is beginning to break down. Mrs. Fry, the mother of seven children, is caught by Karen making love with a deliveryman. Sebastian Fry, who is the curator for Paris Pratt, a wealthy, mysterious benefactor of artists, is in love with her poetic image, while his wife, Patty, a convert to Mormonism, valiantly tries to keep their home together.

Feeling a closeness to the sensitive, creative Sebastian, Karen, in a moment of recklessness, makes love to him on the floor of Mrs. Pratt's bedroom. To Karen, this act is another attempt to free herself. When Mrs. Fry hears of the incident, she chides Karen for not living up to the Mormon role of womanhood and for ignoring the sanctity of marriage. Karen again takes flight, only to return, unable to face the uncertainties of the future on her own.

The climactic scene occurs at one of the Frys' regular Sunday-night dinners. Mrs. Fry insists on eating some suspicious-looking mushrooms, while the others refuse to eat them, signifying a waning of her influence. Suddenly distraught, Mrs. Fry confesses her infidelities in a wild scene. She becomes violently ill and ultimately blames all the dissension on Karen, the outsider, and locks her in the bedroom, telling her that she is not "allowed to walk out on this life." When Garth and the other family members fail to come to her rescue, Karen escapes by climbing out the window, realizing now that she must reassess her life.

Earlier, Mrs. Pratt, another of Johnson's guru-type characters, has told Karen that she looks as if she has "not made the important decision yet"—is it possible to be happy? She tells Karen that she must discover an "organizing motif." In the novel's final scene, Karen and her children are on the beach, totally absorbed in building a sand castle. They know that they are "doing an important thing," and it is "an extraordinary, inspired sand castle." She is not running, not waiting; she is "reorganizing."

Johnson focuses on social institutions in *Burning*, a satiric attack on the Los Angeles subculture and particularly the social-welfare agency. A historic event, the Bel Air fire, is the backdrop for the climax and parallels the social disintegration of this world.

The novel covers one day in the life of Barney and Bingo, a middle-class couple with two children who live in the hills of Bel Air. When the hedge separating them from their neighbors, psychiatrist Hal Harris, his wife, and his patient, Max, is cut down by the fire department as a fire hazard, there is a symbolic breaking down of the barrier between their "calm and orderly" world and that of a guru psychiatrist, drug dependents, an unfit mother, and group therapy. Barney and Bingo go through a rite of passage, gradually losing their illusions in a "jungle" that they cannot comprehend. The point of view alternates between Barney and Bingo; indeed, Barney is one of Johnson's more realized male characters.

The world of this novel is askew. The psychiatrist provides drugs, followed by sex, to his patients, but he really prefers his plants. Having given up on his patients, he gives them drugs to sedate them, insulating them from the life he himself avoids; he has retreated from society because he no longer believes in human improvement. Yet Max, an unfit mother and drug addict, looks up to him as a father, and his other patients depend upon his therapy to keep them going. When Bingo is persuaded to substitute for Max, who must appear at a child-welfare agency hearing, Bingo assumes that because she is stable she will pass the test. Her interview with the child-welfare worker is the incisive satiric scene of the novel. Although Bingo gives honest answers, she fails the test and is declared an unfit mother. She is indignant, but shaken, and further disturbed by the fact that she believes the social worker's judgment. She begins to look at herself with less certainty, feeling isolated and inadequate in this environment.

Barney expresses the central metaphor when he comments that one must experience the "pains and exaltations of life" and likens this to a "hard, gemlike flame." Thus he admonishes Bingo, when, at the end, as the fire is raging and water is needed desperately, she wants to take a shower. He accuses her of not caring, of not being committed.

There is a symbolic moment in the final scene when they are faced with the changes in their lives and the loss of their illusions. She laments, "Terrible, terrible. What shall we do?" He replies: "We have each other." The ironic distance in their responses indicates that they are more apart than they realize; Bingo's ability to deal with the changes in her life is dubious.

The psychology of the woman fearing for her life and beset with other fears and panics is skillfully depicted and escalates in intensity in *The Shadow Knows*. Similar to a detective story, the novel begins with the remembrance of a violent crime and ends with a rape. *The Shadow Knows* covers one week in the life of "N," who is a victim of terror and acts of violence. A young, divorced mother of four, a graduate student, involved in a love affair with a married man, she gradually reveals her uncertainties about herself in her search for the criminal identity of her pursuer. Abandoned by her husband, feeling the pain of loneliness, and resentful of her new situation, she declines into misery and paranoia, nursing a foreboding that something violent is going to happen. Adopting a wryly ironic tone to blunt her fear, she thinks that "murder would spoil everything" and that anticipating one's murder "gives you something to live for." She also imagines the "Famous Inspector," a figure who will investigate the murder, and she fantasizes how it will be reported in the newspaper.

Two black women, Osella and Ev, play significant roles, and the protagonist's attitudes toward them reflect truths about herself. She is suspicious of "mad" Osella, who served as N's housekeeper when she was married. She recognizes similarities between them: they are both left-handed and have the same birthday. There is the implication that she represents an alter ego of N—but N hates her for her dominance over the household, for her power. She also realizes that she does not like "fat and black" people and regards Osella as an "insignificant animal." Still, when Osella calls her a "whore," a "taker," and "hard-hearted" and "cold," she is affected, because she sees truth in these accusations. She knows that Osella's presence enabled her to have the freedom she wanted. Ev, her current housekeeper, also shares qualities with N: her husband has deserted her; she lives in permanent fear, and she feels victimized. Yet N admires Ev's courage, for somehow Ev can face her life calmly in spite of difficulties.

In N's ruminations, she wonders whether if one is an intended murder victim one perhaps deserves to be killed. She accepts that there is some evil in herself. She knows that she has exploited Osella and admits that she wanted her as a "slave." She also realizes that she can act without principles; she has considered inducing an abortion of the child she is carrying. In her self-absorption she thinks of suicide, a "wild card." Yet when she is betrayed by her lover, who returns to the wife he does not love, she knows that she must deal with her misery. In the final climactic moment, when N is raped, the metaphorical implications are suggested by her reactions. She feels a "strange elation" and wonders who the rapist was, but she realizes that she has changed, that she has the "lightness of a shadow, like a ghost" leaving the body.

A sense of foreboding also permeates the lives of three women in *Lying Low*. Theo and her two boarders, Marybeth and Ouida, are women struggling without men in uncertain times; their lives have reached intense levels of frustration and dissatisfaction. Victims of circumstances they cannot control, they look back on the past, struggle in the present, and fear the future. They are engulfed in their problems: Marybeth, a fugitive radical of the 1960's, is wanted for blowing up a napalm plant; Ouida, an alien Brazilian student, fears deportation and has difficulty understanding English; and Theo, a non-conformist, laments the lack of moral values in society and fights against social injustices. Dreams and memories link these women to the past, which becomes more real than the present. Covering four days, the novel conveys a sense of futility and violence, beginning with the death of a chicken, which foreshadows the death of Theo at the end.

Disillusioned women who have lost their identity, Theo and Marybeth have been committed to principles in their past lives but are now both "lying low." Remembering herself as "vital and alive" and "committed to a cause six years ago," Marybeth sees herself now as a "drowning person reviewing [her] life." Although Theo was a talented dancer, she never used that gift to accomplish anything, and she speaks of her past as "withered." The present for Ouida, too, is uncomfortable; she seeks solace in her messianic religion, keeping a candle lit in her room, and in her memories of Brazil. This concern for their lost identity leaves them suspended in apprehension. Marybeth has assumed a new name to protect her from arrest and is always ready to move on when she fears discovery. Ouida's lack of a passport makes her fearful in a strange country. Her passport becomes her security. Theo's concern about her identity is revealed in the end, when she calls out her name to prove that she exists and asks, "Who knows her?"

The final irony for Theo comes when she goes to teach dancing to prison inmates, to give them the "power of dance" and participate in the cleansing of their souls—"black men, graceful, in cages": she becomes a victim of the random violence she laments when she is taken hostage in a van with escaped prisoners. The police's shooting at the van, despite their awareness that it contains explosives, parallels Marybeth's crime when she assisted in blowing up the factory though she knew that a man was inside. Marybeth also recognizes the irony in the fact that Theo is the victim: "I always thought it would be me." In the end, Marybeth considers turning herself in, while Ouida realizes that she does not have the ability to protect herself, that she has "great ignorance."

Chloe Fowler, in *Persian Nights*, is another Johnson character who is faced with uncertainties in her life. Chloe is an attractive wife of an American doctor with two children, living a stable, ordered existence. Arriving alone in Iran—her husband, Jeffrey, has been detained to attend a patient—she is frightened and lonely, although she expects to continue her affair with Hugh Monroe, a colleague of her husband. Although she admits to a few affairs, she also realizes her dependence on her husband and feels more secure because she is married. She is aware that safety is important to her and has always been one of her problems: she stays married because that way she feels safer.

Chloe is linked with other Americans who are satirized in this novel. When she arrives at her quarters in the Azami compound, she is distressed at the shabbiness of the apartment: Americans expect a standard of living that assures their comfort. Americans can also do things in Iran that they would not do at home; they have no respect for Iranian law. Thus, they buy antiques that are illegal to sell to foreigners. Chloe feels guilty because she has taken plants from a neighbor, something she would not do at home, and she wonders why. Like the other residents living in the compound, she is isolated from the real Iran.

As the wild dogs bark at night and the Savak (secret police) make arrests, however, Chloe gradually becomes aware of the intensity of Iran's conflict and begins to feel fear. The suspicions and paranoia around her ironically heighten her sensibilities. She believes that she has no reason to be there, but she begins to be stimulated by her situation.

As the pressures intensify, she admits that she cannot "grasp the tragic," so she goes on "with egotism and vanity." Her actions indicate how well she defines herself in this respect. When her husband, who had no intention of joining her in Iran, writes her that he is getting a divorce, that there is someone else, she feels betrayed. She thinks of herself as abandoned, without a home; yet she also observes that she would like to have been the one who decided to leave the marriage. In a climactic scene at the ruins of Persepolis, Abbas Mowlavi, an Oxford-educated doctor, dies trying to save the treasures from plunderers; Chloe cannot react to the tragedy of his death and wonders whether she is the one who is dead. Earlier in the story, she and Abbas had been attracted to each other and had made love.

Yet Chloe begins to be aware that she is not without purpose, that she is searching for a conclusion. She asks herself questions that show her concerns about moral issues. As she departs on the airplane at the end of the novel, unhappy to be leaving, she believes that in her experience in Iran she had found something, but she does not know what it was. Meanwhile, eating tins of caviar, she is comforted by the thought that she will not save one for Jeffrey.

Diane Johnson's novels present perceptive portrayals of women who are struggling with their feelings of anxiety and frustration and the problems of contemporary life. In attempting to overcome their difficulties, they are forced to make changes in their lives.

Millicent Sharma

Other major works

NONFICTION: *The True History of the First Mrs. Meredith and Other Lesser Lives*, 1972; *Terrorists and Novelists*, 1982; *Dashiell Hammett: A Life*, 1983.

Bibliography

Johnson, Diane. "Diane Johnson." Interview by Marilyn Yalom. In *Women*

Writers of the West, by Marilyn Yalom. Santa Barbara, Calif.: Capra Press, 1983. In a revealing conversation, Johnson speaks of the creative process and some of the main ideas of and influences on her writing.

_____. Interview by Larry McCaffery and Tom LeClair. In *Anything Can Happen: Interviews with Contemporary American Authors*, by Larry McCaffery and Tom LeClair. Urbana: University of Illinois Press, 1983. Here Johnson reflects on her life, the writing of fiction, ideas in her novels, and the fiction of contemporary American novelists.

Ryan, Marjorie. "The Novels of Diane Johnson." *Critique: Studies in Modern Fiction* 16, no. 1 (1974): 53-63. In this critical essay, three of Johnson's novels are assessed: *Fair Game, Loving Hands at Home*, and *Burning*.

SAMUEL JOHNSON

Born: Lichfield, Staffordshire, England; September 18, 1709
Died: London, England; December 13, 1784

Principal long fiction
Rasselas, Prince of Abyssinia: A Tale by S. Johnson, 1759 (originally published as *The Prince of Abissinia: A Tale*).

Other literary forms
As the dominant figure of the mid-eighteenth century English literary world, Samuel Johnson's published works—both what he wrote under his own name and for others under their names—ranged throughout practically every genre and form. In verse, he wrote *London: A Poem in Imitation of the Third Satire of Juvenal* (1738) and *The Vanity of Human Wishes: The Tenth Satire of Juvenal Imitated* (1749); his poem "On the Death of Dr. Robert Levet, A Practiser in Physic" appeared first in *The Gentleman's Magazine* (August, 1783) and later in the *London Magazine* (September, 1783). His *Irene: A Tragedy*, performed at the Theatre Royal in Drury Lane in February, 1749, was printed later that same year.

The prose efforts of Johnson tend to generate the highest degrees of critical analysis and commentary. Biographical studies include *The Life of Admiral Blake* (1740), *An Account of the Life of Mr. Richard Savage* (1744), and *An Account of the Life of John Philip Barretier* (1744). His critical and linguistic works are by far the most important and extensive, of which the best known are *Miscellaneous Observations on the Tragedy of Macbeth* (1745), *The Plan of a Dictionary of the English Language* (1747), *A Dictionary of the English Language* (1755), and *Prefaces, Biographical and Critical, to the Works of the English Poets* (1779-1781). Also, Johnson's periodical essays for *The Rambler* (1750-1752), *The Adventurer* (1753-1754), and *The Idler* (1761) contain critical commentary as well as philosophical, moral, and religious observations.

A Journey to the Western Islands of Scotland (1775) comprises his major travel piece, while his political prose includes such essays as *The False Alarm* (1770), a pamphlet in support of the Ministerial majority in the House of Commons and its action in expelling a member of Parliament; *Thoughts on the Late Transactions Respecting Falkland's Islands* (1771), a seventy-five-page tract on the history of the territory and the reasons why England should not go to war with Spain; *The Patriot: Addressed to the Electors of Great Britain* (1774), in which Johnson defends the election of his friend Henry Thrale as MP for Southwark and writes to vindicate the Quebec Act; and *Taxation No Tyranny: An Answer to the Resolutions and Address of the American Congress* (1775). Finally, he edited the works of Richard Savage (1775) and the plays of William Shakespeare (1765); he also translated Father

Jerome Lobo's *A Voyage to Abyssinia* (1735) and Jean Pierre Crousaz's *Commentary on Pope's Principles of Morality* (1739).

Achievements

The quantity and quality of first-hand biographical material compiled during Johnson's life and immediately following his death have helped considerably in assessing the full measure of his contributions to British life and letters. Particularly through the efforts of James Boswell, John Hawkins, Hester Lynch Thrale Piozzi, and Frances Burney, the remarkable personality began to emerge. Through his early biographers, Johnson became the property of his nation, representing the most positive qualities of the Anglo-Saxon temperament: common sense, honest realism, and high standards of performance and judgment. His critical judgments came forth as honest and rigorous pronouncements that left little room for the refinements and complexities of philosophical speculation; nevertheless, he must be considered a philosopher who always managed to penetrate to the essence of a given subject.

Perhaps Johnson's most significant contribution to eighteenth century thought focused upon what appeared to be a set of powerful prejudices that comprised the theses of his critical arguments. To the contrary, Johnson's so-called prejudices proved, in reality, to have been clearly defined standards or principles upon which he based his conclusions. Those criteria, in turn, originated from concrete examples from the classical and traditional past and actual experiences of the present. Johnson strived to distinguish between authority and rules on one side and nature and experience on the other. As the initial lesson of life, the individual had to realize that not all experience is of equal value—that instinctive and emotional activities, for example, cannot be placed above the authority of rational thought. In literary criticism, especially, Johnson's brand of classicism negated whim and idiosyncracy and underscored the necessity for following universal nature—virtually the same criterion that gave strength to critical criteria during the earlier eighteenth century.

Johnson's domination of London intellectual life during the last half of the eighteenth century would by itself be sufficient to establish his reputation. As a writer, however, Johnson achieved distinction in several fields, and literary historians continue to cite him as a prominent poet, essayist, editor, scholar, and lexicographer. Although he failed to produce quality drama, he did succeed in writing a work of prose fiction that went through eight editions during his own lifetime and continues to be read. Certainly, his *A Dictionary of the English Language* has long since outlived its practical use; yet it, as well as *The Plan of a Dictionary of the English Language* that preceded it, remains an important work in the history and development of English lexicography. Principally, though, the achievement of Samuel Johnson focuses on his criticism, especially his sense of rhetorical balance, which causes his essays to emerge as valid critical commentary rather than as untrustworthy, emotional critical reaction.

Perhaps Johnson's greatest achievement is his prose style, which constitutes the essence of intellectual balance. The diction tends to be highly Latinate; yet, Johnson proved his familiarity with the life-blood of his own language—its racy idiom. He possessed the ability to select the precise words with which to express exact degrees of meaning; he carefully constructed balanced sentences that rolled steadily forward, unhampered by parentheticals or excessive subordination. As writer and as thinker, Johnson nevertheless adhered to his respect for classical discipline and followed his instinct toward a just sense of proportion. His works written prior to 1760 tend to be stiff and heavy, too reliant upon classical and seventeenth century models. Later, however, in *The Lives of the Poets*, Johnson wrote with the ease and the confidence that characterized his oral, informal discussions with the famous intellectuals over whom he presided. Indeed, Johnson rose as a giant among the prose writers of his age when the strength of his style began to parallel the moral and intellectual strength of his own mind and personality.

In late February, 1907, Sir Walter Raleigh—professor of English literature at Oxford and respected scholar and critical commentator—delivered a lecture on Samuel Johnson in the Senate House at Cambridge. The final paragraph of that address is essential to any discussion of Johnson's literary and intellectual achievements. Raleigh maintained, principally, that the greatness of the man exceeded that of his works. In other words, Johnson thought of himself as a human being, not as an author; he thought of literature as a means and not as an end. "There are authors," maintained Raleigh, "who exhaust themselves in the effort to endow posterity, and distil all their virtue in a book. Yet their masterpieces have something inhuman about them, like those jewelled idols, the work of men's hands, which are worshipped by the sacrifice of man's flesh and blood." Therefore, according to Raleigh, mankind really seeks comfort and dignity in the view of literature that characterized the name of Samuel Johnson: "Books without the knowledge of life are useless; for what should books teach but the art of living?"

Biography

Born on September 18, 1709, in Lichfield, Staffordshire, England—the son of Michael and Sarah Ford Johnson—Samuel Johnson spent his formative years devouring the volumes in his father's bookshop. Although such acquisition of knowledge came about in haphazard fashion, the boy's tenacious memory allowed him to retain for years what he had read at a young age. Almost from birth, he evidenced those body lesions associated with scrofula; the malady affected his vision, and in 1710 or 1711, his parents took him to an oculist. Searches for cures even extended to a visit to London in 1712, where the infant received the Queen's Touch (from Anne) to rid him of the disease. The illness, however, had no serious effect upon Johnson's growth; he became a large man with enormous physical strength and, given the hazards of life during the eighteenth century, endured for a relatively long period of time.

Johnson's early education was at Lichfield and Stourbridge grammar schools, followed by his entrance to Pembroke College, Oxford, in 1728. Unfortunately, he remained at the University for only one year, since lack of funds forced him to withdraw. He then occupied a number of tutoring posts in Lichfield and Birmingham before his marriage, in 1735, to Mrs. Elizabeth Jervis Porter, a widow twenty years his senior whom he referred to as "Tetty." The following year, he attempted to establish a school at Edial, three miles to the southwest of Lichfield; despite his wife's money, the project failed. Thus, in 1737, in the company of David Garrick (a former pupil), Johnson left his home and went to London, where he found employment with Edward Cave, the publisher of *The Gentleman's Magazine*. His imitation of Juvenal's third satire, entitled *London*, appeared in 1738, and he followed that literary (but not financial) success with the biography of Richard Savage and *The Vanity of Human Wishes*, another imitation of a satire from Juvenal. By 1749, Garrick had established his reputation as an actor and then as manager of the Theatre Royal in Drury Lane, and he produced Johnson's tragedy of *Irene* as a favor to his friend and former teacher. The play, however, lasted for only nine performances and put to an abrupt end any hopes of Johnson becoming a successful dramatist.

Fortunately, Johnson's abilities could be channeled into a variety of literary forms. *The Rambler* essays appeared twice weekly during 1750 to 1752. In 1752, Elizabeth Johnson died, a severe loss to her husband because of his fear (terror, in fact) of being alone. Nevertheless, he continued his literary labors, particularly his dictionary, sustained in part by his sincere religious convictions and his rigorous sense of order and discipline. His adherence to the Church of England and to the Tory philosophy of government, both characterized by tradition and conservatism, grew out of that need to discover and to maintain stability and peace of mind. *A Dictionary of the English Language* was published in 1755, followed by essays for *The Idler* during 1758 to 1760. Another personal tragedy, the death of his mother in 1759, supposedly prompted the writing of *Rasselas* in the evenings of a week's time so that he could pay for the funeral expenses. By 1762, however, his fortunes turned for the better, motivated initially by a pension of three hundred pounds per year from the Tory ministry of King George III, headed by John Stuart, third Earl of Bute. Simply, the government wished to improve its image and to appear as a sincere but disinterested patron of the arts; the fact that *A Dictionary of the English Language* had become a source of national pride no doubt provided the incentive for bestowing the sum upon Johnson.

In mid-May of 1763, Johnson met young James Boswell, the Scotsman who

destined to become the most responsible for promoting the name of Samuel
Johnson to the world. The following year, the famous literary circle over
which Johnson presided was formed; its membership included the novelist/
dramatist/essayist Oliver Goldsmith, the artist/essayist/philospher Sir Joshua
Reynolds, the politician/philosopher Edmund Burke, and, eventually, the
actor/manager David Garrick and the biographer Boswell. Johnson further
solidified his reputation as a scholar/critic with his edition of Shakespeare's
plays in 1765, the same year in which he began his friendship with Henry and
Hester Lynch Thrale—a relationship that was to remain of utmost importance
for him throughout the next fifteen years. In 1781, Henry Thrale died; shortly
thereafter, his widow married an Italian music master and Roman Catholic,
Gabriel Piozzi, much against the wishes of Johnson. That union and Mrs.
Piozzi's frequent departures from England brought to an end one of the most
noteworthy intellectual and social associations of literary history.

In 1773, Boswell convinced his friend and mentor to accompany him on a
tour through Scotland. Thus, the two met in Edinburgh and proceeded on
their travels, which resulted, in Jaunary, 1775, in Johnson's *A Journey to the
Western Islands of Scotland*. Later that same year (in March), he received
the degree of Doctor in Civil Law (LL.D.) from Oxford University, after
which he spent the three months from September through November touring
France with the Thrales. His last major work—*Prefaces, Biographical and
Critical, to the Works of the English Poets* (known popularly as *The Lives of
the Poets*)—appeared between 1779 and 1781.

Johnson died on December 13, 1784, and he received still one final honor:
burial in Westminster Abbey. The poet Leigh Hunt remarked:

> One thing he did, perhaps beyond any man in England before or since; he advanced by
> the powers of his conversation, the strictness of his veracity and the respect he exacted
> towards his presence, what may be called the personal dignity of literature, and has assisted
> men with whom he little thought of co-operating in settling the claims of truth and
> beneficence before all others.

Analysis

Although technically a work of prose fiction, *Rasselas* belongs to the classification of literature known as the moral tale. In Samuel Johnson's specific
case, the piece emerges as an essay on the vanity of human wishes, unified
by a clear narrative strand. Some critics have maintained that, in *Rasselas*,
Johnson simply continued the same themes that he set forth ten years earlier
in his poetic *The Vanity of Human Wishes* and then later in *The Rambler*
essays. Essentially, in all three efforts, the writer focused on the problem of
what it means to be human and of the psychological and moral difficulties
associated with the human imagination. Johnson, both a classicist and a philosophical conservative, took his cue from the poet of Ecclesiastes, particularly

the idea of the minds' eye not being satisfied with seeing or the ear with hearing. Instead, whatever the human being sees or possesses causes him only to imagine something more or something entirely different. Further, to imagine more is to want more and, possibly, to lose pleasure in that which is actually possessed. The inexhaustible capacity of the imagination (including specific hopes and wishes) emerges as the principal source of most human desires, an indispensible ingredient for human happiness. According to both the poet of Ecclesiastes and Samuel Johnson, however, human happiness must be controlled by reality, which is also the primary source of most human misery. Therefore, the line dividing happiness and enjoyment from pain, suffering, and torment remains thin and sometimes even indistinct.

Johnson chose to clothe his moral speculations in a form particularly popular among fellow eighteenth century speculators: the Oriental tale, a Western genre that had come into vogue during the earlier Augustan Age. Its popularity was based on the Westerners' fascination with the Orient: writers set down translations, pseudotranslations, and imitations of Persian, Turkish, Arabic, and Chinese tales as backdrops for brief but direct moral lessons. Although the themes of Oriental tales tended toward the theoretical and the abstract, writers of the period tried to confront real and typical issues with which the majority of readers came into contact.

Originally published as *The Prince of Abissinia: A Tale*, 1759, Johnson's work of fiction is known simply as *Rasselas*. The common name, however, did not appear on the title page of any British edition published during the author's lifetime. The heading on the first page of both volumes of the 1759 edition, however, reads "The History of Rasselas, Prince of Abissinia." Not until the so-called eighth edition of 1787 does one find the title by which the work is generally known: *Rasselas, Prince of Abyssinia: A Tale by S. Johnson*.

Although Johnson once referred to *Rasselas* as merely a "little story book," the work enjoyed immediate and continuing success, which is an indication of its depth and seriousness of purpose. Literary historians agree that an English or American edition has appeared almost every year since the initial publication, while between 1760 and 1764, French, Dutch, German, Russian, and Italian editions were also released. Indeed, before long, Spanish, Hungarian, Polish, Greek, Danish, Armenian, Bengali, Japanese, and Arabic translations were found, indicating clearly the universality of the piece.

The vanity of human wishes theme contributes heavily to the appeal of *Rasselas*, even though such a theme may tend to suffer from an emphasis upon skepticism. Certainly, Johnson seems to have conveyed to his readers the idea that no single philosophy of life can sustain all cultures and that no particular life-style can become permanently satisfying. This philosophy might lead people to believe that life is essentially an exercise in futility and wasted energy. The vanity of human wishes theme, however, as manipulated by Johnson, also allows for considerable positive interpretations that serve to balance its darker side. In *Rasselas*, Johnson does not deny the value of human experience (including desires and hopes), but he frankly admits to its obvious complexity; man needs to move between conditions of rest and turmoil, and he further needs to experiment with new approaches to life. The admission of that need by the individual constitutes a difficult and complex decision, particularly in the light of the fact that absolute philosophies do not serve all people nor apply to all situations. In joining Prince Rasselas in his search for happiness, the experienced philosopher and poet Imlac reveals his understanding that a commitment to a single course of action constitutes a stubborn and immature attempt to settle irritating problems. Continued movement, on the other hand, is simply a form of escape. The philosopher well knows that all men require a middle ground that considers the best qualities of stability and motion.

What emerges from *Rasselas*, then, is a reinforcement of life's duality, wherein motion and rest apply to a variety of issues and problems ranging from the nature of family life to the creation of poetry. For example, the idea of the Happy Valley dominates the early chapters of the work to the extent that the reader imagines it as the fixed symbol for the life of rest and stability. Within the remaining sections, however, there exists a search for action covering a wide geographical area outside the Happy Valley. Johnson guides his reader over an unchartered realm that symbolizes the life of motion. Eventually, the two worlds unite. Before that can happen, however, Rasselas must experience the restlessness within the Happy Valley, while Pequah, the warrior's captive, must discover order in the midst of an experience charged with potential violence. In the end, Johnson offers his reader the simple but nevertheless pessimistic view that no program for the good life actually exists. In spite of that admission, though, humans will continue to perform constructive acts, realizing full well the absence of certainty. Rather than bemoan life, Johnson, through *Rasselas*, celebrates it.

Typical of the classic novel, the themes and plot of *Rasselas* are supported by its structure. The story is about Prince Rasselas who, with his sister Nekayah, lives in the Happy Valley, where the inhabitants anticipate and satisfy every pleasure and where the external causes of grief and anxiety simply do not exist. Rasselas becomes bored with his prison-paradise, however, and with the help of Imlac, a man of the world, he escapes to search for the sources of happiness. Johnson leads his characters through the exploration of practically every condition of life. The rich suffer from anxiety, boredom, and restlessness; they seek new interests to make life attractive, yet others envy them. Believing political power to be the means for doing good, Rasselas discovers that it is both impotent and precarious in its attempts to change the human condition. Learning, which he had thought of in terms of promise and idealism, suffers, instead, from petty rivalries and vested interests. Rasselas observes a hermit who, after having fled from the social world of emptiness and idle pleasure, cannot cope with solitude, study, and meditation. Finally, Rasselas and his companions return to Abyssinia—but not to the Happy Valley—and hope that they can endure and eventually understand the meaning and responsibilities of life.

Aside from its highly subjective moral issues and the variety of questions that the themes posed, *Rasselas* proved difficult for Johnson to write. Fundamentally an essayist, he belonged to a school of rhetoric that encouraged and even demanded formal argument; the task of developing fictional characters within a variety of settings, arranging various escapes and encounters, and then returning those same characters to or near their place of origin proved bothersome for him. To his credit, however, he carefully manipulated those characters into situations that would display the best side of his peculiar literary talents. As soon as Johnson's characters began to speak, to engage in elaborate dialogues, to position themselves for argument, and to counter objections to those arguments, his style flowed easily and smoothly. Thus, *Rasselas* consists of a series of dissertations, the subjects of which scan the spectrum of human experience: learning, poetry, solitude, the natural life, social amusements, marriage versus celibacy, the art of flying, politics, philosophy. Johnson applied a thin layer of fictional episodes to unify the arguments, similar to such earlier sources as Joseph Addison's *The Spectator* essays, Voltaire's *Candide* (published in the same year as *Rasselas*), and the early seventeenth century series of travelers' tales by Samuel Purchas known as *Purchas: His Pilgrimage.*

As Johnson's spokesman, Rasselas and Imlac express the author's own fear of solitude and isolation, the supernatural, and ghosts. The Abyssinian prince and his philosopher guide also convey Johnson's horror of madness, his devotion to poetry, his thoughts on the relationship between hypocrisy and human grief, and his conviction (since the death of his wife and mother) that, although marriage can produce considerable trial and pain, celibacy evidences little or no pleasure.

In *Rasselas*, the loose fictional structure and the serious philosophic discussions combine to control the pesssimism and to produce an intellectual pilgrimage upon which the travelers' questioning intellects and restless spirits seek purpose and meaning for life. In so doing, however, Johnson's Abyssinian pilgrims mistakenly associate happiness with any object or condition that suggests to them the presence of peace, harmony, or contentment. Rasselas, Nekayah, and even Imlac do not always understand that a human being cannot secure happiness simply by going out and looking for it. Johnson titled the final chapter "The Conclusion, in Which Nothing Is Concluded" probably because he sensed his own inability to suggest a solution to finding happiness, a condition he had not managed to achieve.

Outside the realm of its obvious moral considerations, *Rasselas* succeeds because of its attention to an analysis of a significant, universal, and timeless issue: education. Both Rasselas and his sister, Nekayah, are guided by the teacher, philosopher, and poet Imlac, whose principal qualification is that he has seen the world and thus knows something of it. Whether he serves as the knowledge and experience of the author does not appear as important as the reader's being able to recognize his function within the work and his contribution to the growth of the Prince and the Princess. At the outset, Imlac relates to Rasselas the story of his life, which serves as a prologue to what the young people will eventually come to know and recognize. Johnson knew well that the experience of one individual cannot be communicated to others simply; a person can only suggest to his listeners how to respond should they be confronted with similar circumstances. The Prince and Princess go forth to acquire their own experiences. They proceed to discover at first hand, to observe and then to ask relevant questions. Imlac hovers in the background, commenting upon persons and situations. As the narrative discussion goes forward, Rasselas and his sister gain experience and even begin to resemble, in their thoughts and statements, the sound and the sense of their teacher. Naturally, Imlac's motives parallel those of the titled character, which make him seem more real and more human than if he were only a teacher and commentator. Simply, Imlac believes that diligence and skill can be applied by the moral and intelligent person to help in the battle with and eventual triumph over the life of boredom, waste, and emptiness.

In the development of the eighteenth century English novel, Johnson's contemporaries did not embrace *Rasselas* and accept it on the basis of its having met or failed to meet the standards for fiction. Although not a strong example of the form, Johnson does provide his characters with sufficient substance to support the moral purpose of his effort. Nekayah appears more than adequately endowed with grace, intelligence, and the ability to communicate; in fact, stripped of the fashions and the artificial conventions of her time and place (eighteenth century London), the Princess well represents the actualities of feminine nature. Certainly, the male characters speak and act as pure Johnsonian Londoners, clothed in the intellectual habits and language of the mid-eighteenth century. Johnson's intention was to convey the essential arguments of an intellectual debate, and his contemporary readers understood that *Rasselas* existed as nothing more or less than what its author intended it to be: a fictional narrative used as a vehicle for elevated style and thought.

The noted British essayist of the first half of the nineteenth century, Thomas Babington Macaulay, in his encyclopedic essay on Johnson, observed that a number of those who read *Rasselas* "pronounced the writer a pompous pedant, who would never use a word of two syllables where it was possible to use a word of six, and who could not make a waiting-woman relate her adventures without balancing every noun with another noun, and every epithet with another epithet." When considering the size of *Rasselas*, however, it seems the epitome of compression. By composing the work quickly, Johnson forced himself to ignore doubts or hesitations regarding the vanity of human wishes theme and to depend upon his experiences (as painful as they had been) and his skill in expressing them. The entire project also stood as a challenge to Johnson's imaginative and rhetorical artistry. Thus, he again confronted the major thesis of *The Vanity of Human Wishes* and *The Rambler* essays within the context of his own moral thinking.

Walter Jackson Bate, in his recent biography of Samuel Johnson, claimed that *The Vanity of Human Wishes* served as the prologue to the great decade of moral writing, while *Rasselas* was the epilogue. Indeed, such is the appropriate summation for any discussion of Johnson's moral writing as well as moral thought. The wisdom found within both works—as well as in *The Rambler*, *The Idler*, and *The Adventurer* essays—certainly solidifies a general understanding of Johnson's religious and moral views. *Rasselas*, in particular, however, gives dimension to those views, reflects the writer's acuteness, and displays the depth and meaning of his early disillusion with life. In writing *Rasselas*, Johnson sought to expose the exact nature of human discontent as it existed in a variety of specific contexts. Each episode in *Rasselas* proved worthy of serious consideration, and each instance revealed the extent to which Johnson could creatively apply his wisdom and his experience.

Samuel J. Rogal

Other major works

PLAY: *Irene: A Tragedy*, 1749.

POETRY: *London: A Poem in Imitation of the Third Satire of Juvenal*, 1738; *The Vanity of Human Wishes: The Tenth Satire of Juvenal Imitated*, 1749.

NONFICTION: *Marmer Norfolciense*, 1739; *A Compleat Vindication of the Licensers of the Stage*, 1739; *The Life of Admiral Blake*, 1740; *An Account of the Life of Mr. Richard Savage*, 1744; *An Account of the Life of John Philip Barretier*, 1744; *Miscellaneous Observations on the Tragedy of Macbeth*, 1745; *The Plan of a Dictionary of the English Language*, 1747; *A Dictionary of the English Language*, 1755; *The False Alarm*, 1770; *Thoughts on the Late Transactions Respecting Falkland's Islands*, 1771; *The Patriot: Addressed to the Electors of Great Britain*, 1774; *Taxation No Tyranny: An Answer to the Resolutions and Address of the American Congress*, 1775; *A Journey to the Western Islands of Scotland*, 1775; *Prefaces, Biographical and Critical, to the Works of the English Poets*, 1779-1781 (10 volumes; also known as *The Lives of the Poets*).

TRANSLATIONS: *A Voyage to Abyssinia*, 1735; *Commentary on Pope's Principles of Morality*, 1739.

Bibliography

Bate, Walter Jackson. *Samuel Johnson.* New York: Harcourt Brace Jovanovich, 1977. A magisterial biography which is readable and sympathetic. Frankly Freudian, the book presents a troubled Johnson who remains lovable despite his flaws. Devotes a chapter to *Rasselas*, which is viewed as a sensible, moral treatment of life.

Hansen, Marlene R. "*Rasselas*, Milton, and Humanism." *English Studies* 60 (1979): 14-22. Places Johnson in the humanist tradition and sees *Rasselas* as exploring, without resolving, the question of how imperfect people should behave in an imperfect world.

Jones, Emrys. "The Artistic Form of *Rasselas*." *Review of English Studies* 18 (November, 1967): 387-401. Notes that the work divides neatly into three sections of equal length, but that the last chapter breaks this pattern to reflect nature's refusal to be contained and constrained by art.

Keener, Frederick M. *The Chain of Becoming: The Philosophical Tale, the Novel, and a Neglected Realism of the Enlightenment; Swift, Montesquieu, Voltaire, Johnson, and Austen.* New York: Columbia University Press, 1983. Argues for the psychological realism of philosophical tales like *Rasselas* and relates such works to the novels of Jane Austen.

Sklenicka, Carol J. "Samuel Johnson and the Fiction of Activity." *South Atlantic Quarterly* 78 (1979): 214-223. Johnson demonstrates that absolute happiness is not achievable on earth, but activity and friendship provide palliatives to a life in which there is much to be endured and little to be enjoyed.

Tomarken, Edward. *Johnson, "Rasselas," and the Choice of Criticism.* Lexington: University Press of Kentucky, 1989. After surveying the various critical approaches to *Rasselas*, offers a fusion of formalist and other theories to explain *Rasselas* as a work in which life and literature confront each other. The second part of the book argues that Johnson's other writings support this view.

Wahba, Magdi, ed. *Bicentenary Essays on "Rasselas."* Cairo: Cairo Studies in English, 1959. Issued as a supplement to *Cairo Studies in English*, this work collects a number of useful essays. Included are James Clifford's comparison of Voltaire's *Candide* (1759) and *Rasselas*, Fatma Moussa Mahmoud's "*Rasselas* and *Vathek*," and C. J. Rawson's discussion of Ellis Cornelia Knight's *Dinarbas* (1790) as a continuation of Johnson's work.

Walker, Robert G. *Eighteenth-Century Arguments for Immortality and Johnson's "Rasselas."* Victoria, British Columbia: University of Victoria, 1977. Places Johnson's fiction "in the context of eighteenth century philosophical discussions on the nature of the human soul." Reads the work as an orthodox Christian defense of the soul's immortality and as a demonstration that happiness is not attainable in this world.

Whitley, Alvin. "The Comedy of *Rasselas*." *English Literary History* 23

(March, 1956): 48-70. Sees the work as a satire on deviations from reason and realism. Even in the later, darker sections of *Rasselas*, finds the travelers' reactions comic.

ELIZABETH JOLLEY

Born: Birmingham, England; June 4, 1923

Principal long fiction

Palomino, 1980; *The Newspaper of Claremont Street*, 1981; *Mr. Scobie's Riddle*, 1983; *Miss Peabody's Inheritance*, 1983; *Milk and Honey*, 1984; *Foxybaby*, 1985; *The Well*, 1986; *The Sugar Mother*, 1988; *My Father's Moon*, 1989.

Other literary forms

Elizabeth Jolley's reputation was first established by her short stories, one of which, "Hedge of Rosemary," won an Australian prize as early as 1966. The first works she ever published were her short-story collections *Five Acre Virgin and Other Stories* (1976) and *The Travelling Entertainer and Other Stories* (1979); although her novel *Palomino* won a prize as an unpublished work in 1975, it did not appear in print until 1980. A third volume of short stories, *Woman in a Lampshade*, was published in 1983. Her radio plays have been produced on Australian radio and on the British Broadcasting Corporation (BBC) World Network.

Achievements

Jolley had been writing for twenty years before her first book, a volume of short stories, was published in 1976. In 1975, her novel *Palomino* was given the Con Weickhardt Award for an unfinished novel. *Palomino* was not published, however, until 1980, after a second volume of short stories had already appeared. Not until 1984 was Jolley widely reviewed in the United States.

Sometimes compared to Muriel Spark and Barbara Pym, Jolley is unique in her characterization and tone. Critics variously refer to her novels as fantasy combined with farce, comedy of manners, moral satire, or black comedy. Although most reviewers see a moral dimension beneath the slapstick surface of her work, noting her compassion, her wisdom, and her penetration of complex human relationships, some have insisted that she is merely a comic entertainer. Yet to most thoughtful readers, it is obvious that Jolley's humor often derives from characters who refuse to be defeated by their destinies, who boldly assert their individuality, and who dare to dream and to love, however foolish they may appear to the conformists.

Biography

Elizabeth Monica Jolley was born in Birmingham, England, on June 4, 1923. Her mother, a German aristocrat, the daughter of a general, had married a young Englishman who had been disowned by his father because of his pacifist convictions. Privately educated for some years, Jolley and her sister were then sent to a Quaker school. Later, Jolley was trained as a nurse at Queen Elizabeth Hospital, Birmingham, and served in that capacity during World War II. In 1959, she moved to Western Australia with her husband and three children. After her move, Jolley began increasingly to divide her time between writing, tending to her farm, and conducting writing workshops.

Analysis

In "Self Portrait: A Child Went Forth," a personal commentary in the one-volume collection *Stories* (1984), Elizabeth Jolley muses on the frequency with which the theme of exile appears in her works. Often her major characters are lonely, physically or emotionally alienated from their surroundings, living imaginatively in a friendlier, more interesting environment. Because of their loneliness, they reach out, often to grasping or selfish partners, who inevitably disappoint them. For Jolley's lonely spinster, widow, or divorcée, the beloved may be another woman. Sometimes, however, the yearning takes a different form, and the beloved is not a person but a place, like the homes of the old men in *Mr. Scobie's Riddle*.

If there is defeat in Jolley's fiction, there is also grace in the midst of despair. Despite betrayal, her characters reach for love, and occasionally an unlikely pair or group will find it. Another redeeming quality is the power of the imagination; it is no accident that almost every work contains a writer, who may, as in *Foxybaby*, appear to be imagining events into reality and characters into existence. Finally, Jolley believes in laughter. Her characters laugh at one another and sometimes at themselves; more detached, she and her readers laugh at the outrageous characters, while at the same time realizing that the characters are only slight exaggerations of those who view them.

The protagonist of Jolley's novel *Palomino* is an exile desperate for love. A physician who has been expelled from the profession and imprisoned, Laura lives on an isolated ranch, her only neighbors the shiftless, dirty tenants, who inspire her pity but provide no companionship for her. Into Laura's lonely life comes Andrea Jackson, a young woman whom the doctor noticed on her recent voyage from England but with whom she formed no relationship. Up until this point, Laura's life has been a series of unsuccessful and unconsummated love affairs with women. At one time, she adored a doctor, to whom she wrote religiously; when the doctor arrived on a visit, she brought a husband. At another period in her life, Laura loved Andrea's selfish, flirtatious mother, who eventually returned to her abusive husband. Perhaps, Laura hopes, Andrea will be different. She is delighted when Andrea agrees to run off with her, ecstatic when she can install her on the ranch, where the women live happily, talking, laughing, and making love. In her new joy, Laura does not realize that, like her other lost lovers, Andrea is obsessed with a man— her own brother, Christopher. It is Christopher's marriage and fatherhood which has driven her into Laura's arms, but Andrea continues to desire Chris, even at moments of high passion. When Andrea admits that she is pregnant with Chris's baby and tries to use Laura's love for her to obtain an abortion, Laura is forced to come to terms with the fact that the love between Andrea and her is imperfect, as it is in all relationships, doomed to change or to dwindle. Obviously, loneliness is the human condition.

Although Jolley's characters must face hard truths such as the inevitability of loneliness, often they move through suffering to new understanding. This is the pattern of *Palomino*. The novel derives its title from the horses on a nearby ranch, whose beauty Laura can appreciate even though she does not possess them. Joy is in perception, not possession; similarly, joy comes from loving, not from being loved. When Andrea and Laura agree that they must part, for fear that their brief love will dwindle into dislike or indifference, they know that they can continue to love each other, even though they will never again be together.

In the graphic dialogue of Laura's tenants can be seen the accuracy and the comic vigor which characterize Jolley's later works. *Mr. Scobie's Riddle*, for example, begins with a series of communications between the matron of the nursing home where the novel takes place and the poorly qualified night nurse, whose partial explanations and inadequate reports, along with her erratic spelling, infuriate her superior. At night, the nursing home comes alive with pillow fights, medicinal whiskey, and serious gambling, at which the matron's brother, a former colonel, always loses. In the daytime, the home is a prison: Old people are processed like objects, ill-fed, ill-tended by two rock-and-rolling girls, and supervised by the greedy matron, whose goal is to part her new guest, Mr. Scobie, from his property. Yet if the patients are prisoners, so are their supervisors. Having lost her husband to an old schoolmate, the matron cannot ignore the fact that the couple cavort regularly in the caravan on the grounds; in turn, the lonely matron saddles her schoolmate with as much work as possible. Meanwhile, the matron is driven constantly closer to bankruptcy by her brother's gambling and closer to a nervous breakdown by her inefficient and careless employees.

Some of the most poignant passages in *Mr. Scobie's Riddle* deal with the yearnings of two old men in Room One, who wish only to return to their homes. Unfortunately, one's has been sold and bulldozed down; the other's has been rented by a voracious niece and nephew. As the patients are driven toward their deaths, no one offers rescue or even understanding. There are, however, some triumphs. The would-be writer, Miss Hailey, never surrenders her imagination or her hope; ironically, her schoolfellow, the matron, who has taken all of her money, must at last turn to Miss Hailey for understanding and companionship. In the battle for his own dignity, Mr. Scobie wins. Even though he is returned to the nursing home whenever he attempts to go home, and even though his uncaring niece and nephew finally acquire his beloved home, he wins, for he never surrenders to the matron, but dies before she can bully him into signing over his property.

The unique combination of farcical humor, lyrical description, pathos, and moral triumph which marks Jolley's later work is also exemplified in *Miss Peabody's Inheritance*, published, like *Mr. Scobie's Riddle*, in 1983. In this novel, a woman writer is one of the two major characters. In response to a fan letter from a middle-aged, mother-ridden London typist, the novelist regularly transmits to her the rough episodes from her new novel, a Rabelaisian story of lesbian schoolmistresses and the troublesome, innocent girl whom they escort through Europe. When at last the typist travels to Australia to meet her writer-heroine, she finds that the writer, a bed-bound invalid, has died. Yet her courage, her imagination, and her manuscript remain for Miss Peabody, an inheritance which will enable her to live as fully and as creatively as the novelist.

In *Milk and Honey*, there is no triumph of love, of laughter, or of the imagination. Alone among Jolley's novels, *Milk and Honey* begins and ends in despair. At the beginning, a door-to-door salesman with a poor, unhappy wife expresses his loneliness, his loss of the woman he loved and of the music he enjoyed. The rest of the novel re-creates his life, from the time when he went to live with his cello teacher and his seemingly delightful family, through the salesman's discovery that he was used and betrayed, to the final tragic climax, when his income vanished—his cellist's hand was charred in a fire—and the woman who made his life worth living was brutally murdered. Although many of the scenes in the novel are grotesque, they are devoid of the humor which is typical of Jolley and which often suggests one way of rising above despair. Nor does the protagonist's art—here, performing music, rather than creating fiction—enable him to transcend his situation. His love for his wife is destroyed with his illusions about her, his mistress is destroyed by his wife, and he and his wife are left to live out their lives together without love.

Foxybaby, published in 1985, is as grotesque as *Milk and Honey*, but its characters move through desperation to humor, love, imagination, and hope. The setting is a campus turned into a weight-loss clinic. Typically, the characters are trapped there, in this case by the rascally bus driver, who ensures a healthy wrecker and garage business by parking so that all approaching cars plow into him. The central character of *Foxybaby* is, once again, a woman writer, Alma Porch, who along with a sculptor and a potter has been hired to take the residents' minds off food by submerging them in culture. Miss Porch's mission is to rehearse an assorted group of residents in a film which she is creating as the book progresses. Brilliantly, Jolley alternates the wildly comic events at the campus with the poignant story that Miss Porch is writing, an account of a father's attempt to rescue his young, drug-ruined, infected daughter and her sickly baby from the doom which seems to await them. From his affectionate nickname for her when she was a little girl comes the name of the book.

Like the love story in *Milk and Honey*, the plot in *Foxybaby* illustrates the destructive power of love. Well-meaning though he is, the father cannot establish communication with his daughter. The reason is unclear, even to the writer who is creating the story or, more accurately, is letting the characters she has imagined create their own story. Perhaps the father's love was crushing; perhaps in her own perverseness the daughter rejected it. At any rate, it is obvious that despite his persistence, he is making little headway in reaching the destructive stranger who is now his "Foxybaby" and who herself has a baby for whom she feels nothing.

Meanwhile, like Jolley's other protagonists, Porch considers escaping from the place which is both her prison and her exile but is prevented from doing so by the very confusion of events. Loquacious Jonquil Castle moves in with her; a Maybelle Harrow, with her lover and his lover, invites her to an orgy; and the indomitable Mrs. Viggars brings forth her private stock of wine and initiates Porch into the joys of the school-like midnight feast. Offstage, the bus driver is always heard shouting to his wife or his mistress to drop her knickers. Love, in all its variety, blooms on the campus, while it is so helpless in the story being shaped in the same place.

Although the campus trap will be easier to escape, bus or no bus, than the nursing home in *Mr. Scobie's Riddle*, Jolley stresses the courage of the residents, a courage which will be necessary in the lives to which they will return, whether those lives involve battling boredom and loneliness, like Miss Porch's, or rejection, like that of Jonquil Castle, the doting mother and grandmother, or age and the loss of love, like the lascivious Maybelle Harrow's. Just as they will survive the clinic, though probably without losing any weight, they will survive their destinies. At the end of the novel, there is a triumph of love, when Mrs. Viggars, admitting her loneliness, chooses to take a young woman and her three children into her home, in order to establish a family once again. There is also a triumph of imagination, when Miss Porch actually sees the characters whom she has created. For her loneliness, they will be companions.

At the end of the novel, the bus stops and Miss Porch awakes, to find herself at the school. Jolley does not explain: Has Porch dreamed the events of the book? Will they now take place? Or is the awakening misplaced in time, and have they already taken place? Ultimately, it does not matter. What does matter is the power of the imagination, which, along with humor and love, makes life bearable.

Hester Harper, another spinster protagonist, is somewhat like the doctor in *Palomino* in that she lives on an isolated ranch in Western Australia and yearns for love. In *The Well*, however, the beloved is an orphan girl, whom Hester takes home to be her companion. Refusing to admit her sexual desires, even to herself, Hester persuades herself that her feelings are merely friendly or perhaps maternal; yet she is so jealous of the orphan, Katherine, that she cannot bear to think of the friend who wishes to visit her or of the man who will ultimately take her away. The rival, when he appears, is mysterious, perhaps a thief, perhaps only an animal, whom Katherine hits on a late-night drive and whom Hester immediately buries in the well. Perhaps diabolical, perhaps distraught, Katherine insists that he is calling to her, demanding her love, threatening her and Hester. Although at last his voice is stilled, it is clear that Hester has lost control over Katherine, to whom the outside world of sexuality and adventure is calling with undeniable urgency. Unlike the doctor in *Palomino*, Hester cannot be contented with the memory of love. Imagination, however, once again mitigates the horror of life; at the end of the novel, Hester is making the mysterious nighttime adventure into a story to be told to children.

Because she deals with cruelty, indifference, greed, lust, and, above all, with loneliness, Elizabeth Jolley cannot be considered a superficial writer. The great distances of her Western Australia become a metaphor for the mysterious expanses of time; the small clumps of isolated individuals, trapped together on a ranch, on a weight-loss farm, or in a nursing home, represent society, as did Joseph Conrad's microcosmic ships on an indifferent ocean. Jolley makes it clear that love is infrequent and imperfect, that childhood is endangered by cruelty and that old age leads through indignity to death. Yet most of her works are enlivened by comic characters who defy destiny and death by their very insistence on living. Some of her characters transcend their isolation by learning to love, such as the doctor in *Palomino* or Mrs. Viggars in *Foxybaby*. Others, such as Miss Peabody and Miss Porch, triumph through their imaginations. There is redemption in nature, whether in the beauty of palomino horses or the sunlit shore where Miss Porch sees her characters. There is also triumph in the isolated courage of a human being such as Mr. Scobie, who defies institutionalized and personal greed to save the beloved home to which he can return only in memory. If Elizabeth Jolley's characters are mixtures of the pathetic, the grotesque, and the noble, it is because they are human; if her stories keep the reader off balance between confusion, laughter, and tears, it is because they reflect life.

Rosemary M. Canfield-Reisman

Other major works

SHORT FICTION: *Five Acre Virgin and Other Stories*, 1976; *The Travelling Entertainer and Other Stories*, 1979; *Woman in a Lampshade*, 1983; *Stories*, 1984.

RADIO PLAYS: *Night Report*, 1975; *The Performance*, 1976; *The Shepherd on the Roof*, 1977; *The Well-Bred Thief*, 1977; *Woman in a Lampshade*, 1979; *Two Men Running*, 1981.

Bibliography

Daniel, Helen. "A Literary Offering, Elizabeth Jolley." In *Liars: Australian New Novelists*. New York: Penguin Books, 1988. In this comprehensive study, Jolley's fiction is compared to a musical composition by Johann Sebastien Bach, consisting of component literary fugues. While each of her novels is separate, they all blend together to form a graceful totality, and Jolley's handling of theme, time, characterization, and narrative is discussed in this light. The essay appears in a book devoted to Jolley and seven other contemporary Australian novelists, and includes a primary and selected secondary bibliography.

Howells, Coral Ann. "In Search of Lost Mothers: Margaret Laurence's *The Diviners* and Elizabeth Jolley's *Miss Peabody's Inheritance*." *Ariel* 19, no. 1 (1988): 57-70. This comparison of two novels, one Canadian, the other Australian, places them in the tradition of postcolonial writing by women who are concerned not only with their political dispossession as former colonials but with their gender dispossession as well. After a thorough discussion of the two works in this light, the conclusion is drawn that both writers claim their female literary inheritance by rejecting masculinist-inspired tradition and creating their own aesthetic.

Manning, Gerald F. "Sunsets and Sunrises: Nursing Home as Microcosm in *Memento Mori* and *Mr. Scobie's Riddle*." *Ariel* 18, no. 2 (1987): 27-43. This comparative study takes up the similarities in Muriel Spark's *Memento Mori* and Jolley's *Mr. Scobie's Riddle*. The two novels share setting (a nursing home) and theme (age, loneliness, and alienation), and both authors make imaginative use of tragicomic devices to enrich their tone. These works attempt to discover an answer that will lead to the acceptance of death.

Westerly 31, no. 2 (1986). Entitled "Focus on Elizabeth Jolley," this special issue of an Australian journal provides essays on various aspects of Jolley's work, including one on the way her fiction connects to form a continuum, one on her novel *Milk and Honey*, and another on her handling of displaced persons. Also includes fiction by Jolley.

Willbanks, Ray. "A Conversation with Elizabeth Jolley." *Antipodes: A North American Journal of Australian Literature* 3 (1989): 27-30. While concentrating on Jolley's fiction—its characters, themes, background, and development—this interview offers some interesting information on the author's personal background. Jolley tells about her life in England, where she was born and lived to adulthood until she moved to Australia in 1959. She also recalls the impact Australia made on her when she first arrived and discusses its effect on her writing.

JAMES JONES

Born: Robinson, Illinois; November 6, 1921
Died: Southampton, New York; May 9, 1977

Principal long fiction

From Here to Eternity, 1951; *Some Came Running*, 1957; *The Pistol*, 1959; *The Thin Red Line*, 1962; *Go to the Widow-Maker*, 1967; *The Merry Month of May*, 1971; *A Touch of Danger*, 1973; *Whistle*, 1978.

Other literary forms

James Jones published one much underrated collection of short fiction, *The Ice-Cream Headache and Other Stories*, in 1968. Despite the excellence of several of these stories, he did not return to short fiction, primarily because of the difficulty of writing openly about sex in mass circulation magazines. He wrote two book-length works of nonfiction, *Viet Journal* (1974) and *WWII* (1975). The first is an account of Jones's experiences and observations while a war correspondent in Vietnam. *WWII*, a much more important work, is an analysis of the graphic art produced during World War II. The book contains some of Jones's finest writing, as well as an extended analysis of the central concept underlying his best fiction, "the evolution of a soldier." Jones also contributed essays to *Esquire*, *Harper's*, and the *Saturday Evening Post*, among other journals; the subject matter of these pieces ranges widely, from theories of fiction to skin diving.

Achievements

Jones's first novel, *From Here to Eternity*, was a spectacular success, both with critics and with the popular reading audience. As several reviewers pointed out, its frank treatment of sexuality and military brutality broke important new ground for American literary naturalism. While the novel had its detractors, it won the National Book Award for Fiction. *From Here to Eternity* appeared just in time to ride the crest of the new wave in paperback publishing, and in November, 1953, *Newsweek* reported that the paperback reprint of Jones's novel had gone through five printings of "1,700,000 copies . . . in the past six weeks." The popularity of the novel was augmented by its adaptation into one of the most highly regarded American films of the 1950's. Directed by Fred Zinnemann and with unforgettable performances by Montgomery Clift, Burt Lancaster, and Deborah Kerr among others, the film version won the Best Picture award from the Motion Picture Academy of Arts and Sciences and the New York Film Critics in 1953. Jones himself became an international celebrity.

During the next twenty-five years, Jones remained an enormously popular writer. He and Norman Mailer were sometimes praised for having inspired a revitalized American literary realism. Still, Jones never regained the critical acceptance he enjoyed with his first novel. His much anticipated second novel, *Some Came Running*, was denounced as a failure. Occasionally thereafter, his work received positive and intelligent reviews. His tightly constructed 1959 novella *The Pistol* was seen by some perceptive critics as refuting the recurring charge that Jones could not control his material. Such reviewers as Maxwell Geismar and Lewis Gannett emphasized the structural brilliance and emotional power of his 1962 combat novel *The Thin Red Line*. Even *Time* magazine, a perennially hostile critic of Jones's work, praised his 1975 non-fictional analysis of wartime art, *WWII*. Still, when he died in 1977, Jones had been largely ignored by the critical establishment for some time. Academic critics especially dismissed him as an outdated naturalist no longer relevant in an age of literary innovation and experimentation. To the reading public, however, he remained quite relevant. Indeed, it seems quite likely that Jones's public acceptance was a factor in the academy's dismissal of him as a serious writer.

He was, in fact, a most serious and significant writer. Nevertheless, the critical neglect of Jones at the time of his death cannot be attributed solely to academic hostility toward popular success. The last three novels published in his lifetime, *Go to the Widow-Maker*, *The Merry Month of May*, and *A Touch of Danger*, added little to his total achievement. *A Touch of Danger* is a detective novel in the Dashiell Hammett-Raymond Chandler "hard-boiled" tradition. A competent work, it was never intended as anything more than popular entertainment. In contrast, *Go to the Widow-Maker*, inspired by Jones's devotion to skin diving, and *The Merry Month of May*, focusing on the 1968 Paris student rebellion, are quite ambitious civilian novels. Like *Some Came Running*, each is intended as a serious investigation of the novelist's belief that the American male is devoted to an adolescent cult of masculinity. Jones's vision of American sexual maladjustment, while honest and insightful, was simply not original enough to serve as the primary focus of a long novel, although the concept works well as a major subtheme in his army fiction.

In part because of the time he devoted to civilian novels, the major achievement of Jones's career was unrecognized at the time of his death. *From Here to Eternity* and *The Thin Red Line* were always intended as the first two volumes in a highly innovative trilogy. *Whistle*, the concluding volume of the trilogy, was published posthumously in 1978 and inspired a reappraisal of Jones's lasting contribution to American literature. His army trilogy is beginning to receive its proper recognition as the most important fictional treatment of American involvement in World War II. Moreover, *From Here to Eternity* has attained the status of a modern classic, and *The Thin Red Line* is frequently praised as the best American "combat novel." One can expect that a new appreciation of Jones's shorter fiction, especially *The Pistol*, will be forthcoming as well.

Biography

Born in Robinson, Illinois, on November 6, 1921, James Jones grew up in a proud and socially prominent family. When he was a junior in Robinson High School, however, the family's position abruptly deteriorated, largely because of the Samuel Insull stock scandal. Even though his father, Ramon, was never professionally successful and became an alcoholic before ultimately committing suicide, Jones was fond of him. In sharp contrast, he felt contemptuous of, and rejected by, his mother, Ada Blessing Jones.

After he was graduated from high school in 1939, Jones, on the advice of his father, joined the United States Air Force and was stationed in Hawaii, where he transferred to the Infantry. His army career was not distinguished; he once summarized his record of two promotions and subsequent reductions back to the lowest enlisted grade: "'Apted Cpl 13 May 42 Red to Pvt 3 Dec 43, Apt Sgt 1 Mar 44 Red to Pvt 20 May 44.'" Still, in more than one way, Jones's military experience was crucial in his development as an artist. Primarily, he developed a complex love-hate relationship with the United States Army which later gave his military fiction a unique tension. Moreover, he was present at Schofield Barracks, Hawaii, on December 7, 1941, and witnessed the birth of a new and terrifying world. Later, Jones saw combat on Guadalcanal, the brutality of which inspired his concept of "the animal nature of man."

Wounded on Guadalcanal in 1943, he was sent back to the States and, on July 6, 1944, received his military discharge. Greatly shaken both by the combat horror he had experienced and by the continuing dissolution of his family, Jones met Mrs. Lowney Handy of Marshall, Illinois, in late 1943 or early 1944, and began one of the strangest, and ultimately most publicized, apprenticeships in the history of American letters. A 1953 *Newsweek* essay described Lowney Handy as "a more dynamic version of Sinclair Lewis's Carol Kennicott in 'Main Street,'" and she does appear to have waged a one-woman crusade against small-town Midwestern provincialism. Certainly, she and her husband, Harry Handy, supported Jones during a seven-year period in which he worked at his ambition of becoming a writer.

The young soldier had discovered Thomas Wolfe at the Schofield Barracks Post Library and "realized [he] . . . had been a writer all his . . . life without knowing it or having written." With Lowney Handy's encouragement, Jones wrote a first novel, which he submitted to Maxwell Perkins, the legendary editor at Charles Scribner's Sons. Perkins rejected this first novel but encouraged Jones to concentrate on a work about the old peacetime army. After Perkins' death, Jones profited from the help and encouragement of editor Burroughs Mitchell, and when Scribner's published *From Here to Eternity* in 1951, its author became an instant celebrity. Initially, he used his new wealth to establish a writers' colony at Marshall. Lowney Handy assumed the directorship of the colony and imposed an iron discipline upon her new protégés.

Jones, however, grew bored and skeptical in Marshall, seeing the cynicism of some of the writers and the failure of Mrs. Handy's methods to create universally good writing or even cooperation among the writers. His introduction to the beautiful actress Gloria Mosolino made inevitable a bitter and painful break with the Handys. In 1957, Jones and Gloria Mosolino were married at the Olofson Hotel in Haiti. The couple lived for a few months in New York City before moving to Paris in 1958. For the next sixteen years, the Joneses were the center of the American expatriate community in Paris. Whether his books were critically praised or attacked made no difference to Jones's new status as international celebrity.

Jones's break with Lowney Handy and his love affair with Gloria are fictionalized in his autobiographical novel *Go to the Widow-Maker*, and Paris is the setting of his ambitious 1971 work *The Merry Month of May*. Still, he always wrote best about the army. In 1973, he went to Vietnam as a war correspondent and, the following year, published *Viet Journal*, a nonfictional account of what he had seen in that tragic country. Also, in 1974, he and his wife and two children returned home to the United States. Jones was increasingly determined to complete what he had long envisioned as the central work of his career, a trilogy about the United States Army, of which *From Here to Eternity* and *The Thin Red Line* constituted the first two volumes.

On May 9, 1977, Jones died of congestive heart failure in Southampton, New York. He had not quite completed *Whistle*, the third volume of his trilogy. It was possible, however, for Willie Morris, a writer, editor, and longtime friend, to finish the manuscript from Jones's notes and tapes. When *Whistle* was published in February, 1978, James Jones's army trilogy took its place as the most important American fictional treatment of World War II.

Analysis

Critics, especially academics, have increasingly dismissed James Jones as a "war novelist" committed to outdated naturalistic techniques. Though Ihab Hassan provides an extensive and largely favorable discussion of *From Here to Eternity* in *Radical Innocence*, his 1961 examination of post-World War II American fiction, two important subsequent studies of the contemporary American novel, Tony Tanner's *City of Words* (1971) and Josephine Hendin's *Vulnerable People* (1978), ignore Jones completely. This neglect arises, in part, from oversimplified and incorrect perceptions of his work. For example, as the term is most commonly used, Jones is not strictly a "war novelist." Of his eight novels, only one, *The Thin Red Line*, is primarily devoted to a description of military combat, while four have peacetime civilian settings. While it is true that army life provides the background of his best fiction and World War II its controlling event, his reactions to the army and the war exhibit the complexity and ambiguity essential to meaningful art.

Especially during the 1950's, Jones often permitted himself to be depicted as an advocate of masculine toughness in life and literature. A 1957 *Life* magazine "Close-Up" emphasized the novelist's devotion to knives and boxing and declared his prominence in the literary cult of violence. Yet a careful reader of Jones's fiction will discover an artist deeply concerned about man's capacity for self-destruction. In a 1974 interview, Jones discussed his belief that humanity was doomed by two interrelated forces: its own animal nature and the anonymous power of modern technological society. He stressed "the ridiculous misuse of human strength which can include many subjects, not only physical strength, but technology, and all of the things that we live by." After defining morality as the refusal to give another pain "even though one suffers himself," he forecast the inevitable failure of such an idealistic ethical code: "In all of us, there is this animal portion . . . which is not at all adverse to inflicting cruelty on others. This can be quite enjoyable at times. . . . It's in myself . . . it's in all of us."

Modern man, Jones believed, is caught in both an external and an internal trap. Human strength, which has its source in the "animal nature of man," has been translated into an awesome technology which ironically threatens the extinction of human individuality, if not the actual obliteration of mankind. In his civilian novels, Jones's characters habitually seek the few remaining "frontiers" of individualism (for example, skin diving), only to discover the impossibility of escaping their own "animal" heritage. An element of brutal and destructive competition is thereby introduced into the "frontier," which is perverted and ultimately doomed. It is in his army fiction, however, that Jones most memorably dramatizes the tragic vulnerability of contemporary man.

In a 1967 *Paris Review* interview, Jones said: "I've come to consider bravery as just about the most pernicious of virtues. Bravery is a horrible thing. The human race has it left over from the animal world and we can't get rid of it." His army fiction underscores the destructiveness of this "most pernicious of virtues." Strength and bravery are, of course, essential qualities of the traditional hero. In more romantic ages, these two virtues were often perceived as the very foundation of manhood. Today's all-pervasive technology makes such romantic concepts of heroism archaic and dangerous. The dominant social mechanism of the modern world is bureaucracy, which can hardly permit heroism, since bureaucracy denies individuality. Jones saw modern warfare as the inevitable product of a bureaucratic, highly technological society. In it, death falls from the sky in a totally "random" and "anonymous" manner. For Jones, a fundamental and dismaying truth was implicit in this impersonal rain of death: in such a technological hell, the traditional Western concepts of the individual and the self no longer hold their old importance. The question he examines throughout his most important fiction is whether they still have any validity at all.

The major achievement of Jones's career is his army trilogy: *From Here to*

Eternity, *The Thin Red Line*, and the posthumously published *Whistle*. His novella *The Pistol* and several of the short stories in his collection *The Ice-Cream Headache and Other Stories* also have military settings. The thematic focus in all Jones's army fiction is upon the evolution of the soldier, a concept which is given a full and convincing nonfictional elaboration in *WWII*. In Jones's view, warfare constitutes man's total capitulation to his animal nature. The traditional concepts of the individual and the self must be discarded in combat: the army trains the soldier to function on a primitive, subhuman level of consciousness. This training is a reversal of evolution; it is a process by which the army systematically dehumanizes the enlisted man. Such dehumanization is necessary for the soldier's acceptance of his own anonymity and probable death in combat. In World War II's anonymous, technological warfare, the enlisted man became more clearly expendable and anonymous than he had ever been. Throughout his military fiction, Jones is intent upon describing the manner in which the army, by using technology and its awareness of the enlisted man's inherent animalism, carried out the dehumanization process.

The three novels that constitute the army trilogy depict three major stages in the evolution of a soldier. It is important to note here that Jones intended the three novels to be seen as constituting a special kind of trilogy. He wished that each "should stand by itself as a work alone," "in a way that . . . John Dos Passos' three novels in his fine USA trilogy do not." At least in *From Here to Eternity* and *The Thin Red Line*, the first two novels in his own trilogy, Jones clearly achieved this ambition.

The army trilogy's most innovative feature is the presence of three character types in all three volumes. Of these three character types, two are of overriding importance. First Sergeant Milt Warden of *From Here to Eternity* is transformed into Sergeant "Mad" Welsh in *The Thin Red Line* and into Sergeant Mart Winch in *Whistle*. Private Robert E. Lee Prewitt of *From Here to Eternity* becomes Private Witt in *The Thin Red Line* and Private Bobby Prell in *Whistle*. John W. Aldridge, sometimes a perceptive critic of Jones's fiction, understands a more important reason than Prewitt's death in *From Here to Eternity* for the characters' different names in each of the novels: increasingly brutal experiences, he writes, have "transformed [them] into altogether different people." In other words, as they reach new and more dehumanizing stages in the evolution of a soldier, their inner selves undergo transformation.

Still, there is a fundamental level on which the character types remain constant. Warden/Welsh/Winch is Jones's realist, who comprehends the inevitability of his own destruction as well as that of his fellow enlisted men. He is burdened by a deep concern for others, but he attempts to hide that concern behind a surface cynicism. Just as he anticipates, his inability to deny his compassion ultimately drives him mad. Private Prewitt/Witt/Prell is the determined and increasingly anachronistic individualist who regularly defies army bureaucracy in the name of his personal ethical code. In *From Here to Eternity*, which focuses on the old peacetime army, he is a romantic figure refusing to compromise with a corrupt bureaucracy. In *The Thin Red Line*, a grim account of combat on Guadalcanal, he is reduced to an animalistic level; his defiance seems insane and pointless rather than romantic. Primarily through his analysis of these two character types, Jones analyzes the contemporary validity of the interrelated concepts of the self and the individual.

The central factor in the critical and popular success of *From Here to Eternity* was its vivid characterization. As Maxwell Perkins had anticipated, Sergeant Milt Warden and Private Robert E. Lee Prewitt are unforgettable figures. They are not, however, the novel's only memorable characters. Private Angelo Maggio and "the women," Alma Schmidt and Karen Holmes, are also strong individuals determined to preserve their integrity in an anonymous, bureaucratic world. *From Here to Eternity* is easily Jones's most romantic novel. In it, he depicts a world that ceased to exist on December 7, 1941; the novel's setting is Hawaii, and its climax is the Japanese attack on Pearl Harbor. For most of the novel, modern technological destruction has not made its appearance, and individualism seems a vital concept that is to be preserved in spite of "old Army" corruption. On the surface, the novel's roster of unforgettable characters seems to guarantee the survival of this traditional Western value.

Warden always knows, however, what is coming. He sees the inevitable destruction of the self and struggles to suppress his instinctive sympathy for Private Prewitt's defiance of the army. Prewitt's integrity is so strong that ultimately even Warden has to respect it. Still, the sergeant's admiration for his "bolshevik" private is a largely nostalgic response; he identifies with such defiant individualism while remaining aware that it is doomed.

Because his individualism is related to much that is crucial to Western values, Prewitt does, in fact, emerge as the dominant character in the novel. In the beginning, his quarrel with the army is almost absurdly simple. His commanding officer, Dynamite Holmes, is determined that Prewitt will become a member of the regimental boxing team; the private is equally determined not to box, even if his refusal means that he must give up playing the bugle, his "calling." Prewitt undergoes prolonged and systematic mental and physical abuse without acquiescing to Holmes's insistence that he box. Ultimately, this vicious "Treatment" does force him past his breaking point and into a mistake that enables Holmes to have him sentenced to the stockade, where he experiences further brutality at the hands of Sergeant Fatso Judson. Judson is one of the most unforgettable sadists in American literature, and Prewitt decides that he must be destroyed. The reader can hardly disagree with this decision; still, it assures Prewitt's own doom.

Much of *From Here to Eternity*'s unique power derives from the levels of symbolic meaning contained within the deceptively simple Prewitt-Holmes conflict. Boxing is a metaphor for the animal nature of man, while Prewitt's "calling" to play the bugle comes to represent that uniquely individualistic integrity that makes possible artistic creation. Throughout the novel, Prewitt is something of a romantic folk hero; he is the personification of "the good soldier," the proud enlisted man. When he plays taps on the bugle or helps in the collective composition of "The Re-Enlistment Blues," he is also giving artistic expression to the enlisted man's pain and loneliness. His desire to play the bugle symbolizes the urge to create a distinctive proletarian art. Warden sees the army's destruction of Prewitt as an illustration of animalism negating man's potential for lasting creativity. Yet, because Prewitt's death occurs just after the Japanese attack on Pearl Harbor, the sergeant has no real opportunity to mourn him. Since Warden understands that December 7, 1941, represented the end of traditional individualism and self-expression, Prewitt's death seems to him almost an anticlimax.

The mood of doomed romanticism so vital to *From Here to Eternity* is completely missing from the second volume of Jones's army trilogy, *The Thin Red Line*, a grimly detailed account of brutal combat. The bolshevik private in this novel is Witt, whose defiance has no relevance to art or to any idealistic values. In a real sense, the novel's main character is "C-for-Charlie Company," all the members of which are forced to submerge themselves into an anonymous mass. *The Thin Red Line* has been called the best American combat novel, and such high praise is deserved. The novel offers an unforgettable account of the sheer animalism of war. The sexuality of all the men of Charlie Company is systematically translated into brutal aggression toward the enemy. In fact, the only meaningful difference among the characters is the degree to which they are aware that such a transformation is taking place.

The one most aware is the superficially cynical first sergeant, Edward "Mad" Welsh. Like Milt Warden in *From Here to Eternity*, "the First" continually wonders how much of his basic self can be denied without a resultant loss of sanity. He has come very close to finding an answer to this question; one source of Jones's title is an old Midwestern saying: "There's only a thin red line between the sane and the mad." Welsh's sanity is still intact, but it is being severely strained by his unrelenting awareness of the dehumanization process that he and his men are undergoing. They are threatened not only by the fanatical determination of the Japanese enemy and by the deadly accidents of warfare, but also by the gross incompetence of their own officers. Writing out of a proletarian consciousness, Jones depicted the officer class as incompetent, if not actually corrupt, in all his army fiction.

The Thin Red Line is Jones's most structurally sound novel, focusing upon the American struggle to capture an area of Guadalcanal known as "The Dancing Elephant." The brutality of combat is documented in complete naturalistic detail. Still, a majority of the central characters are alive when the novel ends with Charlie Company preparing to invade New Georgia. It is only here that the reader comes to share with Mad Welsh an awful knowledge—for those men who did not die on Guadalcanal, another Japanese-occupied island awaits, and then another and another. Thus, ultimate survival seems out of the question, and madness becomes a form of escape from too much awareness.

While no one individual American soldier could confidently expect to survive the war, the majority of the soldiers did survive to return home. Such men returned to a country which, Jones believed, was being irrevocably changed by an unprecedented wave of material prosperity. Thus, men who had accepted the inevitability of their own deaths and whose sexuality had been converted into unrestrained animalism returned to a vital, challenging economy that could not afford the time for their reorientation. They faced what Jones, in *WWII*, called "The De-Evolution of a Soldier," the final and most difficult stage of the soldier's evolution: the acceptance of life and healthy sexuality by men who, after a long and excruciating process, had been converted to death-dealing and death-accepting savagery. *Whistle* focuses on this last, and nearly impossible, transformation.

In large part because Jones was unable to finish it before his death in May, 1977, *Whistle* lacks the power of *From Here to Eternity* and *The Thin Red Line*. Still, as completed from Jones's notes, by Willie Morris, it stands as a memorable conclusion to the army trilogy. The novel focuses upon the return home of four characters, all members of Charlie Company and all veterans of the kind of brutal combat depicted in *The Thin Red Line*. The war is not yet over, but the stateside economic boom is well under way. Although Marion Landers is not one of Jones's three major recurring character types, he is nevertheless reminiscent of Geoffrey Fife in *The Thin Red Line* and Richard Mast in *The Pistol*. All three men are stunned by their forced realization that modern technological combat negates the heroism assigned in romantic myth to warfare. John Strange completes the least successful of the three character types introduced in *From Here to Eternity*. Like his predecessors, Maylon Stark and Mess Sergeant Storm, Strange (nicknamed Johnny Stranger) is unable to care for anyone but himself, even though he has perfected a mask of compassion. Stark/Storm/Strange is the exact opposite of First Sergeant Warden/Welsh/Winch.

Jones's Bolshevik private in *Whistle* is Bobby Prell, who has recaptured much of the Prewitt quixotic idealism that had hardened into animal stubbornness in the characterization of Witt. Very seriously wounded, Prell is battling the army that wishes to give him the Congressional Medal of Honor—the army that also insists on amputating his leg. While not convinced that he deserves the medal, Prell is certain that he should keep his leg, even if refusing amputation means certain death. Certainly, his conflict is elemental and significant; still, Prell never attains a stature comparable to that of Prewitt. Given Jones's vision, Prell must, in fact, seem largely anachronistic. Pearl Harbor marked the death of the romantic rebel as hero.

The truly memorable figure in *Whistle* is Sergeant Mart Winch, the culmination of Jones's depiction of "the First." Throughout most of *Whistle*, Winch functions as Warden and Welsh did, secretly protecting his men by elaborate manipulation of army bureaucracy. He is forced to see, however, the severe limitations of his ability to protect anyone in a new and nightmarish world. After Landers and Prell are shattered by their inability to adjust to civilian society, Winch surrenders to insanity. Thus, he crosses "the thin red line" and is destroyed by the madness that had threatened to engulf Warden and Welsh. The cumulative characterization of "the First" is the most brilliant achievement in Jones's fiction; it is the heart of the army trilogy. Jones called the vision underlying his trilogy "quite tragic" and talked of the impossibility of an affirmative contemporary literature. He described a world so thoroughly converted to dehumanizing bureaucracy and technology that it drives to insanity those men who still believe in such traditional Western values as the self and individualism.

James R. Giles

Other major works
SHORT FICTION: *The Ice-Cream Headache and Other Stories*, 1968.
NONFICTION: *Viet Journal*, 1974; *WWII*, 1975.

Bibliography
Aldrich, Nelson W., ed. *Writers at Work: The Paris Review Interviews.* 3d ser. New York: Viking Press, 1967. Jones talks about his methods of composition and defends his novels and his own brand of realistic writing against critical attacks. He also believes that an academic education can hurt a writer. Although he was living in Europe at the time of the interview, he considers himself to be an American.
Giles, James R. *James Jones.* Boston: Twayne, 1981. Examines each of Jones's novels in detail and gives a brief biography of the novelist. Sees a central division between the he-man and the sophisticate in Jones's life and art. Contains an excellent bibliography.
Hassan, Ihab. *Radical Innocence.* Princeton, N.J.: Princeton University Press, 1961. Describes the hero of *From Here to Eternity*, Pruitt, as a passive sufferer and compares his alienation to that of the Negro. Hassan likes the novel but not the subliterary psychology in which Jones indulges.
Jones, Peter G. *War and the Novelist.* Columbia: University of Missouri Press, 1976. Praises James Jones's *From Here to Eternity* and *Thin Red Line* highly, describing them as accurate portrayals of Army life and combat and as possessing psychological insights.
Moore, Harry Thornton, ed. *Contemporary American Novelists.* Carbondale: Southern Illinois University Press, 1964. Places Jones in a literary tradi-

tion, American realism, and from that perspective defends him as an important American novelist.

Morris, Willie. *James Jones: A Friendship.* Garden City, N.Y.: Doubleday, 1978. The friendship between these two writers occurred late in Jones's life. They both lived on Long Island and were drawn into conversations about life and art. Jones reveals much about his early military career.

MADISON JONES

Born: Nashville, Tennessee; March 21, 1925

Principal long fiction

The Innocent, 1957; *Forest of the Night*, 1960; *A Buried Land*, 1963; *An Exile*, 1967; *A Cry of Absence*, 1971; *Passage Through Gehenna*, 1978; *Season of the Strangler*, 1982; *Last Things*, 1989.

Other literary forms

Although Madison Jones is known primarily as a novelist, he has also published short stories and literary criticism. The stories have appeared in journals such as *Perspective* and, more important, the *Sewanee Review*, which figured prominently in his early career. His story "Dog Days" was included by Martha Foley in her collection of *The Best American Short Stories of 1953*. Two years earlier, his 1951 story "The Homecoming" had been listed by Foley on her Roll of Honor. His critical works and reviews have appeared in the *Mississippi Quarterly*, the *South Atlantic Quarterly*, the *Washington Post*, and *The New York Times Book Review*.

Achievements

Despite some early success with the short story, Jones's major literary accomplishments are found in his novels, which range from the spare novella form of *An Exile* to the rich, nightmarish extravagance of *Forest of the Night*, from the contemporary social criticism of *A Buried Land* and *A Cry of Absence* to the timeless allegory of sin and redemption in *Passage Through Gehenna*. Whatever the form he employs, Jones is noted for the care with which he constructs his works; he is a stylist of precision and balance. Conservative in the sense that his values are rooted in the traditional, Jones has never become an apologist for the Southern land and people he has chosen as his subject. He refuses to sentimentalize or romanticize. There are instead a sharp intelligence and undeviating morality that motivate each work. His novels are often too emotionally demanding to be "entertaining" in the popular sense of the word, and he has never achieved wide commercial success, although *An Exile* was made into a motion picture starring Gregory Peck and Tuesday Weld.

Jones has long encouraged the development of Southern writers, both through his own example and through his teaching as writer-in-residence at Auburn University. He believes in the need for cultural and intellectual independence for the South. In his concerns and goals, Jones remains a part of that middle generation of twentieth century Southern writers who carry the rich and often troubling heritage of the traditional past into the changing and sometimes ambivalent society of today.

Biography

Madison Percy Jones, Jr., was born on March 21, 1925, in Nashville, Tennessee, the son of Madison Percy and Mary Temple (Webber) Jones. He attended public and private schools in Nashville. In the early 1940's, Jones farmed and trained horses; the knowledge he gained of the land and people of rural Tennessee would later be reflected in his writings.

From 1944 to 1945, Jones served in the United States Army Corp of Military Police in Korea. Shortly thereafter, he entered Vanderbilt University in Nashville and studied under Donald Davidson. After receiving his B.A. from Vanderbilt in 1949, he continued his studies under Andrew Lytle at the University of Florida and was awarded his M.A. in 1951. Jones married Shailah McEvilley in February of 1951 and spent the next two years in postgraduate study at Florida, learning from Lytle and writing his early fiction.

In 1953, Jones became an instructor of English at Miami University (Oxford, Ohio). In 1954, he received the *Sewanee Review* Fellowship, which enabled him to concentrate more on his writing. From 1955 to 1956, he taught at the University of Tennessee in Knoxville. He then moved to Alabama, where he became a professor of English at Auburn University. In 1957, his first novel, *The Innocent*, was published by Harcourt, Brace.

Jones eventually became a full professor and writer-in-residence at Auburn, where he had remained since 1956. He was awarded a Rockefeller Foundation Fellowship in 1968, a John Simon Guggenheim Foundation Fellowship in 1973-1974, and numerous regional awards. He and his wife are the parents of five children. Jones retired from teaching in 1987.

Analysis

Madison Jones is first and foremost a Southern writer. His books are all set in and around Tennessee, but they encompass the spirit and turmoil of the South in general. His novels, all of which include some aspect of Southern history, range from the pioneer settlers in 1802 to the civil rights marchers of the 1960's. Although he has never written about the Civil War itself, its shadow is seen in a number of his works.

During the 1960's, critics such as Robert Penn Warren and Allen Tate placed Jones at the head of the second generation of twentieth century Southern novelists, those who wrote in the shadow of William Faulkner. Louis D. Rubin, for example, in his 1963 essay "The Difficulties of Being a Southern Writer Today: Or, Getting Out from Under William Faulkner," used Jones's third novel, *A Buried Land*, as an example of a Southern novel which dealt with the problems of the modern South on its own terms and not those established by Faulkner. Rubin believed Jones wrote about a world different from Faulkner's with different loyalties and demands. Although one might question the absoluteness of Rubin's conclusions—Faulkner does, after all, look clearly at the problems of the changing South in his later works such as

The Town (1957) and *The Mansion* (1959)—the fact remains that Jones is more closely aligned with Warren, Lytle, and Tate, and with the Fugitive movement in general, than with writers such as Faulkner or Erskine Caldwell, who tended to remain outside political or social movements. Nevertheless, although Jones's novels cast a suspicious eye on the "benefits" of rapid change, they also question the romanticization of the past, the unthinking devotion to the heritage of a bygone era.

Indeed, what Jones seems to argue for most in his works is the need for balance. Characters such as Duncan Welsh in *The Innocent* and Hester Glenn in *A Cry of Absence*, who attempt to live in a kind of mythic past, do so at the risk of their own humanity by denying their present moral responsibilities. On the other hand, characters such as Percy Youngblood in *A Buried Land* or Judson Rivers in *Passage Through Gehenna*, who attempt to deny their past, are equally likely to find themselves teetering on the edge of damnation because they have no faith or loyalties to support them. Jones suggests that both extremes lead to isolation, both physical and spiritual, which is his version of hell on earth. Jones's novels are structured on such conflicts—between past and present, good and evil, revenge and mercy.

Jones is, in a very real sense, a religious writer, one who believes strongly in the existence of sin and the inevitability of retribution, but who also sees the possibility of redemption. The act of writing itself he sees as a moral commitment. He says he learned from Andrew Lytle that writing was, first of all, a craft to be mastered through demanding work; only then could the writer adequately express his private vision. In his book reviews, Jones has criticized writers who fail to look for answers to man's dilemma, who instead retreat into nihilism or descend into exploitation and sensationalism. He also realizes, however, that man, in an overzealous attempt to do good, to impose order, may ultimately pervert the very goodness he is trying to establish. Self-righteousness is, to Jones, another form of self-ignorance, and it is those characters who are most sure of themselves who come to suffer the greatest trials. They may finally achieve knowledge and salvation, but only after hellish journeys into the darkness of their souls.

The irony in the title of Jones's first novel, *The Innocent*, should not be overlooked. Duncan Welsh, the book's protagonist, is the first of many of Jones's characters who lose their innocence in the attempt to preserve it. Duncan is a young man retreating from a world he finds corrupt, complex, and devious. He wants absolutes in his life—absolute purity, absolute integrity—and he hopes to find them by returning to a past which is more a dream than a reality. The book is set in rural Tennessee in the mid-1930's. Duncan has been absent from the region for seven years, working as a newspaperman in the North, where the lack of tradition and heritage has appalled him. He finds, however, upon his return, that many of the vices he sought to escape have now encroached even into his homeland.

Jones alerts the reader from the first of the impossibility of Duncan's dream. The Prologue describes a wrestling match Duncan observes upon his arrival, a match in which a young boy, who is portrayed in terms of his innocence, is killed by a more experienced fighter. The boy's death anticipates Duncan's own. Moreover, the reader learns that Duncan is blind in one eye, the result of a freak accident, and blindness becomes the central metaphor of the novel: Duncan simply cannot see the truth in his misguided attempts to maintain his "innocence."

Duncan's dream is to re-create the past, a way of life he never actually knew but has long imagined. He finds the family farm in disrepair, his father locked in senility, and his sister engaged to a local preacher, Hiram Garner. Garner represents all that Duncan hates (and much of which Jones himself disapproves): he preaches the social gospel of progress, he disparages the past, and he is contemptuous of those who think otherwise. Despite Garner's cruel arrogance, he is not an evil man, nor are his calls for social change selfishly motivated. He quickly recognizes in Duncan what Duncan cannot see in himself: that his desire to live in the past is based on a fear of the present. Still, because of Garner's self-importance, the reader's sympathies lie with Duncan.

In his quest for an idealized world, Duncan begins to withdraw. After his father dies and his sister marries, he is left alone in the family house. Duncan then sets his hopes on breeding the one remaining horse on the farm, a descendant of an almost legendary stallion once owned by Duncan's ancestors in the glorious past. The newborn colt comes to represent the past to him, and as it grows into a stallion itself, it becomes the embodiment of some vague, romantic cavalier tradition. For a time, Duncan's plans seem within reach. He falls in love with the daughter of a neighbor, and when they are married, she tells him that she is pregnant with his child. When Duncan learns that his wife was once the lover of another neighbor, Dicky Jordan, he rejects her, causing her to lose the unborn child, and he is soon again alone in the world.

From this point on, Duncan becomes a man possessed. When his horse is killed (with justification) by the same Dicky Jordan, Duncan's only companion is a vicious outlaw moonshiner, Aaron McCool. Goaded by Aaron's insinuations and challenges, Duncan murders Jordan and when Aaron is arrested for the crime, Duncan helps him escape. Finally, in the woods, removed from civilization, Duncan and Aaron fight with each other when Aaron tries to kill the sheriff who is tracking them down. In the conflict, Duncan is shot, almost by accident, by Aaron, and he dies, blinded by the sun but afraid of the gathering dark.

Duncan Welsh's fundamental ideas are admirable—he wants to maintain a sense of integrity in a corrupt world—but in order to do so, he turns inward, rejecting the companionship and love that others offer. Jones indicates Duncan's growing isolation and cruelty by means of a doubling motif. Duncan is compared first to his father, the old man trapped in the past. Next, he is paralleled to the stallion, Chief, which has a "glass" eye, as does Duncan. The horse has spirit, but also a meanness which disturbs those who see it. At one point, Chief kicks Nettie, Duncan's wife, anticipating Duncan's own actions toward her. It attacks Dicky Jordan's horse without provocation. For all its fire and independence, the horse has the touch of Satan in it, according to Logan, a black farmhand. When Chief is killed, Duncan draws closer to Aaron McCool, and through Aaron, Duncan's own latent violence is manifested: Duncan becomes a murderer. For all his fascination with the past, the one lesson Duncan fails to learn is the most important. It is found in the motto under his grandfather's sword: "He who conquers himself is greater than he who conquers a city." Because of his blindness, his lack of control, his readiness to hate and unwillingness to forgive, Duncan moves from a man seeking truth to a man fleeing justice. He leaves no heritage but shame.

The Innocent was strongly received for a first novel, especially among Southern critics who admired Jones's sense of place and character. A few objected to the violence of the tale and the strain of morbidness that ran throughout. These same virtues and faults were again in evidence in Jones's second novel, *Forest of the Night*. Set in Tennessee and along the Natchez Trace in the early 1800's, this book moves consciously into the realm of legend and the supernatural.

Jonathan Cannon, the book's protagonist, strongly resembles Duncan Welsh, for he, too, is an idealist and innocent. He has come west from Virginia to find the goodness and purity of the new world. When he discovers a horribly mutilated Indian, scalped and left to die by white settlers, Jonathan attempts to help him but that night he is attacked and almost killed by the dying man. The next morning, weak from loss of blood, Jonathan sees the body of the Indian being eaten by buzzards—a view of nature he has omitted from his dream.

After being taken in and nursed by a nearby family, Jonathan falls in love with the daughter Judith, although he is disturbed by her obsessively religious father and her strange, wizened child. In town he learns that Judith was formerly the companion of Wiley and Micajah Harpe, the brutal and savage bandits who had terrorized the Trace. Despite warnings from the townspeople—and especially from an old woodsman named Eli, who tells him that a man must always consider the consequences of his actions, no matter how well-intended—Jonathan determines to "save" Judith from her past, to restore her to an honorable state.

The path Jonathan takes is essentially that worn by Duncan Welsh before him. He tries to force goodness on Judith, to insist on her salvation. When Judith tells him that the Harpes also came west seeking righteousness and the promised land, and that their failure led to the butchery and horrors they committed, Jonathan is blind to the parallel with himself. By forcing Judith to return to the outlaws' cave in order to face the scene of her depravity, Jonathan calls up the nightmares of her past which she apparently had put behind her. After rumor arrives that Wiley Harpe is still alive and in the vicinity, Judith becomes unbalanced, and one day Jonathan returns to find her and her child gone. In his search to find her, Jonathan begins to isolate himself in a kind of "defiant withdrawal." He becomes the very thing from which he had sought to save her. Indeed, people come to mistake him for Wiley Harpe.

When he does find Judith, her first child is dead, she is again pregnant, and she can no longer distinguish between Jonathan and her former lover. Sick and half-mad himself by this time, Jonathan begins to hate Judith and to fear the child she is carrying. In an episode of unrelenting cruelty, Jonathan forces her to walk until she goes into labor and then abandons her in the woods as she dies in childbirth. Returning to the body the next morning, he sees his "true image" in her dead eyes. In his search for virtue, he has become a monster but, unlike Duncan, he escapes death because of Eli's intervention. Taking him back to civilization, Eli explains that self-knowledge comes hard, but that one can—and must—learn to live with it.

Forest of the Night, with its reference to William Blake's poem "The Tyger," confronts more directly than *The Innocent* the nature of evil in man. Again, it is through the perversion of good impulses that the protagonist is guilty of monstrous wrongdoing. The townspeople sarcastically say that Jonathan considers himself an angel of God, but he becomes the figure of the devil. Indeed, there is a strong sense of the supernatural running throughout the book. At a revival meeting, a preacher warns of Satan in the shape of a bear, and alone in the forest Jonathan is mauled by such a creature. Judith sings of a demon lover coming to take her away, and after forcing her to visit the Harpes' cave, Jonathan has a nightmare vision of her embracing a corpselike figure. Later, when he has grown to hate her, she attempts to hold him in the same embrace. The head of Micajah Harpe, impaled on a stake, counsels Jonathan as he grows more and more insane; and finally there is the spirit of Wiley Harpe himself, which becomes inseparable from Jonathan's own.

Forest of the Night is one of the best modern novels dealing with the American frontier. It depicts a land of cruelty as well as courage, and there is little romantic about it. It is a better book than *The Innocent* because of the richness of its imagination and because of the greater ambiguity with which it portrays Jonathan Cannon's capacity for evil. That his double may be of his own making gives the book a dark and terrifying psychological complexity.

With *A Buried Land*, Jones moved directly into the modern South. The book's action is set in the years just before and immediately after World War II. The Tennessee Valley Authority (TVA) is altering the face of Tennessee, building dams, flooding farms, relocating families. The book begins with a quote from Aeschylus' *Eumenides* (458 B.C.) in which the Furies inveigh against those who ignore or reject the laws of the past. The quote is entirely appropriate, for *A Buried Land* examines the results of such a rejection.

Percy Youngblood comes from a rural family, of which he is now ashamed. He looks with anticipation to the new world, the world of progress. He considers himself a man of vision. Like Hiram Garner of *The Innocent*, he sees the benefits of change, and his motives are not essentially selfish. He has, nevertheless, cut himself off from his heritage—land, family, religion— and has turned for guidance to Edgar Cadenhead, a local lawyer who educates him in the ways of the "New South." After rejecting the old ways, however, Percy finds nothing with which to replace them. When a country girl he has been seeing becomes pregnant (and there is some question whether he is really the father), Percy insists on an abortion, which results in the girl's death. Rather than face his responsibility and confront his guilt, Percy buries the girl in one of the empty graves in his own family's cemetery. Percy assumes that when the land is covered by the new lake the TVA is creating, his crimes will remain forever unknown.

As Jones makes clear in all his works, such guilt can never be completely hidden. Percy's most obvious antagonist is Fowler Kinkaid, the girl's brother, who searches for his missing sister. Violent and withdrawn, Kinkaid strongly resembles Duncan Welsh, and his quest for revenge leads him to murder. Jones shows that both Percy and Kinkaid are driven by their own demons, although Kinkaid, as the displaced wanderer, draws the reader's sympathy. Haunted by fear of discovery (a drought begins to dry up the lake, revealing the grave), Percy kills Kinkaid, almost by accident. Now driven to the brink of madness, Percy finally confesses his guilt to his mother and prepares to face up to his deeds.

Percy Youngblood is among Jones's most tormented protagonists, and the novel achieves much of its power from its unrelenting portrayal of a man destroyed by guilt. The book was Jones's best received to date, and many critics proclaimed him as perhaps the South's leading postwar writer.

Following the emotional Walpurgis Night of *A Buried Land*, *An Exile* was especially impressive for its simplicity. Closer in length to a novella than a full-scale novel, it was first published in a special fiction issue of the *Sewanee Review* (Winter, 1967). Its main character, Sheriff Hank Tawes, is a much more likable man than any of Jones's previous protagonists. Because he displays such a fundamental humanity, his destruction is ultimately more affecting. Tawes has reached middle age when the novel begins. Although he is a good lawman, he is dissatisfied with his life. He longs for a simpler past, but that world has been buried beneath the same lake so prominent in *A Buried Land* (both novels are set in the town of Warrington, Tennessee). Tawes is an exile in his own country, a man facing the failure of his dreams and the truth of his mortality. His first misstep is a minor one—he fails to investigate a car he suspects is hauling moonshine—but once he compromises his duty, he is irrevocably lost. Alma McCain, a passenger in the car, realizes that Tawes has looked away because of her. When she seduces Tawes, the sheriff comes to suspect that her power over him is as insidious as it is alluring. Soon Tawes is involved in escalating corruption, becoming a criminal himself, at least partly responsible for the deaths of two men.

Tawes has a self-knowledge not found in Jones's earlier protagonists, and he is not nearly as self-righteous as they. Thus, he is at least partly aware of his corruption. Although he wants to believe that Alma loves him, as she says, and that her father, Flint McCain, is a good man, he cannot completely deny the evil he senses in them—and in himself. When he faces the falsity of his "goodness," the importance of lies in his life, he is stabbed by Flint and dies reaching out, a final attempt to make contact.

An Exile is a finely crafted work, almost a tour de force. Although it makes no attempt to go beyond Jones's other novels in terms of theme or character development, its cleanness of style, the inevitability of its events, and the goodness of its main character invest it with a powerful sense of tragedy. It was made into a film (*I Walk the Line*, directed by John Frankenheimer) in 1970, and was reprinted in paperback under the film's title in the same year.

In none of the books Jones had written so far had he overtly dealt with the sensitive question of racial discrimination. There were black farmhands in *The Innocent*, but Duncan's treatment of them was presented as merely one aspect of his withdrawal from humanity. Blacks were not at all prominent in the other books. In *A Cry of Absence*, Jones focused on the issue, its social implications and its overall effect on the South.

The year is 1957, the beginning of the integration movement. Jones shows how the racial challenge of established mores and beliefs affects the members of a prominent Tennessee family, the Glenns. Hester, the mother, comes from old stock: the town, Cameron Springs, is named after her family. She is aristocratic, benevolent in her treatment of both blacks and poor whites but basically unyielding in her defense of the traditional ways. Of her two sons, Cam, the younger, accepts his mother's beliefs and attempts to fulfill the image of the young, slightly wild, Southern youth. Ames, the elder brother, is more introspective, less entranced with the world he sees crumbling around him. When a black activist is brutally murdered, Hester and Ames are horrified, especially when they come to suspect Cam of the deed. Throughout the book, Jones studies their contrary methods of dealing with the truth.

Hester at first refuses to accept the possibility of Cam's guilt; after she is convinced, she tries to protect him. Ames is less surprised than his mother, but he is equally uncertain as to what to do. For his part, Cam cannot understand their reaction. After all, he reasons, he simply did what they—the community and especially his mother—wanted done, for all their words of outrage. Hester finally realizes that Cam has, indeed, acted out her anger and latent hatred: he is her creation. Rather than turn him over to the sheriff, Hester tries to kill Cam as he lies drunk in his car. Although she is ultimately unable to go through with it, Cam has roused himself enough to realize her intentions and completes the deed after she leaves. Coming to accept her ultimate responsibility for the deaths of the black activist and her son, Hester at first withdraws into the family mansion and later makes what atonement she can before committing suicide herself.

Ames presents a slightly more complex case. Never able to match his mother's romantic image as had Cam, Ames feels he belongs neither in her traditional world nor in the world racked by violent change. His mother's world is gone, and blind loyalty to it has led to disaster for her and Cam. The alternative, however, is in some ways just as repellent to him, for the forces of progress, of justice, are so caught up in their own self-righteousness that they cannot see the human needs which underlie the outworn creeds they oppose. Ames's final choice is to attempt to compromise: to recognize the virtues of his heritage, but to carry them forward into a new society.

Critical reaction to *A Cry of Absence* was mixed. Many found it a compelling and moving book. Critics such as Allen Tate and Andrew Lytle admired the tragic sense of doom Jones had created about the Glenn family; Tate went so far as to call Jones "the Thomas Hardy of the South." Others—generally of the New York-based critical establishment—were not so impressed. Although they admitted the technical proficiency of the writing, they questioned the relevance of what they considered a 1950's subject in a 1970's novel. Moreover, they suspected that Jones's sympathy finally lay more with Hester than with the other characters in the book. To a certain extent, these criticisms are not ill-founded, for there is something mannered and old-fashioned about the work. Far too many of the characters are unconvincing as people, and the symbolism is often strained. Like *An Exile*, the book is finely crafted, but it finally fails to draw from its readers the pity and understanding that they feel for Hank Tawes.

Jones's decision to publish *Passage Through Gehenna* with the scholarly Louisiana State University Press rather than with a more commercial publishing company may have been partly inspired by the Northern critical reaction to *A Cry of Absence*. Jones explained that he simply had grown tired of having to please New York publishers and critics whose interests and tastes were at variance with his own, and he hoped that this act of independence would encourage other Southern writers to do the same.

Passage Through Gehenna is his most overtly religious novel. It returns, in some ways, to the nightmare world of ghosts and demons found in *Forest of the Night*. Although it is given a modern-day setting, the story retells the basic conflict of good and evil, God and Satan. As a boy, Judson Rivers is healed of a mysterious fever by Virgil Salter, a self-appointed man of God.

Jud soon feels his own calling to follow God and begins to travel with Salter. He becomes convinced of his own salvation. When, however, he moves into town, Jud is slowly corrupted by Lily Nunn, who mocks his religion. Salter quickly recognizes her as a witch. (Her name, with its reference to Lilith, the female demon in Hebrew legends, and its play on the word "none" underscores her essential evil. The "Gehenna" of the book's title—the Hebrew place of misery—further refers the reader to Jones's use of the Hebrew legends.) Lily is supported in her seduction by a mysterious acquaintance of Jud, a boy named Meagher. Opposed to these two threats are Salter and Hannah Rice, the daughter of a local preacher with whom Jud comes to live. As Jud grows more under Lily's spell, he begins to plot against both Salter and Hannah. He secretly convinces a local prostitute to tempt Salter; when the old man succumbs, he kills her in rage and despair and is sent to jail. Jud then seduces Hannah, who gives herself to him almost as a sacrifice. Jud finally receives forgiveness for these deeds, but only after a long and hard journey.

Passage Through Gehenna recapitulates Jones's major themes, but it does so in a parablelike manner. It is the most didactic of his works. There is even a first-person narrator who tells Jud's story and who is perhaps a preacher himself. The dialect of his narrative is unobtrusive but subtly adds to the sense that this is a tale out of the oral tradition. What it lacks, however, is the humor and vigor of this tradition, and the tale becomes all too predictable. Despite its fine writing, *Passage Through Gehenna* is not a satisfying work.

Season of the Strangler is really a loosely connected series of stories, held together by one catalytic occurrence. It is set in the summer of 1969 in the small town of Okaloosa, Alabama. From May to September of that year, five elderly women are strangled and sexually assaulted by an unknown murderer. The only evidence found is one strand of black hair under the fingernail of one victim. Each of the book's twelve chapters examines how the murders affect individual members of the community. People look at their neighbors with growing suspicion. Unusual actions take on ominous overtones. In typical Jones fashion, characters also begin to look at themselves. Faced with the reality of unspeakable evil in their midst, they begin to explore their own secret guilts. Indeed, in every story, the murders are merely background to the individual turmoil made evident by the general sense of dread. Although the killer is never caught, the murders suddenly end, and there is still "nobody to blame."

Season of the Strangler is a strong work. As in Mark Twain's "The Man That Corrupted Hadleyburg," a community's false sense of goodness and respectability is ripped apart. Jones links these murders and rapes with the growing racial unrest in the town, which also reaches its climax during that summer, thus connecting the community's social and sexual guilt with its more general fear of the unknown. He does not simply implicate the white members of the town; his stories illustrate how *all* men can be corrupted and twisted by hatred and fear. It is finally man's inability to love, to trust, to believe, that results in the tragedy of these stories. Every man suspects the other, but in each case, the suspicion is a projection of private guilt. The killer remains a "black shadow" or a "spirit" at work in its "evil season," never caught because, in Jones's world, such a shadow hides within the hearts of all men, waiting for the season of release.

Jones's exploration of guilt and redemption continues in *Last Things*, in which young Wendell Corbin returns to his Southern hometown after his college years and becomes involved in a liaison with a married neighbor. Blackmailed into assisting with a drug-trafficking scheme, Wendell is eventually rescued from his moral decline by an evangelist. Thus Jones holds out the promise of a costly redemption, one that his characters can receive only after a descent into the despair of self-knowledge.

Edwin T. Arnold III

Bibliography
Bradford, M. E. "Madison Jones." In *The History of Southern Literature*, edited by Louis D. Rubin, Jr., et al. Baton Rouge: Louisiana State University Press, 1985. In this thoughtful essay, Bradford places Jones in the tradition of Donald Davidson, Andrew Lytle, and other writers of the 1930's. While pointing out that Jones's view of life has become even darker through the years, Bradford explains that it is in part his depiction of evil in humanity which places the author among the most profound Southern writers.
Morrow, Mark. "Madison Jones." In *Images of the Southern Writer*. Athens: University of Georgia Press, 1985. This brief essay, reporting an informal conversation with Jones on matters ranging from his relationships with other writers to his view of his profession, reveals the blend of humor and sadness which are found in his works. Opposite the essay is an excellent full-page photograph.
Rice, William. Review of *Last Things*, by Madison Jones. *National Forum: Phi Kappa Phi Journal* 70 (Spring, 1990): 47. Comments on the revelations of moral horror in the context of the familiar which make this novel, like Jones's earlier works, both dramatic and memorable. Rice points out how one shock of recognition follows another to the climactic confrontation between father and son.
Rubin, Louis D., Jr. "The Difficulties of Being a Southern Writer Today: Or, Getting Out from Under William Faulkner." *The Journal of Southern History* 29 (1963): 486-494. This interesting essay uses Jones's *A Buried Land* to exemplify the difference in approach which is necessary if Southern writers of the generations after Faulkner are to write honestly and suc-

cessfully about the changing South.

Warren, Robert Penn. "A First Novel." Review of *The Innocent*, by Madison Jones. *Sewanee Review* 65 (1957): 347-352. This review by one of the primary men of letters of his generation predicts an impressive career for Jones, based on the new writer's skill in plotting and his thematic originality. Although he points out occasional confusion as to intention and glaring defects in syntax, Warren ends his review with high praise for Jones's intellectual and technical gifts.

JAMES JOYCE

Born: Dublin, Ireland; February 2, 1882
Died: Zurich, Switzerland; January 13, 1941

Principal long fiction

A Portrait of the Artist as a Young Man, 1914-1915 (serial), 1916; *Ulysses*, 1922; *Finnegans Wake*, 1939; *Stephen Hero*, 1944.

Other literary forms

James Joyce commenced his literary career as a poet, essayist, and dramatist, under the influences of William Butler Yeats and Henrik Ibsen, respectively. His *Collected Poems* (1936) contains *Chamber Music* (1907), thirty-six lyrics written before 1904, and *Pomes Penyeach* (1927), eleven poems written after he had made his commitment to prose fiction. His first published essay, "Ibsen's New Drama" (1900), announced his admiration for the Norwegian dramatist; the same attitude is implied in his only original surviving play, *Exiles* (1918).

Miscellaneous literary essays, program and lecture notes, reviews, journalism, and two broadsides are collected in *The Critical Writings of James Joyce* (1959). Joyce's correspondence is contained in *Letters* (1957-1966), with some additions in *Selected Letters of James Joyce* (1975).

Through the compilation of fifteen short stories in *Dubliners* (1914), written between 1904 and 1907, Joyce discerned his métier. This apparently random, realistic series was the first announcement of its author's singular genius. While the volume retains a "scrupulously mean" accuracy in regard to naturalistic detail, it also incorporates a multiplicity of complex symbolic patterns. An ephemeral story, "Giacomo Joyce" (1918), was written as he completed *A Portrait of the Artist as a Young Man* and began *Ulysses* in 1914. The collaboration of several editors has produced in facsimile almost the entire Joyce "workshop"—notes, drafts, manuscripts, typescripts, and proofs—in sixty-four volumes (*The James Joyce Archives*, 1979), a project of unprecedented magnitude for any twentieth century author.

Achievements

From the beginning of his literary career, Joyce was the most distinctive figure in the renaissance which occurred in Irish cultural life after the death of Charles Stuart Parnell. Despite his early quarrels with Yeats, John M. Synge, and other leaders of the Irish Literary Revival, and his subsequent permanent exile, he is clearly, with Yeats, its presiding genius. From the first, he set himself to liberate Ireland, not by returning to Celtic myths or the Gaelic language and folklore, but by Europeanizing her cultural institutions. His early stories are an exorcism of the spirit of paralysis he felt about himself in the Dublin of his youth. As he gained detachment from these obstacles and knowledge of his own capacities as a writer of prose fiction, he produced two of the undisputed masterworks of modern literature—*A Portrait of the Artist as a Young Man* and *Ulysses*, as well as a final work that is perhaps beyond criticism, *Finnegans Wake*.

Throughout this development, Joyce's themes and subjects remain the same, yet his means become more overtly complex: the fabulous comedy, the multivalent language, and the vast design of *Ulysses* and *Finnegans Wake* are strands in the reverse side of the sedulously restrained tapestry of *Dubliners* and *A Portrait of the Artist as a Young Man*.

Joyce's cast of characters is small, his Dublin settings barely change from work to work, he observes repeatedly certain archetypal conflicts beneath the appearances of daily life, and his fiction is marked by certain obsessions of his class, religion, and nationality. Yet his singlemindedness, his wide learning in European literature, his comprehensive grasp of the intellectual currents of the age, his broad comic vision, his vast technical skills, and above all, his unequaled mastery of language, make him at once a Europeanizer of Irish literature, a Hibernicizer of European literature, and a modernizer of world literature.

Biography

James Augustine Joyce was born in Dublin, Ireland, on February 2, 1882, the first of John Joyce's and Mary Murray's ten children. During the years of Joyce's youth, his father wasted the family's substantial resources based on properties in Cork City; Joyce, at the same time, grew to reject the pious Catholicism of his mother. Except for a brief period, his education was in the hands of the Jesuits: at Clongowes Wood College, the less exclusive Belvedere College, and finally at University College, Dublin, where he was graduated in 1902. Joyce quickly outgrew his mentors, however, so that the early influences of the Maynooth Catechism and Saints Ignatius Loyola and Thomas Aquinas yielded to his own eclectic reading in European literature, especially Dante, Ibsen, Gerhart Hauptmann, and Gustave Flaubert. Politically, he retained his father's Parnellite Irish nationalism, modified by a moderate socialism. Despite his declared abjuration of Catholicism and the Irish political and cultural revivals, he continued to pay to each a proud and private subscription. He considered the professions of music and medicine (briefly attending the École de Medicine in Paris in 1902) before eventually leaving Ireland in October, 1904, for Europe and a literary career. He was accompanied by Nora Barnacle, a Galway-born chambermaid whom he had met the previous June, who became the mother of his two children, Georgio and Lucia, and whom he formally married in 1931.

Between 1904 and the conclusion of World War I, the Joyces lived successively in Trieste, Rome, Pola, and Zurich, where Joyce supported his wife and family by teaching English for the Berlitz schools, bank clerking, and borrowing from his brother Stanislaus, who had joined them in 1905. The *Dubliners* stories, begun shortly before he left Ireland, were finished with "The Dead" in 1907, but it was another seven years of wrangling with Irish and British publishers over details which were considered either libelous or indecent before the volume was published. By then, Joyce had fully rewritten *Stephen Hero*, a loose, naturalistic, and semiautobiographical novel, as the classic of impressionism *A Portrait of the Artist as a Young Man*. Ezra Pound, then the literary editor of *The Egoist*, recognized its permanence, published the novel in serial form, and recommended its author to the patronage of Harriet Weaver, who anonymously provided Joyce with a handsome annuity for the rest of his life.

Based on this material support and the establishment of his literary reputation, Joyce worked on *Ulysses* in Trieste, Zurich, and Paris where he moved in 1920. Meanwhile, beginning in March, 1918, Margaret Anderson and Jane Heap's *Little Review* (New York) was publishing the separate episodes of *Ulysses*. The prosecution and conviction in February, 1921, of its two publishers for obscenity gave the novel a wide notoriety which preceded its publication in Paris by Sylvia Beach's Shakespeare and Company on its author's fortieth birthday.

Joyce then became an international celebrity, and the center of literary life in Paris during the 1920's. Between 1922 and 1939, he worked on *Finnegans Wake*, which, under the title "Work in Progress," appeared in Eugene Jolas' *transition* and other avant-garde journals. During this period of his life, Joyce contended with the pirating and banning of *Ulysses* in the United States, the worsening condition of his eyes, which required eleven separate operations, his daughter's schizophrenia, and the loss of many of his earlier admirers because of their puzzlement with or hostility toward the experimentation of *Ulysses* and especially of "Work in Progress."

As World War II approached, *Finnegans Wake* was published and the Joyces moved once again, to neutral Zurich. Following an operation for a duodenal ulcer, Joyce died there on January 13, 1941. With Nora (died 1951), he is buried in Flüntern Cemetery, Zurich, beneath Milton Hebald's sprightly statue.

Analysis

The leaders of the Irish Literary Revival were born of the Anglo-Irish aristocracy. Very few were Catholics, and none was from the urban middle class, except James Joyce. The emphasis of the Revival in its early stages on legendary or peasant themes and its subsequent espousal of a vaguely nationalistic and unorthodox religious spirit kept it at a certain distance from popular pieties. It did no more than gesture toward Europe, and registered very little of the atrophied state of middle- and lower-class city life.

The first to deal with this latter theme realistically, Joyce made a bold show as a "Europeanizer" and openly criticized "patriotic" art. Despite his disdain for contemporary political and literary enthusiasms, his dismissal of Celtic myths as "broken lights," his characterization of the folk imagination as "senile," and his relative ignorance of the Gaelic language, however, his imaginative works are as thoroughly and distinctively Irish as those of William Butler Yeats, John Millington Synge, or Lady Augusta Gregory.

From his earliest childhood, Joyce was aware of the political controversies of the day, observing the conflict between the idealized Charles Stuart Parnell and the ultramontane Church which permanently marked his outlook on Irish public affairs. His faith in Irish nationalist politics and in Catholicism was broken even as it was formed, and soon he launched himself beyond the pales of both, by exile and apostasy, proclaiming that each had betrayed his trust. The supersaturation of his consciousness with the language, attitudes, and myths of Church and state was formative, however, as all of his work documents: *Dubliners*, *A Portrait of the Artist as a Young Man*, *Ulysses*, and *Finnegans Wake* are unparalleled as a record of the "felt history" of Edwardian Dublin, or indeed of any city in modern literature.

From the beginning, Joyce's scrupulous naturalism belied his symbolist tendencies. The revisions of his early stories, and the transformation of *Stephen Hero* into the impressionistic *Bildungsroman* of *A Portrait of the Artist as a Young Man* indicate that he recognized among his own powers of observation and language a special capacity to decode the socialization process—an aptitude, as he put it, for "epiphany." At certain moments in an otherwise continuous state of paralysis, the truth reveals itself and the spirit is liberated from a conditioned servility. The repeated use of carefully selected words can, without neglecting the obligation to realistic fidelity, have the harmonious and radiant effect of a symbol.

As Joyce's technical skills grew, he extended this principle, so that in *Ulysses*, the structural symbols become one, while at the same time, the demands of realism were superseded. The tendencies implied in this shift have their apotheosis in *Finnegans Wake*. From 1922 to 1939, Joyce was very long removed from the Dublin he had known and had come to understand his own genius for language ("I find that I can do anything I like with it"). Drawing on an encyclopedic range of materials, he wrote this final, most challenging work, in which the world of the unconscious, or the sleeping mind, is represented not by realism but by multivalent language and the timeless action of archetypal characters.

In eschewing the narrow confines set by the Irish revival, Joyce turned to the masters of classical and modern European literature for his models: to Homer for his Odysseus, the hero to set against the Christian Savior and the Irish Cuchulain; to Dante for his multiplex realization of Catholic phantasmagoria; to William Shakespeare for his language and his treatment of family relations; and to Henrik Ibsen for his disciplined criticism of modern bourgeois life. Under these influences, Joyce's art developed along highly formalist lines, and mythological antecedents stalk his modern lower-middle-class characters. The effects of such comparisons are, to various ends, ironic; the ordinary Dublin characters lack the remove, heroism, and familiarity with gods or demons of their classic counterparts. Instead, they exhibit various neurotic symptoms associated with modern urban life—repression, anxiety, fetishism, and the confusion of great and small virtue. In these four respects then—in the predeliction for formalism, mythologization, irony, and the subject of individual consciousness—Joyce establishes the methods and the subject of literary modernism.

A Portrait of the Artist as a Young Man is a semiautobiographical *Bildungsroman* describing the development of the sensibility of Stephen Dedalus from his earliest childhood recollections to the beginnings of manhood. The work evolved from the narrative essay "A Portrait of the Artist" (January, 1904), and its expansion into *Stephen Hero*, an undisguised autobiographical novel in the naturalist tradition. The result of this evolution was a startlingly original composition: a highly structured, symbolic, impressionistic, and ironic treatment of the spiritual formation and reformation of an acutely sensitive young man. Stephen's conscience absorbs the values of his Irish Catholic family; by a progressively more complex use of language and technique through the five chapters of the novel, Joyce portrays that conscience undergoing a process of simultaneous severance and refinement. The conclusion of the process, however, is paradoxical, for as Stephen declares his determination to free himself of the claims of the formative establishments of his family, nation, and religion by setting against them the proud and defiant slogan "silence, exile and cunning," the terms by which that defiance is made have already been set. Like his language, Stephen's conflicts with the virtues advocated by the three establishments are not different in kind but more profound than those of his fellows. It is one of Joyce's many ironies in *A Portrait of the Artist as a Young Man* that Stephen mistakes these conflicts for a radical independence of spirit. Like Icarus, his mythological antecedent, his destiny is not to escape from the paternal labyrinths, but to fall from the heights of supercilious pride.

One of the signal achievements of the novel is Joyce's management of the distance between reader and protagonist: as Stephen grows older, he becomes less amiable. This distance is achieved by a multiplicity of devices: the subtle weighing of names, the acute selection of sensuous detail, the exaggeration of language, the ironic structure, the counterpointing of incidents, and the elaborate systematizing of all devices. The endearing sensitivity and naïveté of the child slowly yield to the self-absorbed priggishness of the young man.

Chapter 1 is composed of four sections: random sensations of early childhood, Stephen's illness (at approximately seven years) at Clongowes Wood

College, the Christmas dinner scene, and Stephen's first victory over injustice—Father Dolan's punishment. Each section gathers materials that dramatize the mysterious interplay of private sensation, communal constraint, and language. Each section culminates in an "epiphany," a metatheological term for "a sudden spiritual manifestation" when a response betrays its socially conditioned origin, and the true feeling or idea radiates forth with the force of a symbol.

The opening section in the language of a preschool child is the kernel out of which the entire work develops. It distinguishes in a rudimentary, purely sensory manner the symbols and themes which will preoccupy Stephen: women, road, rose, paternity, flight, creation, the relationship between experience and the representation of it, his own distinctness, guilt, and the demands of home, religion, and nation.

Stephen's illness at Clongowes Wood College causes him to meditate on the repugnance of physical life and his attraction to mysterious realms of religion and language, an association which is later to prove axial. The Christmas dinner scene, on the other hand, is a brilliant dramatization of the tension between the three establishments and the threats they pose to Parnell and Stephen, heroes alike. In the final section, Stephen successfully protests an unjust school punishment.

Chapter 2 is composed of a series of some dozen epiphanies developing the themes of Stephen's gradual estrangement from his family, particularly his father, and his perception of sexual identification, leading to his liberation from innocence in the embrace of a prostitute. Among the revelations in this chapter is the news of the Rector's real attitude toward Father Dolan's treatment of Stephen; the jocosity of this attitude deflates the climax of Chapter 1. When, in Chapter 3, Stephen repents of his sin with the prostitute, the pattern of reversal repeats itself, and the structural irony in the novel is revealed. This chapter falls into three sections—the states of sin, repentence, and grace mediated by the memorable sermon on hell. This terrifying exposition (based on the procedures for spiritual meditation propounded by the *Spiritual Exercises* of Ignatius Loyola) leads Stephen to contrition, confession, and communion, each treated with a certain degree of irony. Not the least of the ironies here is Stephen's dissociated sensibility, as implied in the final page of Chapter 3 and expanded in the opening section of Chapter 4. The true state of his feelings is elucidated in the course of the succeeding two sections: his consideration and rejection of the priestly vocation and his ecstatic response to the call to the priesthood of the imagination. He rejects the priesthood because of its orderliness and uniformity; the life of community is removed from the risks inherent in secular life, and it denies individual freedom. His response to the muse is, however, heavily overlaid with images of the mysteries of the service of the altar. In this climactic epiphany, Stephen risks loneliness and error to transform in freedom the stuff of ordinary experience into the permanent forms of secular art. In response to the messenger, girl-bird-angel, he accepts a vocation which in the cause of self expression will set him apart from all institutions.

In the final chapter, Stephen attempts an exorcism of each aspect of the culture which would possess his soul. To this end, he engages in a dialogue with a series of companions who advance three claims: McCann and Davin (international and national politics); Father Darlington and Lynch (servile, practical, or kinetic arts); and Cranly (conventional morality and religion). In the course of the perambulations accompanying *apologia pro futura sua*, Stephen sets forth his aesthetic theory, which in its refusal to grant overt moral purpose to art owes more to Walter Pater than to Aquinas. The pallid "Villanelle of the Temptress" comes as an anticlimax on the heels of such brilliant theorizing, and raises the question of Stephen's capacities as a creative artist as opposed to those of an aesthete or poseur. The concluding section, comprising the diary entries from the five weeks preceding Stephen's departure, at once recapitulates the themes of the entire novel and anticipates Stephen's commitment to the proud and lonely life of the committed artist. The impression that this sequence of startling entries makes is of an irony of another kind: Stephen has unknowingly stumbled upon a technique which takes him closer to his creator and to the tenor of twentieth century literature than his self-absorbed and self-conscious villanelle. Thus, at the conclusion of *A Portrait of the Artist as a Young Man*, Stephen has yet to acquire a moral awareness, develop human sympathies, or discern his own voice.

The Stephen Dedalus of *Ulysses* has returned to Ireland after a brief sojourn in Paris. He has acquired a few new affectations from that experience, is intensely guilt-ridden over his mother's suffering and death, teaches ineffectually at a Dublin boys' school, lives with some companions in a Martello tower, makes desultory efforts at writing poetry, speculates sensitively on a variety of epistemological, theological, and metaphysical questions, theorizes ostentatiously on Shakespeare's psychobiography, delivers himself of cryptic remarks and oblique anecdotes, and wastes his salary on prostitutes and drink. Despite his dissolution and moodiness, however, the Stephen of *Ulysses* is considerably more receptive to the world of ordinary experience that whirls around him than the protagonist of *A Portrait of the Artist as a Young Man*. Leopold Bloom is the personification of that world.

Bloom is a thirty-eight-year-old Irish Jew of Hungarian extraction. A family man, he has a wife, Molly, four years his junior, and a daughter Milly, age fifteen; a son, Rudy, died in infancy. Bloom is observant and intelligent despite his lack of higher education. He lives in Eccles Street and works as an advertising salesman for a daily newspaper. The key event of the day on which the action of *Ulysses* takes place—June 16, 1904—is Molly's infidelity (of which Bloom is aware) with an impresario named Blazes Boylan. During the course of the day, between 8 A.M. and approximately 3 A.M. on June 17, the reader follows Bloom's thoughts and movements as he manages to retain an equilibrium between many demands and disappointments.

Bloom serves his wife breakfast in bed, takes a bath, corresponds with an epistolary lover, attends a funeral, attempts to secure an ad from a firm by the name of Keyes, has lunch, is misunderstood over a horserace, is insulted and almost attacked in a bar, becomes sexually aroused by an exhibitionist girl on the beach, and inquires about a friend at a maternity hospital, where he encounters Stephen Dedalus carousing with sundry dissolutes. Feeling protective of Stephen, he pursues him to a brothel and subsequently rescues him from brawlers and police, taking him home for a hot drink. Bloom retires, noting the signs of Blazes Boylan's recent occupation of the marital bed. Throughout these physical events, Bloom's consciousness plays with myriad impressions and ideas serious and trivial, from his wife's infidelity to imperfectly remembered incidents from his childhood. He also proves himself to be a resilient, considerate, humorous, prudent, and even-tempered man. As the novel progresses, Bloom, certainly one of the most completely realized characters in fiction, grows in the reader's affections and estimation.

Molly, as revealed to the reader in the famous soliloquy of the final chapter, is a substantial embodiment of the anima. Born in Gibraltar of a Spanish mother and an English military father who later took her to Dublin, Molly is a superstitious Catholic, a plainspoken, amoral, fertile, sensual, passive beauty. She is a singer of sentimental concert-stage favorites who, despite her adultery with Boylan, loves and admires her own husband. Throughout *Ulysses*, she is offstage, yet constantly on Leopold's mind.

Each of these three main figures in *Ulysses* is characterized by a distinctly individuated stream of consciousness. Stephen's bespeaks a cultivated sensibility, abounds with intellectual energy, and moves with a varying pace between considerations of language, history, literature, and theology in a private language that is learned, lyrical, morose, and laden throughout with multidirectional allusions. Bloom's stream of consciousness, on the other hand, drifts bemusedly, effortlessly, and with occasional melancholia, through a catalog of received ideas, its direction easily swayed by sensual suggestion or opportunities for naïve scientific speculation, yet sometimes revealing a remarkable perspicacity. Molly's, finally, is the least ratiocinative and most fluent and even-paced, an unpunctuated mélange of nostalgia, acidity, and pragmatism.

These three fictional characters share a city with a large cast of figures, some of whom are historical, some based on actual people, and some purely imaginary. All move through the most minutely realized setting in literature. Joyce plotted the action of *Ulysses* so as to conform with the details of the day's news, the typical comings and goings in the city's various institutions, the weather report, and the precise elements of Dublin's "street furniture" on June 16, 1904: the tram schedules, addresses, advertising slogans, theatrical notices, smells and sounds of the city, topics and tone of casual conversation, and so on. At this level, the work is a virtuoso exhibition of realism which challenges the most searching literary sleuths.

On another level, *Ulysses* has an equally astounding system of mythological, historical, literary, and formal superstructures invoked by allusion and analogy. As the title implies, Leopold Bloom is a humble modern counterpart to Odysseus, the archetypal hero of Western civilization. Thus Molly corresponds to Odysseus' faithful wife Penelope, and Stephen to his devoted comrade and son Telemachus. As Joyce first revealed to Stuart Gilbert, his design for *Ulysses* called for the alignment of each of the eighteen chapters of his novel with an episode in Homer's *Odyssey* (c. 800 B.C.), with a particular location in the city of Dublin, with a particular hour in the day of June 16, 1904, with an organ of the human body, an art or science, a color, and an archetypal symbol. Finally, each of these chapters was to be written in a distinctive style. Two generations of readers have discerned further schemata and elucidated hundreds of ingenious and delicious ironies woven into every chapter, so that critical appreciation of Joyce's technical achievement in the writing of *Ulysses* continues to grow. Bloom's peregrinations through Dublin, his temporary usurpation from his marriage bed, his difficulties with customers and sundry citizens, and his befriending of the fatherless Stephen, under such grand auspices, become objects of simultaneous amusement and admiration. Even the most trivial actions of unremarkable modern citizens gain stature, resonance, and dignity; at the same time, a classic work and its heroic virtues are reinterpreted for this age.

In its broadest sense, *Ulysses* deals with a husband's usurpation from and repossession of his home: rivals are routed and an ally—a son—found. From another perspective, the plot expounds the relationship of an intellectual abstraction (Stephen) and a sense experience (Bloom). This aspect has its technical analogue in the complex formal structure by which Joyce organizes the myriad material details of the novel. Joyce draws on an impressive range of masterworks from the Western cultural tradition to elaborate these themes and comparisons. Stephen's preoccupation with Shakespeare's *Hamlet* (1600-1601), especially as it is expounded in the ninth episode ("Scylla and Charybdis"), suggests the father-and-son theme in a manner which complements the Homeric. Similarly, the Blazes Boylan-Molly Bloom relationship is orchestrated by reference to Mozart's *Don Giovanni*. Among other major organizational devices are the Catholic Mass, Dante's *The Divine Comedy* (c. 1320), dialectical time-space progressions, Richard Wagner's Ring Cycle, and a progression of literary techniques. Thus, for example, as one moves from chapter to chapter under the guidance of a third-person omniscient narrator, one encounters a succession of literary procedures modeled after journalism, classical rhetoric, catechesis, popular romance, musical counterpoint, and expressionist drama.

The fourteenth chapter ("Oxen of the Sun"), for example, narrates Bloom's visit at 10 P.M. to the maternity hospital at Holles Street, the revelry of the medical students and their departure for bar and brothel. The forty-five-page chapter broadly alludes to Ulysses' visit to the Isle of the Sun (*Odyssey*, Book 12) and his followers' disobediance of his orders in killing the native oxen, which brings down retribution on them that only the hero survives. Joyce's narrative around the theme of respect for the physical processes of conception, gestation, and childbirth, develops as a nine-part episode tracing simultaneously the development of the human embryo and the historical growth of the English language. A complex motif of references to the successive differentiation of organs in the developing human embryo is paralleled by some two score parodies of successive English prose styles from preliteracy and Anglo-Saxon to contemporary slang and a style very like that of *Finnegans Wake*. These progressions are further enhanced by similar motifs alluding to formal evolution, the events of June 16, 1904, and symbolic identifications of Bloom, the hospital, nurse, and Stephen with the sperm, the womb, the ovum, and the embryo, respectively. The cumulative effect of this encyclopedia of procedures is paradoxical: one marvels at the grandeur, the energy, and the variety of the language and the magisterial control of the writer, while at the same time retaining skepticism about the claims of any single perspective.

On almost every aspect of this great novel, the critics are divided: the literary value of such vast systematization, the significance of Bloom's meeting with Stephen, and the very spirit of the work. Nevertheless, its impact on modern literature is immense, from specific literary influences such as that on T. S. Eliot's *The Waste Land* (1922) to all works which mythologize contemporary experience. The themes of *Ulysses*—the dignity of ordinary persons, the values of family and human brotherhood, the consolation of language and the literary tradition, the interrelationships of theological, psychological, and aesthetic language and ideas, the ambiguity of the most profound experiences and the impact of modern revolutions in politics, science, and linguistics on notions of identity—are approached in a manner of unequaled virtuosity.

For all the virtuosity of *Ulysses*, Joyce considered its form inadequate to accommodate the depth and breadth of his vision of human history, experience, and aspiration. Thus, he spent sixteen years of his life composing *Finnegans Wake*, a baffling expedition into the dream of history for which he devised a "night language" composed of scores of languages superimposed on a Hiberno-English base.

Finnegans Wake sets out to express in appropriate form and language the collective unconscious. Thus, it encompasses all of human experience through the millennia in a cycle of recurring forms through a universal language, the language of dreams. The work has five primary dreamers, is divided into four books, and employs a language with simultaneous reference to multiple tongues, expressing the major theme of the cyclical nature of history.

The title derives from the Irish-American comic ballad "Finnegan's Wake," in which Tim Finnegan, a hod carrier, has fallen to his apparent death, but under the effect of spilt whiskey, leaps out of the bed to join the revelry. The fall of this lowly modern Irish laborer recalls previous falls—Lucifer's, Adam's, Newton's, and Humpty Dumpty's—while his resurrection suggests similar parallels, most notably with Christ and, by extension via the implied words *fin* (French for "end"), "again," and "awake," with the myth of the eternal return of all things.

The five primary dreamers are Humphrey Chimpden Earwicker (HCE), a Dublin pubkeeper, his wife Anna Livia Plurabelle (ALP), their twin sons Shem and Shaun, and their daughter Issy. HCE (Haveth Childers Everywhere/ Here Comes Everybody) is the archetypal husband-father who is burdened with guilt over an obscure indiscretion in the Phoenix Park, an Original Sin, the source of all nightmares in this dreambook of history. News of this sin is carried about by rumors and documents, lectures and arguments, accusations and recriminations. Interrogators appear in fours, and there are twelve onlookers: variously jurymen, apostles, mourners, drinkers, and so on. As HCE is identified with the Dublin landscape—from Chapelizod to "Howth Castle and Environs"—his wife is the personification of the River Liffey flowing through that landscape. She is the universal wife-mother, and like all the rivers of the world, constantly in flux. Joyce lavished special care on the section of *Finnegans Wake* (Book 1, Chapter 8, pp. 196-216) where she is featured, and read its conclusion for a phonograph recording. Their warring twin sons, Shem and Shaun, represent the generally opposite character types of introvert and extrovert, subjective and objective, artist and man of affairs, as well as Joyce himself and various antagonists such as his brother Stanislaus, Eamon deValera, John McCormack, and St. Patrick. Issy is the femme fatale, Iseult *rediviva*, the divisive ingenue of *Finnegans Wake*, in contrast with her mother, whose influence is unitive.

The four books of *Finnegans Wake* recount human history according to the four-phase cycle of Giambattista Vico's *La Scienza Nuova* (1725, 1744): theocratic, aristocratic, democratic, anarchic, and thence via a *ricorso* to the theocratic once again and a new cycle. These four phases of history and the night comprehend the totality of individual and racial development by means of analogies with the four Evangelists of the New Testament, the four Masters of Irish history, the four compass points, and so on. Through a vast elaboration of such correspondences, the Joycean universe of *Finnegans Wake* is populated and structured.

Four decades of attempts to explicate *Finnegans Wake* appear to confirm Joyce's prediction that the work would keep the professors busy for centuries. A general opinion among those who take the work seriously is that as a dreambook and a leading expression of the twentieth century world view, it is indeterminate, untranslatable, irreducible. It is a work in which every single element has a function: it contains no nonsense, yet is finally beyond explication. Critical analyses of *Finnegans Wake* have been either macrocosmic or microcosmic, emphasizing its overall design or attempting to gloss particular passages. To date, however, neither procedure has progressed very far toward the other.

Finnegans Wake is Joyce's most ambitious literary endeavor. He anticipated, yet underestimated, the difficulties his readers would encounter, and was disappointed that so many of those who acclaimed *A Portrait of the Artist as a Young Man* and *Ulysses* as supreme expressions of modernity were unprepared to pursue his explorations to the limits of language in *Finnegans Wake*.

Like the great masters in every discipline, Joyce enlarged the possibilities of the forms he inherited. This is indisputably true of the short story, the *Bildungsroman*, and the mythological-psychological novel. In none of these areas has his achievement been superseded, while in the case of *Finnegans Wake*, as Richard Ellmann puts it in the Introduction to his classic biography, "we are still learning to be James Joyce's contemporaries, to understand our interpreter."

Cóilín Owens

Other major works

SHORT FICTION: *Dubliners*, 1914.

PLAY: *Exiles*, 1918.

POETRY: *Chamber Music*, 1907; *Pomes Penyeach*, 1927; *Collected Poems*, 1936.

NONFICTION: *The Critical Writings of James Joyce*, 1959; *Letters*, 1957-1966 (3 volumes); *Selected Letters of James Joyce*, 1975 (Richard Ellmann, editor); *The James Joyce Archives*, 1977-1979 (64 volumes).

Bibliography

Attridge, Derek, ed. *The Cambridge Companion to James Joyce.* Cambridge, England: Cambridge University Press, 1990. A collection of eleven essays by the younger generation of eminent contemporary Joyce scholars, among them John Paul Riquelme, Margot Norris, Hans Walter Gabler, and Karen Lawrence. Surveys the Joyce phenomenon from cultural, textual, and critical standpoints, with *Ulysses* and *Finnegans Wake* each given a separate essay. A valuable aid and stimulus, containing a chronology of Joyce's life and an annotated bibliography.

Bowen, Zack R., and James F. Carens, eds. *A Companion to Joyce Studies.* Westport, Conn.: Greenwood Press, 1984. Sixteen individual essays on each of Joyce's works, with the exception of *Finnegans Wake*, to which three separate essays are devoted. For the purpose of this anthology, Joyce's works are understood to include his letters and juvenilia. Also includes a biographical sketch of Joyce, an account of his texts' history, and a history of his reputation.

Deming, Robert, ed. *A Bibliography of James Joyce Studies.* 2d rev. ed. Boston: G. K. Hall, 1977. The most important source of information for Joyce scholars.

Ellmann, Richard. *James Joyce.* 1959. Rev. ed. New York: Oxford University Press, 1982. The definitive biography, generally regarded as the last word on its subject's life and widely considered the greatest literary biography of the century. Copiously annotated and well illustrated, particularly in the 1982 edition.

Hart, Clive, and David Hayman, eds. *James Joyce's "Ulysses": Critical Essays.* Berkeley: University of California Press, 1974. A compilation of eighteen essays, each devoted to a single section of *Ulysses.* The contributors are among the foremost of those who made Joyce's academic reputation in the postwar period and, while the volume's quality is variable, it is a valuable resource for students familiar with the subject matter.

Hart, Clive, and Fritz Senn, eds. *A Wake Newsletter,* 1961-   . A periodical devoted to the exploration and explication of *Finnegans Wake.* Indispensable for the aficionado.

Joyce, James. *"A Portrait of the Artist as a Young Man": Text, Criticism, and Notes.* Edited by Chester Anderson. New York: Viking Press, 1968. A helpful guide to Joyce's first novel, including expert critical commentary and explication of Joyce's sometimes recondite allusions.

Kenner, Hugh. *Dublin's Joyce.* London: Chatto & Windus, 1955. The first book on Joyce by a critic who has done more than any other to delimit the aesthetic and cultural terrain in which Joyce's contribution to modern literature was made. Rather acerbic and extravagant in its intellectual processes, it nevertheless has been a very influential study, containing in particular a landmark treatment of *A Portrait of the Artist as a Young Man.*

Levin, Harry. *James Joyce: A Critical Introduction.* Norfolk, Conn.: New Directions, 1941. The first full-length study of all Joyce's works. Some of its critical approaches have been superannuated by more recent work, but it remains impressive and valuable.

McHugh, Roland. *The Sigla of "Finnegans Wake."* Austin: University of Texas Press, 1976. A brief introduction to the compositional character of *Finnegans Wake*, with an informal, refreshing, and valuable guide to approaching Joyce's final work.

Staley, Thomas, ed. *The James Joyce Quarterly,* 1963-   . The most convenient source of current bibliographical information, contemporary critical commentary, and access to the community of Joyce scholars.

ANNA KAVAN
Helen (Woods) Edmonds

Born: Cannes, France; 1901
Died: London, England; December 5, 1968

Principal long fiction

A Charmed Circle, 1929 (as Helen Ferguson); *The Dark Sisters*, 1930 (as Helen Ferguson); *Let Me Alone*, 1930 (as Helen Ferguson); *A Stranger Still*, 1935 (as Helen Ferguson); *Goose Cross*, 1936 (as Helen Ferguson); *Rich Get Rich*, 1937 (as Helen Ferguson); *Change the Name*, 1941; *The House of Sleep*, 1947 (published in Britain as *Sleep Has His House*, 1948); *The Horse's Tale*, 1949 (with K. T. Bluth); *A Scarcity of Love*, 1956; *Eagles' Nest*, 1957; *Who Are You?*, 1963; *Ice: A Novel*, 1967.

Other literary forms

In addition to her novels, Anna Kavan produced five collections of shorter fiction, two of which appeared posthumously. She also wrote occasional reviews for Cyril Connolly's journal, *Horizon*.

Achievements

Kavan's early fiction was rather inconsequential and excited little critical notice. Once she shifted emphasis and themes during the early 1940's, reviewers began to notice her work, though not always favorably. In 1947, for example, Diana Trilling castigated *The House of Sleep* unmercifully, insisting that "nothing makes it worth reading." Alice S. Morris, however, writing at the same time as Trilling, described Kavan as "acutely perceptive and a brilliantly disturbing writer." Since that time, Kavan's reputation has been growing steadily. Her depiction of power, unreality, madness, and the isolated, abused woman as well as her experiments in narrative structure place her in the first rank among the lesser novelists of the twentieth century. Feminists have been particularly interested in Kavan, although critical study of her work is still minimal.

Biography

Anna Kavan was born Helen Woods, in 1901, in Cannes, France. She disliked her wealthy mother, and her rather unhappy childhood was spent in various European countries and in California. Her marriages to Donald Ferguson and Stuart Edmonds both ended in divorce; an only son was killed during World War II. She spent many years with her first husband in Burma and later lived and traveled in Norway, the United States, New Zealand, England, and Africa. Twice institutionalized, Kavan was insecure, depressive, often suicidal, and was enamored of dreams. She suffered from a painful spinal disease, and spent the last thirty years of her life as a heroin addict, dying with a syringe in her hand. She began to write when she was in Burma and continued throughout her life. In the early 1940's, she worked as an assistant editor at Cyril Connolly's *Horizon*. She was, additionally, a talented painter, a breeder of bull dogs, an interior designer, and a dealer in real estate. As late as 1962, however, she still had financial problems.

Kavan was hyperbolic, self-denigrating, and unsure of reality, as is evident in many unpublished journal entries from the 1920's. These self-revelations may clarify some of the more unusual elements in her fiction. From the notes and letters written many years later to her close friend Raymond B. Marriott, poet and theater critic for *The Stage*, there emerges a picture of an insecure, forgetful, disorganized, dependent, but thoughtful person, who feigned toughness, was entirely devoted to her craft, and who, even at the end of her life, could still become excited by creative innovation in others. Although she used her own life as a basis for much of her writing, it is virtually impossible to extract the facts from the fictionalized accounts. Indeed, even in her private notebooks she admits that some entries are falsified. In this, she bears a striking resemblance to Louis-Ferdinand Céline.

Analysis

There is a consistent development in Anna Kavan's fiction from the earliest novels through her last works. The early, less important, romances contain themes that are enlarged upon in the later material. Since Kavan was obsessed with her own life, her fiction consists of a multitude of subtle variations on an unwritten autobiography. Power, evil, unreality, madness, isolation, asexuality, and the subconscious play an increasingly significant role in an often surreal landscape. Her short fiction tends to stress a number of additional topics—guilt, *Angst*, dreams, and drugs—which are not as prevalent in the novels. Certain motifs recur again and again; the colonial rescuer who helps a young girl escape to Burma is especially prominent. The later fiction includes some excellent narrative innovation; the ambiguity of these experimental works is not nearly as disconcerting as the lack of resolution in the earlier more traditional romances. Lack of motivation in a number of novels is also a major problem. Franz Kafka's perhaps negative influence is particularly noticeable: characters with only initials for names, overpowering bureaucracies, rumors, terrifying, inexplicable experiences, and victimization appear with great regularity. Indeed, the very name "Kavan," under which she published all of her novels from 1941 to her death, was based on Franz Kafka's name.

Between 1929 and 1941, Kavan wrote seven traditional "Home Counties Novels," as Rhys Davies has termed them. The plots of these novels generally center on complicated relationships between men and women. They are often long-winded, pedestrian, and uninteresting. Embedded in these early novelistic attempts, however, are the seeds from which the later work grows. Kavan's fiction is often discussed in terms of madness, dreams, and dissociated personalities, and it is certainly these pervasive themes which make her writing so stimulating, but two other recurring preoccupations, rarely mentioned by commentators, demand equal attention: evil is palpably manifested in most of the novels, and virtually every longer work revolves around some form of power. In fact, this latter concept is the true driving force of Kavan's work. Madness and unreality result from the abuse of power in both individual relationships and within larger societal contexts.

The first two novels deal with domineering sisters: In *A Charmed Circle*, Beryl Deane is much stronger than the hesitant Olive, and in *The Dark Sisters*, Emerald Lamond controls Karen. The use of power to control is manifested by other characters as well. More significant, in both of these works individuals succumb to a sense of unreality; Karen, for example, like so many of Kavan's characters, escapes from unpleasant situations by dissociation—she much perfers her private dreamworld. Karen is also the first of Kavan's cold, asexual heroines, whom lovers and husbands find frustrating.

Let Me Alone stands out among Kavan's early novels for three reasons: first, there is James Forrester, one of the well-developed eccentrics who Kavan portrays so acutely. Forrester squanders his inheritance, marries, is widowed, retires to a small farm in Spain with Anna-Marie, his young daughter, and spends his time brooding, reading, and writing in his journals. In order to teach Anna-Marie a lesson, he discharges his pistol at her. Although his eccentricities border on the bizarre, the reader regrets his premature suicide. Second, unlike the other early works, whose plots often consist of insignificant social machinations and petty altercations, *Let Me Alone* unfolds a powerful and meaningful account of Anna-Marie's marriage of convenience to Matthew Kavan, a colonial official, who is ostensibly sensitive and caring, but who turns out to be domineering and vicious. When the couple returns to his Burmese post, there is nothing but strife, sweltering heat, and tennis games in which rats are substituted for balls. Third, this is the only early novel in which virtually all of Kavan's later important themes appear: the domineering and evil protagonist; the isolated, asexual, and abused woman whose depression leads to madness and suicidal tendencies; the apotheosis of unreality; the flirtation with lesbianism; and the incredible descriptions of nature.

Thus, despite frequent repetition, long-windedness, exaggerated reactions, and the unconvincing depiction of madness, *Let Me Alone* is both emotionally moving and important in the context of Kavan's development. It is the chrysalis from which the later work emerges; the independent woman appeals to feminists, although it must be noted that Anna-Marie is certainly not faultless, since her refusal to consummate the marriage appears unmotivated to her husband, with whom she toys in order to see whether his gentle or domineering side will win.

Kafka's influence was noticeable in Kavan's fiction as early as 1930, when Anna-Marie Kavan appeared in *Let Me Alone*, and by 1940, it was so strongly apparent that she assumed the name "Kavan" for the publication of *Asylum Piece and Other Stories*, a collection of experimental short fiction. Following the stylistic and thematic innovations in this collection, however, Kavan published *Change the Name* in 1941, a novel that is typical in all respects of the first group of romances. Even *A Scarcity of Love*, published a full fifteen years later, is a traditional narrative, of unusual interest primarily because of Regina, the most bizzare of Kavan's eccentrics. Regina is a selfish, narcissistic, asexual, manipulative woman who spends most of her time caring for her physical body. She is distraught when she becomes pregnant and the birth of her daughter, Gerda, is such a repulsive experience that she temporarily gets rid of the baby; she then completely ignores the simultaneous suicide of her husband. Much of the first part of the novel focuses on Regina's doctor, to whom she is briefly married, and Mona, the young suicidal girl who takes care of the abandoned Gerda. These characters, ostensibly indispensible to the tale, are dropped about half way through, and are never heard from again.

The second part of the book, which picks up the story fifteen years later, recounts Regina's life with a succession of adulating husbands and admirers, and the sufferings of Gerda, first with her domineering mother and then with her husband, Val, another colonial rescuer, who turns out to be as unloving and asexual as Anna-Marie in *Let Me Alone*. *A Scarcity of Love* depicts a world in which relationships are founded upon convenience and love, which, regardless of the character's sex, is invariably unrequited. It is thus obvious that Kavan's negative, pessimistic attitude is not ideologically motivated; she is not a feminist apologist: power, evil, grotesqueness, dissociation, and asexuality are given in equal shares to both male and female characters. Regina's aberrant and abusive behavior holds the reader's attention, Gerda's dissociating and insistence on the unreality of the distasteful are fascinating, and the nature descriptions are extremely lush. There are, however, many problems, including unmotivated behavior and mood shifts, overreactions, longwindedness, emphasis on unimportant details, too much diverse activity, and an inexplicable lack of resolution: the reader is left wondering about the fates of many important characters.

Not until *Eagle's Nest* did Kavan successfully assimilate the influences of Kafka and modernism to her own concerns. Considerably shorter than the preceding novels, structurally innovative, and concerned with an individualized form of bureaucratic circumlocution, the novel is insistently reminiscent of Kafka's *The Castle* (1926). The narrative concerns a protagonist who leaves a job in a department store to return to work for a patron, called the Administrator. Upon arrival at the Administrator's mansion, the hero lapses into a state divorced from reality. As he awaits the return of the Administrator, he broods about his situation, the machinations of the butler, and the motivations of the secretary, Penny. He ascribes an incommensurate significance to minor activities and petty details. He often overreacts, as does Penny, who is grotesquely distraught when he informs her that he has requested an interview with the Administrator. Ultimately, he is sent away for three ludicrous, untenable reasons.

The last chapter, "The Dream Within," explains that after losing a good job, the hero cataloged a library for the Administrator, but during a chance meeting in which the hero indicates that he would like to be rehired, the Administrator insists that he has never worked for him. The sequence of events in this chapter does not account for part of the main narrative. Thus *Eagle's Nest* ends in multiple ambiguity: the spatial and temporal location of the recollector is unknown, the veracity of the memories is questionable, and the fate of the protagonist is unclear. This ambiguity is reminiscent of the epistemological quagmire of Samuel Beckett's *The Unnamable* (1953). Despite the pervasive uncertainty of the plot and the emphasis on dreamlike states, *Eagle's Nest* is one of Kavan's most controlled works and also one of her best.

Thirty-three years after the publication of *Let Me Alone*, Kavan rewrote the final Burma section of the earlier novel, with a new emphasis and in greater detail. *Who Are You?* is all peroration, since the introductory material is jettisoned. Names are also eliminated; now there are the husband (Doghead), the girl, and Suede Boots. The sweltering jungle, with its snakes, rats, and lizards, is given Conradian prominence. The husband is a vicious, raging madman, who forces the girl to obey, and although she does, she never actually capitulates; she is simply lethargic and indifferent.

In an unpublished letter to Raymond Marriott, Kavan insists that she never read Michel Butor, but her writing indicates that she did read Alain Robbe-Grillet's *Jealousy* (1957). Whether this was a direct influence on her work is a moot point. What really matters is that Kavan simply abjured realistic depiction, as she noted in another letter to Marriott, dated September 20, 1964, shortly after the publication of *Who Are You?* The conclusion of *Let Me Alone* finds Anna-Marie returning from her mad, suicidal walk in the storm, awaiting the visit of an English friend, whom she believes will be her salvation. In *Who Are You?* the girl runs into the storm, a scene that is originally depicted from the servants' point of view. Kavan then doubles back and picks up the story at an earlier point. Everything is repeated once again with a new emphasis, but this time there is no resolution. It is unclear whether the girl leaves the porch and goes off into the storm; it is unclear whether this is a surreal dream sequence or an alternative ending. Unlike so many of Kavan's ambiguous conclusions, however, this one is extremely fulfilling. The reader is left astonished by the narrative power, rather than quizzically annoyed by the protagonist's uncertain fate.

Ice is Kavan's most celebrated novel. In fact, Brian Aldiss voted it the best science-fiction novel of 1967, although it may be a disservice to categorize this disturbing work within such a proscribed framework. *Ice* is a variation on Kavan's favorite theme, the domineering man and the abused female. A group of nameless characters—a male narrator, a powerful warden, and a delicate girl—wend their way across a northern land. The warden has imprisoned the acquiescent girl, and many pages are given to the narrator's obsessive search for her. When he finally finds her, he discovers that she does not want to be rescued. The warden and the girl go off and the chase recommences. These personal machinations are reflected in the chaotic state of the world: war and all of its accompaniments are omnipresent, and a drastic change in the weather results in a shift to extreme cold; everything is becoming encrusted with ice. The conclusion, of course, is ambiguously cataclysmic.

Kavan interestingly begins her career by describing the blistering heat of the tropics and concludes it by presenting images of glacial ice; although there is a brief respite in the warmer East, even this area ultimately is overrun by the encroaching cold. In *Ice*, as in works that employ stream of consciousness, the narrative contains interpolated surreal sequences, sometimes clearly imaginary. At other times, however, these sequences are carefully integrated into the main plot line and it is, therefore, impossible to distinguish fantasy from reality. This is the natural culmination of Kavan's literary development. *Ice*, *Eagle's Nest*, and *Who Are You?* form a fictional trio that demands appreciation as well as critical recognition.

Robert Hauptman

Other major works

SHORT FICTION: *Asylum Piece and Other Stories*, 1940; *I Am Lazarus*, 1945; *A Bright Green Field and Other Stories*, 1958; *Julia and the Bazooka*, 1970; *My Soul in China, a Novella & Stories*, 1975.

Bibliography

Crosland, Margaret. *Beyond the Lighthouse: English Women Novelists in the Twentieth Century.* London: Constable, 1981. Provides some biographic details on Kavan, followed by a commentary of her works. An appreciative study in which Crosland tries to rally support for Kavan's experimental fiction and its importance in contemporary British writing.

Dorr, Priscilla. "Anna Kavan." In *An Encyclopedia of British Woman Writers*, edited by Paul Schlueter and June Schlueter. New York: Garland, 1988. Places Kavan firmly among literary modernists, citing her experimental novels as "cryptic and symbolic." Dorr considers Kavan's most successful novel to be *Ice*, the last of a trilogy that includes *Eagles' Nest* and *Who Are You?*

Nin, Anaïs. *The Novel of the Future.* New York: Macmillan, 1968. Claims that Kavan has entered the world of the divided self in *Asylum Piece and*

Other Stories, which Nin considers equal to the work of Franz Kafka. Nin refers to Kavan as one of the new American novelists who have been neglected. Contains some valuable insights into Nin's sparkling style.

Vannatta, Dennis P., ed. *The English Short Story, 1945-1980: A Critical History*. Boston: Twayne, 1985. The entry on Kavan examines her collection of short stories, *I Am Lazarus*. Vannatta considers Kavan's stories of mental illness and so-called "treatments" valuable but hampered by a lack of range and depth.

THOMAS KENEALLY

Born: Sydney, Australia; October 7, 1935

Principal long fiction

The Place at Whitton, 1964; *The Fear*, 1965; *Bring Larks and Heroes*, 1967; *Three Cheers for the Paraclete*, 1968; *The Survivor*, 1969; *A Dutiful Daughter*, 1971; *The Chant of Jimmie Blacksmith*, 1972; *Blood Red, Sister Rose*, 1974; *Gossip from the Forest*, 1975; *Moses the Lawgiver*, 1975; *Season in Purgatory*, 1976; *A Victim of the Aurora*, 1977; *Passenger*, 1979; *Confederates*, 1979; *The Cut-Rate Kingdom*, 1980; *Schindler's Ark*, 1982 (U.S. edition, *Schindler's List*, 1983); *A Family Madness*, 1985; *The Playmaker*, 1987; *To Asmara*, 1989; *Flying Class Hero*, 1991.

Other literary forms

In addition to his long fiction, Thomas Keneally has written several plays: *Halloran's Little Boat* (1966), *Childermass* (1968), *An Awful Rose* (1972), and *Bullie's House* (1980). He has also written two television plays, *Essington*, produced in the United Kingdom in 1974, and *The World's Wrong End* (1981).

Achievements

Keneally has received international acclaim for his fiction; he has received the Miles Franklin Award (1967, 1968), the Captain Cook Bi-Centenary Prize (1970), the Royal Society of Literature Prize (1982), and the Booker Prize (1982). *The Chant of Jimmie Blacksmith* won for him the Heinemann Award for literature (1973), and *Schindler's Ark* won the *Los Angeles Times* Fiction Prize (1983). Keneally's other honors include the presidency of the National Book Council of Australia and membership in the Australia-China Council.

Biography

Thomas Michael Keneally was born in Sydney, Australia, on October 7, 1935. He studied for the Roman Catholic priesthood in his youth but left the seminary two weeks before he was to take Holy Orders. He completed his education at St. Patrick's College, New South Wales. He married Judith Martin in 1965 and had two children. Before becoming a full-time novelist, he taught high school in Sydney, from 1960 to 1964; from 1968 to 1970, he was a lecturer in drama at the University of New England, New South Wales, after which he moved to London.

Analysis

Thomas Keneally has written books on a variety of subjects. His first novel to attain international readership, *Bring Larks and Heroes*, presents the barbarous life of eighteenth century Sydney; *Three Cheers for the Paraclete* concerns a Catholic priest who attacks the Church for its indifference to social evil; *The Survivor* and *A Victim of the Aurora* are stories about Antarctic expeditions, told in flashback by an aged narrator; *A Dutiful Daughter* is a surrealistic tale of a family in which the parents are bovine from the waist down. One may, however, separate Keneally's work into two parts, albeit roughly: the novels which deal with seemingly ordinary, contemporary individuals, and the wide range of what might be called historical novels.

In a large portion of his work, Keneally concerns himself with European history, examining closely the human beings involved, seeing the past not as the present sees it, as a series of neatly wrapped, complete events, but as the participants experience it: as a jumble of occurrences that seem to have little meaning or purpose. Although some reviewers have commented on the portentousness lurking in the background of such works as *Gossip from the Forest*, a fictionalized re-creation of the 1918 peace talks that led to the disastrous Treaty of Versailles, such "damaging knowingness" is only partly Keneally's fault; after all, the present knows what happened in the past, at least in outline.

It must be emphasized that Keneally's historically based fiction is not about ordinary people set against a celebrity-filled background, in the manner of E. L. Doctorow's *Ragtime* (1975). His works deal with the historical figures themselves, presenting them as human beings embroiled in the quotidian matters from which the historical events reveal themselves gradually. The writer's knowledge of history shapes the delineation of the plot. Furthermore, the protagonist's awareness of his or her importance to posterity comes only in flashes. When such awareness occurs, it is as a result of the character's makeup; Joan of Arc, for example, was a visionary, and it is unavoidable that, as a character, she know something of her eventual fate.

It cannot be denied that what Keneally is attempting to do in his historically based novels is difficult; that he succeeds as well as he does is primarily a result of a spare, objective style that is at times brilliant, such as in the description of Yugoslav partisans from *Season in Purgatory*: "Grenades blossomed like some quaint ethnic ornamentation down the front of their coats." The third-person narration, deceptively simple, pretending to mere description, seems detached (at times too detached): *Schindler's List*, based on a German industrialist's widely successful efforts to save "his" Jews, at times suffers from an almost sprightly tone, as if the author were so determined to be objective that he expunged any sense of moral outrage from his account. At its best, however, the stark simplicity of Keneally's prose throws into sharp relief the horrors of which history is made.

The history examined by Keneally is never pretty, no matter how heroic the subject. The final terrible lesson of *Gossip from the Forest* is that well-meaning, intelligent, civilized men have no place in the twentieth century. Matthias Erzberger, liberal member of the Reichstag, has no success in his negotiations; blind self-interest thwarts his every attempt at justice for his defeated country. He is shot to death several years after the meeting at Compiègne by two young officers, proto-Nazis, as a traitor for his role in the Armistice. Erzberger himself, for all of his excellent qualities and basic decency, seems unequal to the task he has had thrust on him. He is aware of his inadequacy: "Like a cardiac spasm he suffered again the terrible bereft sense that there was nothing in his background that justified this journey. . . . At its most high-flown the true Erzberger's mind wasn't far off steak and red wine and Paula's warm and undemanding bed." His dreamy absentmindedness and his eventual despair seem to remove him from the heroic ranks; it is only toward the end of the novel that the reader realizes the true heroism of the civilian in his struggle against the military mind.

This gradual revelation of heroism is evident also in *Season in Purgatory*, the story of a young British physician, David Pelham, who is sent to the island of Mus to perform emergency surgery on Yugoslav partisans. Pelham arrives on Mus with all the fiery idealism of youth. After being thrust, day after day, into the results of war—both the direct results, such as graphically described wounds, and the indirect, such as Marshal Tito's order that any partisans indulging in sexual relations be summarily executed—he is worn down, no longer convinced of the rightness of any cause: "In his bloodstream were two simple propositions: that the savagery of the Germans did not excuse the savagery of the partisans: that the savagery of the partisans did not excuse the savagery of the Germans."

This final realization that "the masters of the ideologies, even the bland ideology of democracy, were blood-crazed . . . that at the core of their political fervour, there stood a desire to punish with death anyone who hankered for other systems than those approved," does not allow the story to end. It is in this moral vacuum that Pelham becomes a hero, having sacrificed the innocence and illusion of idealism for an embittered realism. Keneally continues to reveal Pelham's personal flaws, as he does with all of his heroic figures: His childishness in love and hate and his typical upper-class British attitudes survive the revelation. Therefore, the apotheosis of the physician at the end of the war comes as much as a surprise to the reader as it must to the character himself.

Pelham's loss of idealism is necessary to Keneally's concept of the heroic figure; idealism bathes reality in a rosy glow that does not fit anything but the usual type of historical novel (or many types of history, for that matter). Generally, Keneally's heroes find themselves chosen to be sacrificial victims, without having wished for it. They are by turns reluctant and filled with fervor, and they are always human, at times perversely flaunting their faults. The positive aspect of their selection is generally far more ephemeral than the certitude of the doom toward which they know they are going. They are often in the situation epitomized by the half-caste protagonist of *The Chant of Jimmie Blacksmith*, the novel on which the 1978 Fred Schepisi film is based: "in tenuous elation and solid desolation between self-knowledge and delirium."

Jimmie Blacksmith has a white father, whom he does not know, and an aboriginal mother. He has been taught Christianity and ambition; he is no longer tribal, but his attempts to show the whites that a black may be as industrious and educated as they are fail to gain for him acceptance in their society. He marries a white girl who has also slept with the station cook (played by Keneally himself in the film); when their baby is born, it is white.

Jimmie has been cheated by the whites, has taken up arms against his tribe in order to be thought white, and has married white to consolidate his ambition, yet he is still rejected by the white society. The birth of the baby makes him explode, and he goes on a methodical rampage, first killing the Newby family, for whom he worked, then taking a sympathetic white schoolteacher as a hostage. He eludes his pursuers for a time, but they catch up with him. Shot in the jaw, delirious, he takes refuge in a convent, where he is eventually captured. His hanging, however, is delayed so that it will not detract from the celebration of the Federation anniversary.

Throughout, Jimmie is seen as a man who might be a bridge between the two cultures, but neither the aborigines nor the whites allow such a resolution; his killing spree seems to represent his only alternative, and while other people die, Jimmie is actually the victim. He wants to become the peaceful link, and when this course proves illusory, he becomes the avenger, knowing that he will not survive. He is doomed, in the way Keneally heroes are usually doomed.

This sense of being the sacrificial victim is most strongly presented in Keneally's retelling of the Joan of Arc story. *Blood Red, Sister Rose* is a fictionalized account of the youth and triumph of Joan of Arc. The novel ends with the few anticlimactic months following the coronation of Charles in Rheims and an epilogue in the form of a letter from her father to the family about his daughter's death. Yet throughout the development of Jehanne's awareness of her destiny, the certitude of her martyrdom is evident, for she is a peasant who knows that Christ's sacrifice was not enough; the king needs one, and she has been chosen. Alternately buoyed and depressed by her fate, she sees herself as a conduit for these forces, the importance of which leaves very little time or passion for Jehanne, daughter of Jacques and Zabillet, to pursue her own humanity.

Described as wide-shouldered and plain, Jehanne goes through adolescence without menstruating, which proves to her that she is not like her sister or her mother, that she is the virgin from Lorraine prophesied by Merlin. She has not chosen her fate, but she must accept it. There are moments when she resents this election: Words of tenderness spoken about another woman, for example, evoke great sadness within her, for she knows that such words will never be spoken about her. The greater part of the time, however, is consumed with her mission, not to France, not to the destruction of the English, not even to stop the slaughter of the farmers who suffered so greatly in the wars of the fifteenth century, but to ensure the consecration of the king, to whom she is mystically bound.

Through ancient ritual, Keneally presents the notion of the human sacrifice. The author's weaving of historical incident with the motivations based in archaic mythologies allows a dimension of verisimilitude to the slippery genre of historical fiction. The inclusion of certain surprising elements of fifteenth century life (for example, the mention that peasants in eastern France plowed their field with a naked woman in the harness so that the earth might be bountiful) reveals a society in which the voices heard by Jehanne cannot be casually dismissed as a frustrated spinster's wishful thinking.

Jehanne is, like her forebears, a mixture of ignorance and hardheaded shrewdness. These qualities, at the service of the obsession that invaded her at the age of nine, ensure her success in reaching the king. Furthermore, the feudal society that she opposes is rapidly approaching dissolution: the battle of Agincourt has demonstrated the impotence of armored knights, Prince Hal has taken to killing noble prisoners instead of ransoming them in the time-honored practice of chivalry, the alliances of dukes and barons have been complicated by the presence of the English, and the ongoing war has caused a near-famine in the countryside. Jehanne's clarity of purpose shines brightly through the morass of confusion and disaster that was fifteenth century France.

Once her objective is reached, however, she becomes an ordinary person again, with no voices telling her the next move. One sees her strength and influence eroding as the king is changed from a timid recluse to a confident monarch. His ingratitude is taken as a matter of course by Jehanne, for she has known all along the fate that awaits the year-king, the sacrificial victim. As if her importance has diminished for the author as well as for Charles, the ending is a mere footnote. One is left with a brilliant picture of a strange and remote past, and a sense of what heroes are—never heroes to themselves, accepting the acclaims of the populace bemusedly, as if the admirers were constantly missing the point. Although there are moments when she is elated by her specialness, more often she sees it as an onus, a word that constantly recurs in Keneally's work.

This realization, in small part exhilarating and in larger part burdensome, is one that recurs in Keneally's work. In the novel *Passenger*, for example, the narrator-fetus views the Gnome as his outside brother and protector; the Gnome is eventually killed in a plane crash, and in dying ensures the birth of the narrator. In *A Victim of the Aurora*, two explorers from a previous expedition have remained in the Antarctic, and one survives by eating the other one; the identities are mixed, so that the one who has survived identifies himself by the name of he who has been eaten. One can see plainly Keneally's Catholic background in the use of the sacrificial victim as theme or motif in many of his works: Christ's sacrifice, rendered bloodless by the sacrament of communion, is constantly reenacted in all its primal violence by either his protagonists or his supporting characters.

This theme links the historical novels with those that deal with supposedly ordinary people. In the latter category, Keneally is more experimental, particularly in the mode of narration employed. The objective third-person narration of the historical novels is replaced by various innovations, such as the second-person, self-addressed narration of *A Dutiful Daughter* or the omniscient first-person narration of *Passenger*. At first glance, there seems to be little similarity between the two types of novels, but the author's concerns form a bridge between them.

Passenger's narrator is a fetus, given consciousness by a laser sonogram. Suddenly, the fetus is no longer happily unaware of anything save the coursing of his blood, an animal faculty that requires a certain kind of innocence; he becomes aware of everything: his mother's thoughts, the historical novel she is writing about her ne'er-do-well husband's ancestor (himself seemingly the prototype of Halloran in *Bring Larks and Heroes*), his father's fear of his birth, the existence of Warwick Jones, the Gnome—"We were Dumas' Corsican twins, the Gnome and I. It was as if we *shared* a placenta and swapped our visions and sensation." Jones feels as though he had never really been born, and that he will be born through the agency of the narrator's own birth. For Jones, however, birth means death, literal death. The narrator also sees his own eventual birth as death, and he resists it, unlike Jones, who actively seeks it.

This notion of the sacrificial double is one aspect that links the two categories of novels. The power of history is another. Keneally's fascination with history and heroes surfaces in *Passenger*. In the narrative is a character who has had the same experiences as David Pelham, the protagonist of *Season in Purgatory*. Maurice Fitzgerald, the eighteenth century ancestor of Brian, the narrator's father, was also a reluctant hero in the penal colony of Sydney. The fight against social injustice that characterizes Maurice Fitzgerald forms the thematic center of Keneally's novel *Three Cheers for the Paraclete*.

In this novel, Keneally treats directly the experience that perhaps influenced his life most strongly: the six and a half years of being a seminarian, bound to the doctrine and ideology of the Catholic Church. Again, Father Maitland, the protagonist, is a reluctant hero, unsure of the purity of his motives even as he preaches, afraid of sounding "like a fashionable priest, the glib kind." He tries earnestly to submit to the authority of his bishop, fearing the disappearance of the comforting certainties, but his conscience does not allow him a quiet life.

His working-class cousin has been cheated out of his savings by an unscrupulous housing development corporation; looking into the affair, Maitland discovers that other people had the same experience with that company, and furthermore, that his own diocese owns stock in the company. He becomes the center of controversy, a position he does not want but must take because of his own convictions. The diocese eventually rids itself of the holdings in the dishonest company, but on the advice of its legal staff; the question of morality has been supplanted by one of expediency for the established Church. Maitland, having indirectly succeeded, submits to the rule of his church: the censorship of his sermons, a ban on further publications, and transfer to a rural parish.

The pervasiveness of social injustice and its force makes its appearance in all of Keneally's novels, in one degree or another. Jehanne of *Blood Red, Sister Rose*, a peasant and a woman, is herself a statement against the class and gender inequities of the fifteenth century, at times bringing a modern flavor to a time when such inequities were seldom questioned. Her liberationist tendencies are diluted by the importance of her vision, but it is impossible for her to witness late medieval war without realizing who suffers the most: The farmers, the peasants who form the major part of the armies, are never held for ransom. They are killed outright when captured. The noncombatants, women and children, are raped and killed by the rampaging armies. The sexism inherent in the way she is treated makes her rage impotently.

Jehanne's story appears in *A Dutiful Daughter*; Barbara Glover, the sister of the narrator, possesses what might be a fifteenth century transcript of Jehanne's first examination by priests, which might have saved her from the stake had it not been lost. Barbara sees in Jehanne's story elements which might explain her own life to her.

The Glover family has settled on a swampy bit of land, Campbell's Reach, and has tried to make a living on it with only minimal success. The son, Damian, who is the narrator, has been sent to college, while Barbara has stayed behind to take care of the parents. In a flashback that is evocative of Jehanne's own awakening to the voices, Barbara runs off into the swamp, pursued by her parents; when they finally come back, the parents have undergone a bizarre metamorphosis: they have been turned into cattle from the waist down, "like centaurs, except that the horse half was a cow half." They seem to have not noticed, but Barbara tells them what has happened; they never forgive her, but from that day forward, she has complete control over them. As Damian writes, "It is the duty of a good child to let his parents know the second they turn into animals."

Barbara's control has its responsibilities, and she finds them onerous. She cannot evade them, however, no more than Jehanne can escape her destiny. She therefore perserveres, although life on Campbell's Reach is dismal at best, and in conjunction with the caring for her parents, absolutely deadening. For the parents are indeed cattle from the waist down; the transformation is literal, and Keneally leaves no doubt about that fact. The mother suffers from mastitis, a bovine disease of the udder that is fatal in cows. Most farmers, it is said, kill the cows that contract it. Obviously, Barbara cannot put her mother out of her misery, so she treats her with massive doses of antibiotics, and her mother querulously suffers nearly all the time.

The father really is a bull from the waist down, and goes out in search of heifers, stricken by suicidal shame every time he succeeds, but driven to repeat his quest by his animal self. It is obvious that Barbara is sacrificing herself: the only love she experiences is the incestuous passion that Damian has for her, and that is consummated only once before she puts a stop to it— for his sake. Eventually, she takes the parents with her so that they may all drown in the flood that is sweeping over Campbell's Reach, and so that her brother may finally be free of his unwholesome family ties.

Family, history, the tormented personalities of those who are present at great events, the sacrificial victim—these are the themes that are interwoven in all of Keneally's works. Perhaps the fact that Australia has very little history of its own has contributed to Keneally's fascination with the topic. His novel *A Family Madness* juxtaposes two families: Terry Delaney's working-class family and that of Radislaw Kabbelski. The Delaneys seem not to be touched by history, but the Kabbelskis, Belorussian refugees, have bathed in it for a long time. The third-person narrative, set in contemporary Australia, is interspersed with the journals of the Kabbelski family. The relative degrees of innocence or experience of the two groups are thus seen as contingent on how deeply one is embedded in history.

Differing perspectives, both cultural and historical, and social injustice also play definitive roles in Keneally's *To Asmara*. The product of several months spent researching at first hand in Eritrea by Keneally, *To Asmara* is a fictional account of the state of the Eritrean rebellion in 1987 (the rebellion began in 1962). Keneally uses thinly disguised characters and organizations to bring touches of reality to what is almost otherwise a philosophical tract.

Timothy Darcy is an Australian journalist whose Chinese-Australian wife, Bernadette, has left him for an Aborigine. In London, Darcy is introduced to an Eritrean rebel who wants Darcy to come to Africa and to cover a special mission. Darcy accepts, hoping that by escaping to Africa, he will find his spiritual place in his coverage of the rebellion. Instead, he becomes part of a traveling party that also includes a French girl looking for her father (who had run away from his family many years before and had become a cameraman for the rebels), an English noblewoman on a crusade to end the brutal custom of female circumcision, and an aid worker trying to free his lover, who is in the hands of the Ethiopians, the Eritreans' mortal enemies. Darcy's other objective is to meet with an Ethiopian major held as a prisoner of war by the Eritreans.

The book is supposedly Darcy's journal combined with transcribed tape recordings of his thoughts and observations, with a few interjected chapters by an objective—though unidentified—third person. Ultimately, Darcy is lost, both metaphorically and physically, after he fails to connect with his fellow human beings and fails to rescue an aid truck, instead driving it over a land mine by accident. Darcy's failure reinforces the ongoing theme in Keneally's work of people divorced from their cultures and their spouses, unable to find solace or refuge in other cultures or others' spouses. With *To Asmara*, Keneally's lost generation continues.

There is a wholeness about Keneally's work that belies one's initial impression of diversity. Not that diversity does not exist: geographically and temporally, his work ranges from the Antarctic to Europe and America, from the dim past to the present. Yet certain themes are always prevalent. In the introduction to an interview with Keneally, Janette Turner Hospital writes, "The protagonists of the novels of Thomas Keneally are Jeremiahs of a sort, reluctant prophets or messiahs . . . prophets by random circumstance only." It is Keneally's fascination with circumstance and its effects that stands out as the major lesson that history has taught him: those who do great deeds, either public or private, are no better or worse than anyone else. If they are holy, they are so in the ancient sense of the word: "different from, other than." It is in revealing the humanity in their holiness that Keneally makes his greatest contribution.

Jean-Pierre Metereau

Other major works

PLAYS: *Halloran's Little Boat*, 1966; *Childermass*, 1968; *An Awful Rose*, 1972; *Bullie's House*, 1980.

TELEPLAYS: *Essington*, 1974; *The World's Wrong End*, 1981.

NONFICTION: *Outback*, 1983.

CHILDREN'S LITERATURE: *Ned Kelley and the City of Bees*, 1978.

Bibliography

Gelder, Ken. " 'Trans-what?' Sexuality and the Phallus in *A Dutiful Daughter* and *The Flesheaters* (Analysis of Novels by Thomas Keneally and David Ireland)." *Southerly* 49 (March, 1989): 3-15. Discusses Keneally's work in the light of his representation of sexuality. Includes some references.

Petersson, Irmtraud. " 'White Ravens' in a World of Violence: German Connections in Thomas Keneally's Fiction." *Australian Literary Studies* 14 (October, 1989): 160-173. Addresses the question of Keneally's "cultural specificity" in his writing. Petersson discusses the historical and naturalist perspectives in Keneally's works such as *Schindler's List* and *A Family Madness*. Includes some reference information.

"Thomas (Michael) Keneally." In *Current Biography Yearbook 1987*, edited by Charles Moritz. New York: H. W. Wilson, 1987. One of the few sources for biographical information on Keneally. Also includes brief references.

Thorpe, Michael. Review of *To Asmara*, by Thomas Keneally. *World Literature Today* 64 (Spring, 1990): 360. Thorpe concentrates on Keneally as a "noncombatant novelist of war." Includes references for further information on Eritrea and on Keneally.

WILLIAM KENNEDY

Born: Albany, New York; January 16, 1928

Principal long fiction

The Ink Truck, 1969; *Legs*, 1975; *Billy Phelan's Greatest Game*, 1978; *Ironweed*, 1983; *The Albany Cycle*, 1985 (includes *Legs*, *Billy Phelan's Greatest Game*, and *Ironweed*); *Quinn's Book*, 1988.

Other literary forms

In addition to the four novels cited above, William Kennedy's nonfiction *O Albany! An Urban Tapestry* (1983), pamphlets for the New York State Library, Empire State College, and the *Albany Tricentennial Guidebook* (1985) largely center on his native Albany, New York. He wrote the screenplays for *The Cotton Club* (1984), with Francis Coppola and Mario Puzo, and *Ironweed* (1987), adapted from his novel of the same title. Kennedy collaborated with his son, Brendan, on a children's book, *Charlie Malarkey and the Belly Button Machine* (1986).

Achievements

Kennedy is a former newspaperman from Albany, New York, a city in which politics plays an important role. He was born there of Irish Catholic heritage, struggled at writing for years while teaching as an adjunct at the State University of New York (SUNY) at Albany. He brings all these traditions to his writing: the bite of the newsman, the literary allusions of the professor, and the mysticism of the American Irishman. His first books— *The Ink Truck*, *Legs*, and *Billy Phelan's Greatest Game*—drew some notice but sold sluggishly, so *Ironweed* was rejected by thirteen publishers until Saul Bellow, Kennedy's teacher and mentor, persuaded Viking to reconsider. Viking reissued the previous two novels along with *Ironweed* as *The Albany Cycle*, and *Ironweed* won the National Book Critics Circle Award in 1983 and the Pulitzer Prize in fiction in 1984. Kennedy received a MacArthur Foundation Fellowship in 1983. This unsolicited "genius" award freed him for creative work; he used part of the proceeds to start a writers' institute in Albany, later funded by New York State with him as director. His novels' characters are drawn from the world of bums and gangsters and have been compared in brilliance to those of James Joyce and William Faulkner. *The Albany Cycle*, with its interlocking characters and spirit of place, has been compared to Faulkner's Yoknapatawpha stories and Joyce's *Dubliners* (1914) and *Ulysses* (1922). Kennedy's style has won praise as a combination of naturalism and surrealism, yet critics have faulted what they call his overwriting and pandering to the public's demand for violence, explicit sex, and scatological detail. Critics generally agree that *Ironweed*, the culmination of *The*

Albany Cycle, is also Kennedy's best, fusing the style, characterization, attention to detail, and mysticism of the other two and focusing them with mastery.

Biography

William Kennedy was born in Albany, New York, on January 16, 1928. He was graduated from Siena College in 1949 and went to work for the Glens Falls, New York, *Post Star*, as sports editor and columnist, followed by a stint as reporter on the Albany *Times Union* until 1956. He went to Puerto Rico to work for the *Puerto Rico World Journal*, then for the *Miami Herald* (1957), returning to Puerto Rico as founding managing editor of the San Juan *Star* from 1959 to 1961. Deciding to make fiction writing his career and Albany his literary source and center, he returned to the Albany *Times Union* as special writer and film critic from 1963 to 1970, while he gathered material and wrote columns on Albany's rich history and its often scabrous past. Upon the success of *Ironweed*, he was promoted to Professor of English at SUNY/Albany in 1983. The university and the city sponsored a "William Kennedy's Albany" celebration in September, 1984.

Analysis

William Kennedy's fiction is preoccupied with spirit of place, language, and style, and a mystic fusing of characters and dialogue. The place is Albany, New York, the capital city, nest of corrupt politics, heritor of Dutch, English, and Irish immigrants, home to canallers, crooks, bums and bag ladies, aristocrats, and numbers-writers. Albany, like Boston, attracted a large Irish Catholic population, which brought its churches, schools, family ties, political machine, and underworld connections.

Kennedy's style has been compared to that of François Rabelais for its opulent catalogs and its ribald scatology. Kennedy is not, however, a derivative writer. As his books unfold, one from another, he makes novel connections, adeptly developing the hallucinations of Bailey, the protagonist of *The Ink Truck*, the extrasensory perception of Martin Daugherty, one of the central consciousnesses of *Billy Phelan's Greatest Game*, and the ghosts of his victims visiting Francis Phelan on his quest for redemption in *Ironweed*.

Kennedy's first published novel, *The Ink Truck*, connects less strongly to these themes and styles than do later works. The novel focuses on the headquarters of a Newspaper Guild strike committee on the one-year anniversary of its strike against the daily newspaper of a town resembling Albany. Only four Guild members remain: Bailey, Rosenthal, Irma, and Jarvis, their leader. Bailey, the proverbial blundering Irish reporter, mixes his libido and marital problems with his earnest belief in the strike, now bogged down in trivialities.

Bailey's relationship with his wife is strained and crazed: She is madly jealous, as she has reason to be. Bailey mixes idealism about the strike with several sexual romps and psychic encounters, punctuated by savage beatings from the scabs and company agents determined to break the strike.

Bailey's fantasy is to open the valve on the ink truck coming to the newspaper plant, bleeding the newspaper's black blood into the snow of the mean streets. In the Guild room near the paper plant, Bailey attempts to revive his affair with Irma, another of the few remaining strikers. Joined by Deek, a collegiate type and an executive's son who wants to join the strike, the four members try to harass the paper's owners, whose representative, Stanley, refuses to grant their demands, which, by this time, have become niggling. As they attempt to block the ink truck in the snow and release the ink, everything goes wrong. When Bailey sets fire to the vacant store where the gypsies congregate, Putzina, the queen, is fatally burned, and she dies in the hospital amid a wild gypsy rite. Antic writing celebrates Bailey's subsequent kidnaping by the gypsies so that they seem comic despite the violence. Bailey escapes after cooperating with the company secretary in her sexual fantasy but is disillusioned when he finds that he must sign an apology to the newspaper company for the action of some members.

More setbacks emerge: Bailey takes back the apology, then finds that the motor has been taken out of his car. Rosenthal's house has been trashed viciously. Bailey, expelled from the Newspaper Guild, goes home to find that his wife, Grace, has put all of his belongings on the curb to be pilfered. His uncle Melvin refuses to help but invites him to an elaborate pet funeral for his cat. Just after this event, the cat's body disappears, a ludicrous culmination of all Bailey has lost: Guild, Guild benefits, apartment, and wife. Going literally underground, Bailey takes a job shelving books in the State Library, where Irma visits him to tell him that despite all setbacks, he, Rosenthal, and Deek are being hailed as the Ink Truck Heroes. In this aspect, Bailey prefigures the gangster hero, Legs Diamond, and the hero as transfigured bum, Francis Phelan, of the later books.

Becoming a media hero, Bailey makes one more futile try at the ink truck. In a grand finale, the orgiastic end-of-strike party hosted by Stanley becomes another humiliation for Bailey. Kennedy's low-key and inconclusive ending leaves the characters where they began: looking at the place on the wall of the Guild Room where a sign hung over the mimeograph machine saying DON'T SIT HERE. Bailey tries to make sense of his experiences, but even the reader cannot understand. Some of the richest of these experiences—a religious pilgrimage by trolley car and a trip backward in time to a cholera epidemic in 1832—seem almost gratuitous, loose ends without much relationship to the rest of the story. Bailey realizes that "all the absurd things they'd all gone through, separately or together. . . were fixed in time and space and stood only for whatever meaning he, or anyone else, cared to give them."

Kennedy's next novel, *Legs*, develops clearer patterns and meanings, though with the same mixture of realism and surrealism as in *The Ink Truck*. Kennedy demonstrates the truth of his 1975 novel's epigraph, "People like killers," a quote from Eugène Ionesco, through his portrayal of John "Jack" Diamond, also known as "Legs," an idolized, flamboyant underworld figure, a liquor smuggler during Prohibition, a careless killer, and a tough womanizer. Finally brought to justice by New York governor Franklin D. Roosevelt, Jack was mysteriously executed gangland style in Albany in December, 1931.

The story begins in a seedy Albany bar, where four of the book's characters meet in 1974 to reminisce about the assassination of their gangster-hero, Jack "Legs" Diamond. The novel is a fictionalization of Jack's life, superimposing fictional characters, fictional names for real people, and Kennedy's imagination on real events. Three of the four in the frame story are minor, therefore surviving, members of Jack's entourage. The fourth member of the group is Marcus Gorman, Jack's attorney, mouthpiece, and friend, who gave up a political career to lend respectability and a capacity for legal chicanery to Jack. Marcus is the narrator of the novel, providing a less-than-intimate portrait, yet one filtered through a legal mind accustomed to the trickery of the profession as it was practiced then in Albany.

The book is tightly crafted, with parallel scenes, apt literary allusions, well-constructed flashbacks, foreshadowing throughout, and, always, the map of Albany and its neighboring Catskills in mind. The sordid historical account is elevated with signs and coincidences: Marcus, employed by Jack after he successfully represented another gangster, visits Jack in the Catskills after speaking at a police communion breakfast in Albany; a copy of Rabelais is in the Knights of Columbus Library frequented by Marcus in Albany; one is in Jack's bookcase at his Catskills hideaway. Literary allusions combined with Bonnie-and-Clyde violence produce Kennedy's most transcendental effects. Marcus seems a divided consciousness: He regrets the straight-and-narrow life of Irish Catholic Albany and a secure role in politics, yet he has a way of suborning witnesses, getting them to pretend insanity, and ignoring obvious hints about Jack's grislier killings (such as the garage murder of an erstwhile ally).

Jack Diamond became a mythical imaginative popular hero, a "luminous" personality who appealed to the crowds, and remained their darling even in his final trials. He survived assassination attempts, though his murder is foretold from the beginning. The story is interwoven with parallels and coincidences. Kiki, Jack's gorgeous mistress, engages in a monologue reminiscent of Molly Bloom's in Joyce's *Ulysses* when she learns (from a newspaper she has hidden in her closet) that Jack really kills people. Then, when Jack is shot in a hotel (he recovers), Kiki leaves for a friend's apartment and hides in her closet from both the police and the rival gangsters.

Finally, Jack comes to trial over his torture of a farmer in the matter of a still. The farmer complains, and a grand jury is called by Roosevelt. Though acquitted of the assault on the farmer, a federal case against him nearly succeeds because of the testimony of an aide Jack betrayed. Following this, Jack is shot and killed in a rooming house in Albany.

Part of the novel's theme relates to the legal profession. Marcus insists that he defends those who pay his fee. In Jack's second trial, he uses an old nun, a courthouse regular, telling the court in a rambling summation that this old nun came to tell him how compassionate Jack Diamond was. Though a complete fabrication, these emotional touches win juries.

Kennedy's manic touch is evident in his portrayal of scenes on an ocean liner as Jack and Marcus try to conclude a drug deal, scenes in the Kenmore bar in Albany in its art deco heyday, and of the singing of "My Mother's Rosary" at the Elk's Club bar in Albany. The final coda is a lyrically written, but puzzling, apotheosis: Jack, dead, gradually emerges from his body, in a transfiguration worthy of a Seigfried or a Njall of Nordic sagas.

Kennedy's next novel, *Billy Phelan's Greatest Game*, tells the story of another of Albany's historical crimes—the real kidnaping of the political boss Dan O'Connell's nephew—through the framework of a series of games of chance played by a young hanger-on of the city's underside. He is Billy Phelan, son of an absent father, Francis, who will be the protagonist of *Ironweed*. The other consciousness of the book is Martin Daugherty, old neighbor of the Phelans and a newspaperman. The time frame covers several days in late October, 1938, the time of the greatest game—the kidnaping.

Family interrelationships loom importantly in this novel. Billy Phelan has lost his father, Francis, by desertion twenty-two years before; Martin's father, a writer with an insane wife and a lovely mistress, now lies senile in a nursing home. The politically powerful McCall family almost loses their only heir, the pudgy, ineffectual Charlie. Martin lusts after his father's mistress, who plays sexual games with him. Similarly, Billy's lady friend, Angie, cleverly outwits him by pretending to be pregnant, to see what Billy will do. They have never, she says, really talked about anything seriously. Billy reminisces about rowing down Broadway in a boat, during a flood in 1913, with his father and uncle. Soon, he finds his father in a seedy bar, along with his companion Helen, and gives Helen his last money for his father.

This novel frames and mirrors an unsavory crime in the lives of ordinary, yet complicated, human beings. Kennedy's wealth of language, his handiness with an anecdote, sometimes leads him to leave loose ends in his otherwise tightly constructed narratives. For example, Martin Daugherty has extrasensory perception; moreover, he lusts after his father's former mistress Melissa, who also has a taste for women. These details are interesting, yet, unlike the appearance of the vagrant Francis Phelan, these anecdotes do not further the plot or embellish the theme.

Still, Kennedy's novels unfold in a profusion of ideas, one from the other, both in language and in plot. The same time frame and some of the same characters appear in *Ironweed*, the final book of the cycle and the Pulitzer Prize winner.

Ironweed takes place immediately after the events in *Billy Phelan's Greatest Game*, on Halloween and All Saint's Day, 1938, just after the radio broadcast of Orson Welles's adaptation of H. G. Wells's *The War of the Worlds* (1898). The dates are not randomly chosen: the story, though on the surface the saga of a failed, homeless man, is actually a religious pilgrimage toward redemption from sin. Ironweed is described in an epigraph as a tough-stemmed member of the sunflower family, and Francis, like the weed, is a survivor. These analogies, like the Welles broadcast, hinge on a question of belief important to this novel.

Unlike Kennedy's previous books, *Ironweed* has no narrator or central consciousness. The main character, Francis Phelan, first left home after he killed a man during a transit strike by throwing a stone during a demonstration against the hiring of scab trolley drivers. Subsequently he returned, but left for long periods when he played professional baseball. Later, he disappeared for twenty-two years after he dropped his infant son while diapering him; the child died, yet Francis' wife, Annie, never told anyone who dropped Gerald. Francis and another bum, Rudy, dying of cancer, get jobs digging in St. Agnes' Cemetery, where Gerald and other relatives are buried.

Reason and fact are supremely important in the book, yet within one page Francis' mother, a disagreeable hypocrite, twitches in her grave and eats crosses made from weeds, and the infant Gerald converses with his father and wills him to perform acts of expiation, as yet unknown, that will cease his self-destructiveness and bring forgiveness. Francis has killed several people besides the scab driver, yet it is not for these crimes that he needs forgiveness but for deserting his family. The rest of the book chronicles his redemption. Throughout, shifts to fantasy occur, triggered by passages of straight memory and detailed history. Ghosts of the men Francis killed ride the bus back to Albany, yet they do not seem as horrible to Francis as a woman he finds near the mission, freezing in the cold. He drapes a blanket around her, yet later he finds her dead, mangled and eaten by dogs.

During the night, Francis meets with his hobo "wife," Helen, a gently educated musician (she once went to Vassar) with enough energy, though dying of a tumor, to sing proudly in a pub on their rounds. In the mission, Francis gets a pair of warm socks; on the street, Helen is robbed of the money given to her by Francis' son Billy. Then follows a nightmare search through the cold streets for shelter for the delicate Helen. In desperation, Francis goes to a friend's apartment, where he washes his genital region in the toilet and begs a clean pair of shorts. The friend refuses them shelter, so Francis leaves Helen in an abandoned car with several men, though he knows she will be molested sexually.

The next day, Francis gets a job with a junkman. While making his rounds, he reads in a paper about his son Billy getting mixed up in the McCall kidnaping. Making the rounds of old neighborhoods, buying junk from housewives, releases a flood of memories for Francis: He sees his parents, his neighbors the Daughertys in their house, now burned, where one day the mad Katrina Daugherty walked out of her house naked to be rescued by the seventeen-year-old Francis. Because of this memory, he buys a shirt from the ragman to replace his filthy one. While he is buying the shirt, Helen goes to Mass, then listens to records in a record store (stealing one). Retrieving money she has hidden in her bra, Helen redeems the suitcase at the hotel. In her room, she recalls her life, her beloved father's suicide, her mother's cheating her of her inheritance, her exploiting lover/employer in the music store. Washing herself and putting on her Japanese kimono, she prepares to die.

Francis, meanwhile, revisits his family, bringing a turkey bought with his earnings from the day's job. He bathes, dresses in his old clothing his wife has saved, looks over souvenirs, meets his grandson, gets his daughter's forgiveness as well as his wife's, and is even invited to return. He leaves, however, finds Rudy, and together they look for Helen. Finding Helen registered at Palumbo's Hotel, Francis leaves money with the clerk for her. The final violent scene occurs in a hobo jungle, as it is being raided by Legionnaires. Francis kills Rudy's attacker with his own baseball bat and carries the fatally injured Rudy to the hospital. Returning to the hotel, Francis discovers Helen dead and leaves swiftly in a freight car.

The ending, typical of Kennedy's novels, is inconclusive. The reader can assume either that Francis leaves on a southbound freight or that he returns to his wife Annie's house and lives hidden in the attic. The use of the conditional in narration of this final section lends the necessary vagueness. Nevertheless, in *Ironweed*, the intricacy of poetry combines with factual detail and hallucinatory fugues to create a tight structure, the most nearly perfect of *The Albany Cycle* and its appropriate conclusion. The parallelism, for example, of a discussion of the temptations of Saint Anthony with the name of the Italian Church of St. Anthony, where Helen hears Mass on her last day of life, shows the craftsmanship of the author. The interconnections of theme, plot, and character in the three Albany novels, their hallucinatory fantasies, their ghostly visitations, ennoble the lowest of the low into modern epic heroes.

Kennedy's next novel, *Quinn's Book*, also centers on Albany. Spanning a period from the late 1840's to the mid-1860's, *Quinn's Book* is a historical novel infused with Magical Realism, deliberately extravagant in style. The narrator and protagonist, Daniel Quinn, an orphan, relates his adventures and his gradual progress toward maturity. Ultimately he becomes a writer, encouraged by his editor on the *Albany Chronicle*, Will Canady (whose name suggests that he is the author's alter ego). Coming-of-age tale, picaresque, novel of education, *Künstlerroman*: *Quinn's Book* partakes of all these genres and more, generally stopping just short of parody. It is Kennedy's most explicit celebration of the transformative power of art.

Anne Mills King

Other major works

SHORT FICTION: "The Secrets of Creative Love," 1983; "An Exchange of Gifts," 1985; "A Cataclysm of Love," 1986.

SCREENPLAY: *The Cotton Club*, 1984 (with Francis Coppola and Mario Puzo); *Ironweed*, 1987.

NONFICTION: *Getting It All, Saving It All: Some Notes by an Extremist*, 1978; *O Albany! An Urban Tapestry*, 1983; *Albany and the Capitol*, 1986.

CHILDREN'S LITERATURE: *Charlie Malarkey and the Belly Button Machine*, 1986 (with Brendan Kennedy).

Bibliography

Allen, Douglas R., and Mona Simpson. "The Art of Fiction CXI: William Kennedy." *The Paris Review* 31 (Winter, 1989): 34-59. Conducted in two sessions, in 1984 and 1988, this wide-ranging interview provides an excellent introduction to Kennedy's work. He discusses his experience as a newspaper writer, the vicissitudes of his literary career, and his development as a novelist. Includes Kennedy's observation that he does not regard *Legs*, *Billy Phelan's Greatest Game*, and *Ironweed* as a trilogy but rather as works in an ongoing "cycle" that also comprises *Quinn's Book*.

Clarke, Peter P. "Classical Myth in William Kennedy's *Ironweed*." *Critique: Studies in Modern Fiction* 27 (Spring, 1986): 167. A thorough and interesting study of *Ironweed*, this criticism sees the novel against a mythological backdrop. Compares the hero Francis Phelan to Odysseus; also assigns mythical counterparts to other characters in the novel. Defines the power of *Ironweed* (and its success) in its transformation of "bums into heroes." According to Clarke, this novel is a fine example of how myth is used effectively in fiction.

Cloutier, Candace. "William Kennedy." In *Contemporary Authors*, edited by Linda Metzger. New Revision Series, Detroit, Mich.: Gale Research, 1987. *Ironweed* is given prominence here, although *O Albany!* and *Billy Phelan's Greatest Game* are also mentioned. In addition to a brief chronology on Kennedy, there are extracts from book reviews on various novels. A crisp, efficient, if dull synopsis on Kennedy. Included, however, is an interesting extract from an interview with the author in the *Boston Globe and Mail*, in which Kennedy talks about the "bums" in *Ironweed*.

Nichols, Loxley F. "William Kennedy Comes of Age." *National Review* 27 (August 9, 1985): 78-79. An excellent short piece on Kennedy with much useful information. Discusses *The Ink Truck*, which Nichols considers Kennedy's most atypical work. Also analyzes Jack Diamond's death in Kennedy's second novel, *Legs*. Explores *Ironweed* in the light of its mythical allusions and describes *O Albany!* in terms of the "pervasive vitality of the past."

JACK KEROUAC

Born: Lowell, Massachusetts; March 12, 1922
Died: St. Petersburg, Florida; October 21, 1969

Principal long fiction

The Town and the City, 1950; *On the Road*, 1957; *The Dharma Bums*, 1958; *The Subterraneans*, 1958; *Doctor Sax*, 1959; *Maggie Cassidy*, 1959; *Tristessa*, 1960; *Visions of Cody*, 1960, 1972; *Big Sur*, 1962; *Visions of Gerard*, 1963; *Desolation Angels*, 1965; *Vanity of Duluoz*, 1968; *Pic*, 1971.

Other literary forms

In addition to his novels, Jack Kerouac published *Mexico City Blues* (1959), a poetry collection intended to imitate the techniques of jazz soloists; *Scattered Poems* (1971); and *Old Angel Midnight* (1976), a prose-poem; the latter two were published posthumously. His nonfiction prose includes *The Scripture of the Golden Eternity* (1960), a homemade sutra written to Gary Snyder; *Book of Dreams* (1961), sketches that recorded his dreams; *Lonesome Traveler* (1960), travel sketches; and *Pull My Daisy* (1961), a screenplay based on his abandoned play, *The Beat Generation*.

Achievements

While some critics have condemned Kerouac as an incoherent, unstructured, and unsound writer, the prophet of a nihilistic movement, his books have continued to be read. The very qualities for which he has been criticized—wildness, sensationalism, and irresponsibility—have been sources of charm to other commentators. He has been described on the one hand as pessimistic and bizarre, and on the other as optimistic and fresh. His most prestigious and enthusiastic reviewer has been Malcolm Cowley, who introduced *On the Road* to Viking after it had been turned down by Ace, Harcourt Brace, and Little, Brown. *On the Road* is still in print, and its current respectability is evidenced by its appearance in excerpt form in *The Norton Anthology of American Literature* and its publication as a casebook in The Viking Critical Library series.

Kerouac's unofficial and unwanted title of "King of the Beats" brought him a great deal of the publicity he shunned. As with other aspects of Kerouac's life and works, there was little agreement about what a "Beat" was. Kerouac's friend, Gary Snyder, has described the Beats as a movement that gathered together the myths of freedom espoused by Henry David Thoreau and Walt Whitman, adding some of the notions of Buddhism. John Holmes defined "Beat" as a "nakedness of soul," as "feeling reduced to the bedrock of consciousness." The Beats, he added, recognized the need for home, for values, and for faith, and they advocated companionship, courage, and mutual confidence. To Kerouac, who is generally credited with the invention of the term, "Beat" meant "beatific"—holy and compassionate. Interviewed by Mike Wallace on CBS television, Kerouac declared that the Beats did not fear death and that they wanted to lose themselves as Christ had advised. In *Pageant* magazine, he wrote that the Beats believed that honesty and freedom would lead to a vision of a God of Ecstacy. In a public forum, Kerouac declared that America was changing for the better, and warned those who wanted to spit on the Beat Generation that the wind would blow the spit back on them. Mass media writers developed the image of a bearded "beatnik" who wore sweat shirts and jeans, played bongo drums, never bathed, and used the word "like" as a ubiquitous conjunction. Even though the beatniks were a far cry from the intellectual Beats, they became associated with them in the public eye.

Although Kerouac's public image endangered his critical reception, recent critics have recognized him as a powerful and talented writer. His work, as he intended it to be, is one long opus.

Biography

Jean Louis Lebris de Kerouac was born in Lowell, Massachusetts, on March 12, 1922. His mother, Gabrielle Ange Levesque Kerouac, and his father, Leo Alcide Kerouac, were both French Canadians whose families had emigrated from Quebec. Gabrielle's father, a mill worker and an owner of a small tavern, had died when she was fourteen, and she then went to work as a machine operator in a Nashua shoe shop. From this moment, and for the rest of her life, "Memere" fought for a higher social status. Leo was an insurance salesman who became a job printer. At the time of Kerouac's birth, his sister Caroline ("Nin") was three, and Gerard, the brother who had been weakened by rheumatic fever, was five.

The year after Kerouac's birth, Leo began publication of *The Lowell Spotlight*, which featured local political and theatrical news. The family was very close; the mother was a teller of tales, and the father was an entertainer who specialized in animal noises. At the age of nine, Gerard became so ill that he was forced to remain in bed. To his younger brother, Gerard was a saint who had once saved a mouse from a trap. As Gerard grew weaker, he grew more angelic in the eyes of everyone in the family, and the lively young Kerouac suffered by comparison. As Gerard's pain grew worse, Kerouac began to feel that he was somehow responsible. After Gerard's death, Kerouac tried futilely to replace him by being especially pious and sensitive.

As he grew older, Kerouac went frequently to the movies on passes given to Leo. The public library also became another favorite haunt, but the biggest outside influence on Kerouac's childhood was the Roman Catholic Church of his forefathers. He attended parochial school, had visions of Christ and the Virgin Mary, memorized the catechism, and worried about his sins and purgatory. When he became an alter boy, his Jesuit teachers thought that he might become a priest, but when he entered a public junior high school, Jean Kerouac became "Jacky," who could write, and whose favorite radio program was "The Shadow"—the forerunner of Dr. Sax.

As he walked to Lowell High School, where he participated in track and football, Kerouac saw the factories and the failures of his French-Canadian neighbors; his father had lost his business and had even been forced to accept a job carrying water buckets for the Works Progress Administration (WPA). Memere, frustrated in her everpresent ambitions, placed all her hopes in her remaining son and urged him to study and to succeed in a way that his father had not. By his senior year, Kerouac was a football star, scoring the winning touchdown for Lowell in the final game against Lawrence High.

Kerouac fell in love with Mary Carney, but he left her behind to accept Columbia University football coach Lou Little's offer to attend Horace Mann Prep School, where he was to add the pounds and knowledge requisite for a Columbia football player. At Horace Mann, Jack wrote papers for his class-mates for pay, some of which he spent on his first prostitute. He published short stories in the *Horace Mann Quarterly*, discovered the jazz world in Harlem, and adopted Whitman as his personal bard.

At Columbia, Kerouac studied William Shakespeare under Mark Van Doren, registered for the draft, found another mentor in the works of Thomas Wolfe, and broke his leg in a freshman football game. One day, to the great distress of his parents, who constantly pleaded with him to "get ahead" in the world, Kerouac left Columbia for Washington, D.C., New Haven, and Hartford, Connecticut, and a series of short-lived jobs. While he was a sports-writer for the *Lowell Sun*, he read Fyodor Dostoevski; who became his prophet. He shipped out of Boston as a merchant seaman on the *Dorchester*, where he started a novel called *The Sea Is My Brother*. In 1943, he entered the navy, which discharged him honorably three months later for "indifferent character." In 1944, Kerouac met Allen Ginsberg, a Columbia student until he was banned from campus, and William S. Burroughs, with whom he wrote a detective story. He also met Edie Parker, whom he married but from whom he separated shortly thereafter.

After his father died of cancer in 1946, Kerouac started taking Benzedrine and writing *The Town and the City*. He also met Neal Cassady, the "brother" he had been seeking since Gerard's death. After Cassady returned to Denver, Kerouac set out to see America, stopping in Denver before going to San Francisco, where he worked as a security guard, sending his savings to Me-mere. On a bus bound for Los Angeles, he met Bea Franco, with whom he took a job in Bakersfield picking cotton. From there, he took a bus to Pitts-burgh and hitched a ride back to Memere's house, where she took care of him while he wrote. Cassady came East again, and he, Kerouac, and Cassady's first wife Lu Anne made their famous "on the road" trip.

At this time, Harcourt Brace announced that they would publish *The Town and the City*. Kerouac used the profits from *The Town and the City* to buy a house for Memere in Colorado, but she left it for New York after seven weeks of misery. Several journeys back and forth from Brooklyn to Colorado followed for Cassady and Kerouac. In 1950, Kerouac married Joan Haverty and began writing *On the Road*, typing it on rolls of teletype paper. In 1952, Janet Michele Kerouac was born to Joan, but it would be ten years before Kerouac admitted paternity.

Kerouac held jobs during the next few years as a brakeman, as a yard clerk, and as a fire watcher, but he depended mostly on his mother for support, despite the gnawing recollection that he had promised his father to take care of her. In 1955, he attended the poetry reading of his six friends held at the Six Gallery in San Francisco. After several rejections, *On the Road* was published in 1957 and was hailed by *The New York Times* critic Gilbert Millstein as a major novel. Within the next six years, Kerouac published twelve more books.

While Kerouac was in New York, he fell in love with Mardou Fox, whose American Indian and black ancestry Memere could never accept. After losing Mardou to the poet Gregory Corso, Kerouac wrote about the affair in *The Subterraneans*. In response to William Burroughs' request, Kerouac typed out "The Essentials of Spontaneous Prose," explaining the writing method he had used.

Kerouac found solace in *Walden: Or, Life in the Woods* (1854) and Thoreau, with whom he shared a rejection of civilization, and he also began to study Buddhism as part of his search for peace from the carping of Memere and the disappointments engendered by nonsympathetic editors. He tried to convert the Cassadys, with whom he lived for a time in California, to Buddhism, but he also expressed to Ginsberg, once more in New York, his fear that charlatans might misuse Buddhism for aesthetic purposes. He meditated daily in an effort to reach Nirvana. When he met poet Gary Snyder, a Zen Buddhist whose approach was prayerful, Kerouac felt a harmony he had not known, even with Cassady.

By the time Kerouac married Stella Sampas, the sister of an old friend who was killed in the war, and settled down again in Lowell, he was suffering from three problems: recurring phlebitis, a dependency upon alcohol, particularly wine, and the adulation of youngsters who invaded his privacy and made him feel old. They expected him to be Dean Moriarity of *On the Road*, but his aging, alcoholic body rebelled.

Meanwhile, Cassady had been arrested for possession of marijuana and sentenced to San Quentin, whence he complained about Kerouac's lack of attention. After his release, Cassady drank tequila and swallowed Seconals at a Mexican wedding party; the combination caused his death. Kerouac never allowed himself to believe that Cassady was actually dead. In October, 1969,

Kerouac's years of heavy drinking caused him to begin to bleed internally, and he died hours later. He had been, in spite of his bizarre habits, a gentle, loving man.

Analysis

Jack Kerouac described himself as "a great rememberer redeeming life from darkness." In one sense, the Beat movement itself issued from his memory. In his June, 1959, *Playboy* essay on "The Origins of the Beat Generation," Kerouac claimed that the guts of the Beats had come from his ancestors: the independent Breton nobles who fought against the Latin French; his grandfather, Jean-Baptiste Kerouac, who used to defy God to put out his kerosene lamp during a thunderstorm; his father, who used to give such loud parties that the Lowell police came for drinks; and from his own childhood—peopled with the Shadow, the Moon Man, and the Marx Brothers.

Kerouac claimed on more than one occasion that his books were actually one book about his entire life. He had intentions to consolidate them, but these plans were not carried out before his death. The areas of life that he remembered and celebrated include the dichotomy between his family and friends in Lowell, Massachusetts, and the Beat friends with whom he carried on such a frenzied, peripatetic relationship. As a rememberer, he never separated the two entirely; the Roman Catholic Bretons and the gentle Leo and Gerard were never far from his consciousness. Kerouac declared that his father had never lifted a hand to punish his children, or even their little pets, and that Gerard had extracted from his younger brother a promise never to hurt or allow anyone else to hurt a living thing. These two strains—the fierceness of the Bretons and the gentleness of his brother and father—culminated in the vitality and the kindness of Jack Kerouac, the ex-football player who cared so much for his pets as a grown man that his mother feared to tell him that his cat had died.

When he was ready to write his first published book, *The Town and the City*, Kerouac found it necessary—or more aesthetically pleasing—to use five boys to present the many facets of his own character. The Kerouac family became the Martins, and Lowell became Galloway, which had a rural settng. The Martins are wealthier than the author's own family; they are also less devout as Catholics. The mother is French, and the rest of the family is Irish. Most of the vignettes serve to illustrate the love that the Martins feel for one another, and Galloway was a town of "wild, self-believing individuals," the kind about which Walt Whitman sang.

The style of the novel is romantic and sprawling, in the vein of Thomas Wolfe. While Kerouac possessed an almost uncanny aptitude for recollecting details, he enhanced his memory by reviewing his old notebooks. The book was to be more than a chronicle of the Martin-Kerouac family; it was to be a microcosm of America. There are three sisters and five brothers in the Martin family, as opposed to the daughter and two sons of the Kerouacs; the loving, compassionate Mrs. Martin recalls Kerouac's own mother. Mickey, the youngest child of the Martins, goes to dinner and the races with his father, just as the young Jack had gone to Rockingham with Leo. He also writes novels and publishes newspapers about his imaginary racehorses and baseball teams.

Two of the sisters, Rose and Ruth, have the characteristics of Kerouac's sister Nin, while the third, Liz, is more like Kerouac's high school sweetheart, Mary Carney. One story of sibling love involves Charley, who had broken a window with his slingshot and is collecting junk to pay for it. Liz and Joe pitch in to help him when they learn of his plight. Liz eventually elopes with a jazz musician, has a stillborn baby, divorces her husband, and becomes a blonde barmaid.

The central character, Peter, is thirteen when the novel begins, and the story of his most spectacular high school game is that of his creator. As a result of his prowess, Peter wins a football scholarship to the University of Pennsylvania, but he leaves to join the merchant marines. As a student, however, he meets a new circle of friends, whose habits dismay George Martin just as Kerouac's marijuana-smoking cronies had bewildered Leo. Peter tries to introduce his mistress Judie to his parents, but their meeting is interrupted by a policeman who wants Peter to identify the body of Waldo Meister, a suicide victim. The gulf between the Martin family and Peter's friends is never closed, but Peter continues to be a loving part of both groups. He nurses his father during his illness and reacts to his death with grief and disbelief.

Peter's brother Francis is a shy, studious Harvard student who fails the Officers' Candidate School aptitude test and rebels at being a soldier. When he is confined for tests, he spots a navy psychiatrist with *The New Republic* under his arm and decides that he has met a kindred spirit. Convinced that Francis is indeed incapable of taking orders, the doctor helps him obtain his discharge.

In one scene, Levinsky (the Allen Ginsberg character) lectures to Peter in a Times Square cafeteria about a "post-atomic" disease of the soul, using words taken from an actual essay by Ginsberg (with permission from Ginsberg).

The novel ends with an unhappy Peter heading West to a new life, on a lonely, rainy night. The family has figuratively died with the father, and Peter will go wherever the roads lead. According to John Clellon Holmes, the book had originally ended with the family together, and the "on the road" ending was a last-minute Kerouac addition, which would lead obviously and naturally into his next book, already in the planning stage.

The Town and the City is frequently compared with Thomas Wolfe's *Look Homeward, Angel* (1929), and, like Wolfe's book, it required considerable editing, which was accomplished by Robert Giroux, who cut one third of the manuscript. In spite of its lukewarm success, Kerouac continued to believe in his own genius. Years later, he learned that the Kerouac family crest included the motto (translated from the French), "Love, Work, and Suffer." He happily noted that these words accurately describe the Martin family.

Both the title and the novel were incubating in Kerouac's mind for four years before he sat down to write *On the Road* on a one-hundred-foot roll of paper, in one 120,000 word, single-spaced paragraph. Six more years passed before its publication, and in the decade between conception and birth, America had changed, and so had the writer.

Sal Paradise, the narrator and the Kerouac figure, received his name when Ginsberg wrote a poem containing the line, "Sad paradise it is I imitate." The carelessly written "d" caused "Sad" to look like "Sal." Sal, whose ideals are both romantic and personal, sets out near the beginning of the tale to search for an Eden. He is at the same time leaving behind all intimacy and responsibility associated with home and family.

Like Geoffrey Chaucer's pilgrims, everyone Sal meets is described with superlatives: he hears "the greatest laugh in the world; he observes the most smiling, cheerful face in the world, and he watches a tall Mexican roll the biggest bomber anybody ever saw. While observing these fellow pilgrims, he thinks of himself and his friends as seeking salvation and the promised land. Sal expects to find a direction and purpose on the road that his life has not previously had.

Sal has studied maps of the West, and when he begins his trip, he wants to repeat as closely as possible the path of the old wagon trains. He glories in the names of such cities as Platte and Cimarron and imagines that the unbroken red line that represents Route 6 on his map duplicates the trail of the early American settlers. After a false start on a rainy day, Sal returns to New York, where he had started, and buys a bus ticket to Chicago; the bus is a mode of travel he uses more than once. In Des Moines, Sal awakens nameless and reborn in what seems to be a turning point in his life. This moment that divides his youth from his future occurs, fittingly enough, in mid-America. He goes from Denver to California, where he meets Dean Moriarity, the central figure of the book and the figure that made Neal Cassady a legend.

Moriarity becomes a part of Sal's life, an extension of his personality, his alter ego; he even insists on sharing his wife with Sal. Three become a crowd, however, and Sal, after several digressions, goes back to the East and his aunt. On the last lap of the journey, he meets a shriveled old man with a paper suitcase who is called "Ghost of the Susquehanna." Sal sees him as an aging reflection of what he himself will become—a bum.

The energy of the book derives from Dean Moriarity, who is never far out of Sal's mind. Dean's accomplishments include skillful driving—often of cars he has stolen for a joyride—talking his way out of any tight situation, seducing women—frequently two at a time—and appreciating jazz. The friends Dean has met in pool halls become the minor heroes of this epic.

In Kerouac's mind, Cassady and America were one entity—vibrant, care-free, and admirable. Through Moriarity, Kerouac chronicles a new kind of existence in postwar America—suggesting a life less dependent upon place and family and more tolerant of impropriety. The hedonist Moriarity loves and leaves his women in the manner of the stereotyped cowboy who rides off into the sunset. Moriarity, never complacent, ever free, can be charac-terized by the fact that he goes to answer his door completely naked. Even when he is employed and has a home address, he seems to be on the move; he is always planning a break from entanglements, often represented by whomever his current wife might be.

Sal sees himself as a disciple to the saint, Moriarity, and he exults in Dean's uniqueness and eccentricity. Dean's mysticism consists of belief in his father, in God, and IT, which can be communicated by jazz musicians and which has somehow been communicated to Dean through his missing father, who had been a drunk. The search for Dean's father is one of the book's themes, along with the search for God. The roaders are seeking someone to shelter them from life and responsibility, and they approve of those pilgrims (Montana Slim and Remi Boncoeur) who are respectful toward their own fathers.

Perhaps the story would not have been told if Moriarity had not been such an extraordinary driver, absolutely at home on the road. Sal has no driver's license and when allowed at the wheel guides the car off the road and onto a muddy shoulder. Even though Dean's chief contribution to the conversation seems to be "Wow," he expresses himself eloquently while in control of a car. Never mind if he wears it out; he delivers the car exhausted to its owner, while he travels on jauntily in another vehicle willing to respond to his touch.

Women respond to Dean in the same way, and he sees sex as essential and holy. His problem is that he wants to love several women simultaneously. He sees them as part of his self-improvement schedule, which is not induced by remorse for crimes committed or prison terms spent, but by the demands imposed by his search for a better life. Sal forgives Dean his thefts and other transgressions, reasoning that all Americans are like that.

On the Road is a love story: Sal loves Dean Moriarity, and their movements back and forth across the continent represent in some ways their relationship. Sal sees Dean at first as a source of hope, and he moves toward him, fasci-nated. He finally assumes some of the responsibility for his friend, and he becomes his defender. After Dean's thumb becomes infected as a result of hitting one of his women, Sal sees him as a mad Ahab. When Dean, Sal, and a friend go to Mexico City, on what is significantly their first North-South journey, Sal becomes ill and is abandoned by Dean, who has to go home to straighten out one of his recurring domestic crises. Sal never denies Dean, but he is less enamored of his sometimes childish friend by the book's end.

Most of the characters Sal meets on the road are attractive in some way; as Huck Finn found people on the river to be sympathetic, Sal feels a communion with the hobos, who eschew competition and jobs for a sense of brotherhood and a simple life. He is disappointed, however, when he sees his first cowboy, whose apparel is his only claim to authenticity. Like Stephen Crane before him, Sal sees that the West is merely trying to perpetuate dead traditions, and that Central City is simply a tourist attraction. Nothing can be as fine as his dreams of the West, and he eventually begins to conclude that the East, after all, may be the place to find contentment and salvation. He returns home in his favorite month of October, realizing that he has acted out an adventure, but that he has experienced no rebirth.

The point of view of *On the Road* is consistently that of Sal, but as he tells the reader about his experiences as they occurred at the time, he also comments on the same events as he sees them now, with a more mature, more disillusioned, more objective eye. Saddened by the realization that the road itself is all-important to Dean, he repudiates the idea of movement with no purpose.

Recognizing the vastness and shapelessness of the experience he was about to put on paper, Kerouac sought a suitable form and style. He began to write the book in a conscious imitation of Thomas Wolfe, but he finally decided to emulate Cassady's amorphous, joyous style. He added to that a new, free-association method that he called "sketching," suggested to him by Ed White, who thought it possible to paint with words. Sketching, comparable in Kerouac's view to the improvisation of the jazz musicians he greatly admired, was new, but the story he told was a repetition of the ageless initiation theme. *On the Road* is, however, not simply another *Tom Jones* (Henry Fielding, 1749) or *The Adventures of Huckleberry Finn* (Mark Twain, 1884); it reflects the confusion, the sense of search, and the troubled spirit of the Kerouac generation.

The title of *The Subterraneans* comes from Ginsberg's name for Greenwich Villagers; its setting is New York, disguised with San Francisco place-names. Kerouac claimed that the book is a full confession of the incidents surrounding his love affair with Mardou Fox, a part black, part Indian subterranean who had been hanging out with junkies and musicians. Kerouac fell in love with her, he said, even before they were introduced.

The book, consciously modeled after Fyodor Dostoevski's *Notes from the Underground* (1864), contains Mardou's private thoughts as she has whispered them to Leo Percipied (the Kerouac figure). She imagines herself walking naked in the Village, crouching like a feline on a fence experiencing a private epiphany, and then borrowing clothes and money to buy herself a symbolic brooch.

Leo (as Kerouac himself always did) sympathizes with minority races and listens to Mardou's thoughts about blacks, Indians, and America with a keen perception. The story carries Leo and Mardou on their frenzied movements through the Village in scenes that include meetings with bop musicians, poets, and novelists. A central scene describes Yuri Gligoric's (Gregory Corso) theft of a vendor's pushcart, in which he transports his friends to the home of Adam Moorad (Allen Ginsberg), who is angry at Yuri because of the prank.

Both Mardou and Leo become dissatisfied with their life together, and when Yuri and Leo bicker over her, Leo chooses the incident as an excuse to separate from Mardou. Afterward, he wanders alone to a freight yard, where he has a vision of his mother. Leo finally admits that he felt inadequate sexually in the presence of Mardou, and he concludes, "I go home, having lost her love, and write this book."

Fortified by Benzedrine, Kerouac sat at his typewriter with yet another teletype roll and wrote his confession in "three full moon nights of October." The style of the novel is remarkable for its faithful reproduction of Mardou's syntax and her drawn-out syllables. Kerouac heard in her speech a similarity to bop music, and he found in it what he called the "prose of the future." Impressed by this remarkable language, Burroughs and Ginsberg asked Kerouac to write a description of his spontaneous method of composition, and the result was the essay "The Essentials of Spontaneous Prose."

Reviews of *The Subterraneans* were not favorable. The only affirmation came from Henry Miller, who admired Kerouac's forthrightness. When an editor tried to cut some of the book, Kerouac refused to let him print it, and it was finally published in its original form in March of 1958.

The Dharma Bums, a book which Kerouac himself once described as a potboiler, is perhaps the most representative expression of the Beat sensibility in a work of fiction. Its focus is the close intellectual and religious relationship of Ray Smith (Kerouac) and Japhy Ryder (Gary Snyder). Snyder called *The Dharma Bums* a real statement of synthesis, through Kerouac, of the available models and myths of freedom in America: Whitman, Thoreau, and the bums—with Buddhism added as a catalyst. Unlike *The Subterraneans*, *The Dharma Bums* is not purely confessional, and the literary hand is much more evident in the later work. For example, the author includes an encounter on a freight train with a bum who reads daily the prayers of St. Theresa, who had been much beloved by Kerouac himself since childhood. He includes this character because the ascetic hobo adds to the book's religious ambience, but he pointedly omits mention of a meeting with an earthy, blonde female that occurred the same day and is recounted in his notebook.

Ray Smith remembers an evening of peaceful happiness when he and Japhy sat together on a big glacial rock, elated, hallucinated, yet serious, and surrounded by yellow aspens. It was a cold evening in late autumn, and snow was on the ridges. It was on such an evening that Smith earned the sobriquet of the "Buddha Known as the Quitter," because he failed to climb a mountain.

Ryder is another kind of coward. Because he has been a "poor guy" all of his life, he is afraid to enter a restaurant that might have an expensive menu.

The picture of Japhy is painted through faithful reproduction of Gary Snyder's speech and recollections of his poetry. The haiku Japhy composes on the mountainside are repeated verbatim, and one poem addressed to Sean Monahan (actually written by Snyder to Kerouac) is stuck on a nail of his cabin. Monahan is a twenty-two-year-old carpenter whose wife is adept at keeping him and their two children alive and happy on vegetable soup. The Monahans' life is described as "joyous," and they live in their woodland cottage furnished with Japanese straw mats, while they amuse themselves by studying sutras.

The way of life to which Ryder introduces Smith is a religious way, punctuated with prayer, laughter, and poetry, and it is espoused by the social minority who belong to the rucksack revolution. Both Smith and Ryder long to explain the Dharma, or the truth of religion and life, to others. The Dharma is associated with a nobility of body, mind, spirit, and speech that is surely worthy of their missionary zeal, if it can be attained.

Through Ryder, Smith learns of ecology and earth consciousness. The two discuss their own private religious beliefs. After he learns about the life-style of the "rucksack saints" through observation and listening, Smith delineates the mode of living for any would-be followers, listing the spiritual and physical equipment necessary: submission, acceptance, expectancy, rucksacks, tents, and sleeping bags.

Three books, then, shaped Kerouac's public image: *On the Road*, *The Subterraneans*, and *The Dharma Bums*. Each of them centers on a close relationship between a Kerouac figure and another person, and in each case, an intense dependency is involved. All are testaments of love; all concern America and Americans; all suggest an opportunity to develop emotional maturity, and all describe the existence of a subculture which anticipated the "counterculture" of the 1960's. Yet despite these similarities, there is a progression. Certainly Ray Smith of *The Dharma Bums* is a wiser figure than Sal Paradise of *On the Road*. Smith admires Japhy Ryder, who teaches him about faith, hope, and charity, whereas Sal had worshiped Dean Moriarity, whose human relationships—especially with women—had been characterized by thoughtlessness and selfishness, for all of his charm. Ryder studies Japanese and reads Ezra Pound, whereas Moriarity had parroted Arthur Schopenhauer, often without understanding. The Buddhist sympathy for all beings and the notion that man is but a speck in the universe are a contrast to Moriarity's selfishness and vanity. In Gary Snyder, the gentle Jack Kerouac found the brother he had lost, and *The Dharma Bums* offers a calmer, more benevolent, albeit less sweeping picture of the country Kerouac wanted his works to celebrate than does the more famous *On the Road*.

Sue L. Kimball

Other major works

POETRY: *Mexico City Blues*, 1959; *Scattered Poems*, 1971; *Old Angel Midnight*, 1976.

NONFICTION: *Lonesome Traveler*, 1960; *The Scripture of the Golden Eternity*, 1960; *Book of Dreams*, 1961; *Satori in Paris*, 1966.

Bibliography

Cassady, Carolyn. *Heart Beat: My Life with Jack and Neal.* Berkeley: Creative Arts, 1976. Chronicles Cassady's relationship with Kerouac from 1952 through 1953, and the *ménage à trois* between the Cassadys and Kerouac. Reprinted here are letters of Allen Ginsberg, Kerouac, Neal Cassady, and Carolyn Cassady.

—————. *Off the Road: My Years with Cassady, Kerouac, and Ginsberg.* New York: William Morrow, 1990. A personal account, with many anecdotes and recollections written from Carolyn Cassady's perspective. Important for its inside view of the Beat movement.

Hart, John E. "Future Hero in Paradise: Kerouac's *The Dharma Bums*." *Critique: Studies in Modern Fiction* 14, no. 3 (1973): 52-62. This critical essay acknowledges the spontaneity for which Kerouac has been praised and ridiculed, but emphasizes the classical structure of *The Dharma Bums*, arguing that it has been carefully thought out. Discusses at length the novel's hero, Ray Smith, noting the autobiographical elements. Hart calls the novel both "personal and universal," which gives it a classical framework.

Montgomery, John. *Jack Kerouac.* Fresno, Calif.: Giligia Press, 1970. A short biography of Kerouac which also discusses some of his novels, including *The Dharma Bums, On the Road*, and *Desolation Angels.*

Nicosia, Gerald. *Memory Babe: A Critical Biography of Jack Kerouac.* New York: Grove Press, 1983. A comprehensive, biographical account of Kerouac's life. Highly regarded for background information on Kerouac and the process of his writing.

KEN KESEY

Born: La Junta, Colorado; September 17, 1935

Principal long fiction
One Flew over the Cuckoo's Nest, 1962; *Sometimes a Great Notion*, 1964.

Other literary forms
When Stewart Brand was the editor of *The Last Whole Earth Catalog* in 1971, he asked Ken Kesey to edit *The Last Supplement to the Whole Earth Catalog*. Somewhat reluctant, Kesey agreed if Paul Krassner would be the coeditor. Krassner accepted, and it took almost two months to write, edit, and lay out the five-hundred-page final issue, which contained the best selections from previous issues as well as some new writings by Kesey. The final issue had a total press run of 100,000 copies and is now out of print.

Viking Press and Intrepid Trips jointly published *Kesey's Garage Sale* (1973), a volume based on an American phenomenon: the rummage, yard, or garage sale. The book is a miscellany of essays, poetry, letters, drawings, interviews, prose fiction, and a film script. Although much of the writing was Kesey's, "Hot Item Number 4: Miscellaneous Section with Guest Leftovers" contained a letter by Neal Cassady and poems by Allen Ginsberg and Hugh Romney. Kesey's "Who Flew over What," "Over the Border," and "Tools from My Chest" supply interesting insights into Kesey's beliefs and personality, and more important, they supplement the biographical details in Tom Wolfe's *The Electric Kool-Aid Acid Test* (1968), an informative biographical account of Kesey's Merry Pranksters exploits.

In "Who Flew over What," Kesey answers some of the most common questions about *One Flew over the Cuckoo's Nest*. He admitted that he wrote the novel while a night attendant at the Menlo Park Veterans Hospital, that he wrote part of it while under the influence of drugs, and that Randle Patrick McMurphy, the protagonist, was a fictional character "inspired by the tragic longing of the real men" on the ward. Kesey not only included his only sketches of McMurphy but also provided interesting facts and insights to his job and the actual life on the ward.

"Over the Border" is an innovative film script based on Kesey's second arrest, his flight to Mexico, the arrival of his family and some of the Merry Pranksters, their sojourn in Mexico, and the decision to return to the United States. The characters are easily recognizable: Devlin and Betsy Deboree are Kesey and his wife Faye; Sir Speed Houlihan is Neal Cassady; Claude and Blanch Muddle are Ken Babbs and his wife Anita; the Animal Friends are the Merry Pranksters; Behema is Carolyn Adams. The script contains examples of Kesey's writing techniques, especially as he switches from scene to scene, as he describes the annual land-crab migration, and as he narrates Deboree's encounter with the Lizard, a Federales prison guard. Augmenting Wolfe's biographical account, the script also reveals Kesey's altered attitudes toward drugs as a means of changing society.

Another interesting section is "Tools from My Chest," parts of which were published originally in either *The Last Whole Earth Catalog* or *The Last Supplement to the Whole Earth Catalog*. These "tools" were figuratively those persons and things that had an impact on Kesey's own life and beliefs and, ultimately, on his writings. Kesey commented on such things as the Bible, the I Ching, mantras, the North Star, alcohol, and flowers; about such writers as Ernest Hemingway, William Faulkner (Kesey's declared favorite), Larry McMurtry, and William Burroughs; about radicals such as Malcolm X and Eldridge Cleaver; about entertainers such as Woody Guthrie, Joan Baez, the Jefferson Airplane, and the Beatles. Finally, there are two powerfully written parables about Devlin Deboree.

Another miscellany, *Demon Box*, was published in 1986, and in 1990 Kesey and thirteen of his students published a collaborative novel, *Caverns*, under the pseudonym O. U. Levon. *The Further Inquiry*, also published in 1990, recounts the Merry Pranksters' 1964 cross-country bus trip and memorializes Neal Cassady.

Achievements

Tom Wolfe remarked that Kesey was one of the most charismatic men he had ever met, and others have likewise commented upon Kesey's charisma. In fact, social critics affirmed that there were two important leaders of the 1960 counterculture revolution: Timothy Leary and his devotees on the East Coast and Kesey and his Merry Pranksters on the West Coast. Leary and his Leary-ites took themselves seriously, advocated passively dropping out of society, and rejected much that was American, especially American gadgetry. In contrast, Kesey and his Merry Pranksters were pro-America, were more interested in the spontaneous fun of the twentieth century neon renaissance, and took LSD, not to become societal dropouts, but rather to lead society to new frontiers of social communality.

As a novelist, Kesey achieved both notoriety and distinction as a major voice of his generation. Yet some critics argue that his achievement goes further. They point to his complex characters, rollicking humor, and creative manipulation of point of view as Kesey's enduring contribution to American literature.

Biography

Ken Elton Kesey was born in La Junta, Colorado, on September 17, 1935, to Fred A. and Geneva Smith Kesey. Kesey's father shrewdly foresaw that the West Coast would be ideal for business ventures, and he moved his family to

Springfield, Oregon, where he founded the Eugene Farmers Cooperative, the largest and most successful dairy cooperative in the Willamette Valley. The father taught his sons, Ken and Joe—the latter being called Chuck—how to box, wrestle, hunt, fish, swim, and how to float the Willamette and McKenzie rivers on inner-tube rafts.

After attending the Springfield public schools and being voted most likely to succeed, Kesey enrolled in the University of Oregon at Eugene. In 1956, he married his high school sweetheart, Faye Haxby. During his undergraduate years, Kesey was an adept actor and seriously considered pursuing that career. He was also a champion wrestler in the 174-pound division and almost qualified for the Olympics. He received his Bachelor of Arts degree in 1957, and wrote *End of Autumn*, an unpublished novel about college athletics. In 1958, he enrolled in the graduate school at Stanford University on a creative writing scholarship and studied under Malcolm Cowley, Wallace Stegner, Frank O'Connor, and James B. Hall.

During his graduate years, two important things occurred which would influence Kesey's life and writing. The first occurred when he moved his family into one of the cottages on Perry Lane, then the bohemian quarters of Stanford. He met other writers, including Larry McMurtry, Kenneth Babbs, Robert Stone, and Neal Cassady. The second event was that Kesey met Vic Lovell, to whom he would dedicate *One Flew over the Cuckoo's Nest*. Lovell not only introduced Kesey to Freudian psychology but also told Kesey about the drug experiments at the veterans' hospital in Menlo Park, California. In 1960, Kesey volunteered, earned twenty dollars per session, and discovered mind-expanding drugs which included Ditran, IT-290, and LSD. Kesey thus experienced LSD two years before Timothy Leary and Richard Alpert began their experiment at Harvard. Lovell also suggested that Kesey become a night attendant on the Menlo Park Veterans Hospital psychiatric ward so that he could concentrate on his writing. While a night aide, Kesey completed "Zoo," an unpublished novel about San Francisco's North Beach. Kesey became intensely interested, however, in the patients and their life on the ward, and he began writing *One Flew over the Cuckoo's Nest* during the summer of 1960 and completed it in the spring of 1961. More important, as a volunteer and an aide, Kesey stole all types of drugs—especially LSD—which he distributed to his Perry Lane friends.

In June, 1961, Kesey moved his family to Springfield, Oregon, to help his brother start the Springfield Creamery and to save enough money for researching his next novel. Having saved enough money, the Kesey family moved to Florence, Oregon, fifty miles west of Springfield, and Kesey began gathering material for *Sometimes a Great Notion*. His research included riding in the pickup trucks, called "crummies," which bussed the loggers to and from the logging sites. At night Kesey frequented the bars where the loggers drank, talked, and relaxed.

One Flew over the Cuckoo's Nest was published in 1962 and was critically acclaimed. In the late spring of 1962 the Kesey family returned to Perry Lane, where he began writing his second novel and where he renewed his drug experiments. When a developer bought the Perry Lane area for a housing development, Kesey purchased a home and land in La Honda, California, and invited a dozen or so of his closest Perry Lane friends to join him so that they could continue their drug experiments. This group would eventually become Kesey's famous Merry Pranksters or the Day-Glo Crazies.

Sometimes a Great Notion was scheduled for publication in July, 1964, and Kesey and Ken Babbs, who had just returned from Vietnam, had planned a trip to the New York World's Fair to arrive there for the publication of Kesey's second novel. Kesey bought a converted 1939 International Harvester school bus for the trip; it had all the conveniences for on-the-road living. The trip mushroomed and was the final impetus for forming the Merry Pranksters. Besides painting the bus various psychedelic colors, the Pranksters wired it with microphones, amplifiers, speakers, recorders, and motion-picture equipment: the sign on the front proclaimed "Further" (sic), and the sign on the back warned: "Caution: Weird Load." Prior to departing for New York, Kesey established the only rules for the trip—everyone would "do his own thing," would "go with the flow," and not condemn anyone else for being himself. As an adjunct to the trip, the Pranksters recorded their entire odyssey on tape and film, which would eventually become a film entitled "The Movie," the first acid film recorded live and spontaneously. When the journey ended, there were more than forty-five hours of color film, large portions of which were out of focus, an obvious effect of the drugs. Kesey devoted much of the 1964 spring and the 1965 fall to editing the film.

On April 23, 1965, federal narcotic agents and deputies raided Kesey's La Honda commune. Out of the seventeen people arrested, only Kesey and Page Browning were officially charged with possession of marijuana. When the San Francisco newspapers proclaimed Kesey as a great writer, new leader, and a visionary, Kesey became a celebrity, and people flocked to his La Honda commune. Jerry Rubin and the Vietnam Day Committee even invited him to speak at an antiwar rally at Berkeley in October, 1965. After the fiery speeches the protesters would march *en masse* to the Oakland Army Terminal and close it down. Waiting his turn to speak, Kesey realized that the speaker before him sounded like the Italian dictator Benito Mussolini, and Kesey was appalled. When he spoke, Kesey told the audience simply to turn their backs on the Vietnam War, and then he played "Home on the Range" on his harmonica. Instead of inciting the crowd, Kesey's speech had the opposite effect, and the march ended quietly in the Berkeley Civic Center Park.

Kesey later met August Owsley Stanley III, who was known as the "Ford of LSD" because he was the first mass manufacturer of quality LSD; this was, of course, before LSD was officially declared illegal. With unlimited supplies of LSD, Kesey and his Merry Pranksters could conduct their famous "Can You Pass the Acid Test" experiments. Amid rock music, Day-Glo decorations, strobe lights, and reels from "The Movie," the Pranksters invited everyone—the straight people and the hippies—to come and try LSD.

While Kesey's lawyers were fighting the original possession charge, he was arrested in San Francisco on January 10, 1966, again for possession of marijuana; the second arrest carried an automatic five-year sentence without parole. After a clumsily planned suicide hoax (Kesey was high on drugs), he fled to Mexico and was later joined by his family and some of his Prankster friends.

Tired of being a fugitive and of life in Mexico, Kesey disguised himself and entered the United States at Brownsville, Texas. Arrested by the FBI in San Francisco on October 20, 1966, Kesey was tried twice in San Francisco, once on November 30, 1966, and again in April, 1967; both trials ended in hung juries. His lawyers appealed a *nolo contendere* sentence of ninety days, but Kesey dropped the appeal and served his sentence, first at the San Mateo Jail and then at the San Mateo County Sheriff's Honor Camp. He completed his sentence in November, 1967.

In 1968, Kesey moved his family to Pleasant Hill, Oregon, where he began a book based on his jail experiences; the book, "Cut the Mother-Fuckers Loose," was never published. In August, 1968, Tom Wolfe's *The Electric Kool-Aid Acid Test* was published, and also during this year some of Kesey's letters and other writings appeared in underground publications. Between March and June, 1969, he lived in London and wrote for *Apple*. He also revised the play version of *One Flew over the Cuckoo's Nest*, which had opened in New York but had closed after only eighty-five performances. Early in 1970, however, Lee D. Sandowich, a prominent figure in San Francisco theater circles, saw an amateur production of the play, decided it had potential, and professionally produced the play again at the Little Fox Theatre in San Francisco, where it was a success; the play reopened successfully in a New York off-Broadway theater. During 1971, Kesey, Babbs, and Paul Foster edited selections for *Kesey's Garage Sale*, and in the spring of 1971, Kesey and Krassner coedited *The Last Supplement to the Whole Earth Catalog*. Late in 1971, the film version of *Sometimes a Great Notion* was released.

In 1974, Kesey was instrumental in organizing the Bend in the River Council, a unique people-politics experiment based on the concept of a town meeting. The council featured about two hundred delegates and various experts who discussed a variety of environmental issues in a forum carried on both radio and television, and listeners telephoned their comments and votes on certain issues. In 1976, the film version of *One Flew over the Cuckoo's Nest* was released. During 1978, Kesey edited a magazine called *Spit in the Ocean,* in which he serialized portions of a work-in-progress, a novel entitled "Seven Prayers by Grandma Whittier." Devlin Deboree is a secondary character in the work. He remained content to work on his Pleasant Hill, Oregon, farm and produce his yogurt, which was marketed in Oregon, Washington, and northern California. In the 1980's, a three-term teaching assignment with graduate students in the creative writing program at the University of Oregon resulted in the collaborative novel *Caverns* (1990).

Analysis

To understand some of the ideas behind the counterculture revolution is to understand Ken Kesey's fictional heroes and some of his themes. Originating with the 1950 Beat generation, the 1960 counterculture youth were disillusioned with the vast social injustices, the industrialization, and the mass society image in their parents' world; they questioned many values and practices—the Vietnam War, the goals of higher education, the value of owning property, and the traditional forms of work. They protested by experimenting with Eastern meditation, primitive communal living, unabashed nudity, and nonpossessive physical and spiritual love. At the core of the protest was the value of individual freedom. One of the main avenues to this new type of life and freedom was mind-expanding drugs, which allowed them to *grok*, a word from Robert A. Heinlein's *Stranger in a Strange Land* (1961) which means to achieve a calm ecstasy, to contemplate the present moment. In that it emphasized some major problems in the United States, the counterculture had its merits, but it was, at best, a child's romantic dreamworld, inevitably doomed, because it did not consider answers to the ultimate question: "After the drugs, what is next?"

From Kesey's counterculture experiences, however, he learned at least two important lessons. First, he learned that drugs were not the answer to changing society and that one cannot passively drop out of life. In "Over the Border," for example, Deboree realizes, as he bobs up and down in the ocean's waves, that man does not become a superman by isolating himself from reality and life. Instead, he must immerse himself in the waves so that he can "ride the waves of existence" and become one with the waves.

Second, Kesey detested the mass society image which seemed to dominate life in twentieth century America. Although Kesey was pro-America and admired American democracy per se, he abhorred those things in society which seemed to deprive man of his individuality and freedom. For Kesey, mass society represents big business, government, labor, communication, and religion and thus subordinates the individual, who is stripped of his dignity, significance, and freedom. One of the counterculture's protest slogans underscored this plight: "I am a human being. Do not fold, spindle, or mutilate." The system, preachments, and methodologies of the twentieth century had indeed betrayed man and left him with only two choices: he could either passively conform and thus lose his individuality or find some way to exist in the modern wasteland without losing his dignity and freedom.

Kesey believes that man must not and cannot isolate himself from life; man must meet life on its own terms and discover his own saving grace. Kesey's solution is similar to the solutions found in J. D. Salinger's *Catcher in the Rye* (1951), Joseph Heller's *Catch-22* (1961), Saul Bellow's *Mr. Sammler's Planet* (1973), and even in John Irving's *The Hotel New Hampshire* (1981). Having their archetypes in the comic book and Western heroes, Kesey's McMurphy in *One Flew over the Cuckoo's Nest* and Hank Stamper in *Sometimes a Great Notion* are vibrant personalities who defy the overwhelming forces of life by constantly asserting their dignity, significance, and freedom as human beings. Each one learns also that no victories are ever won by passively isolating oneself from life or by being self-centered. They, therefore, immerse themselves in life, ask no quarter, and remain self-reliant. McMurphy and Stamper may not be able to save the entire world, but, Kesey believes, they can save themselves and perhaps even part of the world. Their victories may be slight, but they are, nevertheless, victories.

In *One Flew over the Cuckoo's Nest*, the oppressive power of the mass society is evident in its setting—a mental ward dominated by the tyrannical Miss Ratched, the big nurse, whom Chief Bromden, the schizophrenic narrator, describes in mechanical metaphors. Her purse is shaped like a toolbox: her lipstick and fingernail polish are "funny orange" like a glowing soldering iron; her skin and face are like an expensively manufactured baby doll's; her ward is run like a computer. If a patient dares disrupt her smoothly running ward, Nurse Ratched has the ultimate threats—electroshock treatments—and if these fail, she has prefrontal lobotomy operations which turn men into vegetables. Bromden says that the ward is only a "factory for the Combine," a nebulous and ubiquitous force which had ruthlessly destroyed Bromden's father and which is responsible for the stereotyped housing developments along the coast.

Kesey's metaphors are clear. The Combine, the macrocosm, and the hospital ward, the microcosm, are the twentieth century world gone berserk with power; it uses the miracles of modern science, not to free man and make his life better, but rather to compel him to conform. It is the mass society that will not tolerate individuality and that will fold, spindle, or mutilate any person who fails to conform.

Into the ward boils McMurphy, the former Marine, logger, gambler, and free spirit who is intimidated by neither the nurse nor her black ward attendants, and who immediately becomes a threat to Nurse Ratched and her ward policies. McMurphy has had himself committed for purely selfish reasons— he disliked the manual labor on the prison work farm, and he wants the easy gambling winnings from the patients, two facts which he candidly admits. Outraged at Ratched's power, McMurphy bets the other patients that he can get the best of her. Certain that he can win his wager, he sings and laughs on the ward, conducts poker games in the tub room, and disrupts the group therapy sessions. He finally succeeds in destroying her composure when he leads the men watching the blank television screen after Nurse Ratched cuts the power source during the first game of the World Series.

These scenes are crucial because they reveal the typical Kesey conflict. A physically powerful, free, and crucible-tested hero comes into conflict with an equally powerful force. It is simply, as most critics have noted, the classic struggle between good and evil, or the epic confrontation reminiscent of Western films. Yet the dichotomy is not so simple, because the Kesey hero must learn a further lesson. McMurphy has won his wager, but he has not yet won significant victory, because his actions are selfish ones.

Several important incidents transform McMurphy into a champion of the patients. McMurphy is *committed*, which means that Ratched can keep him on the ward as long as she wishes. Instead of jeopardizing his relatively short sentence, McMurphy conforms and does not disrupt the therapy sessions or life on the ward. When Charles Cheswick argues with the nurse about the cigarette rationing, he gets no support from McMurphy, despairs, and drowns himself in the hospital swimming pool. Cheswick's death plagues McMurphy, even though he is not actually responsible. McMurphy cannot understand why the other patients, who are there voluntarily, do not leave the hospital. Billy Bibbit finally tells McMurphy that they are not big and strong like McMurphy, that they have no "g-guts," and that it is "n-no use." McMurphy begins to realize that he must do something to convert the patients into responsible men again. At the next group therapy session, when Ratched is supposed to win her final victory over him, McMurphy rams his hand through the glass partition in the nurses' station and thereby renews the struggle.

A key quotation occurs earlier that not only summarizes Kesey's view of man in the modern world but also provides a clue to McMurphy's actions. Scanlon, who is also committed, says that it is a "hell of a life," and that people are damned if they do and damned if they do not. Scanlon adds that this fact puts man in a "confounded bind." At this point, McMurphy is damned either way. If he does nothing, then Ratched has the final victory and McMurphy will become another victim of the Combine, a nonentity like the other patients. If he renews the struggle, he must remain on the ward until the nurse discharges him or kills him. McMurphy chooses, however, the higher damnation, selflessly to give of himself, and in so doing, he also reaffirms his own dignity and significance.

Dedicated to the patients' cause, McMurphy continues to disrupt the ward and ward policy by using what can only be termed McMurphy's therapy. He continues the poker games and organizes basketball games and even a deep-sea fishing trip, during which the men finally learn to laugh at themselves, Nurse Ratched, and the world in general. He fights with an attendant who was bullying one of the patients, and as a result he is given a series of electro-shock treatments. Finally, McMurphy physically attacks the nurse when she ironically accuses him of "playing" and "gambling" with the men's lives. When a prefrontal lobotomy turns McMurphy into a vegetable, Bromden sacrificially murders him and then escapes from the hospital.

In Kesey's world, an individual may indeed be damned either way when he or she encounters the overwhelming forces of the mass society, but through accepting responsibility and acting one can still win an important victory. McMurphy's death is not futile, because he has saved his soul by losing it to a higher cause. He did not save or even change the entire world, but he did save and change part of it: the other patients are no longer cowed and intimidated by Nurse Ratched, and several of them voluntarily check out of the hospital. Bromden, as McMurphy had promised, has been "blown back up" to his full size. There is, then, a slight but significant victory.

Kesey remarked that he wanted his style to be a "style of change," since he wished neither to write like anyone else nor to be part of any movement. Even though *One Flew over the Cuckoo's Nest* was innovative in style and technique, Kesey's second novel is even more innovative. Even though some critics faulted it for being too rambling and disjointed, *Sometimes a Great Notion* is not only much longer than but also superior to his first novel. It is Kesey at his best. Ultimately, what makes the novel superior is its technical complexity.

More than six hundred pages in length, *Sometimes a Great Notion* is reminiscent of *Light in August* (1932) and *Absalom! Absalom!* (1936) by William Faulkner, Kesey's favorite author. As did Faulkner, Kesey begins his novel at its climax, with a scene in a bus depot where Jonathan Bailey Draeger, a labor union official, asks Vivian Stamper, Hank's wife, about the nature of the Stamper family. This interview between Viv and Draeger frames the entire narrative. The narrative then shifts to the past, at times as far back as 1898, when the first Stamper left Kansas to move west. Through these past scenes, Kesey establishes the family background and relationships, which in turn provide the psychological makeup of the characters. Having rejected traditional narrative forms, Kesey thus moves freely from past to present time. Complementing the time shifts are the complex points of view. Bromden is the single narrator in *One Flew over the Cuckoo's Nest*, but in *Sometimes a Great Notion* Kesey uses several points of view. There is the traditional omniscient viewpoint, then there are the first-person points of view in the stories of Henry Stamper, Sr., Hank, and Leland Stanford Stamper, Hank's half brother. Kesey freely shifts abruptly from one viewpoint to another, and several shifts may occur in one paragraph. In addition, Kesey presents several incidents which are separated in space but which are actually simultaneous actions.

Even the conflict in *Sometimes a Great Notion* is more complicated than that of *One Flew over the Cuckoo's Nest*. The forces aligned against McMurphy are clearly delineated; it is McMurphy versus Nurse Ratched and the

Combine, and it is clear who is good and who is evil. On the other hand, in *Sometimes a Great Notion*, Hank confronts more subtle and complex forces. He pits himself against the logging union and the Wakonda, Oregon, community, both of which represent mass society. Hank must also contend with two natural forces—the weather and the Wakonda River, the latter being one of the major symbols in the novel. The most important conflict, however, is between Hank and Lee (Leland, his half brother).

Like McMurphy, Hank is a physically powerful man who is self-reliant, answers to no one but himself, and cherishes his freedom. Like McMurphy, Hank defies those forces of life which would strip him of his dignity, significance, and freedom. For Hank, then, the dictatorial pressures of the union and the Wakonda community are the dictates of the mass society. Having signed a contract with Wakonda Pacific, Hank becomes a strike breaker who is harassed and threatened by union leaders and the townspeople. Literally, Hank breaks the strike to save the Stamper logging business; symbolically, he breaks the strike because to do so will assert his independence and freedom. The results of *any* action Hank chooses to take are undesirable, and he, like McMurphy, chooses the course of a higher morality.

Kesey uses three major symbols to underscore Hank's bullheaded defiance. The first is the Stamper house itself, which "protrudes" into the Wakonda River on "a peninsula of its own making." The second is the "Never Give an Inch" plaque, painted in yellow machine paint over the plaque's original message: "Blessed Are the Meek for They Shall Inherit the Earth." The plaque with its new dictum is nailed to Hank's bedroom wall by old Henry Stamper. The third symbol is old Henry's severed arm, which is a hanging pole, with all of its fingers tied down except the middle one. As part of Kesey's complex technique, these symbols fuse with the characters' historical and psychological background, with the various narrative viewpoints, and with the major conflicts.

Of the conflicts, the one between Hank and Leland is potentially the most destructive, and it is also important in terms of Hank's and Lee's character development. Through a crack in the bedroom wall, Lee watched his mother and Hank commit adultery, an act which eventually results in the mother's suicide after she and Lee move back East. Lee returns to Wakonda, not to help the Stampers' failing lumber business, but actually to take revenge against Hank. Lee decides that he can best hurt Hank by having an affair with Viv, who, even though she loves Hank, cannot tolerate his "teeth-gritting stoicism in the face of pain." She wants to be both loved and needed, and Lee seems to love and need her. Ironically, after the drowning of Joe Ben, Hank swims across the Wakonda instead of using the motorboat, quietly enters the house, and through the same crack in the bedroom wall, sees Lee and Viv in bed together. Temporarily overwhelmed by the death of Joe Ben, his father's horrible maiming, the bad weather, and Viv's adultery, Hank decides that he is "tired of being a villain" and that he will fight the union no longer. His surrender is implied, moreover, in the song lyrics from which the title of the novel is taken: "Sometimes I take a great notion/ To jump into the river an' drown." Immediately after the fistfight with Lee, however, Hank decides to take the logs down river, and Lee joins him.

The fight between Hank and Lee embodies the novel's central theme. Hank understands that Lee has arranged events so cleverly that Hank is damned either way, or as Hank says, "whipped if I fight and whipped if I don't." Hank chooses the greater notion and fights. During the fight, his inner strength is rekindled, and he later tells Viv that "a man is always surprised just how much he can do by himself." Concomitantly, during the fight, Lee realizes that he too has regained the strength and pride which he thought had been lost. Each has a new respect for the other, a respect that is based on love— love for the Stamper name, love for individual freedom. Lee and Hank may be defeated by the river, the weather, or the strike itself, but the significant fact is that they, like McMurphy, are acting. They have not saved the entire world, but they have saved themselves, have regained their own dignity and significance; and that, in itself, is a victory.

Edward C. Reilly

Other major works

NONFICTION: *The Further Inquiry*, 1990.

MISCELLANEOUS: *The Last Supplement to the Whole Earth Catalog*, 1971 (edited with Paul Krassner); *Kesey's Garage Sale*, 1973; *Demon Box*, 1986.

Bibliography

Porter, M. Gilbert. *The Art of Grit: Ken Kesey's Fiction*. Columbia: University of Missouri Press, 1982. In this first full-length study of Kesey, Porter penetrates Kesey's drug-culture image to reveal his accomplishments as an author in the traditional "American mold of optimism and heroism." A highly regarded critical study which offers an astute commentary on Kesey's fiction.

Sherwood, Terry G. "*One Flew over the Cuckoo's Nest* and the Comic Strip." *Critique: Studies in Modern Fiction* 13, no. 1 (1971): 97-109. Sherwood explores Kesey's references to popular culture, particularly comic strip materials, which are not just "casual grace notes but clear indications of his artistic stance." Contains some appreciative criticism, but faults Kesey for his belief in the escapist world of the comic strip and his oversimplification of moral dilemmas.

Tanner, Stephen L. *Ken Kesey*. Boston: Twayne, 1983. This study affirms Kesey as a significant writer and a leader of a cultural movement despite his scant output. Presents some biographical details of Kesey's early years and accomplishments, followed by a critical study of major works. Gives particular attention to *One Flew over the Cuckoo's Nest* and *Sometimes a Great Notion*. Selected bibliography is provided.

Vogler, Thomas A. "Ken Kesey." In *Contemporary Novelists*, edited by James Vinson. London: St. James Press, 1976. Describes Kesey's work as "Richly north-western and regional in quality." Presents some critical appraisal of *One Flew over the Cuckoo's Nest* and *Sometimes a Great Notion*. Also refers to *The Last Supplement to the Whole Earth Catalog*, for which Kesey wrote numerous reviews and articles.

Wolfe, Tom. *The Electric Kool-Aid Acid Test*. New York: Farrar, Straus & Giroux, 1968. A notable work in its own right, here Wolfe confers on Kesey the charismatic leadership of a cultural movement. Provides important background information on Kesey, the Merry Pranksters, and the milieu of psychedelic experimentation.

STEPHEN KING

Born: Portland, Maine; September 21, 1947

Principal long fiction

Carrie, 1974; *'Salem's Lot*, 1975; *The Shining*, 1977; *Rage*, 1977 (as Richard Bachman); *The Stand*, 1978, revised 1990; *The Dead Zone*, 1979; *The Long Walk*, 1979 (as Bachman); *Firestarter*, 1980; *Roadwork*, 1981 (as Bachman); *Cujo*, 1981; *The Running Man*, 1982 (as Bachman); *Christine*, 1983; *Pet Sematary*, 1983; *Cycle of the Werewolf*, 1983 (novelette, illustrated by Berni Wrightson); *The Talisman*, 1984 (with Peter Straub); *Thinner*, 1984 (as Bachman); *The Eyes of the Dragon*, 1984, 1987; *The Bachman Books: Four Early Novels by Stephen King*, 1985 (includes *Rage, The Long Walk, Roadwork*, and *The Running Man*); *It*, 1986; *Misery*, 1987; *The Tommyknockers*, 1987; *The Dark Half*, 1989.

Other literary forms

Stephen King has published more than one hundred short stories (including the collections *Night Shift*, 1978, and *Skeleton Crew*, 1985) and the eight novellas contained in *Different Seasons* (1982) and *Four Past Midnight* (1990). Two of these novellas are central to his work. In *The Body*, a boy's confrontation with mortality shapes his developing identity as a writer. In *The Mist*, King in his satirical and apocalyptic mode brings Armageddon to the Federal Foods Supermarket as an assortment of Grade B movie monsters that inhabit a dense fog.

The relations of King's fiction with the electronic media are many and complex. Much of his fiction has been adapted to film, although it usually plays best in the mind's eye. He has written several mediocre screenplays, four of which have been produced, including *Maximum Overdrive* (1986), which he directed. A relatively successful mixed-media venture was his collaboration with George Romero on *Creepshow* (1982), a film anthology inspired by the E. C. Comics' blend of camp and gore and based on King's own book version. *Creepshow II*, written by Romero and based on King's stories, appeared in 1987. King has published numerous articles and one critical book, *Danse Macabre* (1981).

Achievements

King is perhaps the most widely known American writer of his generation, yet his distinctions include publishing as two authors at once: From 1977 to 1984, he wrote five novels under the pseudonym Richard Bachman. Special World Fantasy and British World Fantasy awards for his contributions to the field in 1980 and 1981 only begin to indicate his achievement. At first ignored and then scorned by mainstream critics, by the late 1980's his novels were reviewed regularly by *The New York Times Book Review* and with increasing favor. Beginning in 1987, most of his novels were main selections of the Book-of-the-Month Club, which in 1989 created the Stephen King Library, committed to keeping King's novels "in print in hardcover." Still, King's most appropriate distinction was the October 9, 1986, cover of *Time* magazine, which depicted a reader, hair on end, transfixed by "A Novel by Stephen King." The cover story on the "King of Horror" correctly suggested that his achievement and the "horror boom" of the 1970's and 1980's are inseparable. Yet, like Edgar Allan Poe, King turned a degenerated genre—a matter of comic-book monsters and drive-in movies—into a medium embodying the primary anxieties of his age.

King's detractors attribute his success to the sensational appeal of his genre, whose main purpose, as he readily confesses, is to scare people. He is graphic, sentimental, and predictable. His humor is usually crude and campy. His novels are long and loosely structured, and increasingly so: *It* comprises 1,138 pages. In an environment of "exhaustion" and minimalism, King's page-turners are the summit of the garbage heap of a mass, throwaway culture. Worst of all, he is "Master of Postliterate Prose"—as Paul Gray put the issue in 1982—of writing that takes readers mentally to the movies rather than making them imagine or think.

On the other hand, King has provided the most genuine example of the storyteller's art since Charles Dickens. He has returned to the novel some of the popular appeal it had in the nineteenth century and turned out a generation of readers who vastly prefer some books to their film adaptations. As Dickens drew on the popular culture of his time, King reflects the mass-mediated culture of his own. His dark fantasies, like all good popular fiction, allow readers to express within conventional frames of reference feelings and concepts they might not otherwise consider. In imagination, King is not merely prolific; his vision articulates universal fears and desires in terms peculiar to contemporary culture.

Biography

The second son of Donald and Nellie King, Stephen William King has lived most of his life in Maine, the setting for most of his fiction. Two childhood traumas, neither of which he remembers, may have been formative. In 1949, when he was two years old, his parents separated and his father disappeared. In 1951, he apparently saw a train dismember a neighborhood friend.

King's conservative Methodist upbringing was supplemented early with a diet of comic books and *Weird Tales*. When twelve, he began submitting stories for sale. In 1970, he was graduated from the University of Maine at Orono with a B.S. in English and a minor in dramatics. He encountered two lasting influences, the naturalist writers and contemporary American mythology. He also met Tabitha Jane Spruce, whom he married in 1971.

After graduation, he worked in an industrial laundry until 1971, when he became an English instructor at a preparatory school in Hampden, Maine. He wrote at night in the trailer he shared with his wife and two children. In the early 1970's, he sold stories to men's magazines. Then, in 1974, he published *Carrie*, which was followed by several best-sellers and motion-picture rights. King makes his home in Maine with his wife, Tabitha King, novelist of *Small World* (1981) and *Caretakers* (1983), and their three children.

Analysis

Stephen King may be known as a horror writer, but he calls himself a "brand name," describing his style as "the literary equivalent of a Big Mac and a large fries from McDonald's." His fast-food version of the "plain style" may smell of commercialism, but that fact perhaps makes him the contemporary American storyteller without peer. From the beginning, his dark parables spoke to the anxieties of the late twentieth century. As a surrogate author in *The Mist* explains King's mission, "when the technologies fail, when . . . religious systems fail, people have got to have something. Even a zombie lurching through the night" is a "cheerful" thought in the context of a "dissolving ozone layer."

King's fictions are naturalized fantasies. They begin with premises accepted by middle Americans of the television generation, opening in suburban or small-town America—Derry, Maine, or Libertyville, Pennsylvania—and have the familiarity of the house next door and the Seven Eleven store. The characters have the trusted two-dimensional reality of kitsch: They originate in clichés such as the high school "nerd" or the wise child. From such premises, they move cinematically through an atmosphere resonant with a popular mythology taken from brand names, the electronic media, and comic strips as well as traditional sources. King applies naturalistic methods to an environment created by popular culture. This reality, already mediated, is translated easily into preternatural terms, taking on what A. D. Hutter calls the quality of a "shared nightmare."

King's imagination is above all archetypal: His "pop" familiarity and his campy humor draw on the collective unconscious. In *Danse Macabre*, a study of the contemporary horror genre which emphasizes the cross-pollination of fiction and film, he divides his subject according to four "monster archetypes": the ghost, the "thing" (or man-made monster), the vampire, and the werewolf. As in his fiction, his sources are the classic horror films of the 1930's, inherited by the 1950's pulp and film industries. He hints at their derivations from the gothic novel, classical myth, Brothers Grimm folktales, and the oral tradition in general. In an anxious era both skeptical of and hungry for myth, horror is fundamentally reassuring and cathartic; the tale-teller combines roles of physician and priest into the witch doctor as "sin eater," who assumes the guilt and fear of his culture. In the neoprimitivism of the late twentieth century, this ancient role and the old monsters have taken on a new mystique.

In this light, *The Eyes of the Dragon*, advertised as "a fairy tale for adults," is not exceptional. In *The Uses of Enchantment* (1976), Bruno Bettelheim argues that the magic and terrors of fairy tales present existential problems in forms children can understand. King's paranormal horrors have similar cathartic and educative functions for adults; they externalize the traumas of later life, especially adolescence.

Stephen King's first published novel, *Carrie*, is such a parable of adolescence. Sixteen-year-old Carrie White is a lonely ugly duckling, an outcast at home and at school. Her mother, a religious fanatic, associates Carrie with her own "sin"; Carrie's peers hate her in a mindless way and make her the butt of every joke. *Carrie* concerns the horrors of high school, a place of "bottomless conservatism and bigotry," as King explains, where students "are no more allowed to rise 'above their station' than a Hindu" above caste. The novel is also about the terrors of passage to womanhood. In the opening scene, in the school shower room, Carrie experiences her first menstrual period; her peers react with abhorrence and ridicule, "stoning" her with sanitary napkins, shouting "Plug it up!" Carrie becomes the scapegoat for a fear of female sexuality as epitomized in the smell and sight of blood. (The blood bath and symbolism of sacrifice will recur at the climax of the novel.) As atonement for her participation in Carrie's persecution in the shower, Susan Snell persuades her popular boyfriend Tommy Ross to invite Carrie to the Spring Ball. Carrie's conflict with her mother, who regards her emerging womanhood with loathing, is paralleled by a new plot by the girls against her, led by the rich and spoiled Chris Hargenson. They arrange to have Tommy and Carrie voted King and Queen of the Ball, only to crown them with a bucket of pig's blood. Carrie avenges her mock baptism telekinetically, destroying the school and the town, leaving Susan Snell as the only survivor.

As in fairy tales, there is a consolation: The bad die and the good survive. As in most folk cultures, initiation is signified by the acquisition of special wisdom or powers. King equates Carrie's sexual flowering with the maturing of her telekinetic ability. Both cursed and empowered with righteous fury, she becomes at once victim and monster, witch and White Angel of Destruction. As King has explained, Carrie is "Woman, feeling her powers for the first time and, like Samson, pulling down the temple on everyone in sight at the end of the book."

Carrie catapulted King into the mass market; it immediately went into paperback and was adapted into a critically acclaimed film directed by Brian De Palma. The novel touched the right nerves. Feminism was one. William Blatty's *The Exorcist* (1971), which was adapted into a powerful and controversial film, had touched on similar social fears in the 1960's and 1970's with its subtext of the "generation gap" and the "death of God." Although Carrie's destructive power, like that of Regan in *The Exorcist*, is linked with monstrous adolescent sexuality, the similarity between the two novels ends there. Carrie's "possession" is the complex effect of her mother's fanaticism, her peers' bigotry, and her newly realized, unchecked female power; it is the combined failure of nature and civilization. Like Anne Sexton's *Transformations* (1971), a collection of fractured fairy tales in sardonic verse, King's novel explores the social and cultural roots of its evil.

King's *Carrie* is a dark modernization of "Cinderella," with a bad mother, cruel siblings (peers), a prince (Tommy Ross), a godmother (Sue Snell), and a ball. King's reversal of the happy ending is actually in keeping with the Brothers Grimm; it recalls the tale's folk originals, which enact revenge in bloody images: The stepsisters' heels, hands, and noses are sliced off, and a white dove pecks out their eyes. As King knows, blood flows freely in the oral tradition.

King represents that oral tradition in a pseudodocumentary form which depicts the points of view of various witnessess and commentaries: newspaper accounts, case studies, court reports, and journals. Pretending to textual authenticity, he alludes to the gothic classics, especially Bram Stoker's *Dracula* (1897). *'Salem's Lot*, King's next novel, is a bloody fairy tale in which Dracula comes to Our Town.

By the agnostic and sexually liberated 1970's, the vampire had been demythologized into what King called a "comic book menace." In his most significant departure from tradition, he diminishes the sexual aspects of the vampire. He reinvests the archetype with meaning by basing its attraction on the human desire to surrender identity in the mass. His major innovation, however, was envisioning the mythic small town in *American Gothic* terms and then making it the monster; the vampire's traditional victim, the populace, becomes the menace as mindless mass, plague, or primal horde. Drawing on Richard Matheson's grimly naturalistic novel *I Am Legend* (1954) and Jack Finney's novel *The Body Snatchers* (1955), King focused on the issues of fragmentation, reinvesting the vampire with contemporary meaning.

The sociopolitical subtext of *'Salem's Lot* was the ubiquitous disillusionment of the Watergate era, King has explained. Like rumor and disease, vampirism spreads secretly at night, from neighbor to neighbor, infecting men and women, the mad and the senile, the responsible citizen and the infant alike, absorbing into its zombielike horde the human population. King is especially skillful at suggesting how small-town conservatism can become inverted on itself, the harbored suspicions and open secrets gradually dividing and isolating. This picture is reinforced by the town's name, 'Salem's Lot, a degenerated form of Jerusalem's Lot, which suggests the city of the chosen reverted to a culture of dark rites in images of spreading menace.

King's other innovation was, paradoxically, a reiteration. He made his "king vampire," Barlow, an obvious reincarnation of Stoker's Dracula that functions somewhere between cliché and archetype. King uses the mythology of vampires to ask how civilization is to exist without faith in traditional authority symbols. His answer is pessimistic, turning on the abdication of Father Callahan, whose strength is undermined by secret alcoholism and a superficial adherence to form. Representing external authority without inner resources, he leaves on a Greyhound bus. The two survivors, Ben Mears and Mark Petrie, must partly seek, partly create their talismans and rituals, drawing on the compendium of vampire lore—the alternative, in a culture-wide crisis of faith, to conventional systems. (At one point, Mears holds off a vampire with a crucifix made with two tongue depressors.) The traditional paraphernalia, they find, will work only if the handler has faith.

It is significant that the two survivors are, respectively, a "wise child" (Mark Petrie) and a novelist (Ben Mears, King's self-portrait); only they have the necessary resources. Even Susan Norton, Mears's lover and the gothic heroine, succumbs. As in *The Shining*, *The Dead Zone*, and *Firestarter*, the child (or childlike adult) has powers which may be used for good or for evil. Mears is the imaginative, nostalgic adult, haunted by the past. The child and the man share a naïveté, a gothic iconography, and a belief in evil. Twelve-year-old Mark worships at a shrinelike tableau of Aurora monsters that glow "green in the dark, just like the plastic Jesus" he was given in Sunday School for learning Psalm 119. Mears has returned to the town of his childhood to revive an image of the Marsten House lurking in his mythical mind's eye. Spiritual father and son, they create a community of two out of the "pop" remnants of American culture.

As in fairy tales and Dickens' novels, King's protagonists are orphans searching for their true parents, for community. His fiction may reenact his search for the father who disappeared and left behind a box of *Weird Tales*. The yearned-for bond of parent and child, a relationship signifying a unity of being, appears throughout his fiction. The weakness or treachery of a trusted parent is correspondingly the ultimate fear. Hence, the vampire Barlow is the devouring father who consumes an entire town. In *The Shining*, King domesticated his approach to the issue, focusing on the threat to the family that comes from a trusted figure within it. Jack Torrance is the abused child who, assuming his father's aggression, in turn becomes the abusing father. The much beloved "bad" father is the novel's monster: The environment of the Overlook Hotel traps him, as he in turn calls its power forth. King brilliantly expands the haunted-house archetype into a symbol of the accumulated sin of all fathers who were one-night stands. In the epic fantasy *The Stand*, King explores the issue in the terms of an apocalyptic Western, as survivors of a superflu struggle across the continent, rebuilding civilization out of the new wilderness, the open future. The haunting and haunted father is the "Walkin'

Dude" named Flagg who draws loners and outlaws to Las Vegas, thwarting community and growth; he is opposed by the idealized tribal Mother Abigail, who is also the childlike seer. Then, in *Cujo*, King naturalizes the issue, making the monster the family dog after it contracts rabies—the objective correlative for a spectrum of domestic and social ills: marital problems, wife beating, business failure, food additives.

In *Christine*, King examines the same threat by way of American popular culture. The setting is Libertyville, Pennsylvania, in the late 1970's. The monster is the American Dream as embodied in the automobile. The epigraph to chapter 14, a song ("Less than Zero") by punk rock artist Elvis Costello, makes the point: "about a couple/ living in the U.S.A." who "traded in their baby/ for a Chevrolet:/ Let's talk about the future now,/ We've put the past away."

King gives *Christine* all the attributes of a fairy tale for "postliterate" adolescents. *Christine* is another fractured "Cinderella" story—*Carrie* for boys. Arnie Cunningham, a nearsighted, acne-scarred loser, falls "in love with" a car, a passionate (red and white) Christine, "one of the long ones with the big fins." An automotive godmother, she brings Arnie, in fairy-tale succession, freedom, success, power, and love: a home away from overprotective parents, a cure for acne, hit-and-run revenge on bullies, and a beautiful girl, Leigh Cabot. Soon, however, the familiar triangle emerges, of boy, girl, and car, and Christine is revealed as a femme fatale—driven by the spirit of her former owner, a malcontent named Roland LeBay. Christine is the vehicle for its death wish on the world, for its all-devouring, "everlasting Fury." LeBay's aggression possesses Arnie, who reverts into an older, tougher self, then into the "mythic teenaged hood" that King has called the prototype of 1950's werewolf movies, and finally into "some ancient carrion eater," or primal self.

As automotive monster Christine comes from a variety of sources, including the folk tradition of the "death car" and a venerable techno-horror premise. King's main focus, however, is the mobile youth culture that has come down from the 1950's by way of advertising, popular songs, film, and national pastimes. Christine is the car as a projection of the cultural self, Anima for the modern American Adam. To Arnie's late 1970's–style imagination, the Plymouth Fury, in 1958 a mid-priced family car, is an American Dream. Her sweeping, befinned chassis and engine re-create a fantasy of the golden age of the automobile: the horizonless future imagined as an expanding network of superhighways and unlimited fuel. Christine recovers for Arnie a prelapsarian vitality and manifest destiny.

Christine's odometer runs backward and she regenerates parts. The immortality she offers, however—and by implication, the American Dream— is really arrested development in the form of a *Happy Days* rerun and by way of her radio, which sticks on the golden oldies station. Indeed, *Christine* is a recapitulatory rock musical framed fatalistically in sections titled "Teenage Car-Songs," "Teenage Love-Songs," and "Teenage Death-Songs." Fragments of rock-and-roll songs introduce each chapter. Christine's burden, an undead 1950's youth culture, means that most of Arnie's travels are in and out of time, a deadly nostalgia trip. As Douglas Winter explains, *Christine* reenacts "the death," in the 1970's "of the American romance with the automobile."

The novel's uncanny narrative perspective is best described as déjà vu. Early New Year's Day, 1979, Arnie takes the narrator, Dennis, on a last ride. "We went back in time," he says, "but did we?" The present-day streets look "like a thin [film] overlay" superimposed on a time "somehow more real" whose "dead hands" reach out to draw them in forever. The epilogue from four years later presents the fairy-tale consolation in a burned-out monotone. Arnie and his parents are buried, Christine is scrap metal, and the true Americans, Leigh and Dennis, are survivors, but Dennis, the "knight of Darnell's Garage," does not woo "the lady fair"; he is a limping, lackluster junior high teacher and they have drifted apart, grown old in their prime. Dennis narrates the story in order to file it away, all the while perceiving himself and his peers in terms of icons from the late 1950's. In his nightmares, Christine appears wearing a black vanity plate inscribed with a skull and the words, "ROCK AND ROLL WILL NEVER DIE." From Dennis' haunted perspective, *Christine* simultaneously examines and is a symptom of a cultural phenomenon: a new American gothic species of anachronism or déjà vu, which continued after *Christine*'s publication in films such as *Back to the Future* (1985), *Peggy-Sue Got Married* (1986) and *Blue Velvet* (1986). The 1980's and the 1950's blur into a seamless illusion, the nightmare side of which is the prospect of living an infinite replay.

The subtext of King's adolescent fairy tale is another coming of age, from the opposite end and the broader perspective of American culture. Written by a fortyish King in the final years of the twentieth century, *Christine* diagnoses a cultural midlife crisis and marks a turning point in King's career, a critical examination of mass culture. The dual time frame reflects his awareness of a dual audience, of writing for adolescents who look back to a mythical 1950's and also for his own generation as it relives its undead youth culture in its children. The baby boomers, King explains, "were obsessive" about childhood. "We went on playing for a long time, almost feverishly. I write for that buried child in us, but I'm writing for the grown-up too. I want grown-ups to look at the child long enough to be able to give him up. The child should be buried."

In *Pet Sematary*, King unearthed that child, which is the novel's monster. *Pet Sematary* is about the "*real* cemetery," he told Winter. The focus is on the "one great fear" all fears "add up to," "the body under the sheet. It's our body." The fairy-tale subtext is the magic kingdom of our protracted American childhood, the Disney empire as mass culture—and, by implication, the comparable multimedia phenomenon represented by King himself. The grimmer, truer text-within-the-text is Mary Shelley's *Frankenstein: Or, The Modern Prometheus* (1818).

The novel, which King once considered "too horrible to be published," is also his own dark night of the soul. Louis Creed, a university doctor, his wife Rachel, and their two children (five-year-old Ellie and two-year-old Gage) move to Maine to work at King's alma mater; a neighbor takes the family on an outing to a pet cemetery created by the neighborhood children, their confrontation with mortality. Additionally the "sematary," whose "Druidic" rings allude to Stonehenge, is the outer circle of an Indian burial ground that sends back the dead in a state of soulless half life, resurrecting with primitive simplicity. Louis succumbs to temptation when the family cat Church is killed on the highway; he buries him on the sacred old Indian burial grounds. "Frankencat" comes back with his "purr-box broken." A succession of accidents, heart attacks, strokes, and deaths—of neighbor Norma Crandall, son Gage, Norma's husband, Jud, and wife Rachel—and resurrections follow.

The turning point is the death of Gage, which his father cannot accept and which leads to the novel's analysis of modern medical miracles performed in the name of human decency and love. Louis is the heavy father as baby boomer who cannot relinquish his childhood. The larger philosophical issue is Louis' rational, bioethical *creed*; he believes in saving the only life he knows, the material. Transferred into an immoderate love for his son, it is exposed as the narcissistic embodiment of a patriarchal lust for immortality through descendants, expressed first in an agony of sorrow and rage, then ghoulishly, as he disinters his son's corpse and makes the estranging discovery that it is like "looking at a badly made doll." Later, reanimated, Gage appears to have been "terribly hurt and then put back together again by crude, uncaring hands." Performing his task, Louis feels dehumanized, like "a subhuman character in some cheap comic-book."

The failure of Louis' creed is shown in his habit, when under stress, of taking mental trips to Orlando, Florida, where he, Church, and Gage drive a white van as Disney World's "resurrection crew." In these waking dreams, which echo the male bond of "wise child" and haunted father from as far back as *'Salem's Lot*, Louis' real creed is revealed: Its focus is on Oz the Gweat and Tewwible (a personification of death to Rachel) and Walt Disney, that "gentle faker from Nebraska"—like Louis, two wizards of science fantasy. Louis' wizardry is reflected in the narrative perspective and structure, which flashes back in part 2 from the funeral to Louis' fantasy of a heroically "long, flying tackle" that snatches Gage from death's wheels.

In this modernization of *Frankenstein*, King demythologizes death and attacks the aspirations toward immortality that typify the 1980's. King's soulless Lazaruses are graphic projections of anxieties about life-support systems, artificial hearts, organ transplants, Baby Faye—what King has called "mech-

anistic miracles" that can postpone the physical signs of life almost indefi-
nitely. The novel also indicts the "waste land" of mass culture, alluding in
the same trope to George Romero's "stupid, lurching movie-zombies," T. S.
Eliot's poem about the hollow men, and *The Wizard of Oz*: "headpiece full of
straw." Louis worries that Ellie knows more about Ronald McDonald and
"the Burger King" than the "*spiritus mundi*."

If the novel suggests one source of community and culture, it is the form
and ritual of the children's pet "sematary." Its concentric circles form a
pattern from their "own collective unconsciousness," one that mimes "the
most ancient religious symbol of all," the spiral. In *It*, a group of children
similarly create a community and a mythology as a way of confronting their
fears, as represented in It, the monster as a serial-murdering, shape-shifting
boogey that haunts the sewers of Derry, Maine. In 1958, the seven protagonists, a cross-section of losers, experience the monster differently, for as in
George Orwell's *Nineteen Eighty-Four* (1949), It derives its power through its
victim's isolation and guilt and thus assumes the shape of his or her worst
fear. (To Beverly Rogan It appears, in a sequence reminiscent of "Red Riding
Hood," as her abusive father in the guise of the child-eating witch from
"Hansel and Gretel.")

In a scary passage in *Pet Sematary*, Louis dreams of Disney World, where
"by the 1890s train station, Mickey Mouse was shaking hands with the
children clustered around him, his big white cartoon gloves swallowing their
small, trusting hands." To all of *It*'s protagonists, the monster appears in a
similar archetypal or communal form, one that suggests a composite of devouring parent and mass-culture demigod, of television commercial and fairy
tale, of 1958 and 1985: as Pennywise, the Clown, a cross between Bozo and
Ronald McDonald. As in *Christine, Pet Sematary*, and *Thinner*, the monster
is mass culture itself, the collective devouring parent nurturing its children on
"imitations of immortality." Like Christine, or Louis' patched-up son, Pennywise is the dead past feeding on the future. Twenty-seven years after its
original reign of terror, It resumes its seige, whereupon the protagonists, now
professionally successful and, significantly, childless yuppies, must return to
Derry, like the ex-hippies of *The Big Chill* (1983), to confront as adults their
childhood fears. Led by surrogate horror writer Bill Denborough, who now
stutters only in his dreams, they defeat It once more, individually as a sort of
allegory of psychoanalysis and collectively as a rite of passage into adulthood
and community.

It was attacked in reviews as pop psychology and by King himself as a
"badly constructed novel," but the puerility was partly intended. The book
summarizes King's previous themes and characters, who themselves look
backward and inward, regress and take stock. The last chapter begins with an
epigraph from Dickens' *David Copperfield* (1849-1850) and ends with an allusion to William Wordsworth's "Intimations of Immortality," from which

King takes his primary theme and narrative device, the look back that enables one to go forward. In the 1970's, King's fiction was devoted to building a mythos out of shabby celluloid monsters to fill a cultural void; in the postmodern awareness of the late 1980's, he began a demystification process. *It* is a calling forth and ritual unmasking of motley Reagan-era monsters, the exorcism of a generation and a culture.

As for King the writer, *It* was one important rite in what would be a lengthy passage, he notes in 1990 while "looking back over the last four years" and seeing "all sorts of cloture." After *It*'s extensive exploration of childhood, however, he took up conspicuously more mature characters, themes, and roles. In *The Eyes of the Dragon* (written for his daughter), he returned to the springs of his fantasy, the fairy tale. He told much the same story as before but assumed the mantle of adulthood. This "pellucid" and "elegant" fairy tale, says Barbara Tritel in *The New York Times Book Review* (February 22, 1987), has the "intimate goofiness of an extemporaneous story" narrated by "a parent to a child." In *The Tommyknockers*, King again seemed to leave familiar territory for science fiction, but the novel more accurately applies technohorror themes to the 1980's infatuation with technology and televangelism. In *The Dark Tower* cycles, he combined the gothic with Western and apocalyptic fiction in a manner reminiscent of *The Stand*. Then with much fanfare in 1990, King returned to that novel to update and enlarge it by some 350 pages.

The process of recapitulation and summing up was complicated by the disclosure, in 1984, of Richard Bachman, the pseudonym under whose cover King had published five novels over a period of eight years. Invented to control King's problem of overproduction, Bachman soon grew into an identity complete with a biography and photographs (he was a chicken farmer with a cancer-ravaged face), dedications, a narrative voice (of unrelenting pessimism), and if not a genre, a naturalistic mode in which sociopolitical speculation combined or alternated with psychological suspense. In 1985, when the novels (with one exception) were collected in a single volume attributed to King *as* Bachman, the mortified alter ego seemed buried. Actually Bachman's publicized demise only raised a haunting question of what "Stephen King" really was.

The alter egos multiplied as books about King and his fiction emerged. The crucial issue and primary tale of terror, for King as well as his readers, was inherent in fantasy itself, in writing, reading, and living in that "strange no man's land that exists between what's real and what's make-believe" (*Four Past Midnight*). *Misery*, which was conceived as Bachman's book, was King's first novel to explore the subject of fiction's dangerous powers. After crashing his car on an isolated road in Colorado, romance writer Paul Sheldon is "rescued," drugged, and held prisoner by a psychotic nurse named Annie Wilkes, who is also the "Number One Fan" of his heroine Misery Chastain (of whom he has tired and whom he has killed off). This "Constant Reader" becomes Sheldon's terrible "Muse," forcing him to write (in an edition especially for her) Misery's *Return* to life. Sheldon is the popular writer imprisoned by genre and cut to fit fan expectations (signified by Annie's amputations of his foot and thumb). Like Scheherazade, the reader is reminded, Sheldon must publish or literally perish. Annie's obsession merges with the expectations of the page-turning real reader, who demands and devours each chapter, and as Sheldon struggles (against pain, painkillers, and a manual typewriter that throws keys) for his life, page by page.

Billed ironically on the dust jacket as a love letter to his fans, the novel is a witty satire on what King has called America's "cannibalistic cult of celebrity": "[Y]ou set the guy up, and then you eat him." The monstrous Reader, however, is also the writer's muse, creation, and alter ego, as Sheldon discovers when he concludes that *Misery Returns*—not his "serious" novel *Fast Cars*—was his masterpiece. Just as ironically, *Misery* was King's first novel to please most of the critics. It was not a complete surprise, then, when in 1989 he examined the issue from the other side, in *The Dark Half*, publishing an allegory of the writer's relation to his genius.

The young writer-protagonist Thaddeus Beaumont has a series of headaches and seizures, and a surgeon removes from his eleven-year-old brain the incompletely absorbed fragments of a twin—including an eye, two teeth, and some fingernails. Nearly thirty years later, Beaumont is a creative writing professor and moderately successful literary novelist devoted to his family. For twelve years, however, he has been living a secret life through George Stark, the pseudonym under which he emerged from writer's block as the author of best-selling crime novels. Stark's purely instinctual genius finds its most vital expression in his protagonist, the professional crime boss Alexis Machine. Like King, Beaumont is forced to disclose and destroy his now self-destructive pseudonym, complete with gravesite service and papier mâché headstone. A series of murders (narrated in Stark's graphic prose style) soon follows. The pseudonym has materialized, risen from its fictional grave literally to take Thad's wife and children (twins, of course) hostage. What Stark wants is to live in writing, outside of which writers do not exist. Yet the writer is also a demon, vampire, and killer in this dark allegory, possessing and devouring the man, his family, friends, community.

Drawing on the motif of the double and the form of the detective story—on Robert Louis Stevenson's *The Strange Case of Dr. Jekyll and Mr. Hyde* (1886) and Sophocles' *Oedipus Rex* (as well as *Misery* and *Pet Sematary*)—King flouts fans expectations by glutting the first half of the book with Stark/Machine's gruesome rampages. The last half is psychological suspense and metafiction in biological metaphor: the struggle of the decently introspective Beaumont against the rawly instinctual Stark for control of both word and flesh, with the novel taking shape on the page as the true author reclaims the "third eye," King's term for both child's and artist's inward vision. Once again, the man buries the terrible child in order to possess himself and his art. The book ends in a "scene from some malign fairy tale" as that child and alter ego is borne away by flocks of sparrows to make a last appearance as a black hole in the fabric of the sky.

In dramatizing the tyrannies, perils, powers, and pleasures of reading and writing, *Misery* and *The Dark Half* might have been written by metafictionists John Fowles (to whose work King is fond of alluding) or John Barth (on whom he draws directly in *It* and *Misery*). Anything but abstract, however, *The Dark Half* is successful both as the thriller that King's fans desired and as an allegory of the writer's situation. Critic George Stade, in his review of the novel for *The New York Times Book Review* (October 29, 1989), praised King for his tact "in teasing out the implications of his parable." Forgoing the overt literary allusions his fictions had lately imported in large quantities, *The Dark Half* contains epigraphs instead to the novels of George Stark, Thad Beaumont, and "the late Richard Bachman," without whom "this novel could not have been written." Thus reworking the Gothic cliché of the double, King allows the mythology of his own life story to speak wittily for itself, lending a subtle level of self-parody to this *roman à clef*. In this instance, his blunt literalness ("word become flesh, so to speak," as George Stark puts it), gives vitality to what in other hands might have been a sterile exercise.

By the early 1980's, King was fast becoming the mass-media guru who could open an American Express commercial with the rhetorical question "Do you know me?" At first prompted to examine the "wide perceptions which light [children's] interior lives" (*Four Past Midnight*) and then the cultural roots of the empire he had created, he proceeded to explore the phenomenon of fiction, the situations of reader and writer, and through these his own darker selves. Most critics approve his shift from the supernatural projections of childhood to a mature imagination. King is still perceived as having direct access to those dark places, and he is still thought to have *no* style. What he evidently has in that department is a narrative voice whose vitality suggests the presence of the oral storyteller.

Linda C. Badley

Other major works

SHORT FICTION: *Night Shift*, 1978; *The Dark Tower: The Gunslinger*, 1982 (illustrated by Michael Whelan); *Different Seasons*, 1982; *Skeleton Crew*, 1985; *The Drawing of the Three*, 1987; *Four Past Midnight*, 1990.

SCREENPLAYS: *Creepshow*, 1982 (with George Romero; adaptation of his book); *Cat's Eye*, 1984; *Silver Bullet*, 1985 (adaptation of *Cycle of the Werewolf*); *Maximum Overdrive*, 1986 (adaptation of his short story "Truck"); *Pet Sematary*, 1989.

NONFICTION: *Danse Macabre*, 1981.
MISCELLANEOUS: *Creepshow*, 1982 (adaptation of the E. C. Comics).

Bibliography

Beahm, George, ed. *The Stephen King Companion*. New York: Andrews and McMeel, 1989. This comprehensive resource guide includes more than one hundred articles, interviews, profiles, and checklists. It is divided into four parts: the first is biographical, with a chronology, interviews, and profiles; the second concerns publishing, fans, critics, and writing; the third provides background information on King's books; the fourth is a reference section of primary and secondary bibliographies, checklists of films, videotapes, audiotapes, and price guides.

Collings, Michael. *The Stephen King Phenomenon*. Starmont Studies in Literary Criticism 14. Mercer Island, Wash.: Starmont House, 1987. The sixth of Collings' continuing series of books on King, this study examines King from multiple perspectives, summarizing images, themes, and characters. Chapters on King as a publishing phenomenon and *It* are of special value. Collings was the first to demonstrate King's literary merits by applying scholarly textual analysis.

Hoppenstand, Gary, and Ray B. Browne, eds. *The Gothic World of Stephen King: Landscape of Nightmare*. Bowling Green, Ohio: Popular Press, 1987. The first collection of academic criticism of King includes an introduction by Hoppenstand and essays on themes ("Adolescent Revolt," "Love and Death in the American Car"), characters ("Mad Dogs and Firestarters," "The Vampire"), genres (King's "Gothic Western," techno-horror), technique ("Allegory"), and individual works.

Magistrale, Tony. *Landscape of Fear: Stephen King's American Gothic*. Bowling Green, Ohio: Popular Press, 1988. Placing King in an American Gothic tradition with Edgar Allan Poe, Nathaniel Hawthorne, Herman Melville, and William Faulkner, this study treats sociopolitical themes such as "The Betrayal of Technology" (chapter 3), individual accountability (chapter 4), innocence betrayed (chapter 5), and survival (chapter 6) in the novels through *It*. The text is supplemented by a bibliography of scholarship from 1980 to 1987.

Reino, Joseph. *Stephen King: The First Decade*. Boston: Twayne, 1988. This book-by-book analysis, from *Carrie* to *Pet Sematary*, attempts to show King's literary merits, stressing subtle characterization and nuances of symbolism and allusion. Reino's King is subversive and projects a pessimistic, apocalyptic vision in fictions with a deceptive complacency of surface. The text is supplemented by a chronology, notes, and primary and secondary bibliographies.

Underwood, Tim, and Chuck Miller, eds. *Fear Itself: The Horror Fiction of Stephen King*. New York: N. A. L. 1984. This first anthology of commentaries on King accounts for him as a popular genre phenomenon, bringing together notables in the field, with an introduction by Peter Straub, foreword by King, afterword by George Romero, and articles by Charles L. Grant, Alan Ryan, Douglas Winter, and King's professor Burton Hatlen. See Underwood and Miller's second anthology, *Kingdom of Fear* (1986), for essays by Robert Bloch, Ramsey Campbell, Whitley Strieber, Clive Barker, Harlan Ellison, Michael McDowell, and Leslie Fiedler. The same editors have published a collection of King interviews, *Bare Bones* (1988).

Winter, Douglas. *Stephen King: The Art of Darkness*. Rev. ed. New York: N. A. L., 1986. This first book on King remains the best introduction and appreciation. Combining biography and analysis and based on exclusive interviews and correspondence, the text is supplemented with a chronology, appendices summarizing the short fiction and listing film and television adaptations, notes, primary and secondary bibliographies, and an index.

RUDYARD KIPLING

Born: Bombay, India; December 30, 1865
Died: Hampstead, London, England; January 18, 1936

Principal long fiction

The Light That Failed, 1890; *The Naulahka: A Story of East and West*, 1892 (with Wolcott Balestier); *Captains Courageous*, 1897; *Kim*, 1901.

Other literary forms

Best-known for his short fiction, Rudyard Kipling wrote more than 250 stories. His style of leaving a story open-ended with the tantalizing phrase, "But that's another story," established his reputation for unlimited storytelling. Although the stories are uneven in quality, W. Somerset Maugham considered Kipling to be the only British writer to equal Guy de Maupassant and Anton Chekhov in the art of short fiction.

His early stories both satisfied and glorified the Englishman in India. The empire builder, the man who devotes his life to "civilize the sullen race" comes off in glowing colors, as in the story "The Bridge Builders." Some of his best stories skillfully blend the exotic and the bizarre, and "The Man Who Would Be King" (1888), which is about two drifters and their fantastic dream to carve out a kingdom for themselves in Central Asia, best illustrates such a story. "A Madonna of the Trenches," with its strange, occult atmosphere, "The Children of the Zodiac," about a young poet who dreads death by cancer of the throat; and "The Gardener" (1926), with its unrelieved sadness and autobiographical reflections on the death of his son, reflect the pain, the suffering, and the dark melancholy of Kipling's later life.

The stories that make up *The Jungle Book* (1894) and *The Second Jungle Book* (1895) were written in Brattleboro, Vermont, when Kipling's mind "worked at the height of its wonderful creative power." They are in the class of animal and folktales that make up such world literary creations as the ancient folktales of *Aesop's Fables* and *The Jataka Tales*. Into the Jungle Book stories, Kipling not only incorporated the clear and clean discipline of the public school but also his favorite doctrine of the natural law. This law had a great impact on the Boy Scout movement and the origins of the Wolf Cub organization, found in the Mowgli tales.

Kipling was a prolific writer, and, as a journalist, he wrote a considerable number of articles, stories, and poems not only for his own newspapers but also for a variety of literary journals in England and the United States. In addition, he was a prolific letter-writer and carried on lengthy literary and political correspondence with such men as Theodore Roosevelt, Cecil Rhodes, and H. Rider Haggard. His correspondence with Haggard has been collected in *Rudyard Kipling to Rider Haggard: The Record of a Friendship*, edited by

Morton N. Cohen (1965). Two volumes of his *Uncollected Prose* were published in 1938 and even some of his desultory writing, such as *American Notes*, concerned with his travels in the United States in 1891, has been recently reissued with editorial notes. In 1932, Kipling personally supervised the publication of the Sussex edition of his work in thirty-five volumes. The Kipling Society, founded in 1927, publishes the quarterly Kipling Journal which keeps Kipling enthusiasts informed of publications about Kipling. Biographical material on Kipling—including his autobiography, *Something of Myself: For My Friends Known and Unknown*, published posthumously in 1937—is considerable, and the record of his literary achievement is now complete.

Achievements

Kipling's first book of fiction appeared in 1888. Since then, his works have undergone several editions, and several of his short stories and poems have found a permanent place in anthologies. Although England and India have both changed enormously since the turn of the century, Kipling's stories continue to attract and fascinate new readers. He was a best-selling author during his lifetime—one of his animal stories, *Thy Servant, a Dog* (1930), sold 100,000 copies in six months in 1932—and he continues to be extremely popular in the English-speaking countries of the world. Several of his works, notably *Captains Courageous*, *Kim*, *The Jungle Book*, and some short stories have been made into motion pictures.

Throughout his lifetime, and soon after his death, Kipling had been associated with the British empire. He had become the laureate of England's vast imperial power, his first book was praised by the Viceroy in 1888, and the King used Kipling's own words to address the empire on Christmas Day in 1932. The day Kipling's ashes were interned at Westminster Abbey—January 23, 1936—King George V's body lay in state in Westminster Hall and the comment that "the King has gone and taken his trumpeter with him" appropriately described the image Kipling had projected.

Kipling wanted to serve the empire through the army or the civil service. Because he had neither family connections with which to obtain a civil service job, nor strong eyesight which barred him from military service, Kipling turned to writing. He wrote with a passionate intensity coupled with admiration for the soldiers, the bridge builders, the missionaries, and the civil servants in remote places who served the empire under "an alien sky." Many of the phrases he used to narrate their tales—"What do they know of England who only England know?," "East is East and West is West," "the white man's burden," "somewhere east of Suez"—have become part of the English language and are often repeated by those who are unfamiliar with his writings. To have used the pen in place of a gun to serve the imperial vision and have such lasting impact on British thinking constitutes a major achievement.

In 1890, Kipling published or republished more than eighty stories, including the novelette *The Light That Failed*. At twenty-five, he had become a famous literary figure. At forty-two, he became the first Englishman to win the Nobel Prize in Literature for "the great power of observation, the original conception and also the virile comprehension and art of narrative that distinguish his literary creations." He had also become a controversial personality since critics and readers saw in his work the effort to mix the roles of the artist and the propagandist. Kipling continues to be controversial and generates extremes of admiration or condemnation. He generates a love-hate response and no year passes without another Kipling study to evaluate and interpret his writings from a new perspective. He is neither neglected nor ignored, which is a true testimony to his importance as a writer.

Biography

Rudyard Kipling was born in Bombay, India, on December 30, 1865. His father, John Lockwood Kipling of Yorkshire, was a scholar and an artist. The elder Kipling went to India as a professor of architectural sculpture in the Bombay School of Fine Arts and later became the Curator of the Lahore Museum, which Kipling was to describe meticulously in *Kim*. He also served as the Bombay correspondent of *The Pioneer* of Allahabad. In 1891, he published *Beast and Man in India* with the help of A. P. Watt, his son's literary agent. The book contains excerpts from Rudyard Kipling's newspaper reports to *The Civil and Military Gazette*. The book provided inspiration for Kipling's Jungle Books and several of the stories: "The Mark of the Beast," "The Finances of the Gods," and "Moti Guj, Mutineer" are some examples.

Kipling's mother, Alice Macdonald, was one of five Macdonald sisters, three of whom married into prominent families. Georgina Macdonald married the distinguished pre-Raphaelite painter Sir Edward Burne-Jones; Agnes Macdonald married another painter Sir Edward Poynter who was influential in helping John Kipling obtain a position in India; and a third sister married Alfred Baldwin, the railroad owner, whose son Stanley Baldwin became Prime Minister of England. Kipling was therefore connected with creative and intellectually stimulating families through his mother, while from his father, he inherited a strong Wesleyan tradition.

Rudyard and his sister, Trix, spent the first six years of their lives in India. Surrounded by Indian servants who told them Indian folktales, Kipling absorbed the Indian vocabulary and unconsciously cultivated the habit of thinking in that vocabulary, as illustrated in his short story "Tod's Amendment." Kipling recalls these early years in his posthumously published autobiography, *Something of Myself*, in which he recalls how he and his sister had to be constantly reminded to speak English to his parents, and that he spoke English "haltingly translated out of the vernacular idiom that one thought and dreamed in." This contributed to the great facility with which he uses Indian words as part of his style. Edmund Wilson in his essay "The Kipling

That Nobody Read," writes that Kipling even looked like an Indian as a young boy.

Like other Anglo-Indian children who were sent home to England for their education, Kipling and his sister were shipped to London to live with a relative of their father in Southsea. The pain and agony of those six years under the supervision of this sadistic woman in what Kipling calls "The House of Desolation," is unflinchingly re-created in the early part of his novelette *The Light That Failed* and in the short story, "Baa, Baa, Blacksheep." According to Edmund Wilson the traumatic experiences of these six years filled Kipling with hatred for the rest of his life.

Kipling studied at the United Services College, a public school for children from families with a military background or with the government civil service. Kipling served as editor of the school newspaper, *The United Services College Chronicle*, to which he contributed several youthful parodies of Robert Browning and Algernon Charles Swinburne. One poem, "Ave Imperatrix," however, with its note of patriotism and references to England's destiny to civilize the world, foreshadows Kipling's later imperial themes. Although Kipling makes fun of flagwaving in "The Flag of Their Country," in *Stalky & Co.* (1899), he did imbibe some of his imperial tendencies at the school because there was an almost universal desire among the boys to join either the army or the civil service for the glory of the empire.

In 1882, when Kipling was sixteen, he returned to India and his "English years fell away" and never "came back in full strength." Through his father's connections, Kipling had no difficulty in becoming assistant editor on *The Civil and Military Gazette* of Lahore at the age of eighteen. Two horror stories written during this period, "The Phantom Rickshaw" and "The Strange Ride of Morrowbie Jukes, C. E." have found a place among his best-known stories.

After four years on *The Civil and Military Gazette*, Kipling moved to Allahabad as assistant editor to *The Pioneer*, and his writings began to appear in four major newspapers of British India. Young, unattached, with servants and horses at his disposal, enfolded in the warmth of his family, these years proved to be Kipling's happiest and most productive. He wrote to a friend, "I'm in love with the country and would sooner write about her than anything else." *Departmental Ditties* was published in 1886 and *Plain Tales from the Hills* in 1888. Soon, Kipling was known all over India and a favorable review in the *Saturday Review* also created a demand for his writings in London.

In March, 1899, he left Lahore on a leisurely sea journey to London by way of Rangoon, Singapore, Hong Kong, Japan, and San Francisco. After making several stops across the United States, the twenty-four-year-old Kipling arrived in London in October, 1899. He has described this journey in *From Sea to Sea*, published the same year. In London, Kipling came into contact with the American Wolcott Balestier whom he met in Mrs. Humphrey Ward's drawing room. He collaborated with him on the novel *The Naulahka*.

Wolcott's sister Caroline was later to become Kipling's wife. Befriended by the poet W. E. Henley, Kipling published *Barrack-Room Ballads and Other Verses* in 1892. It was a completely new poetic voice in style, language, and content. Kipling won an audience, startled and shocked, but fascinated and hypnotized by his style.

Kipling left for America in June, 1891, and the short visit brought him into conflict with certain members of the American press. He returned to England and went on a long sea voyage with a sentimental stopover in India, his last visit to the subcontinent. He returned to London hurriedly because of Wolcott Balestier's death, and a few weeks later, on January 18, 1892, he married Caroline Balestier. Henry James gave away the bride.

The newly married couple returned to the Balestier home in Brattleboro, Vermont, where Kipling wrote *The Jungle Books* and other stories. He also became a friend of Mark Twain. His desire for privacy, his recurrent conflicts with the press, the death of his eldest daughter, Josephine, his own illness, and the notorious publicity as a result of a quarrel with his brother-in-law, all contributed to his decision to leave America in 1897, never to return.

Kipling went to South Africa during the Boer War and became a good friend of another empire builder, Cecil Rhodes. It was during the war that Kipling completed his most important novel *Kim*. Published in 1901, it was Kipling's farewell to India. In 1907, Kipling received the Nobel Prize. During World War I, Kipling lost his only son, John, and his melancholy deepened. The poem "My Boy Jack" (1916) articulates the grief and pain of that loss. In writing other works, he turned to the strange and the macabre, as in "A Madonna of the Trenches," "The Wish House," and "The Eyes of Allah."

Plagued by ill health during the last years of his life, he relied on his wife for support, but she also lost her health to the crippling effects of diabetes and rheumatism. Kipling published his last collection of stories, *Limits and Renewals*, in 1932, and continued to show interest in Britain and world affairs, angry at the complacency of his countrymen toward the growing Fascism outside England. He died January 18, 1936, and his ashes were buried in Westminster Abbey.

Analysis

Rudyard Kipling wrote four novels, one of them *The Naulahka*, in collaboration with Wolcott Balestier. Kipling was essentially a miniaturist, and his genius was for the short story, a single event dramatized within a specific time frame. His novels reflect an episodic quality, while Kipling brings to them a considerable amount of technical information—about cod fishing in *Captains Courageous*, army and artistic life in *The Light That Failed*, authentic topography and local color in *The Naulahka*, he fails in the development of character and in evoking an emotional response from his readers. *Kim*, however, is an exception.

The Light That Failed, dedicated to his mother, has often been described by critics as "the book that failed." Kipling acknowledged a debt to the French novel *Manon Lescaut* (1731) by Abbé Prévost in writing the novel. It was first published in the January, 1891, issue of *Lippincott's Monthly Magazine* and was later dramatized and filmed. When Macmillan and Co. published it two months later, there were four new chapters and the story concluded with a tragic ending and the note, "This is the story of *The Light That Failed* as it was originally conceived by the writer." The difference between the magazine version, with its more conventional ending, and the book version, with the sad ending, caused some consternation among readers and critics.

The Light That Failed has many autobiographical elements. The novel opens with two children brought up by a sadistic housekeeper; Kipling drew upon his own early life in "The House of Desolation" for some of the harrowing experiences of Dick and Maisie in the novel. Dick and Maisie are not related but have an adolescent crush on each other. They are separated, and while Dick goes to the Far East to serve on the frontiers of the empire, Maisie pursues her dream of becoming an artist. Dick wants Maisie to travel with him but Maisie, committed to her art, remains in England. Dick later moves to Egypt as a war artist. He returns to London, and after a period of frustration, he enjoys fame and success. Kipling draws on his familiarity with the art world to describe the life of Dick in London. He had never been to Africa, however, and for the realism of his African scenes, Kipling relied on information he got from his friends. When Dick expresses fury and anger at unscrupulous art dealers, Kipling is lashing out at the publishers in America who boldly pirated his works.

In Dick's and Maisie's doomed love and its impact on Dick, readers see echoes of Kipling's own unrequited love for Violet Flo Garrard. Flo, too, was a painter like Maisie and in the words of Kipling's sister, Flo was cold and obsessed with "her very ineffective little pictures." Angus Wilson, in his study of Kipling, believes that Kipling found in Flo the quintessential *femme fatale*, "the vampire that sucks man's life away." Kipling has transferred some of the intensity of this feeling to Dick Heldar, almost his alter ego at certain times in the novel. Dick Heldar's obsession with the single life and his desire for military life also expresses Kipling's own passions. When Dick goes blind after being spurned by Maisie, Kipling is again drawing upon his own anxiety about the possible loss of his own vision.

The Light That Failed ends very melodramatically with Dick's death in the Sudanese battlefield amid bloody carnage. Apart from the autobiographical elements in the novel, *The Light That Failed* has little interest for the contemporary student of Kipling.

Subtitled "A Story of East and West," and written in collaboration with Wolcott Balestier, *The Naulahka* compares the ways of the East, represented by the princely state of Rhatore in Central India, to those of the West, represented by the village of Topaz, Colorado. Balestier supplied the Western elements of the novel and Kipling wrote the Eastern chapters. The result is a poorly written, melodramatic, and lackluster novel.

Naulahka is a priceless necklace owned by the Maharaja of Rhatore. Tarvin, an aggressive American entrepreneur, wants to bring the railroad to feudalistic Rhatore; he enlists the services of Mutrie, the wife of the president of the railroad company, to influence her husband. He promises to get her the Naulahka as a gift. Tarvin's fiancée, Kate, is also in India to help the Indian women. With her help, Tarvin tries to influence the Maharaja's son. Kate wants a hospital; Tarvin wants the railroad. Kate then breaks off her relationship with Tarvin; he secures the necklace but returns it in order to save Kate's life, which is threatened by a mad priest. Finally, Kate and Tarvin return to the United States.

The characters in *The Naulahka* are one dimensional and the narrative style is very episodic. Kipling has drawn heavily from his earlier book *Letters of Marque* (1891), lifting entire passages and incidents.

A better novel than *The Light That Failed*, *Captains Courageous* is Kipling's only completely American book in character and atmosphere. Kipling made several visits to Gloucester, Massachusetts, with his friend Dr. John Conland to saturate himself with considerable technical information about cod fishing. He has used this information extravagantly in telling the story of *Captains Courageous*. The novel was published serially in *McClure's Magazine*, and Kipling was not pleased with its publication. In a letter to a friend, he wrote that the novel was really a series of sketches and that he had "crept out of the possible holes by labelling it a boy's story."

Captains Courageous is the story of Harvey Cheyne, the spoiled only son of a millionaire. On a voyage to Europe, Harvey falls overboard and is picked up by a fishing boat. He bellows out orders and insults the skipper, Disko. Disko decides to teach the boy a lesson and puts Harvey under a strict program of work and discipline. The plan succeeds, and Harvey emerges stronger and humanized. When the boat reaches Gloucester, laden with salted cod, a telegram is sent to Harvey's father who rushes from San Francisco to retrieve his son. Harvey returns with his father to resume his studies and prepare himself for taking over his father's business empire.

"Licking a raw cub into shape," the central theme of *Captains Courageous*, is a favorite of Kipling. The technical knowledge about cod fishing is impressive but the characters themselves have no individuality. Harvey Cheyne's transformation from a stubborn, spoiled young man into a mature, responsible individual is acheived too speedily. Kipling has used the story merely to illustrate what Birkenhead describes as "the virtue of the disciplined life upon a spoiled immature mind."

T. S. Eliot considered *Kim* to be Kipling's greatest work. Nirad C. Chaudhury, an Indian scholar, considers *Kim* to be "not only the finest novel in

English with an Indian theme but also one of the greatest of English novels in spite of the theme." Kipling wanted to write a major book about India, and he started the project in 1885, in *Mother Maturin: An Anglo-Indian Episode*. That work concerned itself with the "unutterable horrors of lower class Eurasian and native life as they exist outside reports and reports and reports." It was the story of an old Irishwoman who kept an opium den in Lahore but sent her daughter to study in London where she marries and returns to Lahore. Kipling's father did not like it, however, and Kipling dutifully abandoned the project. *Kim* emerged instead.

Published in 1901, *Kim* is Kipling's last book set in India. In *Something of Myself*, he tells readers how he had long thought of writing about "an Irish boy born in India and mixed up with native life." Written under the influence of his demon—Kipling's word to describe his guardian muse—*Kim* takes in all of India, its rich diversity and intensity of life.

In growing old and evaluating the past, Kipling turned to the best years of his life, his years in India. In *Kim*, Kipling relives his Indian years when everything was secure and his family intact. Kim's yearning for the open road, for its smells, sights, and sounds is part of the longing of Kipling himself for the land that quickened his creative impulse and provided his literary success.

Kim is the story of an Irish orphan boy in India, a child of the streets. He grows up among Indian children and is aware of all the subtle nuances of Indian life. Yet, at the same time, he has the spirit of adventure and energy of his Irish ancestry. His joining the Red Lama from Tibet on his quest for the River of Healing, and Kim's fascination for the British Indian secret service, "the Great Game," results in his own self-discovery.

Kim has the characteristic features of a boy's story, the lovable boy involved in a quest filled with adventure and intrigue. One is reminded of Robert Louis Stevenson's *Treasure Island* (1883) and *Kidnapped* (1886) and Mark Twain's *The Adventures of Tom Sawyer* (1876). *Kim*, however, rises above the usual boy's story in that it has a spiritual dimension. By coming into contact with the Lama, Kim emerges a sadder and wiser being at the end of the novel. Kim's racial superiority is emphasized throughout the novel, but after his association with the Lama, Kim is able to say, "Thou hast said there is neither black nor white, why plague me with this talk, Holy One? Let me rub the other foot. It vexes me, I am *not* a Sahib. I am thy chela, and my head is heavy on my shoulders." This is an unusual admission for Kim and Kipling.

Many of Kipling's earlier themes are elaborated and incorporated into *Kim*. There is the vivid picture of the Indian army; the tale of "Lispeth," from *Plain Tales from the Hills*, repeated in the story of the Lady of Shamlegh; and the Anglo-Indian, the native and the official worlds providing backgrounds as they did in the short stories. Administering medicine in the guise of a charm to soothe and satisfy the Indian native, Jat, is an echo from the earlier story, "The Tomb of His Ancestors." Buddhism, whose scriptural tales—*The Jataka Tales*—supplied Kipling with a wealth of source material for his two Jungle Books, and *Just So Stories* (1902), supplies the religious atmosphere in *Kim*. Even Kim's yearning for the open road had been expressed previously in the character of Strickland, who, incidentally, makes a brief appearance in *Kim*.

Both Kim and the Venerable Teshoo Lama, the two main characters in *Kim*, emerge as distinctive individual characters and not mere types of the Oriental holy man and the Anglo-Indian boy. They grow and develop an awareness of themselves and their surroundings. Kim realizes that his progress depends upon the cooperation of several people: the Lama, Mukherjee, Colonel Creighton, and Mahbub Ali. The Lama too undergoes a change of character. He realizes that his physical quest for the River of Arrow has clouded his spiritual vision. The River of Arrow is at his feet if he has the faith to see it.

In selecting the Buddhist Lama as the main character, Kipling has emphasized the Middle Way. To the Lama, there is no color, no caste, no sect. He is also the tone of moderation without the extremes of Hinduism and Islam, the two main religious forces on the subcontinent.

In the relationship between Kim and the Lama, Kipling portrays an integral part of Indian spiritual life, the disciple and teacher relationship, the *Guru* and *Chela* interaction. It is not an ordinary relationship between a boy and a holy man, it is a special relationship, as the Lama notes, forged out of a previous association in an earlier life, the result of good Karma. *Kim* is indeed a virtuoso performance; it is Kipling at his best.

K. Bhaskara Rao

Other major works

SHORT FICTION: *In Black and White*, 1888; *The Phantom Rickshaw and Other Tales*, 1888; *Plain Tales from the Hills*, 1888; *Soldiers Three*, 1888; *The Story of the Gadsbys*, 1888; *Under the Deodars*, 1888; *Wee Willie Winkie*, 1888; *Life's Handicap*, 1891; *Many Inventions*, 1893; *The Jungle Book*, 1894; *The Second Jungle Book*, 1895; *The Day's Work*, 1898; *Stalky & Co.*, 1899; *Just So Stories*, 1902; *Traffics and Discoveries*, 1904; *Puck of Pook's Hill*, 1906; *Actions and Reactions*, 1909; *Rewards and Fairies*, 1910; *A Diversity of Creatures*, 1917; *Land and Sea Tales for Scouts and Guides*, 1923; *Debits and Credits*, 1926; *Thy Servant a Dog*, 1930; *Limits and Renewals*, 1932.

POETRY: *Departmental Ditties*, 1886; *Barrack-Room Ballads and Other Verses*, 1892; *The Seven Seas*, 1896; *Recessional and Other Poems*, 1899; *The Five Nations*, 1903; *The Years Between*, 1919; *Rudyard Kipling's Verse*, 1940 (definitive edition).

NONFICTION: *American Notes*, 1891; *Beast and Man in India*, 1891; *Letters of Marque*, 1891; *The Smith Administration*, 1891; *From Sea to Sea*, 1899,

The New Army in Training, 1914; *France at War*, 1915; *The Fringes of the Fleet*, 1915; *Sea Warfare*, 1916; *Letters of Travel, 1892-1913*, 1920; *The Irish Guards in the Great War*, 1923; *A Book of Words*, 1928; *Something of Myself: For My Friends Known and Unknown*, 1937; *Uncollected Prose*, 1938 (2 volumes); *Rudyard Kipling to Rider Haggard: The Record of a Friendship*, 1965 (Morton N. Cohen, editor).

MISCELLANEOUS: *The Sussex Edition of the Complete Works in Prose and Verse of Rudyard Kipling*, 1937-1939 (35 volumes).

Bibliography

Amis, Kingsley. *Rudyard Kipling and His World*. London: Thames and Hudson, 1975. A general biography, anecdotal and chronological in approach, with some critique of Kipling's works in passing. Contains 115 illustrations, with special attention to India, and plates from Kipling's works.

Birkenhead, Lord. *Rudyard Kipling*. London: Weidenfeld & Nicholson, 1978. Some discussion of Kipling's works, but mainly a chronological biography of his life and surrounding influences. Contains thirty-four illustrations, appendices of honors and awards, and a list of major works.

Carrington, Charles. *Rudyard Kipling: His Life and Works*. London: Macmillan, 1978. A standard biography with access to unique inside information. The appendices to the 1978 edition contain information previously suppressed by Kipling's heirs. Includes a chronology of his life and work as well as a family tree. Much stronger on his adult life than his childhood and concentrates on his life and the influences upon it rather than on literary critique.

Fido, Martin. *Rudyard Kipling*. New York: Viking Press, 1974. A general biography with numerous illustrations, some in color. Short on literary critique but contains some commentary on Kipling's works.

Knowles, Frederic Lawrence. *A Kipling Primer*. Reprint. New York: Haskell House, 1974. Chapter 1 concerns biographical data and includes personality traits. Chapter 2 elaborates on Kipling's literary techniques and critically examines the stages of his artistic development. Chapter 3 is an index to his major writings with brief descriptions and criticisms of Kipling's works by other authors.

Wilson, Angus. *The Strange Ride of Rudyard Kipling: His Life and Works*. London: Martin Secker & Warburg, 1977. Primarily a straight biography with the largest text of Kipling's works published after 1970. There is no easy access to critiques or lists of works and no separate biographical time line or appendices.

ARTHUR KOESTLER

Born: Budapest, Hungary; September 5, 1905
Died: London, England; March 3, 1983

Principal long fiction

The Gladiators, 1939; *Darkness at Noon*, 1940; *Arrival and Departure*, 1943; *Thieves in the Night: Chronicle of an Experiment*, 1946; *The Age of Longing*, 1951; *The Call Girls: A Tragi-Comedy with Prologue and Epilogue*, 1972.

Other literary forms

Arthur Koestler's first five novels, along with most of his other books, have been reissued in the Danube edition, published in England by Hutchinson and Company and in America by Macmillan Publishing Company. His non-fiction works include four autobiographical volumes—*Spanish Testament* (1937), abridged in the Danube edition as *Dialogue with Death* (1942); *Scum of the Earth* (1941); *Arrow in the Blue: The First Volume of an Autobiography, 1905-1931* (1952); and *The Invisible Writing: The Second Volume of an Autobiography, 1932-1940* (1954)—as well as an autobiographical essay on his disillusionment with Communism found in *The God That Failed* (1950), edited by Richard Crossman with additional essays by Richard Wright, Ignazio Silone, Stephen Spender, Louis Fischer, and André Gide. Koestler's nonfiction works exceed twenty-five volumes, divided roughly between social-historical commentary and the history of science. He also wrote one play, *Twilight Bar: An Escapade in Four Acts* (1945).

Achievements

Koestler will be remembered as an apostate to the Left who dramatized in *Darkness at Noon* and in his autobiographical works the integrity of many Communist intellectuals in the 1930's and the anguish they suffered under Joseph Stalin. As a novelist, he is generally a skilled storyteller, putting conventional techniques to the service of philosophical themes. Although none of his novels have been best-sellers in the usual sense, *Darkness at Noon*—translated into thirty-three languages—has been reprinted many times, and its appeal shows no sign of slackening. It continues to be read widely in college courses and is probably one of the most influential political novels of the century, despite the fact that comparatively little academic literary criticism has been devoted to it. Indeed, Koestler's novels—even *Darkness at Noon* are perhaps kept alive more by political scientists and historians than by professional students of literature.

Besides being an accomplished novelist of ideas, Koestler was one of the finest journalists of his age, often producing works as controversial as his political fiction. Typical of his best essays is the piece in *The Lotus and the*

Robot (1960) on "Yoga Unexpurgated" (noted as being "far too horrible for me to read" by William Empson in his review); like many other of his best essays, "Yoga Unexpurgated" will maintain its readability. *The Sleepwalkers: A History of Man's Changing Vision of the Universe* (1959), a survey of early scientific thought with emphasis on Renaissance astronomy, is part of a trilogy (with *The Act of Creation*, 1964, and *The Ghost in the Machine*, 1967) on the understanding of the human mind, and it ranks as Koestler's most suggestive effort at research and speculation. Even more controversial than his psychological studies, although a wholly different kind of work, is *The Thirteenth Tribe* (1976), which revived the thesis that the Jews of Eastern Europe are descended from the ancient Khazar Empire. Scholarly reviews of Koestler's research tended to be severe. *The Case of the Midwife Toad* (1971) reveals sympathies for neo-Lamarckian philosophy, and *The Roots of Coincidence* (1972) surveys the claims of parapsychology, ending with a plea "to get out of the straitjacket which nineteenth-century materialism imposed on any philosophical outlook."

Although he flirted with crank notions, to the detriment of his credibility, Koestler was neither a crank nor a dilettante. His renegade vision has enlivened contemporary arts and letters for several decades, and it is likely that this force will continue to be felt for several more.

Biography

Arthur Koestler was born on September 5, 1905, in Budapest, Hungary, the only child of middle-class Jewish parents. He was precocious in math and science, and closer to his mother than to his father, an eccentric, self-taught businessman. When Koestler was in his teens, the family moved to Vienna, and he attended the university there as a science student. After four years, he left school without a degree and went to Palestine, where he joined a Zionist movement for a while before obtaining a correspondent's job with the Ullstein newspapers of Germany. He advanced rapidly in journalism, becoming in 1930, the foreign editor of *B.Z. am Mittag* and the science editor of *Vossische Zeitung* in Berlin, partly as a result of his success as a reporter on the *Graf Zeppelin* flight to the North Pole in 1931.

In December, 1931, Koestler became a member of the German Communist party, and less than a year later he gave up his position with Ullstein's and spent several weeks traveling in the Soviet Union. He then spent three years in Paris working for the Comintern, leaving for Spain at the outbreak of the Spanish Civil War in 1936. His marriage to Dorothy Asher in 1935 lasted only two years before they were separated, eventually to be divorced in 1950. While in Spain for the Comintern in 1937, Koestler was captured by the Nationalists and sentenced to execution. Thanks to the British press, he was freed after three months, and he published an account of his experiences, *Spanish Testament*. By the next year, he was in France again, where he resigned from the Communist Party in disillusionment with Stalinism and the show trials. During that time, he wrote *Darkness at Noon*. After escaping from Nazi internment in France, he fled to Britain and spent 1941 to 1942 in the British Pioneer Corps.

Darkness at Noon was published in 1946, and Koestler was in Paris at the center of the uproar it caused among members of the French Left. (Simone de Beauvoir's *roman à clef*, *The Mandarins*, 1956, makes vivid this period in French intellectual life.) In the late 1940's, Koestler became a leader among anti-Communist voices in the West, twice visiting America to lecture, as well as enjoying an appointment between 1950 and 1951 as a Chubb Fellow at Yale University. After his divorce in 1950, he married Mamaine Paget. In 1952, he took up residence in America for two years, during which time he published his autobiographical volumes *Arrow in the Blue* and *The Invisible Writing*. He was divorced in 1953. One phase in his career ended in 1955, when he indicated in *Trail of the Dinosaur and Other Essays* that he was through writing about politics. At that time, his interest turned to mysticism and science, and he tried in his writings on ESP to narrow the gap between natural and extrasensory phenomena. He married Cynthia Jefferies in 1965. After World War II, Koestler became a naturalized citizen of England and his adopted country honored him by making him a Commander of the Order of the British Empire (C.B.E.) in 1972 and a Companion of Literature (C.Lit.) in 1974.

Koestler died in London, England, on March 3, 1983. His wife was found beside him, both victims of an apparent suicide.

Analysis

All of Arthur Koestler's works, both fiction and nonfiction, reveal a struggle to escape from the oppressiveness of nineteenth century positivism and its later offshoots. *The Yogi and the Commissar and Other Essays* (1945) sums up the moral paradox of political action. The Yogi, at one extreme, represents a life lived by values that are grounded in idealism. The Yogi scorns utilitarian goals and yields to quietism; his refusal to intervene leads to passive toleration of social evil. The Commissar, committed to dialectical materialism, ignores the shallow ethical concerns of the historically benighted middle class and seeks to function as an instrument of historical progress. History replaces God, and human suffering is seen as an inevitable step toward the ultimate historical synthesis, rather than as an element of God's mysterious purpose. For the Commissar the end justifies the means, and it is this ethical position that is debated most effectively in *The Gladiators*, *Darkness at Noon*, and *Arrival and Departure*.

In his Postscript to the Danube edition of *The Gladiators*, Koestler points out that these novels form a trilogy "whose leitmotif is the central question of revolutionary ethics and of political ethics in general: the question whether, or to what extent, the end justifies the means." The question "obsessed" him, he says, during the seven years in which he belonged to the Communist Party and for several years afterward. It was his answer to this question that caused him to break with the Party, as he explains eloquently in his essay in *The God That Failed*. The city built by the rebellious slaves in *The Gladiators* fails because Spartacus does not carry out the stern measures necessary to insure the city's successful continuation. In *Darkness at Noon*, the old revolutionary Rubashov is depicted as trying to avoid the error Spartacus made but ending up lost in a maze of moral and ethical complications that destroy him.

Behaviorist psychology is congenial to the materialism of Communist revolutionary ethics, and Koestler attacks its claims heatedly. Indeed, Koestler's interest in mysticism, the occult, and parapsychology was an attempt to find an escape route from the deadly rationalism that makes man a mere clockwork orange. As far back as 1931, Koestler was investigating psychometry with as much curiosity as he brought to his journalistic accounts of the exploding universe. His answer to the behaviorists is laid out in *The Ghost in the Machine*, and it is clearly a theological answer. Koestler implies here that evolution is purposive, hence the theological nature of his understanding of life. A problem remains, however; Koestler argues that the limbic system of the brain is at odds with its neo-cortex, resulting in irrational decisions much of the time. Man is thus as likely to speed to his own destruction as he is to his fulfillment. Koestler's unorthodox answer to man's Manichaean internal struggle is deliberate mutation by chemical agents. The same topic is fictionalized quite successfully in *The Call Girls*.

Koestler's first novel, *The Gladiators*, was written in German and translated into English by Edith Simon (his later novels were published in his own English). The source of the novel is the sketchy account—fewer than four thousand words all together—of the Slave War of 73-71 B.C. found in Livy, Plutarch, Appian, and Florus. Koestler divides his narrative into four books. The first, entitled "Rise," imagines the revolt led by the Thracian gladiator Spartacus and a fat, cruel Gaul named Crixus. They march through Campania looting and adding more defectors to their band. In Book Two, "The Law of Detours," after the destruction of the towns Nola, Suessula, and Calatia, the rebels are twenty thousand strong, or more, and approaching the peak of their power. The unruly faction, however, has spoiled the movement's idealism, by its ransacking of these towns, and Spartacus is faced with a decision: Should he let this group go on blindly into a foolhardy battle with the forces of the Roman general Varinius, or should he counsel them and enforce a policy of prudence? In his deliberations he is aided by a wise Essene, a type of the imminent Christ, who tells him that of all God's curses on man, "the worst curse of all is that he must tread the evil road for the sake of the good and right, that he must make detours and walk crookedly so that he may reach the straight goal." He further tells Spartacus that for what the leader wants to do now, he needs other counselors.

Despite the Essene's warning, Spartacus follows the "law of detours." Later that night, he confers with Crixus, and although no details of their talk are given, it is clear that Crixus is going to lead the lawless to their unwitting deaths in a confrontation with Varinius. This sacrifice of the unruly faction, however justified, is a cynical detour from honor. Later, however, when the Thracian Spartacus, already pressed by food shortages in the Sun State after a double-cross by the neighboring city, is faced with a rebellion against his policies by the Celts, he proves to be insufficiently ruthless: he still retains the idealism with which he began the revolution. Koestler sums it up in his 1965 postscript: "Yet he shrinks from taking the last step—the purge by crucifixion of the dissident Celts and the establishment of a ruthless tyranny; and through this refusal he dooms his revolution to defeat." Book Three, "The Sun State," recounts the conflicts that lead up to Spartacus' defeat, and the gladiators' humiliation and crucifixion are narrated in Book Four, "Decline." Although Koestler's characters are wooden, *The Gladiators* is a satisfying historical novel; the milieu is well sketched, and Spartacus' dilemmas are rendered convincingly.

Darkness at Noon, Koestler's masterpiece, is the story of an old Bolshevik, Rubashov, who is called before his Communist inquisitors on charges of heresy against the Party. He is interrogated first by Ivanov, who is himself executed, and then by Gletkin, and at the end he is killed by the inevitable bullet in the back of the neck. The novel is divided into three sections, one for each hearing Rubashov is given, and a short epilogue entitled "The Grammatical Fiction." Besides the confrontations between Rubashov and his questioners, there are flashbacks from Rubashov's past and extracts from his diary; the latter provide occasions for Koestler's meditations on history. The narrative is tight and fast-moving, and its lucid exposition has surely made it one of the most satisfyingly pedagogic novels of all time. Many readers shared the experience of Leslie Fiedler, who referred to *Darkness at Noon* in his review of *The Ghost in the Machine*, admitting that "Koestler helped to deliver me from the platitudes of the Thirties, from those organized self-deceptions which, being my first, were especially dear and difficult to escape."

Speaking of the "historical circumstances" of *Darkness at Noon*, Koestler explains that Rubashov is "a synthesis of the lives of a number of men who were victims of the so-called Moscow Trials." Rubashov's thinking is closest to that of Nikolai Bukharin, a real purge victim, and Rubashov's tormentor, Gletkin, had a counterpart of sorts in the actual trial prosecutor Andrei Vishinsky. (Robert Conquest's *The Great Terror*, 1968, provides useful details of the real trials.)

Two main theses are argued in *Darkness at Noon*: that the end does not justify the means; and that the individual ego, the *I*, is not a mere "grammatical fiction" whose outline is blurred by the sweep of the historical dialectic. The events that cause Rubashov great pain and guilt involve two party workers whose devotion is sacrificed to the law of detours. Little Loewy is the local leader of the dockworkers' section of the Party in Belgium, a likable man whom Rubashov takes to immediately. Little Loewy is a good Communist, but he is ill-used by the Party and eventually destroyed in an act of expediency. When the Party calls for the workers to resist the spreading Nazi menace, Little Loewy's dockworkers refuse to handle cargoes going out from and coming into Germany. The crisis comes when five cargo ships from Russia arrive in port. The workers start to unload these boats until they discover the contents: badly needed materials for the German war effort. The workers strike, the Party orders them back to the docks, and most of the workers defect. Two years later, Mussolini ventures into Africa and again a boycott is called, but this time Rubashov is sent in advance to explain to the dockworkers that more Russian cargo is on its way and the Party wants it unloaded. Little Loewy rejects the duplicity, and six days later he hangs himself.

In another tragedy of betrayal, Rubashov abandons his secretary, Arlova, a woman who loves him and with whom he has had an affair. When Arlova's brother in Russia marries a foreigner, they all come under suspicion, Arlova included. Soon after, she is called back to oblivion in Russia, and all of this happens without a word from Rubashov. As these perfidies run through his mind, Rubashov's toothache rages intensely. Ivanov senses Rubashov's human sympathies and lectures him on the revolutionary ethic: "But you must allow that we are as convinced that you and they would mean the end of the Revolution as you are of the reverse. That is the essential point. The methods follow by logical deduction. We can't afford to lose ourselves in political subtleties." Thus, Rubashov's allegiance to the law of detours leads him into a moral labyrinth. He fails to heed that small voice that gives dignity to the self in its resistance to the degrading impersonality of all-devouring history and the behaviorist conception of man.

In *Arrival and Departure*, Koestler's third novel, Peter Slavek, twenty-two, stows away on a freighter coming from Eastern Europe and washes up in Neutralia (Portugal) in 1940. He is a former Communist who has been tortured by Fascists in his home country, and he is faced in Neutralia with four possibilities: reunion with the Party, with whom he is disillusioned; joining the Fascists, who present themselves as the shapers of the true Brave New World; flight to America; or, finally, enlistment with the British, whose culture is maimed but still represents a "brake" on the madness overtaking Europe. Homeless and confused, he meets two women. Dr. Sonia Bolgar, a native of his country and friend of his family, gives him a room and looks after him while she is waiting for the visa that will take her to America. Her lover, Odette, is a young French war widow with whom Peter has a brief affair until Odette leaves for America. Her departure precipitates a psychosomatic paralysis of one of Peter's legs, symbolic of the paralysis of will brought on in him by conflicting urges to follow her and to commit himself again to political action. Sonia, who is an analyst and reduces all behavior to the terms of her profession, leads Peter through a deconstruction of his motives that exposes their origins in childhood guilt feelings. His self-insight cures his paralysis, just as his visa for America is granted. He prepares to leave, but at the last moment dashes off the ship and joins the British, who parachute him back into his own country in their service.

Much of *Arrival and Departure* is artistically inert, but it does have a solid point to make. Although Fyodor Dostoevski's name is never mentioned in *Arrival and Departure*, the novel is Koestler's response to Dostoevski's *The Possessed* (1871-1872), which depicts revolutionaries as warped personalities dramatizing their neuroses and grudges in political action. For Koestler, human motives are more complex: *"You can explain the messages of the Prophets as epileptical foam and the Sistine Madonna as the projection of an incestuous dream. The method is correct and the picture in itself complete. But beware of the arrogant error of believing that it is the only one."* *Arrival and Departure* is, then, a subtle commentary on the motivation of revolutionaries, rejecting any claims to exclusivity by psychoanalysis and psychobiography.

A far more absorbing novel than *Arrival and Departure*, *Thieves in the Night* is an account of the establishment of the commune of Ezra's Tower in Palestine. Many of the events are seen from the perspective of one of the commune's settlers, a young man named Joseph who was born and educated in England. His father was Jewish, his mother English, and this mixed heritage justifies Koestler's use of him as a voice to meditate on the Jewish character and the desirability of assimilation. As a novelistic study of a single character, *Thieves in the Night* is incomplete, but as a depiction of the personal tensions within a commune and as an essay on the international politics wracking Palestine in the period from 1937 to 1939, it is excellent. The British policy formulated in the 1939 White Paper is exposed in all its cruelty. This policy— perhaps influenced by romantic conceptions of the Arab world—shut down the flow of immigrants into Palestine, leaving the Jews exposed and helpless in Europe. At the novel's end, Joseph has joined the terrorist movement and is engaged in smuggling Polish Jews off the Rumanian cattle boats that are forbidden to unload their homeless cargo. In its musings on terrorism, *Thieves in the Night* seems to back off from the repudiation of the doctrine that the end justifies the means. Koestler always faced these issues honestly, and *Thieves in the Night* is as engrossing—and as cogent—in the 1980's as it was in 1946.

Published in 1951 and set in Paris in the the middle 1950's, *The Age of Longing* describes a time of spiritual disillusionment and longing for an age of faith. The narrative opens on Bastille Day and focuses on three characters: Hydie, a young American apostate from Catholicism, who kneels on her priedieu and asks, "LET ME BELIEVE IN SOMETHING"; Fedya Nikitin, a security officer with a rigid commissar mentality, and Julien Delattre, poet and former party member. The relationship between Hydie and Fedya occupies much of the novel, with Hydie's ache for religious solace played off against Fedya's unquestioning faith in Communism. Hydie is American, naïve, and innocent; she is seeking experience on which to base faith. Fedya is the son of proletarian revolutionaries from Baku, a son of the revolution with the instincts of a true commissar. He seems to have been programmed with Party clichés. When the two become lovers, Fedya humiliates Hydie by treating her as a mere collocation of conditioned responses. She then turns against Fedya and, finally understanding his true assignment as a spy, tries to shoot him but botches the job. Whether their relationship has allegorical significance, the unfeeling commissar is one of Koestler's most effective characterizations. At one point, Fedya asks a young school friend why she likes him, and the answer is "Because you are clean and simple and hard like an effigy of 'Our Proletarian Youth' from a propaganda poster."

The third main character, Julien Delattre, is in many ways a self-portrait. He has given up his allegiance to the "God that failed," and he tells Hydie that "My generation turned to Marx as one swallows acid drops to fight off nausea." He finds his mission in warning others about the ideological traps that he has successfully escaped, and one of the best scenes in the novel comes when he takes Hydie to an evening meeting of the Rally for Peace and Progress. The centerpiece of the session is Koestler's satirical depiction of Jean-Paul Sartre, who appears as the pompous theoretician Professior Pontieux. Author of a fashionable work of postwar despair, "Negation and Position," Professor Pontieux "can prove everything he believes, and he believes everything he can prove." *The Age of Longing* ends with an image appropriate to its theme. A funeral party is proceeding past the graves of Jean de La Fontaine, Victor Hugo, and others when air-raid sirens start screaming. "The siren wailed, but nobody was sure: it could have meant the Last Judgment, or just another air-raid exercise."

More than twenty years passed between the publication of *The Age of Longing* and that of *The Call Girls*, Koestler's last novel. During those two decades, Koestler's interests had shifted from ideology to science and human behavior. The "call girls" of the title are prominent intellectuals—mostly scientists but including a poet and a priest—nomads of the international conference circuit. Koestler puts them all together in a Swiss mountain setting and sets them to talking about ideas. They have been summoned by one of their members, Nikolai Solovief, a physicist, to consider "Approaches to Survival" and send a message to the president of the United States. Unfortunately, the meeting degenerates into a series of uncompromising exchanges between behaviorists and nonbehaviorists. Only Nikolai and Tony, the priest, are able to accommodate themselves to the claims of both reason and faith, and rancor replaces the objective search for truth. *The Call Girls* is an enter-

taining exposition of the various options available to those seeking enlightenment today. Readers of *The Ghost in the Machine* and Koestler's work on
ESP will recognize in the arguments of Nikolai and Tony those of Koestler
himself. Koestler has always staged his intellectual dramas in the dress of
irreconcilable opposites—the yogi and the commissar, ends versus means—
and here the protagonist is clearly spirit and the antagonist matter. His call
girls demonstrate that there is still life in this old conflict.

Frank Day

Other major works

PLAY: *Twilight Bar: An Escapade in Four Acts*, 1945.

NONFICTION: *Spanish Testament*, 1937; *Scum of the Earth*, 1941; *Dialogue
with Death*, 1942; *The Yogi and the Commissar and Other Essays*, 1945;
Promise and Fulfillment: Palestine, 1917-1949, 1949; *Insight and Outlook: An
Inquiry into the Common Foundations of Science, Art, and Social Ethics*,
1949; *Arrow in the Blue: The First Volume of an Autobiography, 1905-1931*,
1952; *The Invisible Writing: The Second Volume of an Autobiography, 1932-
1940*, 1954; *Trial of the Dinosaur and Other Essays*, 1955; *Reflections on
Hanging*, 1956; *The Sleepwalkers: A History of Man's Changing Vision of the
Universe*, 1959; *The Lotus and the Robot*, 1960; *Hanged by the Neck: An
Exposure of Capital Punishment in England*, 1961 (with C. H. Rolph); *Suicide
of a Nation? An Enquiry into the State of Britain Today*, 1963 (edited); *The
Act of Creation*, 1964; *The Ghost in the Machine*, 1967; *Drinkers of Infinity:
Essays, 1955-1967*, 1968 (edited with J. R. Smythies); *Beyond Reductionism:
New Perspectives in the Life Sciences*, 1969 (edited with J. R. Smythies); *The
Case of the Midwife Toad*, 1971; *The Roots of Coincidence*, 1972; *The Chal-
lenge of Chance: Experiments and Speculations*, 1973 (with Sir Alister Hardy
and Robert Harvie); *The Heel of Achilles: Essays, 1968-1973*, 1974; *The
Thirteenth Tribe*, 1976; *Life After Death*, 1976 (with Arthur Toynbee, *et al.*);
Janus: A Summing Up, 1978; *Bricks to Babel: Selected Writings with Com-
ments*, 1981.

Bibliography

Day, Frank. *Arthur Koestler: A Guide to Research*. New York: Garland, 1987.
In addition to a listing of Koestler's publications, there are 518 entries for
writings about him, many of them from newspapers and journals. Includes
some foreign-language items, and the latest materials are from 1985.
Hamilton, Iain. *Koestler: A Biography*. New York: Macmillan, 1982. This
lengthy biography, favorable to Koestler, is arranged year by year in the
fashion of a chronicle and breaks off around 1970. Many events have been
retold partly on the basis of interviews, Koestler's papers, and firsthand
accounts.

Harris, Harold, ed. *Astride the Two Cultures: Arthur Koestler at Seventy.* London: Hutchinson University Library, 1975. This collection of essays by authors sympathetic to Koestler provides approximately equal coverage of the writer's involvement in literary and in scientific concerns.

Koestler, Arthur, and Cynthia Koestler. *Stranger on the Square.* Edited by Harold Harris. London: Hutchinson University Library, 1984. What began as a joint memoir was, in the end, written largely by Cynthia, Koestler's third wife. Contains some provocative and revealing passages on events during the 1940's and 1950's, when she served as a personal secretary to the writer.

Levene, Mark. *Arthur Koestler.* New York: Frederick Ungar, 1984. Koestler's own life is discussed in the first chapter, and his major literary works are considered in detail, but relatively little attention has been given to his scientific writings. The chronology and bibliography are useful.

Mikes, George. *Arthur Koestler: The Story of a Friendship.* London: André Deutsch, 1983. The author first met Koestler in 1952, and in this brief account he has set down some anecdotes, by turns whimsical and moving, which provide glimpses of the writer's character and home life.

Pearson, Sidney A., Jr. *Arthur Koestler.* Boston: Twayne, 1978. Although a bit sketchy on matters of biography, this work deals with basic issues in Koestler's writings and has some trenchant and interesting discussion of political themes. Also helpful are the chronology and a selected annotated bibliography.

Sperber, Murray A., ed. *Arthur Koestler: A Collection of Critical Essays.* Englewood Cliffs, N.J.: Prentice-Hall, 1977. Both positive and negative reactions appear in this fine sampling of critical work about Koestler's literary and scientific writings. Among those commentators represented by excerpts here are George Orwell, Saul Bellow, Edmund Wilson, Stephen Spender, and A. J. Ayer, as well as others. A chronology and bibliography have also been included.

JERZY KOSINSKI

Born: Lodz, Poland; June 14, 1933
Died: Manhattan, New York; May 3, 1991

Principal long fiction

The Painted Bird, 1965; *Steps*, 1968; *Being There*, 1971; *The Devil Tree*, 1973 (revised, 1981); *Cockpit*, 1975; *Blind Date*, 1977; *Passion Play*, 1979; *Pinball*, 1982; *The Hermit of 69th Street: The Working Papers of Norbert Kosky*, 1988.

Other literary forms

Jerzy Kosinski was a professional sociologist, educated in Poland and the Soviet Union. His first two books in English were studies of collectivized life in Soviet Russia, *The Future Is Ours, Comrade* (1960), and *No Third Path* (1962), both published under the pen name Joseph Novak. Kosinski has discussed some of his critical views in two short booklets, *Notes of the Author on "The Painted Bird"* (1965) and *The Art of the Self* (1968).

Achievements

Kosinski is among that small group of serious, difficult, absolutely uncompromising writers who have attained critical acclaim, and, at the same time, great popular success; his novels regularly appeared on best-seller lists and have won such prizes as the National Book Award (1969) and the French Prix du Meilleur Livre Etranger (best foreign book, 1966). His first, most popular, and probably best novel, *The Painted Bird*, about a child growing up through sheer determination in a very hostile world, is one of those works, such as Daniel Defoe's *Robinson Crusoe* (1719) or Mark Twain's *The Adventures of Huckleberry Finn* (1884), that immediately touch some basic part of every reader. His later novels expressed contemporary experiences so directly that they seem to have been written out of the day's headlines. The charges of excessive violence and sensationalism are sometimes directed against Kosinski's work, but he argued cogently that life, no matter how much people have numbed themselves to it, is violent and sensational and it is better to face the implications of those realities than to run and hide from them. In fact, it is only in experiencing life fully that one can extract value from it. His existential theme is that only when one lives conscious of the knowledge of one's coming death is one fully alive. Kosinski's reputation will continue to grow as critics and thoughtful readers better understand his intentions.

Biography

Jerzy Nikodem Kosinski was born in Lodz, Poland, on June 14, 1933. His life was as incredible as any of his novels, which are, to some degree, autobiographical. In 1939, when he was six, World War II began. He was

Jewish, and his parents, believing he would be safer in the remote eastern provinces of Poland, paid a large sum of money to have him taken there. He reached eastern Poland, where he was immediately abandoned; his parents thought he was dead. Instead, at this very young age, he learned to live by his wits in an area where the peasants were hostile and the Nazis were in power. The extreme experiences of that time were given artistic expression in his first novel, *The Painted Bird*. Kosinski survived the ordeal and his parents found him in an orphanage at the end of the war. The stress of his experience had rendered him mute, and his irregular, wandering life had left him unfit to live normally with other people. Finally, in the care of his family, Kosinski regained his speech, and, studying with his philologist father, he completed his entire basic formal education in a year and entered the University of Lodz, where he eventually earned advanced degrees in history and political science.

By that time, Poland was an iron-curtain country with a collectivized society. Kosinski, after his youthful years of lone wandering, had developed a fierce independence and could not endure communal life in which the individual was under scrutiny at every step. He knew he could not remain without getting into serious trouble with the government, so he put together an elaborate scheme to escape. Making the cumbersome bureaucracy work in his favor, Kosinski invented a series of sponsors, all highly regarded scientists according to the documents he forged for them, to write him letters of recommendation, which eventually enabled him to get a passport to study in the United States. He arrived in New York on December 20, 1957, twenty-four years old, with $2.80 in his pocket and a good textbook knowledge of English, though little experience in speaking the language. He lived any way he could, stealing food when necessary and constantly studying English. By March, he was fluent in the language, and within three years he had published *The Future Is Ours, Comrade*, a study of Soviet life that sold extremely well. Suddenly he was moderately wealthy, but that was only the beginning. Mary Hayward Weir, the young widow of steel magnate Ernest Weir and one of the wealthiest women in the United States, read his book and wrote him a letter of praise. They met and were soon married. All at once he was wealthy beyond his own dreams, owning villas in several countries, a vast yacht, a private jet. "I had lived the American nightmare," he has said; "now I was living the American dream."

Five years later, in 1968, Mary Weir died of a brain tumor. The wealth, held by her in trust, went back to the estate. Kosinski had, during his marriage, written his first two novels, *The Painted Bird* and *Steps*, and he was a well-known, celebrated author. Needing to earn a living, he taught at Yale, Princeton, and Wesleyan. He continued to write novels; they continued to sell well, so that he was able to leave teaching to write full time. He was remarried, to Katherina von Frauenhofer, in 1987.

Kosinski's life then fell into an active but regular and disciplined pattern. In season, he traveled to Switzerland to ski or to the Caribbean to play polo, and he made extensive American tours, granting innumerable interviews and publicizing his books. He was also internationally active in civil rights cases and served for two terms (the maximum allowed) as president of P.E.N., the international writers organization. The rest of the time he spent working in his small apartment in Manhattan.

On May 3, 1991, Jerzy Kosinski, suffering from a serious heart disorder and discouraged by a growing inability to work, apparently chose to end his own life.

Kosinski often wrote that the world is an arena of violence and pure chance, which was certainly true of his own life. In addition to the numerous violent fluctuations of his early life, on a 1969 trip his baggage was misplaced, by chance, delaying his plane flight. His eventual destination was the home of his friends Roman Polanski and Sharon Tate; had it not been for the delay he would have been there the fateful night the Manson gang murdered everyone in the house.

Always a highly visible figure, Kosinski became in the early 1980's the subject of unwelcome publicity. In an article in *The Village Voice* (June 29, 1982), Geoffrey Stokes and Eliot Fremont-Smith charged that a number of Kosinski's novels had been written in part by various editorial assistants whose contributions he failed to acknowledge and indeed systematically concealed. Stokes and Fremont-Smith further charged that Kosinski's accounts to interviewers of his traumatic childhood experiences, his escape from Poland, and his first years in America have been contradictory and in some cases verifiably untrue. Finally, they suggested that Kosinski's acclaimed first novel, *The Painted Bird*, was actually written in Polish and then rendered into English by an unacknowledged translator. Kosinski denied all the charges. In *The Hermit of 69th Street*, which its protagonist calls a *"roman à tease,"* he responds indirectly to the controversy by reflecting on the writer's craft, which, he concludes, is largely a process of borrowing and recasting narrative material.

Analysis

The themes and techniques of Jerzy Kosinski's fiction are adumbrated in the sociological studies he published within five years of his arrival in the United States. As a highly regarded Polish sociology student in the mid 1950's, Kosinski was granted permission to travel widely in the Soviet Union to interview people about their experiences in collectivized living. It was assumed by the authorities that he would write a thesis praising Communism, but, in fact, he found it abhorrent; his notes provided material for *No Third Path* and *The Future Is Ours, Comrade*, indictments of the system which he could never have published had he remained behind the iron curtain. The studies are diaries of his travels and consist mainly of his interviews with the people he met, people from every walk of life, some of whom were thriving in conformity within the system while others were in trouble because of their opposition to it. The interviews are not arranged chronologically; rather, each is located at the point where it can best support the theme under discussion.

This arrangement is typical of the structure of Kosinski's novels. The protagonist, who often has a great deal in common with Kosinski himself, is a loner, able to travel freely through all walks of life. Because he is secretly at war with his society, he is unable to stop and settle or to have more than a fleeting relationship with each person he encounters. The brief scenes in the novels are not arranged chronologically, but each vignette is one more stone in a mosaic; taken together, these vignettes constitute a powerful statement of Kosinski's recurring theme.

That theme is exactly the same as that of the sociological studies on collective life: the struggle of the individual to retain his individuality in a mass society. Central to Kosinski's novels are the ideas of the German philosopher Martin Heidegger, who profoundly influenced the existentialists. Heidegger said that one has no control over what is given one in life—where and when one is born, whether one is healthy or the reverse, intelligent or the reverse—that is all a matter of chance. It is one's responsibility, however, to make the most of the particular life one is given. Daily life, petty responsibilities, the routine of work and family life, all have the effect of dulling one to the passage of time, and with it, the passage of one's opportunity to make the most of one's brief life. It is soothing, in a way, to be lulled and numbed into inattentiveness to coming pain and dissolution, yet to live in such a state is really not to live at all. According to Heidegger, one only lives fully when confronted by the terror of approaching death. The Kosinski hero purposely and unflaggingly thrusts himself into the terror-ridden present moment of his life, heroically refusing the deceptive and deadening temptations of his society to give up his lonely individuality and crawl under the umbrella of its collective "safety."

While Kosinski was living in immense wealth with his wife Mary Hayward Weir, he began writing *The Painted Bird*, a novel which, in its details, closely parallels his own experience as an orphaned outcast. "It was an attempt to somehow balance the reality of my past with the reality of my present. She [Mary], in turn, learned of my past through my writing." This statement suggests an autobiographical impulse for writing *The Painted Bird*; in other statements, however, Kosinski has made it clear that it was a novel, a work of art he was writing, not a memoir.

The child protagonist of the novel, never named, is dark-haired and dark-eyed, and he speaks the educated dialect. The peasants among whom he is abandoned are blond and blue-eyed and speak a barely comprehensible peasant dialect. He stands out from them at a glance, and they suspect he is a gypsy or a Jew; the penalty for hiding such a person from the Nazis is severe, so they are not pleased to have him around. Further, the peasants are suspicious of strangers, and superstitious, and they believe his dark coloring indicates an evil eye. He has no choice, however, but to live among them, suffer their unmotivated violence, and take the blame for any natural catastrophes, surviving in any way he can.

At one point he lives with Lekh, the bird-catcher. When Lekh is angry, he takes out his anger by capturing a bird, the strongest and handsomest of the flock, painting it in brilliant rainbow colors, and then releasing it among its drab brown congeners. They fall on it at once and peck it to death. The example of the perils of being a "painted bird" are constantly brought home to the boy, who is aware that his visible difference from the others marks him out as a painted bird. In one of Kosinski's nonfiction works, *No Third Path*, he describes a man he met in the Soviet Union who survives because he is able to remain as one of the masses, always staying in the exact center of the crowd, never calling attention to himself. In that way, life could be "waited through," as he phrased it, without too much inconvenience. There is safety, then, in not being a painted bird, yet it is safety gained through a denial of life.

In the winter there is no work for the boy to do in the villages. He is simply another mouth to feed, and his presence is unwelcome. Instead, he wanders freely over the countryside, wrapped in his collection of rags and bits of fur. He is warmed and protected by his "comet," a tin can with a wire handle. The can is punched full of holes so that by swinging it he can force air through it, thus keeping alight the sticks and bits of dry moss he uses to fuel it. No one else ventures out in the deep snow; he can easily break into barns and steal potatoes and other vegetables, then find shelter for the night under the roots of a tree and cook his food with his comet. At these times, even though he is only seven or eight years old, he feels a marvelous happiness at his freedom and independence, his ability to face life directly and survive. In the summer, he is forced to move back into the village, and his torments begin again. His only hope is to try to blend into the society—valuable months of his life need to be "waited through."

Toward the end of the war, when the Germans have retreated, he is found and briefly adopted by a Soviet army battalion. The stresses of his experience have left him mute; he has psychically cut himself off from communication with others. Two soldiers in the army have particularly taken him under care: Gavrila, the political officer, and Mitka the Cuckoo, the sharpshooting instructor. They are the first human beings in memory to treat him kindly, and he worships them and wants to model his life after theirs. He cannot, however, because they are diametrically opposite to each other. Gavrila lectures him daily on the advantages of the collective: no one stands alone, but the entire society is a unit. The individual can make mistakes, but not when he gives himself up to the wise decisions of the community. As long as he is careful to remain within the center of the collective, he will march ahead to a marvelous new future. The boy wants to believe what his hero Gavrila tells him, but he is uneasy. His experiences in the villages, putting himself in the power of the mass, have all been unfortunate, whereas his life seemed fullest and most satisfying when he was by himself, making his own decisions. Mitka the Cuckoo—his name suggesting that he, like the boy, is a painted bird—was a sniper behind enemy lines; because of this, he had to develop to the fullest his instincts to be solitary and to depend on no one but himself. Like the boy, he has always been a loner in an hostile world but able to take care of himself. In the end, of course, it is this philosophy that wins the boy.

The boy survives, when so many other children did not, because of his miraculously tough emotional health. He does not despair or curse his fate. Instead, he accepts his world as it is and desperately tries to learn how to survive in it. In this respect, *The Painted Bird* is a *Bildungsroman* in which the boy, always an empiricist, struggles to find the underlying principle of life. He believes at one time that it might be love, at another time religion, and finally that it might be evil, but each time he is disillusioned. At the end, his speech gone, he believes that hatred and revenge against one's enemies are the keys to survival. The war is over and his parents have found him in an orphanage; it seems he has survived. Yet, hatred and cynicism possess him completely. They give him a certain power: the power to have survived. Yet, one wonders whether he really is a survivor if he has been so deeply scarred that he can no longer relate to other human beings.

How can this story about experiences apparently so remote from those of most of its readers have moved those readers so deeply? Perhaps a clue to this can be found in a statement Kosinski made: "I think it is childhood that is often traumatic, not this or that war." Perhaps the novel is best read as an allegory of childhood, and the war—as so often occurs in works of fiction—is symbolic of the struggle and engagement with life. Children—who are small, weak, powerless, and ignorant of adult ways—are often deeply alienated from the ruling adult society (adults, after all, may be the prototypes for the terrifying giants found in the most powerful children's tales). Learning to live in a society, in enemy territory, can be a deeply scarring struggle. Reconciliation and the reopening of communications come, if at all, with the slow painful dawning of maturity.

Steps was the first novel Kosinski began writing, but feeling too close in time to some of the experiences he was recording in it, he set it aside and instead wrote *The Painted Bird*. *Steps*, which won a National Book Award, is engrossing but puzzling for the reader. The book consists of nearly fifty brief vignettes. Many of the scenes report perverse or violent sexual encounters or ruthless acts of revenge. Each scene is brief, and each has little or no connection with the successive scenes. There is no certain indication that the main character in one scene will reappear in the next one. Kosinski never comments on the action, forcing the reader to decide for himself what or how he is to judge the characters.

These puzzling features are explained by Kosinski's aesthetic and philosophical principles. The short vignettes force the reader to concentrate his attention on the individual scenes themselves, rather than, as in a conventionally plotted book, taking the scene as a whole. Society tries to "plot" one's life, Kosinski suggests, in such a way as to make one look to the future, but while one waits for the future to come, one has missed one's real life, which takes place in the present moment. The protean narrator of the scenes presents another philosophical point. He is different each time he appears; indeed, some critics have claimed that there are several different protagonists, but Kosinski has specifically stated that one protagonist links all the scenes: identity, the nature of the self, is fluid. Finally, there is no authorial judgment of the actions of the protagonist. Kosinski makes it a point in all his novels to give the absolute minimum of advice to the reader, thus implicating the reader continuously in the action, forcing him to examine his own values.

Perhaps an exception to this system is in the scenes of revenge. In many of his novels, Kosinski seems to advocate an ethic of revenge. If a man has hurt one, physically or spiritually, that individual must hurt him back or lose his sense of himself. Selfhood seems to be very much an absolute value to Kosinski. It must be defended against the collective and in personal encounters as well, particularly in sexual encounters. Kosinski believes that man reveals himself most completely in his sexual relations, and therefore these relations play a large role in his novels. The longest series of repeated, connected scenes in *Steps* is a series of thirteen italicized passages, sprinkled throughout the novel, which consist of elaborate pre- and postcoital dialogues between a man and a woman who are trying desperately to sort out their relationship. The difficulty in a relationship is to find the means by which one may give himself to another while still retaining his selfhood. Kosinski presents this problem in terms reminiscent of Jean-Paul Sartre's existential psychology: in any relationship between two people, one must be the subject, and the other the object. To be the object is to give up one's selfhood and be nothing. To be the subject is to manipulate and diminish the other. There is a desperate struggle then for each to retain his selfhood—in other words, to become the subject and make the other the object. If one is successful in the struggle, he survives as an individual, but only at the cost of destroying the other. Relationships in this novel, and in all of Kosinski's novels, tend to be manipulative and destructive. Though the characters do not seem to find a way out of their dilemma, and though the novel offers no solutions, it seems that Kosinski is critical of his characters for their failure, for he has elsewhere defined love as "the attempt to be simultaneously subject and object . . . the willing relinquishment of the single subject to a new subject created from two single ones, each subject enhanced into one heightened self."

Steps is thus Kosinski's purest novel: it has no "plot," but instead it draws the reader's attention to the present moment of each incident as it unfolds; it has a protean narrator who is a new person in relation to each new set of experiences with which he is confronted; it presents man's life as a struggle to maintain selfhood, to avoid being diluted into some larger mass, or, on the individual level, to avoid being dominated and made into an object in personal relationships; and finally, it offers no authorial judgments, throwing the reader entirely on his own resources.

Being There, at twenty-three thousand words, is a novella rather than a novel. Short in length, stripped and pure in language, and simple in outline, the story is told like a parable or moral allegory, which indeed it is. Chance, the protagonist, is consistent as a character because he has no character. Since he is mentally retarded, he is incapable of change or growth. No situation makes an impression on him, and therefore no situation alters him. He has never in his life been outside a rich man's estate, where he has remained to tend the garden. He works in the garden by day and watches television by night. When the rich man dies, however, the executors of the estate release Chance. He is tall, handsome, soft-spoken, and wears his former employer's cast-off suits. The wife of a billionaire financier invites Chance into her house thinking he must be a rich businessman. That night, the president of the United States visits the financier and is introduced to Chance. In every situation, Chance acts the way he has seen someone on television act in a similar situation. Every question he is asked, he answers in terms of gardening, since that is all he knows. His simple statements about flowers growing are taken as profound metaphorical statements about the economy. The president quotes him in his national speech that night, and he is immediately pursued by all the media, invited to talk shows, and courted by foreign ambassadors; by novel's end, there are plans to run him for high office, since he looks good on television and does not seem to have a past which might prove an embarrassment.

This amusingly absurd tale is in fact Kosinski's indictment of the mass media, especially television, which, as a sociologist, he has frequently attacked in lectures and essays. The first evil of television, according to Kosinski, is that it presents viewers with an immediately accessible image, and therefore does not induce them to do any thinking for themselves (an infant child, Kosinski reminds his readers, can watch the same programs they do). This mindless image is ultimately deadly, because it suggests that experience is *outside*, something that happens only to other people. Through lulling viewers into believing that wrecks and bombings and deaths can happen only to others, television robs them of the Angst needed to live life fully. Further, television can make mere images so attractive that it can convince viewers to vote for any well-made-up puppet it puts before them. Into the empty, simplified, television image, viewers pour all their hopes and wishes, as the characters around Chance fill in his blank personality, making him into the person they want him to be. The comedy loses its humor when Kosinski suggests how easily this completely empty puppet could find itself sitting in the oval office, world destruction within the push of a single button.

Unlike television or movies, which present the audience directly with an external image, novels, when they are read properly, force the reader to re-create the scenes inside his head, to generate his own images. This act of re-creation allows the reader to experience directly the action of the novel; when a character dies, the reader must, to an extent, experience that death. Kosinski is so opposed to the way the image falsifies and separates man from experi-ence, that he long refused to have any of his novels made into films. Under extraordinary and repeated persuasion from Peter Sellers, he at last agreed to allow *Being There* to be made into a film, starring Sellers. There is a kind of ironic appropriateness in a story dealing entirely with the effect of visual images being portrayed in visual images.

Blind Date is typical, and indeed is probably the best, of a later group of Kosinski novels (the others in this group are *Cockpit*, *Passion Play*, and *Pinball*). The novel is presented in what can be called a standard Kosinski format: a series of incidents which finds the mobile lone-wolf protagonist in various countries, frequently flashing back to the past, moving from adven-ture to adventure, from woman to woman. In this group of novels, Kosinski begins to move toward more conventional plotting, and his protagonists are softened and made more human, more vulnerable. They are growing older and are no longer capable of some of the feats of their youth. Human rela-tionships become less of a battleground, and at least the possibility of love is present. The theme of revenge, so prominent in earlier novels, begins to diminish. Where it is still present, it has been sublimated. The protagonist, giving up acts of personal revenge, raises himself to be a sort of "scourge of God," taking impersonal revenge against enemies of humanity. The earlier novels made frequent use of autobiographical materials, which these later novels continue to do, but there is a new element. The later novels come more programmatically to represent Kosinski's spiritual biography, and the pro-tagonist, for all the indirection of art, comes more and more to stand for Kosinski himself.

The novel *Blind Date* and its protagonist Levanter are transitional in this scheme. Levanter as a young man is just as egotistic and manipulative as earlier Kosinski heroes have been. In summer camp, for example, he binds and brutally rapes a girl with whom he is infatuated, but he refuses to talk to her because he is too shy. That event, however, is seen in flashback. When the novel opens, Levanter is middle-aged, and though he is still capable of violence, the violence has a social dimension. When he learns that the minister of internal affairs of a small dictatorship, a man famous for tortures and murders, is staying incognito at the same ski resort he is, Levanter manages, through an elaborate scheme, to have him killed. When a champion fencer from an iron curtain country is imprisoned because of information given against him by an informant, Levanter kills the informer by skewering him on just such a sword as the fencer has used.

Levanter, particularly as he grows older, is not so ruthlessly manipulative in his personal relationships as previous protagonists. If Tarden, the protagonist of the previous novel, *Cockpit*, had raped a girl, he would never have looked back. Instead, Levanter again meets the girl he had raped a year later (she had never seen his face), and their relationship continues to the point of true love; when he kisses her in the way the rapist had, however, she recognizes him and leaves in a rage. He feels then that he has missed a real opportunity and regrets his earlier action.

Levanter had met the girl the second time through sheer chance, another in a series of chance events in the novel. For example, in the novel's opening, Levanter meets a woman whose piano playing reminds him of the way his mother once played. By chance, that woman had been instructed under the same teacher as his mother, and Levanter and the woman feel this establishes a link between them. They go their separate ways, but toward the end of the novel, by sheer chance, Levanter meets her again; this time they complete the relationship begun earlier, one of total fulfillment for both. These chance meetings, which have the ironic effect of giving the novel a conventional plot, seem like the most banal and improbable coincidences until the reader realizes that chance is actually the governing principle of the novel. The novel's epigraph is a quotation from Jacques Monod's *Chance and Necessity* (1972) in which he argues that every moment in life is the chance convergence of completely unrelated chains of random events, and therefore there is no "plot" to life, no inevitability, no prediction. *Blind Date* reiterates more directly than any of Kosinski's other novels the Heideggerian notion that man is on earth only through sheer chance, that his time here, whether long or short, must end with death, and therefore he must get the most possible out of each moment as it is lived. What is new in the novel is the social dimension: one way man makes his life meaningful is by trying to make the lives of those around him meaningful as well. The earlier Kosinski protagonists fought desperately and ruthlessly to preserve the self, even if it meant destroying their closest personal relationships. The later protagonists, among whom Levanter again is a transitional figure, take more risks with the self, even hesitantly offering it in love. As a sign of this mellowing, Levanter actually seeks to rectify the cruelty he had practiced as a youth. As a first step he dedicates himself to punishing totalitarians; later, he seeks to undo his own totalitarian act of raping the girl at summer camp. In the novel's greatest coincidence, he realizes that the pianist is that very girl from the summer camp, who, as a result of the rape, has never been able to achieve sexual fulfillment. He binds her now, gently, and, this time with her permission, reenacts the rape, at last freeing her to be fully herself.

At this point a romantic novel might have ended, but such an end would be a falsification. Life can only end with death, which is the only predictable and inevitable conclusion to life's "plot." An aging Levanter is skiing when an unexpected late-season surge of bad weather catches him inadequately dressed. He is lost in the fog and slowly gives in to the cold, feeling he has played life's game very well, and is now perhaps entitled to a rest.

Norman Lavers

Other major works

NONFICTION: *The Future Is Ours, Comrade*, 1960; *No Third Path*, 1962; *Notes of the Author on "The Painted Bird,"* 1965; *The Art of the Self: Essays à Propos "Steps,"* 1968.

EDITED TEXT: *Sociologia Amerykánska: Wybór Prae, 1950-1960*, 1962.

Bibliography

Bruss, Paul. *Victims: Textual Strategies in Recent American Fiction*. Lewisburg, Pa.: Bucknell University Press, 1981. Explores the strategies of three writers, including Kosinski, and their alliance with the idealist tradition. Examines Kosinski's early fiction with regard to his use of language, as well as his novels *Steps, Cockpit*, and *Blind Date*. A selected bibliography of primary and secondary sources is provided.

Coale, Samuel. "The Quest for the Elusive Self: The Fiction of Jerzy Kosinski." *Critique: Studies in Modern Fiction* 14, no. 3 (1973): 25-37. Discusses Kosinski's concern with the consciousness of self in its broader moral and ethical implications. Compares his work to Edgar Allan Poe, Franz Kafka, and Samuel Beckett. Includes critical commentary on *The Painted Bird*, cited here as his best novel, *Steps*, and *Being There*. A generally admiring piece that nevertheless notes flaws in Kosinski's writing.

Fein, Richard J. "Jerzy Kosinski." In *Contemporary Novelists*, edited by James Vinson. London: St. James Press, 1976. Includes comments by Kosinski and critical appraisal of his most distinguished novels. Fein honors the vision of Kosinski and sees his works as "strange hymns to suffering."

Lavers, Norman. *Jerzy Kosinski*. Boston: Twayne, 1982. An appreciative critical study that considers Kosinski a major writer. Discusses his fiction and nonfiction novels with some biographical information and provides considerable critical commentary on *The Painted Bird*. Contains a selected bibliography. A useful introduction to the beginning reader of Kosinski.

Lilly, Paul R., Jr. *Words in Search of Victims: The Achievement of Jerzy Kosinski*. Kent, Ohio: Kent State University Press, 1988. A full-length appreciative critical study of Kosinski's novels with much of interest and value for the Kosinski scholar. Includes a discussion of the controversy with *The Village Voice*, which attacked Kosinski's authenticity and compositional methods.

LOUIS L'AMOUR

Born: Jamestown, North Dakota; March 22, 1908
Died: Los Angeles, California; June 10, 1988

Principal long fiction

Westward the Tide, 1950; *Hondo*, 1953; *Sitka*, 1957; *Last Stand at Papago Wells*, 1957; *The First Fast Draw*, 1959; *The Daybreakers*, 1960; *Sackett*, 1961; *Shalako*, 1962; *Lando*, 1962; *Mojave Crossing*, 1964; *The Sackett Brand*, 1965; *The Broken Gun*, 1966; *Mustang Man*, 1966; *The Sky-Liners*, 1967; *Down the Long Hills*, 1968; *The Lonely Men*, 1969; *The Man Called Noon*, 1970; *Galloway*, 1970; *North to the Rails*, 1971; *Ride the Dark Trail*, 1972; *Treasure Mountain*, 1972; *The Ferguson Rifle*, 1973; *The Man from Skibbereen*, 1973; *Sackett's Land*, 1974; *Rivers West*, 1975; *The Man from the Broken Hills*, 1975; *Over on the Dry Side*, 1975; *To the Far Blue Mountains*, 1976; *Borden Chantry*, 1977; *Fair Blows the Wind*, 1978; *Bendigo Shafter*, 1979; *The Iron Marshal*, 1979; *The Warrior's Path*, 1980; *Lonely on the Mountain*, 1980; *Comstock Lode*, 1981; *Milo Talon*, 1981; *The Cherokee Trail*, 1982; *The Lonesome Gods*, 1983; *Ride the River*, 1983; *Son of a Wanted Man*, 1984; *The Walking Drum*, 1984; *Jubal Sackett*, 1985; *Last of the Breed*, 1986; *The Haunted Mesa*, 1987.

Other literary forms

Although Louis L'Amour has achieved his greatest success as a Western novelist, he began his career as a writer of short pulp fiction, later assembled in a number of collections. He also wrote some hard-boiled detective stories, and early in his career he issued a book of undistinguished poetry. In 1988, the year of his death, a collection of L'Amour quotations entitled *A Trail of Memories* was issued. The following year saw the publication of *Education of a Wandering Man*, an autobiographical work.

Achievements

L'Amour was the most phenomenal Western writer America has ever produced. Each of his eighty-five novels, mostly traditional Westerns, has sold at least a million copies; ten of his novels have doubled that figure. His books have been translated into more than a dozen foreign languages. More than thirty of his plots have been made into motion-picture and television dramas. In 1981, with *Comstock Lode*, L'Amour became a formidable presence in the hardbound-book market; he immediately made the best-seller list; all of his subsequent hardbound novels matched this performance. By 1977, L'Amour had sold fifty million copies of his books. In 1987, the figure was 175 million.

L'Amour also received important awards and honors. He won the Western

Writers of America (WWA) Golden Spur Award in 1969 for *Down the Long Hills* and the Western Writers of America Golden Saddleman Award in 1981 for overall achievement and contributions to an understanding of the American West. When, in 1985, the WWA published a list of the twenty-six best Western novels of all time, L'Amour's *Hondo* made the list. In 1982, the United States Congress awarded him a National Gold Medal, and one year later, President Ronald Reagan awarded him the United States Medal of Freedom.

L'Amour was not averse to peddling his own wares. In June of 1980, he cruised the Midwest and the Mid-South in a leased luxury bus, meeting fans and selling autographed copies of his seventy-five books then available. He also appeared on television to promote his Louis L'Amour Collection of novels. His publisher (Bantam Books) offered L'Amour calendars, audiotape dramas (multivoiced, with sound effects) of certain L'Amour stories, and an audiocassette of their star author's personal reminiscences.

Biography

Louis L'Amour was born Louis Dearborn LaMoore in Jamestown, North Dakota, on March 22, 1908, into a rugged, French-Irish pioneering family. His father, Louis Charles LaMoore, reared by his paternal grandparents in Ontario, was a veterinarian, a Jamestown police chief, and a civic leader. The novelist's mother, Emily, whose father was a Civil War veteran and an Indian fighter, attended the normal school at St. Cloud, Minnesota, and married L. C. LaMoore in 1892. Louis was the youngest of the couple's seven children, four of whom survived to distinguished maturity.

After a healthy early boyhood of outdoor activity and voracious reading, L'Amour moved in 1923 with his family to Oklahoma but soon struck out on his own. An incredible sequence of knockabout jobs followed: sailor, longshoreman, lumberjack, boxer, circus worker, cattle skinner, fruit picker, hay shocker, miner, friend of bandits in China, book reviewer in Oklahoma, lecturer there and in Texas, neophyte writer, and a United States Army tank-destroyer and transportation officer in World War II in France and Germany.

In 1946, L'Amour decided to live in Los Angeles and became a professional writer. Some of his short-story pulps and slicks into the mid-1950's were under the pen names Tex Burns and Jim Mayo. A turning point for L'Amour came with the publication of "The Gift of Cochise" in *Collier's*, the story which formed the basis for *Hondo* a year later. This was not, however, L'Amour's first Western novel, which was the competent *Westward the Tide*, published in London in 1950.

The biography of Louis L'Amour from 1953 onward is largely an account of one popular success after another, adaptations of his plots to the screen, fine efforts at versatility in a career which too many regard as merely capitalizing on the formulaic Western, and steady personal happiness.

With the publication of *Night over the Solomons* (a collection of old pre-war stories) in 1986, L'Amour saw his one-hundredth book into print. Of the many films made from his fiction, the most notable are *Hondo* (1953), *The Burning Hills* (1956), *Apache Territory* (1958), *Heller in Pink Tights* (1960), *Shalako* (1968), and *Catlow* (1971). The best television adaptation from L'Amour fiction was called *The Sacketts* (based on *The Daybreakers* and *Sackett*), which first aired in 1979. Beginning in 1960, L'Amour started the first of three family sagas, novels in multiple numbers featuring generations of families. *The Daybreakers* opened the ongoing Sackett saga, which by 1986 had grown to eighteen volumes. The 1971 publication of *North to the Rails* began another ongoing series, the Chantry family series. In 1975, *Rivers West* began the Talon family sequence.

Abetting L'Amour was the former Kathy Adams, who relinquished her career as an actress to marry him in a gala 1956 ceremony at the Los Angeles Beverly Hilton. In the 1960's, she bore him a daughter, Angelique, and then a son, Beau, and she served as his business manager, informal editor, and chauffeur. L'Amour wrote early in the morning, six hours a day, seven days a week, combining this spartan routine with tough afternoon workouts using a punching bag and weights. Throughout his long career, he lectured and traveled widely and personally scouted locales to make his work more authentic. L'Amour died in Los Angeles in 1988.

Analysis

Louis L'Amour will be remembered for his action-filled Western novels, especially his family sagas. He is appreciated by readers from all walks of life who want to follow the exploits and suffering of heroic men, attractive and dutiful women, and manifestly evil villains, in exciting, well-knit plots, against a backdrop of accurately painted scenery. L'Amour extols the old American virtues of patriotism, respect for the land, go-it-alone courage, stoicism, and family loyalty. He offers his updated vision of the Old West as the locus of increasingly endangered mankind's last, best hope.

Critics should not look to L'Amour for aesthetic subtleties. His unvaried boast was that he was an old-fashioned storyteller, of the sort that sits by a campfire after a hard day's work and spins his tales in a straightforward manner. He did not worry, then, about critics who categorized Western fiction into formulaic narratives, romantic-historical reconstructions, or historical reconstructions. Such critics would probably define his *Hondo* as formulaic, his *Sitka* as romantic-historical, and nothing he wrote as genuinely historical (though he meticulously researched *The Walking Drum*, for example). In addition, critics complain to no avail when they claim that L'Amour's slapdash, unrevised writing betrays compositional errors by the gross.

L'Amour was pleased to be put in the same company as James Fenimore Cooper, Honoré de Balzac, Émile Zola, Jules Romains, and William Faulkner. L'Amour's Tell Sackett bears comparison with Cooper's Natty Bumppo. L'Amour follows Balzac's habit of creating reappearing characters, who help produce both unified, multivolumed fiction and loyal readers. The hero of L'Amour's *Shalako*, between wars in Paris, meets Zola, whose Rougon-Macquart cycle may have inspired L'Amour to build his Sackett/Chantry/ Talon series. Romains employed historical figures, real events, and even specific dates to augment the verisimilitude of his monumental *Les Hommes de bonne volonté* (1932-1946; *Men of Good Will*, 1933-1946); L'Amour, to be sure, deals with three centuries of American frontier Sacketts rather than France in a mere quarter-century, but he uses Romains-like details in doing so. Moreover, Faulkner's love of his native soil, his combination of different races together in weal and woe, his praise of the old virtues of enduring and prevailing, and his construction of interlocked families are echoed in L'Amour's novels.

Since it is impossible to discuss all or even most of L'Amour's fiction, long and short, in a few pages, it seems best to concentrate on several salient titles, which illustrate his peaks of accomplishment, and also to consider his monumental three-family saga. In "Ride, You Tonto Raiders!" (*New Western Magazine*, August 6, 1949; reprinted in *Law of the Desert Born*, 1983), L'Amour prophetically introduced many of his books' most typical features. The broad-shouldered hero is a hard-bitten adventurer with a military, cosmopolitan, cattleman background, and he is now a gunslinger. He kills a bad man in Texas, then delivers the victim's money to his sweet widow and small son. She owns some Arizona land and is aided but also jeopardized by an assortment of L'Amouresque types: rich man, gunslinger, bumbling lawman, codger, literary drunk, Europe-trained pianist, loyal ranch hand, half-breed, and Hispanic. Other ingredients include surrogate fatherhood, dawning love for a red-haired heroine, the taking of the law into one's own hands, berserker fighting lust, hidden documents, place-names aplenty, the dating of the action by reference to historical events, cinematic alternation of close-up and wide-angle lens scenes, the use of key words (especially "alone," "eye," "home," "land," "patience," "shoulder," "silence," and "trouble"), and compositional infelicities. In short, this story is a fine introduction to L'Amour and, in addition, incidentally prefigures *Hondo*.

Hondo remains L'Amour's best Western. It features a typical loner hero, torn between moving on and settling down. It is datable and placeable: Hondo Lane scouts for General George Crook in the Arizona of 1874. Hondo cannot quickly woo and win the fetchingly home-loving heroine, not only because he killed her husband but also because Vittorio's Apaches grab and torture him. Hondo is half in favor of the white man's progress and half in love with violence in Apacheria; similarly, L'Amour mediates between the twentieth century and starker, earlier American epochs.

Last Stand at Papago Wells has an unusually complex set of narrative lines, neatly converging at a desert well and featuring a gallery of characters in varied movement: hero heading west, couple eloping, outraged father of bride-to-be in hot pursuit, survivor of party butchered by Apaches, near-rape victim, frustrated Apaches and two of their chronic enemies, posse remnants, fat woman with heavy saddlebags (is she hiding gold?), and rogue Apache-Yaquis circling and then attacking the forted-up well occupants.

Sitka is L'Amour's first big romantic-historical novel and has a refreshingly different setting. It concerns the Alaska Purchase, features real-life figures such as Secretary of the Treasury Robert Walker and Russian Ambassador Édouard de Stoeckl, and moves scenically from Pennsylvania to the Far West to Pacific Ocean waters (even to Russia)—Jean LaBarge, the hero, is L'Amour's first important fictional sailor—and up by Jean's wheat-laden schooner to Sitka, Alaska. L'Amour charmingly delays an indispensable love affair by having stalwart Jean smitten by a beautiful Russian princess who is demurely wed to a nice old Russian count, whose greasy enemy, another Russian, is Jean's enemy as well. Toward the end of *Sitka*, the plot takes on comic-book coloration, with interludes in Czar Alexander II's court, Washington, D.C., Siberia, and a Sitka prison.

The First Fast Draw never deserved its best-selling celebrity. It is supposedly based on the well-documented life of Cullen Montgomery Baker, the infamous Texas gunman whose bloody career got its impetus from Texas Governor Edmund Davis' vicious Reconstruction laws. L'Amour includes so many other real-life characters and events that naïve readers may think they are reading a historical reconstruction—but this is not so. L'Amour ignores the real Baker's first two marriages, his Quantrill-like antiblack and anti–Union army conduct, and even his death in 1869. L'Amour was enamored enough of thug Baker to shove him tangentially into five later books.

The Daybreakers is the first volume of L'Amour's tremendous, million-word Sackett sequence. It introduces the most famous Sacketts. They are five Tennessee-born brothers: William Tell, Orrin, Tyrel, Bob, and Joe Sackett. An 1866 feud with the evil Higgins family, during which a Higgins kills Orrin's fiancée and is hastily gunned down by narrator Tyrel, obliges both brothers to head out. They go west to gather wild cattle, in spite of dramatic adversities, along the Santa Fe Trail. Once in New Mexico, Orrin marries disastrously: His vicious wife is the daughter of a dishonest and anti-Hispanic politician and land grabber from New England. Tyrel, on the other hand, while on the trail is taught to read by an ex-army officer who later turns alcoholic, jealous, and lethal; Tyrel becomes the gun-handy marshal of Mora and marries a lovely heiress of an old Spanish land grant there. Orrin and Tyrel send for their widowed Ma and younger brothers Bob and Joe. The plot is energized by much violence, though not involving offstage Tell Sackett; having fought in the Civil War, he is now campaigning against the Sioux in the Northwest and is soon to leave Montana for Mora. (Incidentally, Tell was first presented in the story "Booty for a Bad Man," *Saturday Evening Post*, July 30, 1960; reprinted in *War Party*, 1975.) Even while writing much else, L'Amour continued his narrative of these Sackett brothers in six more novels, which, not in order of publication (1961 to 1980) but in chronological order of events (1867 through 1878 or so), are *Lonely on the Mountain*, *Sackett*, *Mojave Crossing*, *The Sackett Brand*, *The Lonely Men*, and *Treasure Mountain*.

During this time, L'Amour was turning his Sackett clock back more than two centuries. In 1974, he published *Sackett's Land*, which introduces Barnabas Sackett of the Welsh fenlands, in 1599. The first of the Sackett dynasty, he and his wife Abigail, daughter of an Elizabethan sea captain, generate a wild brood in the Carolinas: sons Kin Ring, Brian, Yance, and Jubal Sackett, and daughter Noelle Sackett. In the later novels, the three brothers, Kin, Yance, and Jubal (in *To the Far Blue Mountains*, *The Warrior's Path*, and *Jubal Sackett*, respectively), are shown to be different, and their stories shift from the Eastern seaboard, New England, and the Caribbean to the Far West, and advance to the year 1630 or so. In 1983 came *Ride the River*, which tells how a feisty Tennessee girl named Echo Sackett (destined to become the aunt of Tell and his brothers) ventures to Philadelphia to claim an inheritance as Kin Sackett's youngest descendant and gets it home again.

L'Amour has written six other Sackett novels (*Lando*, *Mustang Man*, *The Sky-Liners*, *Galloway*, *Ride the Dark Trail*, and *The Man from the Broken Hills*), which star a dusty array of cousins of Tell and his brothers and bring in still more Sacketts. These cousins, from different parts of Tennessee, Arizona, and New Mexico, include Lando, twins Logan and Nolan, brothers Flagan and Galloway, and Parmalee. The action, ranging through the Southwest and into Mexico, may be dated 1867-1878.

There are about sixty Sacketts in the ambitious Sackett sequence, amid a gallery of more than 750 characters in all. The Chantry/Talon novels, less expansive than the Sackett saga, are usually independent of it but occasionally connect with it. They may be most sensibly read in the chronological order of events narrated. *Fair Blows the Wind* concerns a swashbuckling Rafael Sabatini–like hero-narrator called Tatton Chantry (not his real name, L'Amour oddly insists), in the very late sixteenth century, in Ireland, England, Spain, France, the southern colonies in America, and back to Ireland. *The Ferguson Rifle* tells about a Chantry named Ronan, in the newly acquired lands of the Louisiana Purchase. The picaresque *Rivers West* introduces an early Talon (in the year 1821). He is Jean, hinted to be a descendant of legendary Talon the Claw, a rich old pirate of the glorious Gaspé Peninsula. Western rivers take ambitious builder, lover-manqué Jean Talon to the Louisiana Purchase regions roamed by Ronan Chantry. Enter scholarly, verbose, often violent Owen Chantry in *Over on the Dry Side*, searching in Utah (1866) for his lost brother Clive (dead) and a reputed treasure (really a historical manuscript). The next Talon segment stars Milo Talon, one of Tell Sackett's countless cousins, in *Milo Talon*, a detective story fashioned largely from earlier Western mystery novels by L'Amour, specifically *The Man Called Noon*, *The Man from Skibbereen*, and *The Iron Marshal*, but rendered weird by ridiculous plot improbabilities. Milo does nothing for L'Amour's Talon saga. Then, in 1977, came *Borden Chantry*, perhaps his best Western mystery, because it is direct and gripping. Cleverly, L'Amour makes the victim in the puzzle Joe Sackett, who is the long-unmentioned younger brother of Tell and Tyrell and whose mysterious murder in Colorado (c. 1882), Borden Chantry, storm-ruined cattleman turned town marshal, must solve—or else Tyrel Sackett, who gallops in, will take the law into his own rough hands. The unexceptional *North to the Rails* already featured Borden Chantry's East-softened son Tom and reported that the father had been murdered about 1890, before the action starts, after which young Tom elects to drive cattle from Cimarron, near Santa Fe, north to a railhead for transport east. Obstacles to the hero in his *rites de passage* are varied and absorbing, but the novel is marred by much silliness and an improbable villainess.

As early as 1974, in his preface to *Sackett's Land*, L'Amour informed his public of plans to tell the epic of the American frontier through the westward movement of generations of three families, in forty or so novels. In 1981, he added that he had traced his Sacketts back to the fifteenth century and planned ten more Sackett, five more Chantry, and five more Talon books; further, that his Talons are builders, his Chantrys, educated statesmen, and his Sacketts, frontiersmen. (It has already been seen that L'Amour's practice has often blurred his theoretical distinctions.) Finally, in 1983, the author explained that he saw his three families as periodically linking and splitting. For two tiny examples, in addition to what has already been noticed: In *Ride the River* may be found strong but spoiled Dorian Chantry, whom his splendid old uncle, Philadephia-lawyer Finian Chantry, orders to help heroine Echo Sackett; in the popular but flawed *Son of a Wanted Man*, Borden Chantry is revived and joins forces with Tyrell Sackett in gunning for law and order.

Brief mention may be made of seven of L'Amour's best works, simply to suggest his versatility and undiminished professional ambition. They are *The Broken Gun*, *Down the Long Hills*, *Bendigo Shafter*, *The Cherokee Trail*, *The Lonesome Gods*, *The Walking Drum*, and *Last of the Breed*.

The Broken Gun offers a brilliant translation of nineteenth century Western ingredients—rugged hero, mysterious murder, Hispanic friend, admirable lawman, land-hungry villains, sweet heroine, and villainess—all into twentieth century terms. In addition, the protagonist, a combat veteran and a writer, is partly autobiographical. *Down the Long Hills* is unique in L'Amour's canon: It has strict Aristotelian unities and features a seven-year-old hero saving a three-year-old girl from an assortment of dangers, in a diagrammable plot of villains avoided and rescuers frustrated. *Bendigo Shafter* is L'Amour's classic Western blockbuster—in balanced, numbered thirds, nicely structured, and huge. The admirable hero-narrator describes the establishment in Wyoming's South Pass region (starting about 1862) of a Western community whose inhabitants represent everything from saintly to depraved, young and old, married and single, gauche and nubile. Nearby are Indians good and evil, and assorted white renegades. Nature here can be cruel but rewards those who surrender to its potent beauty. Notable are the hero's return to the East and meeting Horace Greeley there; his rejuvenating visit to the sacred Indian Medicine Wheel in the Big Horns; and L'Amour's skillful depiction of nineteen varied females. *The Cherokee Trail* also dramatizes assorted women's activities: A young widow takes over the management of a Colorado stagecoach station, protects a daughter and an Irish maid there, and has a rich rancher's spoiled daughters for neighbors nearby. *The Lonesome Gods* is epic in its sweep, with a varied plot and such bizarre effects as a disowning, the attempted murder of a little boy, gigantism, an uncannily svelte heroine with an unnecessary Russian background, a wild stallion, ghostly visitations, and—best of all—the loneliness of sad, patient gods in need of human adoration.

The Walking Drum, L'Amour's most ambitious novel, is a sprawling, episodic romp from Brittany through Europe to the Black Sea and beyond, in the years 1176-1180, starring an impossibly talented hero. He is Mathurin Kerbouchard, sailor, horseman, fighter, scientist, magician, caravan merchant, linguist, scholar, and lover. It must be added at once that L'Amour, in days of depraved adult Westerns, is restraint itself: He limns no torrid love scenes on either side of any ocean. In addition, his violence is never offered in splashes of current cinematic gore.

Finally, *Last of the Breed*, another innovative effort, is nothing less than an eastern Siberian Western, cast in contemporary times (Mikhail S. Gorbachev is mentioned). Pitted are a Sioux-Cheyenne United States Air Force superpilot and squabbling Soviet secret police. It has the most elaborately detailed escape since *The Count of Monte Cristo* (1844-1845) by Alexandre Dumas, *père*: here, from a prison camp east of Lake Baikal. Though crafted with care, this novel smacks of the film character Rambo, most of its more than forty characters have hard-to-remember names, the pages are dotted with twice that number of place names, and the hero's success depends on protracted good luck. Sympathetic readers will accept his exploits, however, because they accept the true hero of the novel—hauntingly rendered Siberia.

Louis L'Amour's two most admirable traits were his troubadour wizardry as a narrator and his profound love of Mother Nature and American derring-do. His late-career ambition to broaden his fictive scope, while admirable, can never diminish the significance of what will probably remain his most lasting contribution—namely, his best Westerns, among which the Sackett saga retains a high place. It is certainly to those works that one can attribute his immense popularity.

Robert L. Gale

Other major works

SHORT FICTION: *War Party,* 1975; *Bowdrie,* 1983; *The Hills of Homicide,* 1983; *Law of the Desert Born,* 1983; *Riding for the Brand,* 1986; *The Rider of the Ruby Hills,* 1986; *Night over the Solomons,* 1986; *The Outlaws of Mesquite,* 1990.

POETRY: *Smoke from This Altar,* 1939.

NONFICTION: *Frontier,* 1984 (with photographs by David Muench); *A Trail of Memories,* 1988; *Education of a Wandering Man,* 1989.

Bibliography

Gale, Robert L. *Louis L'Amour.* Boston: Twayne, 1985. Investigates L'Amour as a phenomenon who outsells all competitors with fiction that is low on sex and violence and high on patriotism and family. After sketching L'Amour's life, Gale surveys the range of his fiction from formulaic narrative to historical reconstruction. Presents a chronological perspective on his many novels, which were standard formulas with variations, written to satisfy public demand, from *Westward the Tide* in 1950 to *The Walking Drum* in 1984. Examines in detail the seventeen novels following the Sackett family's adventures, with special attention given to the best five. L'Amour is compared (unfavorably) with predecessors such as James Fenimore Cooper and William Faulkner. Evaluates his strengths (scenic description and character variety) and weaknesses (narrative structure, stereotypes, and clichés). Includes a chronology, notes and references, a selected, annotated bibliography, and an index.

Marsden, Michael T. "The Concept of the Family in the Fiction of Louis L'Amour." *North Dakota Quarterly* 46 (Summer, 1978): 12-21. Claims that concept of the family is a unifying theme in L'Amour's work and his commercial success in America. The Sacketts show how a family can retain its civilized values even when repeatedly uprooted and transplanted in migrations. Although some of L'Amour's heroes are loners, they always act for the good of society in a search for family. The Sacketts, the Talons, and the Chantrys are family groups analyzed in terms of their regions of settlement and the four concepts which make up the family in a L'Amour novel: the Male Principle, the Female Principle, the Hearth (of the Focused Family), and the Family Unit (the Enlarged Family).

——————. "Louis L'Amour (1908-)." In *Fifty Western Writers: A Bio-Bibliographical Sourcebook,* edited by Fred Erisman and Richard Etulain. Westport, Conn.: Greenwood Press, 1982. Explains L'Amour's reception of a congressional gold medallion, sketches his biography, and outlines his major themes. L'Amour emphasizes the importance of history, evoked through descriptions of landscape, and the concept of the family, which provides narrative structure and texture. His treatment of women is sensitive but inconsistent, as he changed his characterizations in response to pressures for women's rights. Other concerns of L'Amour are the environment, the purgatorial value of violence, and the plight of the Indian. Calls for more critical attention for L'Amour and other popular Western writers, and ends with a bibliography of his works and a list of the few critical studies which have been made of them.

_____. "The Modern Western." In *The American Literary West*, edited by Richard W. Etulain. Manhattan, Kans.: Sunflower University Press, 1980. Sets L'Amour's fiction in the tradition of the American Western novels and films. Despite tendencies of the genre since World War II to insist on accuracy of psychology and history, L'Amour continues to emphasize innocence and individual courage as ideals of the old West for modern imitation. Because he thinks of himself as a storyteller in the oral tradition, his novels can best be read aloud, one of the reasons for his success. Another is the strong family ties, expressed through the tales of the Sacketts, the Talons, and the Chantrys. L'Amour continues to write in the spirit of idealism, even as his genre is attacked and changed by many modern revisionists.

Nesbitt, John D. "Change of Purpose in the Novels of Louis L'Amour." *Western American Literature* 13 (Spring, 1978): 65-81. Reprinted in *Critical Essays on the Western American Novel*, edited by William T. Pilkington. Boston: G. K. Hall, 1980. There were three changes in the moral and historical purpose of L'Amour's writing in his career. In the first phase (1953 to the late 1950's), he wrote stories of naked violence and advocated conventional morality. His middle phase (late 1950's to the early 1970's) included more than half of his sixty-or-so novels, which contain either heroes who meet women who walk beside, not behind, them or heroic gentlemen who have been to Europe. In his late phase (1974-1975), L'Amour is chronicler of the movement west and apologist for the settlement of the West, as his heroes become more temperate in character and in their means of solving problems.

_____. "Louis L'Amour: Papier-Mâché Homer?" *South Dakota Review* 19 (Autumn, 1981): 37-48. Criticizes L'Amour's Homeric claims as a maker of epic, a product of advertising which critics have taken seriously. Insists on judging him by the literary tradition of well-crafted narratives, concluding that L'Amour is not rich or deep in vision or method. As he attempted to make his work more serious, he padded his lean narratives with thin philosophy, moralizing, and historical details, but his story remained the same: A superior white man overcomes adversity, wins a vir-

tuous woman, and settles into a community. His compositions and character motivations contain little complexity, but are still valuable for studying
Western American literature and showing how popular literature can achieve
popular versions of the epic.

MARGARET LAURENCE

Born: Neepawa, Manitoba, Canada; July 18, 1926
Died: Lakefield, Ontario, Canada; January 5, 1987

Principal long fiction

This Side Jordan, 1960; *The Stone Angel*, 1964; *A Jest of God*, 1966; *The Fire-Dwellers*, 1969; *The Diviners*, 1974.

Other literary forms

Margaret Laurence published two short-story collections, *The Tomorrow-Tamer* (1963) and *A Bird in the House* (1970), and two children's books, *Jason's Quest* (1970) and *The Christmas Birthday Story* (1980). She also produced a translation of Somali folktales and poems, *A Tree for Poverty: Somali Poetry and Prose* (1954); a travelogue, *The Prophet's Camel Bell* (1963); and a study of Nigerian novelists and playwrights, *Long Drums and Cannons: Nigerian Dramatists and Novelists, 1952-1966* (1968). A collection of her essays, *Heart of a Stranger*, appeared in 1976. Because of her work on Nigerian fiction and drama, she is well known to students of African literature.

Achievements

From the beginning of her writing career, Laurence received much popular and critical recognition. *This Side Jordan* won the Beta Sigma Phi prize for a first novel by a Canadian; *The Stone Angel* received both critical and popular acclaim; *A Jest of God* was awarded the Governor General's Medal in 1966 and was adapted for motion pictures as *Rachel, Rachel*; *The Diviners*, despite less than universal critical acclaim, was at the top of the best-seller list for more than sixty consecutive weeks. Along with her popularity, Laurence enjoyed an international reputation as a consistently accomplished fiction-writer. Her special contribution to the novel was recognized by Jack McClelland of the Canadian publishing house of McClelland and Stewart when he first read *This Side Jordan*. The stories which were gathered in *The Tomorrow-Tamer* and *A Bird in the House* originally appeared separately in such Canadian, American, and British journals as *Prism*, *The Atlantic*, and *Queen's Quarterly*. Laurence also won respect as a lecturer and critic. United College, University of Winnipeg, made her an Honorary Fellow, the first woman and the youngest to be so honored. She received honorary degrees from McMaster, Dalhousie, Trent, University of Toronto, and Carleton University, and served as writer-in-residence at several Canadian universities. Her works have been translated into French, German, Italian, Spanish, Dutch, Norwegian, Danish, and Swedish.

Biography

Margaret Laurence was born Jean Margaret Wemyss on July 18, 1926, in Neepawa, Manitoba. Laurence's mother's family was of Irish descent and her father's Scottish. Although she is separated from the "old country" on both sides by at least two generations, her early memories, like those of Vanessa MacLeod in the short stories in *A Bird in the House* and of Morag Gunn in *The Diviners*, are of a proud and lively Scottish ancestry.

When Laurence was four, her mother died, and her aunt, Margaret Simpson, left a respected teaching career in Calgary and went home to care for her niece. A year later, she and Robert Wemyss were married. They had one son, Robert, born only two years before his father died of pneumonia. In 1938, Margaret Simpson Wemyss took the two children and moved in with her father, the owner of a furniture store. This domestic situation in slightly altered form provides the setting for the Vanessa MacLeod stories in *A Bird in the House*. Laurence lived in Grandfather Simpson's house until she went to United College, University of Winnipeg, in 1944.

John Simpson was a fierce and autocratic man of eighty-two when his widowed daughter and her two children moved in with him. Laurence resented his authority over her and her stepmother; this relationship fostered Laurence's empathy with women struggling toward freedom. All of her heroines— Hagar Shipley, Rachel Cameron, Vanessa MacLeod, Stacey MacAindra, and Morag Gunn—struggle against oppressive forces, and Laurence's recurring theme of the lack of communication between men and women, as well as between women and women, is rooted in the domestic situation in Grandfather Simpson's house. It appears in her first novel, *This Side Jordan*, as the problem between the colonialists and the Africans, between husbands and wives, and between relatives. At the beginning of her latest novel, *The Diviners*, the problem of communication—searching for the right words—is a major frustration which Morag, the protagonist, faces as a writer.

The encouragement and honest criticism given to Laurence by her stepmother were a great help to the girl, who started writing at an early age. At United College, she took honors in English, while her involvement with "The Winnipeg Old Left" during and after her college years reflected her dedication to social reform. Social awareness—the realization that men and women are constrained by social structures and exploit and are exploited by others through these systems—developed from her awareness that the hopes of her parents' generation had been crushed by the Depression and that her own generation's prospects were altered radically by World War II. After she was graduated, she worked for a year as a reporter for the *Winnipeg Citizen*. Her experience covering the local labor news consolidated her social and political convictions and advanced theoretical problems to personal ones.

In 1948, Laurence married Jack Laurence, a civil engineer from the University of Manitoba. They left Canada for England in 1949 and went to the

British Protectorate of Somaliland in 1950, where he was in charge of a dam-building project. In 1952, they moved to the Gold Coast, now Ghana, where they lived until 1957. A daughter, Jocelyn, was born when they were on leave in England in 1952, and a son, David, was born in Ghana in 1955. Out of these African years came several early works, including *The Tomorrow-Tamer*, *This Side Jordan*, the translations of folktales, and the travel journal *The Prophet's Camel Bell*. Of the last, Laurence said that it was the most difficult work she ever wrote because it was not fiction. The importance of this work lies in its theme—the growth in self-knowledge and humility in an alien environment. During the years in Africa, Laurence read the Pentateuch for the first time, and these books of the Bible became a touchstone for her, especially pertinent to the African works and to a lesser extent to her Man-awaka fiction. Here she developed the patience and discipline of a profes-sional writer.

In 1962, Laurence and her children left Jack Laurence in Vancouver and moved to London. They remained in England until 1968, when Laurence returned to Canada to be writer-in-residence at Massey College, University of Toronto. She was affiliated with several other Canadian universities in the years that followed. In 1987, Laurence died in Lakefield, Ontario.

Analysis

The major emphasis of Margaret Laurence's fiction changed considerably between her early and later works. In a 1969 article in *Canadian Literature*, "Ten Years' Sentences," she notes that after she had grown out of her obses-sion with the nature of freedom, the theme of the African writings and *The Stone Angel*, her concern "had changed to that of survival, the attempt of the personality to survive with some dignity, toting the load of excess mental baggage that everyone carries. . . ." In the same article, she remarks that she became increasingly involved with novels of character, that her viewpoint altered from modified optimism to modified pessimism, and that she had become more concerned with form in writing.

The more profound psychological realism of her later novels developed after a general awareness of the intractable problems of emerging African nations had matured both the Africans and their observers. The characters in the African works were products of a now-dated optimism which forced them into preconceived molds. The later novels reveal modified pessimism, but their vitality comes from Laurence's developing concern with psycholog-ical realism, which authenticates the characters and their voices. After *This Side Jordan*, the point of view is consistently in the first person, the protago-nist's, and is strictly limited to the protagonist's consciousness. Although Hagar in *The Stone Angel* and Stacey in *The Fire-Dwellers* are stereotypes, a stubborn old lady and a frantic middle-aged housewife, Laurence makes them both compelling protagonists through accurate psychological portrayals.

A theme of major importance which Laurence did not fully develop until *The Diviners* is the nature of language. Rachel's concern with name-calling in *A Jest of God* anticipates the larger exploration in *The Fire-Dwellers*, in which Laurence experiments with a variety of voices using language in a variety of ways. Exterior voices, many of them bizarre, interrupt and are interrupted by Stacey's inner voices—her monologues, her memories of voices from the past, her challenges, threats, and prayers to God. The exterior voices include radio and television news, snatches of her children's conversations, the characteristic dialects of various socioeconomic groups, the half-truthful promotions of her husband's company, and the meaningfully unfinished conversations between her and her husband. In order to allow language to be discussed explicitly, Laurence makes the protagonist of *The Diviners* a novelist.

In her first three novels Laurence uses biblical allusions to provide a mythic framework for a psychological study of character and situation. All these allusions are from the Old Testament, which made a lasting impression on her when she read it for the first time in Africa. The names she chooses for the characters in the early fiction—Adamo, Jacob, Abraham, Nathaniel, Joshua, Hagar, Ishmael, and Rachel—provide ready-made dilemmas whose traditional solutions appear contrived and psychologically unrealistic. In *This Side Jordan*, Joshua's Ghanian father proclaims that his son will cross the Jordan into the promised land, confidently assumed to be both an independent, prosperous Ghana and a Christian heaven. These allusions contribute to the sacramental overtones in the early works, particularly at the end of *The Stone Angel*.

Biblical myth is replaced in *A Bird in the House* and *The Diviners* by the myths of Scottish immigrants and Canadian pioneers and Indians. Vanessa in *A Bird in the House* lives with the sentimentally mythologized memories of her grandparents. The dispossessed Scots and the dispossessed Metis Indians provide a personal mythology for young Morag Gunn in *The Diviners* which her foster father, Christie Logan, embellishes to give the orphan girl an identity. Christie himself becomes mythologized in the mind of Morag's daughter Pique. The theme of the search for one's true origins plays a prominent part throughout Laurence's fiction, but the issues become increasingly complex. Whereas a clear dichotomy between his Christian and African backgrounds divides Nathaniel Amegbe in *This Side Jordan*, Morag in *The Diviners*, a recognized novelist who was an orphan brought up by a garbage collector, is seriously perplexed by the bases of her identity. Nathaniel hopes for, and apparently receives, both worldly and spiritual rewards in a successful if simplistic reconciliation of his dual heritage. In contrast, Morag painfully learns to reject the heroic Scots ancestress Christie had invented for her without rejecting him; she realizes that she has invented a hopelessly confused web of self-fabricated personal myth which she has to reconcile with her

Canadian roots in her search for self-identity.

Throughout all her works, Laurence explores themes concerning the role of women, the injustices of sex-role stereotyping, and the inequality of opportunity. The changing roles of women in the late twentieth century are a problem for Morag, who is jealous of her daughter's sexual freedom. Although the protagonists of Laurence's later novels are women, women who have not always been treated well by the men in their lives, men are never treated harshly in her work, even though the point of view is limited to the female protagonist's consciousness. Stacey generously concludes that perhaps her uncommunicative husband is tormented by fears and doubts much like her own. Morag never speculates about Jules Tonnerre's motives—a strange lack of curiosity for a novelist. Although Laurence's protagonists are oppressed, they never simply blame the men in their lives or the male-dominated society for their oppression. Men, almost to a man, are given the benefit of the doubt.

Laurence's first novel, *This Side Jordan*, was begun in Ghana in 1955, finished in Vancouver, and published in 1960. The setting of the novel is Ghana just before independence. The protagonist, Nathaniel Amegbe, had boarded at a Roman Catholic mission school since he was seven, and is now caught between two cultures, between loyalty to the fading memory of tribal customs and loyalty to the Christian mission which educated him and gave him the opportunity to better himself, in a European sense, by teaching in the city. His predicament is balanced by that of Johnnie Kestoe, a newly arrived employee of an English-based export-import firm who is trying to forget his slum-Irish background and to rise in the firm despite his antipathy for Africans. Both men have wives expecting their first child. Many of Nathaniel's dilemmas are resolved in the end, even his fears that his father's soul might be assigned to hell. In part, his resolution results from the salvation metaphor of "crossing the Jordan," a feat he hopes his newborn son will accomplish.

Nathaniel's interior monologues reveal the conflicts his dual loyalties have produced. Laurence uses this device more and more in the ensuing novels, and it culminates in *The Diviners* with its complex narrative techniques. Both Johnnie and Nathaniel move through the novel to a greater realization of self by means of humbling experiences, and both achieve worldly success, a naïvely optimistic conclusion made at the expense of psychological realism.

The Stone Angel was published in 1964, two years after Laurence and her children moved to London. Laurence, in "A Place to Stand On" from *Heart of a Stranger*, states that the dominant theme of this novel is survival, "not just physical survival, but the preservation of some human dignity and in the end some human warmth and ability to reach out and touch others." The monument Hagar Shipley's father had built for her mother's tomb in the Manawaka cemetery is a stone angel, gouged out by stonemasons who were accustomed to filling the needs of "fledgling pharaohs in an uncouth land." Laurence's horror at the extravagance of the pharaohs' monuments at Luxor, recorded in "Good Morning to the Grandson of Rameses the Second" in *Heart of a Stranger*, is similar to her reaction to the material ambitions of the stern Scots-Irish prairie pioneers.

The story of Hagar Shipley is told in the first person and covers the three weeks before her death, but in these weeks, long flashbacks depict scenes of Hagar's life in chronological order. Laurence gives sacramental overtones to the events of Hagar's last days: she confesses to a most unlikely priest in a deserted cannery over a jug of wine; in the hospital where she dies, she is able to overcome her pride and to enjoy and empathize with her fellow patients; after she accepts a previously despised minister sent by her son, she has an epiphany—"Pride was my wilderness, and the demon that led me there was fear"; and just before her death, she wrests from her daughter-in-law her last drink. Such sacramental overtones are not unusual in Laurence's works, but in her later works they become more subtle and complex than they are here.

Hagar Shipley is an old woman, an enormously fat, physically feeble old woman, grotesque and distorted in both body and spirit. She is mean-spirited as well as mean about her money and her possessions—almost a stereotype, an unlikely heroine, certainly not one who would seem to attract the sympathy of the reader. Hagar does, however, attract the reader; the genuineness of her portrayal makes her believable because of her total honesty, and the reader empathizes with her plight, which she finally recognizes as self-made. The reader feels compassion for her in spite of and because of her pettiness. Her voice, even in her old age, is still strong, willful, and vital, and the development of her self-awareness and self-knowledge is gripping.

The Stone Angel is the first work in which Manawaka, Laurence's fictionalized hometown of Neepawa, Manitoba, serves as the childhood setting of the protagonist. She makes Manawaka a microcosmic world, the childhood home of all her later protagonists, whose memories and friends carry over from one work to another. The mythic heritage of Hagar in *The Stone Angel*— the Scots-Irish pioneers and Metis Indians in Manitoba—is shared by Vanessa in *A Bird in the House*, Rachel in *A Jest of God*, Stacey in *The Fire-Dwellers*, and Morag in *The Diviners*, although Hagar is old enough to be the grandmother of the other four. Every one of these women leaves Manawaka in a search for identity and spiritual freedom, but none is able to escape her heredity and childhood environment entirely. The effects of environment and heredity were increasingly explored as Laurence became more and more concerned with the nature of identity. The Manawaka setting gave Laurence the opportunity to develop characters whose parents or grandparents engaged in a strenuous battle to open the frontier, founded what they hoped would be dynasties, and lived to see them fall because of the Depression. These stubborn and proud people begot children who had to find their own identities without the visible mansions their fathers had built to proclaim theirs. Pride in personal success became in the next generation pride in family and origin, and Hagar's inheritance from her father showed that the strength of the pioneer generation could destroy as well as build. The recognition of the double-edged nature of this strength enables Hagar, a stone angel in her former blindness, to feel at the end some human warmth for those around her.

A Jest of God was written in Buckinghamshire, England, in 1964 and 1965, and was published the next year. The action takes place during a summer and fall in the 1960's in Manawaka. Laurence creates a woman protagonist learning to break through the entrapments oppressing her.

Only through the first-person point of view could Laurence manage to reenact Rachel Cameron's fearful responses to everything around her and her self-mocking evaluations of her responses; she is afraid even of herself. When she reflects upon the way she thinks, upon her paranoia and her imagination, she warns herself that through her own distortions of reality she will become strange, weird, an outcast. She continues to tell herself that she must stop thinking that way. Her fear about her own responses to ordinary life keeps her in a state near hysteria. Except for the recognizable quality of her perceptions and the color and richness of her imagination, she indeed could be dismissed as a stereotyped old-maid schoolteacher, the butt of the town's jokes. She lives with her widowed mother, renting the upper story of her dead father's former funeral parlor.

The mythic framework for the psychological study of Rachel is the Old Testament story in which she is "mourning for her children"—in the novel, the children she has never had. When she is confident enough to love Nick Kazlik, whom she needs more as a father for her children than as a lover, he tells her that he is not God; he cannot solve her problems. Neither he nor the possibility of the child he might give her can overcome her sense of isolation, of which the lack of children is only the symbol; her sense of isolation seems to be based on her lack of spiritual fulfillment, isolation from God. God's word is evaded in the church she and her mother attend, and she is totally horrified by fundamentalist irrationality. In the end, Rachel recognizes her own self-pity to be a horrendous sort of pride, and starts to learn instead to feel compassion for others because they are as isolated as she.

Rachel's situation could set the stage for a tragedy, but Laurence's heroines do not become tragic. They live through their crises, endure, and in enduring gain strength. Rachel gains strength from the loss of Nick, which she never understands, and from the loss of what she hoped and feared would be Nick's baby. After Rachel has decided not to commit suicide when she thinks she is pregnant, she discovers that what she had thought was a baby was a meaningless tumor, not even malignant—a jest of God. Despite, or perhaps because of, this grotesque anticlimax, Rachel is able to make the decision to leave

Manawaka; she applies for and gets a teaching position in Vancouver. At the end, she is traveling with her mother, her "elderly child," to a new life in Vancouver.

The Fire-Dwellers was written in England between 1966 and 1968; the protagonist of the novel, Stacey MacAindra, is Rachel Cameron's sister. She is an ordinary woman—a middle-class contemporary housewife in Manawaka, anxious over all the possible and impossible perils waiting for her and her family. She overcomes stereotyping through the recognizable, likable, and spontaneous qualities of her narrative voice. Laurence's narrative technique is more complex in *The Fire-Dwellers* than in any of her earlier works. The first-person narration is fragmented by a variety of interruptions—Stacey's inner voices, snatches of Stacey's memories set to the side of the page, italicized dreams and fantasies, incomplete conversations with Mac, her husband, and radio and television news. At times, she is concentrating so completely on her inner voice that she feels a physical jolt when external reality breaks into her inner fantasies.

The title refers, as Stacey's lover Luke implies, to Stacey: she is the ladybird of the nursery rhyme who must fly away home because her house is on fire and her children will burn. Although Sir James Frazer's *The Golden Bough* (1890-1915) lies unopened beside Stacey's bed at the end of the book as it did in the beginning, Stacey seems to understand intuitively the explanation of the primitive sexuality of fire. Stacey burns from sexual frustration and fears the burning of an atomic bomb, a threat ever present on the news. Newspaper pictures from Vietnam of a horrified mother trying to remove burning napalm from her baby's face appear again and again in Stacey's mind. Counterpointing the fire metaphor is that of water, here regenerative as well as destructive, which foreshadows its more important position in *The Diviners*.

Unlike the other Manawaka protagonists, Stacey could never be considered grotesque; she considers herself quite ordinary, and, at first glance, most people would agree, despite her apocalyptic fears. The world around her, however, is grotesque. The frightening events in the lives of Stacey's neighbors and friends are counterpointed by the daily news from the Vietnam War. Almost a symbol of Stacey's inability to communicate her fears, her two-year-old, Jen, cannot or will not speak. No wonder Stacey hides her drinks in the Mix-Master. Her interior dialogue convincingly portrays a compassionate woman with a stabilizing sense of humor which makes the limited affirmation of the conclusion believable; Mac and his equally uncommunicative son Duncan are brought together by Duncan's near-death, and Jen speaks her first words, "Hi, Mum. Want tea?"

Laurence worked on *The Diviners* from 1969 to 1973, at the old house she bought on the Otonabee River near Peterborough, Ontario. Unlike the earlier Laurence protagonists, apparently ordinary women, almost stereotypes who turn out to be extraordinary in their own way, Morag Gunn is an extraordinarily gifted writer who has quite ordinary and common concerns. She is also unlike her Manawaka "sisters" in that she is an orphan reared by the town's garbage collector; thus she is an outsider who bears the scorn and taunts of the town's wealthier children such as Stacey Cameron and Vanessa MacLeod. She shares her humble status with the disreputable half-breed Indians, the Tonnerres, and learns the injustice of the inequality of opportunity at first hand.

The title, *The Diviners*, refers explicitly to gifted individuals, artists such as Morag who contribute to a greater understanding of life, as well as to her friend, Royland, a true water diviner. Indeed, Morag discovers that many of her acquaintances are, in some way, themselves diviners. At the end of the book, when Royland tells Morag he has lost the gift of divining, Morag muses, "At least Royland knew he had been a true diviner. . . . The necessity of doing the thing—that mattered."

The Diviners is the longest and the most tightly structured of Laurence's novels; it has three long parts framed by a prologue and epilogue. The plot is commonplace; Morag spends a summer worrying about her eighteen-year-old dauther Pique, who has gone west to find herself. In this action, Morag is only an observer, as all mothers must be in this situation. Her own story is enclosed within the action in the present, with chronological flashbacks such as those in *The Stone Angel*. The novel is presented in the first person, but with two new techniques: "Snapshots," meditations on the few snapshots Morag has from her youth; and "Memorybank Movies," Morag's memories from her past. The snapshots cover the lives of her parents before Morag was born through her early childhood and their deaths. Aware that she embroidered stories about the snapshots as a child, Morag looks at a snapshot, remembers her make-believe story, and then muses, "I don't recall when I invented that one." This comment, early in the novel, establishes the mythologizing of one's past as an important motif.

Morag's future as a writer is foreshadowed by her retelling of Christie Logan's tales when just a girl, adapting them to her own needs. In the prologue, Morag the novelist worries about diction, the choice of the proper words: "How could that colour be caught in words? A sort of rosy peach colour, but that sounded corny and was also inaccurate." Morag uses her hometown for setting and characters, just as Laurence herself does; the theme of where one belongs is as important to Morag as a writer as it is to Laurence.

The title of Morag's second novel, *Prospero's Child*, foreshadows the motif of the end-frame. Royland loses his gift of witching for water and hopes to pass it on to A-Okay Smith. Morag realizes that she will pass on to Pique her gift, just as Christie Logan's manic prophecies influenced her creativity. Among all Laurence's heroines, Morag Gunn is the closest in experience and interests to Laurence herself. Each successive protagonist, from Hagar and Rachel and Vanessa to Stacy, came closer and closer to Laurence's own identity. She said that she realized how difficult it would be to portray a protagonist so much like herself, but *The Diviners* is a risky novel, an ambitious book which only an established writer could afford to produce.

Because Laurence depicts human problems in terms of sex roles, the gender of the characters in the Manawaka novels is particularly important. The women protagonists of all of these novels clearly demonstrate Laurence's persistent investigation of the role of women in society. The sex lives of Laurence's women are fully integrated parts of their identities without becoming obsessive or neurotic. All of her protagonists enjoy their sexuality but, at the same time, suffer guiltily for it. Laurence did not admit a connection with the women's liberation movement. Morag Gunn, however, a single head of a household with an illegitimate dependent child, could not have been as readily accepted and admired before the feminist movement as she is now.

Similarly, although Laurence employs Christian motifs and themes throughout her fiction, she did not embrace institutional Christianity. Like Carl Jung, Laurence seems to find God in the human soul, defining religion in terms of a Jungian "numinous experience" which can lead to a psychological change. Salvation is redefined as discovery of self, and grace is given to find a new sense of life direction.

Presenting her characters as beings caught between the determinism of history and their free will, as individuals who are torn between body and spirit, fact and illusion, Laurence portrays life as a series of internal crises. Through the development of her protagonists, Laurence celebrates even the crises as she celebrates her protagonists' progress. The search for self involves both the liberation from and the embracing of the past. Survival with dignity and the ability to love, she remarks in *Heart of a Stranger*, are themes inevitable for a writer of her stern Scots-Irish background. Since these themes are of immense contemporary importance, her works explore problems which have universal appeal, a fact that goes far to explain her tremendous popularity.

Judith Weise

Other major works

SHORT FICTION: *The Tomorrow-Tamer*, 1963; *A Bird in the House*, 1970.

NONFICTION: *The Prophet's Camel Bell*, 1963 (published in the United States as *New Wind in a Dry Land*, 1964); *Long Drums and Cannons: Nigerian Dramatists and Novelists, 1952-66*, 1968; *Heart of a Stranger*, 1976.

CHILDREN'S LITERATURE: *Jason's Quest*, 1970; *The Christmas Birthday Story*, 1980.

ANTHOLOGY: *A Tree for Poverty: Somali Poetry and Prose*, 1954.

Bibliography

Buss, Helen M. *Mother and Daughter Relationships in the Manawaka Works of Margaret Laurence*. English Literary Series 34. Victoria, British Columbia: University of Victoria, 1985. This somewhat pretentious study explores female protagonists of Laurence's Manawaka works. Buss's excessively academic style is a drawback.

Gunnars, Kristjana, ed. *Crossing the River: Essays in Honour of Margaret Laurence*. Winnipeg, Manitoba: Turnstone Press, 1988. Twelve previously unpublished essays by Canadian and international writers and critics pay tribute to Laurence's life and work. Includes some interesting new insights.

Kertzer, J. M. "Margaret Laurence and Her Works." In *Canadian Writers and Their Works: Fiction Series*, edited by Robert Lecker, Jack David, and Ellen Quigley. Toronto: ECW Press, 1987. This study is divided into the four parts, "Laurence's Works" being the longest and most thorough section. Despite its scholarliness, this study's clear style and extensive bibliography make it invaluable.

Sorfleet, John R., ed. "The Work of Margaret Laurence." *Journal of Canadian Fiction* 27 (1980). This issue, devoted to Laurence, comprises four stories, a letter and an essay by Laurence, and nine essays by Canadian critics on various aspects of her fiction.

Thomas, Clara. *Margaret Laurence*. Canadian Writers 3. Toronto: McClelland and Stewart, 1969. Thomas' admiring assessment of Laurence's writing covers in five chronologically-arranged chapters the African books, two Manawaka novels, and some of the stories later collected in *A Bird in the House*. This study is still relevant and Thomas' unadorned style is highly readable. The introduction includes illuminating biographical material, and the selected bibliography is thorough.

Verduyn, Christl, ed. *Margaret Laurence: An Appreciation*. Peterborough, Ontario: Broadview Press, 1988. The eighteen essays in this invaluable book chronicle the evolution of Laurence's vision in both her fiction and the chief social concerns of her life. The essay topics range from studies of her early African-experience stories to Laurence's own address/essay, "My Final Hour," in which she movingly states her commitments as a writer and a person.

Woodcock, George, ed. *A Place to Stand On: Essays By and About Margaret Laurence*. Western Canadian Literary Documents Series 4. Edmonton: NeWest Press, 1983. A thorough, rich exploration of Laurence's craft and works, containing essays by Laurence and various critics published over more than twenty years. The book is highlighted by interviews with Laurence. Also includes a useful bibliography.

D. H. LAWRENCE

Born: Eastwood, England; September 11, 1885
Died: Vence, France; March 2, 1930

Principal long fiction

The White Peacock, 1911; *The Trespasser*, 1912; *Sons and Lovers*, 1913; *The Rainbow*, 1915; *Women in Love*, 1920; *The Lost Girl*, 1920; *Aaron's Rod*, 1922; *The Ladybird, The Fox, The Captain's Doll*, 1923; *Kangaroo*, 1923; *The Boy in the Bush*, 1924 (with M. L. Skinner); *The Plumed Serpent*, 1926; *Lady Chatterley's Lover*, 1928; *The Escaped Cock*, 1929 (best known as *The Man Who Died*); *The Virgin and the Gipsy*, 1930; *Mr. Noon*, 1984 (wr. 1920-1922).

Other literary forms

D. H. Lawrence was among the most prolific and wide-ranging of modern writers, a fact all the more remarkable considering that he spent so much time on the move, battling chronic tuberculosis which cut short his life in his forty-fifth year. In addition to his twelve novels, he published more than a dozen books of poetry, collected in *The Complete Poems of D. H. Lawrence* (1964); eight volumes of short fiction, including half a dozen novellas, collected in *The Complete Short Stories of D. H. Lawrence* (1961); and seven plays, collected in *The Complete Plays of D. H. Lawrence* (1965). He also wrote a wide variety of nonfiction, including four fine travel books (*Twilight in Italy*, 1916; *Sea and Sardinia*, 1921; *Mornings in Mexico*, 1927; and *Etruscan Places*, 1932). *Movements in European History* (1921), published under the pseudonym Lawrence H. Davison, is a subjective meditation on historical cycles and Europe's decline, while *Psychoanalysis and the Unconscious* (1921) is a highly original and influential volume of literary criticism. Lawrence's religious vision, in the guise of a commentary on the Book of Revelation, is offered in *Apocalypse* (1931). Many other essays on diverse subjects appeared in periodicals during the last two decades of his life and have been collected posthumously by Edward D. McDonald in *Phoenix* (1936), and by Warren Roberts and Harry T. Moore in *Phoenix II* (1968). Lawrence was also a formidable correspondent, and his letters are invaluable aids to understanding the man and the writer. Some 1,257 of the more than 5,500 known letters are available in a collection edited by Harry T. Moore; a more complete edition, running to eight volumes, is in preparation under the general editorship of James T. Boulton. Several of Lawrence's fictional works—*Sons and Lovers*, *Lady Chatterley's Lover*, "The Rocking-Horse Winner," *Women in Love*, and *The Virgin and the Gipsy*—have been adapted to the motion picture medium, while his life is the subject of the film *The Priest of Love*.

Achievements

The running battle against censorship in which Lawrence engaged through-out most of his career undoubtedly performed a valuable service to subsequent writers and the reading public, though it cost him dearly both emotionally and financially. The essentially symbolic role of sexuality in his writing resembles somewhat that found in Walt Whitman's, but Lawrence's more overt treatment of it—liberating as it was to a generation whose Victorian upbringing had been castigated by the Freudians—led to a general misunderstanding of his work that persisted for almost three decades after his death. The thirty-year suppression of *Lady Chatterley's Lover* backfired as censorship so often does, attracting the public's attention to the object of the prohibition. Unfortunately this notoriety made the novel, far from Lawrence's greatest, the one most commonly associated with his name in the popular mind. His reputation among more serious readers was not helped by the series of sensationalistic memoirs published by some of his more ardent followers in the 1930's and early 1940's. Championed as a prophet of free love and utopianism, repudiated as a crazed homosexual and protofascist, Lawrence the artist all but disappeared from view.

The appearance of several serious and sympathetic studies of Lawrence in the middle and late 1950's, by presenting a more accurate record of his life and a more discriminating assessment of his work, largely succeeded in salvaging Lawrence's stature as a major writer. Among those most responsible for the Lawrence revival were F. R. Leavis, Harry T. Moore, Edward Nehls, and Graham Hough. Subsequent readers have been able to recognize more readily in the best of Lawrence's works what Leavis described as its "marked moral intensity," its "reverent openness before life."

In addition to his prophetic themes, Lawrence's technical innovations are now acknowledged as among the most important in modern fiction. He could convey a "ripping yarn" and portray lifelike characters when he chose, and parts of *Sons and Lovers* and *The Lost Girl*, among many other works, demonstrate his mastery of traditional realism in the representation of his native Midlands. More fundamentally, however, Lawrence's novels are triumphs of mood and sensibility; they seek (as Frank Kermode has said) less to represent life than to enact it. He has no peer in the evocative rendering of place, introducing poetic symbols that carry the meaning without losing sight of their basis in intensely observed, concrete details. His approach to characterization following *The Rainbow* was unconventional in that he avoided "the old stable ego" and pattern-imposed character types in an effort to go beneath the rational and articulate levels of consciousness to the nonhuman being in his characters. As Walter Allen has observed, for Lawrence "the value of people . . . consisted in how far mystery resided in them, how far they were conscious of mystery." The linear, cause-and-effect development of characters controlled by the rational intellect was for him a hindrance. He focused instead on the surging, dynamic forces—sexual impulses, the potency of nature and animals, the terrible allure of death—which in their purest form defy rationality and are communicated by a kind of unmediated intuition. His prose style was similarly subjective in emphasis. The frequent repetitiveness and inflated rhetoric can be tiresome, but at its best the prose is supple and sensuous, its dynamic rhythms incantatory, a powerful vehicle of Lawrence's vision. Further, he avoided the neat resolution of closure of traditional narratives, typically preferring the "open end" in which the vital forces operating in his characters are felt to be continuously and dynamically in process rather than subdued by the authorial imposition of finality. His comment on the bustling activities of Indian peasants on market day, in *Mornings in Mexico*, epitomizes his fictional method as well as his vitalist doctrine: "In everything, the shimmer of creation and never the finality of the created."

Lawrence's approach to fiction involved considerable risks, and many of his novels are seriously flawed. There are those who cannot read him at all. Nevertheless, the integrity of his vision and the sheer power with which he communicated it have made E. M. Forster's estimate (written shortly after Lawrence's death) stand up: "he was the greatest imaginative novelist of his generation."

Biography

David Herbert Lawrence was born on September 11, 1885, in the Midlands coal-mining village of Eastwood, Nottinghamshire. The noise and grime of the pits dominated Eastwood, but the proximity of fabled Sherwood Forest was a living reminder of what Lawrence would later call "the old England of the forest and agricultural past" upon which industrialization had been so rudely imposed. The contrast was to remain an essential element in his makeup. Allied to it was the equally sharp contrast between his parents. Arthur John Lawrence, the father, had worked in the coal-pits from the age of seven. Coarse, semiliterate, intensely physical, a hail-fellow popular with his collier mates, he was prone to drink and to near-poverty. Lydia (née Beardsall) Lawrence, his wife, was a former schoolteacher from a pious middle-class Methodist family which counted among its forebears a noted composer of Wesleyan hymns. Along with his four siblings, young Lawrence was inevitably caught up in the frequent and sometimes violent strife between his mother and father. Delicate and sickly as a child, he could scarcely have emulated his father—not that he was inclined to do so. Instead, he sided with his mother. She in turn doted on him and encouraged him in his studies as a means of escape from the working-class life, thus further alienating him from his father. Only in later life would Lawrence come to see the dangerous liabilities of this overweening maternal bond and the counterbalancing attractiveness of his father's unassuming strength and vitality.

Lawrence was an outstanding student in school and at the age of twelve won a scholarship to Nottingham High School. After graduation in 1901, he worked for three unhappy months as a clerk in a surgical-appliance factory in Nottingham, until he fell seriously ill with pneumonia. About this time, he met Jessie Chambers, whose family lived on a small farm outside Eastwood. Over the next ten years his close relationship with the "spiritual" Jessie (the "Miriam" of *Sons and Lovers*) and her sympathetic family offered further stimulus to his fondness for the beauties of nature, for reading, and for ideas; eventually, with Jessie's encouragement and partial collaboration, he began to write stories and verse. The Chamberses' way of life and the bucolic scenery of Haggs farm, so tellingly unlike the ambience of Lawrence's own home, would later provide him with materials for his first novel *The White Peacock*. After his prolonged convalescence from pneumonia, in 1903 he found a position as a "pupil-teacher" at an elementary school in nearby Ilkeston, Derbyshire. Two years there were followed by a third as an uncertified teacher in the Eastwood British School. In 1906, having won a King's Scholarship competition, he began a two-year course of study for his teacher's certificate at Nottingham University College. By 1908, he qualified to teach at Davidson Road School, a boys' elementary school in the London suburb of Croydon, where he remained until 1911.

Meanwhile Lawrence had published several poems in 1909 in the *English Review*, edited by Ford Madox Hueffer (later Ford), who introduced him to such established writers as H. G. Wells, Ezra Pound, and William Butler Yeats. Soon Lawrence was busily working at two novels, *The White Peacock* and the autobiographical *Paul Morel* (the working title of *Sons and Lovers*). While the former was still in press, his mother died of cancer in December, 1910, an event whose profound impact on him is duly commemorated in his poems and in *Paul Morel*, which he had already begun to rewrite. By this time his relationship with Jessie Chambers had diminished considerably, and he had had several brief affairs with other women. His ill-health and his increasing commitment to writing (*The Trespasser*, his second novel, was to appear the following year) induced him to forego teaching in the winter of 1911-1912. Back in Eastwood, in April, he met and fell in love with Frieda von Richthoven Weekley, the high-spirited daughter of a German baron, wife of a professor of philology at Nottingham University, and at thirty-two the mother of three small children. In May, Lawrence and Frieda eloped to the Continent. There, for the next six months, Lawrence wrote poems, stories, travel-sketches (most of which were later collected in *Twilight in Italy*), and his final revision of the autobiographical novel. This writing, particularly the metamorphosis of *Paul Morel* into *Sons and Lovers* (with which Frieda assisted him by discussing her own maternal feelings and the theories of Freud), marked the true beginning of Lawrence's artistic maturity.

The advent of World War I coincided with what in many ways was the most crucial period of his development as a writer. By the end of 1914,

Lawrence and Frieda had married, the critical success of *Sons and Lovers* had established his reputation, he had formed important associations with Edward Garnett, John Middleton Murry, and Katherine Mansfield, and he had begun to work on what many now consider his greatest novels, *The Rainbow* and *Women in Love* (originally conceived as a single work, *The Sisters*). Yet the triumph that might have been his soon turned to ashes. The official suppression of *The Rainbow* in November, 1916—the charge of "immorality" was leveled on both political and sexual grounds—was followed by a series of nightmarish episodes in which, largely because of Frieda's German origins, the Lawrences were hounded and persecuted as supposed enemy spies. Lawrence was reviled in the "patriotic" English press, and, after *The Rainbow* fiasco, in which many of his literary associates had failed to come to his defense, he found it increasingly difficult to publish his work and hence to make a living. Though he completed *Women in Love* in 1917, it did not appear until 1920 in the United States. Events seemed to conspire against him so that, by the end of the war, he could never again feel at home in his native land. This bitter severance motivated the "savage pilgrimage" that dominated the last decade of his life, driving him feverishly around the globe in search of some "ideal centre" in which to live and work in hope for the future.

Lawrence's travels were as much spiritual as geographical in character, and his quest became the primary focus of his writing after the war. The more than two years he spent in Italy and Sicily (1919-1921) provided him with the materials for the concluding chapters of *The Lost Girl* (which he had begun before the war and set aside to work on *The Sisters*) and for *Aaron's Rod*. Heading for America by way of the Orient, the Lawrences briefly visited Ceylon and then Australia, where he wrote *Kangaroo* in just six weeks. In September, 1922, they arrived in the United States and soon settled near Taos, New Mexico, on a mountain ranch that was to be "home" for them during most of the next three years. Here Lawrence rewrote *Studies in Classic American Literature* (1923; begun in 1917) and produced such important works as "Eagle in New Mexico" and "Spirits Summoned West" (poems), "The Woman Who Rode Away," "The Princess," "St. Mawr," and half of the travel sketches that comprise *Mornings in Mexico*. During this period Lawrence also made three trips to Mexico, staying there a total of about ten months; his travel experiences, embellished by his rather extensive readings in Aztec history and archaeology, provided the sources for his novel of Mexico, *The Plumed Serpent*, his most ambitious creative undertaking of the postwar years. On the day he finished the novel in Oaxaca, he fell gravely ill with acute tuberculosis and nearly died. After convalescing in Mexico City and on the ranch in New Mexico, he returned with Frieda to Europe in the late fall of 1925, settling first in Spotorno on the Italian Riviera and later in a villa outside Florence.

Lawrence's last years were clouded by the inevitable encroachment of his disease, but he remained remarkably active. He toured the ancient Etruscan ruins; took up painting, producing some strikingly original works; and wrote three complete versions of what would become, in its final form, his most famous novel, *Lady Chatterley's Lover*. The book's banning and confiscation in 1928, reviving the old outcry of "obscenity," prompted several of his most eloquent essays on the subject of pornography and censorship. It was his final battle, save that which could not be won. Lawrence died in Vence, France, on March 2, 1930, at the age of forty-four.

Analysis

D. H. Lawrence occupies an ambiguous position with respect to James Joyce, Marcel Proust, T. S. Eliot and the other major figures of the modernist movement. While, on the one hand, he shared their feelings of gloom about the degeneration of modern European life and looked to ancient mythologies for prototypes of the rebirth all saw as necessary, on the other he keenly distrusted the modernists' veneration of traditional culture and their classicist aesthetics. The modernist ideal of art as "an escape from personality," as a finished and perfected creation sufficient unto itself, was anathema to Lawrence, who once claimed that his motto was not art for art's sake but "art for my sake." For him, life and art were intertwined, both expressions of the same quest: "To be alive, to be man alive, to be whole man alive: that is the point." The novel realized its essential function best when it embodied and vitally enacted the novelist's mercurial sensibility. His spontaneity, his limitations and imperfections, and his fleeting moments of intuition were directly transmitted to the reader, whose own "instinct for life" would be thereby quickened. Lawrence believed that at its best "the novel, and the novel supremely," could and should perform this important task. That is why he insisted that the novel is "the one bright book of life." One way of approaching his own novels—and the most significant, by general consensus, are *Sons and Lovers*, *The Rainbow*, *Women in Love*, *The Plumed Serpent*, and *Lady Chatterley's Lover*—is to consider the extent to which the form and content of each in turn rises to this vitalist standard.

To be "whole man alive," for Lawrence, involved first of all the realization of *wholeness*. The great enemy of human (and of aesthetic) wholeness, he believed, was modern life itself. Industrialization had cut man off from the past, had mechanized his daily life and transformed human relations into a power-struggle to acquire material commodities, thereby alienating man from contact with the divine potency residing in both nature and other men and women. Modern Europe was therefore an accumulation of dead or dying husks, fragmented and spiritually void, whose inevitable expression was mass destruction. For Lawrence, World War I was the apotheosis of modernization.

Yet contemporary history provided only the end result of a long process of atomization and dispersion whose seeds lay in ancient prehistory. In *Fantasia of the Unconscious* (1922), Lawrence formulated a myth of origins that sheds light on his quest for wholeness in his travels among "primitive" peoples as well as in his novels. He describes a kind of golden age before the flood, when the pagan world, both geographically and culturally, was a single, unified entity. This *Ur*-culture, unlike the modern fragmented age, had developed a holistic knowledge or "science in terms of life." The primal wisdom did not differentiate between body, mind, and spirit; the objective and the subjective were one, as the reason and the passions were one; man and nature and the cosmos lived in harmonious relation with one another. Men and women all over the earth shared this knowledge. They "wandered back and forth from Atlantis to the Polynesian Continent. . . . The interchange was complete, and knowledge, science, was universal over the earth." Then the glaciers melted, whole continents were drowned, and the monolithic world fragmented into isolated races, each developing its own culture, its own "science." A few refugees from the lost continents fled to the high ground of Europe, Asia, and America. There they "refused to forget, but taught the old wisdom, only in its half-forgotten, symbolic forms. More or less forgotten, as knowledge: remembered as ritual, gesture, and myth-story."

In modern Europe, even these vestiges of the old universal knowledge had largely become extinct, and with them died what was left of the unitary being of man. First Christianity, with its overemphasis on bodiless spirituality, and then modern science, with its excessive dependence upon finite reason as the instrument of control over a merely mechanistic world, had killed it. After the war Lawrence hoped, in traveling to lands where Christianity, modern science, and industrialization had not yet fully taken hold, to uncover the traces of the primal knowledge, if only "in its half-forgotten, symbolic forms." By somehow establishing a vital contact with "primitive" men and women and fusing his "white consciousness" with their "dark-blood consciousness," he hoped to usher in the next phase in the development of the human race. His novels would sound the clarion call—awakening the primordial memory by means of "ritual, gesture, and myth-story"—summoning "whole man alive" to cross over the threshold into the New World of regenerated being.

Although this myth of Apocalypse and rebirth was fully articulated during Lawrence's "wander years" after the war, it was clearly anticipated in his earlier works. There the horror of the modern world's "drift toward death" and the yearning for some "holy ground" on which to begin anew were keenly felt. The initial experience of fragmentation in Lawrence's life was obviously the primal conflict between his mother and father, which among other things resulted in a confusion in his own sexual identity. In the fiction of this period, the stunting of life by fragmentation and imbalance is evident in the portrayal of such characters as Miriam Leivers in *Sons and Lovers*, Anton Skrebensky in *The Rainbow*, and Gerald Crich in *Women in Love*, just as the quest for vital wholeness is exemplified in the same novels by Paul Morel, Ursula Brangwen, and Rupert Birkin, respectively. If the secondary characters in Lawrence's novels tend in general to be static types seen from without, his protagonists, beginning with Ursula in *The Rainbow* and continuing through Constance Chatterley in *Lady Chatterley's Lover*, are anything but static. Rather, they are volatile, inconsistent, and sometimes enigmatic. In *The Plumed Serpent*, Kate Leslie vacillates between intellectual abstraction and immediate sensuous experience; between egotistic willfulness and utter self-abandonment to another; between withdrawal behind the boundaries of the safe and the known, and the passionate yearning for metamorphosis; and so on. There is a constant ebb and flow in Kate's behavior, even a rough circularity, that creates a spontaneous, improvisatory feeling in her narrative. Lawrence's protagonists are always in flux, realizing by turns the various aspects of their natures, and this dynamism is largely what makes them so alive. They are open to life: in themselves, in their natural environment, and in other vital human beings.

Lawrence believed that the novel was the one form of human expression malleable enough to articulate and dramatize the dynamic process of living. In his essay "Why the Novel Matters," he celebrates the novelist's advantage over the saint, the scientist, and the philosopher, all of whom deal only with parts of the composite being of mankind. The novelist alone, says Lawrence, is capable of rendering the whole of "man alive." He alone, by so doing, "can make the whole man alive [that is, the reader] tremble."

The priestly or prophetic function of the novelist is clearly central to this aesthetic doctrine. Lawrence is one of the very few modern writers to assume this role and to do so explicitly. At times, this very explicitness becomes problematic. His novels are quite uneven; most are marred in varying degrees by hectoring didacticism that is less evident in his short fiction. Nevertheless, he needed the amplitude of an extended narrative to give voice to the several sides of his complex sensibility, as if to discover himself in the process. Perhaps that, as much as anything else, was the object of his quest. Collectively his novels represent a restless search for a form capable of rendering that sensibility fully and honestly.

In a letter written a few months after the publication of *Sons and Lovers*, Lawrence made an admission which suggests that "art for my sake" could have been a cathartic as well as a heuristic function. "One sheds one's sickness in books," he wrote, "repeats and presents one's emotions, to be master of them." *Sons and Lovers*, his third novel, was the work that enabled Lawrence to come to terms, at least provisionally, with the traumas of his formative years. The more than two years he spent working and reworking the book amounted to an artistic and psychological rite of passage essential to his development as a man and as a writer.

The novel spans the first twenty-six years in the life of Paul Morel. Because of the obvious similarities between Paul's experiences and Lawrence's, and because the story in part concerns Paul's apprenticeship as an artist—or, more accurately, the obstacles he must overcome to be an artist—the novel has been seen as an example of a subspecies of the *Bildungsroman*, the *Künstler-roman*. Comparison with James Joyce's *Portrait of the Artist as a Young Man* (1916) suggests, however, how loosely the term applies to Lawrence's novel. Where Joyce scrupulously selects only those scenes and episodes of Stephen Dedalus' life that directly contribute to the young artist's development (his first use of language, his schooling, his imaginative transcendence of sex, religion, and politics, his aesthetic theories), Lawrence's focus is far more diffuse. The novel opens with a conventional set-piece description of the town of Bestwood (modeled on Eastwood) as it has been affected by the arrival and growth of the mining industry during the last half-century. This is followed by an account of the courtship and early married life of Walter and Gertrude Morel, Paul's parents. Even after Paul's birth, the main emphasis remains for many chapters on the mother and father, and considerable space is devoted to their first child, William, whose sudden death and funeral conclude Part I of the novel. Paul's interest in drawing is mentioned halfway through Part I, but it is not a major concern until he becomes friends with Miriam Leivers in Part II, and there the companionship itself actually receives more attention. Though the comparison does an injustice to the nature of Lawrence's real achievement in the novel, perhaps *Sons and Lovers* more nearly resembles *Stephen Hero* (1944), the earlier and more generally autobiographical version of Joyce's novel, than it does the tightly constructed *Portrait of the Artist as a Young Man*.

Yet, when in the late stages of revision Lawrence changed his title from *Paul Morel* to *Sons and Lovers*, his motive was akin to Joyce's when the Irishman discarded *Stephen Hero* and began to rewrite. The motive was form, form determined by a controlling idea. The subject of *Sons and Lovers* is not simply Paul's development but his development as an instance of the pattern suggested by the title; that pattern involves the Morels' unhappy marriage, the fateful experiences of Paul's brother William, Paul's frustrated relationship with Miriam, and his later encounters with Clara and Baxter Dawes, as well as Paul's own maturation. For Lawrence, the pattern clearly had wide appli-cation. Indeed, in a letter to Edward Garnett, his editor, written a few days after completing the revised novel, Lawrence claimed that his book sounded "the tragedy of thousands of young men in England."

This claim, along with the change in title and the late revisions designed to underscore a theme already present in the narrative, was probably influ-enced by the discussions which Lawrence and Frieda had had in 1912 regarding Freud's theories, of which Frieda was then an enthusiastic proponent. (There is no evidence of Lawrence's awareness of Freud before this.) In a more general sense, the "tragedy" was rooted historically, as the novel shows, in the disruption of natural human relationships that was one of the byproducts of modernization. Directly or indirectly, the characters in the novel are entrapped by the materialistic values of their society, unable even when they consciously reject those values to establish true contact with one another. Instead they tend to treat one another as objects to be possessed or manipulated for the purpose of self-gratification.

Thus Mrs. Morel, frustrated by her marriage to her coal-miner husband, transfers her affections to her sons, first to William, the eldest, and then to Paul after William's death. Walter Morel, the father, becomes a scapegoat and an outcast in his own home. Whether consciously or not, Mrs. Morel uses her sons as instruments to work out her own destiny vicariously, encouraging them in pursuits that will enable them to escape the socially confining life that she herself cannot escape, yet resenting it when the sons do begin to make a life away from her. Paul's fixation upon his mother—and his hatred of his father—contributes to a confusion of his sexual identity and to his inability to love girls his own age in a normal, healthy way. In the same letter to Edward Garnett, Lawrence characterized this inability to love as a "split," referring to the rupture in the son's natural passions caused by the mother's possessive love. The split causes Paul to seek out girls who perform the psychological role of mother-surrogates: Miriam, an exaggerated version of the spiritual, Madonna-like aspect of the mother image; and the buxom Clara Dawes, who from a Freudian viewpoint represents the "degraded sex-object," the fallen woman, equally a projection of the son's prohibited erotic desires for his mother. Because Paul's feeling for Miriam and Clara are thus compartmentalized and unbalanced, both relationships are unfulfilling, a fact which only reinforces his Oedipal bondage. At the same time, part of the responsibility for the unsatisfactory relationships belongs to Miriam and Clara themselves, both of whom exploit Paul to help them fulfill their own private fantasy lives. The world of *Sons and Lovers* is populated by isolated, fragmentary souls not unlike the inhabitants of T. S. Eliot's *The Waste Land*, 1922 ("We think of the key, each in his prison/Thinking of the key, each confirms a prison").

A decade after the appearance of *Sons and Lovers*, Lawrence declared that of all his books, it was the one he would like to rewrite, because in it he had treated his father unfairly. By then, of course, he was overtly committed to finding embodiments of "whole man alive" and, in retrospect, his father seemed to offer such an embodiment. When he wrote *Sons and Lovers*, however, he had not yet fully come to appreciate the importance of his father's unaffected male vitality. Although occasionally Walter Morel appears in a favorable light, the novel generally emphasizes his ineffectuality as a husband and father. The Oedipal conflict on which the story hinges perhaps made this unavoidable. In any event, the struggle to attain wholeness is centered in Paul Morel.

Because Paul's mother is "the pivot and pole of his life, from which he could not escape," her death amounts to the great crisis of the novel. The terrible spectacle of her agony as she lies dying slowly of cancer torments Paul until, by giving her an overdose of morphine, he commits a mercy-killing. Unconsciously, the act seems to be motivated by his desire to release her from her debilitating "bondage" as wife and mother, the roles that have made her erotically unattainable to Paul. Her death is followed by an eerie, Poe-esque scene in which the shaken Paul, momentarily imagining his mother as a beautiful young sleeping maiden, stoops and kisses her "passionately," as if to waken her like the handsome prince in a fairy tale, only to be horrified by her cold and unresponsive lips. It is a key moment, adumbrating as it does the writer's subsequent shift in allegiances to the "sensuous flame of life" associated with his father. For Paul, however, the loss of his mother induces a period of deep depression (interestingly enough, guilt is not mentioned) in which his uppermost desire is to reunite with his mother in death. This "drift towards death" was what Lawrence believed made Paul's story symptomatic of the times, "the tragedy of thousands of young men in England."

Nevertheless, the novel does not end tragically. Paul, on the verge of suicide, decides instead to turn his back on the "immense dark silence" where his lover/mother awaits him and to head toward the "faintly humming, glowing town"—and beyond it, to the Continent, where he plans to continue his artistic endeavors (just as Lawrence did). Some readers have found this last-minute turnabout implausible, a breakdown in the novel's form. Yet Lawrence anticipates Paul's "rebirth" by having him realize, after his mother's death, that he must finally sever his ties to both Miriam and Clara. For him to have returned to them then for consolation and affection would have meant that, inwardly, he was still cherishing some hope of preserving the maternal bond, even if only through his mother's unsatisfactory substitutes. When Paul effects a reconciliation between Clara and her estranged husband Baxter Dawes, who has been presented throughout in terms strongly reminiscent of Walter Morel, he is (as Daniel A. Weiss and others have observed) tacitly acting out a reversal of the original Oedipal conflict. If the primary emphasis of *Sons and Lovers* is on the tragic split in the emotional lives of the Morels, its conclusion finds Paul taking the steps necessary to begin to heal the split in himself. Only by so doing would Paul, like Lawrence, be able to undertake a quest for vital wholeness. That quest would become the chief subject of the novels following *Sons and Lovers*.

As sometimes happens to a writer after he has successfully struggled to transform autobiography into art, Lawrence reacted against *Sons and Lovers* almost as soon as he had finished it. The process of revaluating the influence of his parents, begun in his revisions of the novel and particularly evident in its concluding chapters, continued apace. His nonfiction of the period exhibits a growing hostility to women as spawners of intellectual and spiritual abstraction and the early traces of his interest in the reassertion of the vital male. Lawrence reacted also against certain aspects of the narrative technique used in *Sons and Lovers*. As he worked on his next novel, initially called *The Sisters*, he found that he was no longer interested in "visualizing" or "creating vivid scenes" in which characters revealed themselves through dramatic encounters and dialogue. The conventions of plot and the "furniture" of realistic exposition bored him. Moreover, the traditional methods of characterization were positively a hindrance to the kind of novel he felt he must write.

Lawrence had in fact embarked on a long and difficult struggle to create a new kind of novel, unprecedented in English fiction. When his publisher balked, Lawrence defended his experiment in an important letter that clarifies his intentions not only in what would eventually become *The Rainbow* and *Women in Love* but in most of his subsequent fiction:

> You mustn't look in my novel for the old stable *ego* of the character. There is another *ego*, according to whose action the individual is unrecognizable, and passes through, as it were, allotropic states which it needs a deeper sense than any we've been used to exercise, to discover are states of the same radically unchanged element. (Like as diamond and coal are the same pure single element of carbon.)

What all this suggests, and what is implicit in the novels themselves, is that the conventions of realism, which were developed preeminently in the English novel of the nineteenth century, are inadequate tools for use by a writer whose aim is the transformation of the very society whose values were embodied in realism. The "old-fashioned human element," "the old stable ego," the "certain moral scheme" prescribing "consistency" and linear development— these were relics of positivism, bourgeois humanism, and other ideologies of a dying culture. Lawrence gropes a bit in the attempt to describe their successors, but it is clear enough that the "other ego," the "physic" or nonhuman in humanity, and the "radically-unchanged element" whose "allotropic" transformations determine a "rhythmic form" along lines unknown, are references to the mysterious source of vital energies capable (he believed) of regenerating both art and society.

The Rainbow applies these ideas in a most interesting way. It is an elegiac study of the dying culture written in Lawrence's revolutionary "new" manner. The story spans three generations of the Brangwen family, beginning with the advent of industrialism around 1840 in the rural Erewash valley—signaled by the construction of canals, the collieries, and the railroad—and continuing up to the first decade of the twentieth century. The theme is the destruction of the traditional way of life and the attempt, by members of the Brangwens, either to accommodate themselves to that loss or to transcend it by discovering a new basis for being.

The novel opens with a rhapsodic prose-poem telescoping two hundred years of Brangwens into archetypal male and female figures, living in "blood intimacy" with one another and with the land: "the pulse of the blood of the teats of the cows beat into the pulse of the hands of the men. [The men] mounted their horses and held life between the grip of their knees." Despite their "vital connection," however, there are opposing impulses in the male and the female principles that become increasingly important as the story proceeds. The Brangwen men, laboring in the fields of the Marsh Farm, are compared with the rim of a wheel revolving around the still center that is hearth and home; the women, like the axle of the wheel, live in the still center but always direct their gaze outward, beyond the wheel's rim toward the road, the village, the church steeple, "the spoken world" that is encroaching on the horizon. This tension between centripetal and centrifugal forces, the rim and the axle, is fruitful so long as the Brangwens live in harmony with the land, for it is a reflection of the cyclical processes of nature in which the clash of opposites generates change and growth. With the second generation, however, the principal Brangwen couple, Will and Anna, leave the land and move to the industrial town of Beldover, where Will works in a shop that produces machine-made lace. The seasonal cycle is replaced by the Christian liturgical calendar, in Lawrence's view a step toward abstraction. The old male-female opposition, having lost its former function as the means by which men and women participate in the dynamic rhythms of nature, becomes a destructive force. The marriage of contraries loses impetus because it now reflects not nature but the mechanisms that are dividing society. Husband and wife settle into a fixed domestic routine, typically Victorian, of piety (on Will's side) and child-rearing (on Anna's). Anna's "outward" impulse is thus sublimated, and like Gertrude Morel in *Sons and Lovers*, she counts on her children to act out her frustrated quest beyond the pale.

Most important of these children is the oldest daughter, Ursula, who, with her sister Gudrun, will also figure prominently in *Women in Love*. Ursula has been called "the first complete modern woman" (Marvin Mudrick) and, even more sweepingly, "the first 'free soul'" (Keith Sagar) in the English novel. It is Ursula, a member of Lawrence's own generation, who finally breaks out of the old circle of life. As she grows into womanhood she challenges and ultimately rejects traditional views of religion, democracy, education, free enterprise, love, and marriage. She is the first Brangwen female to enter a profession and support herself (as a schoolteacher); she attends the university; she travels to London and the Continent. On several levels, then, her "centrifugal" movement takes her far afield. Yet despite her explorations she has no sense of who she really is. The traditional order, which formerly provided a living relationship with nature and with other men and women, has all but collapsed. Motivated only by her isolate will and unreciprocated by any meaningful male contrary—as is amply demonstrated by her unsatisfying love affairs with Winifred Inger, her schoolmistress, and the shallow Anton Skrebensky—Ursula's quest becomes a desperate exercise in redundancy and futility, her vital energies randomly dispersed.

The novel ends as it began, symbolically. In the last of a series of "ritual scenes," in which characters are suddenly confronted with the "physic" or nonhuman "ego" that is the mysterious life-force, Ursula encounters a herd of stampeding horses. Whether hallucinatory or actual, the horses seem to represent the "dark" potencies which she has tried so long to discover on her quest and which have so far eluded her. Now, terrified, she escapes. Soon after, she falls ill with pneumonia, miscarries a child by Skrebensky, and lies delirious with fever for nearly a fortnight. All this is fitting as the culmination of Ursula's abortive, well-driven quest. Her "drift toward death," more like a plunge finally, is even more representative of her generation's crisis than Paul Morel's was in *Sons and Lovers*. As in the earlier novel, furthermore, Lawrence attempts to end *The Rainbow* on a hopeful note. After her convalescence, Ursula awakes one morning on the shores of what appears to be a new world, "as if a new day had come on the earth." Having survived the deluge, she is granted a vision of the rainbow—a symbol related to but superseding the old closed circle—which seems to offer hope for the regeneration not only of Ursula but also of her world.

On both levels, however, the symbolic promise is less than convincing. Unlike Paul Morel, Ursula has not performed any action or had any insight which suggests that her final "rebirth" is more than wishful thinking. As for the modern world's regeneration, when the novel appeared, in September, 1915, nothing could have been less likely. Lawrence hated the war, but like many other modern writers he saw it as the harbinger of Apocalypse, accelerating the advent of a new age. Before long he realized that he had "set my rainbow in the sky too soon, before, instead of after, the deluge." The furor provoked by the novel must have made the irony of his premature hopefulness all the more painful. In the teeth of that furor and the public persecution waged against Frieda and himself as supposed German spies, Lawrence set about writing *Women in Love*, considered by many today his greatest novel and one of the half-dozen or so masterpieces of modern fiction.

Whatever their differences with respect to the emphasis placed upon the operations of the "physic" or nonhuman forces in humanity, *Sons and Lovers* and *The Rainbow* share several important traits that set them apart from most of Lawrence's subsequent novels, beginning with *Women in Love*. For one, they have in common a narrative structure that, by locating the action firmly within a social context spanning generations, subscribes to the novelistic convention of rendering the story of individuals continuous with the larger movements of history. *Women in Love* takes up the story of the "modern" Brangwens about three and one-half years after the end of *The Rainbow* but, in contrast to the earlier novel's sixty-six year span, concentrates attention onto a series of loosely connected episodes occurring within a ten-month period, from spring to winter of 1909 or 1910. One result of this altered focus, at once narrower and relatively looser than that of the earlier novels, is that the social background seems far more static than before. The great transformation of society known as modernization has already occurred, and the characters move within a world whose ostensible change is the slow, inward process of decay. The shift of emphasis is evident also in the protagonists' attitudes toward society. The conclusions of the earlier novels—Paul's turning away from death toward the "humming, glowing town," and Ursula's vision of the rainbow offering hope that a corrupt world would "issue to a new germination"—imply that Western civilization could still respond to the most urgent needs of the individual. In *Women in Love* that assumption has completely vanished. Thus, although Lawrence originally conceived of *The Rainbow* and *Women in Love* as a single work and would later describe them as forming together "an organic artistic whole," the latter novel embodies a far darker view of the world. As Lawrence once said, *Women in Love* "actually does contain the results in one's soul of the war: it is purely destructive, not like *The Rainbow*, destructive-consummating."

The phrase "purely destructive" only slightly exaggerates the despairing nature of the novel's apocalyptic vision. Certainly its depiction of modern society as a dying tree "infested with little worms and dry-rot" suggests that the impetus toward death and destruction is so pervasive as to make the war all but inevitable. In the novel, the working class, far from resisting the dehumanizing mechanism of the industrial system, is "satisfied to belong to the great wonderful machine, even whilst it destroyed them." The leisure class is seen as similarly deluded and doomed. Hermione Roddice's chic gatherings at Breadalby, her country estate (modeled on Lady Ottoline Morrell's Garsington), offer no genuine alternative to the dying world but only a static image of the "precious past," where all is formed and final and accomplished—a "horrible, dead prison" of illusory peace. Meanwhile contemporary art has abdicated its time-honored role as nay-sayer to a corrupt social order. Indeed, in the homosexual artist Halliday, the promiscuous Minette, and the other decadent bohemians who congregate at the Pompadour Café in London, Lawrence clearly implicates intellectual and artistic coteries such as Bloomsbury in the general dissolution of modern society. That the pandering of the modern artist to the death-drive of mechanistic society was a general phenomenon and not limited to England is emphasized near the end of the novel with the appearance of Loerke, a German sculptor whose work adorns "a great granite factory in Cologne." Loerke, who asserts on the one hand that art should interpret industry as it had formerly interpreted religion and on the other that a work of art has no relation to anything but itself, embodies the amorality of modernist aesthetics from Lawrence's viewpoint. Dominated by "pure unconnected will," Loerke is, like Hermione, sexually perverse, and, like the habitués of the Pompadour, he "lives like a rat in the river of corruption."

All of these secondary characters in *Women in Love* exemplify the results of the displacement of the traditional order by industrialization, or what Lawrence terms "the first great phase of chaos, the substitution of the mechanical principle for the organic." Except for Hermione, they are consistently presented from without, in static roles prescribed for them by a static society. Against this backdrop move the four principal characters: Ursula and Gudrun Brangwen, who are sisters, and Rupert Birkin and Gerald Crich, who are friends. The interweaving relationships of these four, highlighted in scenes of great emotional intensity and suggestiveness, provide the "rhythmic form" of the novel. Notwithstanding their interactions with external society and their long philosophical arguments, they are chiefly presented in terms of a continuous struggle among the elemental energies vying for expression within them. Mark Schorer aptly describes the book as "a drama of primal compulsions." The "drama" concerns the conflict between the mechanical will and the organic oneness of being, between the "flux of corruption" or death and the regenerative forces of life, as these are variously embodied in the four main characters and their constantly shifting relationships.

Birkin, full of talk about spontaneity and "pure being" and the "blood-knowledge" available in sensuality, is clearly a spokesman for certain of Lawrence's favorite ideas. Considering this, it is interesting that from the outset the novel emphasizes his involvement in the death-fixation of modern society at large. He has been one of the "mud-flowers" at the Café Pompadour. In addition, he has been for several years involved in an affair with the perverse socialite Hermione, an affair that has degenerated into a hysterical battle of wills, sapping Birkin of his male vitality. As he tells Gerald, he wants above all to center his life on "the finality of love" for one woman and close relationships with a few other friends, but his goal is frustrated by the lingering parody of it represented in Hermione and the London bohemians. It is therefore significant that he is frequently ill, and once goes to the south of France for several weeks to recuperate. His sickness is as much spiritual as physical. Dissatisfied with his prosaic career as a school inspector and frustrated in his relationships, he often finds himself "in pure opposition to everything." In this depressed state he becomes preoccupied with death and dissolution, "that dark river" (as he calls it) which seethes through all modern reality, even love. Not until after his violent break with Hermione, during which she nearly kills him, does Birkin begin to find his way back to life.

Unlike Birkin, Gerald disbelieves that love can form the center of life. Instead he maintains that there is no center to life but simply the "social mechanism" which artificially holds it together; as for loving, Gerald is incapable of it. Indeed the novel everywhere implies that his inability to love derives from his abdication of vital integrated being in favor of mere social fulfillment. As an industrial magnate (he is the director of the local coal mines and has successfully modernized them), Gerald advocates what Birkin calls the "ethics of productivity," the "pure instrumentality of mankind" being for him the basis of social cohesion and progress. If society is essentially mechanistic, Gerald's ambition is to be "the God of the machine" whose will is "to subjugate Matter to his own ends. The subjugation itself," Lawrence adds significantly, "was the point." This egotistic obsession is illustrated in a powerful scene in which Gerald rides a young Arab mare up to a railroad track and, while Gudrun and Ursula look on aghast, he violently forces the terrified mare to stay put as the train races noisily by them. The impact of this cruel assertion of will-to-power registers forcefully on Ursula, who is duly horrified and outraged, and on Gudrun, who is mesmerized by the "unutterable subordination" of the mare to the "indomitable" male.

After abortive affairs with other women, Birkin and Gerald are inevitably attracted to the Brangwen sisters. The protracted ebb and flow of the two relationships is tellingly juxtaposed in a series of scenes richly symbolic of the central dialectic of life and death. Meanwhile, not content with the romantic promise of finding love with a woman only, Birkin proposes to Gerald that they form a vital male bond as of blood brothers pledged to mutual love and fidelity. Whatever its unconscious origins, the intent of the offer is clearly not sexual. As the rest of the novel demonstrates (anticipating a theme that becomes more central and explicit in subsequent novels such as *Aaron's Rod* and *The Plumed Serpent*), Birkin is searching for a kind of pure intimacy in human relationships. He seeks with both men and women a bond of blood and mind and spirit—the integrated wholeness of being that for Lawrence was sacred—that when realized might form the nucleus of a new, vital human community. Because of Gerald's identification with the mechanism of industrial society, Birkin's repeated offer of a *Blutbrüderschaft* amounts to an invitation to a shared rebirth emblematic of epochal transfiguration, an apocalypse in microcosm. Because of that same identification, of course, Gerald, confused and threatened, must refuse the offer. Instead he chooses to die.

The choice of death is brilliantly dramatized in Gerald's impassioned encounters with Gudrun. Despite her earlier identification with the mare he brutally "subordinated," Gudrun might still have offered him the sort of vital relationship that both so desperately need. At any rate, had they been able to pursue their potential for love, the sort of shared commitment to mutual "being" that Birkin offers Gerald and that he eventually discovers with Ursula, regeneration however painful and difficult could have been realized. Rather than accept this challenge, however, Gerald falls back on his usual tactics and tries to subjugate Gudrun to his will. After his father's death, he becomes acutely aware of the void in his life and turns at once to Gudrun—walking straight from the cemetery in the rain to her house, up to her bedroom, his shoes still heavy with mud from the grave—not out of love but desperate need: the need to assert himself, heedless of the "otherness" of another, as if in so doing he could verify by sheer force of will that he exists. Yet, because this egotistic passion is a perversion of love as Lawrence saw it and because Gerald's yearning for ontological security is a perversion of the quest for true being, Gerald's anxieties are only made worse by his contact with Gudrun. For her part, Gudrun, unlike the helplessly dominated mare, never yields herself fully to Gerald. In fact, she does all she can to thwart and humiliate him, and their relationship soon becomes a naked battle of wills. It is redundant to say that this is a battle to the death, for, on the grounds that it is fought, the battle itself is death in Lawrencian terms. In the end, Gerald, whose aim all along as "God of the machine" had been to subjugate Matter to his will, becomes literally a frozen corpse whose expression terrifies Birkin with its "last terrible look of cold, mute Matter." Gudrun, headed at the end for a rendezvous with the despicable Loerke, arrives at a like consummation.

Whatever Lawrence might say about the "purely destructive" forces at work in *Women in Love*, in the relationship of Birkin and Ursula he finds a seed of new life germinating, albeit precariously, within the "dark river of dissolution." After the severance of his nearly fatal tie with Hermione, Birkin finds himself for a time in a quandary. Believing as he still does that the only means of withstanding dissolution is to center his life on close human ties, he casts about him to discover precisely the kind of relation that will best serve or enact his quest for being. The "purely sensual, purely unspiritual knowledge" represented by a primitive statue of an African woman impresses Birkin but finally proves too remote a mystery for him to emulate; in any event, the modern female embodiments of this "mystic knowledge" of the senses are, like Hermione and Gudrun, will-dominated and murderous. A second way is that represented by the proposed bond with Gerald, the "Nordic" machine-god who for Birkin represents "the vast abstraction of ice and snow, . . . snow-abstract annihilation." When these alternatives both reveal themselves as mere "allotropic" variations of the flux of corruption from which he seeks release, Birkin finally hits upon a third way, "the way of freedom." He conceives of it in idealistic terms, as

> the paradisal entry into pure, single being, the individual soul taking precedence over love and desire for union, stronger than any pangs of emotion, a lovely state of free proud singleness, which accepted the obligation of the permanent connection with others, and with the other, submits to the yoke and leash of love, but never forfeits its own proud individual singleness, even while it loves and yields.

It is a difficult and elusive ideal, and when Birkin tries, laboriously, to describe it to Ursula—inviting her to join him in a new, strange relation, "not meeting and mingling . . . but an equilibrium, a pure balance of two single beings" dynamically counterpoised as two stars are—she mocks him for dissimulating. Why does he not simply declare his love for her without "dragging in the stars"? She has a point and Lawrence's art only benefits from such moments of self-criticism. Still, these paradoxical images of separateness in union, of a bond that finds its strength in the reciprocal affirmation of "otherness," do express, like the wheel's axle and rim in *The Rainbow*, Lawrence's essential vision of integrated, dynamic relationships. Furthermore, only by actively pursuing such a marriage of opposites, in which the separateness of each partner is necessary to the indissolubility of the bond, can both parties be caught up in something altogether new: "the third," which transcends individual selves in the oneness of pure being. For Lawrence this is the true consummation, springing up from "the source of the deepest life-force."

So polluted had the river of life become in modern Europe, however, that Lawrence could no longer bring himself to believe that this transcendence, ephemeral as it was to begin with, could survive the general cataract of dissolution. Moreover, even when Birkin and Ursula do find fulfillment together, it is not enough; for Birkin at any rate the new dispensation must involve other people as well as themselves. For both reasons, the quest for integrated wholeness of being, a mystery into which Birkin and Ursula are only new initiates, becomes translated into a pilgrimage through space. They must depart from the old, dying world and, like Lawrence and Frieda after the war, proceed in search of holy ground. The primary focus of subsequent novels, this quest is defined in *Women in Love* simply as "wandering to nowhere, . . . away from the world's somewheres." As *nowhere* is the translation of the word *utopia*, the social impetus of the search is implicit. "It isn't really a locality, though," Birkin insists. "It's a perfected relation between you and me, and others . . . so that we are free together." With this ideal before him, Lawrence was poised at the crossroads of his career.

In the postwar novels, which present fictionalized versions of his and Frieda's experiences in Italy (*Aaron's Rod*), Australia (*Kangaroo*), and Mexico (*The Plumed Serpent*), the quest translates increasingly into a sociopolitical doctrine projected onto whole societies. The bond between men and the fascination of powerful male leaders became more and more of an obsession in these novels. Lawrence tried mightily to remain faithful to the notion that the regeneration of societies should correspond to the "perfected relations" between individuals. The analogy presented difficulties, however, and the struggle to express his essentially religious vision in political terms proved fatal to his art. There are brilliant moments in all of these novels, especially in *The Plumed Serpent*, yet the alien aspects of the foreign lands he visited finally obscured the central issues in what was, at bottom, a quest for self-discovery. *Women in Love*, still in touch with the real motives of that quest and yielding immediate access to its first (and, as it turned out, finest) fruits, offers the richest rendering of both the modern drift toward death and its Lawrencian antidote, "whole man alive."

However ill-defined the object of his protagonists' plans for flight from Europe, ever since the cataclysm of 1914-1918, Lawrence himself had determined to relocate in America. Florida, California, upstate New York, New Mexico—all at one time or another figured as proposed sites of his American dream. In one of these areas, apart from the great urban centers, he would establish a utopian colony to be called Rananim. There he would start over again, free from the runaway entropy of modern Europe. In America, and more particularly aboriginal America, he believed that the Tree of Life remained intact, its potency still issuing "up from the roots, crude but vital." Nevertheless, when the war ended he did not go to America straightaway but headed east, not to arrive on the Western hemisphere until late in 1922. During this prolonged period of yearning, his vision of America as the New World of the soul, the locus of the regeneration of mankind, took on an increasingly definite form. He was imaginatively committed to it even before settling near Taos, New Mexico, where he and Frieda lived on a mountain ranch for most of the next three years.

After studying the classic works of early American literature, he decided that he would write an "American novel," that is, a novel which would invoke and adequately respond to the American "spirit of place." For Lawrence the continent's daemon was the old "blood-and-vertebrate consciousness" embodied in the Mesoamerican Indian and his aboriginal religion. Because of four centuries of white European domination, that spirit had never been fully realized, yet despite the domination it still lay waiting beneath the surface for an annunciation. The terms of this vision, even apart from other factors having to do with his frustrating contacts with Mable Dodge Luhan and her coterie of artists in Taos, all but made it inevitable that Lawrence would sooner or later situate his American novel in a land where the Indian presence was more substantial than it was in the southwestern United States. The Pueblo Indian religion impressed him deeply with its "revelation of life," but he realized that for a genuine, large-scale rebirth to occur in America, "a vast death-happening must come first" to break the hold of the degenerate white civilization. It was natural enough that he turned his eyes south to Mexico, a land which actually had been caught up in revolution for more than a decade—a revolution moreover in which the place of the Indian (who constituted more than thirty percent of the population) in the national life was a central issue. Reading pre-Columbian history and archaeology, Lawrence found in Aztec mythology a ready-made source of symbols and in the story of the Spanish conquest an important precedent for his narrative of contemporary counterrevolution and religious revival.

Yet the writing of his *Quetzalcoatl*, the working title of what would become *The Plumed Serpent*, proved unusually difficult. *Kangaroo* had taken him only six weeks to write; *Aaron's Rod* and *The Lost Girl* were also composed in sudden, if fitful, bursts. In contrast, he worked on his "American novel" off and on for nearly two years, even taking the precaution of writing such tales as "The Woman who Rode Away," "The Princess," and "St. Mawr" (all of which have much in common with the novel), and the Mexican travel sketches in *Mornings in Mexico*, as a kind of repeated trial run for his more ambitious project.

One reason the novel proved recalcitrant was that Lawrence became increasingly aware during his three journeys into the Mexican interior that his visionary Mexico and the real thing were far from compatible. The violence of the country appalled him; its revolution, which he soon dismissed as "self-serving Bolshevism," left him cold; and most important, its Roman Catholic Indians were demonstrably uninterested and seemingly incapable of responding to the sort of pagan revival called for by Lawrence's apocalyptic scheme. Yet, so committed was he to his American "Rananim" that he was unwilling or unable to entertain the possibility of its failure. Rather than qualify his program for world regeneration in the light of the widening breach between his long-cherished dream and the disappointing reality, he elaborated the dream more fully and explicitly than ever, inflating his claims for it in a grandiose rhetoric that only called its sincerity into question. Had he been content with a purely visionary, symbolic tale, a prose romance comparable in motive with W. B. Yeats's imaginary excursions to "Holy Byzantium," such questions would probably not have arisen. Lawrence, however, could not let go of his expectation that in Mexico the primordial spirit of place would answer to his clarion call. At the same time, the realist in Lawrence allowed evidence to the contrary to appear in the form of his extraordinarily vivid perceptions of the malevolence of the Mexican landscape and its dark-skinned inhabitants. Yet, even these were forced into the pattern of New World Apocalypse. In his desperation to have it both ways, doggedly asserting the identity of his own spiritual quest and the course of events in the literal, external world, he contrived a kind of symbolic or mythic formula in which sexual, religious, and political rebirth are not only equated but presented as mutually dependent. The result according to most critics is a complicated muddle in which the parts, some of which are as fine as anything he ever wrote, do not make a whole. Yet for Lawrence the muddle itself would ultimately prove instructive.

In a sense *The Plumed Serpent* begins where *Women in Love* ends. The flow of Birkin and Ursula's relationship in the earlier novel is directed centrifugally away from England toward a nameless "nowhere" of shared freedom in pure being. In *The Plumed Serpent*, the protagonist, Kate Leslie, having heard the death-knell of her spirit in Europe, has arrived at the threshold of the New World of mystery, where a rebirth awaits her "like a doom." That the socialist revolution has addressed only the material needs of Mexicans and left their dormant spirit untouched suggests that Mexico is also in need of rebirth. Disgusted by the tawdry imitation of a modern European capital that is Mexico City, the seat of the failed revolution, Kate journeys westward to the remote lakeside village of Sayula. Sayula also happens to be the center of a new-Aztec religious revival led by Don Ramón Carrasco, who calls himself "the living Quetzalcoatl." The boat trip down the "sperm-like" lake to Sayula begins Kate's centripetal movement toward her destiny, and also Mexico's movement toward an indigenous spiritual reawakening; both movements are directed, gradually but inexorably, toward an "immersion in a sea of living blood."

Unlike Birkin and Ursula of *Women in Love*, Kate, a middle-aged Irish widow, wants at first only to be "alone with the unfolding flower of her own soul." Her occasional contacts with the provincial Indians inspire in her a sense of wonder at their "dark" mystery, but at the same time she finds their very alienness oppressive and threatening. She feels that the country wants to pull her down, "with a slow, reptilian insistence," to prevent her "free" spirit from soaring. Since Kate values her freedom and her solitude, she retreats periodically from the "ponderous, down-pressing weight" which she associates with the coils of the old Aztec feathered serpent, Quetzalcoatl.

Don Ramón explains to her that she must submit to this weight upon the spirit, for by pulling her down into the earth it may bring her into contact with the deep-rooted Tree of Life, which still thrives in the volcanic soil of primordial Mexico beneath the "paleface overlay" on the surface. This injunction is aimed not only at Kate but also at contemporary Mexico itself, which, beckoned by the pulsating drumbeats and hymns of the Men of Quetzalcoatl, is urged to turn its back on the imported white creeds (Catholicism and Bolshevism) and rediscover its indigenous roots. Only by yielding their hold on the conscious will can the "bound" egos of the Mexicans as well as of Kate achieve a transfiguration, symbolized in the novel by the Morning Star. Indeed, as a representative of white "mental consciousness," Kate is destined to perform an important role in the new dispensation in Mexico. Ramón's aim is to forge' a new mode of consciousness emerging from the dynamic tension between the white and dark sensibilities. The new mode is embodied by Ramón himself, in his capacity to "see both ways" without being absorbed by either, just as the ancient man-god Quetzalcoatl united the sky and the earth, and as the Morning Star (associated with Quetzalcoatl) partakes of both night and day, moon and sun, yet remains itself.

Thus described, this doctrine may seem a welcome elaboration of the star-equilibrium theory of human relationships advanced by Birkin in the earlier novel. The transcendent emergence of "the third," at best an elusive idea of divine immanence in *Women in Love*, seems to be clarified by the Aztec cosmogonic symbolism of *The Plumed Serpent*. Undoubtedly the latter novel is the fullest statement of Lawrence's vitalist religion. Yet there is something in the very explicitness of the religion in the novel that renders it suspect. As if in tacit acknowledgment of this, Lawrence, impatient with the slow progress of Ramón's appeal to the spirit, introduces a more overt form of conquest. When both Kate and Mexico fail to respond unequivocally to the invitation to submit voluntarily, Ramón reluctantly resorts to calling on the assistance of Don Cipriano Viedma, a full-blooded Indian general who commands a considerable army. Though Lawrence attempts to legitimize this move by having Ramón induct Cipriano into the neo-Aztec pantheon as "the living Huitzilopochti" (the Aztec god of war) and by having Kate envision Cipriano as the Mexican Indian embodiment of "the ancient phallic mystery, . . . the god-devil of the male Pan" before whom she must "swoon," the novel descends into a pathological nightmare from which it never quite recovers.

It is not simply that Cipriano politicizes the religious movement, reducing it to yet another Latin American literary adventure which ends by imposing Quetzalcoatlism as the institutional religion of Mexico; nor is it simply that Cipriano, with Ramón's blessing, dupes Kate into a kind of sexual subservience that puts Gerald Crich's machine-god efforts with Gudrun (in *Women in Love*) to shame. The nadir of the novel is reached when Cipriano performs a public execution, stabbing to death three blindfolded prisoners who have betrayed Ramón. This brutal act is given priestly sanction by Ramón and even accepted by Kate, in her new role as Malintzi, fertility goddess in the nascent religion. "Why should I judge him?" asks Kate. "He is of the gods. . . . What do I care if he kills people. His flame is young and clean. He is Huitzilopochtli, and I am Malintzi." Their "godly" union is consummated at the foot of the altar in the new temple of Quetzalcoatl. At this point, if not before, the threefold quest for "immersion in a sea of living blood" ceases to serve a metaphorical function and becomes all too chillingly literal.

With its rigidified "mystical" doctrine, its hysterical rhetoric, and its cruelly inhuman advocacy of "necessary" bloodshed and supermasculine dominance, *The Plumed Serpent* offers what amounts to a perfect Lawrencian hell but persists in celebrating it as if it were the veritable threshold of paradise. The novel has found a few defenders among critics enamored of "mythic design," but Harry T. Moore is surely correct in calling it "a tremendous volcano of a failure." Though for a short time he thought it his best novel, by March, 1928, Lawrence himself repudiated *The Plumed Serpent* and the militaristic "leader of men" idea that it embodies.

Nevertheless, *The Plumed Serpent* marks a crucial phase in Lawrence's development, for it carries to their ultimate conclusion the most disturbing implications of the ideas that had vexed his mind ever since the war. Submersion in the "dark blood," as the novel demonstrates, could lead as readily to wholesale murder in the name of religion as to vital and spontaneous relations between men and women. By courageously following his chimerical "Rananim" dream through to its end in a horrific, palpable nightmare, Lawrence accepted enormous risks, psychological as well as artistic. The effort nearly cost him his life, bringing on a severe attack of tuberculosis complicated by malaria. Yet, in the few years that remained to him, he was in a real sense a man reborn, able to return in imagination (in *The Virgin and the Gipsy* and

Lady Chatterley's Lover, among other works) to his native Midlands, where he could once again take up the quest for "whole man alive," happily unencumbered by the grandiose political imperatives of world regeneration. Purging him of this ideological sickness, the writing of *The Plumed Serpent* proved as salutary to his later career as *Sons and Lovers* had been to his period of greatest accomplishment.

When Lawrence settled in southern Europe after leaving America in late 1925, he began to reshape his spiritual map in ways suggestive of his shifting outlook during his last years. The problem with the United States, he decided, was that everyone was too tense. Americans took themselves and their role in the world far too seriously and were unable to slacken their grip on themselves for fear that the world would collapse as a result. In contrast, the Europeans (he was thinking chiefly of southern Europeans rather than his own countrymen) were freer and more spontaneous because they were not controlled by will and could therefore let themselves go. At bottom, the European attitude toward life was characterized by what Lawrence called "insouciance." Relaxed, essentially free from undue care or fret, Europeans were open to "a sort of bubbling-in of life," whereas the Americans' more forthright pursuit of life only killed it.

Whether this distinction between America and Europe has any validity for others, for the post-America Lawrence it meant a great deal. In *The Plumed Serpent*, his "American novel," instead of realizing the free and spontaneous life-flow made accessible by insouciance, he engaged in an almost hysterical striving after life writ large, resorting to political demagoguery and a formalized religion fully armed with rifles as well as rites. Apparently aware in retrospect of his error, he eschewed the strong-leader/submissive-follower relationship as the keynote to regeneration. In its place he would focus on a new relationship: a "sort of tenderness, sensitive, between men and men and men and women, and not the one up one down, lead on I follow, *ich dien* sort of business." Having discovered the virtues of insouciance and tenderness, Lawrence began to write *Lady Chatterley's Lover*, one of his most poignant, lyrical treatments of individual human relations.

As always in Lawrence, the physical setting offers a crucial barometer of sensibility. In this case the treatment of setting is indicative of the novelist's loss of faith in the "spirit of place" as a valid embodiment of his quest. In comparison with his other novels, *Lady Chatterley's Lover* presents a scene much reduced in richness and complexity. Wragby Hall, the baronial seat of the Chatterleys, is described as "a warren of a place without much distinction." Standing on a hill and surrounded by oak trees, Wragby offers a view dominated by the smokestacks of the mines in and around the Midlands village of Tevershall. Like Shortlands, the Criches' estate in *Women in Love*, Wragby and its residents attempt through formal artifice to deny the existence of the pits from which the family income derives. The attempt is futile, however, for "when the wind was that way, which was often, the house was full of the stench of this sulphurous combustion of the earth's excrement," and smuts settle on the gardens "like black manna from skies of doom." As for Tevershall ("'tis now and 'tever shall be"), the mining village offers only the appalling prospect of "the utter negation of natural beauty, the utter negation of the gladness of life, . . . the utter death of the human intuitive faculty." Clearly Wragby and Tevershall are two sides of the same coin minted by the godless machine age. Between the two is a tiny, ever-diminishing remnant of old Sherwood Forest. The wood is owned by the Chatterleys and many of its trees were "patriotically" chopped down during the Great War for timber for the allies' trenches.

It is here that Constance Chatterley and her lover, Oliver Mellors, the gamekeeper, find—or rather create—life together. As Julian Moynihan has observed, the little wood symbolizes "the beleaguered and vulnerable status to which the vital career has been reduced" at the hands of modern civilization. The old centrifugal impulse for a faraway "nowhere" has yielded to a desperate centripetal flight toward refuge from the industrial wasteland. Yet try as they might to find sanctuary within the wood, the lovers must recognize that there is no longer any room in the world for true sanctuary, much less for a Rananim. "The industrial noises broke the solitude," Lawrence writes; "the sharp lights, though unseen, mocked it. A man could no longer be private and withdrawn. The world allows no hermits." The geographical focus of the Lawrencian quest is no longer able to provide a modicum of hope and so yields to a new, scaled-down, more intimate image: the human body.

The sterility and spiritual paralysis of the modern world are embodied by Clifford Chatterley, Connie's husband. A paraplegic victim of the war, Clifford is both literally and symbolically deadened to the life of the passions. All his energy is directed to verbal, abstract, or social undertakings in which actual contact is minimal. Clifford believes in the form and apparatus of the social life and is indifferent to private feelings. A director of mines, he sees the miners as objects rather than men, mere extensions of the pit machinery. For him, "the function determines the individual," who hardly matters otherwise. Clifford also writes fashionably shallow stories and entertains other writers and critics to curry favor. He modernizes the coal mines with considerable success. Thus in broad outline he resembles Gerald Crich of *Women in Love*. Yet, in the far simpler world of *Lady Chatterley's Lover*, Lawrence chooses not to cloud matters by giving his antagonist any redeeming qualities. The reader is never invited to sympathize with Clifford's plight. Motoring around Wragby Hall in his mechanical wheelchair, Clifford coolly urges Connie to have a child by another man—the "sex thing" having been of no particular importance to him even before the war—so that he can have an heir to Wragby. By the end of the novel, he turns to his attendant Mrs. Bolton for the only intimacy left to him: a regressive, perverse form of contact. Such heaping of abuse onto Clifford, far in excess of what is needed to establish his symbolic role, undoubtedly detracts from the novel.

So long as she remains with Clifford, Connie finds herself in a condition of static bondage in which her individuality is circumscribed by the function identified in her title. A "lady" by virtue of her marriage, she is not yet truly a woman. Sex for her is merely a "thing" as it is for Clifford, an instrument of tacit control over men. She is progressively gripped by malaise. Physically she is "old at twenty-seven, with no gleam and sparkle in the flesh"; spiritually she is unborn. Her affair with Mellors is of course the means of her metamorphosis, which has been compared (somewhat ironically) with the awakening of Sleeping Beauty at the Handsome Prince's magical kiss. Less obvious is the overlapping of this fairy-tale pattern with a counter-pattern of male transformation such as that found in the tale of the Frog Prince. For Mellors, too, is trapped in a kind of bondage alone in his precarious refuge in the wood. The "curse" on him is his antipathy to intimate contacts, especially with women, after his disastrous marriage to the promiscuous Bertha Coutts.

The initial encounters between Connie and Mellors in the wood result only in conflict and hostility, as both, particularly Mellors, cling to their socially prescribed roles and resist the challenge of being "broken open" by true contact with another. Yet, when they finally do begin to respond to that challenge, it is Mellors who takes the lead in conducting Connie through her initiation into the mysteries of "phallic" being. With his "tender" guidance she learns the necessity of letting go her hold on herself, yielding to the "palpable unknown" beyond her conscious will. She discovers the importance of their "coming off together" rather than the merely "frictional" pleasures of clitoral orgasm (a notion acceptable within Lawrence's symbolic context if not widely endorsed by the "how-to" manuals of the Masters and Johnson generation, of which Lawrence would no doubt have disapproved). When she tries to get Mellors to tell her that he loves her, he rejects the abstract, overused word in favor of the earthier Anglo-Saxon language of the body and its functions. On one occasion he even introduces her to sodomy so as to "burn out the shames, the deepest, oldest shames, in the most secret places." The result of all this, paradoxically, is that the couple arrives at the state of "chastity." Having broken their ties to the sterile world, they are able to accept an imposed separation until it is possible, after a period of waiting for Mellors' divorce to occur, for them to live together in hope for their future.

In an aside in Chapter 9, Lawrence, asserting that it is "the way our sympathy flows and recoils that really determines our lives," affirms that the great function of a novel is precisely to "inform and lead into new places the flow of our sympathetic consciousness" and to "lead our sympathies away in recoil from things gone dead." As a statement of intention, this will do for all of Lawrence's novels. Of course, even the best of intentions do not necessarily lead to artistic achievement. *Lady Chatterley's Lover*, though in many respects a remarkable recovery after the dead end that was the "leadership novels," is nevertheless flawed by the very directness with which it follows the "flow and recoil" idea. For one thing, the deck is too obviously stacked against Clifford. Lawrence never takes him seriously as a man, by making him the stationary target of so much scorn simply for what he represents, Lawrence in effect replicates Clifford's own treatment of people as mere objects or functions.

Because the "recoil" against Clifford as a "thing gone dead" seems facile and almost glib, Connie's counterflow toward Mellors seems also too easy, despite Lawrence's efforts to render her conflicting, vacillating feelings. Another part of the problem lies in the characterization of Mellors, who after his initial reluctance proves to be a tiresomely self-satisfied, humorless, "knowing" spokesman for the gospel according to Lawrence. Connie, however, is a marvelous creation, far more complex than even Mellors seems to realize. She is a worthy successor to Lawrence's other intriguing female characters: Gertrude Morel, Ursula and Gudrun Brangwen, Alvina Houghton (of *The Lost Girl*), and Kate Leslie.

At his best, in *Sons and Lovers*, *The Rainbow*, and especially *Women in Love*, Lawrence manages to enact the flow and counterflow of consciousness, the centrifugal dilation and the centripetal contraction of sympathies, in a far more complex and convincing way than he does in his last novel. Notwithstanding his battles with Mrs. Grundy, the underlying impulse of all his work is unquestionably moral: the passionate yearning to discover, celebrate, and *become* "whole man alive." The desperateness with which he pursued that elusive ideal in both his life and his art sometimes led him to resort to a bullying, declamatory didacticism, which took the chance of alienating his readers' sympathies.

Lawrence's moral vision was most compelling when embodied and rendered in dramatic or symbolic terms rather than externally imposed by "oracular" utterance and rhetorical bombast. Yet "art for my sake" necessarily involved him in these risks, of which he was fully aware. At a time when aesthetic objectivity and the depersonalization of the artist were the dominant aims of the modernists, Lawrence courageously pursued his vision wherever it might lead.

Through his capacity for outrage against what he considered a dying civilization, his daring to risk failure and humiliation in the ongoing struggle to find and make known the "vital quick" which alone could redeem humanity and to relocate mankind's lost spiritual roots, Lawrence performed the essential role of seer or prophetic conscience for his age. Moreover, because subsequent events in this century have more than confirmed his direst forebodings, his is a voice which readers today cannot afford to ignore. While many are decrying the death of the novel amidst the proliferation of the much-ballyhooed "literature of exhaustion," one could do worse than turn to Lawrence to find again the "one bright book of life."

Ronald G. Walker

Other major works

SHORT FICTION: *The Prussian Officer and Other Stories*, 1914; *England, My England*, 1922; *St. Mawr: Together with the Princess*, 1925; *The Woman Who Rode Away and Other Stories*, 1928; *Love Among the Haystacks and Other Stories*, 1930; *The Lovely Lady and Other Stories*, 1933; *A Modern Lover*, 1934; *The Complete Short Stories of D. H. Lawrence*, 1961.

PLAYS: *The Widowing of Mrs. Holroyd*, 1914; *Touch and Go*, 1920; *David*, 1926; *A Collier's Friday Night*, 1934; *The Complete Plays of D. H. Lawrence*, 1965.

POETRY: *Love Poems and Others*, 1913; *Amores*, 1916; *Look! We Have Come Through*, 1917; *New Poems*, 1918; *Bay*, 1919; *Tortoises*, 1921; *Birds, Beasts, and Flowers*, 1923; *Collected Poems*, 1928; *Pansies*, 1929; *Nettles*, 1930; *The Triumph of the Machine*, 1931; *Last Poems*, 1932; *Fire and Other Poems*, 1940; *Phoenix Edition of Complete Poems*, 1957; *The Complete Poems of D. H. Lawrence*, 1964 (Vivian de Sola Pinto and Warren Roberts, editors).

NONFICTION: *Twilight in Italy*, 1916; *Movements in European History*, 1921; *Psychoanalysis and the Unconscious*, 1921; *Sea and Sardinia*, 1921; *Fantasia of the Unconscious*, 1922; *Studies in Classic American Literature*, 1923; *Reflections on the Death of a Porcupine and Other Essays*, 1925; *Mornings in Mexico*, 1927; *Pornography and Obscenity*, 1929; *À Propos of Lady Chatterley's Lover*, 1930; *Assorted Articles*, 1930; *Apocalypse*, 1931; *Etruscan Places*, 1932; *The Letters of D. H. Lawrence*, 1932 (Aldous Huxley, editor); *Phoenix: The Posthumous Papers of D. H. Lawrence*, 1936 (Edward McDonald, editor); *The Collected Letters of D. H. Lawrence*, 1962 (Harry T. Moore, editor, 2 volumes); *Phoenix II*, 1968 (Harry T. Moore and Warren Roberts, editors).

Bibliography

Bloom, Harold, ed. *D. H. Lawrence.* New York: Chelsea House, 1986. A major compilation of critical commentary on Lawrence's writings, this collection of essays deals largely with his major novels and short stories and makes available varying assessments of philosophical and psychological concerns implicit in Lawrence's works. A chronology and short bibliography are also provided.

The D. H. Lawrence Review, 1968-   . This periodical began publication on the University of Arkansas Press, Fayetteville, with James C. Cowan as editor; since 1984 it has been issued by the University of Delaware Press, Newark, under the editorship of Dennis Jackson. Regularly publishes articles by critics and recognized scholars as well as book reviews and bibliographical notices.

Jackson, Dennis, and Fleda Brown Jackson, eds. *Critical Essays on D. H. Lawrence*. Boston: G. K. Hall, 1988. Various critical insights may be found in this collection of twenty essays, which includes articles by scholars and by well-known writers such as Anaïs Nin and Sean O'Casey. All literary genres in which Lawrence was involved are represented by one or more contributions here. Also of note is the editors' introduction, which deals with trends in critical and biographical literature about Lawrence.

Meyers, Jeffrey. *D. H. Lawrence: A Biography*. New York: Alfred A. Knopf, 1990. The emphasis in this substantial and well-informed biography is on Lawrence's literary milieu and his development of themes and ideas in the broader intellectual context of his own time. Also provides some new interpretations of events in Lawrence's personal life.

Moore, Harry T. *The Priest of Love: A Life of D. H. Lawrence*. Rev. ed. New York: Farrar, Straus & Giroux, 1974. A sympathetic full-scale biography by a major specialist with a deep familiarity for Lawrence's works and writings about him. Remains one of the more consequential and useful studies available.

Preston, Peter, and Peter Hoare, eds. *D. H. Lawrence in the Modern World*. Cambridge, England: Cambridge University Press, 1989. The world-wide dimensions of Lawrence's reputation are illustrated by this collection of papers from an international symposium which included scholars from France, Italy, Israel, and Korea, as well as from English-speaking countries.

Sagar, Keith. *D. H. Lawrence: Life into Art*. Athens: University of Georgia Press, 1985. An important literary biography by a specialist who has written several books about Lawrence, sets forth the events of Lawrence's life alongside an exposition of themes and techniques which characterized the writer's work in several genres.

Schneider, Daniel J. *The Consciousness of D. H. Lawrence: An Intellectual Biography*. Lawrence: University Press of Kansas, 1986. Major themes in Lawrence's works reflected values and subjective responses developed over the course of the writer's life. Traces psychological concerns and modes of belief as they arose during Lawrence's career, without indulging in undue speculation or reductionism.

Squires, Michael, and Keith Cushman, eds. *The Challenge of D. H. Lawrence*. Madison: University of Wisconsin Press, 1990. This group of essays, which deal both with individual works and broader literary contexts, supplies some interesting and provocative insights. Of particular note is the first article by Wayne C. Booth, a self-confessed "lukewarm Lawrentian," who maintains that Lawrence's works are better appreciated upon rereading and reconsideration.

Worthen, John. *D. H. Lawrence and the Idea of the Novel*. London: Macmillan, 1979. Lawrence's personal beliefs and his working habits are traced to show the creative sources of his novels. Worthen, an acknowledged specialist in this field, has also written the more recent *D. H. Lawrence: A Literary Life* (1989).